French Farm and Village Holiday Guide

Self-catering holidays in the famous *gîtes* of rural France

The Publishers wish to thank the Regional and Departmental Tourist Boards in France, the Federation Nationale des Gîtes Ruraux de France, the Animateurs de Relais and the owners of the gîtes included for their assistance and co-operation, without which publication would not be possible.

Farm Holiday Guides Ltd
PAISLEY, GREAT BRITAIN

Acknowledgements

To the Institut Geographique National (IGN) in France which holds the copyright to the map drawings and sections reproduced here with their kind permission.
To the French Government Tourist Office, London, for the use of their photographs.
To the Brittany Tourist Board for the cover photograph by Gratien (Maison Fleure, Rochefort en Terre, Brittany).
To Ted Carden for cover design.

Editorial Director: Peter Clark
Editorial Consultants: J. Henderson McCartney, Martine Benoit
Editors: Elaine Wheeler, Jill Adam
Assistants: Sophie Dufour, Anne Vernière

ISSN 1 85055 042 5 © Farm Holiday Guides Ltd.
Abbey Mill Business Centre, Seedhill, Paisley PA1 1JN (041 887 0428)

PUBLISHED AND PRINTED IN GREAT BRITAIN

All rights reserved. No part of this publication can be reproduced, stored in a retrieval system, or transmitted, in any form or by any means, electronic, mechanical, photocopying, recording or otherwise, without the prior permission of Farm Holiday Guides Ltd.

Publisher's Note

The information in this book is presented in good faith, under the terms of the Trade Descriptions Act. Every effort has been made by the publishers to check the facts, but they do not take responsibility for errors in the information supplied by the owners of gîtes, or the Relais départementaux, or for changes after this guide has been printed, for printer's errors, etc. Nor can any responsibility be taken for deposits, their refund or for cancelled bookings, which must be a matter to be arranged between host and guest or between the various booking services and the prospective holiday-maker.

Type and Graphics by Keyset Composition, Colchester, Essex.
Printed by The Guernsey Press Co. Ltd., PO Box 57, Braye Rd., Guernsey, C.I.
Distributed by Ian Allan Ltd., Coombelands House, Addlestone, Weybridge KT15 1HY (0932 58511).

Some people prefer to spend their holiday on Townsend Thoresen

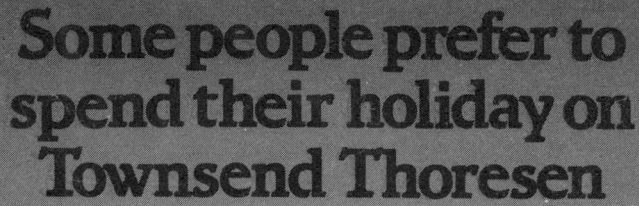

It's funny. We find we have great difficulty getting some people to leave our ships when they get to the other side. It's all so much like a luxury holiday cruise that they want to stay – for a fortnight or more.

It's a surprisingly reasonable cruise too, with low fares even in the high season and special rates if you want to give your caravan or trailer a holiday too.

If you can bear to go ashore, you'll find our carefully planned routes put you well on the way to that other holiday destination. Thousands of sailings, night and day, let you set off whenever you like.

And if you'd like to carry on Townsend Thoresen holiday style – we've some super inclusive motoring packages well worth looking in to. Find out about these and about taking a holiday cruise on the way to your holiday. Get our free colour brochure from Townsend Thoresen Brochure Department, PO Box 12, Dover, Kent CT16 1LD.

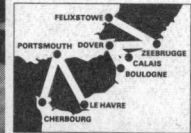

IT'S EASY GOING
TOWNSEND THORESEN

Foreword

Dear Reader,

It is perhaps surprising that it is only relatively recently that British tourists in any great numbers have discovered the many attractions of France as a holiday destination. In the past there were certainly minorities who helped popularise such resorts as Antibes, Nice, Deauville and others were of course drawn by the magnetic appeal of Paris.

But now the variety and interest of all the regions of France are appreciated by a growing majority and the heart of France, the unspoilt country areas, are widely enjoyed. The organisation of the *gîtes ruraux* has played no small part in this and we are pleased to present for 1986 a substantial selection of the accommodation available. By booking directly with the owners or through the *Loisirs Accueil* booking services, you benefit from the lowest possible rates with no booking fees or agency surcharges to increase the cost.

French food and wine again features and those less experienced in travel in France should have no fear in sampling French cuisine – especially in the *fermes auberges*, roadside restaurants and village inns and hotels.

Like English, French is an old and international language. You will enjoy and remember holidays in France all the more if you carry a French dictionary and/or phrasebook and make an effort at local communication! *Courage, mon ami! Et bonnes vacances!*

Peter Clark
J. Henderson McCartney

Contents

Discover Country Food & Wine

France and its Départements		6
Essential Information		9
The French gîtes		
Loisirs Acceuil		12
Central Booking Services		
Holiday Planner		14
Choosing Your Gîte		15
Prices		
Country Food and Wine		17
Symbols		18
1	North – Pas-de-Calais	19
	Nord, Pas-de-Calais	
2	Picardy	30
	Aisne, Oise, Somme	
3	Centre – Val-de-Loire	46
	Cher, Eure-et-Loir, Indre, Indre-et-Loire, Loir-et-Cher, Loiret	
4	Auvergne	76
	Allier, Cantal, Haute-Loire, Puy-de-Dôme	
5	Limousin	91
	Corrèze, Creuse, Haute-Vienne	
6	Midi-Pyrénées	107
	Ariège, Aveyron, Haute-Garonne, Gers, Lot, Hautes-Pyrénées, Tarn, Tarn-et-Garonne	
7	Aquitaine	142
	Dordogne, Gironde, Landes, Lot-et-Garonne, Pyrénées-Atlantiques	
8	Poitou – Charentes	165
	Charente, Charente-Maritime, Deux-Sèvres, Vienne	
9	Western Loire	190
	Loire-Atlantique, Mayenne, Sarthe, Vendée	
10	Brittany	204
	Côtes-du-Nord, Finistère, Ille-et-Vilaine, Morbihan	
11	Normandy	228
	Calvados, Eure, Manche, Orne, Seine-Maritime	
12	Champagne – Ardenne	258
	Ardennes, Aube, Marne, Haute-Marne	
13	Lorraine – Vosges – Alsace	270
	Meurthe-et-Moselle, Meuse, Moselle, Bas-Rhin, Haut-Rhin	
14	Burgundy	282
	Nièvre, Saône-et-Loire, Yonne	
15	Franche-Comté	295
	Doubs, Jura, Haute-Saône	
16	French Alps	308
	Isère, Savoie, Haute-Savoie	
17	Rhône Valley	322
	Ain, Ardèche, Drôme, Loire, Rhône	
18	Provence – Côte d'Azur	339
	Hautes-Alpes, Bouches-du-Rhône, Var	
19	Languedoc – Roussillon	351
	Aude, Gard, Hérault, Lozère	
The Gîtes Federation		365
Addresses. Complaints procedure. Charters		
Bookings and Deposits		370
Prices. Booking by Phone. Sample booking letter.		
Rent Agreement, Inventory		
Relais (departmental gîtes offices) Addresses		376
Loisirs Acceuil Central Booking Addresses		380
Information on French guidebooks		381

France and its départements

Each French department has a number (1–95) which is always the first two numbers of the postcode for any address in that department. All addresses in the department of Somme (80) for example, will have 80 as the first two postcode numbers. Throughout this guide you will find that each gîte has a reference number and this number is also preceded by the department number – all Somme gîtes, therefore, are preceded by 80.

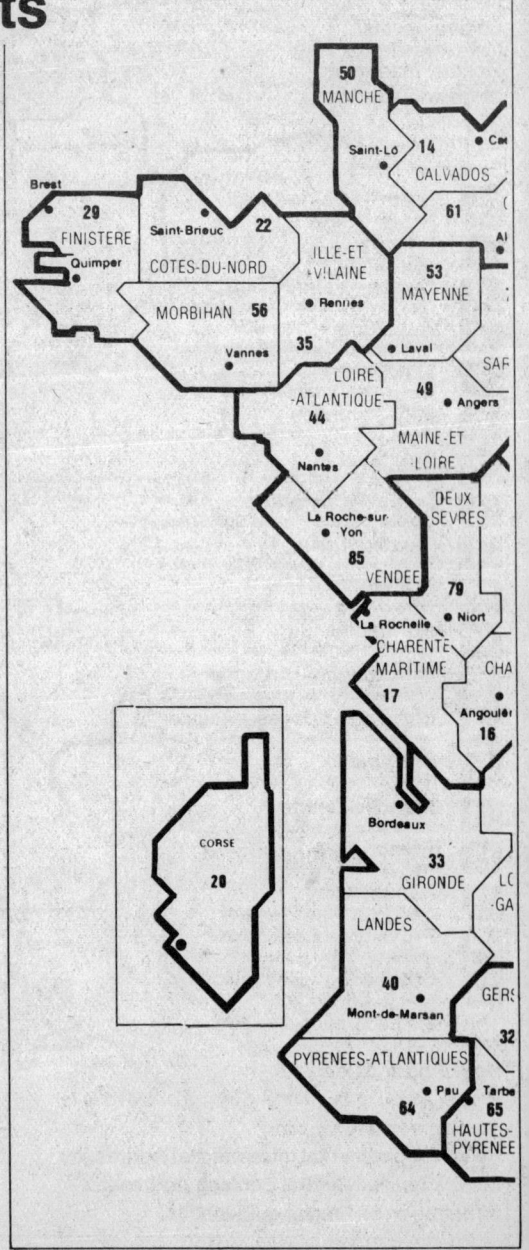

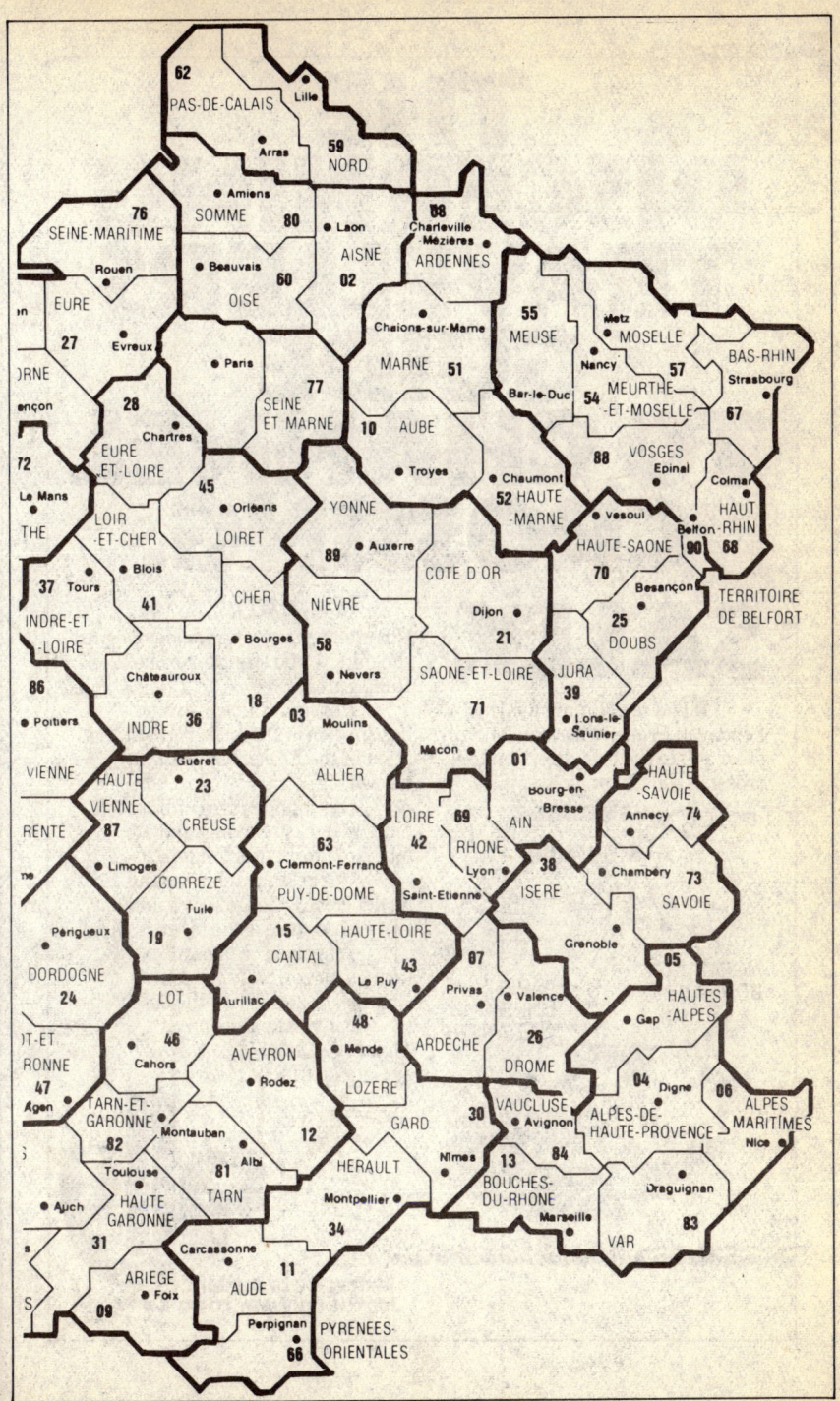

THE DISCERNING TRAVELLERS GUIDE TO CHANNEL CROSSING.

SALLY.

If you're planning a farm holiday in France this year, let Sally steer you in the best direction for crossing the Channel.

Because with Sally cross Channel ferries, your holiday begins the minute you step aboard in Ramsgate.

Leaving Ramsgate our destination is Dunkirk, right at the start of the French Expressway network.

Our lounges are comfortable, our sun decks relaxing, and our bars are most entertaining.

Our restaurant is famous for its delicious 'smorgasbord' and our Duty Free store is the biggest afloat.

When you've chosen your farm, insist on Sally for your Channel crossing – it's the best!

Ring Sally Line on
Thanet 0843 595522
or London 01-858 1127

**Ramsgate to Dunkirk.
It's the only way to go** *with style*

Essential Information

The *French Farm and Village Holiday Guide*, although a fully independent publication, is written in collaboration with the *Fédération Nationale des Gîtes Ruraux de France*. It is about self-catering holidays in the French countryside and is designed to meet the ever-growing demand for realistic holidays in France with a chance to meet the local people and still be within the purse of the average holidaymaker.

All gîtes described in this book are selected by the Relais Départemental which is responsible for the accuracy of the information given. **No** charge is made by the publisher either to the owners or the Relais for these entries.

A **GITE DE FRANCE** is a privately owned, self-contained country holiday home. Often a converted farm cottage or building, this self-catering accommodation has generally been created with the aid of a grant from French Government agencies, and must conform to regulations laid down by the charter of the *Fédération Nationale des Gîtes Ruraux de France*.

A **GITE-CHAMBRE D'HOTE** is the French equivalent of the good, old-fashioned 'bed and breakfast' of the English-speaking world. Many *chambre d'hôte* owners also offer main meals at a reasonable cost on a *table d'hôte* basis. Please note that the minimum stay is generally for one week, although some owners may accept shorter bookings, especially out of season.

A **GITE-CAMPING-CARAVANING A LA FERME** is a camping site on a working farm. Each site has a maximum density of six installations and 20 persons. The minimum area for each installation – tent or caravan – is 300 square metres, except in particular cases. Farm produce and/or farmhouse meals can usually be provided. We are now also including in this category, camp-sites designated **Aire naturelle de camping**. These are similar to *camping à la ferme* sites, but may have up to 25 installations and may be situated further from the farmhouse or on nearby woodland.

GITES EQUESTRES, GITES D'ETAPES and GITES D'ENFANTS. We also try to feature a small selection of *gîtes equestres* (riding centres), *gîtes d'etapes* (stop-over *gîtes*) and *gîtes d'enfants*. The *gîtes equestres* and the *gîtes d'etapes* are an excellent way for walkers and horse lovers to discover the French countryside. The gîtes d'enfants are farm holidays for unaccompanied children. If you are interested in a fuller list of these more specialised facilities, you should contact the appropriate Relais from the list at the back of this book (page 376) or the French Tourist Office in Picadilly, London.

The Gîtes de France Organisation

The *Fédération Nationale des Gîtes Ruraux de France* is a non profit-making organisation, created in 1955, to promote rural tourism. It is supported by various French Ministries, including the Ministry of Agriculture and the State Department for Tourism. The main aim of

FERRY DIRECT

FERRY STYLISH

Our spacious, modern ships with their abundant cabins and berths are the relaxing way to Brittany and Normandy.

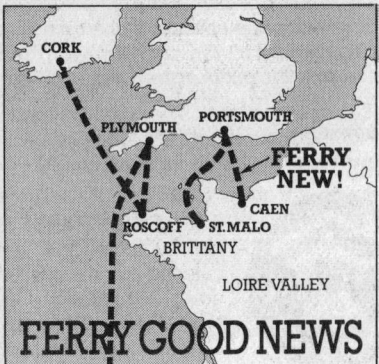

FERRY GOOD NEWS

Our **new** Portsmouth-Caen route to Normandy plus our routes **direct** to Brittany mean we can offer perfect routes to all of holiday France.

FERRY EASY

Our fast, clear, picturesque roads south make driving in France sheer pleasure.

FERRY INCLUSIVE

We've an unbeatable range of value-for-money inclusive Motoring Holidays, Gîte (cottage) Holidays and Short Breaks in France.

Brittany Ferries
The Holiday Ferry

Millbay Docks, Plymouth PL1 3EW. Telephone: (0752) 21321.
The Brittany Centre, Wharf Road, Portsmouth PO2 8RU. Telephone: (0705) 827701.
Tourist House, 42 Grand Parade, Cork. Telephone: (021) 507666.

the *Fédération* is to help country people make use of redundant properties by converting them into holiday accommodation (*Gîtes de France*) and thus promote contact between rural and city dwellers. It supervises the standards of the accommodation offered by its members and ensures that they abide by the rules laid down in the *Fédération*'s Charter.

The Charter and its Sub-Sections

This sets out the basic working rules which the owners must respect to benefit from the guarantees of quality and respectability which the *Fédération* represents in the eyes of the French Government and Public. The Charter and its sub-sections are translated and reproduced in this book (see pages 366–8). Please read them carefully.

The Relais Départemental

The administrative structure of France is based upon 95 *départements*, roughly equivalent to British counties, each one under the administrative authority of an elected *Conseil Général* and a government appointed *Préfet*. The *Fédération* is represented, in each *département*, by a *Relais départemental des Gîtes de France*.

A *Relais départemental* is made up of owners of rural holiday accommodation (*gîtes de France*), representatives drawn from national and local government services and the agricultural, rural, economic and tourist sectors.

The role of these *Relais départementaux* is to:
- inform and help French rural inhabitants to renovate and run their holiday accommodation (*gîtes de France*),
- authorise and regularly check this accommodation,
- act for the owners, in dealing with the local government authorities,
- help to bring together all those who, in a *département*, can, directly or indirectly, help further the organisation,
- publicise the organisation on *départemental* and regional levels,
- help the users, in all ways possible within their means, to book their holiday accommodation (*gîtes de France*),
- participate in all initiatives which help to further rural tourism and bring out contacts between city and country dwellers,
- act for the owners in dealing with the *Fédération Nationale* in Paris.

Each *Relais départemental* generally employs a full-time officer — called an *Animateur* in French — although some are still part-time or voluntary. The *animateur's* office could be in any one of the following: the office of the *Préfet* (county hall); the *Office Départemental de Tourisme* (county tourist office); or the *Chambre d'Agriculture* (roughly similar to a local Farmers Union), or elsewhere.

Though the *animateur* is the backbone of the *Relais départemental*, its success depends on the goodwill, ideas and work of all the people involved and this is also what gives a really unique character to a holiday in a *Gîte de France*.

The Gîtes Organisation guarantees: ● a good welcome ● accommodation with a minimum standard of comfort ● financial respectability through the control exercised by this governmentally recognised organisation ● low prices: you are put directly in contact with the house-owner or a booking service run on a non-profit-making basis by the *Relais départemental* or the region for the benefit of both the user and the proprietor.

You will find a list of all Relais Départementaux at the back of this book on pages 376–379.

Reservation Loisirs Accueil

Special Interest Holidays *Special Interest Holidays* *Special Interest Holidays*

Reservation Loisirs Accueil are centralised departmental booking services for *gîtes ruraux* and special interest holidays. They have been organised with the backing of the official tourist authorities and the *Féderation Nationale des Gîtes Ruraux de France*. There is a Charter and booking conditions to which all Loisirs Accueil booking services must adhere. These booking services have already been set up in many *départements* of France and are planned for several more.

Many of the *gîtes de France* which appear in this guide are bookable through Loisirs Accueil services. We also feature a selection of special interest or theme holidays offered through these services in several *départements*. You may choose for example, a week's canoeing holiday, followed by a more restful week in a *gîte rural* – all bookable at the same time through one booking office. Or you may decide to stay in a *gîte rural* or *chambre d'hôte* and take advantage of one of the non-residential courses offered – cooking or painting for example.

It is important to note that on all courses offered instruction will always be given IN FRENCH (although certain guides or instructors may have a limited knowledge of English). You therefore need to have at least a reasonable knowledge of the language to be able to understand what is going on, and indeed, to get the most from your holiday. This is of course, especially important where personal safety is concerned, for example when canoeing or climbing.

WHAT DO LOISIRS ACCUEIL SERVICES OFFER?

Accommodation

The Loisirs Accueil booking services offer a choice of different types of accommodation: Well equipped **gîtes ruraux** (cottages, chalets or apartments); **chambres d'hôte** (bed and breakfast accommodation); **hotels** (1 to 4 star) with full-board, half-board or just a room. You could also choose to stay in a **holiday village**, offering a variety of events and leisure facilities as well as full-board at an all-inclusive price. If you prefer **camping**, there is a choice here too – on farms, in natural surroundings or on a well-equipped site (1 to 4 star).

Special Interest Holidays

All-inclusive holidays based around a certain theme are becoming increasingly popular with holiday makers who want more from their holiday than just a sun-tan. The Loisirs Accueil services offer a variety of interesting holidays from sports (including canoeing, horse-riding, cycling, ski-ing) to crafts and cookery courses. You may like to choose a holiday afloat on the sea, river or canal, or even spend a weekend in a horse-drawn caravan. If you do not find a particular holiday to suit you in this guide (which includes only a selection), write direct to the Loisirs Accueil booking service in the *département* of your choice for their brochure.

Special Interest Holidays   *Special Interest Holidays*   *Special Interest Holidays*

Guaranteed Prices and Quality Control

The services offered by Loisirs Accueil are completely free and prices are identical to those normally charged by the owners of hotels, *gîtes ruraux* and camp-sites. You can therefore rest assured that you are paying the correct rate and that there will be no "hidden costs" when you arrive at your holiday destination. Regular checks are carried out to ensure that all accommodation and leisure activities come up to required standards.

Local People Who Know Their Region

Staff in the Loisirs Accueil booking services all live locally and can give you the best advice on holiday accommodation and leisure facilities and will make sure that you get the best possible value for money.

All-Year Round Service

Loisirs Accueil booking services are open all year and can also handle bookings for weekends and short stays.

HOW TO BOOK

Most Loisirs Accueil have English speaking staff, so you can telephone or write to the relevant booking service to enquire about a holiday you have selected from the pages of this guide, or to ask for their brochure.
- Once you have made your choice, fill in the booking form, sent by the booking service, giving your order of preference for the holidays and dates selected, and return it to the Loisirs Accueil office.
- The Loisirs Accueil booking service will notify you that your holiday has been provisionally reserved and will be held for you for eight days, during which time you must confirm your booking by sending a deposit of 25% of the total cost of the holiday and returning the signed contract sent by the booking service. If you do not reply promptly, the booking service will automatically withdraw your booking and you will owe them nothing.
- A few days after receiving the deposit, the booking service will send you an invoice indicating the balance due and the date by which full payment must be received, i.e. thirty days before the start of your holiday.
- Finally, having paid the balance due, you will receive a coupon to be given up to the owner or host on arrival at your holiday destination.

An early booking will assure you of a greater chance that the holiday accommodation you choose will be vacant.
For further information on Loisirs Accueil booking services, see the features within the *département* listings of this guide. A full list of the addresses of all Loisirs Accueil booking services featured in this guide is given at the back of the book on page 380.

Holiday Planner

Careful planning helps you avoid delays and other travel problems and allows you more time to relax and enjoy your holiday to the full. We give below some general advice and the addresses of various organisations offering further information.
The French Government Tourist Office at 178 Piccadilly, London W1 publishes a magazine distributed free called, **The Traveller in France** (available to personal callers or by sending 50p to cover postage). This magazine gives useful general information about France and has a handy reference section about routes to France and the ferry companies and airlines that operate them. In the USA tourist information is available from The French Government Tourist Office, 610 Fifth Avenue, New York, NY 10010.

INSURANCE
Fully comprehensive insurance and a green card are strongly advised. Organisations offering advice and special insurance for car driving, medical expenses and personal insurance are the AA, RAC, Routiers (354 Fulham Road, London SW10 9UH, Tel: 01-351-3522) and Europ-Assistance (252 High Street, Croydon CR0 1NF, Tel: 01-680-1234). It is advisable to take with you a European accident statement, available from your insurance broker. These are in common use abroad and will simplify matters in case of an accident.

MEDICAL TREATMENT
Obtain form E111 from your Social Security Office before leaving home and you will save on any medical treatment which may be needed for yourself or family. The owner of your *gîte* will give you the name and address of your nearest doctor and chemist. If you do not qualify for treatment under the reciprocal arrangements we have with France, you should take out private insurance cover.

MONEY
In France you will normally change foreign currency or travellers' cheques in banks, where the rate will be most favourable. It is useful to know however, that exchange is also often available in big hotels, railway stations and even *Syndicats d'Initiative* or *Offices de Tourisme* in major towns. You can obtain £50 cash with Visa or Access at a bank, or pay for goods and services where their signs are displayed. You can also obtain up to £100 cash per day at most banks by cashing sterling cheques backed by a Eurocheque card. Remember always to take your passport with you as identification in any transaction.

DRIVING IN FRANCE
The French Government produces a free map (the Bison Futé), distributed at peak holiday periods at petrol stations, tourist offices, etc., showing alternative routes for those wishing to avoid the often expensive motorways and congested main roads. Maps of the French Ordnance Survey (Institut Géographique National) cover the whole of France in varying scales and are available from good bookshops and by mail order from McCarta Ltd, 122 King's Cross Road, London WC1X 9DS. Tel. 01 278 8278. Send 25p stamp for a catalogue. In the USA, send for a complete catalogue of books and maps of France (including IGN) to Bradt Enterprises Inc., 95 Harvey Street, Box H, Cambridge, MA 02140, USA.

PUBLIC TRANSPORT
A car is not absolutely essential for a *gîte* holiday. It is quite possible to reach many of the *gîtes* listed in the guide by train and then hire a bicycle to get around (enquire about hiring at the railway station or local *Syndicat d'Initiative*). There are also good local bus services, although not many long-distance ones. Timetables are available from local tourist offices and coach stations.

Choosing your gîte

This book is divided into the 19 regions of France and takes in some 78 *départements* (see back cover).

The *gîtes* are listed alphabetically in their respective *départements* according to the name of the village they are situated in or near.

The *gîtes-chambres d'hôte* and *gîtes-camping-caravaning à la ferme* are also listed alphabetically, but separately, after the gîtes and have a specific symbol – a bed or a tent – beside the reference number at the bottom of the description. Occasionally, *gîtes équestres*, *gîtes d'étapes* and *gîtes d'enfants* are listed at the end of the *département*, but have no special symbol.

You can locate your *gîte*, *chambre d'hôte* or *camping-caravaning à la ferme* approximately by using the simple maps given after the introductory page to each region. They are designated in the following manner:

```
•  gîte                    ▲ camping-caravaning à la ferme   ■ gîte équestre
☆ chambre d'hôte          ● main town
```

Each description gives:

The type of house cottage, farmhouse, house in a village, chalet, flat or even a château!

The altitude when over 500 metres.

The number of rooms and beds children's beds are generally only suitable for children up to 5–7 years of age.

The type of heating (not normally included in the rent).

Bed sheets and house linen are not supplied, except where specifically mentioned and, in general, a small charge is made for their hire. However, more and more *gîte* owners are willing to help solve this problem, so do not hesitate to enquire about sheets and linen when booking your *gîte*. Of course, bed linen is supplied in *chambres d'hôte* and *gîtes d'enfants*.

Farm produce: this depends very much on the region, the type and size of farm, and the time of the year. In general, it means milk, eggs and, perhaps, wine, as well as fruit and vegetables in season. Do not forget, however, that these are working farms and that tourism is not the main pursuit of their owners, especially at harvest time! The nearest food shops and restaurants are also given where possible.

The number of people where relevant children are included in the maximum number of people given for each *gîte*.

Map references As the regional map at the beginning of each section is very simplified, we include a map reference for each *gîte* using the **IGN Green Series** Maps (scale 1:100,000, 1 cm to 1 km). The reference is given as *IGN* followed by the sheet no., e.g. *16*, and appears under the number of people given. NB Where there is no photograph for a particular *gîte*, a map extract of the IGN Red Series (1:250,000 scale) is also shown.

Reference numbers: please quote the *gîte* reference numbers on all correspondence. They are given at the bottom left of each description.

Booking Information Prices are given when available (see next page for further information) along with contact addresses and telephone numbers for booking are supplied. **E** indicates that bookings can be made in English.

Prices

Gîtes

Prices for the gîtes are given in French francs for a weekly tenancy. If you stay for two weeks or more, just add it up. Full payment is due for each week of occupation from Saturday to Saturday.

The different prices shown are equivalent to low, high and winter seasons during the French holiday year. The exact periods of these seasons vary a little from region to region, but the prices generally correspond to the following practical examples:

Low season	F 650/690	F 650	October to May
		F 690	June and September
High season	F 850/925	F 850	July
		F 925	August
Winter season	F 780/840	F 780	December to April
		F 840	French winter/spring school holiday periods

Winter season prices apply to gîtes in mountain areas where there is snow and winter sports can be practised. Please note that heating is generally not included in these prices.

French school holidays vary from region to region but are roughly as follows: Christmas 20.12.85 to 3.1.86; Winter 13.2.86 to 3.3.86; Spring 28.3.86 to 10.4.86; Summer 27.6.86 to 8.9.86.

Gîtes-chambres d'hôte

Prices for the *chambres d'hôte* are given per person per night, or where stated, per week, including continental breakfast. **Bookings are normally for a minimum stay of one week.** Midday or evening meals are often available.

Gîtes-camping-caravaning à la ferme

Prices for the *camping-caravaning à la ferme* and *aires naturelles de camping* come under the administrative authorities (*Préfecture*) in each *département*. They are thus subject to government control and are in general not available at the time of going to press. This is, however, a really low-cost way of camping in France and offers all the usual guarantees concerning standards and welcome which figure in the *Gîtes de France* charter.

Gîtes Equestres and Gîtes d'Etape

Prices are either quoted simply for a night's accommodation, or full board, but this is clearly mentioned where appropriate.

Gîtes d'Enfants

Prices given are for full board, normally for one week's stay.

NB The prices quoted are as supplied to us by the *relais* in September 1985. They run for 12 months either from September 1985 or January 1986. In some cases, new prices may arrive too late for publication.)

Country Food and Wine

Perhaps one of the main delights of a holiday in rural France is the opportunity it affords to sample the local food and wine – without spending a fortune.

French cuisine varies quite considerably in different regions, from the rich fare of dishes based on cream and cider in Normandy, to the delicate *foie gras* of the south-west and the delicious seafoods of the Atlantic and Mediterranean coasts. Good restaurants always base their menus on fresh local produce, so do not expect to find a preponderance of seafood restaurants in the heart of the Auvergne.

Prix Fixe Menus

All restaurants should display a menu outside to help you decide where to go and what to choose. "Prix Fixe" menus are usually good value as prices are kept low by using produce available on that day, and you can roughly calculate the cost of a meal before you even enter the restaurant.

New Food and Wine Features

We are including in the guide features on local food and wine in several *départements*. The features vary, but may give details of where to buy fresh produce from farms near your *gîte*; local wine producers offering tastings and direct sales; or even ordering famous Bresse chickens by post (p. 282).

Farm Inns

Of particular interest are the listings of *Fermes Auberges* (farm inns) and *Tables d'Hôtes*. These are privately-run establishments where catering is not normally the main business, but a means of providing extra income for farmers – and superb value for the diners! Menus are based on farm produce and are normally *table d'hôte* although you may be offered a choice of dishes on some courses. Portions are usually exceedingly generous and wine is often included in the very reasonable prices.

Fermes-Auberges are not always open all week, and some may only offer lunch. In any case, the farmers tend to cater only for a limited number of people so it is necessary to telephone and book in advance.

Table d'hôtes are run along similar lines, but are normally part of a *Gîte-Chambre d'hôte* establishment where accommodation is also available.

Apart from enjoying delicious home-cooked meals, based on genuine local produce, these farm inns give the visitor a chance really to get to know and understand the people of rural France and their way of life. When you eat at a *Ferme-Auberge* it is not the same as being in a busy restaurant – you are dining in someone's home and you will be treated more as a welcome guest than a paying customer.

Symbols

The ears of corn give an idea of the comfort of the *gîte* in the same way as stars for hotels. Where there are no ears of corn, the *gîte* has not yet been classified.

The bed designates a *gîte-chambre d'hôte* (bed & breakfast accommodation)

The tent designates a *gîte-camping-caravaning à la ferme* (camping on a farm) or an *aire naturelle de camping*

E   English spoken – you may 'phone and book in English

Reference Numbers: Two reference numbers are given: the figures at the bottom left of the description, e.g. 65/201, is the *gîte* **reference number** which **must** be quoted when booking; the *IGN* number is the Green Series map number to help you locate your *gîte*.

The following symbols give you an idea of the main open-air activities in an area of 10–15 kilometres around your *gîte*.	
🐟	Fishing.
🐴	Riding.
🌳	Walking, forests and woods.
〰	Rivers, lakes or sea.
🐬	Swimming in a river, a lake or the sea.
🏊	A covered or open air swimming-pool.
⛵	All kinds of boating and sailing.
🎾	Tennis.
⛷	Skiing.
🚲	Bicycle hire.

1 NORD / PAS-DE-CALAIS

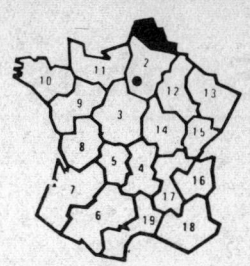

Once joined to England, this region of France is still readily accessible! Many travellers make this a stopping-off place and it has long been associated with short visits across the Channel. However, this northern region, once a land of invasion, has a lot to offer the holidaymaker. The sandy beaches and dunes of the Flemish coastline are backed by a lovely and varied countryside. Here, you can enjoy forest walks and, in particular, "la petite randonnée", short walks lasting the morning, afternoon or a whole day, through valleys, plains and marshlands. Particularly well suited to cycling, the landscape is reminiscent of its close neighbours, Belgium and the Netherlands, with its flowers and windmills.

Many towns in this area have retained great individual charm, despite war damage which obliged the citizens to rebuild and start life again. Of these, Dunkerque, a name well known to the British, now a predominantly modern town, is certainly worth a visit and it still has many quaint old streets and buildings. You can enjoy fresh fish from the fish restaurants near the port itself, or, in town, sample the varied, French and Flemish cuisine. Outings to one of the walled towns or villages, scattered around the port, will bring pleasant surprises.

Calais is a leading Channel port with a long history of English visitors and it is also famous for lace-making. Outside the town hall is Rodin's largest and probably most impressive statue, "The Burghers of Calais", commemorating the six merchants who, in 1347, were prepared to sacrifice themselves to prevent the massacre of the whole town by Edward III. The sister, and rival, port of Boulogne, amongst its other claims to fame, was the port from which Julius Caesar sailed to Britain in 55BC, an exploit almost repeated about 1800 years later by Napoleon!

The regional capital, Lille, is the centre of the French textile industrial and commercial heartland. This is an elegant forward-looking city with the first fully automated metro system in the world and its charming Flemish-style old quarter attracts many visitors.

Historic Armentières, on the river Lys, with its motto 'Poor but Proud' has survived battles throughout the ages and perhaps its inhabitants are justified in their right to feel proud. Arras, Cambrai, picturesque Bergues and many smaller towns are worth a visit — and look out for bell-towers, belfries and of course, windmills.

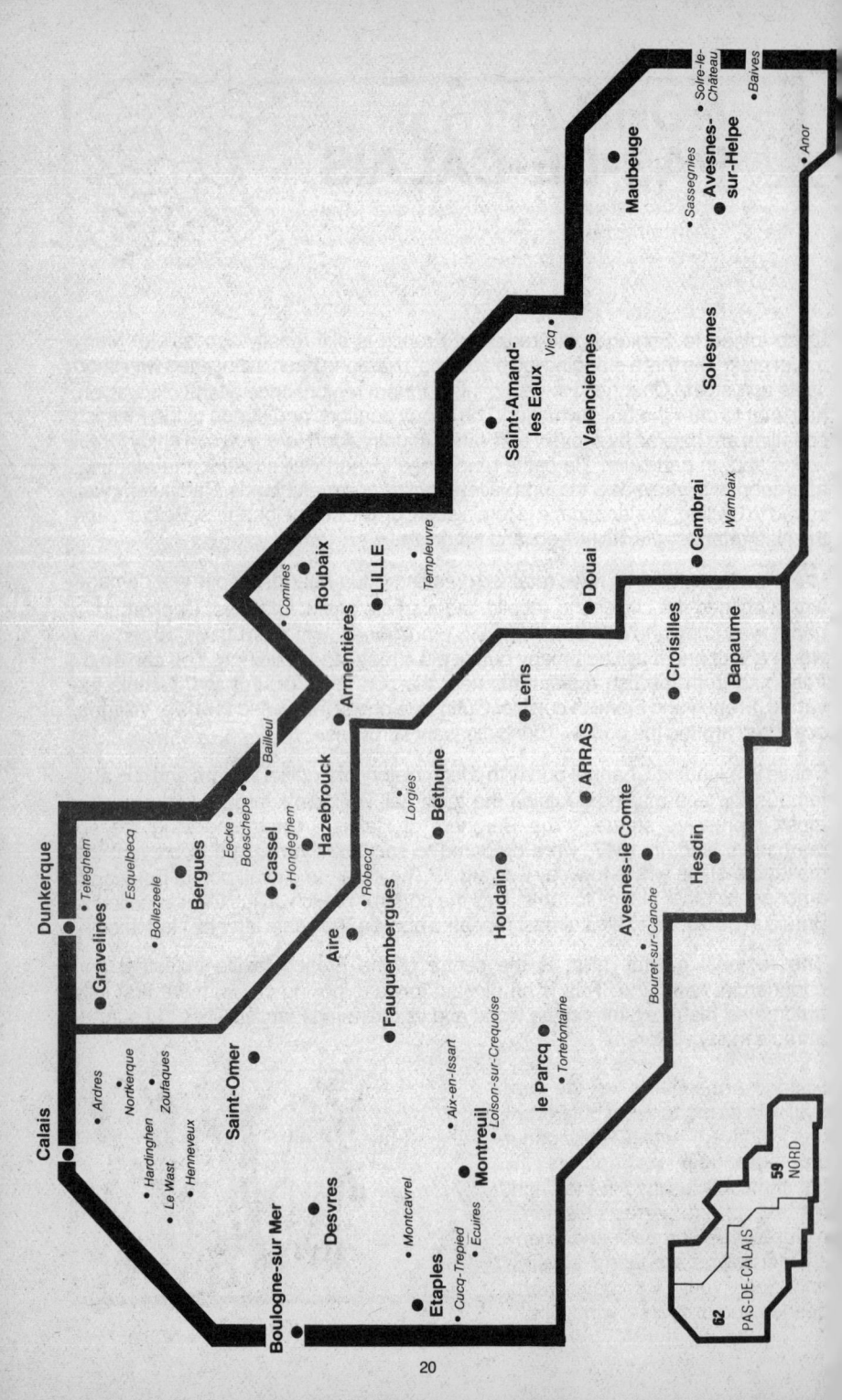

REGION NORD-PAS DE CALAIS
The friendly region

Just across the Channel, the Nord-Pas Calais offers you a great deal in the way of leisure pastimes, and accommodation. Sport, discovery tours, gastronomy and short breaks. Our Shopping centres and craftwork will delight you.

COUNTRYSIDE HOLIDAYS

On the coast, or inland, in *Flanders*, *Artois*, in *Hainaut* or *Avenois* areas, choose from more than 140 gîtes de France, 35 chambres d'hôte (bed and breakfast) and plenty of stopover gîtes for walkers

For further information please contact:
Relais Départemental des Gites Ruraux du Nord
14, square Foch
59800 Lille
Tél. (20) 57.00.61

Relais Départemental des Gites Ruraux du Pas-de-Calais
44, grande rue
62200 Boulogne sur Mer
Tél. (21) 31.66.80

For free brochures on leisure activities, accommodation and tours contact:
Comité Régional de Tourisme
26, Place Rihour
59800 Lille

Nord

ANOR Saint-Clément A neat little house, now renovated and traditionally furnished, standing on a mixed farm 2 km from the village centre. Swimming-pool and bathing in a lake, canoeing, fishing, *boules*, tennis, plus theatre and cinema at Fourmies (5 km). Sailing at 20 km. Living room, kitchen, 2 bedrooms (1 double and 5 single beds), bathroom and shower room, fireplace, electric heating, terrace, enclosed garden with furniture. Farm produce, shopping and restaurant in the village or at Fourmies.

Prices:	low season	F 589/624	**7 people**
	high season	F 676	IGN 5

Booking: M LAMART, Saint-Clément, 02360 Rozoy-sur-Serre. Tel. 23 97 63 40
59/13

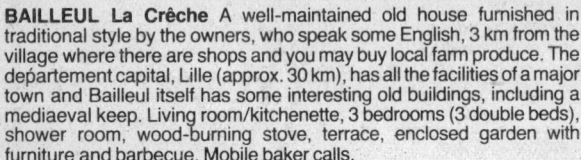

BAILLEUL La Crèche A well-maintained old house furnished in traditional style by the owners, who speak some English, 3 km from the village where there are shops and you may buy local farm produce. The département capital, Lille (approx. 30 km), has all the facilities of a major town and Bailleul itself has some interesting old buildings, including a mediaeval keep. Living room/kitchenette, 3 bedrooms (3 double beds), shower room, wood-burning stove, terrace, enclosed garden with furniture and barbecue. Mobile baker calls.

Prices:	low season	F 624/676	**6 people**
	high season	F 728	IGN 2

Booking: M MOREAU, La Crèche, 59270 Bailleul. Tel. 28 41 10 89
59/11

BAIVES Rue Principale An old house in the centre of the village, now renovated and converted into a rustically furnished gîte. Trélon (5 km) has an eighteenth-century château and a lively series of summer *fêtes*; walks on marked footpaths at Avesnes-sur-Helpe (approx. 20 km). Kitchen, 1 bedroom (2 single and 1 child's bed), shower room, no heating, open garden with furniture. Restaurant, farm produce and shopping in the village.

Prices:	low season	F 550/600	**2/3 people**
	high season	F 650	IGN 5

Booking: M MORIAU, Rue Principale à Baives, 59132 Trélon. Tel. 27 59 70 06
59/24

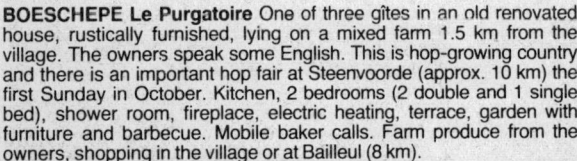

BOESCHEPE Le Purgatoire One of three gîtes in an old renovated house, rustically furnished, lying on a mixed farm 1.5 km from the village. The owners speak some English. This is hop-growing country and there is an important hop fair at Steenvoorde (approx. 10 km) the first Sunday in October. Kitchen, 2 bedrooms (2 double and 1 single bed), shower room, fireplace, electric heating, terrace, garden with furniture and barbecue. Mobile baker calls. Farm produce from the owners, shopping in the village or at Bailleul (8 km).

Prices:	low season	F 468/520	**5 people**
	high season	F 624	IGN 2

Booking: M R. PRUVOST, Le Purgatoire, 59299 Boeschepe. Tel. 28 42 52 44
59/4A

BOLLEZEELE A traditionally furnished gîte in the owners' own renovated house near the village centre. Bicycles can be hired at the gîte. Bergues (14 km) has good sports facilities, some interesting old buildings and typical Flemish houses to see. The sea is at 20 km. Living room/kitchenette (TV), 3 bedrooms (1 double, 4 single and 1 child's bed), bathroom and shower room, electric heating, terrace and balcony, enclosed garden with furniture and barbecue. Farm produce and shopping in the village or at Bergues.

Prices:	low season	F 600	**6/7 people**
	high season	F 600	IGN 2

Booking: M DEQUEKER, 92 Rue de l'Eglise, Bollezeele, 59470 Wormhout. Tel. 28 68 80 58
59/17

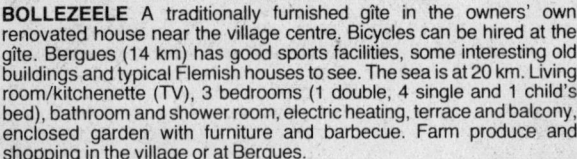

Nord

COMINES Hameau Sainte Marguerite A traditionally furnished ground-floor gîte in a new house on a mixed farm 2 km from the village centre. The Belgian border is just 3 km away. Lille (15 km) has all the facilities of an important town, and the sea is close enough for a day trip at 60 km. Living room (TV), kitchen, 3 bedrooms (1 double and 3 single beds), shower room, fireplace, electric heating, terrace, garden with furniture. Farm produce from the owners, shopping in the village or in Lille.

Prices: low season   F 700   **5 people**
            high season   F 700   *IGN 2*
Booking: M VERMES, Rue de Blanc Coulon, Hameau Sainte Marguerite, 59560 Comines. Tel. 20 39 01 92
59/6

1

EECKE A ground-floor gîte, one of two, in an old house now renovated and traditionally furnished at the village centre. Take a trip to Armentières (approx. 25 km) and try boating on the river Lys; there are several British cemeteries around this famous Flanders town. Living room (1 double divan), kitchen (washing machine), 1 bedroom (1 double and 1 single bed), bathroom, gas central heating, garage, enclosed garden. Mobile baker and fishmonger call, shopping and restaurant in the village or at Steenvoorde (3 km).

Prices: low season   F 550   **5 people**
            high season   F 600   *IGN 2*
Booking: M G. WYCKAERT, Rue du Roi, Eecke, 59114 Steenvoorde. Tel. 28 40 14 08
59/7A

© IGN Red Map 101

ESQUELBECQ An attractive, brick-built house now converted into a gîte with traditional, country-style furnishings a short walk from the village where farm produce is available. Bergues (8 km), designated a rural holiday resort, offers a wide range of activities in season, including guided tours, archery, boating and *carillon* concerts. The sea is at 20 km. Living room, kitchen, 2 bedrooms (2 double, 2 single and 1 child's bed), shower room, fireplace, heating, terrace, garden. Shopping and restaurant in the village or at Bergues.

Prices: low season   F 500   **6/7 people**
            high season   F 600   *IGN 2*
Booking: M DEROI, Rue de la Cloche, Esquelbecq, 59470 Wormhout. Tel. 28 68 93 26.
59/4

HONDEGHEM One of two rustically furnished holiday homes in an old, well-renovated house on a mixed farm; the village centre is 0.3 km. The sea is close enough for a day trip at 35 km. Cassel (approx. 8 km) is a small town with magnificent views across the countryside, a sixteenth-century mill and a folk museum. Living room/kitchenette, 2 bedrooms (1 double and 3 single beds), shower room, electric heating, enclosed garden with furniture. Shopping and restaurant in the village or at Hazebrouck (3 km).

Prices: low season   F 600/650   **5 people**
            high season   F 650   *IGN 2*
Booking: M DEGRAVE, 180 Route d'Hazebrouck, Hondeghem, 59190 Hazebrouck. Tel. 28 41 92 58
59/12

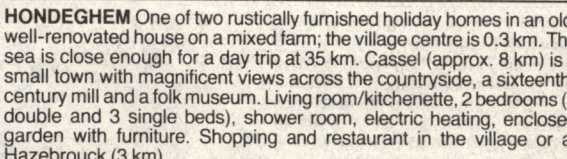

SASSEGNIES One of two gîtes in a substantial old brick-built house, renovated and furnished in country style on a mixed farm with a private pond for fishing. Maubeuge (25 km) is a lively town with plenty of entertainments including a zoo. Living room (TV), kitchen, 2 bedrooms (1 double, 1 single and 1 child's bed), bathroom, heating, terrace, carport, enclosed garden with furniture and barbecue. Linen available F22 per pair per week. Shopping and restaurant in the village (1 km) or at Berlaimont (5 km).

Prices: low season   F 600/650   **3/4 people**
            high season   F 700   *IGN 2*
Booking: M LOCACHE, Sassegnies, 59145 Berlaimont. Tel. 27 67 65 33
59/10

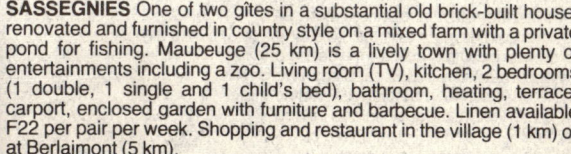

Nord

SOLRE-LE-CHATEAU An attractive, traditionally furnished and renovated stone-built house in its own enclosed garden in the village centre. Avesnes-sur-Helpe (13 km) is a pleasant small town with some old fortifications and walks on marked footpaths, swimming-pool, tennis, table tennis and miniature golf. Living room, kitchen, 3 bedrooms (3 double and 1 child's bed) bathroom, electric heating, terrace, enclosed garden with furniture. Shopping and restaurant in the village or at Avesnes-sur-Helpe.

Prices:	low season	F 600/650	**6/7 people**
	high season	F 700	*IGN 5*

Booking: M MARIANI, 5 Grand Place, 59740 Solre-le-Château.
Tel. 27 61 65 30
59/30

TEMPLEUVE A gîte in an old, simply furnished house standing on a mixed farm 2 km from the village. Lille (approx. 15 km), the département capital, has all the facilities of a large town and Douai (approx. 25 km) has a delightful display of floodlit fountains and pleasant public gardens. Living room, kitchen, 2 bedrooms (2 double beds), shower room, fireplace, electric heating, garden with furniture. Dairy produce and vegetables from the owners, who speak some English, restaurant and shopping in the village.

© IGN Red Map 101

Prices:	low season	on request	**4 people**
	high season	on request	*IGN 2*

Booking: M J.-Y. CHUFFART, 65 Rue de la Caillière, 59242 Templeuve. Tel. 20 34 30 44
59/12

TETEGHEM A rustically furnished, ground-floor gîte, one of three in an old renovated house on a mixed farm just 0.5 km from the village centre where fresh farm produce is available. Dunkerque (5 km) has lovely beaches, museum of contemporary art and a lively nightlife, including cinema, discotheques and a nightclub. Living room (1 double divan), kitchen, 2 bedrooms (1 double and 2 single beds), bathroom, fireplace, electric central heating, terrace, open courtyard with garden furniture. Restaurant and shopping in the village or at Dunkerque.

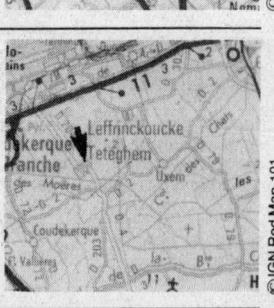

© IGN Red Map 101

Prices:	low season	F 580	**6 people**
	high season	F 580	*IGN 2*

Booking: M J. CATRY, 45 route de Cou de Kerque, 59229 Teteghem.
Tel. 28 61 00 66
59/7

VICQ A gîte in an old, renovated house, furnished in country style and renovated by the owners who speak some English, 2 km from the village. Valenciennes (8 km) is a river port with some interesting old buildings, an art gallery and lace-making school. Grand fairs are held here in May and September. Living room (1 double divan), kitchen, 3 bedrooms (4 double beds), bathroom, fireplace, electric heating, terrace, garage, enclosed garden with furniture. Farm produce, shopping and restaurant in the village where there is a Thursday market.

Prices:	low season	F 550/600	**10 people**
	high season	F 650	*IGN 2*

Booking: Mme MORTIER, 2 rue de la Gare, Vicq, 59970 Fresnes sur Escaut. Tel. 27 27 30 10
59/14

WAMBAIX *Chambre d'hôte* accommodation in the owners' own old renovated home, on a cereal farm just 0.2 km from the village. Cambrai (14 km) has a wealth of old buildings, despite suffering extensive damage in both wars, an art gallery and extensive public gardens. Two rooms available (2 double beds and 2 child's beds), bathroom, electric heating, carport, enclosed garden. Fresh farm produce in the village where there are shops and a restaurant.

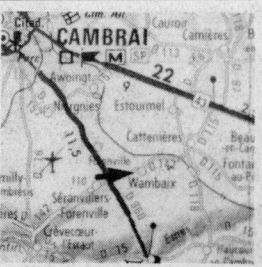

Prices:	low season	F 95	**4/6 people**
	high season	F 95	*IGN 4*

Booking: M BECQUET, 16 Rue de Là Dessous, Wambaix, 59400 Cambrai. Tel. 27 78 73 14

59/15

Pas-de-Calais

AIX-EN-ISSART A pretty little renovated cottage with country-style furnishings near the village centre (0.3 km). Plenty of amenities at the old fortified town of Montreuil (8 km); Bagatelle leisure centre is at 22 km and the coast (sailing facilities) is just 24 km away. Living room/kitchenette (small washing machine), 2 bedrooms (2 double and 1 child's bed), shower room, wood stove, enclosed garden with outdoor furniture. Linen available. Mobile shops call; other shopping and restaurant (3 km) or at Montreuil.

| Prices: | low season | F 650 | 5 people |
| | high season | F 720 | IGN 1 |

Booking: Pas-de-Calais Loisirs Accueil E
62/82

ARDRES La Cauchoise An old, traditionally furnished house, set in its own garden with outdoor furniture and barbecue, 2 km from the village centre. Ardres itself at 7 km, has attractive public gardens and a famous avenue of lime trees planted in the eighteenth-century. The sea is just 12 km away. Living room/kitchenette (1 double divan), 3 bedrooms (1 double, 3 single beds), shower room, heating, garage. Linen available (F28 per set per week). Mobile shops call; other shopping (3 km) or at Ardres; a restaurant at 2 km.

| Prices: | low season | F 750 | 7 people |
| | high season | F 900 | IGN 1 |

Booking: Pas-de-Calais Loisirs Accueil E
62/83

BOURET-SUR-CANCHE One of two gîtes in a well-renovated house with country-style furnishings, surrounded by farmland, near the village centre (0.2 km). Sports facilities at Frévent (2 km) include a swimming-pool and tennis. Take a day trip to the département capital of Arras (40 km approx.). Living room (1 double divan), kitchen (washing machine), 2 bedrooms (1 double, 3 single and 1 child's bed), bathroom, electric central heating, terrace, garage, garden. Mobile shops call; other shopping at Frévent.

| Prices: | low season | F 950 | 8 people |
| | high season | F 1000 | IGN 1 |

Booking: Pas-de-Calais Loisirs Accueil E
62/79

CUCQ-TREPIED La Bergerie One of two purpose-built holiday cottages on an arable farm, 1 km from the village centre. The popular holiday resort of Le Touquet, with its fine sandy beaches and other attractions is just 3 km away. You may hire bicycles there to explore the coastline. Living room/kitchenette (1 double divan), 2 bedrooms (1 double, 5 single and 1 child's bed), shower room, electric heating, enclosed ground. Farm produce and restaurant in the village; shopping at 2 km.

| Prices: | low season | F 1300 | 10 people |
| | high season | F 1300 | IGN 1 |

Booking: M G. DUSANNIER, 301 rue Evariste Dusannier, Trepied, 62780 Cucq. Tel. (21) 94 74 32.
62/55A

ECUIRES A modern chalet with country-style furnishings outside the village and just 2 km from Montreuil. A golf course at the seaside resort of Le Touquet (10 km). Bagatelle leisure park is at 10 km. Take a trip to the Ornithological Park at Rue (20 km). Living room (1 double divan), kitchen, open landing with 1 double, 1 single and 1 child's bed, shower room, heating, verandah, enclosed ground with garden furniture. Linen available (F40 per set per week). Farm produce in the village; other shopping and restaurant at Montreuil.

| Prices: | low season | F 920 | 6 people |
| | high season | F 920 | IGN 1 |

Booking: M P. DELCROIX, 117 rue Fr. Sailly, Ecuires, 62170 Montreuil-sur-Mer. Tel. (21) 06 10 91 E
62/22

Pas-de-Calais

In the Pas-de-Calais we can offer many relaxing itineraries for you to enjoy – through valleys and shady forests where you can travel along quiet roads and experience a rural lifestyle which is still so often completely in tune with nature. Trout are plentiful in our rivers and streams; peaceful forests with welcoming shade skirt the valleys of the département.

Often tourists, lured by the coast road, are surprised at every turn by the natural charm of the landscape. It becomes a pleasant escape to rediscover a certain natural harmony in the passing fields and dark lines of the forest as you travel along.

The diversity of its landscape, along with the many different leisure activities available, make the Pas-de-Calais an ideal choice for your holiday or weekend stay, even outside the tourist season.

To give you a proper welcome and to help you keep in touch with our countryside, we offer several different types of rural holiday accommodation, such as gites, farm camp-sites, hostels, bed and breakfast, etc. . . .

We have something for everyone: youth hostels and camp-sites for young people; an expanding hotel industry and celebrated cuisine (not forgetting the Logis and Auberges de France) for the not-so-young; holiday homes and villages for families and any number of leisure facilities.

Wissant beach

To book your Loisirs Accueil Holiday:
LOISIRS ACCUEIL
44 Grande Rue
62200 BOULOGNE-sur-MER
Tel. (21) 31.66.80.
Telex. CDT PDC 135543 F.

For further information about Pas-de-Calais:
COMITE DEPARTEMENTAL DE TOURISME
44 Grande Rue
62200 BOULOGNE-sur-MER
Tel. (21) 31.98.58.

NB For fuller information about all Loisirs Accueil services, please see pages 12–13 of this guide.

Special Interest Holidays

We show here a sample of activities available in the Pas-de-Calais. All of these can be enjoyed as all-inclusive holidays where the cost covers the activity itself as well as full-board accommodation.

THE SEA Beginner's or more advanced lessons in wind-surfing are available either by the sea or at a lake. Spend an agreeable weekend sea fishing, or try your hand at sand-surfing – a pleasant way of exploring our 120 km of fine sandy beaches. A weekend's sand-surfing holiday would include in the price lessons, insurance, accommodation and meals.

CRAFTS COURSES Come and admire the work done by the many craftsmen and women who exhibit in the département's art and craft galleries and it will inspire you to take up a course. For example, you can spend a week on a beginner's or more advanced course in any of the following crafts: painting on silk or wood; pottery, weaving, lace-making, etc.

FISHING There are many opportunities for freshwater fishing, on rivers or lakes and even in the marshes. For example, a fishing-trip in the Course Valley would include in the price, the fishing permit and a meal.

EXCURSIONS On foot, bicycle, horseback or in a horse-drawn carriage – there are many ways of following the marked paths that allow you to explore our varied landscape with its beaches, dunes, forests, hills and valleys, rivers and marshlands. For example, a 2-day walking tour in the Montreuillois area would be all-inclusive of meals and accommodation.

PAS-de-CALAIS offers accommodation in:
Gîtes de France
Holiday Villages
Chambres d'Hôtes
Logis de France hotels
Hotels
Inns
Group Gîtes
Camp-sites

Pas-de-Calais

HARDINGHEN L'Eau Courte A renovated and rustically furnished cottage in the courtyard of the owners' house, in a peaceful, verdant spot, 3 km from the village. Ideal for those not wanting too long a drive, as it is just 20 km from Calais and Boulogne. Living room (TV, 1 double divan), kitchen, 2 bedrooms (2 double and 1 child's bed), bathroom, fireplace, gas heating. Linen available (F30 per set per week). Farm produce from the owners and in the village where there are shops and a restaurant. Mobile baker calls.

Prices:	low season	F 760	**7 people**
	high season	F 760	*IGN 1*

Booking: Pas-de-Calais Loisirs Accueil **E**
62/64

HENNEVEUX Le Plouy Situated on a mixed farm, this gîte with country-style furnishings is in the owners' old farmhouse, near woodland outside the village. A swimming-pool and tennis and the old fortified town of Desvres (10 km) where there is a colourful fair in October. The coast (16 km). Living room/kitchenette (1 double divan), 1 bedroom (1 double and 1 child's bed), shower room, gas heating, terrace, carport, open ground with garden furniture. Home-made jam from the owners; shopping and restaurant in the village (3 km).

Prices:	low season	F 600	**5 people**
	high season	F 650	*IGN 1*

Booking: Pas-de-Calais Loisirs Accueil **E**
62/65

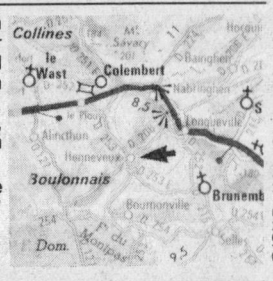

LOISON-SUR-CREQUOISE A modern house in its own enclosed garden near the village centre. Try the owners' home-cooked charcuterie. Visit Hesdin (18 km approx.), a pleasant little town with many historic buildings, a swimming-pool and Flemish tapestry museum. The coast (25 km). Living room/kitchenette, 2 bedrooms (1 double, 2 single beds), bathroom, fireplace, garage. Mobile baker, greengrocer and fishmonger call; other shops at 0.1 km or in Beaurainville (2 km) where there is a restaurant.

Prices:	low season	F 755	**4 people**
	high season	F 850	*IGN 1*

Booking: Pas-de-Calais Loisirs Accueil **E**
62/81

LORGIES A traditionally furnished house on a mixed farm where you may hire bicycles. A tennis court in the village (0.5 km); sailing at a lake (15 km). All the amenities of a major town at Béthune (15 km approx.). The coast is 80 km away. Living room (TV, 1 double divan), kitchen (washing machine), 2 bedrooms (1 double, 1 single bed), bathroom, fireplace, electric heating, garage, enclosed garden with outdoor furniture. Linen available. Mobile butcher and baker call; other shopping in the village or at La Bassée (4 km). A restaurant at 3 km.

Prices:	low season	F 580/650	**5 people**
	high season	F 700	*IGN 2*

Booking: Pas-de-Calais Loisirs Accueil **E**
62/59

MONTCAVREL A rustically furnished and renovated house on a mixed farm where the amenities include table tennis. At Etaples (15 km approx.), visit the house where Napoleon was received by Marshall Ney in 1804. Bathing and sailing at the coast (15 km). Living room/kitchenette (1 single divan), 2 bedrooms (2 double and 2 single beds), shower room, fireplace (wood supplied), electric central heating, open ground with child's swing. Mobile shops call; other shopping and restaurant in the village (2 km) or at Montreuil (6 km).

Prices:	low season	F 800	**7 people**
	high season	F 800	*IGN 1*

Booking: M G. BROUTIER, Ferme de Montéchor, Montcavrel, 62170 Montreuil-sur-Mer. Tel. (21) 06 04 05.
62/73

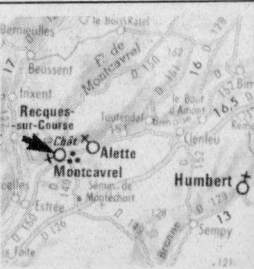

Pas-de-Calais

NORTKERQUE A small gîte, renovated and traditionally furnished, set in open ground, 1.5 km from the village centre. At Tournehem (7 km), the church boasts a very fine organ; there is a leisure park at the town with miniature golf and other attractions. The coast is at 20 km. Living room/kitchenette (1 double divan), 1 bedroom (1 double and 1 single bed), shower room, electric heating, garage, open ground. Mobile baker and butcher call; other shopping at 5 km or at Calais (17 km). A restaurant at 3 km.

Prices: low season   F 630   **5 people**
         high season   F 790   *IGN 1*
Booking: M M. REGNAULT-SAGOT, Haut-Locquin, 62850 Licques. Tel. (21) 39 62 17.
62/70

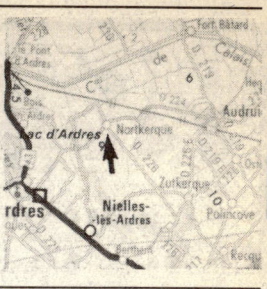

ROBECQ A renovated and rustically furnished gîte on a village farm, near a river where you can hire punts. Bicycles are also available for hire locally. Visit the old cathedral town of Saint-Omer (40 km approx.); other attractions there include an ornithological museum. Living room, kitchen, 1 bedroom (1 double, 6 single and 1 child's bed), shower room, fireplace, electric heating, open garden. Mobile butcher and baker call; farm produce and a restaurant in the village; other shopping at Saint-Venant (4 km).

Prices: low season   F 625/700   **9 people**
         high season   F 750   *IGN 2*
Booking: Mme TRINEL, 1284 rue de la Brasserie, Robecq, 62350 Saint-Venant. Tel. (21) 54 03 88.
62/77

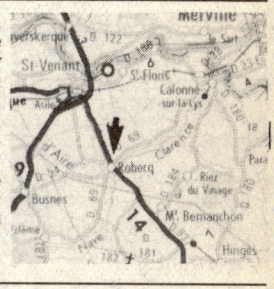

TORTEFONTAINE A spacious, renovated house with country-style furnishings on a mixed farm, 3 km from the village. Many leisure amenities at the interesting old town of Hesdin (8 km). Take a trip to the forest (11 km) or the sea (25 km). Living room (1 single divan), kitchen, 4 bedrooms (2 double, 4 single beds), bathroom, fireplace (wood supplied), electric heating, enclosed ground with garden furniture and barbecue. Shopping and a restaurant in the village.

Prices: low season   on request   **9 people**
         high season   on request   *IGN 1*
Booking: M P. RIGAUX, Tortefontaine, Saint-Josse-au-Bois, 62140 Hesdin. Tel. (21) 86 33 65.
62/84

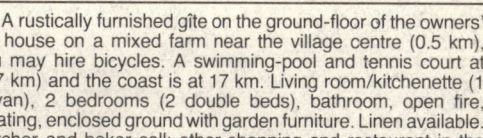

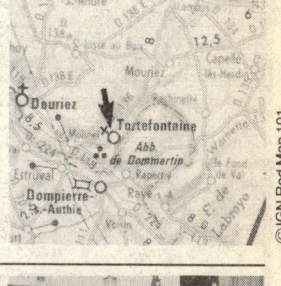

LE WAST A rustically furnished gîte on the ground-floor of the owners' renovated house on a mixed farm near the village centre (0.5 km), where you may hire bicycles. A swimming-pool and tennis court at Desvres (7 km) and the coast is at 17 km. Living room/kitchenette (1 double divan), 2 bedrooms (2 double beds), bathroom, open fire, electric heating, enclosed ground with garden furniture. Linen available. Mobile butcher and baker call; other shopping and restaurant in the village.

Prices: low season   F 750/1000   **6 people**
         high season   F 1100   *IGN 1*
Booking: Mme POYER, 31 rue de Crémarest, 62240 Desvres. Tel. (21) 91 70 06.
62/52

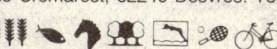

ZOUAFQUES Wolphus A ground-floor gîte with country-style furnishings in the owners' old house, 2 km from the village. The owners have four young children. Amenities at the gîte include table tennis. Tournehem leisure park is just 3 km away and the coast is an easy drive at 20 km. Living room (1 double divan), kitchen, 2 bedrooms (1 double, 3 single beds and a cot), shower room, central heating, terrace, carport, open ground with garden furniture. Linen available. Shops at 2 km or at Ardres (7 km); a restaurant (0.5 km).

Prices: low season   F 840/1050   **8 people**
         high season   F 1260   *IGN 1*
Booking: Pas-de-Calais Loisirs Accueil   **E**
62/78

PICARDY

One or two hours' drive from the channel ports of Calais and Boulogne will bring you to your Gîtes de France holiday house.

The region of Picardy, made up of 3 départements, Aisne, Oise and Somme, remains the closest French countryside for the British visitor.

This vast green region is an ideal starting-point, during your country holiday, for visits to Paris and many other well-known places.

ENQUIRIES:

Picardy Comité régional de Tourisme
    de Picardie
    B.P.0342-80003 AMIENS CEDEX
    Tél. (22) 92.64.64.

    Aisne booking service
    Comité départmental de Tourisme
    de l'Aisne
    1, rue Saint-Martin—02000 LAON
    Tél. (23) 23.24.53
    or (23) 23.34.37 (ext. 22)

    Somme booking service
    Comité départmental de Tourisme
    de la Somme
    21, rue Ernest-Cauvin—80000 AMIENS
    Tél. (22) 92.26.39.

Oise booking service
Comité départmental de Tourisme
de l'Oise
BP222, 1 Rue Villiers de l'Isle Adam
60008 BEAUVAIS Cedex
Tél. (4) 448.16.87

The countryside of Bray

2 PICARDY

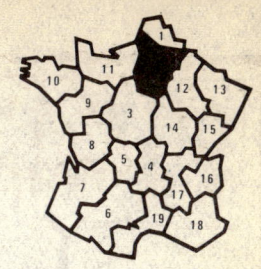

Linking Ile-de-France to the sandy coastline of the Channel, through large forests, green fields and vineyards, this readily accessible region has a diverse landscape of great attraction to both nature-lover and historian.

This is the home of Gothic Art, with six major cathedrals, 'Art Towns', artistic tours through the valleys of Bresle and Liger, châteaux, impressive town halls, stately homes, simple clay cottages, fortresses and the robust, fortified churches of Thiérache.

The varied coastline offers pleasant, family holidays at the resorts of Quend-Plage and Fort-Mahon-Plage, trips to bustling fishing ports such as Le Crotoy and Le Tréport and, in particular, to the port of Saint-Valéry-sur-Somme, from where William the Conqueror set sail in 1066. Ault-Onival and Mers-les-Bains, are attractive stretches of beach, backed by cliffs.

There is much to do and see in this ramblers' paradise, with marked footpaths through the Somme Valley, with its ponds and rivers, and moving inland you can explore the magnificent forests, with amazing Gothic buildings emerging from the landscape, every now and then. Enjoy horse-riding or take advantage of the many bicycle-hire centres and appreciate the scenery at your own pace, in this land of flat, green fields.

Compiègne forest is worthy of inclusion in your itinerary, here you can visit the Armistice Clearing, where signing of the Armistice took place. It was also here, by the town of Compiègne, that Joan of Arc, maid of Orléans, was finally captured. Further South, on the way to Paris, is the little town of Chantilly, which has gained world-wide fame on account of its race-course.

Before you leave, try to see one of the carnivals, which take place throughout the summer months. In May, there is a lively carnival at Amiens, a city renowned for its delicious *ficelle picarde* (savoury pancake) and duck pâté. The lively mediaeval market town of Gerberoy, near Beauvais, with its ancient houses and cobbled streets should not be missed, particularly in June, when its inhabitants celebrate the Festival of Roses and, in September, there is a cheese fair at La Capelle and a splendid mediaeval festival at Laon.

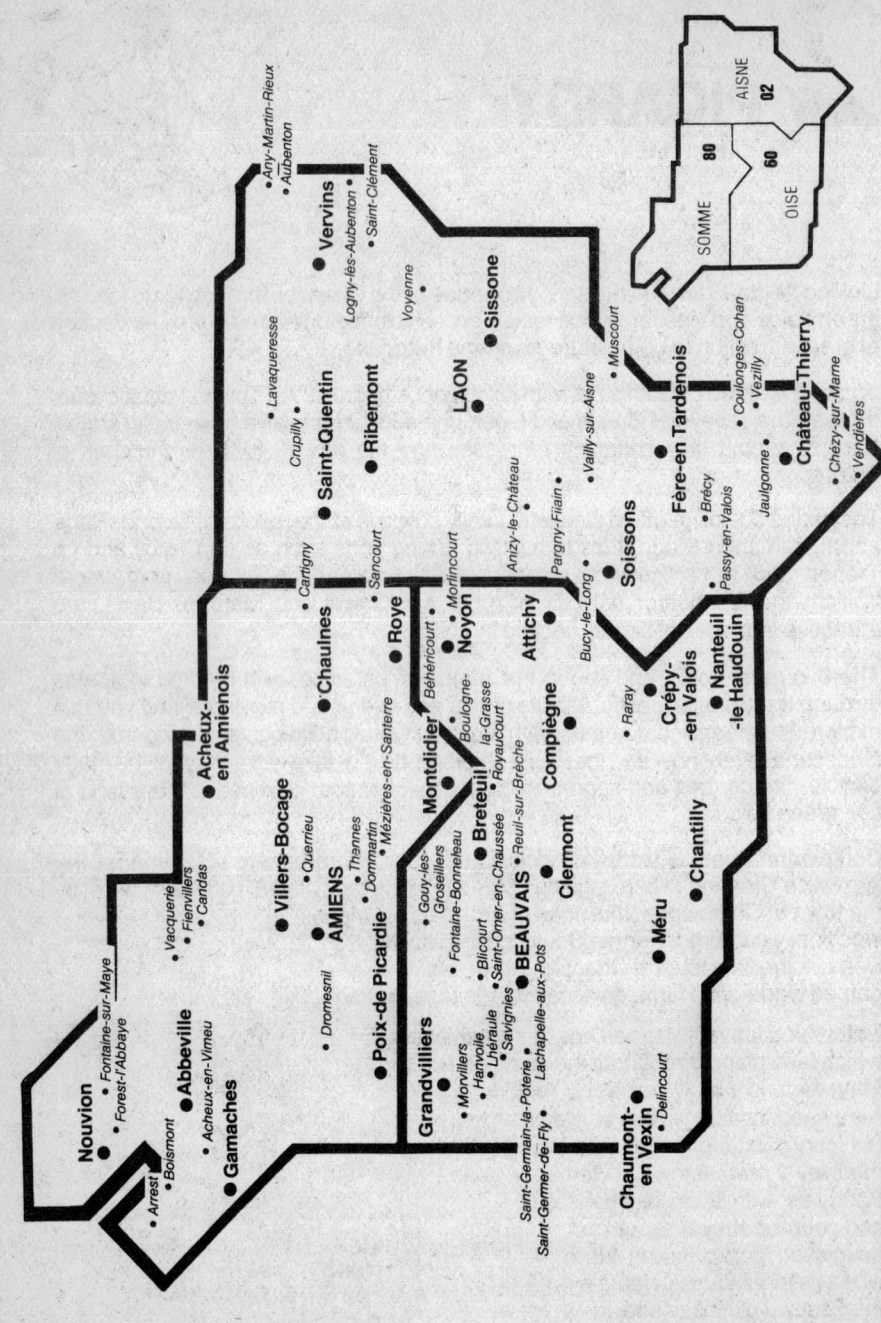

Aisne

ANIZY-LE-CHATEAU Moulin de l'Ocq A stone-built renovated and traditionally furnished mill on a fish farm where the owners have two other gîtes and chambres d'hôte. They may also hire horses. Bathing and sailing (10 km); bicycles for hire at the cathedral town of Laon (18 km). Living room/kitchenette, 2 bedrooms (1 double and 2 single beds), shower room, oil heating, carport, garden with outdoor furniture, children's swings. Mobile shops call; eggs and poultry from the owners, other shopping and restaurant in the village (2 km).

Prices: low season F 525/675   **4 people**
           high season F 675   *IGN 9*
Booking: Aisne booking service   E
02/1

ANY-MARTIN-RIEUX A small gîte, furnished in rustic style in a stone-built house near the village centre. Bicycles for hire at Hirson (10 km); other leisure facilities at Cady Park (13 km). In September, see the cheese festival at nearby La Capelle. Living room (1 double divan), kitchen, 2 bedrooms (2 double, 1 single, 1 child's bed and a cot), shower room, open fire, electric heating, garage, ground with garden furniture. Shopping and restaurant in the village (0.4 km).

Prices: low season F 525/600   **9 people**
           high season F 655   *IGN 5*
Booking: Aisne booking service   E
02/1031

AUBENTON A lovely old gîte with country-style furnishings and its own turret! It is near the village centre with good forest walks nearby (2 km). Visit the abbey church at Saint-Michel, all that remains of an important twelfth-century abbey; this is the Thiérache region, famed for its fortified churches. Living room/kitchenette, 2 bedrooms (4 single beds), shower room (washing machine), fireplace (wood supplied), electric central heating, enclosed ground. Farm produce, other shopping and restaurant in the village (0.2 km) or at Hirson (15 km).

Prices: low season F 510/610   **4 people**
           high season F 695   *IGN 5*
Booking: Aisne booking service   E
02/1049

AUBENTON Val La Caure A rustically furnished gîte on a mixed farm, 2 km from the village centre. There is a lake at 20 km. At the interesting old town of Vervins (30 km approx.), visit the Archaeological Museum of the Thiérache region. Living room/kitchenette (washing machine), 2 bedrooms (2 double, 1 single and 2 child's beds, 1 double divan), shower room, fireplace, electric heating, terrace, carport, ground with garden furniture and child's swing. Mobile baker and grocer call; other shopping in the village or at Hirson (10 km).

Prices: low season F 530/655   **9 people**
           high season F 655   *IGN 5*
Booking: Aisne booking service   E
02/1028

BRECY Ferme du Lucquet A well-renovated gîte on a farm where horses are raised by the owners who speak some English and have two children. It is less than an hour from Paris by motorway in the Marne valley (champagne cellars nearby are open to the public). Living room/kitchenette, 3 bedrooms (2 double and 2 single beds), shower room, open fire, electric heating, terrace, garage, garden with furniture. Linen available (F60 per set per month). Mobile shops call at the village (0.8 km); other shopping (5 km) or at Château-Thierry (15 km).

Prices: low season F 805/915   **6 people**
           high season F 1020   *IGN 9*
Booking: Aisne booking service   E
02/1052

Aisne

BUCY-LE-LONG A renovated cottage with country-style furnishings at the edge of the village and just one hour from Paris. Bicycles for hire at Soissons (5 km), a town almost completely rebuilt since the war, but with a well-restored Gothic cathedral. Sailing at a lake (15 km). Living room (1 double divan), kitchen, 1 bedroom (1 double bed), shower room, fireplace, electric heating, terrace, garden with furniture and barbecue. Linen available. Farm produce at Soissons market; other shopping and restaurant in the village (0.8 km).

Prices: low season   F 545/580   4 people
       high season F 675   IGN 9

Booking: Aisne booking service   E
02/1055

CHEZY-SUR-MARNE Les Roches A stone-built house, renovated and traditionally furnished on a vineyard where the owners will sell their own champagne. It is 2 km from the village and within easy reach of Paris. Château-Thierry (10 km) is the birthplace of "Fables" author, La Fontaine; there is a festival dedicated to him in June. Living room, kitchen, 3 bedrooms (1 double and 3 single beds), bathroom, fireplace, gas central heating, carport. Mobile shops call; other shopping and restaurant in the village or at Charly-sur-Marne (5 km approx.).

Prices: low season   F 630   5 people
       high season F 740   IGN 9

Booking: Aisne booking service   E
02/1018

COULONGES-COHAN A ground-floor gîte, renovated and furnished in simple country-style, in a former farmhouse, at the village centre. At Fère-en-Tardenois (10 km), see the early thirteenth-century château of the Dukes of Montmorency, and the pretty sixteenth-century market halls. Living room (1 double divan), kitchen, 3 bedrooms (4 double beds), bathroom, wood and oil stoves, carport, enclosed ground with garden furniture and child's swing. Mobile shops call; farm produce in the village; other shopping and restaurant at 1.5 km.

Prices: low season   F 525/580   8 people
       high season F 630   IGN 9

Booking: Aisne booking service   E
02/1032

CRUPILLY A delightful renovated house, typical of the region, with comfortable furnishings, situated on a village farm. River fishing (2 km) and bicycle hire at Marly-Gomont (5 km approx.). The gîte is near the verdant Thiérache region with good marked footpaths and horse riding trails. Living room, kitchen, 2 bedrooms (1 double, 3 single beds), shower room, electric heating, garden. Linen available. Mobile baker calls; other shopping at Guise (10 km).

Prices: low season   F 560   5 people
       high season F 715   IGN 4

Booking: Aisne booking service   E

02/37

JAULGONNE This renovated and traditionally furnished house is right at the centre of a village in the Marne valley. Historic Château-Thierry (13 km) is dominated by the ramparts of an eighth-century fort; leisure amenities there include a swimming-pool, water sports, riding and tennis. Living room (1 double divan), kitchen, 3 bedrooms (2 double, 2 single beds and a cot), bathroom, oil-fired central heating, terrace, garden. Farm produce, other shoppping and restaurant in the village.

Prices: low season   F 645   9 people
       high season F 805   IGN 9

Booking: Aisne booking service   E
02/1050

34

Aisne

LAVAQUERESSE A large, renovated house with traditional furnishings at the village centre. Visit the old medieval town of Guise (9 km) which has a fortified château and where you may hire bicycles; Godin stoves are manufactured there. Living room, kitchen, 4 bedrooms (2 double, 3 single and 1 child's bed), bathroom, fireplace, oil central heating, garage, garden. Mobile shops call; other shopping at Guise. A restaurant at 5 km.

Prices:	low season	F 590/630	**7/8 people**
	high season	F 675	IGN 4

Booking: Aisne booking service E

02/1042

LOGNY-LES-AUBENTONS Les Marquets A spacious house, renovated and furnished in rustic fashion, on a mixed farm, 2 km from the village. The vast Hirson forest is at 10 km. Bicycles for hire at the old town of Hirson (15 km) and canoes available for hire at Erloy. Living room (1 double divan), kitchen, 2 bedrooms (3 double, 1 single and 1 child's bed), bathroom, fireplace, electric heating, balcony, garden with outdoor furniture. Linen available. Eggs and poultry available from the owners; other shopping and a restaurant in the village.

Prices:	low season	F 535/580	**9/10 people**
	high season	F 740	IGN 5

Booking: Aisne booking service E

02/29

MUSCOURT A well-renovated, traditionally furnished cottage on a mixed farm outside the village. Fishing and bathing at a river (2 km); sailing at a lake (15 km). You are only 20 km from Reims, the centre of the champagne region and well worth a visit. Living room (TV, 1 single divan), kitchen (washing machine), 3 bedrooms (2 double, 2 single and 1 child's bed), bathroom, electric heating, open fire, garden with furniture. Mobile shops call, farm produce in the village; shopping and restaurant at 2km or at Fismes (10 km).

Prices:	low season	F 535/580	**7/8 people**
	high season	F 705	IGN 9

Booking: Aisne booking service E

02/1024

PARGNY-FILAIN A renovated and rustically furnished cottage set in parkland, right by the Monampteuil lake (0.25 km) where you may bathe and sail. See Vauclerc Abbey and the Caverne du Dragon museum, both at 10 km. Bicycles for hire at the lively town of Laon (13 km). Living room, kitchen, 3 bedrooms (1 double and 4 single beds), shower room, fireplace, oil-fired central heating, carport, garden with barbecue. Mobile shops call and farm produce in the village (0.4 km) which has a restaurant; other shopping at 2.5 km.

Prices:	low season	F 535/580	**6 people**
	high season	F 805	IGN 9

Booking: Aisne booking service E

02/1034

PASSY-EN-VALOIS A renovated and traditionally furnished village house. Visitors in May can see the art and craft fair in the village; there is also an apple fair in October at 6 km. Verdilly rural leisure centre is at 20 km. Living room, kitchen, 5 bedrooms (2 double, 2 single beds and 1 child's bed), bathroom, fireplace, central heating, carport, enclosed garden. Farm produce available; mobile butcher, baker and grocer call; other shopping and restaurant at La Ferté-Milon (6 km).

Prices:	low season	F 670	**7 people**
	high season	F 775	IGN 9

Booking: Aisne booking service E

02/1070

35

Aisne

SAINT-CLEMENT A pretty cottage which has been renovated and furnished in traditional, country style, on a mixed farm near the village centre. There is a local village festival, the last Sunday in May. Montcornet (10 km) boasts one of the finest fortified churches in the region. Living room, kitchen, 3 bedrooms (3 double, 1 single and 1 child's bed), shower room, fireplace, electric central heating, garden with child's swing. Mobile shops call; farm produce in the village and other shopping at Montcornet. A restaurant at 7 km.

Prices: low season F 535/620   8 people
       high season F 745   IGN 5
Booking: Aisne booking service E
02/1021

VAILLY-SUR-AISNE A large old house with traditional furnishings, typical of the region, at the town centre. Recreational facilities near the gîte include table tennis, volley ball and hire of bicycles and archery equipment. Sailing and wind-surfing at a lake (10 km). At historic Laon (21 km), do not miss the splendid twelfth-century cathedral. Living room (TV), kitchen (washing machine), 3 bedrooms (6 single beds), bathroom and shower, fireplace, gas central heating, garage, enclosed ground. Shopping and restaurant in the town or at Soissons (15 km).

Prices: low season F 535/695   6 people
       high season F 835   IGN 9
Booking: Aisne booking service E
02/1054

VENDIERES Villers-sur-l'Eau A spacious, renovated house with modern furnishings, on a sheep farm, 3 km from the village where the owners live with their two sons and will sell their home-made jam. Bicycles for hire at the farm; a swimming-pool at 25 km. Living room (1 double divan), kitchen, 3 bedrooms (2 double, 4 single and 1 child's bed, 1 cot), fireplace, central heating, carport, enclosed ground with garden furniture, barbecue and child's swing. Mobile baker and grocer call; other shopping and restaurant at Montmirail (8 km).

Prices: low season F 620/710   12 people
       high season F 765   IGN 9
Booking: Aisne booking service E
02/1060

VEZILLY A renovated gîte with modern furnishings in the village Mairie (town hall). At Fère-en-Tardenois (13 km) you can see the château originally built by the Duke of Montmorency in 1206 and restored in 1528. See also Dravegny Abbey (10 km). Living room (1 double divan), kitchen, 3 bedrooms (1 double, 4 single beds), shower room, electric central heating, garden and ground. Mobile shops call; farm produce and restaurant in the village or at Fère-en-Tardenois where you can shop.

Prices: low season F 540/505   8 people
       high season F 630   IGN 9
Booking: Aisne booking service E
02/1019

VOYENNE This delightful renovated cottage, with traditional furnishings, lies on a mixed farm in the village. The owners have three children. The medieval cathedral city of Laon, former capital of France where specialities include asparagus and chocolate, is at 20 km. Living room (1 single bed), kitchen, 2 bedrooms (1 double, 2 single and 1 child's bed), bathroom, open fire, electric central heating, open garden. Farm produce (including strawberries); other shopping and restaurant in the village at Marle-sur-Serre (14 km).

Prices: low season F 525   6 people
       high season F 715   IGN 4
Booking: Aisne booking service E
02/35

36

Country Food and Wine in AISNE

La Thiérache, in the north of Aisne with its patchwork landscape of fields and copses, is a region rich in farm produce and traditional country fare. For the discerning visitor, the Aisne Tourism Committee offers the opportunity of enjoying the accommodation, open-air activity and local cuisine of "the Green Walkway" (*l'Axe Vert*) of Thierache.

A former railway track, this is now a 40 km route for ramblers and cyclists which has 3 departmental hostels with 10 to 30 places, a rural *gîte*, and a camping site with low stop-over prices for young people. Bicycles can be hired at Marly-Gomont and canoes at Erloy and Luzoir on the river Oise.

For further details you should contact:

Comité Departemental de Tourisme de l'Aisne,
1 rue Saint-Martin, 02000 LAON.
Tel. 23.23.34.37.

Some of the specialities of La Thiérache can be found as follows:

Maroilles Cheese

Groupement des Producteurs Fermiers,
7 rue Maurice Hédon, 59219 ETROEUNGT.

Thiérache Farm Cider

C.E.A.U.R. Maison de la Thiérache,
7 rue Maurice Hédon, 59219 ETROEUNGT.
Tel. 27.61.19.21.

"Boutons d'Or" Confectionery

02170 LE NOUVION EN THIERACHE.

"Foie-gras"

Monsieur Bourquin,
Ferme Mon Idée,
Route de Baxzy,
02170 LE NOUVION EN THIERACHE.
Tel. 23.98.97.02.

"L'Escavèche"

M. Demaret,
La Neuve Forge,
02500 HIRSON.

FARM INNS

The "fermes-auberges" are farm inns where quality regional menus are offered. Two such inns in this region are recommended here – please note that advance booking by telephone is suggested.

Ferme-Auberge de la Brune

Monsieur Louvet,
Burelles,
02140 VERVINS.
Tel. 23.98.17.72.

Closed Mondays

Ferme-Auberge de Saint-Martin-Rivière

Monsieur Riquet,
Saint Martin Rivière,
02110 BOHAIN EN VERMANDOIS.
Tel. 23.63.18.13.

Open week-ends only

Oise

BEHERICOURT One of two simply furnished gîtes in an old village house, owned by the local council. Noyon (6 km) has a fine cathedral dating back to the twelfth century; Calvin's birthplace there is now a museum and the town boasts many leisure facilities. Living room/kitchenette, 2 bedrooms (1 double and 2 single beds), bathroom, central heating, garden. Mobile butcher, baker and delicatessen call; farm produce in the village; other shopping at Noyon.

Prices:	low season	F 404/477	**4 people**
	high season	F 559	IGN 4

Booking: Oise booking service   E

60/03

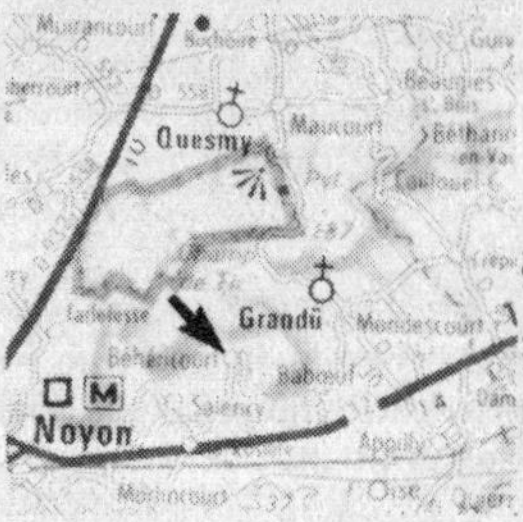

BEHERICOURT An old village house (owned by the local council), simply furnished and situated in its own garden. Tennis, riding and swimming-pool at historic Noyon in the Oise valley (6 km). Visit the ruined Cistercian abbey at Ourscamp nearby. Living room, kitchen, 2 bedrooms and open landing (1 double and 4 single beds), bathroom, central heating, garden. Mobile shops call; farm produce including milk, eggs, poultry and vegetables, in the village; other shopping and restaurant at Noyon.

Prices:	low season	F 404/477	**6 people**
	high season	F 559	IGN 4

Booking: Oise booking service   E

60/04

BLICOURT Regnonval A ground-floor gîte with country-style furnishings in an attractively renovated, half-timbered building in a hamlet, 2 km from the village. Bicycles for hire at Crèvecoeur-le-Grand (4 km) which has a fifteenth-century château. A swimming-pool at 12 km. Living room (TV, 1 double divan), kitchen, 2 bedrooms (1 double and 2 single beds, 1 child's cot), bathroom, fireplace, central heating, terrace, carport, enclosed ground with garden furniture. Linen available. Mobile baker calls; other shopping at Crèvecoeur-le-Grand.

Prices:	low season	F507/580	**7 people**
	high season	F 662	IGN 3

Booking: Oise booking service   E

60/28

BOULOGNE-LA-GRASSE An old, simply furnished gîte near the village centre. River fishing at 4 km; a swimming-pool at the old town of Montdidier (14 km), and other leisure facilities at the lovely old town of Noyon (22 km). Living room, kitchen, 2 bedrooms (1 double, 2 single beds and a child's cot), shower room, electric heating, enclosed garden. Fresh eggs, milk and poultry in the village; other shopping (2 km) or at Ressons-sur-Matz (15 km approx.).

Prices:	low season	F 456/528	**5 people**
	high season	F 610	IGN 4

Booking: Oise booking service   E

60/41

DELINCOURT A simply furnished gîte in an old village house, owned by the local council, where they also offer bed and breakfast accommodation. At Chaumont-en-Vexin (5 km), the sixteenth-century church has fine stained glass windows. A swimming-pool and tennis at 5 km. Living room/kitchenette (1 double divan), 1 bedroom (1 double bed and a child's bed), shower room, central heating, open ground. Linen available. Mobile butcher, charcutier and fishmonger call; shopping in the village and a restaurant at 5 km.

Prices:	low season	F 456/528	**5 people**
	high season	F 610	IGN 8

Booking: Oise booking service   E

60/13

Oise

FONTAINE-BONNELEAU Bonneleau A simply furnished gîte in an old house on a mixed farm where the owners also offer *table d'hôte* meals and have a stop-over gîte for riders and walkers as well as bed and breakfast accommodation. Bicycle hire, river fishing and walking on marked footpaths locally. Living room, kitchen, 2 bedrooms (3 double beds), bathroom, heating, carport, open courtyard with garden furniture. Linen available. Farm produce from the owners; other shopping and restaurant in the village (2.5 km) or at Crèvecoeur-le-Grand (10 km).

Prices:	low season	F 404/477	6 people
	high season	F 559	IGN 3

Booking: Oise booking service   E

60/07

GOUY-LES-GROSEILLERS A simply furnished gîte in the owners' old house on a village farm where you may buy fresh dairy produce. All the amenities of a major town at Beauvais (35 km approx.) where one of the most important sights, the former Bishop's Palace, is now a museum. Living room, kitchen, 2 bedrooms (2 double, 1 single and 2 child's beds), bathroom, coal-stove, carport, enclosed garden. Mobile shops call; other shopping at 2.5 km or at Breteuil (9 km).

Prices:	low season	F 456/528	7 people
	high season	F 610	IGN 3

Booking: Oise booking service   E

60/18

HANVOILE A pretty little cottage, renovated and simply furnished, near the owners' home at the village centre. At Beauvais (25 km approx.) the Saint-Pierre cathedral boasts the highest choir in the world; see also the National Tapestry Museum there. Living room/kitchenette, 2 bedrooms (1 double and 2 single beds), shower room, enclosed ground with garden furniture. Fresh farm produce and other shopping in the village or at Songeons (6 km).

Prices:	low season	F 456/528	4 people
	high season	F 610	IGN 3

Booking: Oise booking service   E

60/19

LACHAPELLE-AUX-POTS A simply furnished gîte in the garden of the owners' house, near the village centre (0.2 km). Saint-Paul leisure park (7 km) has facilities for fishing, pony rides, pedalo boats for hire and other children's amusements. Many other leisure and cultural amenities at Beauvais (15 km). Living room, kitchen, 1 bedroom (1 double and 1 single bed), shower room, central heating, use of the owners' garden. Farm produce, other shopping and restaurant in the village or at Beauvais.

Prices:	low season	F 404/477	3 people
	high season	F 559	IGN 3

Booking: Oise booking service   E

60/20

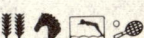

LHERAULE An attractive old house with country-style furnishings at the centre of the village. A swimming-pool, riding and tennis are all within 13 km. Beauvais (13 km) is noted for its manufacture of confectionery: try *Bellevâques* – cherries dipped in Grand Marnier and coated with chocolate. Living room (1 single divan), kitchen, 2 bedrooms (1 double and 3 single beds), bathroom, central heating, terrace, garage, garden with furniture. Linen available. Mobile shops call and farm produce in the village; other shopping and a restaurant at 4 km.

Prices:	low season	F 507/580	6 people
	high season	F 662	IGN 3

Booking: Oise booking service   E

60/21

Oise

MORLINCOURT One of two small, simply furnished gîtes in an old house at the village centre. Local river fishing. Visit the lovely old town of Compiègne (30 km approx.) and see the spot where the Armistice was signed in the forest at the end of the 1914-18 war. Living room/kitchenette, 1 bedroom (1 double bed), bathroom, central heating, enclosed garden. Mobile baker, butcher and delicatessen call; other shopping and restaurant at Noyon (3 km).

Prices:	low season	F 353/435	**2 people**
	high season	F 518	*IGN 4*

Booking: Oise booking service **E**

60/22

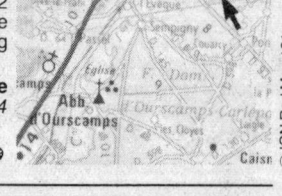

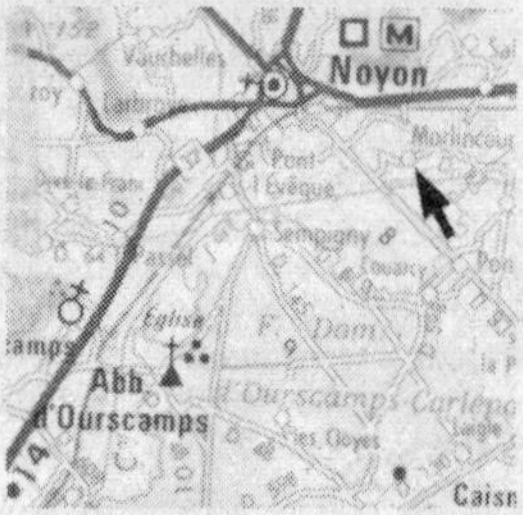

MORLINCOURT A second, simply furnished gîte in the old house described above, near the village centre and just 3 km from Noyon where there are many leisure and cultural amenities. At Compiègne (30 km approx.), see the eighteenth-century Palace, Automobile Museum and other sights. Living room/kitchenette, 2 bedrooms (1 double and 2 single beds), bathroom, central heating, garden. Fresh farm produce (milk, eggs and poultry) in the village; mobile shops call; other shopping and restaurant at Noyon.

Prices:	low season	F 404/477	**4 people**
	high season	F 559	*IGN 4*

Booking: Oise booking service **E**

60/23

MORVILLERS An old house with country-style furnishings at the village centre. Visit the nearby town of Gerberoy, the smallest fortified town in France, where a rose festival is held annually in June. A swimming-pool at 14 km. Living room/kitchenette (1 double divan), 3 bedrooms (2 double and 2 single beds), bathroom, wood stove, carport, enclosed courtyard and ground. Farm produce and other shopping in the village or at Songeons (4 km); a restaurant at 8 km.

Prices:	low season	F 456/528	**8 people**
	high season	F 610	*IGN 3*

Booking: Oise booking service **E**

60/24

RARAY A small, simply furnished gîte in a building which has been renovated by the local council, near the village centre where there is a seventeenth-century château. Senlis (10 km) is a well-preserved old city where sights include Roman ruins, the former royal château, cathedral and a hunting museum. Living room/kitchenette, 1 bedroom (1 double, 2 single and 1 child's bed), bathroom, central heating, enclosed courtyard. Linen available. Mobile shops and farm produce in the village; other shopping and restaurants at Senlis.

Prices:	low season	F 456/528	**5 people**
	high season	F 610	*IGN 9*

Booking: Oise booking service **E**

60/27

REUIL-SUR-BRECHE A well-renovated house with country-style furnishings, set in its own spacious garden in the village. A swimming-pool and riding at 16 km; many other leisure and cultural amenities at the busy department capital of Beauvais (20 km approx.). Living room/kitchenette (1 double divan), 2 bedroroms (1 double and 1 single bed, 1 child's cot), shower room, fireplace, central heating, enclosed garden with child's swing. Mobile shops call; farm produce in the village; other shopping and restaurant at Froissy (5 km).

Prices:	low season	F 507/580	**6 people**
	high season	F 662	*IGN 3*

Booking: Oise booking service **E**

60/29

Oise

ROYAUCOURT An old cottage with rustic furnishings at the village centre. River fishing and riding at 3 km. Take a trip to the lovely old town of Compiègne (35 km approx.) where interesting sights include the Palace where some of Napoleon I's apartments have been restored. Living room, kitchen, 2 bedrooms (2 double, 1 single bed and 2 cots), shower room, fireplace, central heating, carport, garden. Linen available. Farm produce from the owners; mobile shops call; other shopping and restaurant at Montdidier (5 km).

Prices:	low season	F 456/528	**7 people**
	high season	F 610	*IGN 4*

Booking: Oise booking service   **E**

60/31

SAINT-GERMAIN-LA-POTERIE A comfortable village house, renovated and furnished in rustic style. Saint-Paul leisure park is at 2 km; a riding stable at 3 km. Beauvais, on the river Thérain, is within easy reach at 9 km, where you will find plenty more leisure amenities. Living room/kitchenette, 1 bedroom (1 double, 2 single beds), bathroom, fireplace, electric heating, terrace, garage, garden with furniture. Linen available. Farm produce and other shopping in the village (0.5 km) or at Beauvais; mobile butcher calls.

Prices:	low season	F 507/580	**4 people**
	high season	F 662	*IGN 3*

Booking: Oise booking service   **E**

60/32

SAINT-GERMER-DE-FLY A modern house with country-style furnishings near the village centre where there is a *son-et-lumière* display at the abbey church once a month. Many leisure facilities at Gournay-en-Bray (5 km) and at the département capital of Beauvais (30 km approx.). Living room, kitchen, 2 bedrooms (1 double and 2 single beds, 1 child's cot), bathroom, fireplace, central heating, terrace, garage, garden with furniture. Fresh dairy produce, other shopping and restaurant in the village, or at Gournay-en-Bray.

Prices:	low season	F 507/580	**5 people**
	high season	F 662	*IGN 8*

Booking: Oise booking service   **E**

60/34

SAINT-OMER-EN-CHAUSSEE An attractive old house with rustic furnishings, set in its own garden with outdoor furniture, near the town centre. A river where you may fish at the property. See the seventeenth-century château at Marseille-en-Beauvais nearby. Living room (1 double divan), kichen, 3 bedrooms (1 double and 3 single beds), bathroom and shower, fireplace, central heating. Fresh farm produce (milk, eggs and poultry), other shopping and restaurant in the village or at Beauvais (13 km).

Prices:	low season	F 507/580	**7 people**
	high season	F 662	*IGN 3*

Booking: Oise booking service   **E**

60/35

SAVIGNIES A spacious old house, simply furnished and lying at the town centre. Fishing and other facilities at Saint Paul leisure park (5 km). At Beauvais (9 km), visit the fine cathedral, museums and the eleventh-century Saint-Etienne church with its much-admired stained glass windows. Living room (1 double divan), kitchen, 3 bedrooms (2 double, 2 single beds), shower room, heating, enclosed garden. Local farm produce available; other shopping and restaurants at Beauvais.

Prices:	low season	F 353/435	**8 people**
	high season	F 518	*IGN 3*

Booking: Oise booking service   **E**

60/36

Somme

RESERVATION LOISIRS ACCUEIL

With a coastline which alternates between chalk cliffs and sandy beaches and a countryside where pastures and plains, bushes and forests, rivers and ponds exist side by side, the Somme appears like an enormous patchwork tapestry. The unspoilt estuary of the Somme is an ideal place for nature lovers to enjoy the wide variety of plants and wildfowl. The Marquenterre Bird Sanctuary is well worth a visit. Numerous architectural monuments remain in spite of occupations and conflicts: prehistoric and Gallo-Romanic sites, magnificent Gothic buildings, military relics from every epoch. They are evidence of the rich and eventful history of this diverse region.

Close to the channel ports, the Somme offers visitors a whole range of leisure activities from sailing and wind-surfing to exploring the area from the air in a small plane. Anglers will enjoy the many miles of streams and fishing in ponds and lakes. Many craftsmen in the area organize courses for the visitors to learn basket-making, pottery, weaving, carving, or puppet-making. No matter how long you plan to stay in the region, the Somme will offer a wide and varied choice of holiday activities.

For booking and any further information about holidays in the Somme contact:

COMITÉ DÉPARTEMENTAL DU TOURISME DE LA SOMME
21 rue Ernest Cauvin
80000 AMIENS   **Tel.** (22) 92.26.39.
             Telex 140 754.

NB for fuller information about all Loisirs Accueil services, please see pages 12–13 of this guide.

Somme

ACHEUX-EN-VIMEU Frières A renovated house with traditional, country-style furnishings, 1 km from the village centre. Abbeville (12 km approx.) is a busy river port and a pleasant town with modern shopping facilities and good leisure amenities. The coast is just 20 km away. Living room, kitchen, 3 bedrooms (2 double and 2 single beds), bathroom, central heating, enclosed courtyard. Mobile baker, butcher and grocer call; other shopping and a restaurant at Chépy (5 km).

Prices:	low season	F 450/540	**6 people**
	high season	F 750/790	IGN 3

Booking: M G. BOUVET, Frières, 80210 Acheux-en-Vimeu.
Tel. (22) 26 20 15.

80/79.063

ARREST Just 7 km from the sea, this spacious house has been renovated and furnished in traditional, country style. Saint-Valéry-sur-Somme (7 km) is an attractive old fortified town with a fishing and pleasure harbour—William the Conqueror set sail for England from there in 1066. Living room (TV), kitchen, 3 bedrooms (3 double, 1 single and 1 child's bed), bathroom, gas heating, courtyard and lawn with child's swing. Farm produce, shopping and restaurant in the town (0.1 km) or at Saint-Valéry-sur-Somme.

Prices:	low season	F 650	**7/8 people**
	high season	F 750	IGN 1

Booking: M G. CORBEAU, Place Delahaye, 80820 Arrest.
Tel. (22) 27 55 16.
80/78.012

BOISMONT A renovated village house, furnished in traditional, rustic fashion, 4 km from Saint-Valéry-sur-Somme where you may hire bicycles; other leisure facilities there include miniature golf and yachting. There is an ornithological park at 12 km and a forest (12 km). Living room/kitchenette (1 single divan), 2 bedrooms (2 double and 1 child's bed), shower room, open fire, heating, enclosed garden. Farm produce in the village; other shopping and restaurant at Saint-Valéry-sur-Somme.

Prices:	low season	F 480/590	**5/6 people**
	high season	F 800/860	IGN 1

Booking: M J. FORESTIER, 24 rue Louis de Rainvillers, Boismont, 80230 Saint-Valéry-sur-Somme. Tel. (22) 27 56 61.
80/84.008

CANDAS Val Heureux A charming cottage which has been renovated and traditionally furnished in an isolated hamlet where ponies are bred. Fishing in the Authie valley (10 km). A swimming-pool at Doullens (12 km) where you can visit the Lombard Museum of oriental antiquities. The sea (50 km). Living room, kitchen, 4 bedrooms (1 double, 4 single and 1 child's bed), bathroom, fireplace, central heating, enclosed ground. Shopping in the village (4 km) or at Talmas (10 km) where there is a restaurant.

Prices:	low season	F 430/570	**6/7 people**
	high season	F 670/765	IGN 3

Booking: Somme Loisirs Accueil **E**
80/78.027

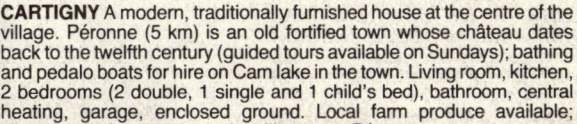

CARTIGNY A modern, traditionally furnished house at the centre of the village. Péronne (5 km) is an old fortified town whose château dates back to the twelfth century (guided tours available on Sundays); bathing and pedalo boats for hire on Cam lake in the town. Living room, kitchen, 2 bedrooms (2 double, 1 single and 1 child's bed), bathroom, central heating, garage, enclosed ground. Local farm produce available; shopping and restaurant in the village or at Péronne.

Prices:	low season	F 420/500	**6 people**
	high season	F 650/750	IGN 4

Booking: Mme JONVILLE, Grand Rue, Cartigny, 80200 Péronne.
Tel. (22) 86 97 04.
80/78.028

Somme

DOMMARTIN A renovated house with traditional, country-style furnishings, bordering a river where you may fish. There is a leisure complex at Ailly-sur-Noye (5 km) in a pleasant spot with a lake (pedalo boats), tennis and miniature golf. A swimming-pool at 12 km. Living room, kitchen, 3 bedrooms (2 double, 1 single and 1 child's bed), bathroom, solid fuel stove, garden. Mobile shops call and farm produce in the village; other shopping and a restaurant at Boves (4 km).

Prices: low season   F 370/480   **6 people**
          high season   F 650   *IGN 4*

Booking: M D. MARTIN, 21 rue Chevalier de la Barre, 80330 Longueau. Tel. (22) 46 32 06.

80/84.001

DROMESNIL A renovated and traditionally furnished gîte at the centre of the village. At Amiens (30 km approx.), see France's largest cathedral with its superb rose window; the département capital also offers all kinds of leisure and cultural amenities. The coast is at 50 km. Living room, kitchen, 2 bedrooms (1 double, 3 single beds), bathroom, fireplace, garden and courtyard. Mobile butcher, grocer and baker call; farm produce in the village; other shopping and restaurant at Hornoy-le-Bourg (5 km).

Prices: low season   F 420/500   **5 people**
          high season   F 710   *IGN 3*

Booking: Mme DE BEAUVILLE, 16 Boulevard Péreire, 75017 Paris. Tel. (1) 763 84 98.

80/81.009

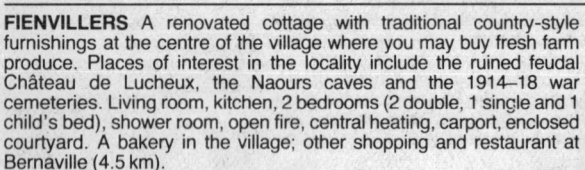

FIENVILLERS A renovated cottage with traditional country-style furnishings at the centre of the village where you may buy fresh farm produce. Places of interest in the locality include the ruined feudal Château de Lucheux, the Naours caves and the 1914–18 war cemeteries. Living room, kitchen, 2 bedrooms (2 double, 1 single and 1 child's bed), shower room, open fire, central heating, carport, enclosed courtyard. A bakery in the village; other shopping and restaurant at Bernaville (4.5 km).

Prices: low season   F 360/490   **6 people**
          high season   F 690/710   *IGN 3*

Booking: Mme L. VAST, 103 rue de la Gare, 80750 Candas. Tel. (22) 77 05 03.

80/78.030

FONTAINE-SUR-MAYE A renovated and traditionally furnished house, situated in a pretty garden at the village centre, 3 km from the Crécy forest, scene of the famous Battle of Crécy (1346). The gîte is just 20 km from the Channel coast, and Abbeville (25 km approx.) offers all the amenities of a large town. Living room, kitchen, 2 bedrooms (2 double and 1 child's bed), shower room, fireplace, oil stove, garage, garden with outdoor furniture. Mobile baker and butcher call; other shopping at Crécy-en-Ponthieu (3 km).

Prices: low season   F 550/580   **5 people**
          high season   F 780/830   *IGN 1*

Booking: M J. MACHY, Fontaine-sur-Maye, 80150 Crécy-en-Ponthieu. Tel. (22) 23 50 47.

80/82.019

FOREST-L'ABBAYE A traditionally furnished gîte in a renovated house on a mixed farm where the owners also offer bed-and-breakfast accommodation and holidays for unaccompanied children. It is situated in the village at the edge of the Crécy forest and just 15 km from the coast. Plenty of leisure amenities at Abbeville (12 km). Living room/kitchenette, 2 bedrooms (1 double, 2 single and 1 child's bed), bathroom, central heating, small enclosed garden. Farm produce available; other shopping at Nouvion-en-Ponthieu (2 km).

Prices: low season   F 370/535   **5 people**
          high season   F 700   *IGN 1*

Booking: M M. BECQUET, 161 rue des Templiers, Forest-l'Abbaye, 80150 Crécy-en-Ponthieu. Tel. (22) 28 30 66.

80/78.032

Somme

MEZIERES-EN-SANTERRE A traditionally furnished gîte in the owners' renovated house on a mixed farm in the village. There is a swimming-pool at Le Castel (6 km); riding and forest walks at 12 km. The gîte is not more than 120 km from Paris. Living room (1 single divan), kitchen, 1 bedroom (1 double bed), bathroom, open fire, central heating, garage, enclosed garden. Farm produce available locally; mobile butcher, baker and grocer call; other shopping at Moreuil (5 km) and a restaurant in the village.

Prices:	low season	F 420	**3 people**
	high season	F 600/620	IGN 4

Booking: Somme Loisirs Accueil E
80/78.009

QUERRIEU A renovated detached house with traditional, country-style furnishings outside the village where there is a golf course. At Amiens (13 km) visit the *hortillonages*—unusual market gardens situated on a network of canals where you may hire a boat to go shopping for fresh fruit and vegetables. Living room, kitchen, 3 bedrooms (1 double, 2 single beds), bathroom, fireplace, heating, enclosed garden. Farm produce, shopping and restaurant in the village (1 km) or at Amiens.

Prices:	low season	F 420/540	**4 people**
	high season	F 720/780	IGN 4

Booking: Mme A. MESNARD, 80115 Querrieu. Tel. (22) 48 00 01.

80/78.048

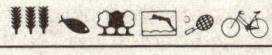

SANCOURT A renovated and traditionally furnished cottage, 0.5 km from the village centre. The owners' children have a duck farm and specialise in the production of *foie gras*. A leisure centre at Offoy (2 km). Ham (3 km) is an important port on the river Somme. Living room (1 single divan), kitchen, 2 bedrooms (2 double beds), bathroom, open fire, garage, open ground. Farm produce (including *foie gras* available), mobile shops call; other shopping and restaurant at Ham.

Prices:	low season	F 412/525	**5 people**
	high season	F 660	IGN 4

Booking: M. DELORMES, rue de l'Eglise, Sancourt, 80400 Ham. Tel. (23) 81 10 21.

80/81.018

THENNES A village gîte, renovated and furnished in traditional country style. There is a leisure complex at Le Castel (5 km) and many other amenities at Amiens (15 km approx.) where you can visit the Madeleine cemetery—actually a very beautiful park—and see the tomb of Jules Verne. Living room, kitchen, 4 bedrooms (2 double, 2 single and 1 child's bed), bathroom, open fire, heating, garage, garden. Farm produce available and mobile shops call; other shopping at Moreuil (4 km) and a restaurant in the village (1 km).

Prices:	low season	F 450/555	**6/7 people**
	high season	F 730/785	IGN 4

Booking: M G. BOUQUEZ, 12 rue Jacques Hodin, Thennes, 80110 Moreuil. Tel. (22) 42 20 31.

80/78.055

VACQUERIE One of two traditionally furnished gîtes in an attractively renovated house on a village farm. The Pré Marquotte leisure complex at Occoches (10 km) offers a swimming-pool, riding and tennis. Amiens is approx. 25 km away and the Channel coast 40 km approx. Living room/kitchenette, 2 bedrooms (2 double, 1 single and 1 child's bed), shower room, fireplace, central heating, carport, enclosed courtyard. Mobile butcher and baker call; fresh dairy produce in the village; other shopping at Bernaville (3 km).

Prices:	low season	F 400/475	**5/6 people**
	high season	F 650/710	IGN 3

Booking: M J. DERAMECOURT, Epecamps, 80370 Bernaville. Tel. (22) 32 71 99.

80/78.058

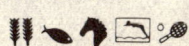

3 CENTRE VAL-DE-LOIRE

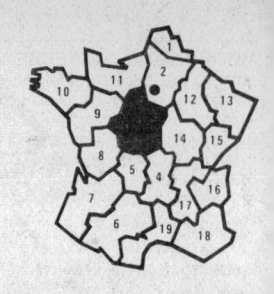

This is the undisputed "Château country" of France which entices visitors to linger much longer than they perhaps originally intended. The fabulous Châteaux of Chenonceaux, Chambord, Amboise, Blois, to name but a handful, are absolutely spell-binding, ranging from mediaeval fortresses to fairytale castles spread the length of the great river Loire which runs all the way from the Massif Central to the Atlantic.

However, apart from its châteaux, the Centre – Val-de-Loire has much of historical interest to offer. In the Middle Ages the main pilgrim routes to Spain and the south passed through here, making Chartres and Tours in particular, important resting places. Angers rose to importance in the twelfth century as the home of the Plantagenets and Orléans is, of course, inextricably associated with the famous "Maid of Orléans", Joan of Arc.

But the Centre — Val-de-Loire is not just a haven for "culture vultures". Not without reason is it called the "Garden of France". Its gentle climate provides the ideal conditions for the production of peaches, pears, apples and, of course, the vines. Loire wines, with their distinctive flavour, are now very much appreciated by the British. A natural accompaniment to the wines is, of course, cheese and a local speciality is the *crottin de Chavignol*, goat's cheese.

Of particular tourist interest in the summer are the many spectacular *son-et-lumière* performances at various châteaux, including Amboise, Azay-le-Rideau, Chinon and many more; the Joan of Arc festival at Orléans and many local festivals.

Map of central France region

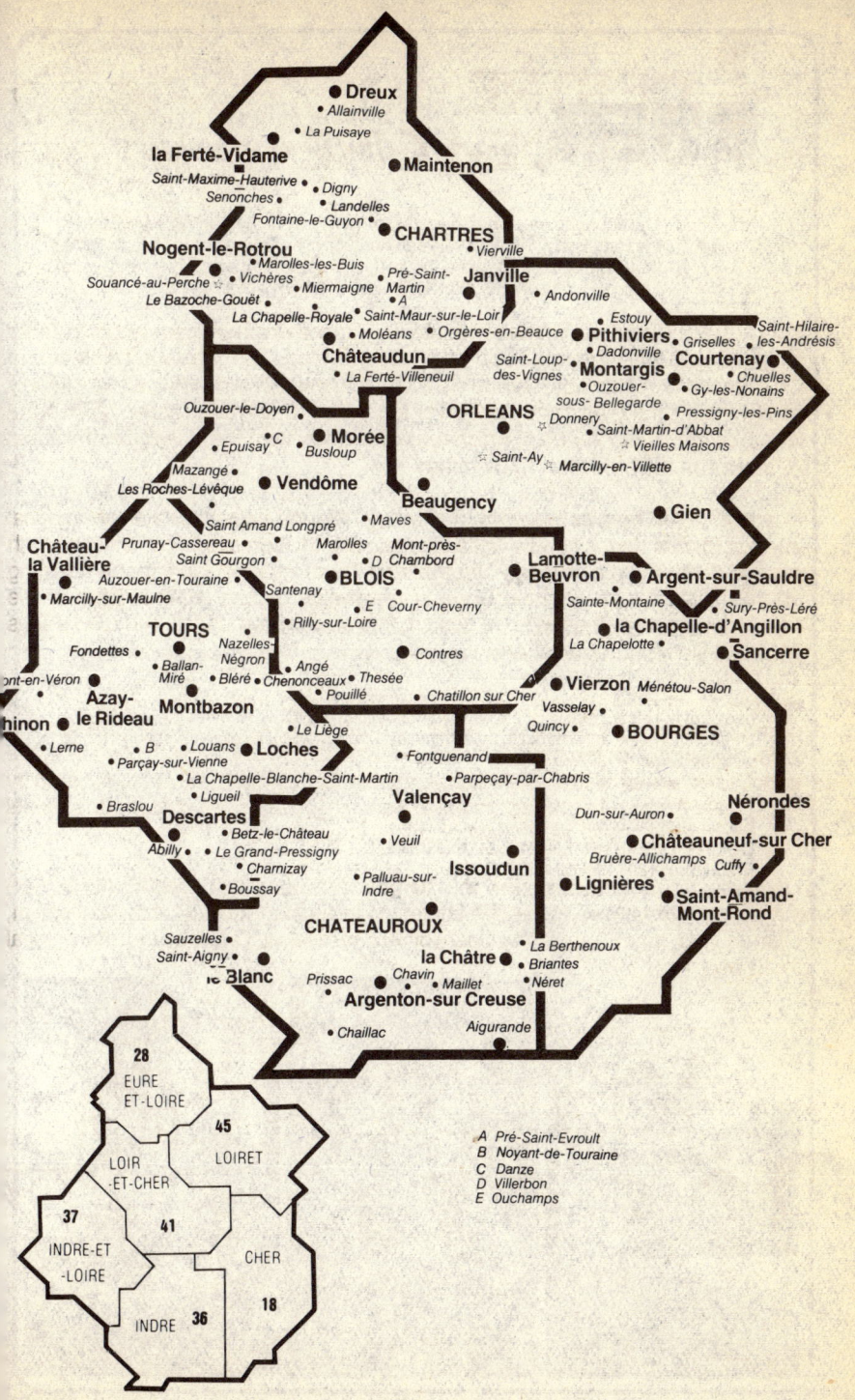

Cities and towns shown on map:

- Dreux
- Allainville
- La Puisaye
- la Ferté-Vidame
- Saint-Maxime-Hauterive
- Maintenon
- Digny
- Landelles
- Senonches
- Fontaine-le-Guyon
- CHARTRES
- Nogent-le-Rotrou
- Vierville
- Marolles-les-Buis
- Pré-Saint-Martin
- Janville
- Souancé-au-Perche
- Vichères
- Miermaigne
- A
- Andonville
- Le Bazoche-Gouët
- Saint-Maur-sur-le-Loir
- Estouy
- Saint-Hilaire-les-Andrésis
- La Chapelle-Royale
- Moléans
- Orgères-en-Beauce
- Pithiviers
- Dadonville
- Grisélles
- Courtenay
- Châteaudun
- Saint-Loup-des-Vignes
- Montargis
- Chuelles
- La Ferté-Villeneuil
- Ouzouer-sous-Bellegarde
- Gy-les-Nonains
- ORLEANS
- Pressigny-les-Pins
- Ouzouer-le-Doyen
- Donnery
- Saint-Martin-d'Abbat
- Morée
- Vieilles Maisons
- Epuisay
- C
- Busloup
- Saint-Ay
- Marcilly-en-Villette
- Mazangé
- Les Roches-Lévêque
- Vendôme
- Beaugency
- Gien
- Château-la Vallière
- Saint Amand Longpré
- Maves
- Marolles
- Mont-près-Chambord
- Lamotte-Beuvron
- Argent-sur-Sauldre
- Prunay-Cassereau
- Saint Gourgon
- D
- Auzouer-en-Touraine
- Santenay
- BLOIS
- Sainte-Montaine
- Sury-Près-Léré
- Marcilly-sur-Maulne
- Rilly-sur-Loire
- E
- Cour-Cheverny
- la Chapelle-d'Angillon
- TOURS
- Nazelles-Négron
- La Chapelotte
- Sancerre
- Fondettes
- Ballan-Miré
- Ангé
- Chenonceaux
- Contres
- Vierzon
- Ménétou-Salon
- ont-en-Véron
- Bléré
- Thésée
- Vasselay
- Azay-le Rideau
- Pouillé
- Chatillon sur Cher
- Quincy
- BOURGES
- hinon
- Lerne
- B
- Le Liège
- Fontguenand
- Montbazon
- Louans
- Parçay-sur-Vienne
- Loches
- Parpeçay-par-Chabris
- Nérondes
- Braslou
- La Chapelle-Blanche-Saint-Martin
- Valençay
- Dun-sur-Auron
- Ligueil
- Veuil
- Châteauneuf-sur-Cher
- Descartes
- Betz-le-Château
- Bruère-Allichamps
- Cuffy
- Abilly
- Le Grand-Pressigny
- Palluau-sur-Indre
- Issoudun
- Lignières
- Saint-Amand-Mont-Rond
- Charnizay
- Boussay
- CHATEAUROUX
- Sauzelles
- La Berthenoux
- Saint-Aigny
- la Châtre
- Briantes
- le Blanc
- Prissac
- Chavin
- Maillet
- Néret
- Argenton-sur-Creuse
- Chaillac
- Aigurande

Legend:
- A Pré-Saint-Evroult
- B Noyant-de-Touraine
- C Danze
- D Villerbon
- E Ouchamps

Departments (inset map):
- 28 EURE-ET-LOIRE
- 45 LOIRET
- 41 LOIR-ET-CHER
- 37 INDRE-ET-LOIRE
- 36 INDRE
- 18 CHER

CHER, *part of the Berry country ...*

The département of the Cher, 200 km from Paris was known in former times as the Haut Berry. Situated between Burgundy, the Touraine and the Auvergne, the Cher offers its visitors the perfect combination for country holidays in France: Rural tourism, cultural tourism and countryside leisure activities.

RURAL TOURISM IN HAUT BERRY
The owners of the 70 varied *gîtes de France* throughout the département will extend a warm welcome in typical Berry style. Here you will find all the countryside's charms as well as peace and fresh air – real holidays in a simple, unsophisticated country setting.

CULTURAL TOURISM IN HAUT BERRY
200 châteaux, the cathedral at Bourges, the Palace of Jacques Coeur, the Abbey of Noirlac – these are just some of the historic sites that will give you a glimpse of the history of this region.

ACTIVITIES IN HAUT BERRY
You will find everything you could wish for in the way of sports and hobbies: you may hunt, fish, swim, go small boating, riding gliding, or play tennis.
If you just wish to relax, then enjoy the green countryside, forests, pools, rivers and lakes that you will find all around you.

Last, but not least, here you can taste the marvellous SANCERRE wines in our *Caves de Dégustation*, and don't forget to try a *crottin de Chavignol*, our local goats' cheese, along with the wine!

For all information, write to:
COMITE DEPARTEMENTAL DE TOURISME DU CHER
Préfecture, 18014 BOURGES, Cedex
France.
Tel. (48) 24 14 95.

Cher

BRUERE-ALLICHAMPS Noirlac A renovated, single-storey gîte in the hamlet of Noirlac which was built up around its Cistercian abbey, founded in 1150, and still inhabited today. Bicycles for hire at Saint-Amand-Mont-Rond (4 km) which has a folk museum and other leisure amenities. Living room (1 single divan), kitchen, 2 bedrooms (1 double, 2 single beds), bathroom, central heating, carport, enclosed garden with furniture. Mobile baker and butcher call; a restaurant in the hamlet; other shopping at Saint-Amand-Mont-Rond.

Prices:	low season	F 675/735	**5 people**
	high season	F 785	IGN 35

Booking: Cher booking service E

18/038.01

LA CHAPELOTTE Les Debains A renovated and traditionally furnished cottage, 3.6 km from the village centre, near a forest. Sancerre (22 km), noted for its white wine, is a lovely old town of narrow winding streets with a fifteenth-century keep and superb views of the Loire and surrounding countryside. Living room/kitchenette, 3 bedrooms (1 double, 3 single and 1 child's bed), bathroom, fireplace (wood supplied), central heating, garage, open courtyard. Shopping and restaurant at Henrichemont (12 km).

Prices:	low season	F 615/765	**6 people**
	high season	F 910	IGN 27

Booking: Cher booking service E

18/051.01

CUFFY Les Fourmis A small, modern gîte with country-style furnishings in a hamlet, 1.8 km from the village. See the floral gardens and museum at Apremont (8 km). Nevers, famous for its porcelain industry, is at 10 km. Visit the European cattle market on Wednesday mornings at Sancoins (23 km). Living room (1 double divan), kitchen, 1 bedroom (1 double, 2 single beds), bathroom, fireplace (wood supplied), enclosed courtyard. Mobile shops call; a restaurant in the village or at Nevers which has good shopping facilities.

Prices:	low season	F 855	**6 people**
	high season	F 965	IGN 36

Booking: Cher booking service E

18/082.02

DUN-SUR-AURON La Douée Situated on an arable crops farm, 5 km from the village centre, this traditionally furnished gîte has been attractively renovated. Saint-Amand-Mont-Rond (21 km) is a lovely agricultural town in the Cher valley which grew up around a ninth-century monastery. Sailing at 25 km. Living room, kitchen, 2 bedrooms (1 double, 2 single beds), central heating, terrace, open garden with furniture. Shopping and restaurant in the village.

Prices:	low season	F 680	**4 people**
	high season	F 790	IGN 35

Booking: Cher booking service E

18/087.01

MENETOU-SALON A spacious gîte in a renovated house at the centre of the town, but with forest walks nearby (0.5 km). Bourges (19 km), capital of the département, is a lovely old town, with a splendid Gothic cathedral, other fine buildings and many leisure amenities. Bathing and sailing at a lake (19 km). Living room, kitchen, 4 bedrooms (2 double, 2 single and 2 child's beds), bathroom, oil-fired central heating, courtyard. Farm produce, shopping and restaurant in the town where the owners also have another gîte.

Prices:	low season	F 750/820	**6/8 people**
	high season	F 1030	IGN 27

Booking: Cher booking service E

18/145.01

Cher

MENETOU-SALON A renovated and traditionally furnished house at the town centre. At Bourges (19 km), see the Palais Jacques Coeur, a mansion built in the fifteenth century with a remarkable degree of comfort for its time; and the Hôtel de Ville (the former Archbishop's Palace) with its garden laid out by Le Nôtre. Living room (1 double divan), kitchen, 2 bedrooms (1 double, 1 single, 1 child's bed), shower room, fireplace, central heating, carport, garden with furniture. Shopping and restaurant in the town.

Prices:	low season	F 615/770	**5/6 people**
	high season	F 830	IGN 27

Booking: Cher booking service   E

18/145.06

QUINCY A renovated and traditionally furnished gîte in a village where wine cellars offer tastings to the public. Bathing and sailing at 4 km. Mehun-sur-Yevre (5 km) is noted for its porcelain. At Vierzon (15 km), see the beautiful gardens of the former abbey. Living room, kitchen, 2 bedrooms (1 double, 2 single and 1 child's folding bed), shower room, heating, enclosed garden with barbecue. Shopping and restaurant in the village.

Prices:	low season	F 445	**4/5 people**
	high season	F 565	IGN 27

Booking: Cher booking service   E

18/190.02

SAINT-MONTAINE Les Clergeries An attractive, traditionally furnished cottage on an arable farm, 3.8 km from the village centre. A swimming-pool and tennis at Aubigny-sur-Nère (13 km) where you should see the sixteenth-century château of the Stuarts and other fine old buildings. Bathing and sailing at a lake (23 km). Living room, kitchen, 3 bedrooms (1 double and 4 child's beds), shower room, fireplace, heating, garage, extensive open grounds with furniture and barbecue. Shopping at 4.5 km; a restaurant in the village.

Prices:	low season	F 870/1055	**2/6 people**
	high season	F 1185	IGN 27

Booking: Cher booking service   E

18/227.01

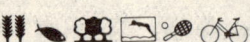

SURY-PRES-LERE Le Petit Mousseret A small, renovated cottage on a cereal crops farm. Good leisure facilities, including sailing, at Saint-Thibault (19 km) on the river Loire. Visit, too, the lovely old town of Sancerre (22 km), perched high above the Loire where the fifteenth-century keep is all that remains of its château. Living room/kitchenette (1 double divan), 2 bedrooms (2 double, 1 single bed), shower room, fireplace (wood supplied), central heating, open ground. Shopping and restaurant in the village (2 km) or at Léré (5 km).

Prices:	low season	F 735	**7 people**
	high season	F 790	IGN 27

Booking: Cher booking service   E

18/257.01

VASSELAY Fontland A renovated, traditionally furnished house on a mixed farm (where you may buy fresh produce from the owners), 3 km from the village. It is just 9 km from the fine old town of Bourges which has a swimming-pool and tennis court amongst its many facilities. Bathing and sailing at a lake (9 km). Living room, kitchen, 3 bedrooms (1 double, 2 single and 1 child's bed; folding bed available), bathroom, electric and wood heating, garage, garden. Mobile butcher, baker and grocer call; other shopping and restaurant in the village.

Prices:	low season	F 850	**4/5 people**
	high season	F 960	IGN 27

Booking: Cher booking service   E

18/271.01

On the Road to the Sun
EURE~ET~LOIRE

- at the crossroads of Normandy, Paris and the châteaux country
- Chartres, its countryside and its magnificent cathedral
- The Perche, green hills and country houses
- The Beauce, a rich prairie land, speckled with windmills
- The Thymerais, and its forests
- The Dunois, watered by the Loire and its tributaries
- The Eure Valley, lying between the great châteaux of Anet and Maintenon

To welcome you in the countryside:

  65 gîtes de France
  15 gîtes-chambres d'hôtes
   2 stopover gîtes in riding centres
   2 gîtes offering special interest holidays –
     pottery and painting
   6 farm camp-sites
   1 riverside camp-site
     luxury hotels, 1–4 star
  33 camp-sites

Rambling in the woods and countryside, fishing in rivers and ponds, sailing centres, music festivals, village fêtes, châteaux, museums, churches, wind- and water-mills, and more and more and . . .

Marcel Proust's house at Illiers-Combray

For further information and booking gîtes ruraux:
Relais Départemental des Gîtes Ruraux de France,
Chambre d'Agriculture d'Eure-et-Loir,
10 rue Dieudonné Costes,
28024 CHARTRES Cédex,
Tel. (37) 34.52.09.

For general tourist information:
Comité Départemental du Tourisme d'Eure-et-Loir,
B.P. 67,
28005 CHARTRES Cédex,
Tel. (37) 21.37.22.

A château on the river Ozanne

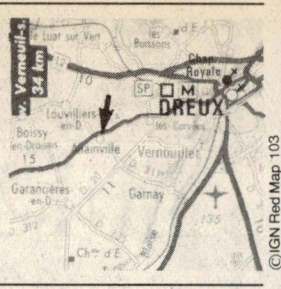

Eure-et-Loir

ALLAINVILLE One of two traditionally furnished gîtes in a renovated farmhouse, 1 km from the village centre, with local marked footpaths. At Dreux (3 km), see the fine belfry and nineteenth-century Saint-Louis royal chapel, burial place of the Orléans family. Living room (1 double divan), kitchen, 3 bedrooms (2 double and 1 child's bed), shower room, electric heating, enclosed ground with garden furniture. Linen available. Shopping and restaurant at Dreux.

Prices: low season F 538/700 **7 people**
high season F 880 *IGN 20*
Booking: M H. AUMONT, 13 rue Claude Debussy, 28500 Vernouillet. Tel. (37) 43 64 74.

28/0165

LA BAZOCHE-GOUET La Billardière A lovingly restored, half-timbered house with country-style furnishings on an arable farm in wooded surroundings, 1 km from the town. Good leisure amenities at the pretty little town of Brou (15 km) including swimming-pool, sailing and riding; see the fifteenth-century Maison de Bois there. Living room (1 double divan available), kitchen (washing machine), 3 bedrooms (2 double, 2 single beds), bathroom, fireplace, electric heating, enclosed ground. Shopping locally or at Brou.

Prices: low season F 880/1185 **8 people**
high season F 1290 *IGN 19*
Booking: M L. ALAIN, Les Livières, La Bazoche-Gouët, 28330 Authon-du-Perche. Tel. (37) 49 22 03. **E**

28/0259

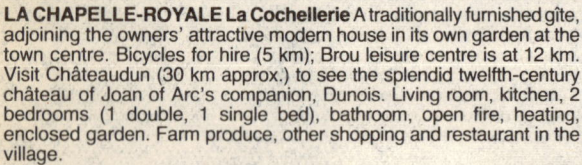

LA CHAPELLE-ROYALE La Cochellerie A traditionally furnished gîte, adjoining the owners' attractive modern house in its own garden at the town centre. Bicycles for hire (5 km); Brou leisure centre is at 12 km. Visit Châteaudun (30 km approx.) to see the splendid twelfth-century château of Joan of Arc's companion, Dunois. Living room, kitchen, 2 bedrooms (1 double, 1 single bed), bathroom, open fire, heating, enclosed garden. Farm produce, other shopping and restaurant in the village.

Prices: low season F 465/518 **3 people**
high season F 675 *IGN 19*
Booking: Mme L. SARRIAC, La Cochellerie, Chapelle Royale, 28290 Arrou. Tel. (37) 49 32 60.

28/0363

DIGNY Le Buisson A renovated and traditionally furnished cottage on a farm where horses are raised in an area particularly suited to riding. There is a riding centre at Senonches (6 km) which also boasts a ruined twelfth-century château and other leisure facilities. The vast Senonches forest is nearby. Living room, kitchen, 3 bedrooms (2 double, 3 single and 1 child's bed), bathroom, fireplace, central heating, carport, open ground (table tennis available). Farm produce in the village (5 km); shopping and restaurant at Senonches.

Prices: low season F 518/630 **7/8 people**
high season F 800 *IGN 19*
Booking: M L. BRIERE, Les Perruches, Digny, 28250 Senonches. Tel. (37) 37 74 14.

28/0431

LA FERTE-VILLENEUIL Grange des Guerets An old, traditionally furnished cottage on a village farm in the picturesque Aigre valley; see the fortified church on the banks of the river. There is a leisure park at Cloyes (9 km). Châteaudun (10 km) has been largely rebuilt after a fire but some fine architecture remains. Living room (1 double divan), kitchen, 1 bedroom (1 double, 1 single, 1 child's bed), shower room, fireplace, heating, use of the owners' garden (outdoor furniture). Linen available. Shopping in the village.

Prices: low season F 465 **6 people**
high season F 570 *IGN 19*
Booking: Mme T. BEAUDOUX, 5 rue Porte Dunoise, La Ferté-Villeneuil, 28220 Cloyes. Tel. (37) 45 09 27. **E**

28/0522

Eure-et-Loir

FONTAINE-LE-GUYON A traditionally furnished gîte in the owners' renovated house at the town centre. It is just 15 km from Chartres, the département capital, dominated by its magnificent cathedral. Visit, too, the former Episcopal Palace, now a museum, and enjoy the many sports and leisure amenities there. Living room/kitchenette, 2 bedrooms (4 single and 1 child's bed), bathroom, central heating, enclosed garden. Shopping and restaurant in the village.

Prices: low season F 465/580 **5 people**
high season F 725 *IGN 19*

Booking: M A. MORLOT, 18 rue Charles Péguy, Fontaine-le-Guyon, 28190 Courville-sur-Eure. Tel. (37) 22 56 44. **E**

28/0668

LANDELLES Château de Landelles A spacious, renovated and traditionally furnished gîte in the wooded grounds of the owners' château at the village centre. Tennis in the village and other amenities at the interesting old town of Courville-sur-Eure (4 km). Wind-surfing (4 km). A visit to Chartres (23 km) is a must. Living room, kitchen, 3 bedrooms (6 single beds and a further single available), 2 bathrooms and shower, fireplace, central heating, enclosed garden. Linen available. Shopping in the village.

Prices: low season F 700/880 **6 people**
high season F 1090 *IGN 19*

Booking: M G. BOSSARD, Château de Landelles, 3 rue du Parc, Landelles, 28190 Courville-sur-Eure. Tel. (37) 23 36 03. **E**

28/0732

MAROLLES-LES-BUIS Maison de l'Institeur An old traditionally furnished gîte, owned by the local council and set in its own garden at the village centre. The market town of Nogent-le-Rotrou (10 km) is dominated by an eleventh-century keep, all that remains of the château of the former Perche counts. Living room/kitchenette, lounge, 3 bedrooms (3 double, 2 single beds), shower room, central heating, children's swings. Shopping and a restaurant at Frétigny (5 km).

Prices: low season F 520/650 **8 people**
high season F 807 *IGN 19*

Booking: Mme HUBERT, Secrétaire de la Maire, La Coterie, Marolles-les-Buis, 28400 Nogent-le-Rotrou. Tel. (37) 52 06 64.

28/0867

MIERMAIGNE La Chicannière A car is essential when staying at this renovated and traditionally furnished cottage, adjoining the owners' home, 2 km from Authon-du-Perche, where the lovely Château de Charbonnières is now used as an hotel. Good leisure amenities (including tennis) at Thiron-Gardais (16 km). Living room (1 double divan), kitchen, 2 bedrooms (2 double, 1 single bed), fireplace, electric heating, garage, enclosed ground. Linen available. Tuesday market and other shopping at Authon-du-Perche.

Prices: low season F 466/600 **7 people**
high season F 790 *IGN 19*

Booking: Mme J. FOUCART, La Chicannière, Route d'Authon, Miermaigne, 28420 Beaumont-les-Autels. Tel. (37) 29 44 59.

28/0945

MOLEANS Valainville A renovated and traditionally furnished house on a cereal crops farm in a town in the picturesque Conie Valley. Châteaudun (7 km) which has been almost destroyed by fire more than once, has a château dating back to the twelfth century, and good sports and cultural amenities. Living room, kitchen, 2 bedrooms (1 double, 2 single beds, 1 double divan), bathroom, fireplace, central heating, open farm courtyard. Linen available. Farm produce, shopping and restaurant in the village.

Prices: low season F 480/600 **6 people**
high season F 755 *IGN 20*

Booking: M B. LAVO, 1 rue du Croc Noir, Valainville, Moléans, 28200 Châteaudun. Tel. (37) 45 16 17.

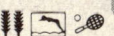

28/1043

Eure-et-Loir

ORGERES-EN-BEAUCE One of two traditionally furnished apartments in the owners' modern home at the town centre. The owner is willing to instruct visitors in yoga, gymnastics and naturopathy. Take a day trip to Chartres (37 km) with its beautiful Gothic cathedral, museums and other places of interest. Living room/kitchenette (1 double divan), 2 bedrooms (1 double, 1 single bed), bathroom, electric heating, garden shared with the owners. Shopping and restaurant in the town or at Patay (13 km).
Prices: low season   F 520/675   **5 people**
          high season   F 790   IGN 20
Booking: M J. DARGERE, 6 rue Henri Dunant, 28140 Orgères-en-Beauce. Tel. (37) 99 74 27.
28/1160

PRE-SAINT-EVROULT Set in its own enclosed ground at the edge of the town, this traditionally furnished house has been recently renovated. Good leisure amenities at the old town of Bonneval (6 km) on the river Loir which was established around the Saint-Florentin abbey (now a hospital). Living room/kitchenette, 2 bedrooms (2 double, 2 single and 1 child's bed), shower room, fireplace, heating, garden furniture. Linen available. Local farm produce; mobile baker and grocer call; other shopping and restaurant at Bonneval.
Prices: low season   F 415/560   **7 people**
          high season   F 705   IGN 20
Booking: M C. HAUDEBOURG, 4 rue des Ecoles, Pré-Saint-Evroult, 28800 Bonneval. Tel. (37) 47 21 91.
28/1226

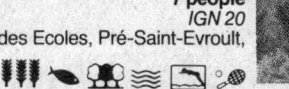

PRE-SAINT-MARTIN A simply furnished farm cottage, less than 10 km from Bonneval. Fishing in the river Loir (6 km); swimming-pool, riding and tennis (7 km). Well situated for day trips to Châteaudun, Chartres and Illiers-Combray (one-time home of Marcel Proust), all within 30 km. Living room (1 single divan), kitchen, 2 bedrooms (2 double, 1 single bed), shower room, fireplace, electric heating, sheltered garden with furniture and swing. Linen available. Mobile shops call; a restaurant at 6 km.
Prices: low season   F 477/620   **6 people**
          high season   F 725   IGN 20
Booking: M D. BARBIER, 5 rue de la Joubardière, Aigueville, Pré-Saint-Martin, 28800 Bonneval. Tel. (37) 47 27 99.
28/1328

LA PUISAYE Gervenne A country cottage, renovated and furnished in traditional fashion, near the Senonches forest (some good walks and picnics), and 6 km from the market town of Senonches where you can see the lovely ruined twelfth-century château. Leisure amenities in the town include a cinema and swimming-pool. Living room/kitchenette (1 double divan), 2 bedrooms (2 double and 1 single bed), shower room, electric heating, garage, garden. Linen available. Dairy produce in the village; other shopping at La Ferté-Vidame (5 km).
Prices: low season   F 485/595   **7 people**
          high season   F 755   IGN 19
Booking: M A. DESLANDES, Dampierre-sur-Blévy, 28170 Châteauneuf-en-Thymerais. Tel. (37) 48 19 84.
28/1440

SAINTE-MAIXME-HAUTERIVE Le Gland A small, renovated and simply furnished gîte on a cereal crops farm in deep countryside, so a car is essential. Interesting sites at Châteauneuf-en-Thymerais (4 km) bear witness to past civilisations; leisure facilities include a swimming-pool, riding and tennis and a delightful forest. Living room/kitchenette (1 single divan), 1 bedroom (3 single beds), shower room, fireplace, electric heating, open ground. Linen available. Shopping and restaurant at Châteauneuf-en-Thymerais.
Prices: low season   F 373/477   **4 people**
          high season   F 570   IGN 19
Booking: Mme M. T. EVAIN, le Gland, Saint-Maixme-Hauterive, 28170 Châteauneuf-en-Thymerais. Tel. (37) 51 68 03.
28/1564

Eure-et-Loir

SAINT-MAUR-SUR-LE-LOIR A renovated traditionally furnished cottage owned by the local council and situated in a village in the lovely Loir valley. Try the country inn (open at weekends) in the village. Swimming-pool, tennis and other amenities at Bonneval (5 km). Living room/kitchenette, 2 bedrooms (1 double, 2 single beds), bathroom, fireplace, electric heating, terrace, open ground. Farm produce in the village; other shopping and restaurant at Bonneval (5 km).

Prices:	low season	F 465/570	**4 people**
	high season	F 725	IGN 20

Booking: M J. DIGER, Secrétariat de la Mairie de Saint-Maur, Le Rouvre, Saint-Maur, 28800 Bonneval. Tel. (37) 47 28 73.

28/1641

SENONCHES La Framboisière A small cottage, renovated and furnished in traditional style, 1 km from the town centre where there is a pony club and a day nursery. Take a day trip to the cathedral city of Chartres or Dreux (both 40 km), and see the historic Chapelle Royale de Saint-Louis. Living room (1 double divan), kitchen, 1 bedroom (1 double, 1 single and 1 child's bed), bathroom, fireplace, heating. Shopping at Senonches (6 km).

Prices:	low season	F 410/525	**5/6 people**
	high season	F 650	IGN 19

Booking: M A. BUISSON, le Grand Village, la Framboisière, 28250 Senonches. Tel. (37) 37 82 62.

28/1733

VICHERES Brieure An attractively renovated cottage, adjoining the owners' home in a hamlet in the picturesque Perche region of woods, rivers and ponds, so plenty of opportunities for pleasant country walks. Other leisure amenities at the market town of Nogent-le-Rotrou (10 km). Living room (1 double divan), kitchen, 1 bedroom (3 single beds), shower room, fireplace, heating, garden. Linen available. Farm produce in the village; other shopping at Nogent-le-Rotrou; a restaurant at 5 km.

Prices:	low season	F 465/570	**5 people**
	high season	F 725	IGN 19

Booking: Mme P. PECCHIOLI, Brieure, Vichères, 28420 Beaumont-les-Autels. Tel. (37) 29 42 96.

28/1861

VIERVILLE A renovated and traditionally furnished gîte on a farm, adjoining the owners' home where they also offer bed-and-breakfast accommodation out of season. It is close to the Dourdan forest, within easy reach of Chartres and just 70 km from Paris. Living room/kitchenette (1 double divan available), 3 bedrooms (1 double, 3 single and 1 child's bed), bathroom and shower, fireplace, electric heating, garage, enclosed garden with furniture. Linen available. Shopping and restaurant at Gouillons (6 km).

Prices:	low season	F 507/630	**7/8 people**
	high season	F 755	IGN 20

Booking: M R. MILOCHAU, 7 rue de Garancière, Vierville, 28700 Auneau. Tel. (37) 24 68 46.

28/1936

SOUANCE-AU-PERCHE La Rosaie *Chambre-d'hôte* accommodation in the owners' renovated and traditionally furnished house on their mixed farm, 2 km from the village. Local fishing and forest walks; swimming-pool, riding and tennis at Nogent-le-Rotrou (7 km) where you can still see the eleventh-century keep of the ruined Château Saint-Jean. One first-floor room available (1 double bed), use of the owners' bathroom, lounge and open ground. Electric heating. Shopping and restaurant in the village.

Prices:	F 115	**2 people**
		IGN 19

Booking: Mme H. CHABOCHE, La Rosaie, Souancé-au-Perche, 28400 Nogent le Rotrou. Tel. (37) 52 37 09.

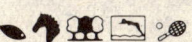

28/20

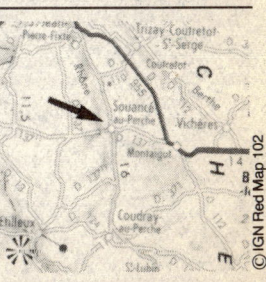

Indre

Indre, in the rural heart of France, offers the visitor the charm of an unspoilt countryside and the interesting atmosphere of a rich heritage.

Nature has endowed Indre with varied and contrasting landscapes which create its own original character: *la Champagne Berrichonne*, fertile cereal-growing plain with sweeping views broken by groves and copses; the undulating *Boichaut-nord*, cattle-rearing country, where meadows alternate with forest; *la Brenne*, the land of a thousand pools, with wild-life whose often rare species live in a free and natural state; and *Boichaut-sud*, a countryside chequered with hedged fields.

But Indre is not only a region of fine landscapes. There are the remains of a past remarkable in its wealth, and castles full of history like Valencay, Bouges, Azay-le-Ferron, Pallau, Nohant, le Bouchet and many others.

Indre is also a lively region where sporting activities such as water-skiing, sailboard, fishing, riding and tennis vie with first-class festivals (Nohant, Gargilesse, Pallau) and high-quality entertainments (Valencay, Cluis, Nohant, Pallau . . .) for your interest and enjoyment.

For further information, please contact:
INDRE TOURISM COMMITTEE
Gare Routière, Rue Bourdillon,
36000 CHATEAUROUX, France.
Tel. 54.22.91.20

Indre

AIGURANDE A neat, renovated and traditionally furnished cottage near the centre of a small town. Visit the old château town of La Châtre, and nearby Nohant, where the author Georges Sand lived and based many of her novels. A lake at 20 km. Living room (1 double divan), kitchen, 2 bedrooms (2 double, 1 single bed), bathroom and shower, electric heating, small enclosed garden. Shopping and restaurant in the town or at La Châtre (20 km approx.). 
Prices: low season   F 600   **7 people**
           high season   F 900   *IGN 35*
Booking: Mairie, Ville d'Aigurande, 36140 Aigurande.
Tel. (54) 30 30 58.   **E**

36/1-2

LA BERTHENOUX Les Cercles An attractively renovated, detached gîte with country-style furnishings, next to the owners' farmhouse where they may offer pony rides. Georges Sand's château at Nohant (6 km) is the setting for many cultural events during the summer. Living room (1 double divan), kitchen, 2 bedrooms (3 double beds), shower room, electric heating, terrace, carport, enclosed ground with garden furniture shared with the owners. Linen available. Restaurant in the village (3 km); shopping at La Châtre (6 km). 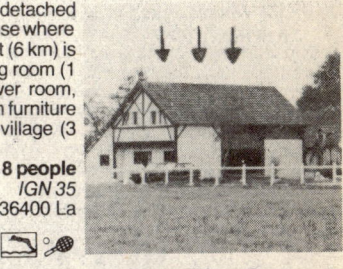
Prices: low season   F 600/700   **8 people**
           high season   F 800   *IGN 35*
Booking: Mme B. GUELTON, Les Cercles, La Berthenoux, 36400 La Châtre. Tel. (54) 30 01 98.   **E**
36/83-1

BRIANTES Le Virolan A small renovated gîte with traditional, country-style furnishings, 2 km from the village centre. There are good restaurants locally: try the goats' cheese and snails. Visit the département capital of Châteauroux (36 km), former home of Napoleon's loyal General, Bertrand. Living room/kitchenette (1 double divan), 1 bedroom (1 double, 1 single bed, cot available on demand), shower room, fireplace (wood supplied), central heating, ground with furniture and barbecue. Linen available. Shopping from mobile stores or at La Châtre (6 km).
Prices: low season   F 450/630   **5 people**
           high season   F 680   *IGN 35*
Booking: M F. COUTURIER, 2 rue Charles Dullin, 36000 Châteauroux. Tel. (54) 36 17 94.
36/23-1

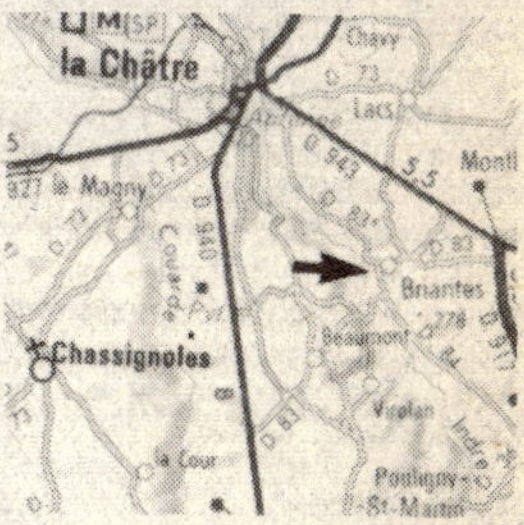

CHAILLAC Brosse A nice old stone-built house now renovated and equipped with simple, traditional furnishings 3 km from the village. Water sports, including sailing, are at 20 km and the countryside around offers beautiful views, a river for fishing and bathing and an eleventh-century château. Living room/kitchenette, 4 bedrooms (2 double and 2 single beds), shower room, wood stove, terrace, garage, enclosed garden. Mobile shops call, restaurant and other shopping in Chaillac where fresh produce is available, or at Saint-Benoit-du-Sault (10 km). 
Prices: low season   F 610
           high season   F 640/715   **6 people**
Booking: Mme R. GIRAUD, Embrimord, 36310 Chaillac.   *IGN 34*
Tel. (54) 25 71 97
36/32-1

CHAVIN Le Bois A rustically furnished gîte in the owners' own spacious, renovated house on a cereal farm just 1.5 km from the village centre. A lake for sailing and other water sports at 17 km and the peaceful countryside around offers woodland walks. Living room/kitchenette, 2 bedrooms (1 double, 3 single and 1 child's bed), shower room, fireplace, electric heating, carport, open grounds. Linen available. Mobile shops call; a restaurant in the village; other shopping (3 km) or at Argenton-sur-Creuse (11 km). 
Prices: low season   F 600/650
           high season   F 700   **5/6 people**
Booking: M R. MERCIER, Le Bois, 36200 Chavin.   *IGN 35*
Tel. (54) 24 02 04   **E**
36/40-1

Indre

FONTGUENAND Tiercerie A ground-floor gîte in a renovated and traditionally furnished building on a farm producing vegetable crops and wine, 2 km from the village. The beautiful Renaissance château at Valençay (6 km) has a museum devoted to Talleyrand and a park with flamingoes and other birds and animals. Living room (1 double divan), kitchen, 2 bedrooms (1 double, 1 single and 1 child's bed), bathroom, fireplace, central heating, open ground. Local farm produce and mobile shops call; other shopping and restaurant at Valençay.

Prices:	low season	F 515/590	**5/6 people**
	high season	F 730	*IGN 26*

Booking: M J. GASGNIER, La Sabotiere, Fontguenand, 36600 Valençay. Tel. (54) 00 10 08.
36/69-1

MAILLET Villerandoux Set on a livestock farm, 2 km from the village, this is a modern, rustically furnished ground-floor gîte. Do not miss the picturesque town of Argenton-sur-Creuse (10 km) whose galleried houses overhang the river; the old Roman city of Argentomagus has been excavated there. Living room (TV, 1 double divan), kitchen, (washing machine), 2 bedrooms (1 double, 2 single and 1 child's bed), bathroom and shower, fireplace, electric heating, enclosed ground with furniture and barbecue. Shopping and restaurant in the village.

Prices:	low season	F 650/850	**6/7 people**
	high season	F 980	*IGN 35*

Booking: M A. BARRE, La Roseraie, Villegongis, 36110 Levroux. Tel. (54) 36 61 81. E
36/121-1

NERET Poirier du Loup A modern, single-storey house with traditional furnishings, 0.5 km from the village centre. See the feudal château, Georges Sand museum and other places of historic interest at La Châtre (15 km approx.). Bathing and sailing at a lake (20 km). Living room (TV), kitchen, bedroom (1 double bed), fireplace (wood supplied), central heating, terrace, enclosed shared ground with garden furniture. Farm produce in the village; mobile baker, butcher and charcutier call; other shopping at Châteaumeillant (4 km).

Prices:	low season	F 700	**2 people**
	high season	F 800	*IGN 35*

Booking: M A. DAUGERON, Lavau, Néret, 36400 La Châtre. Tel. (54) 31 40 07.
36/147-1B

PALLUAU-SUR-INDRE Montgenault A lovely gîte, renovated and furnished in rustic style, adjoining the owners' home on their farm in open countryside. The pretty little town itself (4 km) is dominated by its eleventh-century château which was almost destroyed by the Black Prince. Living room (TV), kitchen (washing machine), 2 bedrooms (1 double, 1 single, 1 child's bed), shower room, fireplace (wood supplied), central heating, terrace, enclosed ground with garden furniture and swing. Linen available. Shopping and restaurant in the town or at Buzançais (12 km).

Prices:	low season	F 800/872	**3/4 people**
	high season	F 930	*IGN 34*

Booking: Mme H. BRUN, Montgenault, 36500 Palluau-sur-Indre. Tel. (54) 38 45 17.
36/158-2

PARPECAY-PAR-CHABRIS Beauvais One of two traditionally furnished gîtes in an old, renovated cottage on a cereal farm 1.5 km from the village. Within reach of the great châteaux of the Loire and 8 km from Valençay where there are *son et lumière* shows in the summer. Living room (1 double divan), kitchen, 2 bedrooms (2 double beds), bathroom, fireplace (wood supplied), electric central heating, terrace, carport, enclosed ground with garden furniture. Linen available. Shopping from mobile shops or at Chabris (5 km) where there is a restaurant.

Prices:	low season	F 530/685	**6 people**
	high season	F 735	*IGN 26*

Booking: M W. BOUET, Pâtines, 36600 Valençay. Tel. (54) 00 21 16.
36/160-1

Indre

PRISSAC Les Rullauds A pretty little country cottage, now renovated and traditionally furnished, situated on a mixed farm 2.5 km from the village where fresh produce is available. Art shows, concerts and country fêtes are features of this area in season. Sailing and water sports at a lake (18 km). Living room, kitchen, 1 bedroom (1 double and 1 single bed), bathroom, fireplace (wood supplied), electric heating, garage, enclosed grounds. Mobile shops call, other shopping (2.5 km) or at Argenton-sur-Creuse (25 km).

Prices:	low season	F 680	**3 people**
	high season	F 720	*IGN 34*

Booking: M R. VAUDEL, Les Rullauds, Prissac, 36370 Belabre.
Tel. (54) 25 71 61 **E**
36/172-1

SAINT-AIGNY Le Terrier A well-renovated gîte with traditional, country-style furnishings, in a hamlet, 4 km from Le Blanc where you could try your hand at parachuting! The town also boasts a château, impressive viaduct and other historic buildings. Try the local *kirsch* and *clafoutis* (cherry pudding). Living room (1 double divan), kitchen, 2 bedrooms (1 double, 2 single beds), bathroom and shower, electric central heating, terrace, garage, enclosed ground with garden furniture. Linen available. Shopping and a restaurant at Le Blanc.

Prices:	low season	F 460/690	**6 people**
	high season	F 796	*IGN 34*

Booking: M PETRAULT, Asnières, Sauzelles, 36220 Tournon-Saint-Martin. Tel. (54) 37 44 20.
36/192-3

SAUZELLES Asnières A small, old farm cottage, traditionally furnished in country style, near the owner's home, 1 km from the village centre. Ideally situated for touring the lovely Creuse valley; visit the magnificent twelfth-century Fongombault Abbey. Leisure pursuits locally include canoeing and climbing (10 km). Living room/kitchenette, 2 bedrooms (3 single, 1 child's bed), shower room, fireplace, central heating, carport, enclosed ground. Shopping from mobile stores or at Le Blanc (10 km).

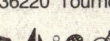

Prices:	low season	F 580	**4 people**
	high season	F 740/780	*IGN 34*

Booking: M G. CAPPELLE, Asnières, Sauzelles, 36220 Tournon-Saint-Martin. Tel. (54) 37 33 09. **E**
36/185-1

VALENÇAY La Petite Vernelle A rustically furnished cottage on a mixed farm, 0.8 km from the town. Valençay boasts a superb château, once owned by Scotsman John Law, the eighteenth-century financier; now the setting for summer concerts and other spectacles. A lake for water sports at 20 km. Living room/kitchenette, 2 bedrooms (2 double, 1 single bed), shower room, electric heating, garage, extensive enclosed ground with garden furniture and swings. Linen available (F 30 per set per week). Shopping and restaurants at Valençay.

Prices:	low season	F 500/550	**5 people**
	high season	F 700/800	*IGN 26*

Booking: M G. BERTHONNET, La Petite Vernelle, 36600 Valençay.
Tel. (54) 00 17 73.
36/232-1

VEUIL La Gravette One of two gîtes with country-style furnishings in a single-storey cottage on a mixed farm 2 km from the village. Water sports at a lake (35 km); the Loire châteaux within touring distance and Valençay (4 km) offers various entertainments in its own château. Living room/kitchenette (1 double divan), 2 bedrooms (2 double and 1 single bed), shower room, fireplace, heating, terrace, open ground with garden furniture. Linen available. Shopping, including farm produce, in the village where there is also a restaurant or at Valençay.

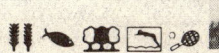

Prices:	low season	F 720/800	**7 people**
	high season	F 850	*IGN 26*

Booking: Indre Booking Service
36/238-2b

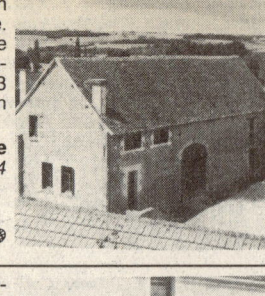

Indre-et-Loire

ABILLY La Chatière A traditionally furnished and renovated cottage in a picturesque setting on a mixed farm, 3 km from the village centre. Descartes (7 km) is named after the philosopher, whose birthplace there is now a museum; leisure amenities there include a swimming-pool and tennis. Living room/kitchenette, 3 bedrooms (1 double and 3 single beds), bathroom, open fire, heating. Shopping and restaurant in the village or at Descartes.

Prices: low season   F 670   **5 people**
        high season   F 1080/1305   *IGN 34*
Booking: M J. M. ARNAUD, La Chatière, Abilly, 37160 Descartes.
Tel. (47) 59 78 44   E

37/001-185

ABILLY Les Forges An attractively renovated gîte with rustic furnishings on a mixed farm where the owners are happy to sell their produce. Forest walks on marked footpaths locally; at Descartes (4 km) enjoy the public gardens on the banks of the Creuse. Riding stables at 7 km. Living room/kitchenette (1 double divan), 2 bedrooms (1 double, 2 single beds), shower room, fireplace, electric central heating, terrace, enclosed ground. Shopping and restaurant in the village (0.5 km).

Prices: low season   F 700/950   **6 people**
        high season   F 1250   *IGN 34*
Booking: M MARNE, Les Forges, Abilly, 37160 Descartes.
Tel. (47) 59 78 29.

37/001-100

AUZOUER-EN-TOURAINE La Haut Villaumay A spacious village house which has been renovated and traditionally furnished. The lovely château at Château-Renault (3 km) dates back to the eleventh century and the town boasts a ninth-century keep tower. Enjoy also the parks in the town, its swimming-pool, tennis court and miniature golf. Living room, kitchen, 4 bedrooms (3 double, 2 single and 1 child's bed), bathroom, fireplace, central heating, enclosed ground. Shopping and restaurant at Château-Renault.

Prices: low season   F 1071   **9 people**
        high season   F 1392   *IGN 26*
Booking: Mme A. GOUJON, La Caherie, Auzouer-en-Touraine, 37110 Château-Renault. Tel. (47) 56 58 18.

37/010-263-1

BALLAN-MIRE Le Moulin Vert A very unusual gîte in a converted mill, with country-style furnishings at the village centre. Local forest walks, bathing and sailing at a lake (2 km). Tours (10 km) is a busy university town with a fine Gothic cathedral and a wine museum. Living room, kitchen, 2 bedrooms (2 double beds), bathroom, fireplace, electric central heating, enclosed ground. Shopping and restaurant in the village or at Tours.

Prices: low season   F 875/1030   **4 people**
        high season   F 1235   *IGN 26*
Booking: Mlle M. SABAT, 76 rue Nationale, 37000 Tours.
Tel. (47) 05 48 21   E

37/018-229

STOP...PRESS...STOP...PRESS...STOP...PRESS...STOP...PRESS...S
Out break of classical swine fever in Belgium . . . hitherto unknown in Northern Europe . . . believed due to illegal personal import of meat products . . . all meat and meat products such as sausages, ham or pâté MUST BE DECLARED TO CUSTOMS IN THE RED CHANNEL . . . . .
STOP...PRESS...STOP...PRESS...STOP...PRESS...STOP...PRESS...S

Indre-et-Loire

BALLAN-MIRE Saulu A lovely old house which has been renovated and furnished in traditional style, 2 km from the village. There is a golf course near the village and many amenities at the département capital of Tours (12 km) where the former Archbishop's Palace is now a fine museum. Living room, kitchen (washing machine), 2 bedrooms (2 double, 2 single beds), shower room, fireplace, heating, open ground. Shopping and restaurant in the village.

Prices:	low season	F 803/857	**6 people**
	high season	F 1070	*IGN 26*

Booking: M E. CLEMENT, Ferme de Château de Vau, Ballan-Miré, 37510 Joué-lès-Tours. Tel. (47) 53 20 83.

37/018-252

BEAUMONT-EN-VERON Grésil A renovated and traditionally furnished house, typical of the region, 1.5 km from the village centre. The lovely old town of Chinon (5 km) is dominated by its splendid fortified château. The area is noted for its wines and many cellars are open for tastings. Living room/kitchenette, 2 bedrooms (2 double beds, 1 double divan), shower room, fireplace, electric central heating, courtyard. Shopping and restaurant in the village.

Prices:	low season	F 721/824	**6 people**
	high season	F 1030	*IGN 25*

Booking: M G. GALLE, La Giraudière, Beaumont-en-Veron, 37420 Avoine. Tel. (47) 58 43 96.

37/022-192

BETZ-LE-CHATEAU La Châtre A small cottage, renovated and traditionally furnished, at the edge of the village (0.8 km). Fishing at a nearby river (0.3 km). The gîte is ideally situated for exploring this region of châteaux and vineyards, justly known as the "Garden of France". Living room/kitchenette, 2 bedrooms (2 double beds), shower room, fireplace, heating, open ground. Shopping and restaurant in the village or at Ligueil (10 km).

Prices:	low season	F 520	**4 people**
	high season	F 700	*IGN 34*

Booking: Mme Y. MIGNE, Les Basses Tailles, Betz-le-Château, 37600 Loches. Tel. (47) 59 65 26.

37/026-214

BLERE Le Bosquet A renovated and traditionally furnished gîte set in its own enclosed ground just 0.7 km from the centre of Bléré. Leonardo da Vinci spent some time at the picturesque château town of Amboise (10 km approx.) and there is a museum dedicated to him there. Living room, kitchen, 3 bedrooms (2 double, 2 single, 1 child's bed, 1 single divan), shower room, gas central heating. Shopping and restaurant in the village.

Prices:	low season	F 800/1000	**8 people**
	high season	F 1200	*IGN 26*

Booking: Mme S. LIMOUX, 16 route de Cigogne, 37150 Bléré. Tel. (47) 57 84 75.

37/027-175-2

BOUSSAY La Maison Colin A renovated and traditionally furnished farm cottage, 2 km from the village centre. A swimming-pool and tennis at Preuilly-sur-Claise (5 km) which boasts a Romanesque church. Châtellerault (30 km approx.) has a fifteenth-century château and motor museum as well as other leisure amenities. Living room/kitchenette, 2 bedrooms (3 double beds), bathroom, open fire, electric central heating. Shopping and restaurant in the village.

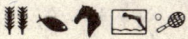

Prices:	low season	F 620	**6 people**
	high season	F 740	*IGN 34*

Booking: M G. BRIOLLET, Le Bourg, Chaumussay, 37350 Le Grand-Pressigny. Tel. (47) 94 54 01.

37/033-102

Indre-et-Loire

BRASLOU La Boistière A renovated and traditionally furnished gîte on a working farm. Historic Richelieu (10 km) was built at Cardinal Richelieu's command and has a museum of the Richelieu family. Take a trip on the tourist steam train from there to Chinon. Living room, kitchen, 2 bedrooms (2 double, 1 single, 1 child's bed, 1 single divan), shower room, gas central heating, carport. Farm produce from the owners; other shopping and restaurant in the village (2 km).

Prices:	low season	F 690/740	**7 people**
	high season	F 890	*IGN 34*

Booking: Mme A. MORON, La Boistière, Braslou, 37120 Richelieu. Tel. (47) 58 15 12.

37/034-161

BRASLOU Le Petit Bois This cottage, which has been renovated and traditionally furnished, is on a former farm, 3 km from the village. Richelieu (8 km), surrounded by moats and with a fine seventeenth-century market hall, was built in 1631 by the architect of the Sorbonne. Living room/kitchenette, 1 bedroom (1 double bed and 1 double divan), shower room, electric central heating, enclosed ground. Shopping and restaurant in the village or at Richelieu.

Prices:	low season	F 520/620	**4 people**
	high season	F 750	*IGN 34*

Booking: M J. M. MARTIN, Le Petit Bois, Braslou, 37120 Richelieu. Tel. (47) 58 25 46.

37/034-298

LA CHAPELLE-BLANCHE-SAINT-MARTIN Grillemont A renovated and traditionally furnished gîte on a farm courtyard near the owners' château in a lovely rural setting. Visit Loches (25 km approx.) to see its former royal château and well-preserved Renaissance quarter which is floodlit on summer evenings. Living room/kitchenette, 2 bedrooms (1 double, 2 single beds, 1 single divan), bathroom, open fire, electric heating, enclosed ground. Shopping and restaurant in the village (3 km) or at Ligueil (7 km).

Prices:	low season	F 1155	**5 people**
	high season	F 1375	*IGN 34*

Booking: Mme C. DE SAINT-SEINE, Grillemont, La Chapelle-Blanche-Saint-Martin, 37240 Ligueil. Tel. (47) 59 62 03   **E**
37/057-274

CHARNIZAY Pouvreau A spacious gîte, renovated and furnished in traditional style, in its own enclosed ground. Local river bathing and fishing and forest walks. Interesting sites in the area include the Château D'Azay-le-Ferron and the spa town of La Roche Posay. Living room (TV), kitchen, 3 bedrooms (1 double, 4 single and 1 child's bed), bathroom, fireplace, central heating, enclosed courtyard. Shopping and restaurant in the village (2 km) or at Preuilly-sur-Claise (10 km).

Prices:	low season	F 870	**7 people**
	high season	F 1125	*IGN 34*

Booking: M S. SAUTIERE, 1 rue de la Bretonnerie, 37000 Tours. Tel. (47) 64 09 95   **E**
37/061-276

CHENONCEAUX A small village house which has been renovated and traditionally furnished, near the river Cher where you may bathe and fish (sailing at 4 km). The superb Renaissance Chenonceaux Château straddles the river and has beautiful gardens. A swimming-pool and tennis at Bléré (7 km). Living room/kitchenette, 2 bedrooms (2 double beds), bathroom, central heating. Shopping and restaurant in the village (0.2 km) or at Bléré.

Prices:	low season	F 453/486	**4 people**
	high season	F 750	*IGN 26*

Booking: M G. CLEMENT, 3 rue de la Roche, Chenonceaux, 37150 Bléré. Tel. (47) 29 94 24.

37/070-127

YOUR HOLIDAY CHOICE IN THE LOIRE VALLEY

Elevage de La Martinière

Mr and Mme Bonetat
LA MARTINIERE
37510 Savonnieres, France
Tel: 47.50.04.46

La Martinière is a pony-breeding Farm and pony-trekking centre well-placed in the ever-popular valley of the Loire. 1 km from the chateau of Villandry and 15 km from historic Tours. Several alternative holiday opportunities are available to you.

La Martinière 'gite'. Self-catering accommodation in a lovely, renovated cottage with rustic furnishings. Set in a quiet position on this equestrian farm where riding is available. 2/3 bedrooms with 1 double and 5 single beds; living room with fireplace and TV; kitchen (washing-machine); shower room; electric heating. Terrace and garden. An ideal base for touring or for a quiet, peaceful holiday. Prices from 1300 FF per week.

La Martinière 'Bed and Breakfast'. Serviced accommodation is available in the farmhouse itself which has been beautifully restored. Rooms for 2, 3 or 4 people at 120 to 190 FF. Breakfast is provided at 18 FF. Shower or bathroom. The absolute calm of the garden is reserved for guests.

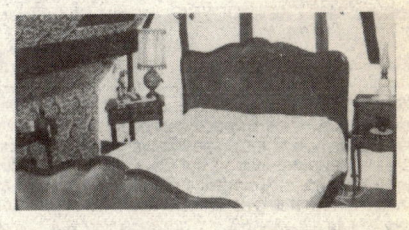

La Martinière 'Chateaux of the Loire' tour. Mr and Mme Bonetat will organise a one-week tour of the famous castles of the Loire for you. In a group of 8 to 10, led by an expert guide, you can visit the magnificent dwellings of the kings of France, travelling by pony along medieval by-ways. Accommodation is arranged each night in the homes of local people in a region renowned for its food, wine and comfortable hospitality.

To book, please write or telephone: Mr and Mme Bonetat, La Martiniere, 37510 Savonnieres, France. (47.50.04.46).

Indre-et-Loire

FONDETTES Clos de la Fremaudière An attractively renovated cottage with rustic furnishings, next door to the owners' home, 2 km from the village. Local forest walks and sailing at a lake (5 km). Tours (5 km) offers all the amenities of a major city; see too the former royal château there. Living room, kitchen, 2 bedrooms (1 double and 3 single beds), shower room, fireplace, electric central heating, terrace, enclosed ground. Shopping and restaurant in the village.

Prices: low season F 800/1030   **5 people**
high season F 1270   *IGN 20*

Booking: Mlle DASQUE, Clos de la Fremaudière, Fondettes, 37230 Luynes. Tel. (47) 42 00 98   **E**

37/109-73

LE GRAND PRESSIGNY Etableau A renovated village gîte with traditional, country-style furnishings, near a river (fishing permitted). A riding stable, tennis court and swimming-pool all at 1 km. Grand Pressigny's fortified château is now a museum; see too the nearby Château de Guerche, built for Charles VII. Living room (TV), kitchen (washing machine), 2 bedrooms (2 double, 2 single beds, 1 single divan), shower room, fireplace, heating, garden. Shopping in the village (1 km) or at Descartes (11 km).

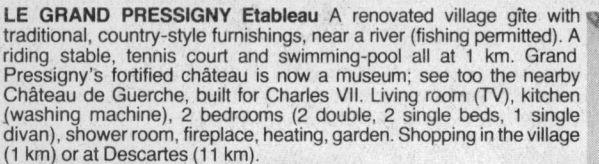

Prices: low season F 580/780   **7 people**
high season F 980   *IGN 34*

Booking: Mme H. MEUNIER, Place des Halles, 37350 Le Grand Pressigny. Tel. (47) 94 91 16 (after 8 pm).

37/113-119

LE GRAND PRESSIGNY Les Imbertières A spacious, well-renovated house, typical of the region, furnished in rustic style and situated 2 km from the village centre. Local forest walks; plenty of leisure facilities in the village itself or at the interesting old town of Descartes (12 km). Living room, kitchen, 3 bedrooms (3 double and 2 single beds), bathroom, fireplace, electric central heating. Shopping and restaurant in the village or at Descartes.

Prices: low season F 855/905   **8 people**
high season F 1180   *IGN 34*

Booking: M Y. LABRACHERIE, Etableau, 37350 Le Grand Pressigny. Tel. (47) 94 90 74.

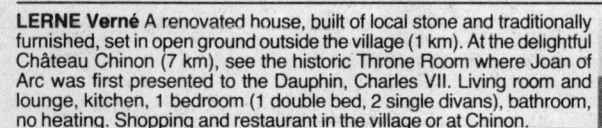

37/113-92

LERNE Verné A renovated house, built of local stone and traditionally furnished, set in open ground outside the village (1 km). At the delightful Château Chinon (7 km), see the historic Throne Room where Joan of Arc was first presented to the Dauphin, Charles VII. Living room and lounge, kitchen, 1 bedroom (1 double bed, 2 single divans), bathroom, no heating. Shopping and restaurant in the village or at Chinon.

Prices: low season F 600/824   **4 people**
high season F 1030   *IGN 25*

Booking: M ROULEUX, 63 Avenue de la Libération, 54000 Nancy. Tel. (83) 96 28 75.

37/126-320

LE LIEGE Set in its own enclosed ground on a working farm, this attractive cottage has been renovated and furnished in traditional fashion. It is at the village centre, 16 km from the lovely château town of Loches on the river Indre. Sailing (10 km). Living room/kitchenette, 1 bedroom (2 double beds, 1 single divan), shower room, fireplace, wood central heating. Shopping and restaurant in the village or at Loches.

Prices: low season F 450/560   **5 people**
high season F 680   *IGN 26*

Booking: Mme C. DELAVOUX, Le Bourg, Le Liège, 37460 Montrésor. Tel. (47) 59 52 20.

37/127-69-2

Indre-et-Loire

LIGUEIL A delightful, ivy-clad cottage which has been renovated and furnished in traditional style, at the town centre. Local forest walks; tennis and swimming-pool in the town which is an ideal starting-point for exploring this lovely region of châteaux. Living room/kitchenette, 1 bedroom (2 double beds), shower room, fireplace, heating, enclosed ground. Shopping and restaurant in the town.

Prices:	low season	F 360/515	**4 people**
	high season	F 670	*IGN 34*

Booking: M R. DELAUNE, 54 rue des Fossés-Saint-Martin, 37240 Ligueil. Tel. (47) 59 63 23 **E**

37/130-183-1

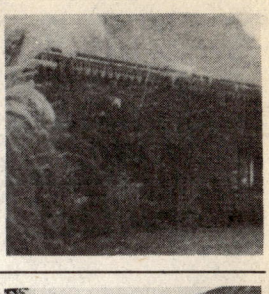

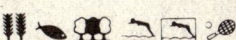

LOUANS A renovated and traditionally furnished gîte on a mixed farm, 1 km from the village centre. Montbazon (10 km) is an old town on the river Indre with ruined eleventh-century château; leisure facilities there include miniature golf, tennis and horse racing. Living room, kitchen, 2 bedrooms (2 double, 1 single bed), bathroom, open fire, heating, enclosed ground. Shopping and restaurant in the village or at Montbazon.

Prices:	low season	F 720	**5 people**
	high season	F 825	*IGN 26*

Booking: Mlle A. VINERIER, La Lande, Louans, 37320 Esvres-sur-Indre. Tel. (47) 92 87 60.

37/134-208

NAZELLES-NEGRON Vallée de Vaubrault An unusual, traditionally furnished house, cut into the cliff-side near the river Loire. Visit the cellars along the river for wine tasting. At Négron, a medieval barn has been converted into a theatre. Do not miss the splendid Amboise Château (7 km). Living room, kitchen, 2 bedrooms (2 double, 1 single bed, 1 single divan), bathroom, heating, open ground. Shopping and restaurant in the village (3 km).

Prices:	low season	F 755	**6 people**
	high season	F 915	*IGN 26*

Booking: M F. ANDRE, 16 Allée de Brédanne, 37400 Amboise. Tel. (47) 57 59 74.

37/163-243

NOYANT-DE-TOURAINE Les Colombelles A former farmhouse, now renovated and traditionally furnished, set in open ground near the village centre (0.5 km). The old town of Sainte-Maure-de-Touraine (10 km) in the Manse valley, is noted for its goats' cheese – buy it at the Friday market in the seventeenth-century market halls. Living room/kitchenette, 2 bedrooms (1 double, 2 single beds, possibility of a child's bed), shower room, heating. Shopping and restaurant in the village.

Prices:	low season	F 561	**4 people**
	high season	F 736	*IGN 34*

Booking: Mme J. THOMAS, La Gare, Noyant-de-Touraine, 37800 Sainte-Maure-de-Touraine. Tel. (47) 65 85 85.

37/176-219

PARCAY-SUR-VIENNE Côteaux de Puchard A spacious, renovated and traditionally furnished house, built of local stone and situated 2 km from the village. At L'Ile-Bouchard there are facilities for motor-boating and sailing as well as tennis courts and a swimming-pool; see the lovely ruined priory there. Living room, kitchen, 4 bedrooms (2 double, 4 single beds), bathroom, open fire, electric heating, open ground. Shopping and restaurant in the village.

Prices:	low season	F 1000	**8 people**
	high season	F 1300	*IGN 34*

Booking: M A. VERNA, 12 rue des Courlis, 37220 L'Ile-Bouchard. Tel. (47) 58 43 46.

37/180-315

Loir-et-Cher

The Loisirs Accueil in Loir-et-Cher offers you:

Numerous activities and courses throughout the Loire Valley!

In order to discover this region in depth and to get to know it better, we suggest: *La Roulotte* (travelling around the region in horse-drawn, gipsy-style caravans) with various things to see and do in Sologne and the Cher Valley.

We also suggest riding about in a horse-drawn carriage in the Parc de Chambord.

For further information and our free catalogue, please write to:

LOISIRS ACCUEIL
11 Place du Château
41000 BLOIS
Tel. (54) 78.55.50.
Telex. 751375.

You can also book your *gîte* or Loisirs Accueil holiday through our booking service and ask us to supply you with information about holidays in Loir-et-Cher.

NB For fuller information about all Loisirs Accueil Services, please see pages 16–17 of this guide.

Special Interest Holidays

RESERVATION LOISIRS ACCUEIL

Blois Château

Loir-et-Cher

ANGE La Foltiere A ground floor gîte in a substantial old cottage, now renovated and furnished in traditional style, set in the owners' vineyard 1.5 km from the village. The area specialises in the production of goats cheese and wine, and Montrichard (4 km) offers good leisure facilities. Living room/kitchenette, 2 bedrooms (1 double and 3 single beds), shower room, electric central heating, terrace, enclosed garden with barbecue and garden furniture. Wine from the owner and mobile baker calls; restaurant in the village and shopping at 3 km.

Prices:	low season	F 482/630	**5 people**
	high season	F 828	IGN 26

Booking: M. A. LECLAIR, La Foltiere, Angé, 41400 Montrichard. Tel. (54) 32 09 72.
41/37

BUSLOUP Le Tertre A pretty, traditionally fuurnished renovated cottage set on a cereal farm overlooking the Loire valley, 1.8 km from the village where there is tennis and river fishing; swimming pool at 12 km and a lake at 20 km. Living room/kitchenette (1 double divan), 2 bedrooms (1 double, 3 single and 1 child's bed), shower room, fireplace, central heating, terrace, carport, enclosed courtyard with garden furniture. Strawberries (in season) from the owner, mobile baker calls; shopping in the village or at Vendôme (12 km).

Prices:	low season	F 660/680	**8 people**
	high season	F 800	IGN 26

Booking: Mme de BOISGROLLIER, Le Tertre, Busloup, 41160 Morée. Tel. (54) 23 43 74.
41/207

CHATILLON SUR CHER La Haie Jallet A newly built, traditionally furnished gîte on a vineyard 3 km from the village centre. Local forest walks, river fishing in the Cher at 1 km, tennis at 3 km and swimming pool at 7 km. Living room/kitchenette, 2 bedrooms (2 double and 1 single bed), shower room, electric heating, balcony, open courtyard. Linen available. Wine from the owners, mobile butcher, baker and fishmonger call. Shopping and restaurant in the village or at Selles sur Cher or Saint-Aignan (7 km).

Prices:	low season	F 465/615	**5 people**
	high season	F 815	IGN 26

Booking: M. J. THOMAS, La Haie Jallet, Chatillon sur Cher, 41130 Selles sur Cher. Tel. (54) 71 05 69
41/43

CONTRES La Presle A renovated ground floor cottage traditionally furnished in rustic style and set on a farm 1.5 km from the town centre. Bathing in the Cher (17 km), sailing on the Lac de Loire and bicycle hire at 20 km. Living room, kitchen (1 single divan), 2 bedrooms (2 double beds), bathroom, fireplace, electric heating, terrace, car port, courtyard. Linen available if necessary. Eggs, vegetables and wine from the owners, shopping and restaurant at Contres.

Prices:	low season	F 433/661	**4/5 people**
	high season	F 942	IGN 26

Booking: Mme. M. GASCHON, La Rouchère, Sassay, 41700 Contres. Tel. (54) 79 53 51

41/24

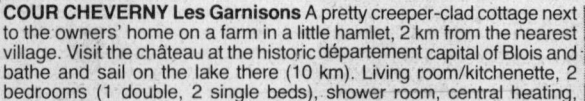

COUR CHEVERNY Les Garnisons A pretty creeper-clad cottage next to the owners' home on a farm in a little hamlet, 2 km from the nearest village. Visit the château at the historic département capital of Blois and bathe and sail on the lake there (10 km). Living room/kitchenette, 2 bedrooms (1 double, 2 single beds), shower room, central heating, terrace, garage, courtyard with garden furniture and barbecue. Mobile baker calls, shopping and restaurant at 2 km or at Blois.

Prices:	low season	F 495/620	**4 people**
	high season	F 884	IGN 26

Booking: M. L. MAULNY, Les Garnisons, Cour Cheverny, 41700 Contres. Tel. (54) 79 91 18

41/30

Loir-et-Cher

DANZE Le Bois-Malon A well-renovated ground floor gîte set in its own enclosed courtyard in a hamlet 1.2 km from the village centre. The châteaux of the Loire are easily accessible (approximately 40 km) and the lovely town of Vendôme with its own château is just 8 km. The traditionally furnished gîte offers living room (1 single divan), kitchen (washing machine), 2 bedrooms (2 double, 2 single and 1 child's bed), shower room, fireplace, electric heating, terrace, garage, enclosed grounds. Linen available. Mobile butcher and baker call, shopping and restaurant in the village or at Vendôme.
Prices: low season   F 385/540   **7/8 people**
           high season   F 810   IGN 26
Booking: M. R. BARRÉ, 37 Route de Danzé, Saint Ouen, 41100 Vendôme. Tel. (54) 77 33 16.
41/57

EPUISAY L'Etang An old gîte with country-style furnishings, situated on a mixed farm at 2 km from the village, where you may hire bicycles. Farm produce is available from the owners. River bathing at 4 km; the lovely town of Vendôme with its château, once the stronghold of the Counts of Vendôme, is at 17 km. Living room/kitchenette (washing machine), 2 bedrooms (1 double, 2 single and 1 child's bed), shower room, fireplace, electric heating, terrace, garage, enclosed ground with furniture. Linen available. Shopping and restaurant in the village.
Prices: low season   F 465/610   **4/5 people**
           high season   F 830/850   IGN 26
Booking: M. J. NORGUET, L'Etang, Epuisay 41360 Savigny-sur-Braye. Tel. (54) 72 01 67. **E**
41/75

EPUISAY La Roussetière A gîte, renovated and furnished in traditional country style, on a mixed farm. Table tennis at the gîte and fishing. See the ruined tenth-century château at Mondoubleau (10 km). Living room (1 double divan), kitchen, 1 bedroom (2 double, 1 child's bed and a cot), shower room, open fire, electric heating, terrace, garage, garden. Linen available. Farm produce from the owners; shopping and restaurant in the village (1 km).
Prices: low season   F 460/620   **6/8 people**
           high season   F 840   IGN 26
Booking: M. G. ODEAU, La Roussetière, Epuisay, 41360 Savigny-sur-Braye. Tel. (54) 72 04 68.
41/76

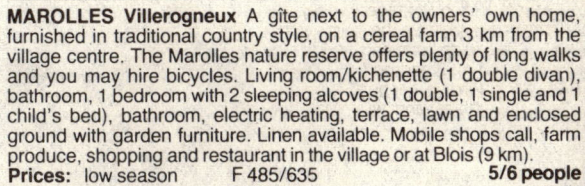

MAROLLES Villerogneux A gîte next to the owners' own home, furnished in traditional country style, on a cereal farm 3 km from the village centre. The Marolles nature reserve offers plenty of long walks and you may hire bicycles. Living room/kichenette (1 double divan), bathroom, 1 bedroom with 2 sleeping alcoves (1 double, 1 single and 1 child's bed), bathroom, electric heating, terrace, lawn and enclosed ground with garden furniture. Linen available. Mobile shops call, farm produce, shopping and restaurant in the village or at Blois (9 km).
Prices: low season   F 485/635   **5/6 people**
           high season   F 830/850   IGN 26
Booking: M. J. CRÉCHE, 2 Rue de Marolles, Villerogneux, 41000 Blois. Tel. (54) 20 03 64
41/129

MAVES Villerussien A renovated and rustically furnished gîte in a hamlet, 3.5 km from the village centre. Historic Blois, with its château, lake for bathing and sailing and riding facilities is at 18 km. Living room, kitchen, 3 bedrooms (2 double, 2 single and 1 child's bed), bathroom, fireplace, central heating, garage, open ground. Shopping in the village or at Blois.
Prices: low season   F 484/824   **6/7 people**
           high season   F 978   IGN 26
Booking: M. D. LEMAIRE, Villerussien, Maves, 41500 Mer. Tel. (54) 87 31 14
41/186

Loir et Cher

MAZANGE Fourmange A ground floor gîte in an old cottage furnished in traditional style on a farm 1.5 km from the village. Riding at 18 km. Vendôme, with château and swimming pool, is 14 km and you may hire bicycles at the gîte. Living room/kitchenette (1 single divan), 2 bedrooms (1 double, 3 single and 1 child's bed), shower room, fireplace, electric heating, carport, open grounds with furniture. Mobile shops call, farm produce and shopping in the village or at Vendôme.

Prices: low season F 366/495 **6/7 people**
high season F 655 *IGN 26*

Booking: M BRETON-DESFORGES, Fourmangé, Mazangé 41100 Vendôme. Tel. (54) 72 03 03.

41/58

MONT-PRES-CHAMBORD A detached, cottage-style gîte in a village, which has been renovated and furnished in traditional fashion. Ideally situated for visiting the Loire Châteaux: Chambord, Blois, Amboise, Chenonceaux and Cheverny. Blois is at 10 km. Living room, kitchen, 2 bedrooms (2 double and 1 single bed), bathroom, open fire, electric central heating, garage, enclosed courtyard with outdoor furniture. Shopping and restaurant in the village.

Prices: low season F 600 **5 people**
high season F 830 *IGN 26*

Booking: Mme F. DEPEZAY, 131 Rue de l'Aumone Mont-près-Chambord, 41250 Bracieux. Tel. (54) 70 71 00.

41/136

OUCHAMPS Les Motteux A gîte in the owners' own renovated farmhouse, furnished in country style and situated in a hamlet 3 km from the village. Ideally placed for visiting the Loire châteaux and a visit to the old town of Blois is highly recommended. Living room (TV), kitchen, 2 bedrooms (3 double, 1 single and 1 cot), shower room, electric heating, terrace, enclosed ground with garden furniture. Linen available. Mobile shops call, shopping and restaurant in the village or at Blois (12 km).

Prices: low season F 485/632 **7/8 people**
high season F 832 *IGN 26*

Booking: M. J. VERNON, Les Motteux, Ouchamps, 41120 Les Montils. Tel. (54) 70 42 62

41/336

OUZOUER-LE-DOYEN La Bruyère An old, cottage-style gîte with rustic furniture, situated on a cereal farm at 1.5 km from the village. The owners will be happy to sell you farm produce. Bathing and sailing at Cloyes-sur-le-Loir (13 km). Living room (TV, 1 double divan), kitchen, 1 bedroom (1 double, 1 child's bed and 2 cots), bathroom, open fire, electric heating, terrace, garage, open courtyard, with lawn, swing and barbecue. Linen available. Mobile shops call; other shopping and restaurant in the village.

Prices: low season F 410/575 **4/7 people**
high season F 820 *IGN 19*

Booking: Mme M. F. HUCHET, La Bruyère, Ouzouer-le-Doyen, 41160 Morée. Tel. (54) 80 49 17.

41/64

POUILLE La Tesnière A traditionally-furnished gîte in the owners' new house on a vineyard 2 km from the village centre. Montrichard (8 km), overlooked by an old castle, is worth a visit and Saint-Aignan (8 km) offers good bathing facilities from a beach on the river Cher. Living room/kitchenette, 2 bedrooms (2 double beds), shower room, electric-central heating, balcony, garage, open grounds with garden furniture. Linen available. Mobile baker calls, farm produce and restaurant in the village, other shopping at Montrichard.

Prices: low season F 480/630 **4 people**
high season F 830 *IGN 26*

Booking: Mme G. MARTEAU COURANT, La Tesnière, Pouillé, 41110 Saint-Aignan-sur-Cher. Tel. (54) 71 45 59

41/38

Loir-et-Cher

PRUNAY-CASSEREAU La Cussonnière A ground floor cottage, renovated and rustically furnished, situated on a farm 3 km from the village. The great châteaux of the Loire are within easy touring distance and there is riding at 15 km. Living room/kitchenette (1 single divan), 3 bedrooms (3 double beds), shower room, fireplace, central heating, enclosed ground, linen available. Farm produce from the owners, mobile baker calls, shopping and restaurant in the village or at Châteaurenault (10 km).
Prices: low season F 487/632 **7 people**
high season F 832 *IGN 26*
Booking: Mme. E. FOURNIER, La Courtairie, Prunay-Cassereau, 41310 Saint Amand Longpré.
41/62

RILLY-SUR-LOIRE La Noirée An attractively renovated gîte near the village centre (0.4 km) and just 0.5 km from the river Loire itself—so plenty of fishing and interesting walks. Join in local summer fêtes; visit the delightful château at Amboise (13 km); other leisure facilities at Montrichard (13 km). Kitchen, 2 bedrooms (2 double and 2 single beds), shower room, fireplace, electric heating, carport, garden with furniture. Linen (F20 per set, per week). Mobile shops call; farm produce, other shopping and restaurant in the village or at Onzain (7 km).
Prices: low season F 395/540 **6 people**
high season F 720 *IGN 26*
Booking: Mme J. PERTHUIS, Rilly-sur-Loire, 41150 Onzain. Tel. (54) 20 97 52.
41/15

LES-ROCHES-LEVEQUE A detached, renovated gîte with traditional furniture on the river's edge, situated in the town. Visit the troglodyte dwellings, near the town. A beach by the river Loir, is at 4 km; a swimming-pool at Montoire-sur-le-Loir (3 km); tennis at 4 km. Living room/kitchenette, 2 bedrooms (1 double, 2 single and 1 child's bed), shower room, open fire, electric central heating, terrace, garden and enclosed ground with furniture. Linen available. Mobile butcher calls; other shopping in the village.
Prices: low season F 406/550 **4/5 people**
high season F 732/760 *IGN 26*
Booking: M. M. DESHAYES, 'Le Bourg', Les Roches-Lévêque, 41800 Montoire-sur-le-Loir. Tel. (54) 85 03 89.
41/88E/3

LES ROCHES L'EVEQUE La Chenaudière A country cottage, renovated and furnished in rustic style on a mixed farm 3 km from the centre of the village. Well situated for touring the beautiful Loire valley and the great châteaux; sailing at 40 km, riding at 20 km. Living room/kitchenette, 2 bedrooms (1 double, 2 single and 1 child's bed), shower room, fireplace, electric heating, terrace, lawned garden with furniture, linen available. Mobile shops call, farm produce, shopping and restaurant at Montoire-sur-le-Loire (4 km).
Prices: low season F 490/636 **4/5 people**
high season F 830/865 *IGN 26*
Booking. M. A. COLAS, Saint Nicolas, 41800 Saint Rimay. Tel. (54) 85 03 89.
41/61E/3

SAINT AMAND LONGPRE Le Moulin de Longpré A small renovated and rustically furnished cottage in a delightful setting with footpaths and a pond where you may fish. The département capital, Blois, is well worth a visit at approximately 30 km. Living room/kitchenette (1 double divan), 1 bedroom (1 double, 1 single bed), shower room, fireplace, central heating, terrace, open grounds with garden furniture, linen available. Farm produce from the owners, mobile shops call, restaurant at 2 km and shopping at Saint Amand Longpré (6 km).
Prices: low season F 502/632 **4/5 people**
high season F 832 *IGN 26*
Booking: M. R. TARU, Le Moulin de Longpré, 41310 Saint Amand Longpré. Tel. (54) 82 83 18
41/67

Loir-et-Cher

SAINT GOURGON La Brosse An old country cottage rustically furnished and all on one level 1.5 km from the village where farm produce is available. The historic town of Vendôme is at 12 km where there is a swimming pool and château; sailing at 20 km. Living room (1 double divan), kitchen, 3 bedrooms (4 single and 1 child's bed), bathroom, fireplace, electric heating, carport, open ground with barbecue and garden furniture, linen available. Shopping and restaurant at 5 km or at Vendôme.
Prices: low season   F 500/690   **6/7 people**
           high season   F 940   *IGN 26*
Booking: M. P. GOSSEAUME, Les Michelinieres, Saint Cyr du Gault, 41190 Herbault. Tel. (54) 46 12 61
41/63

SANTENAY La Basse Prunière A neat little cottage, traditionally furnished and situated on a mixed farm on the edge of the village. The département capital, Blois, is well worth a visit at 18 km and there are local facilities for fishing. Living room (TV), kitchen, 2 bedrooms (2 double and 1 single bed), bathroom, fireplace, gas heating, terrace, garage, enclosed courtyard and extensive grounds with garden furniture. Linen available. Fresh dairy produce and vegetables from the owner, shopping and restaurant in the village or at Herbault (4 km).
Prices: low season   F 473/667   **5 people**
           high season   F 914   *IGN 26*
Booking: M. R. BRETON, La Basse Prunière, Santenay, 41190 Herbault. Tel. (54) 46 12 11
41/6

SANTENAY La Vallée A small, renovated and traditionally furnished gîte in a hamlet, 0.3 km from the village where there is a recommended restaurant. Miniature golf (15 km). Take a trip to Amboise (20 km approx.) and visit the former royal château and the Leonardo da Vinci museum at Clos-Lucé where he once lived. Living room, kitchen, 2 bedrooms (1 double, 3 single and 1 child's bed), shower room, oil central heating, terrace, garage, garden with furniture. Linen available. Farm produce available, shopping at Herbault (4 km).
Prices: low season   F 487/687   **5/6 people**
           high sason   F 887   *IGN 26*
Booking: M. P. BIGUIER, La Vallée, Santenay, 41190 Herbault. Tel. (54) 46 11 91.
41/3

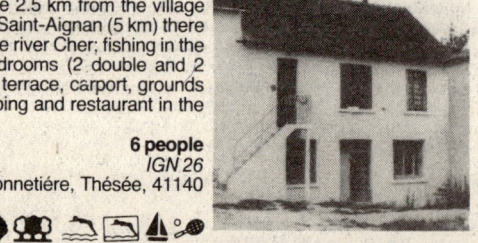

THESEE La Bougonnetiére One of two gîtes in a substantial well-renovated house furnished in traditional style 2.5 km from the village centre where you may buy the local wine. At Saint-Aignan (5 km) there are good bathing facilities from a beach on the river Cher; fishing in the village itself. Living room/kitchenette, 3 bedrooms (2 double and 2 single beds), shower room, electric heating, terrace, carport, grounds with garden furniture. Linen available. Shopping and restaurant in the village or at Saint Aignan.
Prices: low season   F 435/562   **6 people**
           high season   F 715   *IGN 26*
Booking: Mme. C. BARBEILLON, La Bougonnetiére, Thésée, 41140 Noyers sur Cher. Tel. (54) 71 41 23.
41/34

VILLERBON Villejambon A renovated gîte with traditional, country-style furnishings on a cereal crops farm 2 km from the village. Plenty to see and do at Blois (10 km); organised bathing and sailing on the Loire at 10 km. Walks in Blois forest (10 km). Living room, kitchen, 2 bedrooms (2 double, 1 single and 1 child's bed), shower room, electric central heating, terrace, garage, open ground with garden furniture. Linen available. Mobile butcher and baker call; a restaurant in the village and other shopping at 5 km.
Prices: low season   F 520/700   **5/6 people**
           high season   F 915   *IGN 26*
Booking: M. R. LESOURD, Villejambon, Villerbon, 41000 Blois. Tel. (54) 46 83 16.
41/8

Loiret

ANDONVILLE A comfortable gîte with traditional furnishings in a converted presbytery next to its old bell tower in a hamlet. This is a lovely hilly region with good leisure facilities (swimming-pool, tennis and riding all at 12 km). Living room/kitchenette, 3 bedrooms (2 double, 2 single and 2 bunk beds), shower room, central heating, garden with outdoor furniture and a child's swing. Mobile shops call; farm produce in the village; other shopping at Angerville (7 km) or at 13 km.

Prices: low season F 485/640
high season F 800

8 people
IGN 20

Booking: Loiret Loisirs Accueil   E

45/C6

CHUELLES Saint-Abdon An old cottage with a mixture of traditional and modern furnishings, set in its own ground with furniture and a barbecue for outdoor meals. Montargis (20 km) is an unusual town, criss-crossed with numerous canals and some 126 bridges! Enjoy water sports at the lake there. Living room/kitchenette (1 double divan), 1 bedroom (1 double bed), bathroom, open fire, central heating, garage. Mobile fishmonger calls; other shopping in the village (0.5 km).

Prices: low season F 485/645
high season F 805

4 people
IGN 21

Booking: Loiret Loisirs Accueil   E

45/D25

DADONVILLE Denainvilliers A renovated stone cottage with country-style furnishings in a farming hamlet, 1.5 km from the village centre. Fishermen will appreciate the delightful Oeuf Valley. Plenty of leisure facilities at the large market town of Pithiviers (3 km). Try the local patisseries and honey. Living room/kitchenette, 1 bedroom (1 double, 1 single bed, 1 single divan; a cot available on request), shower room, fireplace, gas central heating, carport, enclosed ground. Shops in the village.

Prices: low season F 490/635
high season F 775

4 people
IGN 20

Booking: Loiret Loisirs Accueil   E

45/C10

ESTOUY A sympathetically renovated and traditionally furnished gîte in a quiet street in a village on the river Essonne (good fishing). A swimming-pool and tennis as well as other amenities at Pithiviers (6 km). Orléans with its famous cathedral is an easy day trip at 50 km approx. Living room (1 double divan), kitchen, 1 bedroom (1 single and 2 bunk beds), bathroom, fireplace, electric central heating, garden. Farm produce and other shopping in the village.

Prices: low season F 465/615
high season F 770

5 people
IGN 20

Booking: Mme ROY, 10 Grande Rue, Estouy, 45300 Pithiviers. Tel. (38) 34 20 61 (M. Robiteau).

45/C5

GRISELLES Le Chesnoy A renovated gîte with country-style furnishings, set in its own ground with garden furniture, on a mixed farm where you will receive the warmest welcome. It is just near the beautiful Clairie Valley, 3 km from Ferrieres which has an unusual abbey church, a place of pilgrimage in September. Living room/kitchenette, lounge, 2 bedrooms (2 double and 2 single beds), shower room, fireplace, central heating. Shopping in the village or from mobile shops (fishmonger and greengrocer).

Prices: low season F 525/690
high season F 880

6 people
IGN 21

Booking: Loiret Loisirs Accueil   E

45/D28

Loiret

GY-LES-MONAINS A modern gîte, tastefully furnished and set in enclosed grounds bordering a river (trout fishing possible) at the edge of the village (0.6 km). At Montargis (8 km), see the twelfth-century château which was largely rebuilt in the nineteenth century; enjoy the many leisure amenities there. Living room (TV, 1 single divan), kitchen, 3 bedrooms (3 double and 1 single bed), bathroom, central heating, terrace, garage, garden furniture. Farm produce in the village; other shopping (4 km).

Prices: low season F 680/855
high season F 1070
8 people
IGN 21

Booking: Loiret Loisirs Accueil E
45/D22

OUZOUER-SOUS-BELLEGARDE L'Isle A traditionally furnished gîte in a converted water mill in a lovely setting with a view over the river. The hamlet is 1.5 km from the château town of Bellegarde which has a swimming-pool and tennis court. Orléans forest is at 12 km. Living room, kitchen, 3 bedrooms (4 double, 2 single and 1 child's bed), shower room, oil-fired central heating, enclosed ground. Fresh dairy produce in the village (0.7 km); other shopping and restaurant at Bellegarde.

Prices: low season F 615/805
high season F 1010
11 people
IGN 21

Booking: M R. SEVIN, 13 rue Marcel Sambat, 45200 Montargis. Tel. (38) 93 51 45
45/D1

PRESSIGNY-LES-PINS A renovated and traditionally furnished cottage, on a mixed farm at the edge of the village (1.5 km). At Gien on the river Loire (30 km approx.) the splendid château houses a hunting museum. Living room (1 double divan), kitchen, 1 bedroom (1 double and 1 single bed), shower room, fireplace, carport, enclosed ground with garden furniture and child's swings. Fresh eggs and poultry from the owners; mobile baker calls; other shopping in the village or at Montargis (12 km).

Prices: low season F 460/605
high season F 750
5 people
IGN27

Booking: Loiret Loisirs Accueil E
45/D27

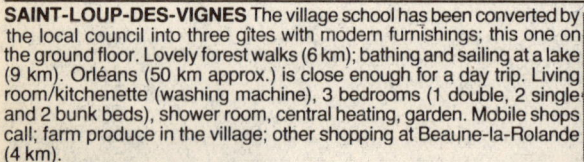

SAINT-HILAIRE-LES-ANDRESIS Les Deniaux This former farm cottage has been renovated and furnished in traditional style. It is set in open ground, some 4 km from the village and 5 km from Courtenay which has a ruined abbey and château and whose museum exhibits a reconstruction of Aristide Briand's cabaret. Living room (1 double divan), kitchen, 3 bedrooms (3 double, 2 single and 1 child's bed), bathroom, central heating, carport. Fresh eggs and poultry from the owners; other shopping in the village.

Prices: low season F 460/575
high season F 775
11 people
IGN 21

Booking: Loiret Loisirs Accueil E
45/D15

SAINT-LOUP-DES-VIGNES The village school has been converted by the local council into three gîtes with modern furnishings; this one on the ground floor. Lovely forest walks (6 km); bathing and sailing at a lake (9 km). Orléans (50 km approx.) is close enough for a day trip. Living room/kitchenette (washing machine), 3 bedrooms (1 double, 2 single and 2 bunk beds), shower room, central heating, garden. Mobile shops call; farm produce in the village; other shopping at Beaune-la-Rolande (4 km).

Prices: low season F 770
high season F 900
winter season F 570
6 people
IGN 21

Booking: Loiret Loisirs Accueil E
45/D16

Loiret

SAINT-MARTIN-D'ABBAT Domaine de Mitouedin A renovated and traditionally furnished house, situated on an estate of woodland and ponds, 2 km from the village. At the château in Châteauneuf-du-Loire (5 km) visit the Orangery and the Marine Museum; leisure facilities in the town include a swimming-pool, tennis and miniature golf. Living room/kitchenette, 3 bedrooms, each with private bath (3 double beds), fireplace, central heating. Farm produce and other shopping in the village.

Prices: low season   F 905
         high season   F 1130
         winter season   F 720

6 people
IGN 27

Booking: Loiret Loisirs Accueil   E
45/A19

DONNERY Les charmettes *Chambre d'hôte* accommodation in the owners' fine old traditionally furnished house at the edge of the Orléans canal. The owners are bee-keepers and happy to sell their honey. At Orléans (20 km), visit the cathedral, Museum of Fine Arts and the delightful floral park. Three rooms available on the first floor: bedroom 1 (2 single, 1 child's bed, private bath); bedrooms 2 and 3 (1 double bed each, shared bathroom). Farm produce, shopping and restaurant in the village (3 km).

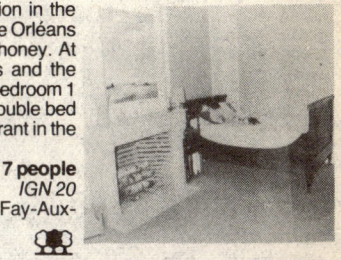

Prices: 1p F 85, 2p F 95, 3p F 115

7 people
IGN 20

Booking: Mme SICOT, Les Charmettes, Donnery, 45450 Fay-Aux-Loges. Tel. (38) 59 22 50.
45/12

MARCILLY-EN-VILLETTE Saint-Michel *Chambre d'hôte* accommodation in the owner's old, traditionally furnished house, lying in its own grounds in the heart of the village where there is a tennis court. Riding and a swimming-pool at La Ferté-Saint-Aubin (8 km) Orléans (approx. 17 km). Three bedrooms available on the first floor: bedroom 1 (1 double and 1 single bed), bedroom 2 (1 double bed and 1 single folding bed), bedroom 3 (2 single beds), oil heating; shared shower room and lounge. Possibility of main meals. Shopping and restaurant in the village or at La Ferté-Saint-Aubin.

Prices: 1p F 90, 2p F 100, 3p F 120

8 people
IGN 27

Booking: Mme PILLOT, Saint-Michel, Marcilly-en-Villette, 45240 La Ferté-Saint-Aubin. Tel. (38) 76 10 34   E
45/GCH14

SAINT-AY *Chambre d'hôte* accommodation in the owners' modern, traditionally furnished house outside the village (1.2 km). The owners are bee-keepers, so try their delicious honey. Orléans, famous for its cathedral and links with Joan of Arc, is at 15 km. Discover also the Sologne forest and lakes and the châteaux of Meung-sur-Loire and Beaugency. Two double rooms available on the first floor (one room also has a child's bed); oil-fired central heating, shared shower room, lounge and garden. Shopping and restaurant in the village.

Prices: 1p F 85, 2p F 95, 3p F 115

5 people
IGN 20

Booking: Loiret Loisirs Accueil   E
45/GCH9

VIEILLES MAISONS Grignon *Chambre d'hôte* accommodation in the owners' large home, a former post-house on the Orléans canal where you can fish. The Orléans forest is at 3 km and Lorris, with its fine Renaissance buildings and old market halls, is 4 km away. Five double bedrooms on the first floor available (two rooms also have a child's bed); central heating, shared bathroom, lounge, carport and grounds at your disposal. Meals available or nearby restaurant. Farm produce in the village (2.5 km); shopping at Lorris.

Prices: 1p F 90, 2p F 100, 3p F 120

12 people
IGN 21

Booking: Loiret Loisirs Accueil   E
45/GCH8

"l'Auvergne un pays neuf"

**FOR YOUR NEXT HOLIDAYS
AUVERGNE, IN THE CENTRE OF FRANCE,
IS WAITING FOR YOU!**

– IF YOU SEEK SPAS AND PURE AIR,
– IF YOU WANT TO HAVE A PLEASANT STAY IN A COUNTRY OF LAKES AND VOLCANOES,
– IF YOU LIKE OUTDOOR SPORTS,
– AND IF YOU DON'T WANT A LONG DRIVE.

ACCOMMODATION: classified hotels, "Logis and Auberges de France", Gites, Holiday Villages, Camping and Caravanning sites. . . . .

VERY INTERESTING PRICES

INFORMATION AND AUVERGNE BOOKING SERVICE "GITES":
COMITE REGIONAL DE TOURISME AUVERGNE
43, avenue Julien - B.P. 395
63011 CLERMONT-FERRAND CEDEX
Tel. (73) 93.04.03 - Telex: AUVTOUR 990529 F

CHOOSE SPRING AND AUTUMN FOR SPECIAL LOWER RATES

4 AUVERGNE

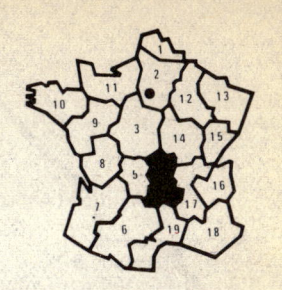

The largest volcanic region in Europe, the Auvergne, is now France's biggest Regional Nature Conservation Park, covering some 780,000 acres of mountains and lakes. This is excellent rambling country, crossed by the long-distance footpaths GR3 and GR4 and many minor paths.

Auvergne's now silent volcanoes have certainly left their mark on the region: apart from the many lakes that have formed in the craters, other natural sites include waterfalls, monumental blocks of basalt and even a fossilized forest buried beneath layers of ash at the Pas de la Margeride (Cantal).

The Auvergne is very popular for another of its volcanic legacies – the many spas with their revivifying mineral springs. There are now ten major resorts (including Vichy) where treatments for rheumatism and many other complaints are offered.

With its mountain peaks of Mont Dore and Monts du Cantal rising to 6,230 ft, the Auvergne is known as a ski resort, where the emphasis is on a relaxed atmosphere and friendly hospitality. Other sports to be enjoyed are riding, cycling, golf and all kinds of water sports.

Auvergne still maintains many of its old customs and traditions such as the celebration of the "ascent" at Besse-en-Chandesse (Puy-de-Dôme) in early June, when cowherds and cattle accompany the "Black Madonna" in solemn ceremony to their highland pastures with singing, dancing and fireworks. A similar "descent" is held in late September.

Not to be missed in the region are the lace shops and museum at Le Puy-en-Velay; Bort-les-Orgues with its curious natural phenomenon of a series of phonolite columns resembling organ pipes; the main town of Clermont-Ferrand and its petrifying springs; and Ambert where paper is still made by hand and where you can visit a museum dedicated to the art: Moulin Richard-le-Bas, 3.5 miles away. And like most parts of France the local meats, cheeses and wines are distinctive and palatable.

Isle-et-Bardais

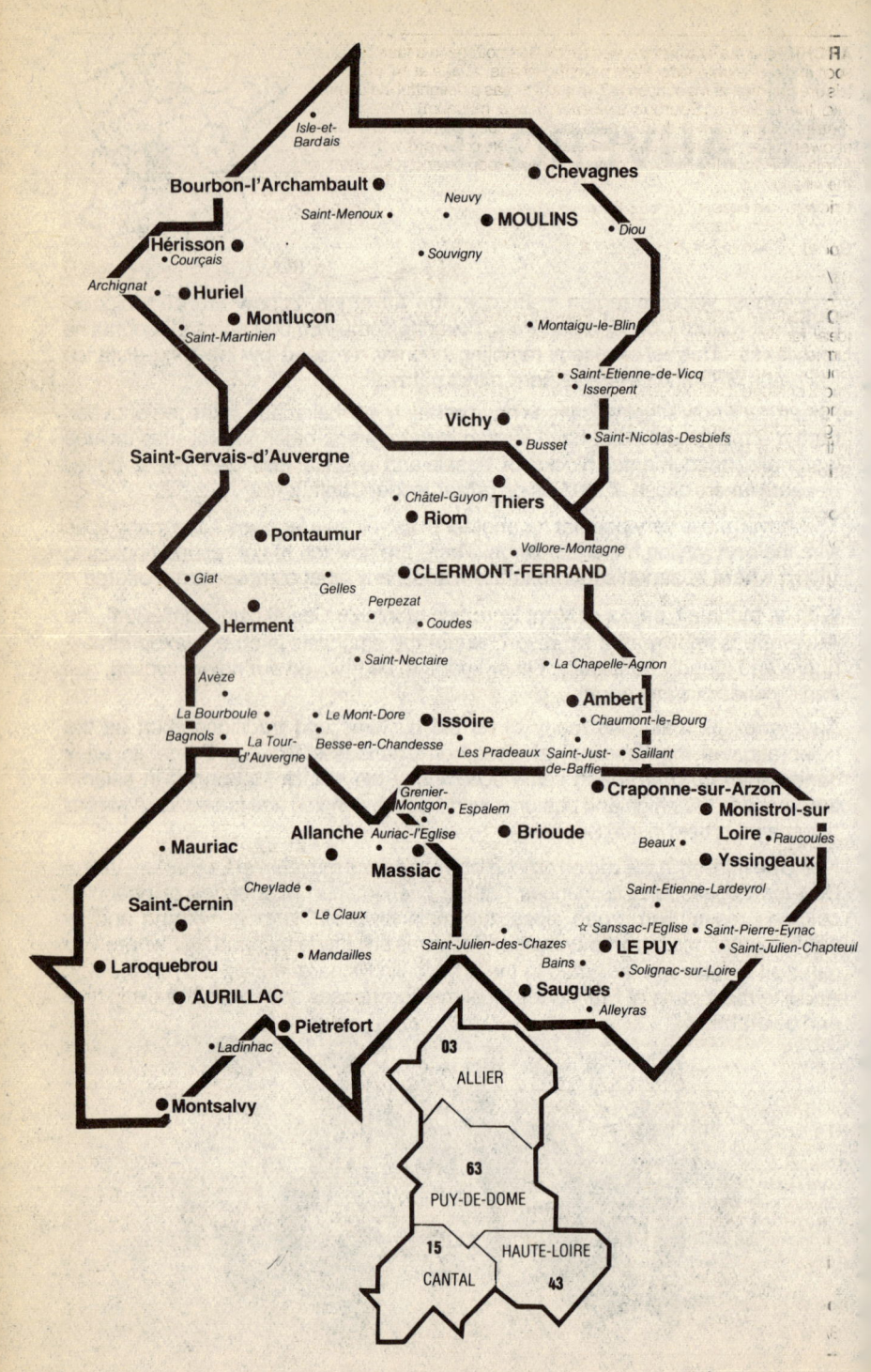

● Bourbon-l'Archambault   ● Chevagnes

  Saint-Menoux   *Neuvy*   ● MOULINS   ● *Diou*

● Hérisson
  Courçais   *Souvigny*

Archignat ● Huriel
             ● Montluçon
  Saint-Martinien   ● *Montaigu-le-Blin*

                                        ● *Saint-Etienne-de-Vicq*
                                        ● *Isserpent*
                          Vichy ●   ● *Saint-Nicolas-Desbiefs*
                                ● *Busset*

Saint-Gervais-d'Auvergne ●

                    ● *Châtel-Guyon* ● Thiers
      ● Pontaumur   ● Riom

                            ● *Vollore-Montagne*
Giat ●   *Gelles* ● CLERMONT-FERRAND
             Perpezat
        ● Herment   ● *Coudes*

              ● *Saint-Nectaire*   ● *La Chapelle-Agnon*

Avèze   ● Ambert
La Bourboule ● ● *Le Mont-Dore* ● Issoire   ● *Chaumont-le-Bourg*
● *Bagnols*   ● *La Tour-*   *Besse-en-Chandesse* *Les Pradeaux* *Saint-Just-* ● *Saillant*
              d'Auvergne   *de-Baffie* ● Craponne-sur-Arzon
                          ● *Grenier-*   ● Monistrol-sur-
                          Montgon *Espalem*   Loire ● *Raucoules*
● Mauriac   ● Allanche ● *Auriac-l'Eglise* ● Brioude   *Beaux* ● Yssingeaux
                    ● Massiac
● Saint-Cernin   *Cheylade*   *Saint-Etienne-Lardeyrol*
                   ● *Le Claux*   ☆ *Sanssac-l'Eglise* ● *Saint-Pierre-Eynac*
                 ● *Mandailles*   *Saint-Julien-des-Chazes* ● LE PUY ● *Saint-Julien-Chapteuil*
● Laroquebrou   *Bains*
                                                    ● Sauges   *Solignac-sur-Loire*
● AURILLAC   *Alleyras*
   ● Pietrefort
   ● *Ladinhac*   ┌─────────┐
                                   │   03   │
● Montsalvy   │ ALLIER │
                                   │   │
                                   │   │
                                   ├─────────┤
                                   │   63   │
                                   │PUY-DE-DOME│
                                   ├────┬────┤
                                   │ 15 │HAUTE-LOIRE│
                                   │CANTAL│ 43 │
                                   └────┴────┘

Allier

ARCHIGNAT La Tannière A well renovated cottage in a fairly isolated spot in deep countryside, 6 km from the village. A lake at 14 km. Good leisure facilities at Montluçon (17 km) which has a delightful old quarter and the Dukes of Bourbon Château (now a museum). Altitude 550 metres. Living room (1 double bed), kitchen, 1 bedroom (1 double bed), shower room, fireplace, electric heating, open courtyard with garden furniture. Possibility of farm produce, other shopping and restaurant in the village.

Prices:	low season	F 582/635	**4 people**
	high season	F 742	IGN 35

Booking: Allier booking service   **E**

03/F499

BOURBON-L'ARCHAMBAULT Feu-d'En-Haut A very large house, ideal for two families holidaying together; it has been renovated and furnished in rustic style. Many leisure amenities at the spa town of Bourbon l'Archambault (2 km) where you can see the ruined mediaeval ducal château. Living room, lounge, kitchen, 8 bedrooms (1 double, 10 single beds and a cot), bathroom and shower, fireplace, oil heating, large enclosed ground with garden furniture. Shopping and restaurant in the village or at Moulins (22 km).

Prices:	low season	F 1360	**13 people**
	high season	F 1680/2220	IGN 36

Booking: Allier booking service   **E**

03/H477

BUSSET Les Murs du Temple A spacious, renovated house with country-style furnishings situated in a hamlet in hilly countryside, 7 km from the village. Vichy (21 km), seat of the French Parliament during the Nazi occupation, has many leisure facilities including a golf course and lake for sailing. Living room, lounge, kitchen, 4 bedrooms (1 double, 6 single beds), shower room, fireplace, oil-fired central heating, small garage, enclosed courtyard with garden furniture. Shopping and restaurant in the village.

Prices:	low season	F 700/900	**8 people**
	high season	F 1125	IGN 43

Booking: Allier booking service   **E**

03/D497

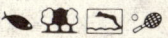

COURCAIS Pitrot An attractively renovated house with modern furnishings, adjoining an empty barn in a hamlet, 3 km from the village. A swimming-pool and tennis court at the château town of Montluçon (18 km). Visit Néris-les-Bains (28 km), a spa town with Gallo-Roman ruins. Living room, lounge, kitchen, 2 bedrooms (2 double, 1 single bed), bathroom, electric central heating, garage, enclosed courtyard with garden furniture. Restaurant and possibility of farm produce in the village, other shopping (5 km).

Prices:	low season	F 620/675	**5 people**
	high season	F 790	IGN 35

Booking: Allier booking service   **E**

03/F459

DIOU Moulin des Prats A renovated and traditionally furnished gîte right by a river (good fishing) and 3 km from the village. Le Pal leisure and zoological park is worth a visit at 15 km. Moulins (35 km) has a fifteenth-century cathedral and many other places of interest. Living room (1 single divan), small kitchen, 2 bedrooms (1 double, 2 single beds), shower room, open fire, central heating, carport, open courtyard with garden furniture. Shopping and restaurant in the village or at Dompierre-sur-Besbre (4 km).

Prices:	low season	F 500/600	**5 people**
	high season	F 700	IGN 36

Booking: Allier booking service   **E**

03/B479

Allier

ISLE-ET-BARDAIS Le Petit Bougimont A renovated cottage, set at the heart of the Tronçais forest, where there are good leisure amenities, including wind-surfing and other water sports on its many lakes. Miniature golf in the village (2 km); archery and bicycle hire at Saint-Bonnet-Tronçais (10 km). Living room, kitchen, 2 bedrooms — one of which is an open landing (4 single beds), bathroom, fireplace, electric heating, open ground. Shopping in the village or at Cérilly (6 km) where there is a restaurant.

Prices:	low season	F 835/875	**4 people**
	high season	F 1250	**IGN 35**

Booking: Allier booking service **E**

03/G501

ISSERPENT Mongenet An attractively renovated gîte with country-style furnishings, 3 km from the village. See Lapalisse Château at 15 km. Many leisure facilities at the lively spa town of Vichy (15 km), including a casino; guided tours of the old quarter of the town are available. Living room (1 single divan), kitchen, 1 bedroom (1 double, 1 single bed), bathroom, oil heating, small garage, enclosed ground with garden furniture. Farm produce from the owners; other shopping and restaurant in the village.

Prices:	low season	F 495/610	**4 people**
	high season	F 755/815	**IGN 43**

Booking: Allier booking service **E**

03/C483

MONTAIGU-LE-BLIN Les Gaumins This gîte is in a lovely tranquil spot; it has been renovated and furnished in rustic fashion. A swimming-pool and tennis at 8 km. Many places of interest at Vichy (20 km), including the old clock tower and the exotic collections at the Missionaries' Museum. Living room/kitchenette, 1 bedroom (1 double, 1 single bed), mezzannine (1 double bed), bathroom, fireplace, electric central heating, terrace, carport, ground. Shopping and restaurant in the village (1 km), or at Varennes-sur-Allier (8 km).

Prices:	low season	F 790/890	**5 people**
	high season	F 1100/1150	**IGN 43**

Booking: Allier booking service **E**

03/B492

NEUVY Château de Thoury A spacious gîte with country-style furnishings in the owners' fairytale château set in parkland, 3 km from the village. Many leisure facilities at the cathedral town of Moulins (5 km) including a swimming-pool, riding and tennis; visit the museum at the Maison de Jeanne d'Arc. Living room, kitchen, 4 bedrooms (2 double, 5 single and 1 child's bed), 2 bathrooms, wood heating, parkland. Farm produce in the village; other shopping and restaurant at Moulins.

Prices:	low season	F 1100	**10 people**
	high season	F 1400	**IGN 36**

Booking: Allier booking service **E**

03/A341

DID YOU KNOW that certain plants, including several species of wildflowers and all forest trees, certain vegetables and fruits may not be brought into Britain without a phytosanitary certificate declaring that they are free from disease? If you intend to bring home such produce please contact the Plant Health Unit, MAFF, Great Westminster House, Horseferry Road, London SW1P 2AE for a list of exceptions.

HELP KEEP BRITISH GARDENS, PLANTS, FIELDS AND TREES FREE OF PESTS FROM OVERSEAS

Allier

SAINT-ETIENNE-DE-VICQ Les Landes An attractive gîte, renovated and furnished in rustic style, set in its own enclosed ground in a hamlet, 2 km from the village. The Château des Comtes de Chabannes at Lapalisse (13 km) is worth a visit for its Flanders tapestries and Italian Renaissance ceilings. Living room/kitchenette, 3 bedrooms (2 double and 2 large single beds), shower room, electric heating, garage, garden furniture. Farm produce (0.5 km); other shopping in the village and a restaurant at 3 km.

Prices:	low season	F 750/800	**6 people**
	high season	F 950	*IGN 43*

Booking: Allier booking service   **E**
03/C419

SAINT-MARTINIEN Les Montées Situated in a hamlet, 1.5 km from the village, this renovated and rustically furnished gîte is built in typical local style. Tennis (1.5 km); fishing at a lake (8 km). Guided visits of Montluçon's old quarter (10 km) are available in summer. Living room, kichen, 2 bedrooms (1 double, 2 single beds), bathroom, open fire, electric heating, garage, enclosed courtyard. Shopping and restaurant (8 km) or at Montluçon.

Prices:	low season	F 650/750	**4 people**
	high season	F 950	*IGN 42*

Booking: Allier booking service   **E**
03/F490

SAINT-MENOUX A small, renovated and traditionally furnished gîte near the village centre. At 8 km is the historic spa town of Bourbon-l'Archambault where you can see the remains of the mediaeval château of the Dukes of Bourbon. Many leisure amenities at Moulins (15 km). Living room (1 single divan), kitchen, 1 bedroom (1 double and 1 single bed), shower room, open fire, electric central heating, enclosed courtyard with garden furniture. Farm produce, shopping and restaurant in the village.

Prices:	low season	F 736/822	**4 people**
	high season	F 958	*IGN 36*

Booking: Allier booking service   **E**
03/H368

SAINT-NICOLAS-DESBIEFS Boffet A modern chalet with rustic furnishings in the area known as the Bourbon Mountains (altitude 900 metres). This comfortable gîte benefits from good views and pleasant forest walks all around. Winter ski-ing at La Loge-des-Gardes (8 km). Living room/kitchenette, 2 bedrooms (4 single beds), bathroom, electric central heating, large balcony, enclosed ground with garden furniture and barbecue. Shopping in the village (0.2 km) or at Le Mayet (16 km).

Prices:	low season	F 650/886	**4 people**
	high season	F 1080	*IGN 43*

Booking: Allier booking service   **E**

03/C246

SOUVIGNY Les Andrets d'En Bas A renovated and traditionally furnished cottage, some 3 km from the town where you can see the splendid tombs of the Bourbon family in the cloisters of the priory church where organ recitals are often performed in summer. Many leisure amenities at Moulins (15 km). Living room (1 double divan), kitchen, 2 bedrooms (3 single beds, 1 cot), fireplace, electric heating, terrace, carport, enclosed courtyard and open ground (garden furniture). Farm produce from the owners; shopping and restaurant in the town.

Prices:	low season	F 536/623	**6 people**
	high season	F 732/752	*IGN 36*

Booking: Allier booking service   **E**
03/H485

Country Food and Wine in AUVERGNE

You will find small restaurants and fermes-auberges everywhere with a simple but tasy menu and reasonable prices but in the Auvergne you will also find 'grand cuisine'.

The regional cooking of the Auvergne derives the secret of remarkable flavour from the freshness and simplicity of its basic ingredients: cream, butter, eggs, meat – all of high quality; fruit and vegetables –all a delight to the eye and palate. The celebrated poultry of the Bourbonnais are themselves an important source of trade. And where woods and forests spread over hundreds of acres, ripe fruits and mushrooms of all sorts abound, while fine-fleshed fish fill the rivers and lakes.

Moreover, the Auvergne table offers all the variety of a traditional fare which is the dream of the gourmet:

Auvergne hotpot is a substantial dish of salted pork and cabbage. Coq au vin from Chanturgue owes its success to slow and careful cooking in the local wine; gigot 'brayaude' simmers for at least 5 hours before being served on a bed of larded potatoes flavoured with herbs. Trout is prepared in cheese or bacon fat. Edible fungi accompany meats but are also cooked in creamy sauces or omelettes. Nor should the salted meats be overlooked: locally cured ham, meat loaf, or sausage with lentils from Puy.

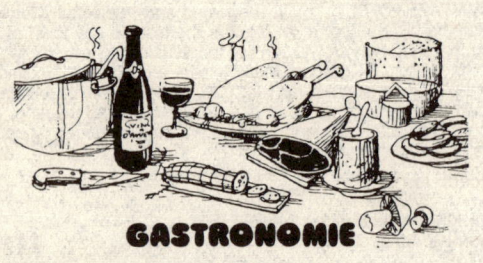

Pastry and cakes are excellent. 'Millard aux cerises' is a kind of creamy fruit tart which is eaten warm, as is the bilberry pie and apple 'pompe', the apple pie of the Auvergne.

Thanks to the abundance and quality of its fruits, fruit compotes and jams made in Limagne are justifiably renowned.

In addition to the established wines of 'appelation controlée' quality, you can sample the lesser-known local wines where they are actually produced and also liqueurs and special aromatic spirits from gentian, verveine, juniper etc.

But it is cheese which is the real glory of the Auvergne table. Cantal, Saint-Nectaire, Bleu de Laqueuille, Fourme d'Ambert . . . . these are cheeses which figure in the best menus all over the world.

For further information or enquiries: please contact:

COMITE REGIONAL DE TOURISME AUVERGNE,
43 Avenue Julien, B.P. 395,
63011 CLERMONT FERRAND
Cedex, France.
Tel: 73.93.04.03.

Cantal

CHEYLADE Fouilloux A stone-built gîte, lying on a farm in a delightful, lush valley. Cheylade (4 km) has a twelfth-century church, museum and cinema; see the nearby waterfalls in the regional Parc des Volcans. Cross-country ski-ing at 4 km; traditional ski-ing (40 km). Altitude 1000 metres. Kitchen, dining-room, 4 bedrooms (2 double, 3 single and 1 child's bed), bathroom, oil-fired central heating, open courtyard with garden furniture. Mobile baker and grocer call; other shopping in the village or at Riom-ès-Montagne (15 km).

Prices:	low season	F 1157/1357	**8 people**
	high season	F 1557	IGN 49
	winter season	F 1357	

Booking: Auvergne booking service E
15/550

LE CLAUX An attractive gîte in the owners' home in a village on the river Rhue (fishing permitted), where you can visit a pottery workshop (altitude 1080 metres). Local cross-country ski-ing; sailing at Cheylade lake (5 km). Guided walks available of this interesting volcanic region, studded with fine chestnut trees. Kitchen/diner, 2 bedrooms (2 double and 1 single bed), bathroom, oil-fired central heating, enclosed courtyard with garden furniture. Shopping at Cheylade or Riom-ès-Montagne (18 km).

Prices:	low season	F 800/850	**5 people**
	high season	F 1100	IGN 49
	winter season	F 1050	

Booking: Auvergne booking service E
15/373

LADINHAC Valette A modern gîte with traditional furnishings, built in local style, on a livestock farm where you may buy produce and take meals (including local specialities) with the owners who also have chambres d'hôte and a farm camp-site. Swimming-pool and tennis at Montsalvy (12 km). Altitude 630 metres. Living room/kitchenette (1 double divan), 1 bedroom (1 double and 1 single bed), shower room, fireplace, electric central heating, carport, open ground. Shopping and restaurant in the village (4 km).

Prices:	low season	F 657/700	**5 people**
	high season	F 950	IGN 58
	winter season	F 657	

Booking: Auvergne booking service E
15/136

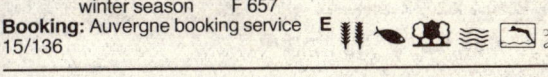

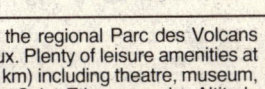

MANDAILLES A small village gîte in the regional Parc des Volcans which is dotted with numerous châteaux. Plenty of leisure amenities at the département capital of Aurillac (25 km) including theatre, museum, swimming-pool and tennis; visit Château Saint-Etienne nearby. Altitude 950 metres. Living room/kitchenette (1 double divan), 1 bedroom (1 double, 1 single and 1 child's bed), shower room, electric heating, enclosed courtyard with garden furniture. Farm produce and other shopping in the village.

Prices:	low season	F 607	**6 people**
	high season	F 1057	IGN 49
	winter season	F 1057	

Booking: Auvergne booking service E
15/392

Haute-Loire

ALLEYRAS A delightful, traditionally furnished gîte adjoining other buildings in picturesque village overlooking the River Allier (1 km). Le lac du Bouchet (15 km) has varied leisure activities. Le Puy-en-Velay (32 km) is a most interesting historic city. Altitude 750 metres. Living room (TV, 1 double divan), kitchen, 2 bedrooms (2 double beds), bathroom, gas heating, terrace, garage, courtyard (child's swing). Mobile shops and farm produce in village. Shops and restaurant at 2 km.

Prices:	low season	F 1000	**6 people**
	high season	F 1150	*IGN 50*

Booking: M J. GIBERT, 43570 Alleyras. Tel. (71) 57 57 31 **E**
43/448

BAINS Montbonnet A detached house with traditionally furnished accommodation all on the ground floor, situated on a mixed farm. Forest nearby; bathing at a lake (10 km) and swimming-pool and tennis at the département capital of Le Puy-en-Velay (15 km). Altitude 1000 metres. Living room, kitchen, 2 bedrooms (1 double and 2 single beds), bathroom, heating, terrace, enclosed ground. Linen available. Mobile baker, grocer and butcher call; farm produce and other shopping in the village (3 km).

Prices:	low season	F 724/780	**4 people**
	high season	F 1095/1191	*IGN 50*

Booking: M PLANTIN, Montbonnet-de-Bains, 43570 Solignac-sur-Loire. Tel. (71) 57 51 63.
43/504

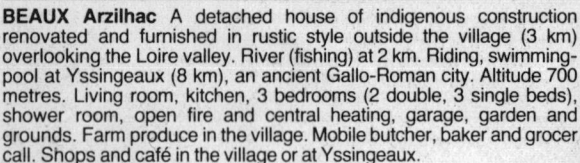

BEAUX Arzilhac A detached house of indigenous construction renovated and furnished in rustic style outside the village (3 km) overlooking the Loire valley. River (fishing) at 2 km. Riding, swimming-pool at Yssingeaux (8 km), an ancient Gallo-Roman city. Altitude 700 metres. Living room, kitchen, 3 bedrooms (2 double, 3 single beds), shower room, open fire and central heating, garage, garden and grounds. Farm produce in the village. Mobile butcher, baker and grocer call. Shops and café in the village or at Yssingeaux.

Prices:	low season	F 625/668	**7 people**
	high season	F 780/880	*IGN 50*

Booking: M P. COULOMB, Arzilhac-Beaux, 43200 Yssingeaux.
43/431

CRAPONNE-SUR-ARZON La Monatte One of two gîtes, in a renovated house with traditional furnishings. It lies 1 km from the centre of Craponne, an old town with some fine Renaissance and medieval architecture. Try the local charcuterie and liqueurs. Altitude 920 metres. Living room, kitchen, 2 bedrooms (2 double, 1 single bed), shower room, central heating, carport and open courtyard. Linen available (F 22 per set per week). Shopping and restaurant in Craponne or at Le Puy-en-Velay (40 km).

Prices:	low season	F 615	**5 people**
	high season	F 820	*IGN 50*

Booking: M POUGNET-JOURDE, La Monatte, 43500 Craponne-sur-Arzon. Tel. (71) 03 35 17.
43/373

ESPALEM La Baraque A renovated and traditionally furnished gîte on a sheep farm, in a tiny hamlet, 2.5 km from the village (altitude 650 metres). A quiet spot with views of the Auvergne mountains. Visit the interesting old village of Blesle (6 km). Living room/kitchenette, 2 bedrooms (1 double, 2 single and 1 child's bed), shower room, oil-fired central heating, balcony, enclosed ground shared with the owners. Linen available. Farm produce available; mobile shops call, other shopping at Blesle; a restaurant at 4 km.

Prices:	low season	F 570/685	**5 people**
	high season	F 770/910	*IGN 49*

Booking: M C. DELAIR, La Baraque, Espalem, 43450 Blesle. Tel. (71) 76 20 50.
43/73

Haute-Loire

GRENIER-MONTGON Fleurival An unusual and very spacious gîte with traditional country furniture in the wing of a manor house near the Allagnon river. Swimming-pool, tennis and riding at 3 km and there is a lake at 30 km. Altitude 550 metres. Living room (TV), kitchen, 2 bedrooms (2 double, 1 single bed and 1 child's cot), bathroom, fireplace, gas central heating, grounds with garden furniture. Linen available. Mobile butcher and local farm produce; shopping in the village (0.6 km), other shopping and restaurant at Massiac (3 km). 
Prices: low season F 800/900 **6 people**
   high season not available IGN 49
Booking: M SOULIE, Fleurival, 43450 Grenier-Montgon.
Tel. (71) 76 22 26 **E**
43/610

RAUCOULES Rochette One of two gîtes with country-style furnishings on a farm at the edge of the village (0.7 km). Good local walks; a swimming-pool, riding and tennis all within 10 km. Visit the former Roman town of Yssingeaux (20 km approx.). Altitude 960 metres. Living room, kitchen, 3 bedrooms (2 double and 1 large single bed), shower room, fireplace (wood supplied), oil heating, enclosed ground with child's swings. Farm produce from the owners or in the village; other shopping at Montfaucon (2 km). 
Prices: low season F 550/600 **5 people**
   high season F 720/750 IGN 50
Booking: Mme A. SOUVIGNHEC, Rochette, Raucoules, 43290 Montfaucon. Tel. (71) 59 94 01.
43/407

SAINT-ETIENNE-LARDEYROL Fougères A renovated, stone-built house, traditionally furnished, lying near the owners' house, 4 km from the village (altitude 800 metres). Swimming-pool, tennis and other leisure facilities at Yssingeaux (12 km); riding at 15 km. Living room, kitchen, 3 bedrooms (2 double and 2 single beds), shower room, open fire, enclosed ground. Linen available. Mobile shops call. Other shopping and restaurant in the village. 
Prices: low season F 500/700 **6 people**
   high season F 800/850 IGN 50
Booking: M A. PAULIN, Fougères, Saint-Etienne-Lardeyrol, 43260 Saint-Julien-Chapteuil. Tel. (71) 03 01 97.

43/721

SAINT-JULIEN-CHAPTEUIL A substantial old house, renovated and furnished in traditional fashion, lying near the village centre (altitude 815 metres). Ideally situated for exploring the Auvergne's volcanic landscape. Cross-country ski-ing (1 km). Living room, kitchen, 4 bedrooms (1 double, 4 single, 1 child's bed), bathroom, open fire (wood supplied), gas heater, garage, garden with furniture. Shopping and restaurant in the village (0.3 km) or at Le Puy-en-Velay (18 km). 
Prices: low season F 800 **7 people**
   high season F 1000/1150 IGN 50
Booking: M H. JEAN, 24 rue Charles VII, Espaly, 43000 Le Puy-en-Velay. Tel. (71) 09 55 25.
43/866

SAINT-JULIEN-CHAPTEUIL Les Fromentaux A newly built detached house with rustic furnishings. Bicycle hire at the local tourist office (2 km). Also in the town are a ruined château and prehistoric caves. Altitude 830 metres. Living room, kitchen, 2 bedrooms (1 double and 2 single beds), shower room, open fire, gas central heating, terrace, enclosed ground. Shopping in Saint-Julien (2 km) or at Le Puy-en-Velay (18 km). 
Prices: low season F 1165 **4 people**
   high season F 1165 IGN 50
   winter season F 1425
Booking: M P. LIMAGNE, 24 rue Vibert, 43000 Le-Puy-en-Velay.
Tel. (71) 05 45 72 **E**
43/361

Haute-Loire

SAINT-JULIEN-DES-CHAZES Le Monteil A renovated and tastefully furnished gîte, one of two, lying at an altitude of 750 metres. Allier River with its splendid fishing (4 km); swimming-pool, tennis and riding at Langeac leisure centre (10 km). Lounge/kitchenette, 3 bedrooms and attic room (2 double, 3 single and 1 child's bed), bathroom, oil-fired central heating, terrace, courtyard. Restaurant (2 km). Shopping at Langeac market (10 km) or from mobile stores.

Prices: low season   F 780   **8 people**
          high season   F 1040/1050   IGN 50

Booking: M A. VALENTIN, Plaine de Von, 43300 Langeac. Tel. (71) 77 07 83.

43/423

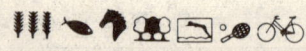

SAINT-JULIEN-DES-CHAZES Le Monteil A second gîte, furnished in traditional country style, in the charming, renovated house described above, approx. 3 km from the village. Langeac (10 km) is a delightful old château town where the colourful St Gal festival is celebrated on the first Sunday of July. Living room/kitchenette, 4 bedrooms (4 double beds), attic room (1 double divan), bathroom, fireplace (wood supplied), terrace, enclosed ground with furniture and barbecue. Shopping at Langeac.

Prices: low season   F 780   **10 people**
          high season   F 1170/1240   IGN 50

Booking: M A. VALENTIN, Plaine de Von, 43300 Langeac. Tel. (71) 77 07 83.

43/712

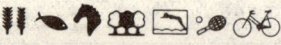

SAUGUES Le Rouve A traditionally furnished, semi-detached house in a quiet spot, surrounded by fields and woods, some 4.5 km from Saugues where a very active tourist office offers many leisure pursuits. Bathing at a lake and tennis courts at Saugues. Altitude 1000 metres. Living room/kitchenette (washing machine), 3 bedrooms (2 double, 2 single beds), bathroom, open fire and electric central heating, terrace, enclosed ground. Farm produce and restaurant nearby; other shopping at Saugues.

Prices: low season   F 630   **6 people**
          high season   F 800/900   IGN 50

Booking: Mme A. LEBRAT, rue des Roches, 43170 Saugues. Tel. (71) 77 82 72   **E**

43/615

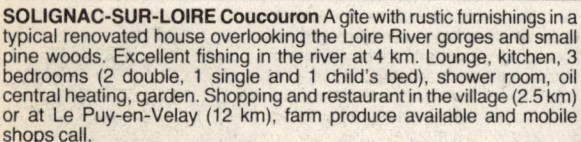

SOLIGNAC-SUR-LOIRE Coucouron A gîte with rustic furnishings in a typical renovated house overlooking the Loire River gorges and small pine woods. Excellent fishing in the river at 4 km. Lounge, kitchen, 3 bedrooms (2 double, 1 single and 1 child's bed), shower room, oil central heating, garden. Shopping and restaurant in the village (2.5 km) or at Le Puy-en-Velay (12 km), farm produce available and mobile shops call.

Prices: low season   F 650   **6 people**
          high season   F 948/1010   IGN 50

Booking: M J. B. MATHIEU, Le Val-de-Mialaure, Route de Saugues Espaly, 43000 Le Puy-en-Velay. Tel. (71) 09 62 78   **E**

43/330

SANSSAC-L'EGLISE Domaine de Barret Chambre d'hôte accommodation in the owners' substantial farmhouse which has been renovated and traditionally furnished, in a quiet spot, 10 km from Le Puy-en-Velay where you can visit the cattle market; winter sports, 38 km. Two rooms available, each with 1 double, 2 single and 1 folding bed, shared bathroom, lounge, kitchen, central heating, terrace, garage and open ground. Meals available; a restaurant in the village (1 km). Shopping at Le Puy-en-Velay.

Prices: on request   **10 people**
          IGN 50

Booking: M J. GARNIER, Domaine de Barret, Sanssac-l'Eglise 43320 Loudes. Tel. (71) 08 64 78.

43/15

Puy-de-Dôme

AVEZE Les Plantades This gîte is surrounded by farmland and lies in its own garden, 4 km from the small mountain town of Avéze (altitude 850 metres). Local sites include the Gorges d'Avéze and the Château de Chazelles. Canoeing (4 km); ski-ing at 26 km. Living room, kitchen, 3 bedrooms (2 double and 3 single beds), bathroom, open fire, electric central heating, ground with garden furniture. Mobile butcher and baker call; other shopping at Tauves (5 km).

Prices:	low season	F 820/1100	**7 people**
	high season	F 1600	IGN 42

Booking: Auvergne booking service E

63/888

BAGNOLS Chassagnoux A ground-floor gîte in the owners' holiday home, on farmland, 2 km from the village (altitude 850 metres). La Tour d'Auvergne lake (10 km) has facilities for bathing and fishing. Traditional and cross-country ski-ing at Chambourget (14 km); riding at 18 km. Living room, kitchen, 2 bedrooms (2 double and 1 child's bed), shower room, heating, garden with outdoor furniture. Linen available. Shopping in the village.

Prices:	low season	F 860	**5 people**
	high season	F 1060	IGN 42

Booking: Auvergne booking service E

63/795

BESSE-EN-CHANDESSE Les Janiauts One of three gîtes in a modern terrace in an old town of the Monts-Dore Regional Park, where there is a cheese market on Mondays. A lake for sailing and bathing, skating-rink and ski-ing at Super-Besse (7 km). Altitude 950 metres. Living room/kitchenette, 3 bedrooms (2 double and 3 single beds), bathroom, oil-fired central heating, terrace, enclosed ground with garden furniture. Shopping in the village or at Murol (11 km).

Prices:	low season	F 967/1020	**7 people**
	high season	F 1463	IGN 42
	winter season	F 1717	

Booking: Auvergne booking service E

63/901

LA BOURBOULE L'Etable du Prégnoux One of two gîtes in the owners' unusual old house at the edge of this spa town where the many leisure facilities include a golf course, leisure park, tennis, swimming-pool and a casino. Sites to see in the region include lakes, waterfalls and mountain peaks. Altitude 950 metres. Living room/kitchenette, 2 bedrooms (1 double and 2 single beds), shower room, oil-fired central heating, terrace, garden with furniture. Linen available. Shopping and restaurant in the town (1.5 km).

Prices:	low season	F 757/1025	**4 people**
	high season	F 1309	IGN 42
	winter season	F 1365	

Booking: Auvergne booking service E
63/777

CHATEL-GUYON Rochepradière One of a group of twenty-four modern chalets in a holiday village set in pleasant wooded surroundings, 2.5 km from the spa town of Châtel-Guyon. Leisure amenities in the town include swimming-pool, riding, miniature golf, cinemas and a casino. You are just 20 km from the département capital of Clermont-Ferrand. Living room, kitchen, 1 bedroom (4 single beds), bathroom, gas heating, terrace, open ground (shared with the other gîtes). Linen available. Shopping in the town.

Prices:	low season	F 789/955	**4 people**
	high season	F 1109	IGN 50

Booking: Auvergne booking service E
63/820

Puy-de-Dôme

CHATEL-GUYON A second, larger gîte in the holiday village described above where you will not be bored with all the amenities in the town nearby (2.5 km), and many châteaux and other sites to see. Clermont-Ferrand, the home of Michelin tyres, is well worth a visit (20 km). Living room, kitchen, 2 bedrooms (1 double and 3 single beds), bathroom, gas central heating, terrace, open grounds with garden furniture. Linen available. Shopping in the town.

Prices:	low season	F 898/1062	**5 people**
	high season	F 1226	*IGN 50*

Booking: Auvergne booking service   **E**
63/836

CHAUMONT-LE-BOURG One of two adjoining gîtes at the centre of the village (altitude 650 metres). Arlanc (6 km) has a lace museum and a lake for bathing and fishing. Early risers may find mushrooms to pick in the forest nearby. Swimming-pool, tennis and riding at Ambert (13 km). Living room/kitchenette, 3 bedrooms (2 double and 2 single beds), shower room, open fire, carport, open courtyard. Shopping at the château town of Marsac-en-Livradois (4 km).

Prices:	low season	F 600/750	**6 people**
	high season	F 1000	*IGN 50*

Booking: Auvergne booking service   **E**
63/870

COUDES A small gîte situated at the edge of the village, lying on the river Allier where there is salmon fishing. The village also has mineral waters and such attractions as a ruined château and gothic bridge. There is a wax museum, swimming-pool and other leisure facilities at Issoire (11 km); ski-ing at 37 km. Living room (1 double divan), kitchen, 1 bedroom (1 double bed), bathroom, open fire, electric central heating, garage, enclosed ground. Mobile baker calls; other shopping in the village (1.5 km).

Prices:	low season	F 750/900	**4 people**
	high season	F 1150	*IGN 42*
	winter season	F 1000	

Booking: Auvergne booking service   **E**
63/687

GIAT Route d'Herment A small gîte adjoining another house at the centre of this small town which has a regular market (altitude 780 metres). Local riding and forest walks. There is an interesting tumulus nearby and Condat-en-Combraille (10 km) has a lake where you may bathe. Living room (1 double divan), kitchen, 1 bedroom (1 double bed), bathroom, electric heating, balcony, garage, courtyard with garden furniture. Farm produce and other shopping in the village.

Prices:	low season	F 817	**4 people**
	high season	F 918	*IGN 42*
	winter season	F 817	

Booking: Auvergne booking service   **E**
63/775

LE MONT-DORE Le Rigolet-Haut An attractive cottage on a mixed farm, ideal for summer or winter visitors (altitude 1175 metres). At the ski resort and spa town of Le Mont-Dore (3 km) you can see the old Roman baths and enjoy the many modern amenities and, of course, ski-ing. Living room/kitchenette (washing and washing-up machines), 3 bedrooms (2 double and 3 single beds), bathroom, fireplace, electric central heating, open ground with garden furniture. Farm produce and shopping in the town.

Prices:	low season	F 1874/2052	**7 people**
	high season	F 1988	*IGN 42*
	winter season	F 2150	

Booking: Auvergne booking service   **E**
63/225b

Puy-de-Dôme

LES PRADEAUX One of two gîtes near a river (1 km) where you can go canoeing. Issoire (7 km), an old town on the rivers Allier and Couze (salmon fishing), has tennis courts, swimming pool and facilities for gliding and riding. See the Perrier caves nearby. Ski-ing at 39 km. Living room/kitchenette, 2 bedrooms (1 double and 1 single bed), shower room, electric central heating, open courtyard and ground. Shopping at Issoire.

Prices:	low season	F 525/640	**3 people**
	high season	F 740	IGN 42
	winter season	F 640	

Booking: Auvergne booking service E
63/914

ROCHE-CHARLES-LA-MAYRAND La Mayrand One of two gîtes in a house situated on open ground on a mountain farm (altitude 1050 metres). Cross-country ski-ing at 6 km; fishing and boating at Pavin lake (22 km). Many facilities for winter and summer visitors at the ski resort of Super-Besse (25 km). Living room/kitchenette (2 single divans), 2 bedrooms (1 double and 2 single beds), bathroom, fireplace, electric central heating, open ground with garden furniture. Shopping at Compains (6 km) or at Ardes-sur-Couze (16 km).

Prices:	low season	F 770/890	**6 people**
	high season	F 1005	IGN 49
	winter season	F 890	

Booking: Auvergne booking service E
63/884

SAILLANT One of five small gîtes in a large, attractive house standing at the village centre (altitude 930 metres). The old town of Viverols (8 km) has a medieval château and a museum. Ambert (25 km) is a centre of paper production and has a museum tracing the history of the industry. A zoological park at 26 km. Living room/kitchenette, 2 bedrooms (1 double and 2 single beds), shower room, open fire, electric central heating, courtyard shared by all the gîtes. Mobile butcher calls; farm produce and other shopping in the village.

Prices:	low season	F 750	**4 people**
	high season	F 860	IGN 50
	winter season	F 750	

Booking: Auvergne booking service E
63/281

SAINT-GERVAIS-D'AUVERGNE Etang des Ouches A small gîte, ideal for fishermen, as it lies near a small lake where the owners have another gîte, 2 km from the village (altitude 720 metres). Tennis in the village; see the Fades viaduct at 7 km and many châteaux in the area. Sailing at Besserve lake (20 km). Living room, kitchen, 2 bedrooms (1 double and 2 single beds), bathroom, no heating, open fields with garden furniture. Linen available. Shopping in the village.

Prices:	low season	F 692	**4 people**
	high season	F 827	IGN 42

Booking: Auvergne booking service E

63/812

SAINT-NECTAIRE Freydefond A gîte situated 4 km from the spa town of Saint-Nectaire, a town noted for its cheese of the same name. It lies in the Mont-Dore Regional Park, where sites include standing stones, caves, waterfalls and curious petrifying fountains. Chambon lake (10 km); ski-ing at 17 km. Altitude 900 metres. Living room/kitchenette (TV washing machine), 4 bedrooms (2 double, 3 single and 2 child's beds), bathroom, electric central heating, balcony, garage, ground, Linen available. Mobile baker and grocer call; other shopping in the town.

Prices:	low season	F 867/1068	**9 people**
	high season	F 1591	IGN 49
	winter season	F 1330	

Booking: Auvergne booking service E
63/757

Puy-de-Dôme

SAINT-NECTAIRE Freydefond A spacious gîte, situated 4 km from the spa town of Saint-Nectaire where leisure amenities include a casino, tennis, riding and children's amusement park. It lies in the Mont-Dore Regional Park at the heart of the Auvergne region of volcanoes, lakes and châteaux. Ski-ing (17 km). Altitude 930 metres. Living room/kitchenette, 4 bedrooms (4 double and 1 child's bed), shower room, electric central heating, courtyard. Shopping and restaurants in the town.

Prices:	low season	F 1060/1250	**9 people**
	high season	F 1636	IGN 49
	winter season	F 1609	

Booking: Auvergne booking service E
63/871

SAINT-NECTAIRE Saillant One of two gîtes in a renovated house at the edge of the town (altitude 700 metres). Saint-Nectaire is an interesting spa town with caves where the local cheese is matured (available at the weekly market) and a fountain containing minerals which can set to stone objects put into it. Bed-sitting room (2 double beds), kitchen, electric central heating, terrace. Shopping and restaurants in the town.

Prices:	low season	F 695/746	**4 people**
	high season	F 1140	IGN 49
	winter season	F 790	

Booking: Auvergne booking service E
63/793

LA TOUR-D'AUVERGNE Le Parc Saint-Pardoux A gîte in the owners' holiday home near the village centre which has a ruined feudal château and a lake for bathing and fishing. The surrounding countryside is dotted with waterfalls; see the Gorges de la Burande. Ski-ing (11 km) and La Bourboule leisure centre is at 13 km. Altitude 950 metres. Living room/kitchenette (TV), 2 bedrooms (2 double and 1 single bed), shower room, electric central heating, balcony, garden with outdoor furniture. Linen available. Shopping in the village.

Prices:	low season	F 825/985	**5 people**
	high season	F 1210	IGN 49
	winter season	F 1110	

Booking: Auvergne booking service E
63/886

VOLLORE-MONTAGNE Le Verdier One of six purpose-built holiday homes owned by the local commune and situated 2 km from the village (altitude 900 metres). Tennis at Noirétable (9 km); other leisure facilities at Saint-Rémy-sur-Durolle (20 km) which has a large lake with sandy beaches. Ski-ing at 30 km. Living room/kitchenette (1 single divan), 2 bedrooms (1 double and 2 single beds), shower room, electric central heating, carport, open ground and barbecue shared by all the gîtes. Shopping in the village or at Noirétable.

Prices:	low season	F 560/631	**5 people**
	high season	F 975	IGN 43
	winter season	F 560	

Booking: Auvergne booking service E
63/861

VOLLORE-MONTAGNE Le Verdier Another of the gîtes described above, set in the Forez mountains (altitude 900 metres). Local riding and forest walks; cross-country ski-ing at Col de la Loge (15 km). Leisure amenities at Saint-Rémy-sur-Durolle lake (20 km) include sailing, miniature golf, pedalo boats etc. Living room/kitchenette (1 single bed, 1 single divan), 1 bedroom (1 double bed), shower room, electric central heating, carport, open ground with barbecue shared by all the gîtes. Shopping in the village or at Noirétable (9 km).

Prices:	low season	F 516/521	**4 people**
	high season	F 745	IGN 43
	winter season	F 521	

Booking: Auvergne booking service E
63/866

5 LIMOUSIN

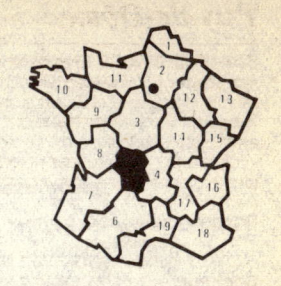

A peaceful, traditional way of life is offered to visitors in this charming, historic land of hills and valleys, forests and plains, rivers and picturesque, ancient cities where the old, almost forgotten skills of tapestry weaving and quality pottery are still going on.

Fording the river Vienne, lies Limoges, synonymous with ceramics, fine enamelwork, chinaware and porcelain which are on display both in museums and shops. At the Adrien-Dubouché Museum you can follow the industrial development of pottery in Limousin. The Municipal Museum also contains examples of local enamelwork from its early beginnings to the present day. Not far away is the small market town of St. Léonard-de-Noblat, where November visitors can enjoy the 'Quintaine' ceremony, in memory of the patron saint of prisoners, a spectacle where horsemen demolish a symbolic wooden castle. Wherever you go in Haute-Vienne, you will never be far from the road taken by pilgrims on the way to St. Jacques-de-Compostelle and the fine Romanesque and Gothic churches and castles, constructed in a wide variety of styles, remarkable considering the almost compulsory use of granite.

The wide valley along the river Creuse provides grazing land for the sheep whose wool is used for the splendid tapestries exhibited in the town hall at Aubusson during the summer. Weavers at tapestry workshops will be pleased to show their fine work in wool, silk and even gold and silver threads. You can also visit the "Maison du Vieux Tapissier" and relive the story of the Corneille Family who for centuries made their living from weaving. A splendid mediaeval fortress situated at the meeting point of the rivers Creuse and Sédelle,
gives the village of Crozant a very imposing approach
and has been named "the key to the Limousin".

Restaurant du Lac

Mme & M. Solignac, Camps, 19430 Mercoeur, Correze
Tel: 55.28.51.83

Camps is a little village in the south of Correze with typical houses and pleasant walks, swimming and tennis available. There are worthwhile visits nearby to Padirac, Rocamedour, Reygade, Argentat and les Tours de Merle. The Hotel/Restaurant du Lac offers full or half board accommodation and an excellent cuisine with such specialities as fresh duck's liver with grapes; grilled 'magret' of duck with green pepper sauce; omelettes and chocolate sweet. Full board for two persons from 308 FF and half board for two from 208 FF. *(Please book by letter or phone, in English if you wish.)*

Map

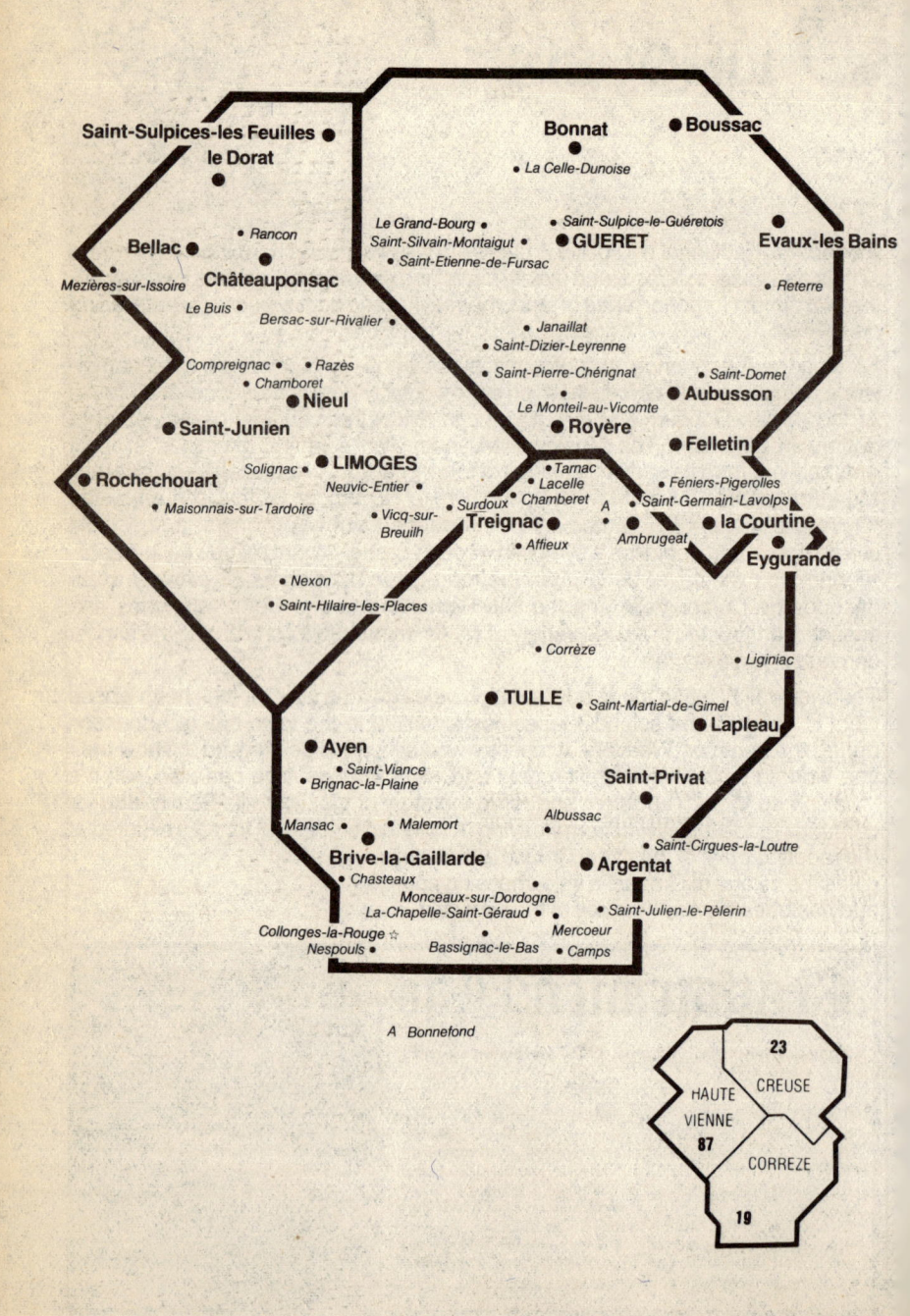

Haute-Vienne (87), Creuse (23), Corrèze (19)

- Saint-Sulpices-les-Feuilles
- le Dorat
- Rancon
- Bellac
- Châteauponsac
- Mezières-sur-Issoire
- Le Buis
- Bersac-sur-Rivalier
- Compreignac
- Razès
- Chamboret
- Nieul
- Saint-Junien
- Solignac
- LIMOGES
- Rochechouart
- Neuvic-Entier
- Maisonnais-sur-Tardoire
- Vicq-sur-Breuilh
- Surdoux
- Nexon
- Saint-Hilaire-les-Places

- Bonnat
- Boussac
- La Celle-Dunoise
- Le Grand-Bourg
- Saint-Sulpice-le-Guéretois
- Saint-Silvain-Montaigut
- GUERET
- Saint-Etienne-de-Fursac
- Evaux-les-Bains
- Reterre
- Janaillat
- Saint-Dizier-Leyrenne
- Saint-Pierre-Chérignat
- Saint-Domet
- Le Monteil-au-Vicomte
- Aubusson
- Royère
- Felletin
- Tarnac
- Lacelle
- Féniers-Pigerolles
- Chamberet
- Saint-Germain-Lavolps
- Treignac
- Ambrugeat
- la Courtine
- Affieux
- Eygurande

- Corrèze
- Liginiac
- TULLE
- Saint-Martial-de-Gimel
- Lapleau
- Ayen
- Saint-Viance
- Saint-Privat
- Brignac-la-Plaine
- Albussac
- Mansac
- Malemort
- Brive-la-Gaillarde
- Saint-Cirgues-la-Loutre
- Chasteaux
- Argentat
- Monceaux-sur-Dordogne
- La-Chapelle-Saint-Géraud
- Saint-Julien-le-Pèlerin
- Collonges-la-Rouge ☆
- Mercoeur
- Nespouls
- Bassignac-le-Bas
- Camps

A Bonnefond

```
       23
    CREUSE
HAUTE
VIENNE
  87
       CORREZE
       19
```

Limousin
Take the road to discovery

Limousin is a region where you will always find something new.

Discover the rich and fascinating secrets of its countryside: the wide open spaces of Creuse, the red sandstone of Corrèze, the forests of Haute-Vienne.

Delve into Limousin's past — you will find its spirit lingering in its old buildings, Romanesque churches, Limoges porcelain and Aubusson tapestries.

Experience Limousin today through its lively people and the many leisure facilities they have to offer: fishing, sailing, riding, tennis, cycling.

Enjoy the Limousin way of life — it is such a dynamic yet delightful area. The more you get to know it, the more you will grow to love it.

To organize your holiday in Limousin, send for our free brochure to:

Comité Régional de Tourisme du Limousin (FFVHG),
8 cours Bugeaud,
87000 Limoges.
Tel. (55) 79.57.12.

Le Limousin
Tous ses chemins mènent à la découverte

Corrèze

AFFIEUX Balème One of three traditionally furnished gîtes in a renovated house outside the village (altitude 540 metres). Ideal for ramblers as it lies near the Millevaches Plateau footpath (GR440). Many summer activities are organised at Treignac-sur-Vezère (3 km); bathing and sailing at a lake (4 km). Living room, kitchen, 2 bedrooms (2 double and 1 single bed), shower room, open fire, electric heating, open communal ground. Farm produce in the village (2 km); shopping and restaurant at Treignac.

Prices:	low season	F 460/580	**5 people**
	high season	F 870/1030	*IGN 48*

Booking: Corrèze Loisirs Accueil **E**
19/3.001

AMBRUGEAT Le Bourg One of two traditionally furnished gîtes in a converted village school, looked after by the local mayor. Local fishing; bathing and sailing at a large lake within walking distance (1 km). Other leisure facilities at the interesting old town of Meymac (4 km). Altitude 680 metres. Living room (1 double divan), kitchen, 2 bedrooms (1 double and 2 single beds), bathroom, electric central heating, carport, open ground shared with the other gîte. Farm produce in the village; other shopping and restaurant at Meymac.

Prices:	low season	F 430/540	**6 people**
	high season	F 860/1040	*IGN 48*

Booking: Corrèze Loisirs Accueil **E**
19/3.131

BASSIGNAC-LE-BAS La Flamanchie A simply furnished gîte, in a large old house in a delightful wooded setting of the Dordogne valley, 2 km from the village. Visit the lovely town of Beaulieu-sur-Dordogne, the 'Riviera Limousine' and see the Gorges de la Dordogne. Living room (1 single divan), kitchen, 4 bedrooms (4 double beds), bathroom and shower, no heating, terrace, large open ground with garden furniture. Shopping and restaurant at Beaulieu-sur-Dordogne (5 km).

Prices:	low season	F 825	**9 people**
	high season	F 1235/1340	*IGN 48*

Booking: Corrèze Loisirs Accueil **E**

19/6.001

BONNEFOND Le Bourg An attractively renovated stone cottage with country-style furnishings, set in its own enclosed ground in a fairly isolated little village (altitude 850 metres). The elderly owners live close by. Local cross-country ski-ing. Sailing and bathing at Viam lake and other leisure amenities in Bugeat (10 km). Living room/kitchenette, 4 bedrooms (3 double and 1 single bed), bathroom, fireplace, oil-fired central heating. A grocer in the village; other shopping at Bugeat; farm produce from the owners.

Prices:	low season	F 615/820	**7 people**
	high season	F 1165	*IGN 48*

Booking: Corrèze Loisirs Accueil **E**
19/3.018

BRIGNAC-LA-PLAINE La Cabane A comfortably furnished and well-renovated house in a fairly isolated spot (although the owners' parents live nearby). Tennis in the village (2 km); all kinds of water sports at the Causse-Corrézien lake (15 km). The interesting old town of Brive-la-Gaillarde (22 km) is well worth a visit. Living room, kitchen, 3 bedrooms and open landing (2 double, 3 single beds, 1 single divan), bathroom and shower, fireplace, electric central heating, terrace, open ground. Shopping in the village or at La Rivière-de-Mansac (9 km).

Prices:	low season	F 650/700	**8 people**
	high season	F 1100/1410	*IGN 48*

Booking: Corrèze Loisirs Accueil **E**
19/2.027

Corrèze

CAMPS Maison Neuve Situated on a livestock farm, this renovated stone house with country-style furnishings is typical of the Limousin (altitude 550 metres). The interesting old town of Argentat-sur-Dordogne in the Dordogne valley (15 km) has a swimming-pool, tennis courts and other leisure facilities including sailing at Sablier lake. Living room/kitchenette, 3 bedrooms (2 double, 1 single and 1 child's bed), shower room, electric heating, open ground. Farm produce, shopping and restaurant in the village (3 km).

Prices: low season   F 540/650   **6 people**
high season   F 960/1040   *IGN 48*

Booking: Corrèze Loisirs Accueil   **E**

19/6.003

CHAMBERET Moulin de Bonnac This large, simply furnished gîte has been converted from a former water-mill. It stands in a slightly isolated spot amongst a few other farm buildings, 4 km from the village. Tennis and riding in the village. Sailing at Treignac lake (12 km); see the Gallo-Roman ruins at Les Cars (20 km approx.). Living room, kitchen (washing machine), 5 bedrooms (4 double and 1 single bed), bathroom, no heating, garage, open ground. Shopping and restaurant in the village, or at Treignac.

Prices: low season   F 700/780   **9 people**
high season   F 1180/1260   *IGN 41*

Booking: Corrèze Loisirs Accueil   **E**

19/3.029

LA-CHAPELLE-SAINT-GERAUD Le Bourg A semi-detached village house (altitude 580 metres), renovated and traditionally furnished. See the reservoirs in the Dordogne valley; the picturesque town of Beaulieu (10 km approx.) has an abbey church and lies in the delightful region known as the Limousin Riviera. Hall (1 double divan), living room, kitchen, 2 bedrooms (2 double beds), bathroom, electric central heating, garage, garden (opposite the gîte) with furniture. Mobile shops call, other shopping and restaurant in the village or at Argentat (7 km).

Prices: low season   F 470/535   **6 people**
high season   F 795/915   *IGN 48*

Booking: Corrèze Loisirs Accueil   **E**

19/6.012

CHASTEAUX Rozier A simply furnished ground-floor gîte, one of two in a converted watermill near the village centre. All water sports at the Causse-Corrézien lake (1 km); bicycles for hire and plenty to see and do at Brive (15 km), a town which is a delightful blend of old and new. Living room, kitchen, 2 bedrooms (2 double, 1 single bed), shower room, terrace and open grounds. Farm produce in the village (0.2 km), other shopping at Larche (8 km).

Prices: low season   F 430/560   **5 people**
high season   F 770/910   *IGN 48*

Booking: Corrèze Loisirs Accueil   **E**

19/2.038

CORREZE Le Cayre A very comfortably furnished and well-renovated house at the heart of the countryside and well situated for exploring the rest of the département. Sailing at a lake (6 km), and all the facilities of a large town at the département capital of Tulle (20 km). Altitude 550 metres. Living room, kitchen, 3 bedrooms (2 double, 1 single bed and a child's cot), shower room, fireplace, electric central heating, carport, large open ground. Farm produce, shopping and restaurant in the village (2 km).

Prices: low season   F 555/860   **5/6 people**
high season   F 1120/1300   *IGN 48*

Booking: Corrèze Loisirs Accueil   **E**

19/1.040

Correze
IN LIMOUSIN

Collonges-la-Rouge

CORREZE

Situated in Central France, the Corrèze neighbours on Dordogne and Quercy, with a similar climate and peaceful life style. It's a region of great natural beauty, a land of tranquil rivers abounding in fish, vast tracts of open countryside, sloping hills and valleys, lakes, pools and forests full of quiet charm.

The Correze people know how to welcome visitors and offer their best home-grown products – foie gras, truffles, trouts, cherry flan – ("clafoutis").

You will get there quickly with the new French Railways Motorail which will whisk you and your car to BRIVE. When you walk by the Dordogne River, on the Millevaches Plateau or on the Causse Corrézien, you will want to come back.

HISTORY

The main town, BRIVE, built in 200 BC, is a town steeped in history. Many interesting buildings from past centuries still remain, including the Ernest Rupin Museum. Indeed the whole of Corrèze bears witness to its past be it through museums, old castles built along the Dordogne river, Romanesque churches or lovely villages such as Pompadour, Collonges-la-Rouge or Uzerche, built on a rock and surrounded on three sides by the river Vézère.

Special Interest Holidays

RESERVATION LOISIRS ACCUEIL

SPORTS AND LEISURE

Enjoy all kinds of water sport in the many natural and artificial lakes. Selected and varied country holidays packages and itineraries for walking, cycling, canoeing, horse-drawn caravans or for riding are also available.

ACCOMMODATION

- a range of Tourist hotels from one to four stars, with competitive prices including many "Logis de France" and "Auberges rurales" known for their warm welcome and traditional cooking.
- well-equipped camping grounds.
- "gîtes ruraux" comfortable, self-catering country dwellings situated near farms or villages.
- "chambres d'hôtes" which offer a bed for the night and breakfast in the morning and where farmers organise week-ends to teach you how to preserve "confits d'oie et canard", how to use precious truffles and make country bread.
- holiday villages in the Dordogne Valley.

For booking and any further information about holidays and accommodation contact:

RESERVATION LOISIRS-ACCUEIL CORREZE
Comité Départemental de Tourisme
Quai Baluze
19000 TULLE
Tél. (55) 26.46.88
Télex: CCITUL 590-140 F (Gîtes ruraux)

Corrèze

LACELLE Magadoux A former farmhouse which has been renovated and traditionally furnished, surrounded by empty buildings on a farm, 5 km from the village (altitude 700 metres). For real country-lovers, this gîte is on the rugged Millevaches Plateau, a region of forests, fields and streams (good for fishing). Living room/kitchenette, 4 bedrooms (2 double, 2 single beds), shower room, fireplace, gas central heating, enclosed ground. Farm produce, shopping and restaurant in the village or at Bugeat (10 km).

Prices:	low season	F 600	**6 people**
	high season	F 880/940	*IGN 41*

Booking: Corrèze Loisirs Accueil   **E**

19/3.051

LAPLEAU Laporte A rustically furnished gîte on an arable farm, surrounded by woodland just outside the village (1.5 km). All kinds of water sports at Marcillac-la-Croisille lake (12 km); see too the Rochers Noirs viaduct and the sixteenth-century Château de Burc nearby. Altitude 550 metres. Living room/kitchenette, 2 bedrooms (2 double and 1 child's bed), bathroom, gas central heating, terrace, garage, enclosed ground with garden furniture. Linen available. Farm produce, shopping and restaurant in the village or at Egletons (12 km).

Prices:	low season	on request	**4/5 people**
	high season	on request	*IGN 48*

Booking: Corrèze booking service

19/4.024

LIGINIAC Job One of two traditionally furnished gîtes in a stone cottage outside the village (altitude 650 metres). At Neuvic (7 km), there is a golf links and a lovely lake with facilities for water ski-ing, wind-surfing and sailing, as well as pedalo boat hire for the less adventurous! Living room/kitchenette (washing machine), 3 bedrooms (3 double beds), bathroom, open fire (wood supplied), carport, enclosed ground with garden furniture and barbecue. Shopping and restaurant in the village (3 km); mobile shops call.

Prices:	low season	on request	**6 people**
	high season	on request	*IGN 49*

Booking: Corrèze booking service

19/4.029

MALEMORT Roumegoux A renovated house with country-style furnishings, situated on a livestock farm, 3 km from the village centre. It is just 5 km from Brive where you can visit the attractive old quarter of the town and take advantage of its many leisure amenities. Living room (2 double divans), kitchen, 2 bedrooms (1 double, 1 large single bed), bathroom, fireplace (wood supplied), electric central heating, open ground with garden furniture and barbecue. Linen available. Farm produce, shopping and restaurant in the village.

Prices:	low season	on request	**7 people**
	high season	on request	*IGN 48*

Booking: Corrèze booking service

19/2.071

MERCOEUR Causinille An old stone house, renovated and simply furnished, on a slightly isolated farm, some 7 km from the village (altitude 500 metres). Local forest walks; fishing and riding within 13 km. Argentat (15 km) in the Dordogne valley is an interesting old town with swimming-pool and tennis courts. Kitchen, 2 bedrooms (2 double, 1 single bed), shower room, no heating, open ground. Mobile baker and butcher call; farm produce, other shopping and restaurant in the village or at Bretenoux (13 km).

Prices:	low season	F 360/420	**5 people**
	high season	F 645/790	*IGN 48*

Booking: Corrèze Loisirs Accueil   **E**

19/6.020

Corrèze

MERCOEUR Rioubazet A modern, simply furnished gîte, surrounded by forests and situated 3 km from the village (altitude 520 metres). The owners' children speak English. At the village restaurant, try the local specialities of river trout and omelettes with delicious cepes mushrooms. Sailing at 16 km. Living room, kitchen, 4 bedrooms (4 double, 2 single and 2 child's beds), bathroom and shower, fireplace, heating, garage, enclosed ground. Linen available. Mobile baker calls; other shopping in the village or at Argentat (15 km).

Prices:	low season	on request	**10/12 people**
	high season	on request	*IGN 48*

Booking: Corrèze booking service

19/6.021

MONCEAUX-SUR-DORDOGNE Le Chambon A ground-floor gîte, one of two in an attractive, renovated house with modern furnishings, near the village centre where you can hire a canoe. In the vicinity: see the Murel waterfall and the *son et lumière* at the ruins of the Merle Towers. Living room (TV, 1 double divan), kitchen, 2 bedrooms (2 double beds), bathroom, electric heating, open ground (garden furniture and barbecue). Mobile shops call, a grocer in the village; other shopping and a restaurant at Argentat-sur-Dordogne (3 km).

Prices:	low season	F 650/800	**6 people**
	high season	F 1320	*IGN 48*

Booking: Corrèze Loisirs Accueil   E

19/4.042

NESPOULS Le Bourg This lovely former presbytery at the village centre has been converted into four gîtes with traditional furniture (this small one on the ground floor). Nearby you can visit the Fage chasm and the Lamouroux caves. Bicycle hire at Brive (15 km). Living room/kitchenette (1 single bed), 2 bedrooms (2 double beds), shower room, no heating, open communal ground. Grocer, baker and restaurant in the village, other shopping at 4 km.

Prices:	low season	F 570	**5 people**
	high season	F 850/920	*IGN 48*

Booking: Corrèze Loisirs Accueil   E

19/2.091

SAINT-CIRGUES-LA-LOUTRE La Borde A detached house, built in typical local style and furnished in rustic fashion. It lies in the midst of fields on a cattle farm where there is another gîte to share the table tennis and the private swimming-pool. Horse-riding (3 km); other attractions at Saint-Privat (7 km). Living room/kitchenette, 3 bedrooms (2 double, 1 single bed), shower room, open fire, electric heating, enclosed ground. Linen available. Farm produce from the owners; shopping and restaurant in the village (0.5 km).

Prices:	low season	F 725/800	**5 people**
	high season	F 1225/1445	*IGN 48*

Booking: Corrèze Loisirs Accueil   E

19/6.024

SAINT-GERMAIN-LAVOLPS Endevaysse A pretty little country cottage which has been well renovated and furnished in rustic fashion, some 4 km from the village, but just 50 metres from the owners' house (altitude 815 metres). At Meymac (10 km), see the old market halls and abbey church. Sechemailles lake is at 11 km. Living room/kitchenette (washing machine), 2 bedrooms (2 double, 1 single bed), shower room, fireplace, central heating, terrace, garage, open ground. Shopping and restaurant at Meymac.

Prices:	low season	F 550/665	**5 people**
	high season	F 1105/1220	*IGN 41*

Booking: Corrèze Loisirs Accueil   E

19/3.091

Corrèze

SAINT-JULIEN-LE-PELERIN Sagnemoussouze A very attractive old house, with a fine view over the Cère Gorge. It has been renovated and furnished in rustic fashion and is 4 km from the village (altitude 620 metres). At Camps (6 km), see the so-called 'Painter's Rock' (Rocher du Peintre); Sablier lake (18 km). Living room/kitchenette (TV), 2 bedrooms (1 double, 3 single, 1 child's bed), shower room, fireplace, electric central heating, open ground with garden furniture. Shopping and restaurant at Goulles (6 km); local farm produce.

Prices:	low season	F 740/880	**5/6 people**
	high season	F 1240/1420	IGN 48

Booking: Corrèze Loisirs Accueil E

19/6.049

SAINT-MARTIAL-DE-GIMEL Les Pleaux An attractive house, renovated and divided into two simply furnished gîtes. Tourist attractions in the area include a lake for bathing and sailing (10 km); the Gimel waterfall, Sédières Château and the delightful Dordogne valley. Swimming-pool and tennis in the cathedral town of Tulle (15 km). Living room, kitchen, 2 bedrooms (2 double, 1 single bed), shower room, fireplace, carport, enclosed ground shared with the other gîte. Farm produce, shopping and restaurant in the village (1 km).

Prices:	low season	F 400/500	**5 people**
	high season	F 750/900	IGN 48

Booking: Corrèze Loisirs Accueil E

19/1.118

SAINT-VIANCE Les Rebières Blanches A detached house, renovated and furnished in country style, standing in its own grounds with garden furniture. Bicycle hire, a skating rink and museums are some of the facilities at the lively town of Brive (12 km). Visit Pompadour (15 km) for its château and national stud farm. Living room, hallway (1 single divan), kitchen, 3 bedrooms (3 single beds), bathroom, electric heating, terrace, carport, ground. Shopping, farm produce and restaurant in the village (1 km), or at Varetz (4 km).

Prices:	low season	F 600/660	**4 people**
	high season	F 930/980	IGN 48

Booking: Corrèze Loisirs Accueil E

19/2.141

TARNAC Javeaux Set in its own open ground on a livestock farm near the owners' home, this renovated and traditionally furnished gîte is just outside the village. At Bugeat (12 km), enjoy the tennis court, miniature golf and water sports facilities at Viam lake. Altitude 800 metres. Living room/kitchenette (1 double divan), 2 bedrooms (2 double beds), shower room, electric central heating. Shopping and restaurant in the village or at Peyrelevade (11 km).

Prices:	low season	F 510/620	**6 people**
	high season	F 1000	IGN 41

Booking: Corrèze Loisirs Accueil E

19/3.111

COLLONGES-LA-ROUGE La Raze *Chambre d'hôte* accommodation in a well-renovated and traditionally furnished building next to the owners' home in a hamlet at the edge of the village (0.8 km). Collonges is a picturesque little mediaeval village built of red sandstone, with a Romanesque church. Five rooms available: 2 double rooms with private showers, 1 room with 1 double and 1 single bed, 1 room with 2 double beds, 1 room with 2 singles; shared shower room and lounge; electric central heating; open ground. Restaurant in the village; shopping at Meyssac. Possibility of evening meals.

Prices: 1p F 95, 2p F 105, 3p F 140, 4p F 160   **13 people**
IGN 48

Booking: Corrèze Loisirs Accueil E
19/2.700

Creuse

LA CELLE-DUNOISE A stone-built house in the village, which offers pleasant walks along the banks of the River Creuse where fishing, bathing and canoeing are possible. In Dun-le-Palestel (12 km) you will find mediaeval and vestiges of neolithic architecture. Tennis and swimming-pool (25 km). Living room/kitchenette, (TV), 2 bedrooms (2 double and 1 single bed), bathroom, enclosed ground, garage, no heating. Shopping, farm produce and café in the village.

Prices:	low season	F 655/765	**5 people**
	high season	F 945	IGN 41

Booking: Creuse Loisirs Accueil   E

23/43

FENIERS-PIGEROLLES Soulières An old farmhouse with rustic furniture on a cattle farm, 2 km from the village. Felletin (18 km) has a château. Local cross-country ski-ing, tennis and swimming-pool (18 km), sailing at a lake (25 km). Altitude 900 metres. Living room/kitchenette, 3 bedrooms (3 double beds), bathroom, fireplace, electric central heating, carport, garden and ground. Shopping from mobile stores or in the village, restaurant at Saint-Setiers (8 km).

Prices:	low season	F 880	**6 people**
	high season	F 1050	IGN 41
	winter season	F 750	

Booking: Creuse Loisirs Accueil   E

23/104

LE GRAND-BOURG L'Age-au-Fils A renovated gîte with modern and country-style furniture, some 5 km from the town, in the Gartempe valley. Local fishing; La Souterraine (6 km) which has buildings dating back to the twelfth century, has a swimming-pool, tennis and other amenities. Visit, too, the château town of Guéret (15 km). Living room, kitchen (washing machine), 2 bedrooms (1 double, 3 single and 1 child's bed), shower room, fireplace, electric central heating, terrace, open ground with garden furniture. Farm produce and other shopping in the town; a restaurant at La Souterraine.

Prices:	low season	F 490/515	**6 people**
	high season	F 780/910	IGN 41

Booking: Creuse Loisirs Accueil   E

23/127

JANAILLAT Les Mats A large old house on a mixed farm where there is one other gîte, 2 km from the village (altitude 550 metres). Swimming-pool, riding and tennis (18 km). Guéret (22 km) is a château town with an interesting museum. Living room (TV), kitchen, 4 bedrooms (3 double and 1 child's bed), bathroom, open fire, electric central heating, garage, enclosed ground. Farm produce and restaurant in the village; other shopping at Pontarion (6 km).

Prices:	low season	F 590	**7 people**
	high season	F 805/970	IGN 41

Booking: Creuse Loisirs Accueil   E

23/141

JANAILLAT Pierrefitte A single-storey house with country-style and modern furniture, adjoining other buildings on a cattle farm 2 km from the village. Local fishing (1 km); swimming-pool, riding, tennis within 22 km. Altitude 550 metres. Living room, kitchen, 1 bedroom (1 double bed and 1 child's bed), bathroom, fireplace, terrace, garage, open ground. Shopping and restaurant in the village or at Bourganeuf (16 km). Farm produce available from the owner.

Prices:	low season	F 445/510	**3 people**
	high season	F 595/685	IGN 41

Booking: Creuse Loisirs Accueil   E

23/123

Creuse

LE MONTEIL-AU-VICOMTE Le Moulin A ground-floor gîte with rustic furniture in an old stone cottage built against a wooded slope 2.5 km from the village. Trout fishing locally; lake for bathing and sailing and tennis (12 km). Aubusson, famous for its tapestries, is at 18 km. Living room, kitchen, 2 bedroroms (1 double, 2 single, 1 child's bed); bathroom, electric central heating, open ground bordering the river. Shopping in the village. A restaurant at Chavanat (1.2 km).

Prices:	low season	F 580	**5 people**
	high season	F 805/850	IGN 41

Booking: Creuse Loisirs Accueil   E

23/157

RETERRE Les Périchoux A detached house with traditional furniture and enclosed grounds with garden furniture, 3 km from the village. Evaux-les-Bains (6 km) is a small town, once a Roman spa with numerous chafeaux in the surrounding countryside. Altitude 500 metres. Living room, kitchen, 3 bedrooms (3 double and 1 single beds), bathroom, wood stove, fireplace, garage. Shopping and restaurant in Evaux-les-Bains.

Prices:	low season	F 370/570	**7 people**
	high season	F 740/830	IGN 42

Booking: Creuse Loisirs Accueil   E

23/182

SAINT-DIZIER-LEYRENNE Le Monteil An old two-storey house with rustic furniture, adjoining another gîte, 5 km from the village. Bourganeuf (12 km) is an old Gallo-Roman town set in a dramatic landscape. Swimming-pool (18 km). Altitude 600 metres. Living room/kitchenette (TV), 2 bedrooms (2 double beds), bathroom, electric central heating, fireplace, open courtyard shared with the other gîte. Shopping and restaurant in the village or at Bourganeuf, local farm produce available.

Prices:	low season	F 605/685	**4 people**
	high season	F 820/895	IGN 41

Booking: Creuse Loisirs Accueil   E

23/199

SAINT-DOMET Le Prieuré An old, detached house nestled among trees in its own garden 1 km from the village. It is renovated and has rustic furniture. Fishing, bathing and tennis (1 km), riding (10 km), and swimming-pool (15 km). Living room/kitchenette, 2 bedrooms (2 double and 1 single bed), shower room, fireplace, electric central heating, terrace, garage, enclosed garden. Shopping in the village, or at Aubusson (15 km). Local farm produce available. Restaurant at 2 km.

Prices:	low season	F 455/535	**5 people**
	high season	F 720/810	IGN 42

Booking: Creuse Loisirs Accueil   E

23/202

SAINT-ETIENNE-DE-FURSAC Belleville Situated some 3.5 km from the village, this spacious house has been furnished in country fashion. Fishing and sailing in the river Gartempe (4 km). See the nearby ruined Château de Chamborand and the Sainte Hélène rocks. Summertime *Son et Lumière* concerts are held at La Souterraine (15 km). Living room/kitchenette (washing machine), 3 bedrooms (4 double beds), shower room, electric central heating, garage, enclosed ground. Shopping and restaurant in the village.

Prices:	low season	F 595/740	**8 people**
	high season	F 855/910	IGN 41

Booking: Creuse Loisirs Accueil   E

23/243

Creuse

SAINT-ETIENNE-DE-FURSAC La Chérade A detached, renovated house with country-style furniture, set in its own enclosed ground 4 km from the village. Fishing (3 km); swimming-pool, tennis, sailing and bathing (4 km). At Bénévent-L'Abbaye (15 km approx.) see the lovely Romanesque church, once an abbey. Living room, kitchen, 3 bedrooms (3 double beds), shower room, fireplace, heating, enclosed ground. Farm produce in the village; other shopping at Fursac (4 km) where there is a restaurant.

Prices:	low season	F 595/660	**6 people**
	high season	F 925/1050	IGN 41

Booking: Creuse Loisirs Accueil E

23/204

SAINT-PIERRE-CHERIGNAT Lestrade A two-storey renovated cottage in its own garden, furnished in rustic fashion, 2 km from the village. There is a lake for swimming, sailing and water ski-ing at 15 km. Bourganeuf (18 km) has a splendid château and Gallo-Roman remains. Living room/kitchenette, 2 bedrooms (3 double and 1 child's bed), shower room, no heating, balcony, garden. Shopping at St. Martin-Ste Catherine (2 km), local farm produce available. Restaurant at Chatelus-le-Marcheix (5 km).

Prices:	low season	F 590/650	**7 people**
	high season	F 845/920	IGN 41

Booking: Creuse Loisirs Accueil E

23/223

SAINT-PRIEST-LA-FEUILLE Le Breuil A nicely renovated and traditionally furnished house on a mixed farm, 3 km from the village. Swimming-pool and tennis at La Souterraine (10 km). Guéret (20 km approx.), the département capital, has a fifteenth-century château and a museum (closed on Tuesdays) with noted Aubusson and Felletin tapestries. Living room, kitchen, 2 bedrooms (1 double and 3 single beds), bathroom, fireplace, oil-fired central heating, terrace, garage, enclosed ground. Other shopping at La Souterraine; restaurant at Fursac 4 km.

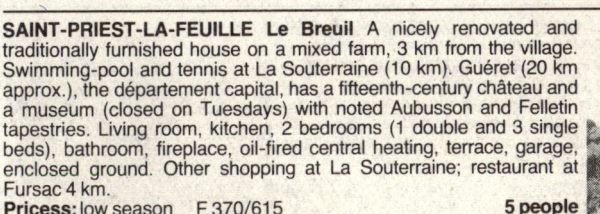

Prices:	low season	F 370/615	**5 people**
	high season	F 805/930	IGN 41

Booking: Creuse Loisirs Accueil E
23/300

SAINT-SULPICE-LE-GUERETOIS La Ribière A rustically furnished, stone-built cottage, adjoining other farm buildings at the edge of the village (1.5 km). Wind-surfing (7 km) and many other leisure facilities at Guéret (7 km). Sites in the vicinity include megaliths in Chabrière forest. Las Peyras fountain and mediaeval châteaux. Living room/kitchenette, 2 bedrooms (2 double and 1 single bed), shower room, fireplace, electric central heating, garage, open courtyard and enclosed ground. Farm produce in the village; other shopping at Guéret; restaurant at 6 km.

Prices:	low season	F 590/730	**5 people**
	high season	F 940	IGN 41

Booking: Creuse Loisirs Accueil E

23/238

SAINT-SYLVAIN-MONTAIGUT Le Masbonson A recently built gîte with country-style furnishings, situated outside the village (2 km). Fishing at 1 km. Riding, tennis and swimming-pool at Guéret (10 km), an old château town. Altitude 500 metres. Living room, kitchen (small washing machine), 3 bedrooms (2 double and 2 single beds), bathroom, open fire, electric central heating, terrace, garage, parkland. Shopping and restaurant at 5 km or in Guéret.

Prices:	low season	F 765	**6 people**
	high season	F 995/1060	IGN 41

Booking: Creuse Loisirs Accueil E

23/233

Haute-Vienne

BERSAC-SUR-RIVALIER La Salesse A stone-and-plaster house, 2 km from the village with its own open ground. Walking in the locality; tennis at 3 km; river fishing (6 km); bicycle hire and bathing (9 km). Lounge, kitchen, 2 bedrooms (2 double beds), shower room, fireplace, electric heating. Shopping in the village, at Bessines (6 km) or at Limoges (40 km).

Prices: low season   F 620/680   **4 people**
         high season   F 920/1030   IGN 41

Booking: Haute-Vienne Loisirs Accueil   E

87/4031

LE BUIS An old traditionally furnished house on farmland in the village. Many summer festivals take place around Saint-Pardoux (9 km). Tennis, fishing and bicycle hire, all within 11 km. Try your hand at wind-surfing (11 km). Living room/kitchenette, 3 bedrooms (4 double and 2 single beds), bathroom, fireplace, enclosed ground. Shopping and restaurant at Nantiat (5 km).

Prices: low season   F 380/515   **10 people**
         high season   F 610/680   IGN 41

Booking: Haute-Vienne Loisirs Accueil   E

87/3200

CHAMBORET Château de Corrigé One of two rustically furnished gîtes in a wing of a former manor house which the owner, who is a vet, uses as a holiday home, outside the village. Private fishing and tennis in the grounds (supplement), a lake at 8 km and bicycle hire at Saint-Pardoux (14 km). Living room/kitchenette (washing-machine), 3 bedrooms (3 double and 1 child's bed), shower room, fireplace, heating, carport, garden furniture and child's swing. A restaurant in the village (1 km); shopping at Nantiat (4 km), or Limoges (30 km).

Prices: low season   F 940/1030   **7 people**
         high season   F 1160/1240   IGN 41

Booking: Haute-Vienne Loisirs Accueil   E

87/2121

COMPREIGNAC Villebert One of two gîtes with modern furnishings in a renovated house, right at the edge of Saint-Pardoux lake and 5 km from the village. Many tourist activities are organised at the lake; bicycles for hire at 3 km; tennis (5 km) and riding (10 km). Living room/kitchenette, 2 bedrooms (5 single beds), bathroom and shower, fireplace, electric central heating, ground. Shopping and restaurant in the village or at Nantiat (8 km approx.).

Prices: low season   F 565/740   **5 people**
         high season   F 790/900   IGN 41

Booking: Haute-Vienne Loisirs Accueil   E

87/3150

MAISONNAIS-SUR-TARDOIRE Chadelais A lovely old stone house with country-style furnishings outside the village (3 km). Several wood-working studios to visit in the vicinity. Local fishing and tennis at 4 km. Saint-Mathieu (13 km) has a lake for bathing and children's boating. Living room/kitchenette, 2 bedrooms (2 double and 1 single bed) and 2 single beds on a mezzanine landing, bathroom, open fire, electric central heating, open ground. Shopping and restaurant at 10 km.

Prices: low season   F 600/650   **7 people**
         high season   F 780/950   IGN 41

Booking: Haute-Vienne Loisirs Accueil   E

87/7315

Haute-Vienne

MEZIERES-SUR-ISSOIRE Darvizat One of two gîtes in a former farmhouse which has been renovated and furnished in traditional style, some 4 km from the village which has fortnightly sheep markets. Visit the Château de la Côte in the neighbouring hamlet of Sainte-Anne. Bellac (16 km) is a beautiful old city on the river Vincou with a twelfth-century hump-backed bridge. Living room, kitchen, 3 bedrooms (2 double, 4 single beds), bathroom, fireplace, electric heating, open courtyard shared with other gîte. Shopping and restaurant in Mezieres.

Prices:	low season	F 527/633	**8 people**
	high season	F 844/950	IGN 41

Booking: Haute-Vienne Loisirs Accueil   **E**

87/1210

NEUVIC-ENTIER Picq An attractive, old, rustically furnished gîte, 2 km from the village. Fishing in a nearby river; bathing at a lake; tennis and interesting walks in lovely Châteauneuf forest with panoramic views, all at 4 km. See, too, the Espinassou fountain. Living room, kitchen, 2 bedrooms (2 double and 2 single beds), bathroom, electric heating, carport, open ground. Shopping and restaurant at Châteauneuf-la-Forêt (3 km).

Prices:	low season	F 465/560	**6 people**
	high season	F 780/850	IGN 41

Booking: Haute-Vienne Loisirs Accueil   **E**

87/5270

NEUVIC-ENTIER Le Veytisou A new house, traditionally furnished, in a hamlet; very suitable for a family. Fishing and bathing in the lake at Châteauneuf-la-Forêt (6 km). Swimming-pool at 8 km. Not far away are the Eymoutiers hills. Altitude 500 metres. Living room, kitchen, 2 bedrooms (2 double and 1 child's bed), shower room, heating, garden. Shopping in Neuvic-Entier (4 km).

Prices:	low season	F 450/585	**5 people**
	high season	F 825/930	IGN 41

Booking: Haute-Vienne Loisirs Accueil   **E**

87/5271

NEXON Combrouze A large, attractive old farmhouse situated among other buildings in a farming hamlet 4 km from Nexon. The owners, who live nearby, will welcome you warmly. Country-style furniture, and large open spaces adjoining the house. Fishing in a pond; bathing and riding within 5 km. Living room (1 double divan), kitchen, 2 bedrooms (2 double and 4 single beds), bathroom, fireplace, central heating, garage. Shopping and restaurant in Nexon; local farm produce available.

Prices:	low season	F 500/700	**10 people**
	high season	F 900	IGN 41

Booking: Haute-Vienne Loisirs Accueil   **E**

87/6310

RANCON Villenue A well-renovated house with modern furnishings, near a hamlet, 3 km from the village. Châteauponsac (8 km), formerly a fortified town, overlooks the river Gartempe and has Romanesque church and chapel, museum in the old priory, terraced gardens and craftwork studio. Sailing at Saint-Pardoux lake (18 km). Living room/kitchenette, 3 bedrooms (1 double, 4 single beds), shower room, fireplace, electric central heating, enclosed ground. Shopping and restaurant in the village.

Prices:	low season	F 500/650	**6 people**
	high season	F 800/830	IGN 41

Booking: Haute-Vienne Loisirs Accueil   **E**

87/3261

Haute-Vienne

RAZES La Roche A lovely old stone-built house, furnished in country style. Saint-Pardoux lake (bathing, sailing and riding) is at 5 km. Bicycle hire (11 km). At 12 km is Bessines, a little town in the Gartempe valley, birthplace of Suzanne Valadon, mother of Utrillo and a painter in her own right. Living room/kitchenette, 1 bedroom on an open landing (1 double and 2 single beds), shower room, fireplace, heating, enclosed ground. Shopping and restaurant in the village (2 km) or at Bessines.

Prices:	low season	F 370/470	**4 people**
	high season	F 700/820	IGN 41

Booking: Haute-Vienne Loisirs Accueil   E

87/3300

SAINT-HILAIRE-LES-PLACES Lac de Plaisance A very attractive old cottage with rustic furnishings, one of three in converted farm buildings by a small lake where you may bathe and fish. Local tennis and forest walks; other leisure facilities at Saint-Yrieix-la-Perche (20 km approx.) where the discovery of kaolin in the eighteenth century led to the development of the Limoges porcelain industry. Living room/kitchenette, 2 bedrooms (2 double, 2 single beds), shower room, electric heating, enclosed ground. Shopping and restaurant in the village (1 km).

Prices:	low season	F 482/846	**6 people**
	high season	F 876/897	IGN 41

Booking: Haute-Vienne Loisirs Accueil   E

87/6393

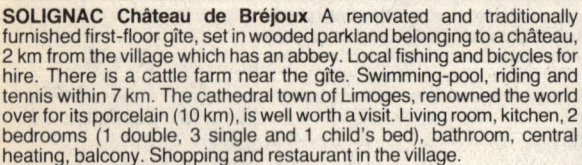

SOLIGNAC Château de Bréjoux A renovated and traditionally furnished first-floor gîte, set in wooded parkland belonging to a château, 2 km from the village which has an abbey. Local fishing and bicycles for hire. There is a cattle farm near the gîte. Swimming-pool, riding and tennis within 7 km. The cathedral town of Limoges, renowned the world over for its porcelain (10 km), is well worth a visit. Living room, kitchen, 2 bedrooms (1 double, 3 single and 1 child's bed), bathroom, central heating, balcony. Shopping and restaurant in the village.

Prices:	low season	F 550/700	**6 people**
	high season	F 1000/1100	IGN 41

Booking: Haute-Vienne Loisirs Accueil   E

87/9461

SURDOUX Le Peyrol A small but comfortable house, renovated and furnished in rustic fashion, lying in extensive grounds in a hamlet at the heart of the picturesque Plateau de Millevaches (altitude 600 metres). Good walking and fishing within 7 km; bathing at a lake, and tennis within 9 km. Living room/kitchenette, 2 bedrooms (1 double and 1 single bed, 2 bunk-beds and 1 single for children), bathroom, open fire, electric central heating, enclosed ground. Shopping and restaurant at Chamboret (8 km).

Prices:	low season	F 545/595	**6 people**
	high season	F 860/900	IGN 41

Booking: Haute-Vienne Loisirs Accueil   E

87/5460

VICQ-SUR-BREUILH Combas One of two gîtes with country-style furnishings in a lovely old annexe of a château on a livestock farm, 2 km from the village. At Limoges (20 km) see the ruined Roman arena in the Orsay Gardens and the porcelain museum. Living room/kitchenette (1 double divan), 3 bedrooms (7 single beds), bathroom and shower, fireplace, central heating, garage, open ground with garden furniture shared with the other gîte. A restaurant in the village; shopping at 10 km.

Prices:	low season	F 885/970	**9 people**
	high season	F 1385/1620	IGN 41

Booking: Haute-Vienne Loisirs Accueil   E

87/6478

6 MIDI-PYRENEES

Midway between the Atlantic and the Mediterranean, the Midi-Pyrénées enjoys a particularly pleasant climate. Here, in the largest region of France, you can really appreciate the wide open spaces, rolling hills and snow-capped mountains. Such a diverse landscape offers all kinds of holiday opportunities – from ski-ing and mountaineering to walking, riding and pot-holing. You can even try panning for gold in the rivers of Ariège!

Over such a wide geographical area, the architecture too varies considerably: from solid stone houses and fortified villages in the north and west, to the delicate pink brick of Toulouse and Albi and the distinctive "fish scale" roofs of the Pyrénées.

The history of the region is rich and fascinating stretching back to the paleolithic hunters and their famous cave paintings in Ariege in the foothills of the Pyrénées. Full of the mysterious stories of Cathar heresies, the romance of the troubadours and the Langue d'Oc, and the passion of the Albigensian Crusades, the religious tradition of the region lingers on in the pilgrimages to Lourdes. But the region's most famous son is surely d'Artagnan, hero of Alexandre Dumas' Musketeers, whose statue stands proudly in Auch – at the heart of Armagnac country.

Grapes (for wine and Armagnac) are just one of the products of this most prolific fruit-growing area: try for instance local plums, pears and melons.

Not to be missed during your visit are the fascinating sites of Rocamadour and Padirac in Lot; the mediaeval village of Cordes-sur-Ciel in Tarn; Albi with its museum of Toulouse-Lautrec's work; Toulouse with its traditional festival, *Gaston Phébus*, in June. In the south there is delightful Pau with Henri IV's château and, whether religious or not, Lourdes can be quite awe-inspiring.

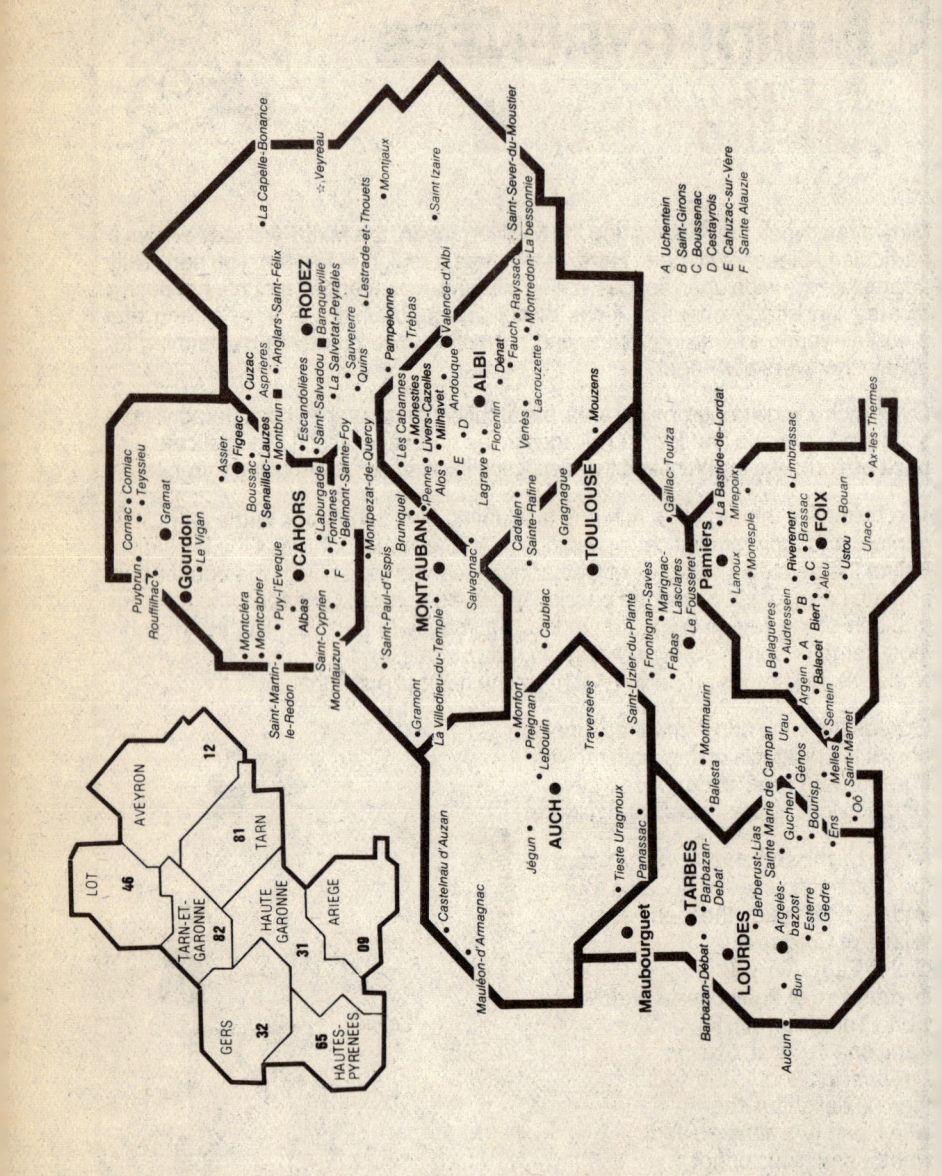

A Uchentein
B Saint-Girons
C Boussenac
D Cestayrols
E Cazouac-sur-Vère
F Sainte Alauzie

MIDI-PYRENEES
and the rural world

The **Midi-Pyrénées** region is outstanding by its size and its low population (one and a half times the size of Belgium, its population is 5 times smaller!). This is the chosen land of lovers of nature and vast open spaces.

Home of **Lourdes** and the Pyrénées mountains, our region is also the true home of rural tourism, founded on its many country communities and their fields, rivers, lakes, fishing and craft traditions...

Here you will find a dream climate and multiple landscapes, untouched by urbanisation; a rich historical past, a wealth of gastronomical pleasures, (fois gras, cassoulet, roquefort armagnac, vins de pays...).

And among the many means of accommodation found in our region — camping, rural inns, holiday villages — the **2000 Gîtes de France** come first.

Comité Régional
de Tourisme
12 rue Salambo
31000 TOULOUSE
Tel. (61) 47.11.12
or 21.88.00

Ariège

ALEU Le Moulin A very distinctive two-storey house, furnished in the local style, in a group of houses near that of the friendly owner who speaks English and also offers *chambres d'hôte* in his home. There is a surrounding park and swimming-pool, nearby river fishing, hunting and forests. Altitude 500 metres. Living room/kitchenette, 1 bedroom (1 double bed and 1 double divan), bathroom, electric heating, ground. Linen available. Shopping in the village (0.5 km), at Massat (14 km) or at Saint Girons (18 km).

Prices:	low season	F 902/972	**4 people**
	high season	F 972	*IGN 71*
	winter season	F 972	

Booking: Ariège booking service   E
09/68

ARGEIN An attractive, modern village house with a large garden (altitude 600 metres). At Castillon-en-Couserans (5 km) which has a park with twelfth-century Calvary chapel, leisure facilities include tennis and a nightclub. The interesting old town of Saint-Girons (18 km approx.) is well worth a visit. Living room (1 single bed), kitchen, 2 bedrooms (2 double beds), shower room, oil heating, garden. Farm produce and grocer's shop in the village, other shopping and restaurant at Castillon.

Prices:	low season	F 624/878	**5 people**
	high season	F 1111	*IGN 71*
	winter season	F 878	

Booking: Ariège booking service   E
09/164

AUDRESSEIN A renovated house, furnished in traditional country style in a lovely village. The owner, a clog-maker, has his studio next to the gîte. Local fishing and forest walks; tennis at Castillon-en-Couserans (1 km); a swimming-pool and riding at 14 km. Altitude 600 metres. Living room, kitchen, 3 bedrooms (3 double beds), shower room, oil-fired central heating, courtyard. Fresh eggs and vegetables from the owner, mobile grocer and baker; other shopping and restaurant at Castillon.

Prices:	low season	F 601/722	**6 people**
	high season	F 974	*IGN 71*
	winter season	F 694	

Booking: Ariège booking service   E
09/129

AX-LES-THERMES Petches This old cottage with rustic furnishings is ideally situated for exploring the area. It is just 3 km from the delightful spa town of Ax-les-Thermes (popular both summer and winter); 5 km from a ski station and close to Andorra and the Spanish border. Altitude 900 metres. Kitchen, 2 bedrooms (3 double beds), shower room, fireplace, electric heating, garden. Mobile grocer and baker and farm produce in the village; other shopping and restaurant at Ax-les-Thermes.

Prices:	low season	F 594/715	**6 people**
	high season	F 836	*IGN 71*
	winter season	F 826	

Booking: Ariège booking service   E
09/143

BALACET A well-renovated, terraced house with country-style furnishings, at the centre of a small mountain village (altitude 909 metres). Sentein (3 km) is a lively town with many tourist activities organised in summer. Bethmale lake is at 9 km; a swimming-pool and riding (24 km). Living room/kitchenette (3 single beds), 1 bedroom (1 double and 1 single bed), bathroom, fireplace, electric central heating, open ground. Linen available. Mobile baker and grocer call; farm produce in the village; other shopping and restaurant at Sentein.

Prices:	low season	F 905/1090	**6 people**
	high season	F 1230	*IGN 71*
	winter season	F 1090	

Booking: Ariège booking service   E
09/B16a

Ariège

BALAGUERES Agert Set in a little mountain farming hamlet with lovely views, is this renovated gîte with country-style furnishings (altitude 600 metres). Visit Saint-Lizier (15 km approx.), an old Gallo-Roman city with cathedral and an interesting old pharmacy (guided visits), and neighbouring Saint-Girons. Living room/kitchenette, 2 bedrooms (1 double and 2 single beds), shower room, fireplace, balcony, open ground. Farm produce available, mobile baker and grocer call, other shopping at Castillon-en-Couserans (6 km).

Prices:	low season	F 495/687	**4 people**
	high season	F 957	*IGN 71*
	winter season	F 495	

Booking: Ariège booking service E
09/137

BALAGUERES Alas This renovated and traditionally furnished gîte is one of two owned by the proprietor, who is particularly friendly. It occupies the end building of a terrace in a quiet village street. Fishing, walking, tennis within 5 km; swimming and riding within 12 km. Altitude 500 metres. Living room/kitchenette, 4 bedrooms (4 double and 2 single beds), shower room, oil central heating, separate grounds. Linen available. Café in the village. Mobile baker and grocer call. Shops at Castillon-en-Couserans 4 km away.

Prices:	low season	F 627/660	**10 people**
	high season	F 968	*IGN 71*
	winter season	F 627	

Booking: Ariège booking service E
09/85

LA BASTIDE-DE-LORDAT One of two adjoining gîtes, rustically furnished and situated on the edge of the village (3 km). Pamiers (12 km) is an attractive, mediaeval cathedral town on the river Ariège, and has one of the oldest churches in the Pyrenees; leisure facilities there include a swimming-pool and tennis. Living room (1 single divan), kitchen, 4 bedrooms (4 double and 2 single beds), shower room, fireplace, garage, open ground. Mobile baker calls; farm produce, other shopping and restaurant in the village or at Pamiers.

Prices:	low season	F 760/1000	**11 people**
	high season	F 1300	*IGN 71*
	winter season	F 1000	

Booking: Ariège booking service E
09/1

BIERT One of four traditionally furnished gîtes in a renovated building owned by the local council, in a small mountain village where you should try the local cheese. A lake at 10 km; bicycle hire at 24 km. Visit Saint-Lizier (30 km approx.) for its fine Romanesque cathedral. Altitude 585 metres. Living room/kitchenette (1 single divan), 2 bedrooms (1 double and 2 single beds), shower room, electric central heating, open ground. Farm produce available in the village; other shopping and restaurant at Massat (3 km).

Prices:	low season	F 497/650	**6 people**
	high season	F 875	*IGN 71*
	winter season	F 650	

Booking: Ariège booking service E
09/81

BOUAN One of two gîtes with country-style furnishings in a large village house (altitude 500 metres). Visit Tarascon-sur-Ariège (8 km approx.), a particularly sunny town surrounded by high mountains, with swimming-pool and tennis; see the Niaux prehistoric caves; ski-ing (25 km). Living room/kitchenette (1 single bed), 3 bedrooms (2 double and 1 single bed), shower room, electric central heating, terrace, garden. Mobile shops call, other shopping and restaurant at Les Cabannes (3 km).

Prices:	low season	F 647/705	**6 people**
	high season	F 988	*IGN 71*
	winter season	F 705	

Booking: Ariège booking service E
09/14

Ariège

BOUSSENAC Jacoy A traditionally furnished gîte, one of two in a former presbytery (altitude 900 metres). This is a particularly lovely region of the Pyrenees, just a few kilometres from the Col de Port (1200 metres). Tennis at the old town of Massat (7 km). Living room/kitchenette, 2 bedrooms (2 double and 3 single beds), bathroom, gas central heating, terrace, open ground. Mobile baker and grocer call; farm produce in the village, other shopping and restaurant at Massat.

Prices:	low season	F 363/506	**7 people**
	high season	F 550/830	IGN 71
	winter season	F 506	

Booking: Ariège booking service   **E**
09/22.

BOUSSENAC Touron-de-Louis An attractively renovated house with country-style furnishings in a mountain hamlet of the Massat valley (altitude 796 metres). Tennis, riding and cross-country ski-ing at Massat (7 km); a lake at 16 km. Visit the pleasant château town of Foix (20 km approx.), capital of the département. Living room, kitchen, 3 bedrooms (1 double and 2 single beds), shower room, fireplace, electric central heating, terrace, open ground. Farm produce from the owners next door, mobile shops call; other shopping and restaurant at Massat.

Prices:	low season	F 844	**4 people**
	high season	F 1259	IGN 71
	winter season	F 1023	

Booking: Ariège booking service   **E**
09/7

BRASSAC Les Martis A large house, renovated and furnished in country style, in a small but very active mountain hamlet where the local people organise many social activities (altitude 600 metres). The lovely old city of Foix, with its feudal château, swimming-pool, tennis and cinema, is just 7 km away. Living room/kitchenette, 3 bedrooms (3 double beds, a child's bed on request), shower room, fireplace, garden. A baker calls, other shopping in the village (1 km).

Prices:	low season	F 885	**6 people**
	high season	F 1140	IGN 71

Booking: Ariège booking service   **E**

09/103

BRASSAC Les Martis A recently renovated house, furnished in traditional, country style, set in a farming hamlet (altitude 600 metres). It is just 7 km from Foix where there are many leisure and cultural amenities. Take a boat trip through the strange illuminated, subterranean river at Labouriche (14 km approx.). Living room, kitchen, 2 bedrooms (3 double and 1 child's bed), shower room, fireplace, electric heating, open ground. Mobile shops call; other shopping and restaurant in the village (0.5 km).

Prices:	low season	F 737/825	**6/7 people**
	high season	F 1100	IGN 71
	winter season	F 825	

Booking: Ariège booking service   **E**
09/108

LANOUX A traditionally furnished gîte, one of three in this fine château, standing in parkland, 3 km from the village where a local fair is held in June. See the fortified mediaeval church at Le Fossat (3 km). Visit the mediaeval city of Foix (approx. 25 km) dominated by its famous thirteenth-century château. Living room/kitchenette (washing machine), 2 bedrooms (2 double beds), shower room, electric central heating, carport, ground. Mobile shops call; other shopping, farm produce and restaurant at Le Fossat.

Prices:	low season	F 288/662	**4 people**
	high season	F 852	IGN 71

Booking: Ariège booking service   **E**
09/93

Ariège

LIMBRASSAC Endaillou A gîte in the owner's attractive, turreted house, entirely renovated and furnished in the local style, 1 km from the village. River fishing (1 km), riding and a swimming-pool (10 km). Altitude 500 metres. Living room, kitchen, 3 bedrooms (3 double and 1 single bed), bathroom and shower, oil heating, fireplace, balcony, terrace, ground. Mobile shops call, other shopping and restaurant at Laroque-d'Olmes (8 km).

Prices:	low season	F 822/892	7 people
	high season	F 1178	IGN 71
	winter season	F 1046	

Booking: Ariège booking service E
09/2

MIREPOIX Le Mas de Terride A renovated and traditionally furnished gîte, overlooking a valley. It is just 2 km from the cathedral town of Mirepoix which boasts a château and fifteenth-century Bishop's palace; also good fishing and canoeing on the river L'Hers, a swimming-pool and tennis. Living room (1 folding single bed), kitchen, 2 bedrooms (1 double and 2 single beds), shower room, open fire, electric central heating, terrace, large open ground. Shopping and restaurant at Mirepoix.

Prices:	low season	F810/948	5 people
	high season	F 1215	IGN 71
	winter season	F 925	

Booking: Ariège booking service E
09/60

MONESPLE Berdot An old house, typical of the region, which has been renovated and rustically furnished on a hill in an abandoned farming hamlet where there are two or three other holiday homes. The delightful little town of Pamiers with its mediaeval architecture is at 14 km. Living room (1 double and 1 single bed), kitchen, 3 bedrooms (2 double and 1 single bed), shower room, fireplace, electric central heating, enclosed ground with garden furniture and barbecue. Farm produce in the village (3 km); shopping and restaurant at Pailhes (5 km).

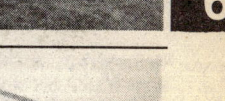

Prices:	low season	F 489/715	8 people
	high season	F 1015	IGN 71
	winter season	F 775	

Booking: Ariège booking service E
09/127

RIVERENERT A detached house with simple, traditional furnishings, in its own extensive grounds at the edge of the village (altitude 800 metres). The small town of Saint-Girons (7 km) is well known for its paper-making industry; leisure facilities there include a swimming-pool and tennis court. A lake at 16 km and ski-ing (30 km). Kitchen, 2 bedrooms (2 double and 1 single bed), shower room, oil stove, open ground. Mobile grocer calls; other shopping and restaurant at Saint-Girons.

Prices:	low season	F 632/753	5 people
	high season	F 1001	IGN 71
	winter season	F 753	

Booking: Ariège booking service E
09/158

SAINT-GIRONS La Chicane A gîte with rustic furnishings in an attractively renovated building on a mixed farm where you will receive a warm welcome from the young farmers who live there (but do not own the gîte). Swimming-pool and tennis in the town (2 km). Altitude 500 metres. Living room/kitchenette, 2 bedrooms (1 double and 2 single beds), bathroom, open fire, electric central heating, terrace, garden and extensive park. Farm produce available, mobile baker calls; other shopping and restaurant in Saint-Girons.

Prices:	low season	F 658/782	4 people
	high season	F 1058	IGN 71
	winter season	F 782	

Booking: Ariège booking service E
09/98

Ariège

SENTEIN Estouéou One of two gîtes in an attractive cottage with country-style furnishings, in a farming hamlet, 4 km from the lively town of Sentein (altitude 745 metres). Bethmale lake is at 10 km and interesting visits in the area could include Bethmale Museum of Folklore, and a local cheese factory. Living room/kitchenette (3 single beds), 1 bedroom (1 double and 2 single beds), shower room, fireplace, electric central heating, open ground. Linen available. Mobile baker and grocer call; other shopping and restaurant at Sentein.

Prices: low season   F 970/1160   **7 people**
high season   F 1300   *IGN 71*
winter season   F1160
Booking: Ariège booking service E
09/B40D

SENTEIN Eylie-d'en-Haut This attractive gîte is one of a number of houses that has been specially renovated to bring back life to the magnificent Ariège valley. There are many activities organised during the summer at Sentein. This gîte is slightly isolated, enjoying space and mountain air (altitude 900 metres). Living room (2 single beds), kitchen, 2 bedrooms (1 double and 4 single beds), bathroom and shower, fireplace, electric central heating, ground. Linen available. Mobile shops call; farm produce available; other shopping in the village (5 km).

Prices: low season   F 1160/1365   **8 people**
high season   F 1480   *IGN 71*
winter season   F 1365
Booking: Ariège booking service E
09/B38

UCHENTEIN A small cottage, with country-style furnishings, near another gîte, but otherwise in a slightly isolated spot, outside the village (altitude 930 metres). At Audressein (8 km approx.) you can see one of the last remaining traditional clog makers at work. A swimming-pool and riding at 22 km. Living room/kitchenette (4 single beds), 1 bedroom (1 double bed), bathroom, open fire, electric central heating, open ground. Linen available. Mobile baker calls; farm produce available in the village; other shopping and restaurant at Sentein (4 km).

Prices: low season   F 905/1090   **6 people**
high season   F 1230   *IGN 71*
winter season   F 1090
Booking: Ariège booking service E
09/B17a

UNAC A spacious, renovated village house with country-style furnishings, enjoying fine mountain views (altitude 650 metres). It is close enough to Andorra and the Spanish border for a day trip and the spa town and winter sports resort of Ax-les-Thermes is at just 9 km. Living room, kitchen, 3 bedrooms (2 double and 1 single bed), shower room, fireplace, oil-fired central heating, terrace, garage, courtyard. Shopping and restaurant at Luzenac (1 km).

Prices: low season   F 731/803   **5 people**
high season   F 1090   *IGN 71*
Booking: Ariège booking service E

09/59

USTOU Saint-Lizier d'Ustou A renovated and traditionally furnished terraced house, at the heart of a mountain village (altitude 739 metres). Local sites include the Fontsainte caves, the Cirque de Cagateille and some interesting dolmens. A lake nearby (1 km) and ski-ing at 6 km; other leisure amenities at the spa town of Seix (12 km). Living room/kitchenette, 3 bedrooms (2 double and 2 single bunk beds), shower room, electric central heating, open ground. Mobile butcher and baker call; restaurant in the village; shopping at Ustou (1 km) or at Seix.

Prices: low season   F 594/808   **6 people**
high season   F 1130/1188   *IGN 71*
winter season   F 1903
Booking: Ariège booking service E
09/192

Aveyron

ANGLARS-SAINT-FELIX A small, renovated cottage at the village centre. There is a swimming-pool and tennis court at 3 km. Local sites include the Châteaux of Belcastel and Peyrusse. The lovely old town of Villefranche-de-Rouergue (30 km) is also worth a visit. Kitchen, 2 bedrooms (1 double and 1 single bed), shower room, electric and wood heating, terrace. Farm produce in the village; mobile grocer and baker call; other shopping at Rignac (3 km) and a restaurant within walking distance (0.8 km).

Prices:	low season	F 397/550	**3 people**
	high season	F 768	*IGN 58*

Booking: Aveyron booking service E

12/1664

LA CAPELLE-BONANCE Le Navech A renovated gîte, lying near open fields, some 4.5 km from the village. It is just 0.4 km from the river Lot (good fishing) and 7 km from the interesting old town of Saint-Geniez-d'Olt where there is a swimming-pool and tennis court. Ski-ing at 30 km. Kitchen, 2 bedrooms (1 double, 1 large single bed, 1 cot, 1 folding single bed), shower room, electric heating, carport, barbecue. Mobile shops call; other shopping and restaurant at Saint-Geniez-d'Olt.

Prices:	low season	F 495/765	**4 people**
	high season	F 877	*IGN 58*

Booking: Aveyron booking service E

12/1289

CUZAC Gours A detached, modern house, with traditional furniture, in a hamlet at 2 km from the village itself. Fishing and bathing at the Lot river nearby, swimming-pool and tennis at Capdenac (6 km); riding at 8 km. Living room (TV, 1 single divan), kitchen, 4 bedrooms (2 double, 3 single and 1 cot), shower room, electric heating, terrace, enclosed ground and courtyard. Shopping and restaurant at Capdenac.

Prices:	low season	F 703/1019	**9 people**
	high season	F 1342	*IGN 57*

Booking: Aveyron booking service E

12/1529

ESCANDOLIERES Les Laquets A renovated gîte with country-style furnishings, 2 km from the village. Visit Belcastel Château, or, more unusually, the "Découverte" (an open coal mine) at Décazeville (15 km). The fascinating old Roman town of Conques is at 25 km approx. Living room/kitchenette, 2 bedrooms (1 double and 3 large single beds), shower room, fireplace, courtyard and meadowland. Mobile shops call and local farm produce; other shopping at Rignac (12 km); a restaurant in the village.

Prices:	low season	F 522/697	**5 people**
	high season	F 893	*IGN 58*

Booking: Aveyron booking service E

12/1270

LESTRADE-ET-THOUELS An attractive gîte in a modern apartment above the owners' garage, with another gîte next door, at the village centre (altitude 750 metres). At Villefranche-de-Panat (6 km) there is a lake with a sailing school and facilities for other water sports. Living room (TV, 1 double divan), kitchen, 2 bedrooms (2 double beds), bathroom, oil-fired central heating, garage. A grocery in the village and mobile shops call; other shopping at Villefranche-de-Panat.

Prices:	low season	F 516/721	**6 people**
	high season	F 1016	*IGN 58*

Booking: Aveyron booking service E

12/131

Aveyron

MONTJAUX A renovated village gîte furnished in rustic fashion in the centre of a picturesque village overlooking the beautiful Tarn valley. Altitude 650 metres. Marked footpaths, fishing (5 km), river sailing (10 km), riding, swimming-pool, bathing in a lake within 26 km. Living room/kitchenette, 2 bedrooms (1 double, 2 single beds), shower room, open fire, electric stoves, grounds. Farm produce available. Baker and butcher call. Shops and restaurant in the village or in Millau or Sainte-Affrique (25 km).

Prices: low season   F 499/725   **4 people**
           high season   F 937   *IGN 58*
Booking: Aveyron booking service   **E**

12/1602

PAMPELONNE A gîte in a charming old house which has been renovated and furnished in traditional rustic style. The house is situated in calm surroundings at 0.5 km from the town centre. Altitude 500 metres. Pampelonne is named after Pamplona in Navarre, and has lovely views over the Viaur gorge and is overlooked by the ruins of a château. River bathing at 3 km. Living room, kitchen, 3 bedrooms (2 double and 2 single beds), bathroom, fireplace, electric heating, carport, enclosed ground. Shopping and restaurant in the town or at Carmaux (14 km).

Prices: low season   on request   **6 people**
           high season   on request   *IGN 58*
Booking: Aveyron booking service   **E**

12/1562

QUINS La Prade-Haute-de-Sauveterre A renovated house on a livestock farm, some 5 km from the village. Local sites include the splendid Viaur Viaduct and the Château du Bosc. For nightlife, visit the "Le Valadier" discotheque (3 km). The fine cathedral town of Rodez (33 km) is well worth a visit. Kitchen, 3 bedrooms (1 double, 4 large single beds and 1 single folding bed), shower room, solid-fuel stove, terrace, garage, open ground with child's swing. Farm produce in the village; other shopping and restaurant at Naucelle (4 km).

Prices: low season   F 543/819   **6 people**
           high season   F 993   *IGN 58*
Booking: Aveyron booking service   **E**

12/1049

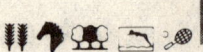

SAINT-IZAIRE Faveyrolles A pleasant, modern, first-floor gîte adjacent to the owner's living quarters with simple furniture outside the village (5 km). Fishing, riding, swimming-pool, tennis, cinemas at Sainte-Affrique (22 km) from where you can go and visit the surrounding sites and ancient monuments. Living room (TV), kitchen, 2 bedrooms (2 double, 1 single bed, and cot), shower room, central heating, balcony, ground. Farm produce in the village. Baker and butcher call. Grocer's shop in the village, a restaurant at Broquies (15 km).

Prices: low season   F 491/771   **6 people**
           high season   F 893   *IGN 65*
Booking: Aveyron booking service   **E**

12/9

FIREKILLSFIREKILLSFIREKILLSFIREKILLSFIREKILLS

FIRE — spreads rapidly
take care with matches and cigarettes!

Aveyron

LA SALVETAT-PEYRALES La Guionie de Pradials A renovated gîte surrounded by farmland, some 6 km from the village (altitude 570 metres). Local sites include the ruined Château de Roumegoux and the Viaur Viaduct. A small lake, tennis and swimming-pool at Rieupeyroux (8 km) and other amenities at Villefranche-de-Rouergue (20 km). Living room, kitchen, 2 bedrooms (3 double beds), shower room, gas stove, enclosed ground with garden furniture. Mobile baker and grocer; local farm produce; other shopping in the village.

Prices:	low season	F 482/715	**6 people**
	high season	F 893	IGN 57

Booking: Aveyron booking service E

12/221

LA SALVETAT-PEYRALES La Pendarie An attractively renovated cottage, 6 km from the village (altitude 550 metres). The owner also has a farm camp-site and you may be interested in joining in his craft courses (in ironwork). Fishing at a pond on the property; a day nursery available in the village 15th July–15th August). Kitchen, 2 bedrooms (1 double, 2 single beds), shower room, wood stove, carport, open ground with child's swing. Farm produce from the owner; other shopping and restaurant in the village.

Prices:	low season	F 412/604	**4 people**
	high season	F 744	IGN 57

Booking: Aveyron booking service E

12/736

SAUVETERRE La Taurelle An old, isolated stone house with simple country-style furnishings some 5 km from the village centre, where you can visit a thirteenth-century royal blockhouse, and join in the quaint traditional celebrations, in October, of chestnut harvest and cider festival. Altitude 550 metres. Living room/kitchenette, 3 bedrooms (1 double, 3 single beds), shower room, electric heating, terrace, garage, open ground with garden furniture. Baker and grocer call, farm produce, and restaurant in the village; shops at Naucelle (12 km).

Prices:	low season	F 339 /480	**5 people**
	high season	F 621	IGN 58

Booking: Aveyron booking service E

12/266

TREBAS Saint-Pierre-de-Trebas A modern, purpose-built gîte, set in open countryside, overlooking the river Tarn, 0.8 km from the village centre (a car is essential). Take a trip to the lovely old town of Albi (40 km) and visit the famous museum dedicated to Toulouse-Lautrec. Living room, kitchen, 2 bedrooms (2 double and 1 single bed), oil stove, terrace, open ground with garden furniture. Farm produce, other shopping and restaurant in the village or at Requista (15 km).

Prices:	low season	F 554/831	**5 people**
	high season	F 1016	IGN 65

Booking: Aveyron booking service E

12/1449

SAINT-SEVER-DU-MOUSTIER Chambre d'hôte accommodation in a well-renovated local house (with fourteenth-century tower) and furnished in rustic fashion. Altitude 550 metres. It lies close to a little river and there are marked footpaths or you may borrow bicycles. Swimming-pool, riding and tennis (10 km). Four bedrooms available on the first and second floor, each with 1 double bed. Bathroom and shower room shared. Dining room and reading room with open fire at your disposal. Shops at Belmont-sur-Rance (approx. 10 km).

Prices: on request   **8 people**
IGN 65
12370

Booking: Mme M.-H BEZIAT, Saint-Sever-du-Moustier, Belmont-sur-Rance. Tel. (65) 99 90 35. E

12/6

Aveyron

VEYREAU *Chambre d'hôte* accommodation in the owners' beautifully renovated former convent, with country-style furnishings at the village centre. There is a private swimming-pool in the grounds. Try your hand at hang-gliding or canoeing at Millau (28 km). Two double bedrooms available; shared lounge with open fireplace, bathroom, central heating, enclosed courtyard with garden furniture. Farm produce and other shopping in the village where there is a restaurant.

Prices: on request

4 people
IGN 58

Booking: Mme C. PLANTROU, Veyreau, 12100 Millau.
Tel. (65) 62 62 84   **E**

12/CH50

Camping à la ferme Five farms spread over four villages provide camping accommodation in the district known as Pays de l'Alzou. Many streams and rivers for fishing; marked footpaths; local fairs and markets for bric-à-brac and craft products; Peyrusse-le-Roc has a fancy-dress fête in August. All within a radius of 16 km from Villefranche-de-Rouergue.

Prices: on request

IGN 57

Booking: M MAUREL, S.I. des Pays de l'Alzou, Mairie de Lanuéjouls, 12350.

12/17

Camping à la ferme Fifteen farms spread over eight villages, some at an altitude of 650 metres around Naucelle which is on the Toulouse-Rodez rail line (Rodez 37 km). Many opportunities for unusual pastimes. Craft courses in pottery, basket-making, clay modelling; plenty of marked footpaths; riding and pond fishing; village fêtes and dancing. Orienteering.

Prices: on request

IGN 58

Booking: Mme COTTE, Comité d'action et de rénovation rurale du Naucellois (C.A.R.R.N.A.U.), Hôtel de ville, 12800 Naucelle.
Tel. (65) 47 04 32.

12/18

ASPRIERES Ranch des Trois Marie A *gîte équestre* open all the year round, for horse-riding enthusiasts. Accommodation in rooms at the gîte, or hotel, inn or camping near-by. Rides in groups of 6 or 12 riders organised for 3, 4 or 6 days, and in August for a special circuit of 4 weeks stopping in bivouacs or gîtes. Different circuits organised on request. The little town of Montbazens (approximately 10 km) has tennis courts and swimming-pool as well as shops and restaurant.

Prices: on request

12 people
IGN 57

Booking: M P. NAYROLLES, La Remise, Asprières 12700 Capdenac Gare.
Tel. (65) 64 85 81

12/19

BARAQUEVILLE Le Moulinou Accommodation for horse-riders in a purpose-built *gîte équestre* in the heart of the country (altitude 600 metres). Riding, forest walks, fishing, disco and tennis locally, swimming-pool (12 km). There are 7 bedrooms available, 2 with a double bed each, the other 5 with 2 single beds each, 2 bathrooms and 2 showers are shared. If preferred you may camp there. Set riding programmes or special rides organised on request. Shops and restaurant in the village (3.5 km) or in Rodez (23 km).

Prices: on request

14 people
IGN 58

Booking: M G. PUECH, Le Moulinou, 12160 Baraqueville.
Tel. (65) 69 02 68.

12/20

Haute-Garonne

BALESTA A renovated house, typical of the region, furnished in rustic style and situated at the heart of the village. Sailing at a lake, miniature golf and other amenities at Boulogne-sur-Gesse (15 km), a fortified town which dates back to the thirteenth century. Living room (TV), kitchen, 4 bedrooms (2 double and 2 single beds), bathroom, fireplace, central heating, terrace, garage, garden with outdoor furniture. Farm produce from the owners; other shopping in the village.

Prices:	low season	F 875	**6 people**
	high season	F 1030	*IGN 70*

Booking: Haute-Garonne Loisirs Accueil **E**

31/330

CAUBIAC Basseillac This renovated gîte with traditional, country-style furnishings is set in open ground, some 3 km from the village. Visit Toulouse (25 km approx.), called *La Ville Rose* because of the old quarter's faded red brick; see in particular, the delightful Jacobins church. Living room (TV), kitchen (washing machine), 2 bedrooms (4 double, 1 single bed), bathroom, fireplace, central heating, terrace, open ground with garden furniture. Mobile baker calls; farm produce in the village; shopping at Cadours (3.5 km).

Prices:	low season	F 900 (4 persons)	**9 people**
	high season	F 1200 (4 persons)	*IGN 64*

Booking: Haute-Garonne Loisirs Accueil **E**

31/342

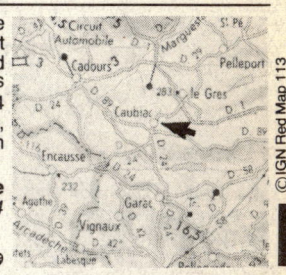

FABAS One of two gîtes with traditional rustic furnishings in a renovated house, 3 km from the village. L'Isle-en-Dodon (9 km) has a lovely fourteenth-century church; see the nearby Gallo-Roman villa at Montmaurin. Sailing at a lake (25 km). Living room, kitchen, 2 bedrooms (2 double, 1 single bed), bathroom, fireplace, oil stove, open ground. Farm produce available in the village; other shopping and restaurants at L'Isle-en-Dodon.

Prices:	low season	F 715	**5 people**
	high season	F 915	*IGN 63*

Booking: Haute-Garonne Loisirs Accueil **E**

31/100

LE FOUSSERET Le Coustala A modern holiday home with traditional furnishings, in a pleasant rural setting, 2 km from the village. Sailing and water ski-ing on the river Garonne at the picturesque town of Cazères (12 km) which holds a flower festival on Whit Monday; see the nearby Château de Palminy (fifteenth century). Living room, kitchen, 2 bedrooms (4 single beds), shower room, fireplace, central heating, terrace, carport, enclosed ground with child's swings. Shopping in the village and a restaurant within walking distance.

Prices:	low season	F 995	**4 people**
	high season	F 1240	*IGN 63*

Booking: Haute-Garonne Loisirs Accueil **E**

31/305

FRONTIGNAN-SAVES This renovated and traditionally furnished gîte lies at the centre of the village where there is a swimming-pool. Good leisure amenities at the rural holiday resort of L'Isle-en-Dodon (7 km) which has a remarkable church. Riding at 10 km. Living room/kitchenette, 2 bedrooms (1 double, 2 single beds), shower room, no heating, terrace, open ground with garden furniture. Farm produce available in the village; other shopping and restaurants at L'Isle-en-Dodon.

Prices:	low season	F 775	**4 people**
	high season	F 915	*IGN 63*

Booking: Haute-Garonne Loisirs Accueil **E**

31/316

Country Food and Wine in HAUTE-GARONNE

FARM INNS

Farm inns in Haute-Garonne welcome their guests with traditional cooking using locally produced ingredients. It is advisable to phone in advance to make a booking. Below are several farm inn addresses in Haute-Garonne:

Mr Robert DENCAUSSE
Saint Oule
Castelbiague 31160 Aspet
Tel. 61.97.53.45 and 61.97.52.47
(1.5 km from the village de Castelbiague)
Regional cuisine based on local
farm produce. Meals to order.

Madame David COURTOT
Ferme de Montgay
31560 Nailoux
Tel. (61) 81.31.62.
(3 km from Nailloux, 0.8 km from Lac de la Thésauque)
Open: July and August
Camping à la Ferme also available

Monsieur Joseph BONNEMAISON
Esplanade P. Campech
31260 Fronton
Tel. (61) 82.43.59.
(12 km from Villemur, 25 km from Toulouse)
Closed the last week in August and the first week in September
Chambres d'Hôtes also available

Madame SCHMITT
Ferme au Village d'Auzas
31360 St. Martory
Tel. (61) 90.23.61.
Closed Sunday evening and Monday
Farm produce available

Monsieur Claude LEGENDRE
La Ferme de Naudon
31370 Rieumes
Tel. (61) 91.84.97.
(2 km from Rieumes, 30 km from Toulouse)
Open: at the end of the week
Farm produce available – speciality *foie gras*

FARM PRODUCE

Local farm produce and locally produced wines may be bought at MAISON DE LA HAUTE-GARONNE, which is a large shop incorporating a tourist information service and tourist souvenirs, as well as a large selection of locally produced food and wine. It is accessible from the Autoroute des Deux Mers as well as the Canal du Midi.

MAISON DE LA HAUTE-GARONNE
Aire de Port-Lauragais
Autoroute A 61
31290 AVIGNONET-LAURAGAIS
Tel. (61) 81.69.46.
Open: all year round

Haute-Garonne

GAILLAC-TOULZA Rey A large renovated house with country-style furnishings, set in open countryside, some 6 km from the village where you may buy local farm produce. Fishing at a nearby lake (0.5 km). Visit the delightful medieval town of Pamiers (20 km approx.) with its fourteenth-century cathedral and other sights. Living room (TV), kitchen (washing machine), 4 bedrooms (2 double, 2 single, 1 child's bed and a cot), fireplace, terrace, carport, ground. Shopping from mobile stores; other shops (5 km) or at Auterive (12 km).

Prices:	low season	F 1300	**8 people**
	high season	F 1805	IGN 64

Booking: Haute-Garonne Loisirs Accueil   **E**

31/341

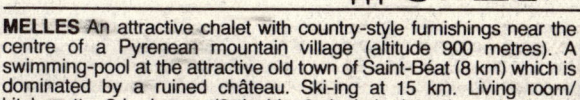

GENOS A ground-floor gîte with traditional, country-style furnishings in a renovated house, near the village centre. A swimming-pool and lake at the small spa town of Barbazan (10 km); organ recitals are performed during the summer in the splendid cathedral at nearby Saint-Bertrand-de-Comminges. Altitude 520 metres. Living room/kitchenette, 3 bedrooms (3 double, 2 single beds), bathroom, fireplace, central heating, enclosed ground with swings. Mobile butcher and baker; other shopping and restaurant at Barbazan.

Prices:	low season	F 690	**8 people**
	high season	F 865	IGN 70

Booking: Haute-Garonne Loisirs Accueil   **E**

31/156

6

GRAGNAGUE La Tuilerie One of three small, traditionally furnished gîtes in a renovated house, typical of the region, set in open ground, 1 km from the village centre. Toulouse (18 km) is a lovely old town with Renaissance church (les Jacobins), old paved quarter and good modern shopping facilities. Living room/kitchenette (2 single divans), 1 bedroom (1 double bed), shower room, central heating, open ground. A restaurant nearby; shopping (7 km) or at Toulouse.

Prices:	high season	F 650	**4 people**
			IGN 64

Booking: Haute-Garonne Loisirs Accueil   **E**

31/283

MARIGNAC-LASCLARES A renovated gîte with traditional furnishings, 1.5 km from the village centre. Tennis and sailing at a lake (5 km). Visit the picturesque town of Montesquieu-Volvestre (15 km approx.) with its old market halls and reputed restaurants. Living room (TV, 1 double divan), kitchen, 3 bedrooms (2 double, 2 single beds), bathroom, fireplace, central heating, terrace, garage, enclosed ground with garden furniture and children's swings). Farm produce from the owners; mobile baker and grocer; other shopping at Le Fousseret (5 km).

Prices:	low season	F 980	**8 people**
	high season	F 1300	IGN 64

Booking: Haute-Garonne Loisirs Accueil   **E**

31/326

MELLES An attractive chalet with country-style furnishings near the centre of a Pyrenean mountain village (altitude 900 metres). A swimming-pool at the attractive old town of Saint-Béat (8 km) which is dominated by a ruined château. Ski-ing at 15 km. Living room/kitchenette, 3 bedrooms (2 double, 3 single beds and a cot), shower room, fireplace, gas central heating, terrace, carport, open ground with garden furniture and barbecue. Mobile shops call; other shopping at Saint-Béat.

Prices:	low season	F 1135	**8 people**
	high season	F 1500	IGN 70

Booking: Haute-Garonne Loisirs Accueil   **E**

31/91

Haute-Garonne

MONTMAURIN A spacious, attractive modern house with traditional furnishings near the village centre (0.5 km) which boasts a Roman villa and museum of ancient history. Sailing at a lake at the old fortified town of Boulogne-sur-Gesse (8 km). Living room, kitchen, 5 bedrooms (3 double, 4 single and 2 child's beds), bathroom, fireplace, central heating, terrace, garage, open ground. Mobile shops call; farm produce in the village; other shopping and restaurants at Boulogne-sur-Gesse.

Prices:	low season	F 955	**12 people**
	high season	F 1250	*IGN 70*

Booking: Haute-Garonne Loisirs Accueil   E

31/280

OÔ One of two traditionally furnished gîtes in a renovated house near the village centre (0.3 km). Luchon (9 km) is an attractive spa town, popular in summer and with good winter sports facilities at nearby Superbagnères. Altitude 950 metres. Living room, kitchen, 2 bedrooms (1 double, 2 single beds), shower room, central heating, enclosed ground. Mobile shops call and restaurant in the village; other shopping at Luchon.

Prices:	low season	F 810	**4 people**
	high season	F 1000	*IGN 70*

Booking: Haute-Garonne Loisirs Accueil   E

31/234

SAINT-MAMET A gîte with country-style furnishings, one of two in a well renovated house, set in enclosed ground, just 10 km from the Spanish border. A swimming-pool and tennis at the popular spa resort of Luchon (0.7 km). Ski-ing at 10 km. Altitude 600 metres. Living room/kitchenette, 2 bedrooms (2 double, 1 single bed), bathroom, fireplace, central heating. Shopping and restaurants at Luchon.

Prices:	low season	F 1025	**5 people**
	high season	F 1190/1300	*IGN 70*

Booking: Haute-Garonne Loisirs Accueil   E

31/247

SAINTE-RAFINE Les Anchous An attractively renovated house with traditional, country-style furnishings, set in open ground with garden furniture for *al fresco* meals, 1 km from the village centre. Local fishing and forest walks, a swimming-pool and tennis within 3 km. Toulouse is an easy day trip at 25 km approx. Living room/kitchenette (1 single divan), 2 bedrooms (2 double and 1 single bed), fireplace, central heating, terrace, carport. Shopping and restaurant at Villemur-sur-Tarn (3 km).

Prices:	low season	F 755/1080	**6 people**
	high season	F 1190/1210	*IGN 64*

Booking: Haute-Garonne Loisirs Accueil   E

31/299

URAU Noustens A spacious renovated and traditionally furnished former farmhouse in an attractive garden, outside the village (3 km). This is an attractive region at the foothills of the Pyrenees. The spa town of Salies-du-Salat (12 km) has many leisure facilities, including miniature golf and a casino; see the nearby prehistoric caves at Marsoulas. Living room, kitchen, 3 bedrooms (2 double, 1 single bed), bathroom, fireplace, electric central heating, terrace. Farm produce from the owners; other shopping and restaurant at Salies-du-Salat.

Prices:	low season	F 800	**5 people**
	high season	F 1060	*IGN 71*

Booking: Haute-Garonne Loisirs Accueil   E

31/271

Gers

CASTELNAU D'AUZAN La Paloumerou A renovated house with traditional furniture on a vineyard outside the village. Swimming-pool and tennis in the village (2.5 km). The spa-town of Barbotan-les-Thermes (14 km) has a lake for swimming and sailing and other leisure facilities. Living room (2 single divans), kitchen, 2 bedrooms (1 double, 2 single and 1 child's bed), shower room, no heating, grounds (field) with garden furniture. Farm produce from the owners; shopping and restaurant in the village.

Prices:	low season	F 750	**6/7 people**
	high season	F 1060	IGN 63

Booking: Gers booking service E

32/726

JEGUN Bordes A gîte adjoining the owner's house which has been renovated and furnished in traditional rustic style 2.5 km from the village on a mixed farm. Fishing and pleasant walks locally. Only 3 km away the little spa town of Castera-Verduzan where there are riding stables and a lake. At Vic-Fezensac there is a swimming-pool, tennis court and cinema. Living room/kitchenette, 3 bedrooms (1 double and 2 large single beds), shower room, open fire, oil central heating, garden and shaded ground with garden furniture. Farm produce from the owner. Shopping in the village or at Vic-Fezensac (13 km).

Prices:	low season	F 820	**4 people**
	high season	F 1170	IGN 63

Booking: Gers booking service E

32/346

LEBOULIN This detached house on an arable farm has been renovated and traditionally furnished. It lies at the edge of the village, just 8 km from the lovely old town of Auch, capital of the département, where you will find d'Artagnan's statue, a beautiful cathedral and interesting exhibitions. Many leisure facilities at Taybosc farm (15 km). Living room, kitchen, 2 bedrooms (1 double and 2 single beds), shower room, central heating, ground. Farm produce in the village (0.5 km); shopping and restaurants at Auch.

Prices:	low season	F 710	**4 people**
	high season	F 1020	IGN 63

Booking: Gers booking service E

32/306

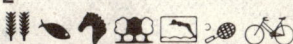

MAULEON-D'ARMAGNAC This pleasantly renovated and simply furnished gîte lies next to the owners' home on their vineyard where Armagnac is produced – you will be welcome to buy some. The village is at 1.5 km. Swimming-pool at Panjas (10 km); fishing, bathing, and sailing at a lake in Cazaubon (10 km). Living room, kitchen, 2 bedrooms (4 single beds), shower room, electric and wood heating, grounds (field). Shopping and restaurant at Estang (5 km).

Prices:	low season	F 740	**4 people**
	high season	F 1060	IGN 63

Booking: Gers booking service E

32/153

MONFORT La Queyrouse A renovated gîte adjoining the owner's house and modestly furnished just outside the village (2.5 km). Local river fishing and pleasant walks. Tennis in the village. Taybosc (11 km) has a farm with leisure facilities including bicycles, pony rides, swimming-pool and an inn. Living room/kitchenette (1 double divan) with small washing machine, 2 bedrooms (1 double, 2 single beds), bathroom, electric heating, garage, garden and large grounds with garden furniture. Farm produce and shops in the village. More shops and restaurant at Mauvezin (10 km).

Prices:	low season	F 920	**6 people**
	high season	F 1310	IGN 63

Booking: Gers booking service E

32/573

Gers

GERS: A LAND OF SUBTLE CHARMS

Gers covers 6300 square kilometres of hilly countryside, away from the main roads of France. Gascony, historically an agricultural region, is still today completely oriented towards the work of the land.
The landscape is gentle and welcoming: grassy hills, clusters of chestnut trees, rocky ledges, hidden footpaths.
Visitors can explore at leisure and enjoy one of the main agricultural départements of France.
Wine production is an important part of this agriculture . . . Madiran, Pacherenc and Côtes-du-Mont number among its noted wines; try too the apéritifs Floc and Pousse-Rapière and Armagnac brandy.
Poultry breeding is an equally important activity: fattened ducks and geese, black turkeys . . .

The rolling Gers countryside

Auch

GERS – a region warmed by the south wind and rich in colours filtered by a gentle light.

For booking and any further information about holidays in Gers, contact:
LOISIRS ACCUEIL GERS
Découverte de la Gascogne
Maison de l'Agriculture
Route de Mirande B.P. 99
32003 AUCH Cedex.   **Tel.** (62) 63.16.55.   **E**

NB For fuller information about all Loisirs Accueil services, please see pages 12–13 of this guide.

Gers

PANASSAC L'Arrabé A detached renovated gîte with country-style furnishings standing in its own extensive grounds at the edge of the village (1 km). Local river fishing and walks, a swimming-pool and tennis court (0.5 km), riding and a lake for sailing, wind-surfing and bathing at 5 km; the Pyrenees are just 40 km away. Living room (1 double divan), kitchen, 2 bedrooms (2 double beds), bathroom, electric heating, terrace, garden and grounds with outdoor furniture. Shops in the village or at Masseube (5 km).

Prices:	low season	F 1050	**6 people**
	high season	F 1490	*IGN 63*

Booking: Gers booking service **E**

32/273

PREIGNAN A single-storey gîte of recent construction standing in its own ground 2 km from the village, and furnished with traditional and modern equipment. River fishing in the village, swimming-pool, riding, tennis, cinemas and many other attractions at the important town of Auch (10 km). Living room (TV), kitchen, 2 bedrooms (1 double, 2 single and 2 single folding beds), bathroom, oil-fired central heating, garden with furniture and barbecue. Farm produce in the village and a good inn only 1 km away. Shops and restaurant in Auch.

Prices:	low season	F 1050	**6 people**
	high season	F 1490	*IGN 63*

Booking: Gers booking service **E**

32/334

6

SAINT-LIZIER-DU-PLANTE Les Lauriers Roses One of four gîtes (this one on the ground floor) in the owner's large and imposing manor house which has been renovated, with antique furniture, 3 km from the village. There is a games room and a lake on the property with wind-surfer and pedalo boat, local fishing, tennis, riding and a swimming-pool at Samatan (10 km). Living room, kitchen, 2 bedrooms (2 double, 2 single beds, child's bed on request), shower room, heating, garden and grounds. Shops and restaurant at Frontignan (1 km) or at Samatan.

Prices:	low season	F 1090	**6 people**
	high season	F 1550	*IGN 63*

Booking: Gers booking service **E**

32/444

TIESTE-URAGNOUX La Roseraie A gîte in a renovated village house with traditional furnishings. Fishing in lake or river (1 km), swimming-pool, riding and tennis at Plaisance (6 km). Miélan (10 km) has a large lake for bathing and sailing. Living room/kitchenette, 2 bedrooms (2 double and 1 single bed), shower room, open fire, electric central heating, terrace and grounds. A good inn 3 km away. Shops in Plaisance.

Prices:	low season	F 710	**5 people**
	high season	F 1020	*IGN 63*

Booking: Gers booking service **E**

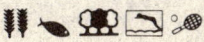

32/642

TRAVERSERES This attractive house, which has been renovated and traditionally furnished, lies on a farm not far from the local town hall. Local walks; swimming-pool and fishing at Seissan (7 km), tennis (11 km), other leisure facilities, including a lake, at Miélan (20 km). Living room, kitchen (washing machine), 2 bedrooms (1 double, 3 single beds), 1 double divan on the landing, another single bed on request, shower room, fireplace, oil and electric heating, ground. Mobile shops call; farm produce available; shopping and restaurant at Seissan.

Prices:	low season	F 840	**7/8 people**
	high season	F 1210	*IGN 63*

Booking: Gers booking service **E**

32/429

Lot

ALBAS Cambau A charming old cottage which has been renovated and traditionally furnished. It lies in its own enclosed ground, 1.5 km from the village centre. The old town of Luzech (3 km) has Roman ruins and a ruined mediaeval château, a swimming-pool and tennis court Cahors (17 km) is well worth a visit. Living room, kitchen, 2 bedrooms (2 double and 1 single bed), shower room, no heating, terrace, carport, enclosed ground with garden furniture. Farm produce available; other shopping and restaurant in the village.

Prices:	low season	F 467/556	**5 people**
	high season	F 956/1056	IGN 57

Booking: Lot Loisirs Accueil **E**

46/984

ASSIER A renovated and traditionally furnished house, next to the church in a village which boasts a ruined Renaissance château and has facilities for fishing, riding and tennis. Bicycles for hire and swimming-pool at Lacapelle-Marival (6 km) which has a château and interesting old market halls. Living room (TV), kitchen, 2 bedrooms (2 double and 2 single beds), bathroom, fireplace, terrace, enclosed courtyard. Farm produce, shopping and restaurant in the village.

Prices:	low season	F 690	**6 people**
	high season	F 988/1050	IGN 57

Booking: Lot Loisirs Accueil **E**

46/268V

BELMONT-SAINTE-FOY An attractive, modern holiday cottage with country-style furnishings in a hamlet where you may buy local farm produce. Bicycles for hire, a swimming-pool and tennis at Lalbenque (8 km). Visit Cahors (35 km approx.) and see the historic Valentry bridge and taste its noted wines. Living room/kitchenette (1 single divan), 2 bedrooms (1 double and 2 single beds), bathroom, no heating, terrace, open ground with garden furniture and barbecue. Shopping at Lalbenque; a restaurant at 4 km.

Prices:	low season	F 500/584	**5 people**
	high season	F 834/912	IGN 57

Booking: Lot Loisirs Accueil **E**

46/1087

BOUSSAC Le Paunchu An old house with rustic furnishings, surrounded by woodland and meadows in a slightly isolated spot, 2 km from the village. River fishing and bathing near the gîte; tennis, swimming-pool and riding at Figeac (10 km), an interesting old town. Living room/kitchenette (1 single bed), 2 bedrooms (2 double beds), shower room, open fire, electric heating, terrace, carport, enclosed ground with garden furniture and table tennis. Mobile shops call and farm produce in the village. Other shopping and restaurant at Figeac.

Prices:	low season	F 723	**5 people**
	high season	F 867/912	IGN 57

Booking: Lot Loisirs Accueil **E**

46/126V

COMIAC Proupech A spacious, old stone cottage with rustic furnishings, set in its own enclosed ground with garden furniture for *al fresco* meals. It lies 9 km from the château town of Souseyrac (swimming-pool, tennis court and bicycle hire) and is an ideal base for exploring the famous sites of Rocamadour, Padirac, etc. Living room (TV), kitchen, 3 bedrooms (1 double and 3 single beds), shower room, oil-fired central heating, carport. Farm produce from the owners; other shopping and restaurant at Sousceyrac.

Prices:	low season	F 1000	**5 people**
	high season	F 1223/1445	IGN 48

Booking: Lot Loisirs Accueil **E**

46/190V

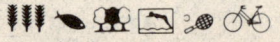

Lot

CORNAC Soulhol An old cottage with rustic furnishings, set in its own grounds on a livestock farm, 8 km from the small, but lively town of Saint-Céré, which has a swimming-pool, tennis, riding and sailing facilities. The surrounding countryside is extremely pleasant and popular with walkers. Living room/kitchenette, 3 bedrooms (3 double beds), shower room, electric heating, enclosed ground. Farm produce in the village; other shopping and restaurants at Bretenoux (8 km) or Saint-Céré.

Prices: low season   F 532/578   **6 people**
         high season   F 945/1075   *IGN 48*

Booking: Lot Loisirs Accueil   **E**

46/933

FIGEAC Les Fraisies A ground-floor gîte, one of two in a well-renovated and traditionally furnished house on a livestock farm, 3 km from the fine old town of Figeac which offers many tourist attractions. Hire bicycles there to explore this delightful area at your leisure. Living room/kitchenette (1 double divan), 2 bedrooms (1 double and 4 single beds), bathroom, fireplace, open ground. Shopping and restaurant in the town.

Prices: low season   F 556   **8 people**
         high season   F 1000/1112   *IGN 57*

Booking: Lot Loisirs Accueil   **E**

46/1092

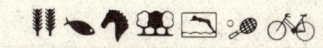

FIGEAC Les Fraisies A second gîte, this one on the first-floor, of the attractively renovated house described above, so ideal for two families holidaying together. It lies in its own enclosed ground on a farm, 3 km from the town centre. Local fishing and farm produce available. Living room (1 double divan), kitchen, 2 bedrooms (1 double and 4 single beds), bathroom, no heating, open ground. Shopping and restaurant in Figeac (3 km).

Prices: low season   F 556   **8 people**
         high season   F 1000/1112   *IGN 57*

Booking: Lot Loisirs Accueil   **E**

46/1093

FONTANES Les Martinets A lovely old, traditionally furnished gîte, typical of the region, on a mixed farm, 0.5 km from the centre of a village in the rugged Causses region. Bicycle hire and other leisure facilities at Lalbenque (6 km). Visit the famous wine producing centre of Cahors (15 km approx.). Living room/kitchenette, 2 bedrooms (2 double and 1 single bed), shower room, no heating, open ground with garden furniture. Farm produce in the village; other shopping and restaurant at Lalbenque.

Prices: low season   F 745/800   **5 people**
         high season   F 1156/1212   *IGN 57*

Booking: Lot Loisirs Accueil   **E**

46/1148

GRAMAT Gibert A very large, attractively renovated house with country-style furnishings, whose owners speak a little English. Plenty of leisure facilities in Gramat itself (4 km), but do not miss the famous sites of Rocamadour (15 km approx.), the Gorges du Tarn and the medieval town of Gourdon (30 km approx.). Living room, kitchen, 4 bedrooms (3 double and 2 single beds), bathroom, open fire, gas heating, open ground. Farm produce, other shopping and restaurant in Gramat.

Prices: low season   F 834/887   **8 people**
         high season   F 1278/1389   *IGN 57*

Booking: Lot Loisirs Accueil   **E**

46/799

Lot

LABURGADE Le Pech A pretty little cottage, renovated and traditionally furnished, where the English-speaking owners offer private fishing, horse riding and bicycle hire. It is 0.8 km from the village centre and just 5 km from Lalbenque, an interesting old town with galleried houses and a winter truffle market! Living room (TV, 1 double divan), kitchen, 2 bedrooms, (1 double and 2 single beds), bathroom, electric heating, terrace, carport, enclosed ground. Shopping and restaurant at Lalbenque.

Prices: low season   F 667/867   **6 people**
          high season   F 1223/1389   *IGN 57*

Booking: Lot Loisirs Accueil   **E**

46/41R

MONTBRUN A simply furnished old farm cottage, surrounded by cultivated fields, 2 km from the village centre. The gîte has private access for fishing and bathing on the river Lot. A swimming-pool and tennis at the château town of Cajarc (8 km). Visit historic Villefranche-de-Rouergue (25 km approx.). Living room/kitchenette, 2 bedrooms (3 double and 1 single bed), shower room, no heating, garage, open ground. A restaurant in the village; shopping at Cajarc.

Prices: low season   F 712/945   **7 people**
          high season   F 1167   *IGN 57*

Booking: Lot Loisirs Accueil   **E**

46/977

MONTCABRIER Cayrol A renovated gîte with country-style furnishings on a mixed farm where the owners will sell their produce (including wine). It lies a little outside the village and 5 km from the historic town of Puy-l'Evêque which overlooks the Lot valley and offers many leisure facilities, including miniature golf. Living room/kitchenette, 2 bedrooms (3 double beds), bathroom, fireplace, garage, open ground. Shopping and restaurant at Puy-l'Evêque.

Prices: low season   F 945/1112   **6 people**
          high season   F 1667   *IGN 57*

Booking: Lot Loisirs Accueil   **E**

46/845

MONTCABRIER Le Mas d'Amour A traditionally furnished gîte on the ground-floor of the English-speaking owners' farmhouse outside the village. Plenty of delightful walks on marked footpaths locally; the charming town of Puy-l'Evêque (5 km) offers a swimming-pool, tennis court and other facilities. Bathing at a lake (13 km). Living room/kitchenette, 1 bedroom (1 double, 1 single bed), shower room, no heating, terrace, enclosed ground. Farm produce from the owners; other shopping at Puy-l'Evêque.

Prices: low season   F 445/500   **3 people**
          high season   F 723/778   *IGN 57*

Booking: Lot Loisirs Accueil   **E**

46/5V

MONTCLERA Les Gunies This spacious gîte has been carefully renovated and furnished in traditional style, in a hamlet, 3 km from the village. Bathing and fishing at a small lake at Frayssinet (4 km); there is a swimming-pool at Salviac (15 km) which boasts a fine thirteenth-century Romanesque church. Living room/kitchenette, 3 bedrooms (1 double and 4 single beds), bathroom and shower, fireplace, electric heating, garage, open ground. Shopping and restaurant at Frayssinet.

Prices: low season   F 812/867   **6 people**
          high season   F 1100/1223   *IGN 57*

Booking: Lot Loisirs Accueil   **E**

46/1101

Lot

MONTLAUZUN A gîte in a substantial house owned by the local community and next to a country church. This is pleasant countryside for walking, fishing in the neighbourhood and the gîte lies in extensive open ground. Aero club and gliding at Moissac (30 km). The départe-ment capital, Cahors (approx. 30 km) has a remarkably mild climate and the tourist office offers guided tours round the old quarters. Living room (1 double divan), kitchen, 3 bedrooms (2 double and 4 single beds), shower room, electric heaters may be available, carport. Farm produce locally, shopping and restaurant at Montcuq (7 km).

Prices: low season   F 845/1023   **10 people**
          high season   F 1512/1594   *IGN 57*
Booking: Lot Loisirs Accueil   **E**
46/71V

PUYBRUN A fine old house, renovated and furnished in traditional style, at the edge of the village. Tennis and bicycle hire in the village, fishing and bathing nearby on the river Dordogne. The gîte is ideally situated for visiting the famous sites of Rocamadour, Sarlat and others. Living room, kitchen, 5 bedrooms (3 double, 2 large single, 1 single bed and a cot), bathroom, terrace, enclosed ground. Farm produce, other shopping and restaurant in the village (0.1 km) or at Bretenoux (5 km).

Prices: low season   F 612/712   **10 people**
          high season   F 1245/1312   *IGN 48*
Booking: Lot Loisirs Accueil   **E**

46/263V

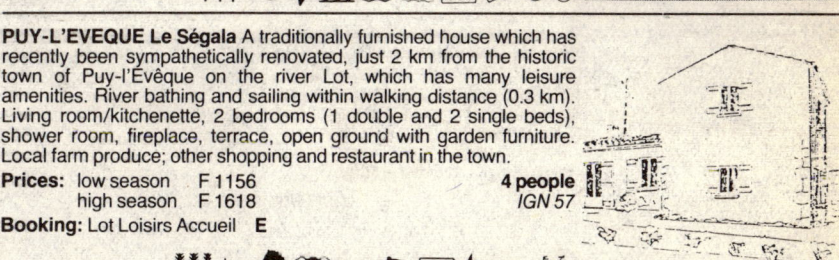

PUY-L'EVEQUE Le Ségala A traditionally furnished house which has recently been sympathetically renovated, just 2 km from the historic town of Puy-l'Evêque on the river Lot, which has many leisure amenities. River bathing and sailing within walking distance (0.3 km). Living room/kitchenette, 2 bedrooms (1 double and 2 single beds), shower room, fireplace, terrace, open ground with garden furniture. Local farm produce; other shopping and restaurant in the town.

Prices: low season   F 1156   **4 people**
          high season   F 1618   *IGN 57*
Booking: Lot Loisirs Accueil   **E**

46/51R

ROUFFILHAC Les Granges This modern, rustically furnished gîte stands in its own enclosed ground near the owners' house in open countryside. Gourdon (6 km) is a well-preserved medieval town where leisure facilities include tennis, swimming-pool and bicycle hire. Sailing at a lake (8 km). Living room (TV, 1 double divan), kitchen, 3 bedrooms (1 double and 2 large single beds), shower room, open fire, electric heating, terrace, garage, enclosed ground with garden furniture. Local farm produce; shopping and restaurant at Gourdon.

Prices: low season   F 556/667   **7 people**
          high season   F 1334   *IGN 48*
Booking: Lot Loisirs Accueil   **E**
46/162V

SAINTE ALAUZIE Les Fontenelles A gîte situated near the owner's home in extensive, open ground where visitors may swim and fish in the private lake. Castelnau-de-Montratier (10 km) is picturesquely sited on a rocky spur and offers swimming-pool and riding facilities. The département capital, Cahors (approx. 25 km), is an old fortified city on the Lot with much to interest the historian. Living room (2 single beds), kitchen, 3 bedrooms (2 double and 1 single bed), bathroom, fireplace, garage. Farm produce at 2 km, shopping and restaurant at Castelnau-de-Montratier.

Prices: low season   F 667/778   **7 people**
          high season   F 112/1333   *IGN 57*
Booking: Lot Loisirs Accueil   **E**
46/223V

Lot

SAINT-CYPRIEN La Paille A sympathetically renovated house, furnished in traditional style, outside the village, with river fishing nearby. Visit the département capital of Cahors (20 km approx.) with its fascinating old buildings (guided tours available) and many other leisure facilities; try the local wine and foie gras. Living room/kitchenette, 4 bedrooms (3 double and 2 single beds), bathroom, open fire, carport, open ground. Farm produce in the village; mobile baker, butcher and charcutier call; other shopping at Lauzerte (8 km), a restaurant at Montcuq (10 km).

Prices: low season   F 578/809   **8 people**
         high season   F 1177/1415   IGN 57
Booking: Lot Loisirs Accueil   E
46/86R

SAINT-MARTIN-LE-REDON La Grangette An attractively renovated cottage with traditional furnishings, situated at the edge of the village with local tennis, fishing and marked footpaths. Hire bicycles at Puy-l'Evéque (10 km) to explore the many famous sites in this area. Visit too, the historic wine-producing town of Cahors (50 km approx.). Kitchen, 3 bedrooms (1 double and 4 single beds), shower room, open fire, open ground. A mobile baker calls, a grocery and farm produce available in the village; other shopping and restaurant at Duravel (4 km).

Prices: low season   F 667/723   **6 people**
         high season   F 1045/1212   IGN 57
Booking: Lot Loisirs Accueil   E
46/1062

SENAILLAC-LAUZES Artix A delightful old stone house with country-style furnishings, set in its own enclosed grounds in a slightly isolated position, 2 km from the village in the rugged Causses region. Swimming-pool and tennis at the old château town of Labastide-Murat (7 km); fishing in the Célé river at 12 km. Living room/kitchenette, 3 bedrooms (2 double and 3 single beds), shower room, fireplace, enclosed ground. Fresh dairy produce from neighbouring farms, mobile grocer calls; other shopping and restaurant at Labastide-Murat.

Prices: low season   F 578   **7 people**
         high season   F 867   IGN 57
Booking: Lot Loisirs Accueil   E
46/636

TEYSSIEU Ussel This spacious, recently renovated house has traditional furnishings and stands quite alone in a pleasant wooded area. There is a small lake (bathing and fishing) and tennis courts at Leval-de-Cère (6 km); a swimming-pool at the small town of Bretenoux (13 km). Living room (TV), kitchen, 3 bedrooms (1 double, 2 single and 1 child's bed), bathroom, fireplace, electric heating, terrace, open ground with garden furniture. Mobile shops and farm produce in the village; other shopping at Bretenoux.

Prices: low season   F 636/808   **5 people**
         high season   F 1213/1271   IGN 48
Booking: Lot Loisirs Accueil   E
46/271V

LE VIGAN Le Peyrès A renovated and traditionally furnished house, built in typical local style, in a hamlet, 5 km from the town where there is a fishing lake. Many other leisure facilities, including swimming-pool, tennis and bicycle hire available at the beautifully preserved medieval town of Gourdon (7 km). Living room (TV, 1 double divan), kitchen, 2 bedrooms (1 double and 2 single beds), bathroom, open fire, terrace, open ground. Local farm produce available and mobile shops call; other shopping and restaurant in the town.

Prices: low season   F 667/1000   **6 people**
         high season   F 1667   IGN 57
Booking: Lot Loisirs Accueil   E
46/2R

Hautes-Pyrénées

AUCUN A gîte in an attractive house with mountain views shared with the owner on a farm 2 km from the village. The gîte has its own entrance and there is a courtyard and garden. Altitude 850 m. Plenty of opportunity for mountain walks nearby and cross-country skiing at 12 km. Argelès-Gazost (approx. 12 km) is a spa town with good winter and summer sports facilities and various entertainments, including casino and cinema. Living room/kitchenette, 2 bedrooms (2 double beds), 1 single bed available (supplement), shower room. Shopping at Aucun.

Prices:	low season F 850	**4/5 people**
	high season F 1050	IGN 70
	winter season F 850	

Booking: Hautes-Pyrénées Loisirs Accueil E
65/1

BERBERUST-LIAS A gîte in the owner's own substantial house in a peaceful village, altitude 700 m. Lourdes (8 km), world famous as a centre for pilgrims, also offers good sporting facilities including swimming-pool, windsurfing, pedalo hire, tennis and walks on marked footpaths. Skiing at Hautacam (25 km). Kitchen, 2 bedrooms (2 double, 1 single and 1 child's bed), shower room, courtyard and garden. Shopping at Lourdes or at Argelès-Gazost (approx. 15 km).

Prices:	low season F 850	**5/6 people**
	high season F 1000	IGN 70
	winter season F 900/1000	

Booking: Hautes-Pyrénées Loisirs Accueil E
65/2

BARBAZAN-DEBAT A charming gîte with rustic furnishings, situated in the owners' home, with a separate entrance, in a house dating from the eighteenth century, lying in parkland, at 1 km from the village. Tennis, riding and a swimming-pool all within 2 km. Living room (1 double divan and 1 single folding bed), kitchen, lounge, 1 bedroom (2 single beds), bathroom and shower, fireplace, open ground and garden. Shopping in the village.

Prices:	low season	on request	**5 people**
	high season	on request	IGN 70

Booking: Hautes-Pyrénées Loisirs Accueil E

65/LA2

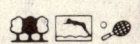

BOURISP One of two gîtes in a pretty stone house in the village, altitude 800 m. Saint-Lary-Soulan (2 km) is on the edge of the national park and is an excellent starting-point for walks through the lovely Aure valley – contact the tourist office for guided tours. This whole area is renowned for stunning mountain scenery, rivers and waterfalls and highly recommended for touring. Living room/kitchenette (1 double divan), 2 bedrooms (2 double beds), bathroom, fireplace. Shopping at Saint-Lary-Soulan.

Prices:	low season	on request	**6 people**
	high season F 1500		IGN 70
	winter season F 2000		

Booking: Hautes-Pyrénées Loisirs Accueil E
65/4

BUN One of two gîtes in an attractive house in its own grassy grounds and set by itself at the edge of the village amongst mountain scenery. Argelès-Gazost (approx. 7 km) is a small spa town with facilities for tennis, mini-golf, swimming-pool, and other entertainments include cinema and casino. The town is also an ideal starting-point for touring the Cauteret and Bareges valleys. Skiing at approx. 17 km. Kitchen, 3 bedrooms (3 double beds and a cot), bathroom. Shopping at Argelès-Gazost.

Prices:	low season F 1400	**6 people**
	high season F 1400	IGN 70
	winter season F 1400	

Booking: Hautes-Pyrénées Loisirs Accueil E
65/5

Hautes-Pyrénées

RESERVATION LOISIRS ACCUEIL

SITUATED ON THE SPANISH BORDER, A DEPARTMENT WHICH LINKS PLAINS, HILLS AND HIGH MOUNTAINS

Far from industry and the cities, close to the Spanish frontier, the département of Hautes-Pyrénées gathers together mountain, hill and plain. Perhaps because of its privileged situation, the natural splendours of the Pyrénées have been better protected than those of other regions. This splendidly isolated situation has no doubt helped to preserve a landscape rich in species of flora and fauna which are now extremely rare or have even died out in other parts of France and Europe.

The département of Hautes-Pyrénées offers tourists many distinctive attractions: long-established spas, pilgrimages to Lourdes, mountaineering and winter sports, are all certainly enhanced by the beauty of their surroundings, but it is also the appeal of the rural life and traditions which draws holiday-makers to the Hautes-Pyrénées. If what you are looking for is to get back to nature, to rediscover the joys of the country and a way of life that is warm, simple and direct, then come to the countryside of Bigorre.

SPECIAL ATTRACTIONS
Néouvielle Nature Reserve — Cirque de Gavarnie — the glaciers at Néouvielle, Mont Perdu, Roland's Breach, Vignemale and Balaïtous.

LOURDES: the grottoes, the Saint-Pie X basilica, the Gemmail and Pyrenean museums, the lake, the Grotte du Loup, the Subercarrère forest and the fortified castle.

SCENIC ROUTES: the passes of Soulor, Tourmalet, Aspin, Peyresourde; the high peaks — Pic du Midi, Pic de Capdelong, Pic de Troumouse.

CAVES: Massabielle, Bétharram (5 km from St-Pé-de-Bigorre), Medous, Béout, Gargas (near Aventignan).

To book the gîtes on the following page and for any further information about holidays in the Hautes-Pyrénées, contact:

LOISIRS ACCUEIL HAUTES-PYRENEES
Comité Départemental du Tourisme
6 rue Eugene Tenot
65000 TARBES
Tel. (62) 93.03.30.   E
Telex 530 535 COMTOUR

NB For fuller information about all Loisirs Accueil services, please see pages 12–13 of this guide

Hautes-Pyrénés

ENS A gîte in the owner's own house with southerly views over the mountains. Saint-Lary-Soulan (5 km) offers excellent winter and summer sporting facilities including skating, tennis, swimming-pool and riding and is renowned as a ski resort. Bagnères-de-Bigorre (approx. 50 km) is a lively spa town and well worth the trip through some impressive scenery. Living room/kitchenette (1 double divan), 3 bedrooms (2 double and 2 single beds), bathroom, fireplace. Shopping at Saint-Lary-Soulan.

Prices: low season F 1500
high season F 1650
winter season F 2200

8 people
IGN 70

Booking: Hautes-Pyrénées Loisirs Accueil   E
65/6

ESTERRE One of several purpose-built village gîtes with courtyard, garden and private parking. The village is close to Luz-Saint-Sauveur, a spa town with a magnificent twelfth-century fortified church and winter sports facilities at Luz Ardiden. Summer visitors can enjoy walks in the national park, tennis, mini-golf, craft exhibitions and special summer entertainments. Living room/kitchenette (1 double divan), 1 bedroom (1 double bed), bathroom. Shopping at Luz-Saint-Sauveur.

Prices: low season F 750
high season F 1150
winter season F 1050/1680

4 people
IGN 70

Booking: Hautes-Pyrénées Loisirs Accueil   E
65/7

GEDRE One of two gîtes in a renovated house with modern furniture at the heart of a typical mountain village (altitude 1000 metres). The Cirq de Gavarnie (6 km) has ski-ing facilities and you can enjoy exploring the Pyrénées National Park on rambles organised from there. Living room/ kitchenette, 2 bedrooms (1 double and 2 single beds), shower room, electric heating, garden with outdoor furniture. Farm produce, shopping and restaurant in the village or at Luz-Saint-Sauveur (12 km).

Prices: low season   on request
high season   on request
winter season on request

4 people
IGN 70

Booking: Hautes-Pyrénées Loisirs Accueil   E
65/LA4

GUCHEN A gîte in a detached village house with its own courtyard and garden. Saint-Lary-Soulan (6 km), a typical Pyrenean village with a mild climate, is a good starting-point for mountain walks – either on the gentle lower slopes or the more challenging high mountains: guides are available – contact the tourist office. Why not take a day-trip to Spain through the Aragnouet tunnel? Lounge, living room, kitchen, 2 bedrooms and an attic (3 double and 1 single bed), bathroom.

Prices: low season F 1050
high season F 1575
winter season F 1500/2300

7 people
IGN 70

Booking: Hautes-Pyrénées Loisirs Accueil   E
65/9

SAINTE MARIE DE CAMPAN A gîte in an attractive house with southerly views and its own grounds 2 km from the village in the Haut Adour valley. Altitude 750 m. The lively spa town of Bagnères-de-Bigorre (7 km) offers all kinds of sports, and various entertainments include museums and a casino. Windsurfing and cross-country skiing at 7 km to ski slopes at La Mongie (13 km). Living room, dining room, kitchen, 3 bedrooms (3 double and 1 single bed), bathroom, fireplace. Shopping at Bagnères-de-Bigorre.

Prices: low season F 1050
high season F 1575
winter season F 1260/1680

7 people
IGN 70

Booking: Hautes-Pyrénées Loisirs Accueil   E
65/10

Tarn

ALOS Gauginelles A modern holiday home with country-style furnishings on a mixed farm, 1 km from the village centre. Trout fishing at 0.5 km; sailing at Pont-de-Laure leisure centre in Castelnau-de-Montmiral (8 km). Bicycle hire and forest walks at 10 km. Living room/kitchenette, 2 bedrooms (2 double and 1 single bed), shower room, no heating, terrace, carport, open field with garden furniture and barbecue. Local farm produce available; mobile shops call; other shopping and restaurant (6 km) or at Gaillac (16 km).

Prices:	low season	F 530/660	**5 people**
	high season	F 880/985	IGN 57

Booking: Tarn booking service

81/352

ANDOUQUE Puech Autenc This lovely old house, renovated and furnished in traditional style, stands in its own garden outside the village. Fishing (0.1 km), a pine forest at 1 km; riding (4 km); sailing at 20 km. Living room (TV), kitchen (small washing machine), 2 bedrooms (2 double beds), shower room, no heating, garage, open ground. Farm produce locally, shopping and restaurant in the village (4 km) or at Carmaux (10 km).

Prices:	low season	not available	**4 people**
	high season	F 1308	IGN 64

Booking: Tarn booking service

81/371

LES CABANNES La Vedillerie One of two simply furnished gîtes (this one on the ground floor) in an old house on a farm where the owners also have an inn, so good home-cooked meals available. A visit to the beautifully preserved mediaeval town of Cordes, a few kilometres away, is a must. Living room/kitchenette, 2 bedrooms (4 double and 1 child's bed), shower room, fireplace, balcony, open ground. Linen available. Shopping and restaurant in the village (3 km) or at Monestiés (15 km approx.).

Prices:	low season	F 1148/1152	**8/9 people**
	high season	F 1469/1619	IGN 57

Booking: Tarn booking service

81/316

CADALEN Petite Mareye One of two gîtes with country-style furnishings, in a large renovated building on a farm near the village centre and where the owners will be pleased to sell their produce. Sailing on the river at 4 km and a skate-board park at 8 km. Living room, kitchen (washing machine), 3 bedrooms (2 double and 3 single beds), shower room, fireplace, terrace, open ground with garden furniture. Mobile baker calls; other shopping and a restaurant in the village (0.3 km) or at Gaillac (15 km approx.).

Prices:	low season	F 595/742	**7 people**
	high season	F 903/1164	IGN 64

Booking: Tarn booking service

81/261

CAHUZAC-SUR-VERE An attractively renovated gîte in a hamlet with river fishing, tennis and bathing nearby. Gaillac (11 km) is an old town at the heart of one of France's most ancient wine-producing regions. Sailing and bathing at Aiguelèze lake (15 km). Living room, kitchen, 3 bedrooms (3 double and 1 child's bed), shower room, fireplace. Farm produce, including wine, eggs and jam, available locally; other shopping and restaurant in the village or at Gaillac.

Prices:	low season	F 450/579	**6/7 people**
	high season	F 866/1078	IGN 64

Booking: Tarn booking service

81/412

Tarn

CESTAYROLS A traditionally furnished gîte in the owners' village house. Take a day trip to the picturesque old town of Albi (20 km) with its remarkable pink brick cathedral dating from the thirteenth century; see too the museum dedicated to Toulouse-Lautrec. Living room, kitchen, 3 bedrooms (3 double, 2 single beds), bathroom, fireplace, shady courtyard with garden furniture. Farm produce available locally; other shopping at 6 km or at Albi. A restaurant at 10 km.

Prices:	low season	F 860	**8 people**
	high season	F 1094/1201	IGN 64

Booking: Tarn booking service

81/356

CESTAYROLS A renovated and traditionally furnished house, set in open countryside, 2.5 km from the village. Aiguelèze lake (sailing) is at 10 km. At Gaillac (20 km), see the lovely gardens at Foucauld Park, set out by Le Nôtre, France's answer to Capability Brown. Living room/kitchenette (1 double divan), 3 bedrooms (3 double and 1 single bed), no heating, garage, open ground with garden furniture. Farm produce in the village and shops (6 km) or at Gaillac.

Prices:	low season	F 860	**9 people**
	high season	F 1094/1201	IGN 64

Booking: Tarn booking service

81/414

DENAT La Peyrade A renovated gîte on a mixed farm, 2 km from the village. Réalmont (5 km) is a lively market town and the surrounding countryside offers many attractions including a mediaeval château and Rassisse reservoir, for water sports. Swimming-pool and tennis at 8 km; riding at 16 km. Living room (TV), kitchen, 2 bedrooms (2 double and 1 single bed), shower room, electric heating, open ground with garden furniture. Shopping and restaurant at 3 km.

Prices:	low season	F 410/520	**5 people**
	high season	F 740/930	IGN 64

Booking: Tarn booking service

81/345

LACROUZETTE Thouy A charming old house, renovated, with country-style furniture, on a mixed farm, 6 km from the village (a car is essential). River fishing and forest walks near the gîte. (Altitude 500 metres.) Swimming-pool and tennis in the village. Riding facilities and a lake for sailing within 5 km. Living room/kitchenette, 3 bedrooms (3 double and 1 child's bed), shower room, heating, terrace, own ground with barbecue. Fresh farm produce, shops and restaurant in Lacrouzette or at Castres (15 km approx.).

Prices:	low season	F 547/663	**6/7 people**
	high season	F 1186/1250	IGN 64

Booking: Tarn booking service

81/49

LIVERS-CAZELLES A gîte on the first floor of the owners' traditionally furnished house. Do not miss the well-preserved mediaeval village of Cordes (3 km approx.) perched high above the Cérou valley with lovely views over the surrounding countryside. Visit too the historic pink-brick département capital of Albi (15 km approx.). Living room, kitchen, 2 bedrooms (2 double and 1 single bed), bathroom and shower, fireplace, central heating, carport, open ground with furniture for outdoor meals. Shopping at Noailles (5 km).

Prices:	low season	F 580/922	**5 people**
	high season	F 1168	IGN 57

Booking: Tarn booking service

81/515

Tarn

MILHAVET Capendu A typical old local house with traditional furniture on the edge of the village (1 km). River fishing, swimming-pool, riding and tennis within 5 km. The little mediaeval town of Cordes (8 km), has many craft workshops (stone cutters, painting on wood and silk, embroidery, etc.) and holds a festival of ancient music. Living room/kitchenette, 2 bedrooms (1 double, 3 single beds), shower room, fireplace, enclosed, shady ground. Fresh farm produce (4 km) and shopping at Cordes.

Prices:	low season	F 480/546	**5 people**
	high season	F 806/1062	*IGN 57*

Booking: Tarn booking service

81/327

MONESTIES Le Canabel One of two traditionally furnished gîtes in an old house, standing in a pleasant garden with barbecue and furniture for outdoor meals, 4 km from the village. A lake, fishing and sailing at 3 km. Museums and other amenities at the fine old town of Carmaux (10 km). Living room, kitchen, 2 bedrooms (2 double, 1 single and 1 child's bed), shower room, central heating. Shopping and restaurant in the village or at Carmaux.

Prices:	low season	F 508/651	**5/6 people**
	high season	F 957/1138	*IGN 57*

Booking: Tarn booking service

81/382

MONTREDON-LABESSONNIE Le Barthas A traditionally furnished gîte, one of two in a renovated house outside the village. At Castres (30 km), see the former Bishop's Palace (built by Mansart in the seventeenth century) with gardens laid out by Le Nôtre; see also the Museum dedicated to Goya and the Spanish school. Living room, kitchen, 2 bedrooms (2 double and 2 single beds), shower room, wood stove, terrace, enclosed ground with child's swing. Mobile baker calls; other shopping and restaurant at Montredon-Labessonnie (8 km).

Prices:	low season	F 610	**6 people**
	high season	F 770/990	*IGN 64*

Booking: Tarn booking service

81/08

PENNE Aurifeuilles A ground-floor gîte in the owners' attractively renovated old house, 4 km from the village centre and near a forest (2 km). The pretty little town of Saint-Antonin-Noble-Val on the river Aveyron (12 km) has preserved its mediaeval character and offers good leisure facilities. Living room/kitchenette, 2 bedrooms (1 double and 2 single beds), shower room, fireplace, open ground. Farm produce from the owners; other shopping in the village or at Saint-Antonin-Noble-Val and a restaurant at 4 km.

Prices:	low season	F 391/519	**4 people**
	high season	F 738/913	*IGN 57*

Booking: Tarn booking service

81/388

PENNE Le Ségala This old, simply furnished house is typical of this region and is situated on a mixed farm, 2 km from a village in the Aveyron valley. The magnificent forest of Grésigne is 5 km away. A visit to the mediaeval town of Cordes (12 km) is a must. Living room/kitchenette (small washing machine), 2 bedrooms (1 double and 2 single beds), shower room, open fire, balcony, garage, small garden with furniture. Farm produce and shopping in the village or at Vaour (6 km).

Prices:	low season	F 455/646	**4 people**
	high season	F 753/913	*IGN 57*

Booking: Tarn booking service

81/186

Tarn

RAYSSAC Le Viala A ground-floor gîte, with traditional furnishings, one of two in a renovated house on a mixed farm, in the village. Bathing and sailing at a lake at Raississe leisure centre (8 km); riding and tennis at 21 km. Altitude 600 metres. Living room, kitchen, 2 bedrooms (2 double, 1 child's bed and a double divan), shower room, no heating, terrace, open ground. Farm produce available in the village; other shopping and a restaurant at Saint-Paul-de-Trivisy (8 km).

Prices:	low season	F 500/525	**6/7 people**
	high season	F 740/965	IGN 64

Booking: Tarn booking service

81/41

RAYSSAC Le Viala A second gîte in the renovated and traditionally furnished house described above and situated in open ground on a village farm (altitude 600 metres). The gîte is well sited for exploring this fascinating region: Albi and Castres are both within easy reach by car (approx. 40 km). Living room, kitchen, 3 bedrooms (4 double and 1 child's bed), shower room, open fire, terrace. Farm produce in the village and mobile shops call; other shopping and restaurant at Saint-Paul-de-Trivisy (8 km).

Prices:	low season	F 499/575	**8/9 people**
	high season	F 850/1062	IGN 64

Booking: Tarn booking service

81/42

SALVAGNAC Les Braguards A ground-floor gîte with country-style furnishings in the owners' old house on their mixed farm, 2 km from the village centre. A swimming-pool at the interesting old fortified town of Rabastens (12 km), overlooking the river Tarn. Riding stables at 25 km. Living room/kitchenette, 1 bedroom (2 double and 1 child's bed), shower room, gas central heating, carport, meadowland with garden furniture. Shopping at Rabastens; a restaurant at 2 km.

Prices:	low season	F 430/580	**4/5 people**
	high season	F 910/1080	IGN 64

Booking: Tarn booking service

81/102

VALENCE-D'ALBI Peyrelaus A lovely old stone house, renovated and furnished in country style, on a mixed farm, 2 km from the town. Take a drive along the exhilarating Gorges du Tarn (12 km approx.). Riding and sailing at a lake (20 km). Living room, kitchen, 2 bedrooms (1 double and 1 single bed), shower room, no heating, carport, enclosed ground and garden furniture. Fresh produce available from neighbouring farms; other shopping and restaurant in the town or at Albi (25 km approx.).

Prices:	low season	F 509	**3 people**
	high season	F 753/914	IGN 58

Booking: Tarn booking service

81/248

VENES La Brugue A rustically furnished gîte, one of two in a renovated house on farmland, 3 km from the village. It is 7 km from the market town of Réalmont where you may hire bicycles, and you should visit the nearby Gorges du Dadou. Sailing at a lake and forest walks at 16 km. Living room, kitchen, 3 bedrooms (2 double and 1 single bed), shower room, open fire, garage, open ground. Mobile baker calls; other shopping and a restaurant at Réalmont.

Prices:	low season	F 621/629	**5 people**
	high season	F 821/1179	IGN 64

Booking: Tarn booking service

81/488

The church and tower of St. Pierre in Gaillac (Tarn).   Photo: Feher

Tarn-et-Garonne

BRUNIQUEL A lovely, half-timbered house which has been renovated and furnished in traditional style at the village centre. Bruniquel is a pretty village dominated by a twelfth-century château and overlooking the Aveyron valley. Montauban (24 km) offers all the facilities of a large town. Living room (1 double divan), kitchen, 1 bedroom and mezzanine landing (1 double, 1 single bed), bathroom, fireplace, electric heating. Linen available. Farm produce available; shopping and restaurant in the village.

Prices:	low season	F 630/780	5 people
	high sason	F 1050/1260	IGN 57

Booking: Tarn-et-Garonne Loisirs Accueil

82/532

GROMONT Latroque A well-renovated stone cottage with country-style furnishings at the edge of a lovely little village where there is a château (open to the public). This area is noted for its garlic and Saint-Clar (5 km) has a weekly garlic market. Lectoure (16 km) has a fine cathedral and a large lake (wind-surfing). Living room, small kitchen, 2 bedrooms (1 double, 2 single beds), shower room, open fire. Fresh farm produce (including eggs, poultry and vegetables); other shopping and restaurant in the village (1 km).

Prices:	low season	F 714	4 people
	high season	F 892/945	IGN 63

Booking: Tarn-et-Garonne Loisirs Accueil

82/476B

6

MONTPEZAT-DE-QUERCY Le Cruzel A ground-floor gîte in a renovated house with rustic furnishings, at the edge of a wood, 3 km from the village centre. At the château town of Molières (9 km), there is a lake (bathing and sailing). A swimming-pool at 14 km and riding stables at 21 km. Living room/kitchenette, 2 bedrooms (1 double, 2 single beds), shower room, open fire, electric heating, enclosed ground with garden furniture. Farm produce from the owners; other shopping and restaurant in the village or at Caussade (14 km).

Prices:	low season	F 551/681	4 people
	high season	F 908/1021	IGN 57

Booking: Tarn-et-Garonne Loisirs Accueil

82/503A

SAINT-PAUL-D'ESPIS Bilot Situated on a mixed farm, this renovated house with country-style furnishings, has its own open ground with garden furniture and barbecue for outdoor meals. There are musical concerts at Moissac (20 km approx.) during the summer. Sailing at a lake at Saint-Nicolas-de-la-Grave (7 km). Living room, kitchen, 2 bedrooms and open landing (2 double, 5 single and 1 child's bed), bathroom and shower, fireplace, electric heating, garage, Shopping and restaurant at Melouse (4 km); mobile baker.

Prices:	low season	F 618/721	10 people
	high season	F 1030/1133	IGN 57

Booking: Tarn-et-Garonne Loisirs Accueil

82/538

LA VILLEDIEU-DU-TEMPLE Choisy-Haut An attractively renovated cottage with country-style furnishings on a mixed farm where the owners will sell fresh produce. There is a Jazz Festival at Montauban (10 km), the first fortnight of July; see too the Ingres Museum in the town. Living room/kitchenette (1 single divan), 2 bedrooms (1 double, 1 single and 2 bunk beds), bathroom, fireplace, electric heating, garage, open garden with outdoor furniture. Mobile grocer and baker call; other shopping in the village (2 km).

Prices:	low season	on request	6 people
	high season	on request	IGN 57

Booking: Tarn-et-Garonne Loisirs Accueil

82/533

Tarn-et-Garonne

In the heart of the South-West, Tarn-et-Garonne is situated to the north of Toulouse. From the Gorges de l'Aveyron to the Coteaux de Gascogne, along the Garonne valley, the Coteaux du Bas-Quercy and the Causse du Quercy, the countryside is extremely varied.

Tarn-et-Garonne is also a famous gastronomic region; in the markets you can buy poultry, *foie gras*, fragrant Lomagne garlic, melons, Moissac grapes, peaches, pears, apples, plums and numerous other fruits.

HISTORY Moissac, reflecting Roman art at its peak, welcomes to its cloister and abbey-church the pilgrims of Saint Jacques de Compostelle.

At Montauban, a twelfth-century town, the main square and old hotels bear witness to the prosperity of the town through past centuries; In the Ingres Museum, built on the site of the Black Prince's castle, you will find Ingres' paintings and drawings and Bourdelle's sculptures.

The old villages in the region have preserved the traces of their history; mediaeval houses surround their arcaded squares

ACCOMMODATION Choose from rural gîtes, campsites on the lakeshores, hotel-restaurants specialising in regional cuisine (*foie gras*, cassoulet, *confit d'oie* or *confit de canard*), camping on farms.

LEISURE ACTIVITIES Go riding, sailing or wind-surfing; try painting, drawing or sculpture courses, learn about traditional Quercy cooking or hire a boat and sail along the canals.

For booking and any further information about holidays in Tarn-et-Garonne, contact:

LOISIRS-ACCUEIL TARN-ET-GARONNE
Hôtel des Intendants
Place du Maréchal Foch
82000 MONTAUBAN   **Tel:** (63) 63.31.40.
                  Telex: 531705

NB For fuller information about all Loisirs–Accueil services, please see pages 12–13 of this guide.

Special Interest Holidays

RESERVATION LOISIRS ACCUEIL

Free colour Brochure

7 DAYS OF FREEDOM

Atlantique / Moissac / Rocamadour / Albi / Toulouse-Lautrec / L'Armagnac / Toulouse / Les Pyrénées / Méditerranée

A new formula for discovering the South-West of France

F 840 per person
7 nights half-board
accommodation in a
hotel with a swimming-pool

For example: one week half-board
accommodation in a 1-star hotel
at Vaissac:
F 840 per person

F 550 to F 1021
7 nights for 4 people
in a Gîte de France

For example: one week in
a Gîte de France for 4 people
at Montpezat-de-Quercy:
JUNE: F 680
JULY: F 910
AUGUST: F 1021
OCT to MAY F 550

For booking and further information, please write or telephone:

LOISIRS ACCUEIL – TARN-ET-GARONNE
Hôtel des Intendants – Place du Maréchal Foch – 82000 Montauban
Tel. (63) 63.31.40. Telex 531 705 F

CARCANS MAUBUISSON
des Vraies Vacances

The resort of Carcans-Maubuisson, full of happy activity, is situated alongside the largest lake in France. Only 3 km away are the huge beaches of the Atlantic coast and all round about are picturesque pine forests.

Bordeaux is nearby and this is a country of fine wine and good food.
A wide range of sporting activities is available – tennis, cycling, sailing, windsurfing etc. – and plenty of entertainment with the cinema, theatre and music.
Carcans-Maubuisson offers a choice of quality accommodation. There are holiday villages or you can book into serviced accommodation with either full or half board.

For further information, complete the Coupon or contact: Maison de la Station,
33121 CARCANS-MAUBUISSON, France
Tel: 56.03.34.94

To: Maison de la Station, 33121 Carcans-Maubuisson, France
Name
ADDRESS
Please send details of holidays and accommodation

7 AQUITAINE

'Land of Water' as named by the Romans, who were attracted to this region, with a 150-mile stretch of sandy beaches, lagoons in the northern inland areas and river after river. It is a land much fought over during the Anglo-French conflict in the Middle Ages and if you are interested in history you will be aware of the many *bastides* (fortified towns) built during the conflict, around the time of the marriage between Eleanor of Aquitaine and Henri Plantagenet. There are many beautiful châteaux reminding us of the troubled Middle Ages and fortresses which withstood the Hundred Years War.

However, this fertile land, with its successful agriculture, was appreciated long before the arrival of the Romans. It was inhabited by Palaeolithic man, who found the climate suitable and that food, in the form of bison and deer, was plentiful. It is here, according to records, that we have our earliest evidence of man the artist. Visitors should certainly make a point of seeing the many cave-paintings and engravings, found in the Dordogne Valley at Lascaux and Les Eyzies.

In the south, by the coast and in the Pyrénées, there are villages and even the town of Bayonne, where the inhabitants proudly retain their own culture, neither French nor Spanish, although the Spanish influence is strongly felt. This is the French Basque country with similar people living just over the border. Learn more about their history and customs at the Basque Museum in Bayonne or at the Bayonne Festival in August.

Sample some of the region's fine cuisine and you will know more of the customs. One of the delicacies, a truffle, known as the black diamond of Périgord, is a variety of underground mushroom, sniffed out by pigs in winter, when it is at its best. More widely known dishes include Périgord's *pâté de foie gras* and oysters. Bordeaux, surrounded by vineyards, is the home of the famous Claret, but try also the *Médoc* and the reasonably priced *Cahors*.

Enjoy the bustling towns, the peaceful countryside, the villages with their games of *boules* and *pelota* and the health-giving waters of Aquitaine.

Map of Southwest France

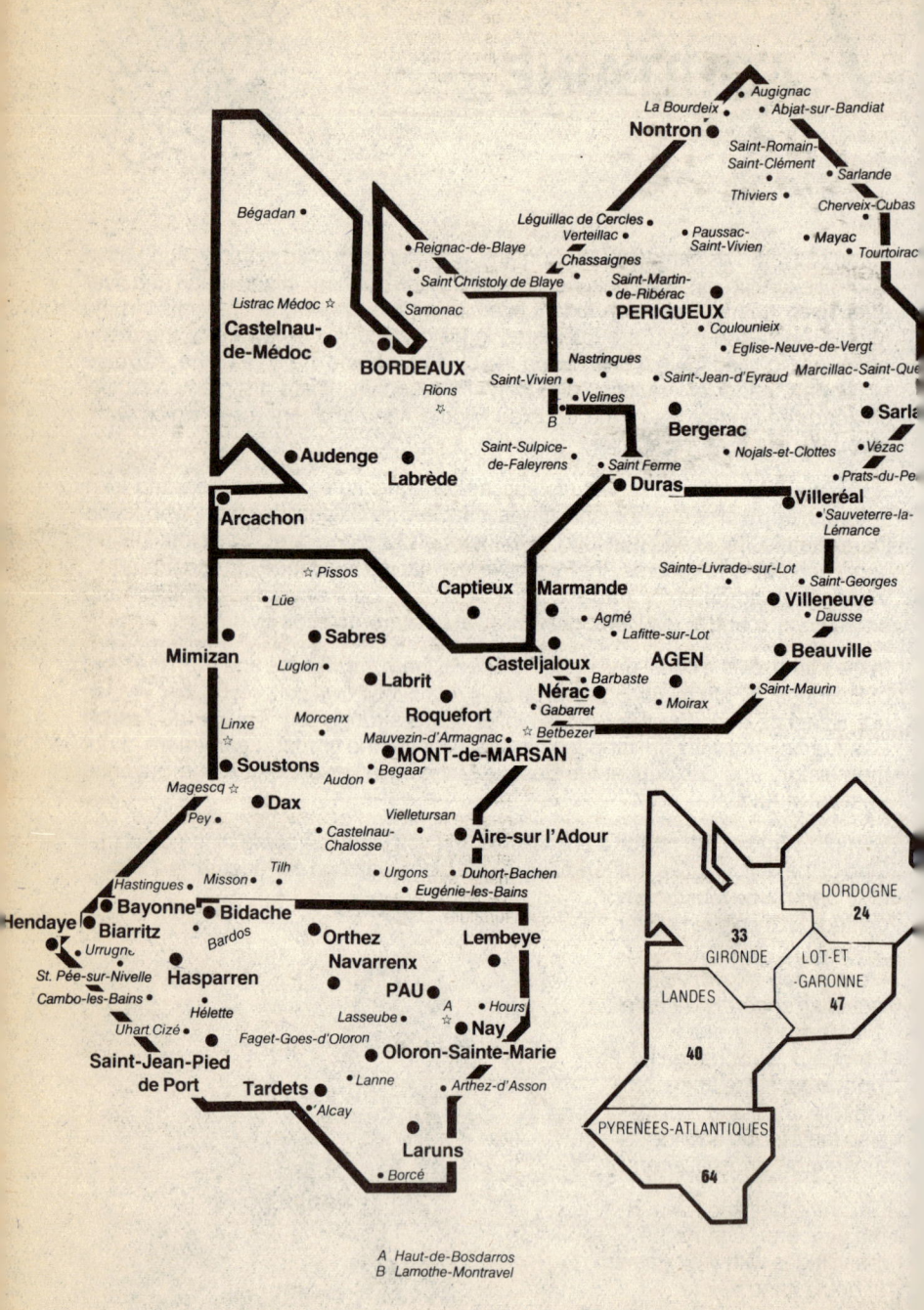

Départements:
- GIRONDE 33
- DORDOGNE 24
- LOT-ET-GARONNE 47
- LANDES 40
- PYRÉNÉES-ATLANTIQUES 64

Cities and towns:

- Augignac
- La Bourdeix
- Abjat-sur-Bandiat
- **Nontron**
- Saint-Romain-Saint-Clément
- Sarlande
- Thiviers
- Cherveix-Cubas
- Léguillac de Cercles
- Verteillac
- Paussac-Saint-Vivien
- Mayac
- Tourtoirac
- Bégadan
- Reignac-de-Blaye
- Chassaignes
- Saint-Martin-de-Ribérac
- Saint Christoly de Blaye
- **PÉRIGUEUX**
- Samonac
- Listrac Médoc ☆
- Coulounieix
- Église-Neuve-de-Vergt
- **Castelnau-de-Médoc**
- Nastringues
- Saint-Jean-d'Eyraud
- Marcillac-Saint-Qu...
- **BORDEAUX**
- Saint-Vivien
- Vélines
- **Sarla...**
- Rions ☆
- B
- **Bergerac**
- Vézac
- **Audenge**
- Saint-Sulpice-de-Faleyrens
- Nojals-et-Clottes
- Prats-du-Pe...
- **Labrède**
- Saint Ferme
- **Villeréal**
- **Duras**
- Sauveterre-la-Lémance
- **Arcachon**
- Sainte-Livrade-sur-Lot
- Saint-Georges
- **Captieux**
- **Marmande**
- **Villeneuve**
- ☆ Pissos
- Agmé
- Lafitte-sur-Lot
- Dausse
- Lüe
- **Beauville**
- **Sabres**
- **Castejaloux**
- **AGEN**
- **Mimizan**
- Luglon
- **Labrit**
- Barbaste
- Saint-Maurin
- **Roquefort**
- **Nérac**
- Morcenx
- Gabarret
- Moirax
- Linxe
- Mauvezin-d'Armagnac
- ☆ Betbezer
- Magescq ☆
- **Soustons**
- Audon
- **MONT-de-MARSAN**
- Begaar
- Pey
- **Dax**
- Vielletursan
- Castelnau-Chalosse
- **Aire-sur-l'Adour**
- Tilh
- Urgons
- Duhort-Bachen
- Hastingues
- Misson
- Eugénie-les-Bains
- **Hendaye**
- **Bayonne**
- **Bidache**
- **Biarritz**
- Bardos
- **Orthez**
- **Lembeye**
- Urrugne
- **Navarrenx**
- St. Pée-sur-Nivelle
- **Hasparren**
- **PAU**
- Cambo-les-Bains
- Hélette
- A · Hours
- Lasseube
- ☆ **Nay**
- Uhart Cizé
- Faget-Goes-d'Oloron
- **Saint-Jean-Pied de Port**
- **Oloron-Sainte-Marie**
- Lanne
- **Tardets**
- Arthez-d'Asson
- Alcay
- **Laruns**
- Borcé

A Haut-de-Bosdarros
B Lamothe-Montravel

Dordogne

ABJAT-SUR-BANDIAT La Roderie A renovated house with country-style furnishings in a hamlet, 2 km from the village itself. There is a private lake near the property; swimming-pool, tennis and riding within 8 km. The old château town of Nontron (8 km) has a lively market (every Saturday) and a good gastronomic reputation. Living room, kitchen (small washing machine), 2 bedrooms (2 double and 3 single beds), fireplace, electric central heating, terrace, ground. Farm produce, shopping and restaurant in the village.

Prices: low season   F 880/1100
           high season   F 1320

7 people
IGN 47

Booking: Dordogne Loisirs Accueil   E
24/848

AUGIGNAC Maine du Bost A lovely old stone-built house which has been renovated and traditionally furnished, set in a hamlet. Fishing, bathing and pedalo boats for hire at Saint-Estèphe lake (6 km). The museum at Nontron (8 km approx.) has a fine collection of antique dolls. Living room (1 double divan), kitchen, 2 bedrooms (1 double and 2 single beds), bathroom and shower, electric central heating, terrace, open ground. Farm produce in the village; other shopping at Piegut Pluviers (3 km).

Prices: low season   F 693/808
           high season   F 979/1039

6 people
IGN 47

Booking: Dordogne Loisirs Accueil   E
24/752

LE BOURDEIX A gîte with modern furniture above the vilage's *Salle des Fêtes,* where the local fête is held on the last weekend of June. A swimming-pool and tennis court at Nontron (9 km) where local gastronomic treats include '*confit*' (duck, turkey or goose preserved then roasted in its own fat). Living room (1 double divan), kitchen, 2 bedrooms (1 double and 2 single beds), shower room, fireplace, electric heating. Shopping and restaurant at Nontron.

Prices: low season   F 440/660
           high season   F 825

6 people
IGN 47

Booking: Dordogne Loisirs Accueil   E

24/714

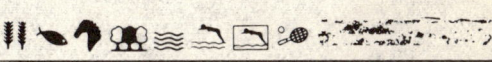

CHASSAIGNES A renovated house with country-style furnishings, 2 km from the village centre. Ribérac (10 km approx.), a busy town on the river Dronne where you may bathe, has a market every Friday and a twelfth-century Faye church. Living room/kitchenette, studio room (1 double divan), 2 bedrooms (1 double, 2 single beds), shower room, fireplace, electric heating, courtyard with garden furniture. Shopping at Lanouaille (4 km).

Prices: low season   F 605/715
           high season   F 935

6 people
IGN 47

Booking: Dordogne Loisirs Accueil   E

24/55

CHERVEIX-CUBAS Mouneix Set in its own large garden with furniture for outdoor meals, this renovated house with country-style furnishings is ideally situated for exploring the lovely countryside of the Dordogne. The Château d'Hautefort is 5 km away; Périgueux, the département capital and historic Sarlat both 40 km. Living room (1 double divan), kitchen, 3 bedrooms (2 double, 3 single and 1 child's bed), fireplace, electric radiators, terrace, garage. Shops at 4 km or at Tourtoirac (6.5 km).

Prices: low season   F 924
           high season   F 1375

10 people
IGN 48

Booking: Dordogne Loisirs Accueil   E
24/711

Dordogne

In south-west France, between the Massif Central and the Atlantic coast, Dordogne is ready to offer you a delightful holiday.

The beauty of Dordogne's varied landscapes will enchant you: from stark rocky hills and plateaux to gently sloping green valleys; fine views over the Dordogne river — much favoured by anglers and overlooked by splendid châteaux; beautiful forests, resplendent in autumn in shades of red and gold. Dordogne's fine sunshine makes all this even more appealing.

The Dordogne is an area steeped in history and prehistory: the most famous site being the caves in the region of Les Eyzies; later centuries have provided much fine architecture — in medieval fortified villages, Romanesque churches and numerous well-kept châteaux.

The Dordogne offers more to the tourist than history lessons! Modern hotels and camp-sites, swimming-pools, riding centres and other sports facilities are all there for you to enjoy, as are the many gastronomic specialities of the region, including foie gras and truffles, as well as the fine wines of Monbazillac and Bergerac.

For booking and further information about the holidays listed opposite, contact:
LOISIRS ACCUEIL DORDOGNE PERIGORD
Office Départemental du Tourisme de la Dordogne
16 rue Wilson
24000 PERIGUEUX   **Tel.** (53) 53.44.35   E
Opening hours: 9.30 to 11.30
14.30 to 16.30 (French time)

NB for fuller information about all Loisirs Accueil services, please see pages 12–13 of this guide.

Special Interest Holidays

RESERVATION LOISIRS ACCUEIL

Loisirs Accueil Dordogne has many different types of holiday for you to choose from:
- Horse riding holidays (6 days with full board)
- Horse riding holidays for unaccompanied children (1 week with full board accommodation in a gite d'enfants)
- Camping/caravanning on a farm with full or half board accommodation
- Art and craft courses, including pottery, weaving, wrought iron work (each 1 week's stay with full board accommodation)
- Stay in a gite rural or chambre d'hôte (see listings)
- Stay in a family-run Logis de France hotel.

HORSE DRAWN CARAVANS A holiday to really get away from city life: trotting along the byways of the Dordogne in a horse-drawn caravan. Spend a week or two with family or friends in a horse-drawn caravan well equipped for up to four people. You will be provided with maps, suggested routes, and overnight stops and much more practical advice.
Availability: all year
Price: from F 3200 per week
Cost includes: bedding and kitchen utensils for 4 people; maps and other documents.

Dordogne

COULOUNIEIX Petite Borie A renovated gîte with country-style furnishings on a mixed farm in the village. It is 5 km from Périgueux where you may visit some fascinating Roman sites, including the amphitheatre and a villa; and take advantage of the many leisure facilities there. Living room/kitchenette, 3 bedrooms (2 double and 2 single beds), shower room, fireplace, electric central heating, terrace, ground with garden furniture. Farm produce in the village; other shopping and restaurant in Périgueux.

Prices:	low season F 1045	**6 people**
	high season F 1320	*IGN 47*

Booking: Dordogne Loisirs Accueil **E**
24/643

EGLISE-NEUVE-DE-VERGT La Juillerie A small gîte, adjoining the owners' renovated farmhouse where you may buy fresh produce, including strawberries in season. Visit the old quarter of Périgueux (10 km approx.) and see the beautifully preserved Renaissance houses, Saint-Front cathedral and the military museum. Living room/kitchenette, 2 bedrooms (1 double, 2 single and 1 child's bed), bathroom, central heating, terrace, open ground with garden furniture and swing. Shopping and restaurant at Vergt (7.5 km).

Prices:	low season F 569/683	**5 people**
	high season F 896	*IGN 47*

Booking: Dordogne Loisirs Accueil **E**
24/724

LAMOTHE-MONTRAVEL Rateau One of two gîtes (this one on the ground-floor), in a modern house on a mixed farm, 1.5 km from the village centre. There is an important gallo-roman archaeological site at Montcaret (3 km). Bergerac (30 km approx.) is noted for its wines and has an unusual tobacco museum. Living room, kitchen, 2 bedrooms (1 double and 2 single beds), no heating, ground with garden furniture. Wine from the owners; other shopping in the village.

Prices:	low season F 640/720	**4 people**
	high season F 875	*IGN 47*

Booking: Dordogne Loisirs Accueil **E**
24/111

MARCILLAC-SAINT-QUENTIN La Vergne A ground-floor gîte, one of two, in an attractively renovated house with country-style furnishings, 3 km from the village centre. Sarlat (7 km) is a beautiful, well-preserved old town with buildings dating back to the twelfth century. It holds an annual drama festival (mid July-mid August). Living room/kitchenette, 2 bedrooms (2 double and 1 single bed), shower room, fireplace, electric heating, terrace, carport, open ground with garden furniture. Shopping at Sarlat.

Prices:	low season F 880/1017	**5 people**
	high season F 1095	*IGN 48*

Booking: Dordogne Loisirs Accueil **E**
24/122

LEGUILLAC DE CERCLES La Gauterie One of two gîtes in an attractively renovated stone-built house 2 km from the village, with fishing in the owner's pond nearby. The lovely old town of Mareuil (10 km) has a fortified château and other historic monuments. Living room/kitchenette, 2 bedrooms (1 double and 2 single beds), shower room, fireplace, open ground with furniture for outdoor meals. Farm produce from the owners; other shopping and restaurant at Mareuil.

Prices:	low season F 737/830	**4 people**
	high season F 895	*IGN 47*

Booking: Dordogne Loisirs Accueil **E**
24/116

Dordogne

MAYAC Pomerède A renovated house with country-style furnishings, in a farming hamlet, 2 km from Savignac-les-Eglises where there is a tennis court. Visit the lovely old town of Saint-Jean-de-Côle (20 km approx.) with its interesting museum and art gallery. Périgueux is just 35 km approx. away. Living room/kitchenette (1 single divan), 3 bedrooms (2 double, 2 single beds), shower room, fireplace, electric heating, terrace, open ground with swing and garden furniture. Shopping and restaurant at Savignac.

Prices: low season   F 980/1055
          high season   F 1330

7 people
IGN 48

Booking: Dordogne Loisirs Accueil   **E**

24/125

NASTRINGUES Chantegros A well-renovated house with country-style furnishings on a mixed farm, 2 km from the village. A swimming-pool at 7 km and sailing at a lake (10 km). Try the local wines at the Maison des Vins (near the statue of Cyrano) in Bergerac (25 km approx.). Living room/kitchenette, 2 bedrooms (1 double and 2 single beds), bathroom and shower, fireplace, electric heating, carport, open ground with garden furniture. Shopping and restaurant at Velines (2 km).

Prices: low season   F 715/960
          high season   F 1025

4 people
IGN 47

Booking: Dordogne Loisirs Accueil   **E**

24/884

NOJALS-ET-CLOTTES Videpot A renovated stone cottage, typical of the region, with rustic furnishings. Beaumont (3 km) is an old town with much English-influenced architecture and a fortified church; see too the Château de Bannes 2.5 km away. A swimming-pool and riding facilities at 12 km. Living room/kitchenette, 2 bedrooms (4 single beds), shower room, fireplace, garage, enclosed ground with garden furniture and child's swing. Shopping and restaurant at Beaumont.

Prices: low season   F 495/605
          high season   F 1045

4 people
IGN 57

Booking: Dordogne Loisirs Accueil   **E**

24/442

PAUSSAC-SAINT-VIVIEN One of two gîtes in a renovated, traditionally furnished house on a mixed farm. Visit Brantôme (10 km approx.) with its many ancient buildings (floodlit on summer evenings) and enjoy leisure facilities such as pedalo boats, tennis and miniature golf. Living room, kitchen, 2 bedrooms (1 double, 1 single and 1 child's bed), shower room, no heating, open ground. Shopping and restaurant at Lisle (3 km).

Prices: low season   F 595/695
          high season   F 825

4 people
IGN 47

Booking: Dordogne Loisirs Accueil   **E**

24/143

PRATS-DU-PERIGORD A charming old village house which has been renovated and furnished in rustic fashion. Local forest walks on marked footpaths and a tennis court in the village. Visit the medieval town of Belvès (15 km approx.) with its many fine old buildings and good leisure facilities. Living room/kitchenette, 2 bedrooms (3 double and 1 child's bed), shower room, no heating, balcony, enclosed ground with garden furniture and barbecue. Shopping and a restaurant at Villefranche-du-Perigord (8 km).

Prices: low season   F 600/1000
          high season   F 1000

7 people
IGN 57

Booking: Dordogne Loisirs Accueil   **E**

24/875

Dordogne

SAINT-JEAN-D'EYRAUD Le Pey A traditionally furnished and renovated cottage, lying in its own ground, 1 km from the village centre. This is a very picturesque region of châteaux, lovely valleys, gastronomic specialities and fine wines. Swimming-pool and Monday market at Villamblard (8 km) and plenty of amenities at Bergerac (15 km approx.). Living room, kitchen, 2 bedrooms (2 double and 2 single beds), bathroom and shower, no heating, garage, open ground. Shopping and restaurant at Villamblard.

Prices:	low season	F 737/795	6 people
	high season	F 1078	IGN 47

Booking: Dordogne Loisirs Accueil E
24/838

SAINT-ROMAIN-SAINT-CLEMENT A very attractive old house which has been well renovated and furnished in rustic fashion. It is 5 km from the important town of Thiviers, which has many leisure facilities. Thiviers is noted for its *foie gras* and truffles – its famous truffle markets take place November–February. Living room (1 double divan), kitchen (washing machine), 2 bedrooms (2 double beds), bathroom and shower, fireplace, gas central heating, terrace, courtyard with garden furniture. Shopping and restaurant at 3 km.

Prices:	low season	F 786/869	6 people
	high season	F 990	IGN 48

Booking: Dordogne Loisirs Accueil E
24/657

SAINT-VIVIEN La Reynaudie An old stone cottage with country-style furnishings on a farm where there is a tennis court and fishing pond nearby. A riding stable at 10 km and swimming-pool at 15 km; see the lovely ruins of the château at nearby Gurson. Living room/kitchenette (1 single divan), 3 bedrooms (1 double and 4 single beds), shower room, no heating, garage, open ground. Shopping and restaurant at Velines (3 km).

Prices:	low season	F 470/924	7 people
	high season	F 1045	IGN 47

Booking: Dordogne Loisirs Accueil E
24/547

SAINT-VIVIEN La Reynaudie A very attractive and unusual gîte with country-style furnishings, on a vineyard where the owners will sell their wine. Interesting sites in the vicinity include the huge church at Velines (3 km), the Château de Montazeau and Gurson lake. Living room/kitchenette, 1 bedroom (1 double, 1 single bed and a cot), no heating, terrace, open ground with garden furniture. Shopping and restaurant at Velines.

Prices:	low season	F 412/565	4 people
	high season	F 687	IGN 47

Booking: Dordogne Loisirs Accueil E
24/548

SARLANDE A gîte with country-style furnishings in the owners' renovated house in the village. Bathing and sailing at a lake (5 km). Plenty to see and do at Thiviers (25 km approx.) and you should take a trip to Hautefort Château (30 km approx.). Living room/kitchenette (1 double divan), 2 bedrooms (2 double and 1 child's bed), bathroom and shower, fireplace, terrace, enclosed ground with garden furniture. Shopping in the village or at Angoisse (5 km).

Prices:	low season	F 960	7 people
	high season	F 1100/1400	IGN 48

Booking: Dordogne Loisirs Accueil E

24/563

Dordogne

THIVIERS Pierrefiche A spacious modern house with country-style furnishings, set in the countryside some 5 km from Thiviers. Walking on marked footpaths locally, river fishing at 1 km and a lake at 12 km. Thiviers itself is a busy town with good cultural and leisure amenities. Living room, kitchen, 3 bedrooms (3 double beds), shower room, fireplace, central heating, balcony, open ground with garden furniture. Shopping and restaurant in Thiviers; farm produce available locally.

Prices:	low season	not available	**6 people**
	high season	F 1050	*IGN 48*

Booking: Dordogne Loisirs Accueil **E**

24/906

TOURTOIRAC Laudenie A village house which has been renovated and furnished in rustic fashion near Auvezère river (good fishing). Local sites include the Clautre fountain, Lafarge Château and the park and beautiful Hautefort Château (extensively rebuilt since a fire in 1968) at 8 km. Living room (1 single divan), kitchen, 2 bedrooms (1 double and 1 single bed), shower room, no heating, carport, courtyard with garden furniture. Shopping and restaurant in Tourtoirac or at Excideuil (10 km approx.).

Prices:	low season	F 695	**4 people**
	high season	F 1045	*IGN 48*

Booking: Dordogne Loisirs Accueil **E**

24/239

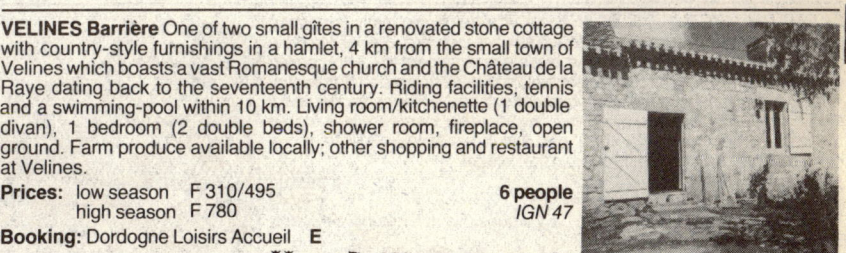

VELINES Barrière One of two small gîtes in a renovated stone cottage with country-style furnishings in a hamlet, 4 km from the small town of Velines which boasts a vast Romanesque church and the Château de la Raye dating back to the seventeenth century. Riding facilities, tennis and a swimming-pool within 10 km. Living room/kitchenette (1 double divan), 1 bedroom (2 double beds), shower room, fireplace, open ground. Farm produce available locally; other shopping and restaurant at Velines.

Prices:	low season	F 310/495	**6 people**
	high season	F 780	*IGN 47*

Booking: Dordogne Loisirs Accueil **E**

24/242

VERTEILLAC Puynozac A renovated gîte, typical of the region, with rustic furnishing, 1.5 km from the village centre. See the nearby Château de la Mefrénie, the Cluzeau caves, the Chatillon fountain and other sites. Visit Ribérac (12 km) a lively town where *foie gras* is a speciality on restaurant menus. Living room and lounge, kitchen (small washing machine), 2 bedrooms (2 double and 3 single beds), bathroom, two fireplaces, electric heating, open ground with garden furniture and child's swing. Shopping and restaurant in the village (1.5 km).

Prices:	low season	F 880	**7 people**
	high season	F 1100	*IGN 47*

Booking: Dordogne Loisirs Accueil **E**

24/754

VEZAC Le Luc A ground-floor gîte, one of two in a modern house with country-style furnishings near the village centre. River fishing (0.2 km) and a lake at 0.3 km. It is just 10 km from the beautifully preserved mediaeval town of Sarlat. Living room/kitchenette, 2 bedrooms (2 double beds), shower room, no heating, terrace, open ground with garden furniture. Farm produce and other shopping in the village (0.2 km) or at Domme (5 km approx.).

Prices:	low season	F 935/1008	**4 people**
	high season	F 1288	*IGN 48*

Booking: Dordogne Loisirs Accueil **E**

24/244

Gironde

BEGADAN Le Bourg A renovated house with simple furniture, situated on a village vineyard. In the vicinity you may visit châteaux, wine cellars and join in a wine festival in August at Lesparre (7 km). Sports facilities in the busy commercial town of Lesparre; the sea (25 km). Living room, kitchen, 2 bedrooms (1 double, 3 single beds), shower room, fireplace (wood supplied), oil and electric heating, garden with furniture. Shopping at 7 km.

Prices:	low season	F 600/700	5 people
	high season	F 800	IGN 46

Booking: Mme J. BIBEY, Begadan, 33340 Lesparre. Tel. (56) 41 50 43.

33/111

REIGNAC-DE-BLAYE Allaire A traditionally furnished gîte on the ground floor, one of two in a renovated two-storey house situated near woods 2 km from the village. Swimming-pool at 5 km, the sea and Royan (50 km). Living room/kitchenette, 3 bedrooms (3 double and 1 child's bed), shower room, oil heating, fireplace, garden. Linen available. Mobile shops call; shopping and restaurant at Etauliers (2 km) or at Blaye (15 km).

Prices:	low season	F 500/650	6/7 people
	high season	F 850	IGN 47

Booking: Mme G. RENAUD, La Comteau, Etauliers, 33820 Saint-Ciers-sur-Gironde. Tel. (57) 64 72 71.

33/55

SAINT CHRISTOLY DE BLAYE au Afaine A modestly furnished ground-floor gîte in a small, old house set in a vineyard. Blaye (11 km) is a rural holiday resort amongst vineyards and pinewoods with its own port and fishing facilities; good markets on Wednesdays and Saturdays. The sea is 70 km. Living room/kitchenette, 2 bedrooms (2 double and 1 single bed), shower room, no heating, garage, garden with outdoor furniture. Linen available (F35 per pair per week). Wine from the owners, shopping and restaurant in the village.

Prices:	low season	F 700	5 people
	high season	F 940	IGN 46

Booking: M R. MERIOCHAUD, La Verguée, Saint Christoly de Blaye, 33920 St Savin. Tel. 57 42 51 72

33/66

SAINT FERME La Garenne A gîte in the owners' renovated house, simply furnished in traditional style on a farm 3 km from the village. Libourne (35 km approx.) is a busy town set on the confluence of the rivers Isle and Dordogne with renowned vineyards. The sea is 120 km. Living room/kitchenette, 2 bedrooms (2 double and 1 single bed), shower room, electric heating, carport, garden. Linen available (F25 per pair per week). Mobile baker calls, farm produce from the owners, restaurant and shopping in the village or at Monsegur (5 km).

Prices:	low season	F 700/750	5 people
	high season	F 800	IGN 56

Booking: Mme G. DUBOIS, Château Bellgrave, Saint Lambert, 33250 Pauillac. Tel. 56 59 05 53

33/193

SAINT-SULPICE-DE-FALEYRENS Cour d'Argent A large, renovated house with two traditionally furnished gîtes on a farm by the River Dordogne. Bicycles for hire and other facilities at Libourne (10 km). The sea (100 km). Living room, kitchen, 3 bedrooms (2 double, 1 single and 1 child's bed), shower room, fireplace (wood supplied), electric heating, garage, ground with garden furniture. Shopping and restaurant at Branne (2 km).

Prices:	low season	F 650/700	5/6 people
	high season	F 850	IGN 47

Booking: Mme LASSERRE, Le Bourg, Saint-Sulpice-de-Faleyrens, 33330 Saint-Emilion. Tel. (57) 24 75 54.

33/124

Gironde

SAINT-SULPICE-DE-FALEYRENS Cour d'Argent The second gîte in the house described above, with simple, traditional furniture. Swimming-pool and bathing at a lake (10 km); tennis, riding and other facilities at the large town of Libourne (10 km). The sea at 100 km. Living room, kitchen, 2 bedrooms (2 double, 1 single bed), shower room, fireplace (wood supplied), electric heating, garage, ground with garden furniture. Shopping in the village (5 km) or at the important commercial centre of Branne (2 km).

Prices: low season   F 600/650   **5 people**
         high season   F 750   *IGN 47*
Booking: Mme LASSERRE, Le Bourg, Saint-Sulpice-de-Faleyrens, 33330 Saint-Emilion. Tel. (57) 24 75 54.
33/138

SAMONAC Beaulieu A ground-floor gîte in the owners' fine old house on a mixed farm 3.5 km from the village. Swimming-pool in the grounds; sailing at Bourg-sur-Gironde (3.5 km); painted caves at Pair-Non-Pair. The sea (80 km). Living room (2 single divans), kitchen, 2 bedrooms (1 double, 3 single and 1 child's bed), bathroom, central heating, terrace, garage, garden with furniture and barbecue. Linen available. Shopping and restaurant at Bourg; milk, vegetables and wine from the owners, who speak English.

Prices: low season   F 666/800   **7/8 people**
         high season   F 950   *IGN 47*
Booking: Mme E. GRONEMAN-DOYER, Château Beaulieu, Samonac, 33710 Bourg-sur-Gironde. Tel. (57) 68 43 93   **E**
33/58

SAMONAC Tourteau A detached, renovated house with rustic furniture on a vineyard 3.5 km from the village. Sailing on the river at the lovely old town of Bourg-sur-Gironde (4 km). Living room, kitchen, 3 bedrooms (2 double, 3 single and 1 child's bed), bathroom, fireplace, heating, terrace, ground with barbecue and garden furniture. Linen available. Baker calls; farm produce available, other shopping and restaurant in Bourg. English spoken.

Prices: low season   F 666/800   **7/8 people**
         high season   F 950   *IGN 47*
Booking: Mme E. GRONEMAN-DOYER, Château Beaulieu, Samonac, 33710 Bourg-sur-Gironde. Tel. (57) 68 43 93   **E**
33/144

LISTRAC MEDOC Donissian Capléon Vérin *Chambre d'hôte* and *table d'hôte* accommodation in the owners' lovely old renovated and rustically furnished house on a mixed farm 3 km from the village. Living room, 5 bedrooms available: bedroom 1 (1 double and 2 single beds); bedroom 2 (1 double and 1 single bed): bedrooms 3 and 4 (1 double bed); bedroom 5 (1 single bed); shower room and toilet for use of guests, open fire and central heating, garden with furniture. Fresh produce from the owners, shopping and restaurant in the village or at Saint Laurent (5 km).   **12 people**

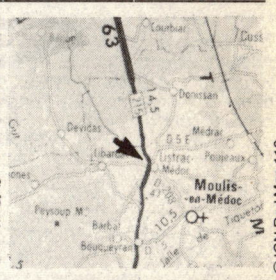

Prices: 1p F 150, 2p F 170, 3p F 190 per night all, year.   *IGN 46*
Booking: Mme M. MEVRE, Donissian Capléon Vérin, 33480 Listrac Médoc. Tel. 56 58 07 28   **E**
33/378

© IGN Red Map 110

RIONS Le Broustaret *Chambre d'hôte* accommodation in the owners' château on a vineyard. Swimming-pool and tennis at Cadillac (6 km). Four rooms available on the first floor: 2 bedrooms sleeping 2/3, private bathroom and toilet; 2 bedrooms sleeping 2/3 with private toilet. Lounge, central heating, and grounds. Evening meals available. Wine from the owners, shopping and restaurant in the village (6 km).

Prices: 1p F92/119   **4/6 people**
         2p F108/135   *IGN 56*
Reducations for stays of 4 days and over.
Booking: M J. GUILLOT-DE-SUDUIRAUT, Le Broustaret, Rions, 33410 Cadillac. Tel. (56) 62 96 97.   **E**
33/176

Landes

AUDON Au Haoü A detached gîte situated on a farm at 0.6 km from the village in a modern, white-washed house. Local river fishing; a swimming-pool at the nearby town of Tartas (5 km) where there is also horseback riding. A lake with water sports at 30 km. Living room, kitchen, 2 bedrooms (1 double, 1 single and 1 child's bed), shower room, no heating, terrace, carport, ground and garden. Shopping and restaurants at Tartas.

Prices:	low season	F 700	**3/4 people**
	high season	F 990	**IGN 62**

Booking: Landes booking service

40/633

AUDON Peyzé A detached house at the edge of a farming village (0.8 km) which has been renovated and traditionally furnished. Nearby fishing and forest walks; at Tartas (5 km) you will find tennis courts and a swimming-pool, while the sea at 50 km is near enough for a day trip. Living room, kitchen, 3 bedrooms (1 double, 2 single and 1 child's bed), bathroom, no heating, open ground. Farm produce in the village, other shopping at Tartas.

Prices: on request   **4/5 people**
   IGN 62

Booking: Landes booking service

40/540

BEGAAR Pas-dou-Bas An attractive gîte, situated on a farm at 0.8 km from the village and only 3 km from the town of Tartas. The house is completely detached and has traditional furniture. Various activities at Tartas include tennis, a swimming-pool, fishing, riding and sight-seeing. The sea is close enough for a day-trip at 55 km. Living room, kitchen, 3 bedrooms (1 double and 3 single beds), shower room, wood-burning stove in the living room, garage and ground. Shopping and restaurants at Tartas.

Prices:	low season	F 760	**5 people**
	high season	F 1050	**IGN 62**

Booking: Landes booking service

40/669

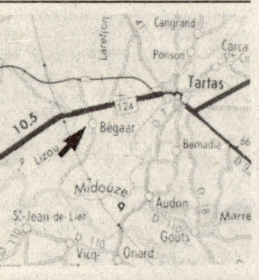

CASTELNAU-CHALOSSE Mora A traditionally furnished, ground-floor gîte in the owners' renovated house on a mixed farm, near the village centre (0.5 km). Dax (20 km) is a large town on the river Adour which was first established as a spa in Roman times (especially for treatment of rheumatism). The sea (50 km). Living room/kitchenette, 2 bedrooms (2 double beds), shower room, no heating, carport, open ground. Farm produce available; other shopping and restaurant at Pomarez (4 km).

Prices:	low season	F 820	**4 people**
	high season	F 1010	**IGN 62**

Booking: Landes booking service

40/18

DUHORT-BACHEN A renovated house, typical of the region, with rustic furniture, on a mixed farm where there is another gîte. The old cathedral city of Aire on the river Adour (7 km), has many tourist amenities and has a large fruit and poultry market every Tuesday. Living room (1 single bed), kitchen, 3 bedrooms (2 double, 1 single and 1 child's bed), bathroom, fireplace, electric central heating, carport, open ground with garden furniture. Farm produce and shopping in the village (1.5 km).

Prices:	low season	F 680/890	**6/7 people**
	high season	F 1200	**IGN 62**

Booking: Landes booking service

40/398

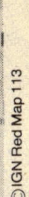

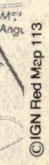

Landes

EUGENIE-LES-BAINS A detached gîte, built in cottage style, situated in the village surrounded by lovely countryside with forests and rivers nearby. There is a tennis court and a swimming-pool at 12 km. There is a living room/kitchen, 3 bedrooms (1 double, 1 single and 1 child's bed), shower and bath, no heating, and linen is available for a supplement. Shopping and restaurants at 10 km.

Prices:	low season	F 890	**3/4 people**
	high season	F 1200	**IGN 62**

Booking: Landes booking service

40/679

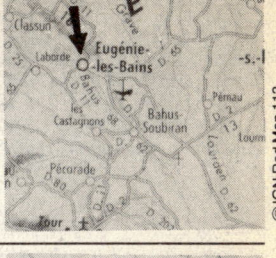

GABARRET A lovely gîte lying at 0.8 km from the village, which has old, traditional furnishings. Ideally situated for forest walks, local fishing or tennis courts, virtually on the door-step; a swimming-pool at 9 km and the nearest large town is Eauze (20 km), once the capital of the Roman Province *Aquitaine Tertia* and worth a visit. Living room (1 double bed), kitchen, 2 bedrooms (1 double and 1 single bed), bathroom, oil heating, garden and ground. Shopping can be done in the village and there is a choice of restaurants at 20 km.

Prices:	low season	—	**5 people**
	high season	F 725	**IGN 63**

Booking: Landes booking service

40/612

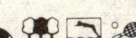

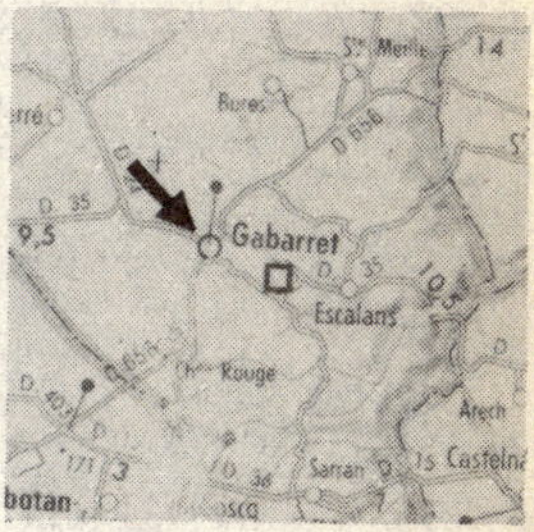

HASTINGUES Jouandot An old farmhouse, surrounded by fields, 4 km from the village. Local footpaths; a swimming-pool and tennis at 6 km. A short drive through the delightful Landes forest will bring you to the Atlantic coast (30 km). Living room/kitchenette, 2 bedrooms (2 double and 1 single bed), child's bed available on request, shower room, oil stove, garden. Baker and grocer call; other shopping at Bidache (3 km).

Prices:	low season	F 490/675	**5 people**
	high season	F 1110	**IGN 62**

Booking: Landes booking service

40/541

LUGLON Barail One of two gîtes, this one on the ground floor, in this very attractive half-timbered house, typical of the region, with modest furnishings. It is situated in a forest, 0.5 km from the village. Visit the Ecomuseum, Marquèze, in the forest. Swimming and tennis (6 km); fishing (28 km); the sea (40 km). Living room/kitchenette, 2 bedrooms (2 double beds), shower room, electric heating, ground. Shopping in the village or at Sabres (6 km).

Prices:	low season	F 635/765	**4 people**
	high season	F 950	**IGN 62**

Booking: Landes booking service

40/366

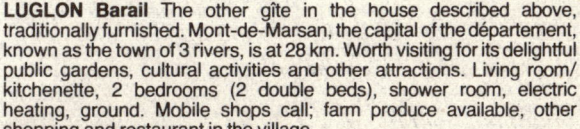

LUGLON Barail The other gîte in the house described above, traditionally furnished. Mont-de-Marsan, the capital of the département, known as the town of 3 rivers, is at 28 km. Worth visiting for its delightful public gardens, cultural activities and other attractions. Living room/kitchenette, 2 bedrooms (2 double beds), shower room, electric heating, ground. Mobile shops call; farm produce available, other shopping and restaurant in the village.

Prices:	low season	F 635/765	**4 people**
	high season	F 950	**IGN 62**

Booking: Landes booking service

40/354

Landes

LUE Gaillard A detached, renovated house containing two gîtes, among a group of holiday homes. Traditionally furnished, 3 km from the village, it lies in a grassy field, shaded by oak trees. The sandy beaches of the Atlantic just 25 km away. Living room/kitchenette, 2 bedrooms (1 double bed and 4 singles), shower room, fireplace, gas heating, ground. Shopping in the village or at Labouheyre (4 km).

Prices:	low season	F 460/610	**6 people**
	high season	F 1015	IGN 55

Booking: Landes booking service

40/74

MAUZEVIN-D'ARMAGNAC A modern holiday home with traditional furnishings situated at the edge of the vast Landes forest, 1 km from the village. The popular spa resort of Barbotan-les-Thermes (6 km) enjoys an exceptionally mild climate, permitting the cultivation of all kinds of exotic plants; leisure facilities there include tennis and horse racing. Living room/kitchenette, 3 bedrooms (1 double and 4 single beds), bathroom, fireplace, electric central heating, open ground with garden furniture. Shopping at Barbotan.

Prices:	low season	F 1320	**6 people**
	high season	F 1515	IGN 62

Booking: Landes booking service

40/622

MISSON Grand Pré One of two gîtes, next door to each other in a large, renovated and traditionally furnished house. The house is situated on extensive farmland with a nursery, 2 km from the village. The cathedral town of Dax, popular for its hot springs, was a British possession for 300 years from 1152. Living room, kitchen, 2 bedrooms (2 double, 2 single and 1 child's bed), shower room, garage, ground. Shopping in the village.

Prices:	low season	F 605/720	**6/7 people**
	high season	F 905	IGN 62

Booking: Landes booking service

40/98

MORCENX Bourg A ground-floor gîte, one of four in a house converted and let by the local commune. It is situated by a stream at the village centre. A swimming-pool, tennis and cinema in the village (4 km). Other leisure facilities at the département capital of Mont-de-Marsan (38 km). Living room/kitchenette (1 single bed), 2 bedrooms (1 double and 2 single beds), shower room, electric heating. Shopping at Morcenx-Gare (4 km).

Prices:	low season	—	**5 people**
	high season	F 1090	IGN 62

Booking: Landes booking service

40/626

MORCENX Bourg A second ground-floor gîte in the house described above in very pleasant surroundings at the village centre. Local leisure facilities include forest, tennis and swimming-pool, with the sea just 45 km away. Mont-de-Marsan (38 km) has a famous arena where bull-fights are staged in summer, and a race-course. Living room/kitchenette (1 single bed), 2 bedrooms (1 double and 2 single beds), shower room, electric heating. Shopping at Morcenx-Gare (4 km).

Prices:	low season	—	**5 people**
	high season	F 1090	IGN 62

Booking: Landes booking service

40/627

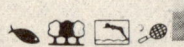

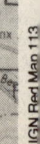

156

Ferme Auberge Maison 'César'
40700 HAGETMAU LANDES
Tel: 58.79.41.45

Just outside the town of Hagetmau, a pleasant country resort, on the route D933, you will find a worthwhile stop at the family small-holding of Pierre and Clotilde Castaignos.

Maison 'Cesar' is a ferme aubege which also offers bed and breakfast accommodation. Enjoy the traditional cuisine with delicious local produce, including foie gras and wood-fired grills.

With half or full board at the farm, you can visit the nearby Atlantic coast (one hour approx.), the Pyrenees or simply enjoy the warm and green countryside. There are many leisure activities available nearby as well as castles and crypts to explore.

For a full, enjoyable and tasty holiday, please phone 58.79.41.45 or write to M and Mme Castaignos, Miason 'Cesar', 40100 Hagetmau.

A flock of geese at Barthe de Saubusse (Landes).

Landes

PEY Au Basta A charming house, recently built and traditionally furnished, lying 1 km from the village centre and just 20 km from the Atlantic coast. Walking locally in the magnificent Landes forest; swimming-pool and tennis at 12 km. Living room, kitchen, 3 bedrooms (4 double beds), bathroom, open fire, electric central heating, carport, garden. Shopping in the village or at Saint-Vincent-de-Tyrosse (20 km).

Prices:	low season	F 820/1085	**8 people**
	high season	F 1515	*IGN 62*

Booking: Landes booking service

40/556

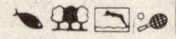

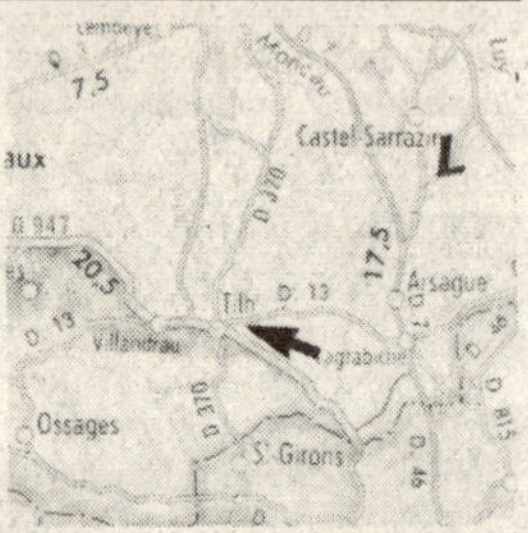

TILH A gîte with country-style furnishings in the owners' old house near the village centre (0.1 km). Fishing and bathing at a lake (12 km). Leisure facilities at the spa town of Dax (24 km) include a casino and you can watch the locals play the Basque game of *Pelota*. Living room, kitchen, 4 bedrooms (3 double and 1 single bed), bathroom, no heating, courtyard. Shopping and restaurant in the village or at Dax.

Prices:	low season	F 550/720	**7 people**
	high season	F 950	*IGN 62*

Booking: Landes booking service

40/545

TILH Poussedit An old two-storey detached house traditionally furnished in the local manner, in a village, with fishing and forests nearby (1 km). A swimming-pool (12 km), a lake (15 km). The pine-fringed Atlantic coast with lovely sandy beaches and high dunes 60 km away. Living room, kitchen, 4 bedrooms (3 double, 1 single bed), no heating, ground. Shopping and restaurant in the village or at Dax (24 km).

Prices:	low season	F 740	**7 people**
	high season	F 910	*IGN 62*

Booking: Landes booking service

40/360

URGONS Lespalière A gîte of modern design with traditional furnishings, on a mixed farm where you can buy fresh produce, outside the village (3.5 km). Enjoy nearby forest walks; swimming-pool and tennis at the interesting old town of Geaune (4 km). Living room, kitchen, 3 bedrooms (3 double, 1 single bed, a further single bed available on request), bathroom, oil central heating, carport, garden and ground with garden furniture. Linen available. Shopping at Geaune.

Prices:	low season	F 750	**7 people**
	high season	F 1200	*IGN 62*

Booking: Landes booking service

40/487

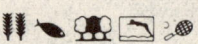

VIEILLE TURSAN Rey Situated on a mixed farm, 5 km from the village, this gîte has been renovated and furnished in traditional style. Local river fishing (0.5 km). At the lovely old town of Saint-Sever (12 km), see the eleventh-century Benedictine abbey and the seventeenth-century Jacobin monastery; leisure amenities there include a swimming-pool, tennis and canoeing. Living room, kitchen, 3 bedrooms (3 double beds), bathroom, fireplace, open ground. Farm produce from the owners; other shopping at Saint-Sever.

Prices:	low season	F 785	**6 people**
	high season	F 1120	*IGN 62*

Booking: Landes booking service

40/678

Landes

BETBEZER Château Jouhan *Chambre d'hôte* accommodation in a small château on a farm. The owners will sell produce such as Armagnac and *foie gras* and also offer *table d'hôte* meals. Bicycle hire; leisure centre at Barbotan (12 km). Four bedrooms available, each with private washing facilities: bedroom 1 (2 single beds, bathroom), bedroom 2 (1 double bed), bedroom 3 (2 single beds), bedroom 4 (1 single bed); shared bathroom, lounge and open grounds; electric heating. Shopping in the village (1.5 km).
Prices: 1p F 60, 2p F 100, 3p F 115   **7 people**
                                            IGN 62

Booking: Mme PLOUVIER, Château Jouhan, 40240 Betbezer.
Tel. (58) 44 81 58.
40/33-6

LINXE *Chambre d'hôte* accommodation in the owners' large, modern village house with traditional furnishings. The owners are retired farmers with grown-up children. Village festivals are held in summer; bicycle hire at 1 km and the old spa town of Dax (30 km) is well worth a visit. Two bedrooms available: bedroom 1 (1 double and 1 single bed), bedroom 2 (1 double, 1 single and 1 child's bed); shared shower room and lounge; central heating and garden. Farm produce and other shopping in the village (0.5 km).
Prices: 1p F 60, 2p F 100, 3p F 115   **7 people**
                                            IGN 62

Booking: Mme R. LAVIGNE, Lotis. Communal, 40260 Linxe.
Tel. (58) 42 93 64.
40/5-6

LINXE Lahourate *Chambre d'hôte* accommodation in a renovated, simply furnished building on the owners' mixed farm and 25 metres from the farmhouse where meals are available. It lies in a pine forest, 2.5 km from the village. Bicycles for hire; lake for bathing and sailing (5 km). Two rooms with shared shower room: bedroom 1 (2 double beds), bedroom 2 (2 single beds); lounge, kitchen and grounds at your disposal; electric heating. Shopping and restaurant in the village or at Dax (35 km).
Prices: 1p F 60, 2p F 100, 3p F 115   **6 people**
                                            IGN 62

Booking: Mme F. LARTIGUE, Lahourate, 40260 Linxe.
Tel. (58) 42 92 59.
40/10-11

MAGESCQ *Chambre d'hôte* accommodation in a very modern house where the owners live with their teenage children. It lies in a large park, 1 km from the village where bicycles are for hire and there are summer festivals. The lovely old town of Dax (15 km) has many tourist amenities. The sea (15 km). Two rooms available each with 1 double and 1 single bed; bathroom, lounge and open grounds at your disposal; central heating. Shopping and restaurant in the village.
Prices: 1p F 60, 2p F 100, 3p F 115   **6 people**
                                            IGN 62

Booking: Mme M. DESBIEYS, 40140 Magescq. Tel. (58) 57 71 55.

40/12-13

PISSOS *Chambre d'hôte* accommodation in a modern, traditionally furnished house in a village where you will find several craft workshops (woodworking, weaving) and bicycles for hire. Swimming-pool, fishing and forest walks at Ecomusée (1 km); the sea at Mimizan (35 km). Two double bedrooms each with private washing facilities; use of bathroom, lounge and garden. Meals available or restaurant at 1 km. Shopping in the village (0.5 km).
Prices: 1p F 60, 2p F 100, 3p F 115   **4 people**
                                            IGN 55

Booking: Mme BROT, Route de Trensacq, 40410 Pissos.
Tel. (58) 07 70 50.
40/37-9

Lot-et-Garonne

AGME Bretou A renovated and traditionally furnished house, set in an open garden, 1 km from the village. A swimming-pool (13 km) and a lake (15 km). Marmande (20 km) is a bustling market town with plenty of sports and leisure amenities and an attractive old quarter. Kitchen, 2 bedrooms (1 double, 2 single beds), shower room, fireplace, central heating, covered verandah, carport, open garden. Shopping and restaurant at 5 km.

Prices:	low season	F 442/730	**4 people**
	high season	F 993	IGN 56

Booking: Lot-et-Garonne booking service

47/170B

BARBASTE Sacot An attractive modern house with traditional furnishings, 7 km from the small town of Barbaste whose impressive ruined château is in a picturesque river setting. Bathing at a lake (5 km) and good shopping and leisure amenities at Nérac (15 km) whose own fifteenth-century château is now a museum. Living room, kitchen, 2 bedrooms (1 double, 2 single beds and a single divan in the large hallway), shower room, fireplace, balcony, garage, open ground. A grocery at 1 km; other shopping and restaurant in the town.

Prices:	low season	F 600/900	**5 people**
	high season	F 1100/1200	IGN 56

Booking: Lot-et-Garonne booking service

47/287A

DAUSSE Clos de Bérès A spacious, detached house in its own garden near the village centre. The interesting old market town of Villeneuve-sur-Lot (20 km approx.) was built in the thirteenth century as a bastide with its streets in the old centre in the usual grid pattern; see the old chapel near the river. Living room, kitchen, 3 bedrooms (2 double, 2 single beds), bathroom, garage, enclosed garden. Shopping in the village.

Prices:	low season	F 1040/1240	**6 people**
	high season	F 1540	IGN 57

Booking: Lot-et-Garonne booking service

47/285

LAFITTE-SUR-LOT Pont-de-Roussanes A detached house, in a quiet spot right by the river Lot (good fishing). Bathing and sailing facilities on the river at 5 km. In the centre of the département, the gîte is ideally situated for trips to the old town of Agen, Nérac, Villeneuve-sur-Lot, etc. Dining room/bedroom (separated by a curtain, 1 double bed), kitchen, 2 bedrooms (2 single beds), shower room, carport, enclosed garden with outdoor furniture. Shopping in the village (2.5 km) or at Clairac (5 km).

Prices:	low season	F 694	**4 people**
	high season	F 948/1005	IGN 56

Booking: Lot-et-Garonne booking service

47/253

MOIRAX Le Cap du Bosc A ground-floor gîte, one of two on a working farm where there is a swimming-pool at your disposal. Bathing, pedalo boats and wind-surfing at Lamontjoie lake (10 km). At 13 km is Agen, the département capital whose old quarter around the cathedral is particularly attractive. Living room, kitchen, 2 bedrooms (3 double beds), bathroom, fireplace, gas central heating, carport, open ground. Linen available. Shopping at Laplume (6 km).

Prices:	low season	F 627/783	**6 people**
	high season	F 977/1020	IGN 56

Booking: Lot-et-Garonne booking service

47/164A

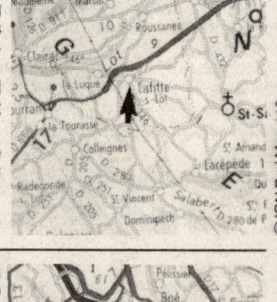

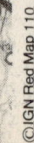

Lot-et-Garonne

MOIRAX Jean de Videau A large house, near the town centre in a region noted for its fruit production, particularly plums. See the recently restored Cistercian abbey nearby. The owners live at Agen (10 km) a busy town on the river Garonne with good modern shopping facilities. Living room, kitchen, 3 bedrooms (2 double, 1 single bed), bathroom, open garden. Farm produce and restaurant in the town (0.5 km); other shopping at 8 km.

Prices:	low season	F 617/761	**5 people**
	high season	F 1018/1040	*IGN 56*

Booking: Lot-et-Garonne booking service

47/295A

SAINT-GEORGES Foulanon Nord An old stone house, typical of the region, renovated and furnished in traditional rustic style, on a livestock farm, some 5 km from the village. Enquire at the tourist office in Fumel (10 km approx.) for guided visits to the remarkable fortified Château de Bonaguil. Living room, kitchen, 3 bedrooms (2 double, 1 single, 1 child's bed), bathroom, terrace, carport, open ground with garden furniture. Farm produce from the owners; other shoping and restaurant in the village or at Villeneuve-sur-Lot (23 km).

Prices:	low season	F 658/1070	**5/6 people**
	high season	F 1173/1276	*IGN 57*

Booking: Lot-et-Garonne booking service

47/289

SAINT-MAURIN Naudy An attractively renovated and traditionally furnished gîte, set in open ground, 2 km from the village centre. At Nérac (10 km approx.) see the remaining wing of the fine Renaissance château, erstwhile home of Henry IV of Navarre, in the pleasant old quarter of the town. Living room/kitchenette, lounge (1 single divan), 2 bedrooms (1 double, 1 single bed), shower room, terrace, carport, open ground. Farm produce from the owners; shopping and restaurant in the village, at Nérac or at Agen (20 km).

Prices:	low season	F 560/737	**4 people**
	high season	F 955/995	*IGN 57*

Booking: Lot-et-Garonne booking service

47/278A

SAINTE-LIVRADE-SUR-LOT Septfonds A large, modern house with contemporary furnishings in the Lot valley, 4.5 km from the town centre. Local river fishing; a swimming-pool and tennis in the town. See the Château de Tombebouc-Fongrave nearby and do not miss the interesting old town of Villeneuve-sur-Lot (10 km). Living room, kitchen, 3 bedrooms (2 double, 2 single beds), bathroom, fireplace, oil stove, terrace, garage, large enclosed ground with garden furniture and swings. Shops and a restaurant at 1.8 km.

Prices:	low season	F 1100/1250	**6 people**
	high season	F 1355	*IGN 56*

Booking: Lot-et-Garonne booking service

47/252

SAUVETERRE-LA-LEMANCE Guillouti A delightful old house, renovated and furnished in traditional rustic style, with large airy rooms, 2 km from the village. Do not miss the imposing fortified Château de Bonaguil (20 km approx.) and the interesting old town of Puy-l'Evêque, overlooking the Lot valley (25 km approx.). Lounge, kitchen, 2 bedrooms (3 double, 1 single, 1 child's bed), bathroom, fireplace, balcony, open courtyard with garden furniture. Farm produce, other shopping and restaurant in the village (2 km) or at Fumel (17 km).

Prices:	low season	F 1440	**7/8 people**
	high season	F 1540/1640	*IGN 57*

Booking: Lot-et-Garonne booking service

47/301

Pyrénées-Atlantiques

ALCAY One of two traditionally furnished and renovated gîtes outside the village (3 km), ideal for walkers as it is close to the Iraty and Arbaille forests and the GR10 long-distance footpath. A swimming-pool and tennis at 18 km. Living room/kitchenette, 2 bedrooms (1 double, 2 single beds), bathroom, open fire, open ground. Shopping and restaurant at the pretty little town of Tardets (7 km).

Prices:	low season	F 1080/1296	**4 people**
	high season	F 1296	IGN 69

Booking: Pyrénées-Atlantiques Loisirs Accueil E

64/6

ARTHEZ-D'ASSON A rustically furnished gîte on a mixed farm, 3 km from the village at the foot of the Béarn mountains in the Ouzom valley. Visit Asson Zoo at 1 km and the Bétharram caves (9 km). Bicycles for hire (10 km) and a lake at 30 km. Living room/kitchenette (washing machine), 2 bedrooms (1 double, 2 single beds), bathroom, electric heating, balcony, open garden. Shops at Asson (7 km) or Nay (10 km) and a restaurant at 6 km.

Prices:	low season	F 988	**4 people**
	high season	F 1212	IGN 70

Booking: Pyrénées Atlantiques Loisirs Accueil E

64/2

BARDOS Daguerrenia A small, second-floor gîte, one of several apartments in the owners' fine old house at the village centre. Local river fishing; tennis and swimming-pool at 10 km and the Atlantic coast is an easy day trip at 35 km. Living room/kitchenette (1 child's bed), 1 bedroom (1 double bed), bathroom, no heating. Linen available. A restaurant at 2 km; shopping at Labastide-Clairence (10 km).

Prices:	low season	F 648	**2/3 people**
	high season	F 864	IGN 69

Booking: Pyrénées Atlantiques Loisirs Accueil E

64/8

BORCE One of two gîtes with traditional furnishings at the centre of the village where there is a refuge for a Pyrenean bear! It is in the Béarn mountain range (altitude 625 metres) in the Pyrénées National Park, just 20 km from the Spanish border. Living room, kitchen, 3 bedrooms (2 double and 1 single bed), bathroom, no heating, enclosed courtyard. Shopping in the village (0.2 km) or at Accous (6 km); a restaurant at 2 km.

Prices:	low season	F 918	**5 people**
	high season	F 918	IGN 69

Booking: Pyrénées-Atlantiques Loisirs Accueil E

64/1

CAMBO-LES-BAINS A gîte in the owner's traditionally furnished Basque-style house with views over the Nive Valley, Basque country and the Pyrénées. Fishing locally; visit the local church built in a traditional style. Swimming-pool and tennis (2 km), and the coast (22 km). Living room/kitchenette, 2 bedrooms (1 double, 2 single beds), shower room, heating, courtyard and enclosed ground. Shopping and restaurant in the village (2 km) or at Bayonne (18 km).

Prices:	low season	F 540/594	**4 people**
	high season	F 702/756	IGN 69

Booking: Pyrénées-Atlantiques Loisirs Accueil E

64/12

Pyrénées-Atlantiques

FAGET-GOES-D'OLORON A recently renovated barn with traditional furnishings, just outside the village overlooking the Gave d'Oloron valley. Salmon fishing and other leisure amenities at the lovely old town of Oloron-Sainte-Marie (7 km) which has a twelfth-century cathedral. The coast (100 km). Living room, kitchen, 3 bedrooms (2 double, 1 single bed), bathroom, fireplace (wood supplied), electric heating, carport, open ground. Eggs and milk available locally; other shopping and restaurant at Oloron-Sainte-Marie.

| Prices: | low season | F 756 | **5 people** |
| | high season | F 1080 | *IGN 69* |

Booking: Pyrénées-Atlantiques Loisirs Accueil   **E**

64/4

HELETTE Zalundea A traditionally furnished, first-floor gîte, one of two in the owners' lovely old house, 2 km from the village centre, set on wooded hills with views over the Pyrénées. A swimming-pool and tennis at Hasparren (12 km); the coast and lovely Saint-Jean-de-Luz (35 km). Living room, kitchen, 2 bedrooms (2 double, 1 single bed), bathroom, no heating, balcony, enclosed ground. Linen available. Fresh milk and eggs available locally; other shopping at Hasparren; a restaurant in the village.

| Prices: | low season | F 648 | **5 people** |
| | high season | F 864 | *IGN 69* |

Booking: Pyrénées-Atlantiques Loisirs Accueil   **E**

64/9

HELETTE Zalundea A second gîte in the house described above, on a farm, 2 km from the centre of the village in the Basse Navarre region. Interesting day trips could include the Basque coast (35 km) and the lovely old town of Saint-Jean-Pied-de-Port at the foot of the Roncesvalles Pass in the Pyrénées. Living room, kitchen, 2 bedrooms (1 double, 2 single beds), bathroom, open fire (wood supplied), balcony, enclosed ground shared with the other gîte. Shopping at Hasparren (12 km); a restaurant in the village.

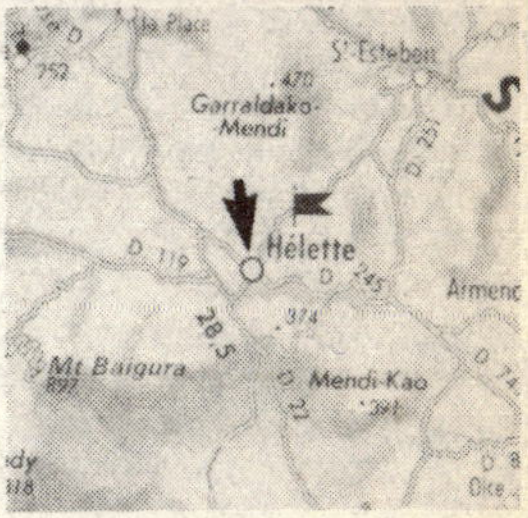

| Prices: | low season | F 702 | **4 people** |
| | high season | F 918 | *IGN 69* |

Booking: Pyrénées-Atlantiques Loisirs Accueil   **E**

64/10

© IGN Red Map 113

HOURS An old, traditionally furnished gîte, 1 km from the village centre. It is just 20 km from the lovely old town of Pau (see Henry IV's splendid château which is open to the public) and Lourdes, which receives nearly 3 million pilgrims each year. Living room, kitchen, 3 bedrooms (2 double and 2 single beds), bathroom, no heating, garage, enclosed ground. Local farm produce; other shopping and a restaurant at Soumoulou (6 km).

| Prices: | low season | F 648/756 | **6 people** |
| | high season | F 864 | *IGN 70* |

Booking: Pyrénées-Atlantiques Loisirs Accueil   **E**

64/5

LANNE A ground-floor, traditionally furnished gîte, one of two apartments in a modern house at the village centre which has a swimming-pool, tennis court and river fishing. Ski-ing at 30 km. It is 18 km from the ancient town of Oloron-Sainte-Marie which boasts two cathedrals. Living room (1 double, 1 single bed), kitchen, 1 bedroom (1 double bed), shower room, electric heating, enclosed ground. Shopping and restaurant in the village.

| Prices: | low season | F 648 | **5 people** |
| | high season | F 810 | *IGN 69* |

Booking: Pyrénées-Atlantiques Loisirs Accueil   **E**

64/7

Pyrénées-Atlantiques

LASSEUBE Cambuse, Le Chêne Lière A traditionally furnished gîte in the owners' old house on a livestock farm on the banks of the river Baïse, 3 km from the village centre. This is in the small area which produces Jurançon wine. A swimming-pool at the attractive old town of Oloron-Sainte-Marie (10 km). Living room/kitchenette, 2 bedrooms (1 double, 1 single bed), shower room, open ground. Local farm produce; other shopping at Oloron-Sainte-Marie and a restaurant in the village.

Prices:	low season	F 432/540	3 people
	high season	F 810/918	IGN 69

Booking: Pyrénées-Atlantiques Loisirs Accueil **E**

64/3

SAINT-PEE-SUR-NIVELLE Chabaten Etcheberria An apartment in the owners' typical Basque house, 1 km from the town centre which boasts a ruined fifteenth-century château and an artificial lake. It is in the picturesque Nivelle valley, just 6 km from the Spanish border and 14 km from the coast. Living room, kitchen, 4 bedrooms (4 double and 1 single bed), bathroom, no heating, balcony, open ground. Shopping and restaurant in the town or at Saint-Jean-de-Luz (10 km approx.).

Prices:	low season	F 816/1049	9 people
	high season	F 1566/1782	IGN 69

Booking: Pyrénées-Atlantiques Loisirs Accueil **E**

64/13

UHART-CIZE A ground-floor gîte, one of two rustically furnished apartments in an old house in a wooded setting outside the village and on the route of the GR10 long-distance footpath. Plenty to see and do at the lovely old town of Saint-Jean-Pied-de-Port (1 km) and in the surrounding villages. Living room/kitchenette (1 single divan), 2 bedrooms (1 double, 2 single beds), bathroom, no heating, balcony, open ground. Linen available. Farm produce, other shopping and restaurant in the village (1 km).

Prices:	low season	F 702	5 people
	high season	F 972	IGN 69

Booking: Pyrénées-Atlantiques Loisirs Accueil **E**

64/11

URRUGNE Bi Anaiak A traditionally furnished gîte in the owners' modern house, 3 km from the ancient village of Urrugne. At 6 km is the delightful old fishing port of Saint-Jean-de-Luz, now very popular with tourists who enjoy its lively night-life and good selection of restaurants. Living room, kitchen, 2 bedrooms (1 double, 4 single beds), bathroom, no heating, open ground. A restaurant in the village and shopping at Saint-Jean-de-Luz.

Prices:	low season	F 734	6 people
	high season	F 1188/1296	IGN 69

Booking: Pyrénées-Atlantiques Loisirs Accueil **E**

64/14

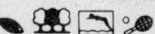

HAUT-DE-BOSDARROS *Chambre d'hote* accommodation in the owners' well-renovated house on a farm which has its own swimming-pool. The owners, who speak some English, also offer the use of a sauna and thalassotherapy treatment. Do not miss Pau whose Boulevard des Pyrénées offers a view over the whole mountain range and whose château has a fine collection of tapestries. Four double rooms available, each with private bath and WC. Electric heating, garden. Meals available; shopping at Nay (8 km).

Prices:	on request		8 people
			IGN 69

Booking: M M. PUCHEU, Loutarès, Haut-de-Bosdarros, 64800 Nay. **E**

64/15

8 POITOU – CHARENTES

From pleasant countryside to the bustling ports and harbours, from mysterious marshes and canals to the sandy, pine fragrant beaches and from the islands of Ré, Aix and Oléron to the sleepy vineyards of Cognac, this is a region of great richness. Here, the country dwellers hurry, slowly; people and land alike are soothed by a mild climate.

Angoulême, chief town of Charente, is largely industrial, but the old quarter, sitting on a hill above the river Charente, is of interest with its mediaeval, Romanesque and Byzantine architecture. Cognac, the town that gives its name to that famous French drink, is the centre of the wine-growing area where cognac has been distilled since the seventeenth century. A visit to one of the local cognac producers' establishments is a must.

La Rochelle, a bustling port, is the chief town of Charente-Maritime. This was a thriving maritime town between the fourteenth and eighteenth centuries, trading with North America from an early period and has preserved much of its character with its old harbour defences and arcaded houses. The old harbour is used by fishing boats while the large seagoing ships use the new harbour, La Pallice. A few miles inland is the Marais Poitevin, the coastal marshland, sometimes called "Green Venice", where boatmen are happy to take you on a cruise, imparting their knowledge of life and habitat of the marshes. Do not miss the islands of Oléron and Ré. Ile d'Oléron is the second largest island in France and is joined to the mainland by a bridge. There are several pleasant beaches and Saint-Trojan-les-Bains is a popular seaside resort.

Old traditions of the region include weaving, tapestry and lace from Charente and Deux-Sèvres; pottery from Saintonge; ceramics and woodwork from Charente-Maritime; beautiful embroidery from Angles-sur-l'Anglin in the Vienne. Do not leave this abundant region before sampling some of the local cuisine, where the varied countryside provides a wide range of menus. Try the Marennes-Oléron oysters; the famous goat cheeses, such as the "chabichou"; and Pineau, a mixture of grape juice and cognac.

Map of localities

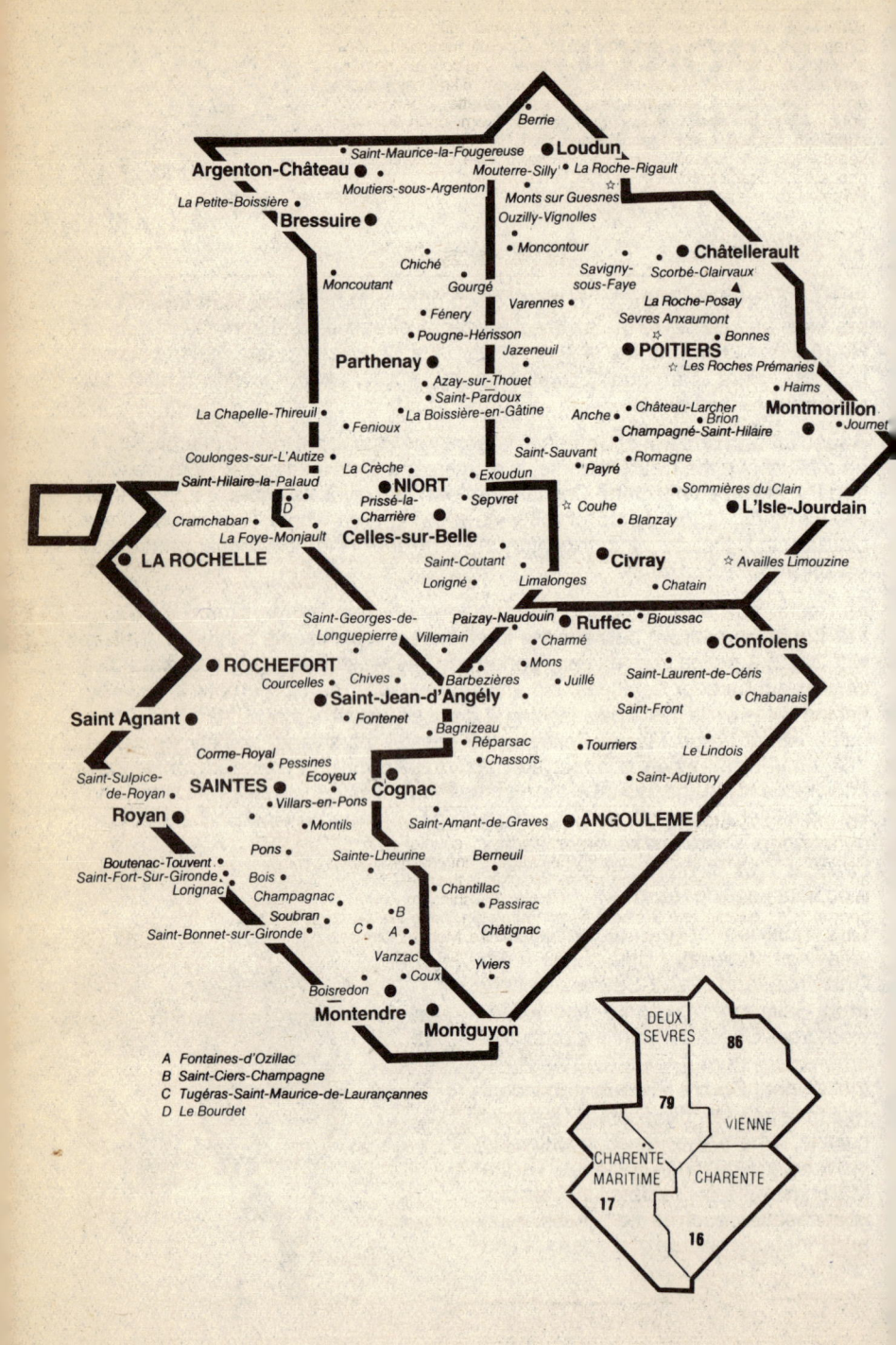

- Berrie
- Loudun
- Argenton-Château
- Saint-Maurice-la-Fougereuse
- Mouterre-Silly
- La Roche-Rigault
- Moutiers-sous-Argenton
- Monts sur Guesnes
- La Petite-Boissière
- Ouzilly-Vignolles
- Bressuire
- Moncontour
- Châtellerault
- Chiché
- Savigny-sous-Faye
- Scorbé-Clairvaux
- Moncoutant
- Gourgé
- La Roche-Posay
- Fénery
- Varennes
- Sevres Anxaumont
- Pougne-Hérisson
- Bonnes
- Parthenay
- Jazeneuil
- POITIERS
- Azay-sur-Thouet
- Les Roches Prémaries
- Saint-Pardoux
- Haims
- La Chapelle-Thireuil
- La Boissière-en-Gâtine
- Château-Larcher
- Montmorillon
- Anche
- Brion
- Fenioux
- Saint-Sauvant
- Champagné-Saint-Hilaire
- Journet
- Coulonges-sur-L'Autize
- La Crèche
- Payré
- Romagne
- Saint-Hilaire-la-Palaud
- Exoudun
- Sommières du Clain
- NIORT
- Sepvret
- Couhe
- L'Isle-Jourdain
- Cramchaban
- Prissé-la-Charrière
- Blanzay
- La Foye-Monjault
- LA ROCHELLE
- Celles-sur-Belle
- Civray
- Saint-Coutant
- Availles Limouzine
- Lorigné
- Limalonges
- Chatain
- Saint-Georges-de-Longuepierre
- Paizay-Naudouin
- Ruffec
- Bioussac
- Villemain
- Confolens
- ROCHEFORT
- Charmé
- Courcelles
- Chives
- Mons
- Saint-Laurent-de-Céris
- Barbezières
- Juillé
- Saint Agnant
- Saint-Jean-d'Angély
- Chabanais
- Fontenet
- Bagnizeau
- Saint-Front
- Corme-Royal
- Réparsac
- Tourriers
- Le Lindois
- Saint-Sulpice-de-Royan
- Pessines
- Chassors
- SAINTES
- Ecoyeux
- Saint-Adjutory
- Royan
- Villars-en-Pons
- Cognac
- ANGOULEME
- Pons
- Montils
- Saint-Amant-de-Graves
- Boutenac-Touvent
- Sainte-Lheurine
- Berneuil
- Saint-Fort-Sur-Gironde
- Bois
- Lorignac
- Champagnac
- Chantillac
- Passirac
- Soubran
- Châtignac
- Saint-Bonnet-sur-Gironde
- C A
- Vanzac
- Yviers
- Coux
- Boisredon
- Montendre
- Montguyon

A Fontaines-d'Ozillac
B Saint-Ciers-Champagne
C Tugéras-Saint-Maurice-de-Laurançannes
D Le Bourdet

DEUX SEVRES 86
79 VIENNE
CHARENTE MARITIME CHARENTE
17 16

166

Charente

SAINT-AMANT-DE-GRAVES Chebrat A small gîte in a typical Charentais-style house, renovated and traditionally furnished, lying on a vineyard, 2 km from the village, owned by a young couple who offer a very warm welcome. At picturesque Châteauneuf (6 km) enjoy boating on the lovely river Charente. Living room/kitchenette, 2 bedrooms (1 double, 2 single and 1 child's bed), shower room, open fire (wood supplied), terrace, carport, enclosed ground. Farm produce (including vegetables and cognac) from the owners; mobile shops call, other shopping and restaurant at 4 km or at Jarnac (8 km).

Prices:	low season	F 700	**5 people**
	high season	F 700/750	IGN 40

Booking: Charente Loisirs Accueil E
16/4.36

SAINT-FRONT Chez Brouty A renovated and traditionally furnished house near another gîte, both owned by an Englishman, lying by a river where you may bathe and fish in a quiet, shady hamlet, 1.5 km from the village. Swimming-pool and other distractions at Mansle (9 km). Living room/kitchenette, 2 bedrooms (2 double and 2 child's beds), bathroom, fireplace (wood supplied), electric heating, terrace, garage, garden with furniture and games. Mobile shops call; other shopping and restaurant at 5 km.

Prices:	low season	on request	**6 people**
	high season	on request	IGN 40

Booking: Charente Loisirs Accueil E
16/1.63

SAINT-LAURENT-DE-CERIS La Jarnaud A carefully renovated and traditionally furnished country cottage in its own shady garden close by a river (good for fishing) just 3 km from Saint-Laurent-de-Céris, where there are shops and tennis. Confolens (15 km) has a folk festival in the middle of August. Living room (1 double divan), kitchen, 3 bedrooms (1 double, 5 large single beds), bathroom, open fire, oil stove, garage, open garden. Mobile shops call, shopping at Saint-Claud (7 km) where there is a restaurant.

Prices:	low season	F 490/735	**9 people**
	high season	F 980	IGN 40

Booking: Charente Loisirs Accueil E
16/2.32

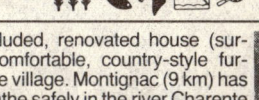

TOURRIERS Bouffanais A nice, secluded, renovated house (surrounded by a walled garden) with comfortable, country-style furnishings. It is in a hamlet, 1.5 km from the village. Montignac (9 km) has an old abbey and a keep and you can bathe safely in the river Charente there. Living room (1 single divan), kitchen (washing machine), 3 bedrooms (1 double and 3 single beds), bathroom, open fire (wood supplied), electric heating, garage, outdoor furniture. Mobile shops call; other shopping and restaurant in the village or at Mansle (9 km).

Prices:	low season	F 900/1100	**6 people**
	high season	F 1300	IGN 40

Booking: Charente Loisirs Accueil E
16/1.67

YVIERS Les Aireaux A renovated and traditionally furnished gîte in a hamlet, right in the south of the département, close to the popular Perigord region. The attractive château town of Chalais is at 3.5 km and Brossac, with its lake and many leisure amenities, is just 8 km away. Living room/kitchenette, 2 bedrooms (1 double and 3 single beds), bathroom, open fire (wood supplied), terrace, garage, garden with barbecue, outdoor furniture and games. Farm produce in the village, mobile butcher and baker call; other shopping and restaurant at Chalais.

Prices:	low season	F 525	**5 people**
	high season	F 575	IGN 47

Booking: Charente Loisirs Accueil E
16/3.73

Charente

The Charente, an essentially rural département, is situated between the Poitou and Aquitaine. The landscape is highly varied and stretches from the plains of Poitou to the heathlands of the Landes; and from the Périgord hills to the foothills of the Massif Central. Its architecture, craftsmanship and gastronomy illustrate this variety. And with the sea only 100 km away there is a dominant Atlantic climate. Last but not least, slowly maturing on old Charente farms, is our famous Cognac and its by-product Pineau, which we drink as an aperitif.

HISTORY The traces of the first Charente inhabitants date over 100,000 years. Important ruins bear witness to the Gallo-Roman era; each Charente village contains an eleventh- or twelfth-century Romanesque church. Our many châteaux and museums will help you form a full picture of the development of our département.

ACCOMMODATION Gîtes ruraux, chambres d'hôtes and many small family-run country hotels assure a pleasant stay in our region. Our fermes-auberges (farmhouse inns) and restaurants will help you discover the delights of our Charente cuisine, made even more delicious by Cognac and Pineau.

SPORTS AND LEISURE Along with our many tennis courts, swimming-pools, lakes, footpaths and riding centres, we offer our country holiday packages: exploring the Charente by bicycle, canoe or on horseback.

For booking and any further information about holidays in Charente, contact:
LOISIRS-ACCUEIL CHARENTE
Office Départemental du Tourisme
Place Bouillaud
16021 ANGOULEME **Tel.** (45) 92.24.43.   E
             Telex. 791-607

NB For fuller information about all Loisirs Accueil services, please see pages 12–13 of this guide.

Special Interest Holidays

RESERVATION LOISIRS ACCUEIL

FISHING The river Charente is very popular for fishing. This holiday offers full-board accommodation in the 2-star hotel, L'Orangerie at Jarnac, a small town and important centre of the Cognac industry. Other leisure facilities include tennis, bathing, country walks.
Availability: April–July (minimum stay: 3 days)
Price: on request
Cost includes: half-board accommodation.

HORSE-RIDING An 8-day trek, taking you from the Limousin foot-hills through Cognac country, the Charente valley and the Périgordian forests. At each stop along the way in Charente farmhouses, where once the horse was highly regarded as an essential tool, you will be assured of a warm welcome. The accommodation provided will be bed and breakfast and *table d'hôte* meals.
Availability: (all year; 1 holiday only per month from September to July)
Price: on request
Cost includes: hire of horse and equipment; full-board accommodation; services of a guide.

PAPER-MAKING COURSE The Moulin de Fleurac workshop is now one of the few remaining places where hand-made paper is produced using methods of the eighteenth century. This 5-day course (Monday–Friday) allows you to learn all about this craft (instruction in French only). Accommodation will be arranged according to your choice (hotel, gîte, etc.).
Availability: May–June–September; 6 people per course.
Price: on request
Cost includes: instruction and materials, but not accommodation or meals.

BOATING HOLIDAYS ON THE CHARENTE RIVER A week's holiday, boating on the river Charente: 160 km of navigable waterway with 21 locks. Departing from Cognac, the river passes through the cognac vineyards and famous towns and cities with a rich heritage – Cognac, Saintes, Rochefort. The boats are fully equipped with bedding and cooking facilities for 2-6 people.
Availability: May-October.
Price: on request
Cost includes: hire of fully-equipped boat, insurance, quantity of camping gas; F 1000 deposit against damages.

Charente

BARBEZIERES An old farm building, renovated and furnished in country style, adjoining other buildings on a mixed farm close to the village centre (0.1 km) where there is a restaurant. The owners provide three bicycles for the use of guests. Living room/kitchenette, 2 bedrooms (1 double, 2 single and 1 child's bed), shower room, open fire (wood supplied), carport, courtyard and enclosed ground with garden furniture, barbecue. Mobile shops call, other shopping in the village or at Aigre (8 km).

Prices:	low season	F 450/900	**5 people**
	high season	F 800/900	IGN 40

Booking: Charente Loisirs Accueil   E

16/1.49

BERNEUIL Chez Marquis This pleasant, renovated and traditionally furnished gîte lies on a family-run farm near the village centre. You can visit an agricultural centre; tennis, riding, fishing, bathing at a lake and bicycle hire at Brossac (9 km); swimming-pool at the château town of Barbezieux (12 km). Living room (1 double bed), kitchen, 3 bedrooms (2 double, 5 single beds), bathroom, fireplace, garage, enclosed grounds. Shopping at Brossac, and restaurant in the village (0.4 km).

Prices:	low season	F 450	**11 people**
	high season	F 600/700	IGN 47

Booking: Charente Loisirs Accueil   E

16/3.2

BIOUSSAC Bois-Regnier A traditionally furnished gîte, renovated with care by the owners who also provide 2 bicycles, a barbecue and sun lounge in the large well-kept garden. It is in a hamlet, 2.5 km from the village and 9 km from Ruffec with its many leisure facilities. Living room (1 double divan), kitchen (washing machine), 2 bedrooms (1 double, 3 single beds), bathroom, fireplace, electric heating, carport, garden. Mobile shops all; other shopping and restaurant at Ruffec.

Prices:	low season	F 450/700	**7 people**
	high season	F 905/1030	IGN 40

Booking: Charente Loisirs Accueil   E

16/1.68

CHABANAIS Domaine de Grène A small but attractive rustically furnished gîte on a livestock farm, 500 metres from a river where you may fish. There are Gallo-Roman ruins at 5 km, and Etagnac Château houses a museum (6 km). Living room/kitchenette, 2 bedrooms (1 double, 2 single and 1 child's bed), shower room, open fire (wood supplied), carport, open ground. Shops and restaurant in the village (1.5 km) or at Rochechouart (15 km approx.).

Prices:	low season	F 800	**5 people**
	high season	F 900	IGN 40

Booking: Charente Loisirs Accueil   E

16/2.36

CHANTILLAC Chez Cerclet Substantial old stone-built house, now renovated and traditionally furnished, 0.5 km from the village centre. Brossac (20 km) offers a wide range of leisure activities including pleasant walks, lake for bathing, riding and bicycle hire. The ground-floor gîte provides living room, kitchen, 3 bedrooms (2 double, 3 single and 1 child's bed), shower room, open fire (wood supplied), electric heating, carport and open ground with barbecue. Linen available. Mobile shops call, other shopping (2 km), and restaurant at Chantillac or Chevanceaux (both 4 km).

Prices:	low season	F 580/650	**8 people**
	high season	F 850/900	IGN 47

Booking: Charente Loisirs Accueil   E

16/3.52

Charente

CHARME Les Inchauds An attractively renovated house with traditional country-style furnishings, lying on a mixed farm. Ruffec (13 km) has a ruined Romanesque church with richly decorated façade, a swimming-pool and riding facilities. Living room (1 single divan), kitchen (washing machine), 2 bedrooms (1 double, 2 single and 1 child's bed), shower room, gas central heating and open fire (wood supplied), carport, garden with furniture. Shopping from mobile stores or in the village (3 km); a restaurant at 5 km.

Prices: low season F 620/640 **6 people**
high season F 850 IGN 40
Booking: Charente Loisirs Accueil E
16/1.64

CHASSORS La Cadois A lovely old ivy-clad gîte, renovated and traditionally furnished in rustic style. It lies in its own quiet garden (with tennis court and furniture for outdoor meals) on a vineyard, 1 km from the village. At Jarnac (4 km) visit the Cognac distilleries and barrel-makers and try the local product! Living room/kitchenette, 3 bedrooms (3 double and 1 child's bed), shower room, open fire and electric heating, enclosed ground. Mobile baker and fishmonger call; other shopping and restaurant at Jarnac.

Prices: low season F 750/775 **7 people**
high season F 1000 IGN 40
Booking: Charente Loisirs Accueil E
16/4.27

CHATIGNAC Le Faix de Néraud A large renovated gîte, furnished in traditional country style in a lovely peaceful spot, some 5 km from the village. There is a leisure centre based around a lake at Brossac (5 km) and the château town of Chalais at 12 km has a swimming-pool. Living room (1 double divan), kitchen, 5 bedrooms (4 double and 2 single beds), bathroom, open fire (wood supplied), oil-fired central heating, carport, garden and open ground with furniture, child's swing and barbecue. Shopping and restaurant in the village.

Prices: low season F 1300 **12 people**
high season F 1700 IGN 47
Booking: Charente Loisirs Accueil E
16/3.49

JUILLE A renovated gîte with traditional furnishings lying in enclosed grounds at the heart of a quiet village. Leisure facilities at Mansle (8 km) include a swimming-pool, boating on the Charente river and a tennis court. There are marked footpaths in the Saint-Amant forest (10 km). Living room/kitchenette, 2 bedrooms (3 double beds), shower room, electric heating, garage, garden with furniture. Mobile shops call; other shopping and restaurant at Mansle.

Prices: low season F 630 **6 people**
high season F 800 IGN 40
Booking: Charente Loisirs Accueil E
16/1.48

LE LINDOIS La Garde A renovated gîte with traditional, rustic furnishings, situated in a hamlet, surrounded by forests, 4 km from Montemboeuf which has a swimming-pool and tennis. Visit the interesting old cathedral town of Angoulême (approx. 35 km), capital of the département. Living room (1 single divan), kitchen, 2 bedrooms (2 double and 2 single beds), bathroom, fireplace (wood supplied), electric heating, terrace, carport, enclosed ground. Mobile shops call. Shopping in the village (1 km) and restaurant at Montemboeuf.

Prices: low season on request **7 people**
high season on request IGN 40
Booking: Charente Loisirs Accueil E
16/2.34

Charente

MONS This gîte, which has been renovated and furnished in traditional rustic style, lies on a vineyard where the owners are happy to sell their produce – Cognac and its aperitif, Pineau. The hamlet is 12 km from the rural holiday resort of Rouillac which boasts a Gallo-Roman theatre and various leisure facilities. Living room/kitchenette (1 double divan), 2 bedrooms (1 double, 2 single beds, 1 single divan), shower room, no heating, carport, enclosed ground. Mobile shops call; other shopping and restaurant at Aigre (3 km).

Prices: low season   not available
          high season F 740
7 people
IGN 40

Booking: Charente Loisirs Accueil   **E**

16/1.50

PAIZAY-NAUDOUIN Les Delfonds An attractively renovated and well-equipped gîte with traditional, country-style furnishings in a hamlet, with river fishing at 2 km, a swimming-pool (15 km) and riding (20 km). Visit the lively town of Ruffec (18 km) with its many leisure and tourist attractions. Living room (TV, 1 double divan), kitchen, 3 bedrooms (3 double, 1 single and 1 child's bed), bathroom, fireplace, electric heating, terrace, garage, garden with barbecue, table tennis and other games. Shopping in the village (0.5 km); restaurant at Villefagnan (8 km).

Prices: low season   F 800/850
          high season F 1150
10 people
IGN 40

Booking: Charente Loisirs Accueil   **E**

16/1.56

PASSIRAC Chez Gabard This long, low old house with comfortable rustic furnishings lies on a cereal crops farm 2 km from the village centre. At Brossac leisure centre (4 km) you can ride and play tennis. Visit the château at Barbezieux (17 km) where there is also a race course. Living room, kitchen, 4 bedrooms (3 double, 1 single and 2 child's beds), shower room, open fire, central heating (wood supplied), carport, garden (with furniture). Shopping and restaurant at Brossac.

Prices: low season   F 1000
          high season F 1000
9 people
IGN 47

Booking: Charente Loisirs Accueil   **E**

16/3.51

REPARSAC A large old stone-built detached house situated right in the centre of the village and appropriately furnished in traditional, country style. Good leisure facilities at Cognac (11 km) include a swimming-pool. Living room (1 single divan), kitchen, 3 bedrooms (2 double, 3 single and 1 child's bed), bathroom, open fire (wood supplied), electric heating, carport, enclosed courtyard and ground with garden furniture. Shopping in the village or at Jarnac (7 km), where there are restaurants.

Prices: low season   F 520/650
          high season F 780
9 people
IGN 40

Booking: Charente Loisirs Accueil   **E**

16/4.10

SAINT-ADJUTORY L'Epardelière This renovated gîte with rustic furnishings lies in its own grounds on a mixed farm, in a hamlet, 3 km from the village. Swimming-pool and tennis at Chasseneuil-sur-Bonnieure (5 km) which has a seventeenth-century château and a memorial to the Resistance Movement. Living room/kitchenette, 2 bedrooms (1 double, 2 single and 1 child's bed), shower room, fireplace (wood supplied), carport, courtyard, and open ground. Mobile shops call; other shopping and restaurant at Chasseneuil.

Prices: low season   not available
          high season F 700
5 people
IGN 40

Booking: Charente Loisirs Accueil   **E**

16/2.27

Charente-Maritime

BAGNIZEAU An old village house, with traditional furnishings in a wine-growing area. The historic town of Saintes, with its Roman amphitheatre and many other distractions, is close enough for a day trip (35 km); the sea (70 km). Living room/kitchenette (1 double divan), 5 bedrooms (4 double, 2 single and 1 child's bed), bathroom, oil central heating, carport, enclosed garden with outdoor furniture. Mobile baker and butcher call; shopping and restaurant at Matha (3 km).

Prices:	low season	F 977/1136	12/13 people
	high season	F 1189	IGN 40

Booking: Charente-Maritime booking service   E

17/180

BOIS La Martinière A very pretty, well-renovated gîte, furnished in traditional country style, on a farm, 2.5 km from the village. Bicycles available. Plenty to see and do at Pons (12 km), a centre for the manufacture of Cognac and its apéritif, pineau; the sea (35 km). Living room/kitchenette (1 double divan), 1 bedroom (2 double beds), shower room, fireplace, heating, carport, ground with garden furniture and child's swing. Shopping in the village and restaurant at Saint-Genis (5 km); mobile baker, grocer and butcher call.

Prices:	low season	F 690/743	6 people
	high season	F 775	IGN 46

Booking: Charente-Maritime booking service   E

17/1214

BOUTENAC-TOUVENT Boutenac An old gîte with traditional rustic furnishings at the village centre. Pons (20 km) is an old château town, once a resting place for pilgrims on the road to Compostella – the pilgrims' hostel is still standing. The popular resort of Royan is at 20 km. Living room, kitchen, 3 bedrooms (2 double and 2 single beds), shower room, gas heating, garden. Shopping at Saint-Genis (10 km) or Pons, restaurant at Mortagne (4 km).

Prices:	low season	F 658/711	6 people
	high season	F 870/934	IGN 46

Booking: Charente-Maritime booking service   E

17/747

CHAMPAGNAC Chauvreau A single-storey renovated gîte with traditional furniture on a farm near the village (1 km). Local fishing and many beautiful footpaths. Jonzac (5 km) has swimming-pool and tennis court as well as a Romanesque church and a château. The sea (40 km). Living room/kitchenette (1 single divan), 2 bedrooms (3 double beds), shower room, no heating, garage, garden with barbecue. Shopping in the village and restaurant at 4 km.

Prices:	low season	not available	7 people
	high season	F 764/817	IGN 46

Booking: Charente-Maritime booking service   E

17/256

CHIVES Le Magnoux Situated at the edge of a small village (0.5 km) is this delightful, renovated and rustically furnished gîte. Much interesting Romanesque architecture in the region: Aulnay (18 km) has a twelfth-century church and ruined château. Swimming-pool and tennis at 15 km and the sea (70 km). Living room/kitchenette, 3 bedrooms (3 double, 1 single and 1 child's bed), shower room, open fire, gas heating, terrace, carport, enclosed courtyard and open ground with garden furniture. Mobile butcher, baker and grocer call; shopping in the village; a restaurant at Néré (10 km).

Prices:	low season	F679/786	7/8 people
	high season	F 977	IGN 40

Booking: Charente-Maritime booking service   E

17/57

Charente-Maritime

CORME-ROYAL A delightful, comfortable gîte in a former priory at the village centre where there is a remarkable twelfth-century church. The owners speak good English. Saintes (18 km) dates back to Roman times and the amphitheatre and Roman arch should not be missed; there are also some good museums. The Atlantic coast is at 18 km. Living room (1 single divan), kitchen, 2 bedrooms (1 double and 2 single beds), 2 bathrooms, fireplace, electric heating, garden with outdoor furniture. Restaurant and shopping in the village.

Prices:	low season	F1083/1189	**5 people**
	high season	F1719/1878	IGN 39

Booking: Charente-Maritime booking service   **E**

17/899

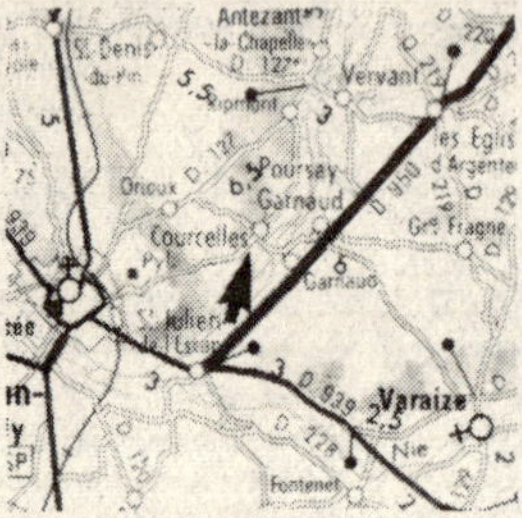

COURCELLES Orioux A newly built gîte in a hamlet 2 km from the village centre where you may buy fresh farm produce. Saint-Jean-d'Angély (approx. 8 km), a small harbour town on the river Boutonne, grew up around an old monastery founded by Pépin, King of Aquitaine. The sea is easily accessible at 54 km. Living room (TV), kitchen (washing machine), 3 bedrooms (2 double and 2 single beds) and 1 double divan), electric central heating, garden with lawn. Shopping and restaurant in the village.

Prices:	low season	F 799	**8 people**
	high season	F 1159	IGN 40

Booking: Charente-Maritime booking service   **E**

17/48

COUX Jean Vérat A comfortable gîte, renovated and furnished in traditional country style, 2 km from the village centre. Leisure facilities at the château town of Montendre-les-Pins (2 km) include a swimming-pool and tennis, and Baron Desqueyroux lake is at 6 km. The sea is close enough for a day trip at 70 km. Living room (1 double divan), kitchen (washing machine), 4 bedrooms (3 double and 2 single beds), shower room, open fire, electric heating, terrace, enclosed ground with garden furniture. Shopping and restaurant at Montendre.

Prices:	low season	F 643/849	**10 people**
	high season	F 1055	IGN 46

Booking: Charente-Maritime booking service   **E**

17/277

CRAM CHABAN Chaban A pretty, renovated house with traditional furnishings at the edge of a little village (1 km) near the Marais Poitevin region – the half-aquatic flatland known as 'Green Venice'. Leisure facilities at Mauzé-sur-le-Mignon (4 km) include tennis and swimming-pool. The sea (37 km). Living room/kitchenette, 3 bedrooms (2 double and 1 single bed), shower room, open fire, garage, open ground. Mobile baker, grocer and butcher call; other shopping and restaurant at Mauzé-sur-le-Mignon.

Prices:	low season	F 775/828	**5 people**
	high season	F 872	IGN 39

Booking: Charente-Maritime booking service   **E**

17/347

ECOYEUX A gîte in the friendly owners' old house, furnished in traditional style in the village. At 13 km, Saintes, erstwhile capital of the former Saintonge province, and still an important town with a wealth of sites and monuments. Try the local cognac. The sea (45 km). Living room/kitchenette (1 double divan), 2 bedrooms (2 double and 1 child's bed), shower room, fireplace, electric heating, shared garden. Shopping in the village and restaurant at Saintes.

Prices:	low season	F 595/658	**6/7 people**
	high season	F 796	IGN 40

Booking: Charente-Maritime booking service   **E**

17/109

Charente-Maritime

FONTAINES D'OZILLAC La Chaume A renovated and rustically furnished gîte on a working farm, 1 km from the village. There are several small recommended restaurants in the locality, serving regional specialities. Swimming-pool and tennis at Jonzac (8 km) which also has a château and Romanesque church. The coast (50 km). Living room (1 double divan), kitchen, 4 bedrooms (4 double and 3 single beds), 2 shower rooms, open fire, enclosed ground. Shopping and farm produce in the village; restaurant at 8 km.

Prices: low season   F 643/797   **13 people**
         high season   F 952   IGN 46
Booking: Charente-Maritime booking service   E
17/285

FONTENET A gîte with traditional, rustic furnishings in the English-speaking owners' delightful, renovated manor house with extensive grounds and private swimming-pool at the edge of the village (0.1 km). Canoes for hire at Saint-Jean-d'Angély (6 km) which has picturesque winding streets and a Renaissance fountain. The sea (67 km). Living room, kitchen, 3 bedrooms (2 double and 1 single bed), bathroom, heating, grounds with garden furniture and barbecue. Mobile grocer calls. Shopping in the village or at Saint-Jean-d'Angély where there is a restaurant.

Prices: low season   F 770   **5 people**
         high season   F 1078   IGN 40
Booking: Charente-Maritime booking service   E
17/35

FONTENET A detached, renovated house with traditional, rustic furnishings in the grounds of the property described above with private swimming-pool, at the edge of the village. Riding and tennis at Saint-Jean-d'Angély (6 km), a historic town dating back to Roman times. A forest at 18 km. Living room, kitchen, 2 bedrooms (1 double and 2 single beds), shower room, electric heating, grounds with garden furniture and barbecue. Mobile grocer calls. Shopping in the village or at Saint-Jean-d'Angély where there is a restaurant.

Prices: low season   F 763   **4 people**
         high season   F 827   IGN 40
Booking: Charente-Maritime booking service   E
17/39

LORIGNAC Rigal A single-storey gîte on a farm at the edge of the village (0.6 km), where you may buy fresh farm produce. Jonzac (20 km) is a centre for the manufacture of cognac and has several craft industries including pottery and porcelain decoration and good sports facilities. Pons (20 km) has opportunities for boating, swimming and tennis. Living room/kitchenette, 2 bedrooms (2 double, 1 single and 1 child's bed), shower room, open fire, electric heating, carport, ground. Shopping and restaurant in the village.

Prices: low season   F 748/841   **6 people**
         high season   F 934   IGN 46
Booking: Charente-Maritime booking service   E
17/167

MONTILS Jarlac A renovated and traditionally furnished gîte in a village of the Seugne valley, 10 km from Pons and 10 km from the historic city of Saintes. Boating on the Charente river nearby; the sea is 30 km away. Try the local cognac and pineau – the lesser known apéritif of the region. Living room (TV), kitchen, 2 bedrooms (1 double, 3 single and 1 child's bed), bathroom, heating, garage, garden with furniture. Mobile butcher, grocer and baker call; shopping (3 km) or at Pons where there are restaurants.

Prices: low season   F 849   **5/6 people**
         high season   F 952   IGN 40
Booking: Charente-Maritime booking service   E
17/170

Charente-Maritime

MONTILS Les Trois Ormeaux A gîte in an old renovated stone house, furnished in country style, 1 km from the centre of a quiet little village. At Cognac (10 km) see the *son-et-lumière* spectacle at François I's château and visit the Cognac distilleries. The sea is 40 km away. Living room, kitchen, 2 bedrooms (1 double, 3 single and 1 child's bed), shower room, electric heating, garage, courtyard. Shopping in the village.

Prices: low season   F 700/733   **5/6 people**
           high season   F 950/1058   *IGN 40*
Booking: Charente-Maritime booking service   **E**

17/136

PESSINES Le Repéré One of two gîtes in an old, renovated building in a hamlet a short walk from the village (2 km). Saintes (8 km) has a Roman amphitheatre and arch, good museums, cinemas, a theatre and a magnificent total of 38 restaurants! Look out for special summer entertainments here and at Royan (approx. 30 km). Living room/kitchenette, 2 bedrooms (1 double and 2 single beds), shower room, open fire, ground with garden furniture. Farm produce and shopping in the village, restaurant at 8 km.

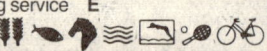

Prices: low season   F 1074   **4 people**
           high season   F 1203   *IGN 39*
Booking: Charente-Maritime booking service   **E**

17/198A

PESSINES Le Repéré A second gîte in the old renovated building described above. Royan (approx. 30 km) is a seaside resort with fine sandy beaches, extensive pine forests, riding, golf, tennis, nightclubs and a casino. Try the local seafood and butter. Both Royan and the old Roman town of Saintes (8 km) have a special summer programme of entertainments. Living room/kitchenette, 2 bedrooms (1 double and 2 single beds), shower room, fireplace, ground with garden furniture. Fresh farm produce and shopping in the village; restaurant at Saintes.

Prices: low season   F 1074   **4 people**
           high season   F 1203   *IGN 39*
Booking: Charente-Maritime booking service   **E**

17/198

PONS Fondurand A recently built gîte with traditional and rustic furnishings, outside the château town of Pons (2 km) where leisure facilities include a swimming-pool and tennis; see the nearby Renaissance Château d'Ussons. Do not miss historic Saintes (25 km) and the coast is 35 km away. Living room, kitchen, 3 bedrooms (2 double and 1 single bed), bathroom, electric heating, terrace. Shopping and restaurant in the village.

Prices: low season   F 993   **5 people**
           high season   F 1426/1642   *IGN 40*
Booking: Charente-Maritime booking service   **E**

17/114

SAINT-BONNET-SUR-GIRONDE Le Boucaud A gîte in a single-storey renovated old house, furnished in rustic style, standing 3 km from the village near the Poitevin marshes. Within a radius of 9 km you can enjoy river fishing, tennis and swimming-pool. The sea and beaches only 35 km away. Living room, kitchen, 2 bedrooms (2 double and 2 single beds), shower room, fireplace, electric heating, ground with garden furniture. A baker and butcher call. Other shopping in the village or at Mirambeau (8 km) where there is a restaurant.

Prices: low season   F 605/764   **6 people**
           high season   F 870   *IGN 46*
Booking: Charente-Maritime booking service   **E**

17/1208

Charente...

SAINT-CIERS-CHAMPAGNE Chez Cardot A renovated and traditionally furnished house lying in its own grounds, some 5 km from the village. At Jonzac (12 km), see the Château and Romanesque church and visit the cognac distilleries. A lake at 25 km; the sea (70 km). Living room (1 double divan), kitchen, 3 bedrooms (2 double and 3 single beds), shower room, open fire, electric heating, terrace, carport, garden, garage. Shopping and restaurant in the village.

Prices: low seasoon F 552/643
high season F 743

9 people
IGN 46

Booking: Charente-Maritime booking service E

17/1211

SAINT-FORT-SUR-GIRONDE Pradelle A well-renovated and maintained house standing on a farm 0.8 km from the village centre. At Jonzac (20 km) you can see the cognac distilleries, take a bicycle tour round the old churches or the craft workshops, and try boating on the Seugne. The sea is at 25 km. Living room, kitchen, 3 bedrooms (1 double and 6 single beds), bathroom, fireplace, electric central heating, terrace, carport, large grounds. Shopping and restaurant in the village, at Jonzac or Pons (20 km).

Prices: low season F 800/903
high season F 1057

8 people
IGN 46

Booking: Charente-Maritime booking service E

17/862

SAINT-GEORGES-DE-LONGUEPIERRE A village gîte, renovated and traditionally furnished, 3 km from the small town of Aulnay which has a twelfth-century church and ruined château. Saint-Jean-d'Angély (approx 23 km) is an old port on the river Boutonne and is set in undulating, woody countryside. The sea is at 60 km. Living room/kitchenette (1 double divan), 2 bedrooms (1 double and 3 single beds), shower room, fireplace, electric heating, enclosed ground with garden furniture. Farm produce in the village, shopping and restaurant at Aulnay.

Prices: low season F 774/881
high season F1042/1117

7 people
IGN 40

Booking: Charente-Maritime booking service E
17/903

SAINT-LHEURINE Chez Palisse A renovated gîte furnished in local style on a vineyard just 0.2 km from the village centre. Local river fishing and tennis; swimming-pool at 5 km and the interesting town of Pons (18 km) with its many historic buildings and municipal gardens laid out by Le Nôtre. Living room/kitchenette, 2 bedrooms (2 double and 2 single beds), 1 single divan on a mezzanine, shower room, electric central heating, garden. A restaurant in the village. Shopping at Archiac (5 km).

Prices: low season F 643/705
high season F 766/869

7 people
IGN 46

Booking: Charente-Maritime booking service E

17/244

SAINT-SULPICE-DE-ROYAN La Lande An interesting gîte in a well-renovated house with traditional furnishings, 1 km from the village centre. Local fishing, forest walks; the sea, beaches, and the cultural and sporting centre of Royan only 5 km away. Living room (1 double divan), kitchen, 1 bedroom and open landing (3 single beds), shower room, no heating, garage, ground. Shopping and restaurant in the village or at Royan.

Prices: low season F 669/674
high season F 880

5 people
IGN 39

Booking: Charente-Maritime booking service E

17/821

Charente-Maritime

SAINT-SULPICE-DE-ROYAN La Lande A traditionally furnished gîte on open ground where there is one other gîte. It is in a quiet position just 5 km from the popular seaside resort of Royan with its fishing and pleasure harbour, covered market, casino and other attractions. Living room/kitchenette, 2 bedrooms (1 double and 3 single beds), shower room, open fire, garage, garden and furniture. Shopping and restaurant in the village (1 km) or at Royan.

Prices:	low season	F 669	**5 people**
	high season	F 849	IGN 39

Booking: Charente-Maritime booking service   E

17/781

SOUBRAN Les Simons An old, traditionally furnished stone house which has been renovated 1.5 km from the village centre. The château town of Montendre (12 km) has a lake, open-air theatre and unusual market halls designed by Eiffel's nephew. The sea (55 km). Living room/kitchenette (TV, 1 single divan), 2 bedrooms (1 double, 2 single and 1 child's bed), shower room, fireplace, electric heating, garage, garden. Shopping and restaurant at Mirambeau (6 km).

Prices:	low season	F 828/1003	**5/6 people**
	high season	F 1055/1106	IGN 46

Booking: Charente-Maritime booking service   E

17/299

TUGERAS-SAINT-MAURICE-DE-LAURANCANNES Saint Maurice A picturesque renovated gîte furnished in local country style near the village centre. The little town of Montendre at 9 km not only offers historic monuments to visit but a lake, a château, swimming-pool, tennis, riding, cinema, dancing and local wine and cognac. Living room/kitchenette (washing machine), 3 bedrooms (3 double, 1 single and 1 child's bed), shower room, open fire, terrace, garage, private garden with outdoor furniture. Grocer and baker call. Shops and restaurant in the village.

Prices:	low season	F 605/690	**7/8 people**
	high season	F 828	IGN 46

Booking: Charente-Maritime booking service   E

17/231

VANZAC Petit Moulin A traditionally furnished and renovated gîte on a mixed farm in the village. Visit the cognac distilleries at Jonzac (12 km) and the château and Romanesque church. A lake and pine forest at Montendre (7 km). The sea and beaches (60 km). Living room/kitchenette, 2 bedrooms (1 double and 2 single beds), shower room, fireplace, gas central heating, garage,, garden with furniture and child's swing. Shopping in the village (0.5 km) and restaurant at Jonzac.

Prices:	low season	F 632	**4 people**
	high season	F 764	IGN 46

Booking: Charente-Maritime booking service   E

17/282

VILLARS-EN-PONS La Rangearderie A spacious, old, traditionally furnished house near the village centre. The château town of Pons (6 km), set on a hill above the river Seugne, has a remarkable twelfth-century keep and other sites; leisure amenities there include a swimming-pool and tennis. The Atlantic coast is just 35 km away. Living room, kitchen, 3 bedrooms (1 double and 4 single beds), shower room, gas heating, garden with furniture. Farm produce in the village; other shopping and restaurant at Pons.

Prices:	low season	F 817	**6 people**
	high season	F 977	IGN 39

Booking: Charente-Maritime booking service   E

17/616

Deux-Sèvres

AZAY-SUR-THOUET La Jaufrère A renovated house with traditional furnishings in a hamlet, 3 km from the village. Local river fishing. A swimming-pool and Les Effres lake (bathing, sailing, pedalos and miniature golf) at Secondigny, the magnificent Secondigny forest (good for picincs) (5 km). The sea (80 km). Living room, kitchen, 2 bedrooms (2 double and 2 single beds), shower room, fireplace, oil central heating, garden. Linen available. Farm produce and shopping in the village; mobile baker calls; other shopping at Secondigny.

Prices:	low season	F 640/780	**6 people**
	high season	F 875/955	IGN 33

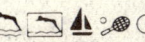

Booking: Deux-Sèvres booking service E
79/602

AZAY-SUR-THOUET La Jousselinière An attractively renovated cottage with traditional country-style furnishings in a hamlet, 3 km from the village. Plenty of leisure facilities in this region of lakes and forests. Parthenay (10 km) is a lovely old town with a ruined thirteenth-century château and half-timbered houses. Living room/kitchenette (TV), 3 bedrooms (2 double and 1 single bed), bathroom, terrace, garden with outdoor furniture. Linen available. Mobile baker calls; farm produce, other shopping and restaurant in the village or at Secondigny (4 km).

Prices:	low season	F 510/780	**5 people**
	high season	F 875/975	IGN 33

Booking: Deux-Sèvres booking service E
79/603

LA BOISSIERE-EN-GATINE A substantial old house, simply furnished with private fish pond, near the village centre. Secondigny forest (9 km) has marked footpaths; Les Effres lake at Secondigny offers sailing, bathing, fishing and tennis. Living room, kichen, 4 bedrooms (3 double and 4 single beds), bathroom and shower, fireplace, central heating, carport, garden and enclosed ground. Mobile shops call; fresh milk and eggs from the owners; other shopping and restaurant in the village or at the château town of Mazières-en-Gatine (6 km).

Prices:	low season	F 690	**10 people**
	high season	F 870/930	IGN 33

Booking: Deux-Sèvres booking service E
79/606

LE BOURDET A spacious, renovated house with traditional furnishings, adjoining the owners' home, near the village centre. The fascinating Marais Poitevin, the beautiful verdant marshland where punts are the main form of transport, is just 8 km away. Visit too, Chizé forest (12 km) and the coast at 45 km. Living room, kitchen, 4 bedrooms (1 double and 4 single beds), shower room, oil-fired central heating, garden. Farm produce in the village; other shopping and restaurant at Mauzé-sur-le-Mignon (6 km).

Prices:	low season	F 630/800	**6 people**
	high season	F 920/980	IGN 39

Booking: Deux-Sèvres booking service E
79/701

LA CHAPELLE-THIREUIL An attractively renovated and traditionally furnished semi-detached house at the village centre. Bicycles for hire at Beugnon (6 km). Take a trip to the vast marshland of the Marais Poitevin (25 km), a work of land reclamation which started way back in the thirteenth century. Secondigny lake and forest are within 16 km. Living room (1 double divan), kitchen, 2 bedrooms (2 double beds), bathroom, fireplace, terrace with outdoor furniture. Mobile butcher, baker and other shopping in the village or at Coulonges-sur-L'Autize (10 km) where there is a restaurant.

Prices:	low season	F 350/600	**6 people**
	high season	F 700	IGN 33

Booking: Deux-Sèvres booking service E
79/608

Deux-Sèvres

LA CHAPELLE-THIREUIL Moulin de Billette This delightful traditionally furnished gîte is an eighteenth-century mill. It is in a slightly isolated spot, 2 km from the village. Fishing in the mill stream. A large covered market each Tuesday at Coulonges-sur-l'Autize (8 km); Mervent-Vouvant forest (18 km) has a zoo and picnic sites; the sea (65 km). Living room, kitchen (washing and washing-up machines), 3 bedrooms (1 double, 4 single and 1 child's bed), shower room, open fire, electric central heating, enclosed ground. Linen available. Farm produce and other shopping in the village or at Fenioux (4 km).

Prices: low season F 650/700
high season F 825/940
7 people
IGN 33
Booking: Deux-Sèvres booking service E
79/611

LA CHAPELLE-THIREUIL La Ronfraire A small gîte, renovated and simply furnished, just outside the village (1 km). Swimming-pool and good market at Coulonges-sur-l'Autize (11 km), which has a Renaissance château; sailing at Mervent lake (20 km). The Atlantic coast (100 km). Living room/kitchenette, 1 bedroom (2 double and 1 single bed), shower room, fireplace, central heating, garage, garden. Linen available. Mobile baker calls; farm produce from the owners; other shopping in the village or at Fenioux (6 km).

Prices: low season F 385/495
high season F 585/655
5 people
IGN 33
Booking: Deux-Sèvres booking service E
79/610

CHICHE La Gorge A detached, renovated and traditionally furnished gîte on a working farm, some 6 km from the village which boasts a twelfth-century church. Bressuire (12 km) also has many places of historical interest including a ruined feudal château. Les Effres lake (20 km). Living room (1 double divan), kitchen, 2 bedrooms (2 double, 1 child's bed), shower room, central heating, terrace, garage, enclosed ground with garden furniture. Linen available (F40 per set per week). Shopping and restaurant in the village.

Prices: low season F 455/540
high season F 700/740
7 people
IGN 33
Booking: Deux-Sèvres booking service E
79/402

COULONGES-SUR-L'AUTIZE Pain Perdu A large, traditionally furnished gîte, adjoining the owners' home at the edge of the town (1 km). Coulonges' large Tuesday market offers fresh eggs and poultry. Visit the old town of Niort (22 km), whose history is closely linked with England; see the fine twelfth-century keep, now a museum. The sea (70 km). Living room, kitchen, 3 bedrooms (3 double, 2 single and 1 child's bed), bathroom, open fire, central heating, garage, enclosed ground. Linen available. Shopping and restaurant in the town or at Secondigny (20 km).

Prices: low season F 515/605
high season F 755/830
9 people
IGN 33
Booking: Deux-Sèvres booking service E
79/617

LA CRECHE Tressauves This renovated and traditionally furnished house has the benefit of a large, well-kept garden. Le Lambon lake and leisure park (7 km) has sailing facilities (tuition available) and a restaurant. Plenty of cultural and leisure amenities at the département capital of Niort (14 km). Living room (1 double divan), kichen, 2 bedrooms (1 double, 1 single bed), bathroom, open fire, gas central heating. Linen available (F40 per set per week). Shopping and restaurant in the village (3 km); mobile baker calls.

Prices: low season F 515/660
high season F 780/810
5 people
IGN 33
Booking: Deux-Sèvres booking service E
79/719

Deux-Sèvres

EXOUDUN La Maisonnette A well-renovated cottage, adjoining the owners' home, 3 km from the centre of Exoudun, a typical Poitevin village. At La Mothe-Saint-Héray (2 km), you can visit the dairy and try their *tourteau fromager*, a kind of cake made with cheese. Living room, (TV, 1 double divan), kitchen (washing machine), 3 bedrooms (1 double, 2 single and 1 child's bed), bathroom, oil-fired central heating, garden with outdoor furniture. Linen available. Mobile baker calls; other shopping and restaurant at La Mothe-Saint-Héray.

Prices:	low season	F 560/630	**7 people**
	high season	F 690/830	IGN 33

Booking: Deux-Sèvres booking service **E**

79/805

FENERY La Baudrière A renovated and simply furnished gîte, adjoining the owners' home on their mixed farm where you may buy fresh eggs and milk, 1 km from the village centre. Parthenay (10 km) boasts the largest weekly cattle market in France. See the town's imposing ruined château, and ramparts and towers built by the English in 1202. Living room (1 double divan), kitchen, 3 bedrooms (4 double beds), shower room, oil heating, carport, garden with furniture. Linen available. Mobile shops call; other shopping at Clesse (4 km).

Prices:	low season	F 410/585	**8 people**
	high season	F 705/820	IGN 33

Booking: Deux-Sèvres booking service **E**

79/619

FENIOUX La Butaudrie A modern gîte with traditional furnishings near the owners' home and another gîte, at the heart of the village. Bicycles for hire, table tennis, pony rides and child's swings at the gîte. Secondigny forest (5 km) and lake (9 km). The sea (90 km). Living room/kitchenette (TV and washing machine available), 2 bedrooms (1 double, 2 single and 1 cot), shower room, central heating, terrace, garage, garden. Linen available. Shopping from mobile shops, in the village or at Secondigny (9 km). Owners offer evening meals.

Prices:	low season	F 515/625	**5 people**
	high season	F 775/845	IGN 33

Booking: Deux-Sèvres booking service **E**

79/620

LA FOYE-MONJAULT Le Puyroux A small, renovated house with traditional furnishings, close to another gîte, 2.5 km from the village centre. Chizé forest at 8 km has picnic areas, marked footpaths and a zoo. Le Grand Mauduit leisure complex at Marigny (7 km) offers pony rides, miniature golf and a museum. The coast (45 km). Living room/kitchenette (TV, small washing machine, 1 double divan), 1 bedroom (1 double, 1 single bed), shower room, central heating, small garden with furniture. Shopping at Beauvoir-sur-Niort (6 km).

Prices:	low season	F 490/595	**5 people**
	high season	F 655/695	IGN 39

Booking: Deux-Sèvres booking service **E**

79/706

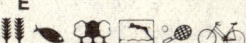

GOURGE La Chagnelle Anglers will enjoy this little gîte as it has a private fishing pond. Renovated and traditionally furnished, it lies in its own garden near the owners' farm. Wind-surfing at Cebron reservoir (1 km); a swimming-pool and tennis at the picturesque old town of Airvault (9 km). Living room, kitchen, 1 bedroom (2 double beds, 1 cot), bathroom, fireplace, central heating. Linen available. Dairy produce from the owners; other shopping and restaurant in the village (2 km) or at Saint-Loup-sur-Thouet (5 km).

Prices:	low season	F 470/605	**5 people**
	high season	F 725/795	IGN 33

Booking: Deux-Sèvres booking service **E**

79/625

Deux-Sèvres

LIMALONGES Chez Dorange One of two renovated gîtes with traditional furnishings in a house, situated near a wood, outside the village (2.5 km). Sauzé-Vaussais (8 km) has a leisure complex with miniature golf, swimming-pool, tennis and bicycle hire. Ruffec forest is at 10 km. Living room/kitchenette, 3 bedrooms (1 double and 3 single beds), bathroom, open fire, central heating, enclosed ground (shared with the other gîte). Mobile butcher and baker; fresh eggs, milk and poultry in the village; other shopping at Civray (7 km).

Prices:	low season	F 505/640	**5 people**
	high season	F 850/910	IGN 40

Booking: Deux-Sèvres booking service   E

79/807

LORIGNE Le Petit Portail An attractive gîte, renovated and traditionally furnished, 2 km from the village and just 4 km from Sauzé-Vaussais leisure centre where you may hire bicycles to explore the area. Visit the ancient Abbey at nearby Celles-sur-Belle and the Merovingian tombs at Pers. Living room (TV, 1 double divan), kitchen, 2 bedrooms (2 double and 1 single bed), bathroom, open fire, central heating, carport, garden with barbecue and extensive enclosed ground. Linen available. Shopping at Sauzé-Vaussais.

Prices:	low season	F 545/735	**7 people**
	high season	F 920/975	IGN 40

Booking: Deux-Sèvres booking service   E

79/808

MONCOUTANT Le Puy Cadoré A spacious sixteenth-century house which has been well-renovated and furnished in rustic fashion – ideal for a large family. Private fishing available in its extensive grounds. Bathing at La Tardière lake (18 km) and the Atlantic is just close enough for a day trip at 80 km. Living room (TV), kitchen (washing machine), 5 bedrooms (2 double, 3 single and 2 child's beds), bathroom, fireplace, terrace, garden furniture. Shopping and restaurant in the village (4 km) or at Bressuire (14 km).

Prices:	low season	F 900	**9 people**
	high season	F 1035	IGN 33

Booking: Deux-Sèvres booking service   E

79/414

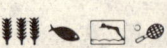

MOUTIERS-SOUS-ARGENTON La Grange A traditionally furnished, renovated house lying in a hamlet, 2 km from the village. Private fishing on the property and bicycles for hire. Argenton-Château (10 km) has a lake and tennis courts; the lovely château town of Thouars (14 km) on the river Thouet, has a museum of local history. Living room (2 single beds), kitchen, 4 bedrooms (2 double, 3 single and 1 cot), 2 shower rooms, open fire (wood supplied), oil-fired central heating, extensive ground with garden furniture. Shopping in the village.

Prices:	low season	F 565/670	**10 people**
	high season	F 810/920	IGN 33

Booking: Deux-Sèvres booking service   E

79/407

LA PETITE-BOISSIERE Le Tillac A renovated and traditionally furnished gîte, right by a river (fishing nearby at a lock), 3 km from the village. The château town of Mauléon has an abbey, ruined during the religious wars but restored in the eighteenth century and now housing a museum. Bathing and sailing at Pouzauges (18 km). Living room/kitchenette (1 double divan), 2 bedrooms (1 double and 2 single beds), bathroom, fireplace, oil central heating, carport, garden. Mobile baker calls: farm produce in the village, and other shopping at Mauléon (3 km).

Prices:	low season	F 605/755	**5 people**
	high season	F 845/965	IGN 33

Booking: Deux-Sèvres booking service   E

79/409

Deux-Sèvres

POUGNE-HERISSON Le Patis A traditionally furnished gîte in a renovated house, 2 km from the village centre. There are four lakes, all with good facilities, within a radius of 22 km. The busy town of Parthenay (14 km) has retained much of its medieval character. Living room/kitchenette (washing machine), 2 bedrooms (3 double and 1 single bed), shower room, fireplace, heating, terrace, enclosed garden. Mobile baker calls; shopping in the village or at Secondigny (4.5 km) where there is a restaurant.

Prices:	low season	F 565	**7 people**
	high season	F 745/875	IGN 33

Booking: Deux-Sèvres booking service **E**
79/630

PRISSE-LA-CHARRIERE Le Petit Bousseau A pretty cottage, renovated and traditionally furnished, 1.5 km from the village centre. Chizé forest and zoo at 2 km has good picnicking areas. Explore the Marais-Poitevin, the country of the "great green silence" and a paradise for fishermen (20 km). Kitchen, bed-sitting room (1 double, 1 single bed), 1 bedroom (1 double bed), bathroom, open fire, oil-fired central heating, garden with outdoor furniture. Shopping in the village or at Beauvoir-sur-Niort (3 km) where there is a restaurant.

Prices:	low season	F 795	**5 people**
	high season	F 960/1050	IGN 40

Booking: Deux-Sèvres booking service **E**
79/710

SAINT-COUTANT Germain A very unusual gîte with traditional furnishings in a fifteenth-century tower where the owners have another gîte next door. It is 2 km from the village and 4 km from Lezay (a swimming-pool and tennis courts) where you should try the local cheese and *Torteau Fromager* (cake made with cheese). Living room, kitchen, 2 bedrooms (1 double, 1 single and 1 child's bed), bathroom and shower, open fire, electric heating, garden and courtyard (shared with the other gîte). Shopping and restaurant at Lezay or at Melle (13 km).

Prices:	low season	F 425/515	**4 people**
	high season	F 680/775	IGN 40

Booking: Deux-Sèvres booking service **E**
79/815

SAINT-HILAIRE-LA-PALUD Montfaucon A very attractive house which has been renovated and traditionally furnished, 1 km from the village in the lovely Marais Poitevin region. The popular resort of La Rochelle, a delightful harbour town on the Atlantic coast is an easy day trip at 45 km. Living room/kitchenette, 3 bedrooms (2 double and 2 single beds), shower room, fireplace, central heating, terrace, garage, garden with outdoor furniture, barbecue and punt available. Shopping in the village or at Mauzé-sur-le-Mignon (9 km).

Prices:	low season	F 700/830	**6 people**
	high season	F 950/970	IGN 39

Booking. Deux-Sèvres booking service **E**
79/712

SAINT-HILAIRE-LA-PALUD Montfaucon A large, renovated and traditionally furnished house, situated in the Marais Poitevin, that green marshy wonderland, where a punt (available from the owners) is the main way to get around. Bicycles for hire and tennis in the village (1 km) and leisure centre (miniature golf, swimming-pool, etc.) at La Garette (14 km). Living room, kitchen, 3 bedrooms (3 double beds), shower room, fireplace, electric central heating, garage, garden. Mobile baker calls; farm produce and other shopping in the village or at Mauzé-sur-le-Mignon (9 km).

Prices:	low season	F 620/795	**6 people**
	high season	F 910/970	IGN 39

Booking: Deux-Sèvres booking service **E**
79/713

8

Deux-Sèvres

SAINT-MAURICE-LA-FOUGEREUSE La Fougereuse A ground-floor gîte with traditionall furnishings in a former abbey that dates from the time of Charlemagne! It lies in its own ground, 1.6 km from the village centre. Try wind-surfing at Beaurepaire lake (6 km) or visit the Loire châteaux, just 40 km away. Living room/kitchenette, 3 bedrooms (3 double beds), shower room, fireplace, heating. Linen available (F40 per set per week). Shopping in the village or at Argenton-Château (7 km) where there is a restaurant.

Prices: low season F 650
high season F 760/875

6 people
IGN 33

Booking: Deux-Sèvres booking service E
79/412

SAINT-PARDOUX Le Bois Set near a mixed farm is this renovated and traditionally furnished cottage, some 4 km from the village. Fishing in river Thouet (3 km); Secondigny forest and Les Effres lake (bathing, sailing, pedalos, etc.) are at 12 km. Visit historic Niort, capital of the département (25 km approx.). Living room/kitchenette (1 single divan and 1 single bed), 2 bedrooms (3 double beds), shower room, fireplace, central heating, enclosed ground. Linen available. Farm produce and other shopping in the village or at Parthenay (8 km).

Prices: low season F 435/560
high season F 700/750

8 people
IGN 33

Booking: Deux-Sèvres booking service E
79/634

SAINT-PARDOUX Russeil A renovated gîte with country-style furnishings, in a very peaceful farming hamlet of just two houses. The mediaeval town of Parthenay (11 km) was once a resting place for pilgrims on the road to Compostella in Spain; leisure amenities there include a swimming-pool and tennis. Living room/kitchenette (1 single divan), 2 bedrooms (1 double and 2 single beds), shower room, fireplace, electric heating, garage and enclosed ground. Linen available. Mobile butcher, baker and produce from a neighbouring farm; other shopping in the village (4 km); restaurants at Parthenay.

Prices: low season F 490/735
high season F 805/875

5 people
IGN 33

Booking: Deux-Sèvres booking service E
79/635

SEPVRET Logis de Brégion A gîte with traditional, country-style furnishings in a former gatehouse near the owners' mixed farm, 2 km from the village. Try the local speciality, *Tourteau Fromager* a cake made of goats' cheese and eggs. Visitors to Niort (40 km approx.) in May, can see the agricultural show. Living room (1 double divan), kitchen (washing machine), 4 bedrooms (2 double and 5 single beds), shower room, open fire, heating, carport, open ground. Mobile shops, and milk and eggs from the owners; other shopping and restaurant at Lezay (7 km).

Prices: low season F 650/890
high season F 995/1100

11 people
IGN 40

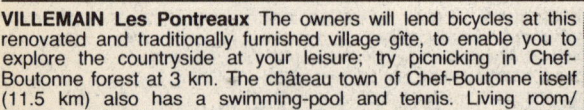

Booking: Deux-Sèvres booking service E
79/827

VILLEMAIN Les Pontreaux The owners will lend bicycles at this renovated and traditionally furnished village gîte, to enable you to explore the countryside at your leisure; try picnicking in Chef-Boutonne forest at 3 km. The château town of Chef-Boutonne itself (11.5 km) also has a swimming-pool and tennis. Living room/kitchenette (washing machine, 1 double divan), 2 bedrooms (2 double, 1 single and 1 child's bed), shower room, fireplace, central heating, carport, garden with furniture. Linen available. Shopping at Couture-d'Argenson (3 km).

Prices: low season F 465/545
high season F 655/755

8 people
IGN 40

Booking: Deux-Sèvres booking service E
79/830

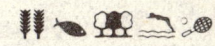

Vienne

ANCHE Fonsalmois A first-floor gîte furnished in traditional style in a renovated building on a farm where the owners raise sheep and boar. The village is 2.5 km. Vivonne (8 km) is a rural holiday resort and riverside leisure facilities there include bathing, children's games, pedalos and tennis. Living room (1 double divan), kitchen, 2 bedrooms (4 single and 1 child's bed), bathroom, electric central heating, carport, ground with garden furniture. Milk from the owners, mobile baker calls and shopping in Vivonne.

Prices:	low season	F 485/540	**6/7 people**
	high season	F 710/745	*IGN 40*

Booking: Vienne Loisirs Accueil E
86/432

BERRIE Le Haut Nueil A ground-floor gîte in an old, renovated house, simply furnished and lying in a hamlet 2 km from the village. There is a lake for sailing and bathing at 24 km, riding at 18 km and the Loire châteaux are within touring distance. Living room, kitchen, 2 bedrooms (2 large single and 1 single bed, 1 child's bed), shower room, electric central heating, carport, enclosed ground with garden furniture. Eggs and wine in the village, mobile shops call, shopping and restaurant at 6 km.

Prices:	low season	F 500/590	**3/6 people**
	high season	F 685/705	*IGN 33*

Booking: Vienne Loisirs Accueil E
86/299

BLANZAY La Cotterie A ground-floor gîte in an extension of the owners' house which has been renovated and traditionally furnished, situated on a livestock farm outside the village (2 km). Civray (9 km), a rural tourist centre in the Charente valley, has prehistoric caves, a swimming-pool, tennis, riding and fishing. Living room, kitchen, 2 bedrooms (4 large single beds, 1 child's bed and a cot), bathroom, gas central heating, terrace, garden with furniture. Shopping in the village; mobile butcher, greengrocer and baker call; farm produce from the owners.

Prices:	low season	F 580/675	**4/9 people**
	high season	F 785/825	*IGN 40*

Booking: Vienne Loisirs Accueil E
86/108

BRION Le Chilloc An old detached house simply furnished in traditional style 4 km from the village. Gençay (11 km) has thirteenth-century and Renaissance chateaux to see and, being situated at the confluence of two rivers, has good watersports facilities and pleasant walks. Living room (1 double divan), kitchen, 2 bedrooms (1 double and 2 single beds), shower room, wood central heating, carport, large enclosed ground. Linen available, F25 per pair per week. Mobile baker calls, shopping and restaurant at 7 km or at Gençay.

Prices:	low season	F 470/540	**6 people**
	high season	F 710/725	*IGN 34*

Booking: Vienne Loisirs Accueil E
86/442

CHAMPAGNE-SAINT-HILAIRE Chaumes A gîte in an old, lovingly restored house, with rustic furniture, next-door to the owners' home, on a mixed farm at 5 km from the village, in a peacefully isolated setting. River bathing (3 km); fêtes nearby throughout the summer and interesting abbeys to visit. Living room/kitchenette (1 double divan), 1 large bedroom (2 double and 1 single bed), bathroom, electric heating, garage, courtyard and open prairie land. Farm produce from the owners; other shopping and restaurant in the village.

Prices:	low season	F 465/490	**7 people**
	high season	F 620/650	*IGN 40*

Booking: Vienne Loisirs Accueil E
86/170

Vienne

CHATEAU-LARCHER An old semi-detached village house, simply furnished in traditional style, in its own enclosed ground and owned by the local butcher. Vivonne (5 km) is a rural holiday resort with good river fishing. Poitiers (approx. 25 km) is the regional capital, an old university town with a long history, and not to be missed! Living room (1 double divan), kitchen (washing machine), 2 bedrooms (1 double, 1 large single and 1 child's bed), shower room, fireplace, oil and gas heating, enclosed garden. Mobile greengrocer and fishmonger call, shopping and restaurant in the village or at Vivonne.

Prices: low season   F 485/540   **5/7 people**
          high season   F 710/745   *IGN 34*
Booking: Vienne Loisirs Accueil   **E**
86/308

JAZENEUIL La Quinterie A smart, renovated house with rustic furniture. Bicycles for hire and games at the gîte. Good local fishing; swimming-pool at 9 km. Conducted walks in Saint-Sauvant forest available (8 km). Living room (TV), kitchen (washing machine), 3 bedrooms (1 double and 3 single beds), bathroom and shower, open fire, electric heating, terrace, garage, garden with furniture and barbecue. Linen available. Shopping and restaurant in the village or at Lusignan (5 km).

Prices: low season   F 835/915   **5 people**
          high season   F 1025/1075   *IGN 34*
Booking: Mme R. BERTRAND, La Quinterie, Jazeneuil, 86600 Lusignan. Tel. (49) 53 50 18.   **E**
86/188

JOURNET A substantial old, renovated house in the village centre with its own small, private courtyard, owned by local farmers. This is a most attractive region with lush, hilly countryside and particularly rich in ecclesiastical architecture. Fishing at La Trimouille (6 km) and a lake for sailing at 30 km. Living room, kitchen, 3 bedrooms (4 double and 1 child's bed), bathroom, oil and electric heating. Mobile butcher and baker call, shopping in the village or at La Trimouille.

Prices: low season   F 695/800   **8/9 people**
          high season   F 930/975   *IGN 34*
Booking: Vienne Loisirs Accueil   **E**

86/39

MONCONTOUR Montjean A ground-floor gîte in an old mill beside the river Dive, now renovated and rustically furnished, near the village centre (0.8 km). Loudun (19 km) is an interesting town with much old architecture and Guesnes (16 km) offers miniature golf, fishing and go-karting amongst other activities. Living room/kitchenette, 3 bedrooms (2 double and 2 single beds), bathroom, fireplace, electric heating, carport, open ground with furniture. Linen available (F25 per pair per week). Farm produce, shopping and restaurant in the village.

Prices: low season   F 620/775   **6 people**
          high season   F 860/900   *IGN 33*
Booking: Vienne Loisirs Accueil   **E**

86/455

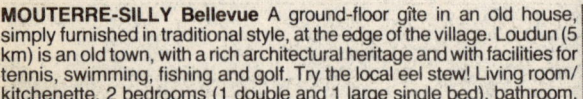

MOUTERRE-SILLY Bellevue A ground-floor gîte in an old house, simply furnished in traditional style, at the edge of the village. Loudun (5 km) is an old town, with a rich architectural heritage and with facilities for tennis, swimming, fishing and golf. Try the local eel stew! Living room/kitchenette, 2 bedrooms (1 double and 1 large single bed), bathroom, electric heating, enclosed ground with garden furniture. Mobile shops call, farm produce in the village, shopping and restaurant at Loudun.

Prices: low season   F 455/525   **3/4 people**
          high season   F 675/705   *IGN 34*
Booking: Vienne Loisirs Accueil   **E**

86/436

Vienne

MOUTERRE-SILLY Beaussay A simply furnished gîte in the owners' renovated house in a hamlet in a lovely wine-producing region within easy reach of the Loire châteaux. The fine old town of Loudun (5 km) is rich in historic monuments and has many leisure amenities, including swimming-pool, riding and tennis. Living room/kitchenette, 2 adjoining bedrooms (1 double and 2 large single beds), bathroom, oil-fired central heating, balcony, small courtyard. Linen available. Mobile baker calls; farm produce in the village, shopping at Loudun where there are restaurants.

Prices:	low season	F 455/525	**4/6 people**
	high season	F 675/705	IGN 34

Booking: Vienne Loisirs Accueil E
86/250

OUZILLY-VIGNOLLES Sauzeau A very old, wattle and daub cottage, renovated and simply furnished, on a farm in a hamlet which dates back to the thirteenth century. Moncontour (3 km) is a pleasant village in the Dive valley with a fine lake for bathing, sailing and fishing (especially trout). Living room/kitchenette, 2 bedrooms (3 large single beds), shower room, open fire, wood stove, garage, enclosed ground. Linen available (F 25 per set, per week approx.). Mobile butcher calls; farm produce available; other shopping and restaurant in Moncontour.

Prices:	low season	F 455/525	**3/6 people**
	high season	F 675/705	IGN 34

Booking: Vienne Loisirs Accueil E
86/127

LA ROCHE-RIGAULT La Raye A simply furnished, renovated gîte adjoining the bachelor owner's own home on his farm where he grows tobacco, cereal crops and raises poultry. Riding and tennis at 6 km; Moncontour, with its superb lake for bathing and sailing, is at 23 km. Living room/kitchenette, 2 bedrooms (1 double, 2 single and 1 child's bed), bathroom, electric heating, terrace, garden with outdoor furniture. Mobile shops call and farm produce in the village where there is a restaurant; other shopping (7 km) or at Loudun (10 km).

Prices:	low season	F 540/650	**4/5 people**
	high season	F 740/775	IGN 34

Booking: Vienne Loisirs Accueil E
86/219

SAINT SAUVANT La Teilleé An old detached house, simply furnished in traditional style 4 km from the village. Lusignan (15 km) is on the river Vonne and offers bathing, tennis, riding, canoeing, and local crafts include basketmaking, pottery and weaving. There are guided walks with the ranger through the St Sauvant forest. Living room (1 single divan, kitchen, 3 bedrooms (1 double, 2 single beds and a cot), bathroom, fireplace, carport, large grounds. Mobile baker calls, farm produce, shopping and restaurant in the village.

Prices:	low season	F 695/800	**5 people**
	high season	F 930/975	IGN 34

Booking: Vienne Loisirs Accueil E
86/381

SAINT SAUVANT Vitré A ground-floor gîte in an old, renovated house, furnished in simple country style 2 km from the village. Lusignan (11 km) offers walks on marked footpaths, public gardens with children's games, canoeing and tennis. Guided forest walks in the St Sauvant forest. Living room (2 single divans), kitchen, 1 bedroom (1 double and 1 single bed), shower room, fireplace, garage, large grounds. Farm produce (including goats' cheese), shopping and restaurant in the village.

Prices:	low season	F 435/480	**5 people**
	high season	F 575/605	IGN 34

Booking: Vienne Loisirs Accueil E
86/85

Vienne

SAVIGNY-SOUS-FAYE A large old house, renovated and simply but fairly comfortably furnished, near the village centre. Châtellerault (20 km) has a motor museum and many leisure amenities, including sailing and other water sports, swimming-pool, etc. Visitors in August can enjoy the melon festival at Vendeuvre (15 km approx.). Living room/kitchenette, 3 bedrooms (2 double and 1 single bed), bathroom, open fire, balcony, garage, garden. Farm produce, shopping and restaurant in the village (0.25 km) or at Lencloitre (8 km).

Prices:	low season	F 565	**5 people**
	high season	F 735/775	*IGN 34*

Booking: Vienne Loisirs Accueil   **E**

86/155

SCORBE-CLAIRVAUX Les Terrasses This charming house recently built and furnished in traditional, country style lies in a little wood on a country road with no traffic – so peace and quiet are assured. Châtellerault (10 km) with its fifteenth-century château and many leisure amenities, is well worth a visit. Living room (1 double divan), kitchen, 1 bedroom (1 double bed), shower room, open fire, central heating, terrace, garden and open ground. Linen available. Shopping and restaurant in the village (1 km). Farm produce available locally.

Prices:	low season	F 505/585	**4 people**
	high season	F 680/710	*IGN 34*

Booking: Vienne Loisirs Accueil   **E**

86/316

SOMMIERES DU CLAIN A gîte in the owners' large old renovated village house furnished in country style. Gençay (12 km) is a pleasant town lying on the confluence of the rivers Clouere and Belle and offers good fishing, walks and tennis. Swimming-pool at 16 km and riding at 18 km. Living room, kitchen, 2 bedrooms (1 double and 1 single bed), shower room, electric heating, shared garden and field. Linen available. Local dairy produce, shopping and restaurant in the village.

Prices:	low season	F 540	**3 people**
	high season	F 710/745	*IGN 40*

Booking: Vienne Loisirs Accueil   **E**

86/396

VARENNES Les Touches A ground-floor gîte in an old house, now renovated and simply furnished in traditional style. Mirebeau (5 km) offers summer fêtes and donkey racing and there are good weekly markets and sports facilities at Poitou (12 km). A lake for sailing and bathing at 20 km. Living room/kitchenette (1 double divan), 2 bedrooms (2 double and 1 single bed), bathroom, fireplace, electric heating, enclosed ground. Mobile butcher, baker, grocer and fishmonger call, farm produce and restaurant in the village, shopping at Mirebeau.

Prices:	low season	F 540/650	**7 people**
	high season	F 740/775	*IGN 34*

Booking: Vienne Loisirs Accueil   **E**

86/278

AVAILLES LIMOUZINE Logis de la Mothe *Chambre d'hôte* accommodation in a substantial old house standing in its own shady walled garden in a village. L'Isle Jourdain (14 km) is a pretty little town offering fishing, canoeing, sailing, windsurfing, tennis, swimming, riding and walks on marked footpaths. Four rooms available: 3 rooms with 1 double bed each and 1 room with 1 double and 1 single bed. Private shower room and bathroom available (supplement), other 2 rooms share a bathroom; shared living room. Open all year. Shopping and restaurant at Confolens (14 km) or St Saviol (30 km).

Prices: 1p F 88/98, 2p F 108/118, 3p F 128   **9 people**
IGN 40
Booking: Vienne Loisirs Accueil   **E**

86/CH/86/27

Vienne

COUHE Valence *Chambre d'hôte* accommodation in a fine old villa standing in its own large enclosed garden with children's games at the edge of the village. Fishing, bathing, swimming-pool and tennis in the village. Poitiers (32 km) stands on a promontory overlooking the rich agricultural land watered by the rivers Clain and Boivre and has all the amenities of an old university town. Three bedrooms available: bedroom 1 (2 double beds); bedrooms 2 and 3 (1 double and 1 single bed each). One bedroom has a private bathroom, the other two share a shower room; shared living room. Open all year. Shopping at Couhe (3 km) or Ruffec (30 km).
Prices: 1p F 88, 2p F 108, 3p F 128, 4p F 148   **10 people**
Booking: Vienne Loisirs Accueil   E   IGN 40
86/CH/86/6

MONTS SUR GUESNES Bourgville *Chambre d'hôte* accommodation in a lovely renovated village house in its own grounds overlooking the countryside where the owner also manages three gîtes. Children are very welcome and are provided with special menus; baby-sitting can be arranged. Bicycles for hire on site. Five rooms available, all with private shower: bedroom 1 (1 double and 2 single beds); bedrooms 2 and 3 (2 double beds); bedroom 4 (2 single beds); bedroom 5 (1 single bed). Child's bed on request. Shared living room. Full board, half board and meals available all year. Shopping and restaurant at Loudun (15 km).
Prices: 1p F 100, 2p F 120, 3p F 150, 4p F 180   **11 people**
Booking: Vienne Loisirs Accueil   E   IGN 34

86/CH/86/4

LES ROCHES PREMARIES Raboué *Chambre d'hôte* accommodation in the owner's old, tastefully renovated house set in its own large grounds at the edge of a hamlet. Plenty of facilities close by including riding, forest walks, swimming-pool and fishing within 2 km, tennis at 4 km and an ice rink at Poitiers (13 km) where there are shops and restaurants. Two rooms available, sleeping 3 and 4 respectively. Child's bed available on request. Private bathroom shared between the two rooms, shared living room and lounge.
Prices: 1p F 88, 2p F 108, 3p F 128, 4p F 148   **7 people**
Booking: Vienne Loisirs Accueil   E   IGN 34

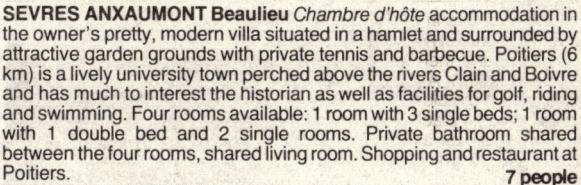

86/CH/86/31

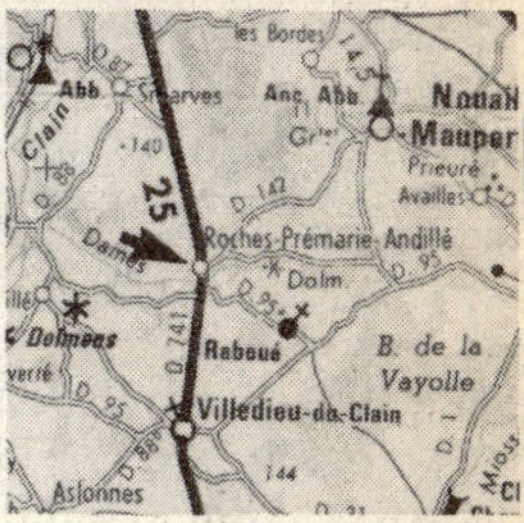

SEVRES ANXAUMONT Beaulieu *Chambre d'hôte* accommodation in the owner's pretty, modern villa situated in a hamlet and surrounded by attractive garden grounds with private tennis and barbecue. Poitiers (6 km) is a lively university town perched above the rivers Clain and Boivre and has much to interest the historian as well as facilities for golf, riding and swimming. Four rooms available: 1 room with 3 single beds; 1 room with 1 double bed and 2 single rooms. Private bathroom shared between the four rooms, shared living room. Shopping and restaurant at Poitiers.
                                                       7 people
Prices: 1p F 78, 2p F 98, 3p F 118   IGN 34
Booking: Vienne Loisirs Accueil   E
86/CH/86/15

LA-ROCHE-POSAY Fonsemort *Camping à la ferme* on a mixed farm at 5 km from the village. The site is flat prairie-land in a partially shaded meadow and there are 5 sites available. La-Roche-Posay is a picturesque town, above the river Creuse and famous for its mineral springs. One hot shower, electricity, washing machine, swings and table tennis. Restaurant and shops at La-Roche-Posay.
Prices: F 6.60 per person, (F 2.80 child);   **7 people**
          F5.40 per site.   IGN 34
Booking: M PARE, Fonsemort 86270 La-Roche-Posay.
Tel. (49) 86 27 18.   E

86/25

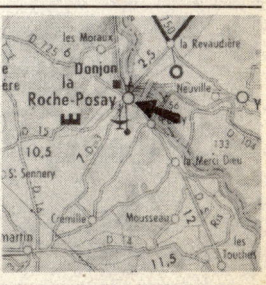

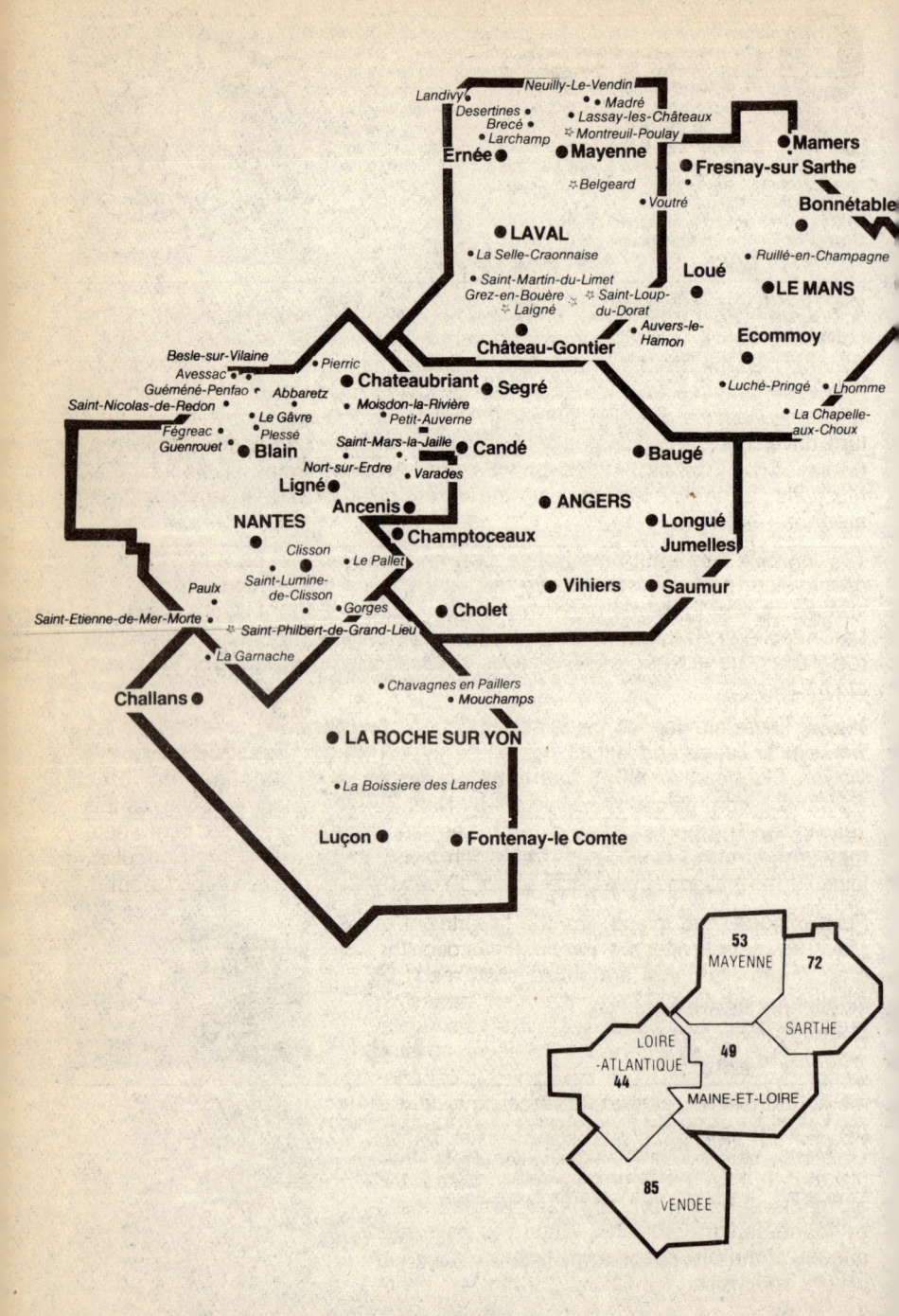

Neuilly-Le-Vendin
Landivy • Madré
• Desertines • Lassay-les-Châteaux • Mamers
• Brecé • Montreuil-Poulay
• Larcham • Mayenne Fresnay-sur Sarthe
Ernée Bonnétable
• Belgeard • Voutré

LAVAL Loué • Ruillé-en-Champagne
• La Selle-Craonnaise LE MANS
Saint-Martin-du-Limet Saint-Loup-
Grez-en-Bouère du-Dorat Ecommoy
Laigné Auvers-le-
Château-Gontier Hamon
Besle-sur-Vilaine • Luché-Pringé • Lhomme
Avessac • • Pierric • La Chapelle-
Guéméné-Penfao Chateaubriant aux-Choux
Saint-Nicolas-de-Redon Abbaretz • Moisdon-la-Rivière • Segré
Fégréac • Le Gâvre • Petit-Auverne Baugé
Guenrouet Plessé Saint-Mars-la-Jaille • Candé
Blain Nort-sur-Erdre
Ligné • Varades ANGERS Longué
Ancenis Jumelles
NANTES Champtoceaux
Clisson • Vihiers • Saumur
Paulx Saint-Lumine- • Le Pallet
de-Clisson Gorges Cholet
Saint-Etienne-de-Mer-Morte Saint-Philbert-de-Grand-Lieu
• La Garnache

• Chavagnes en Paillers
Challans • • Mouchamps

• LA ROCHE SUR YON

• La Boissière des Landes

Luçon • • Fontenay-le Comte

```
        53
      MAYENNE    72
               SARTHE
   LOIRE    49
 -ATLANTIQUE
    44    MAINE-ET-LOIRE

        85
      VENDEE
```

190

9 WESTERN LOIRE

A temperate land where the river Loire flows west into the Atlantic Ocean, off the coast of Brittany. The soft countryside, with its splendid châteaux and fine wines contrast with the beaches, wild, rocky coastline and the thriving industrial port of Nantes. The largest town in Brittany, Nantes dates back to the Gallo-Roman era, when the Romans defeated the Gallic inhabitants of Brittany, who were in their turn, driven out four centuries later by the Celts who came from Britain, themselves displaced by invading Angles and Saxons. Around Nantes is the home of Muscadet, a fine wine to accompany the fish and shell-fish dishes particular to this area.

To the north, lies the Brière Nature Conservation Park, an unusual stretch of countryside, near the sea, whose fascination lies in its marshes, canals and villages, clustering on what once were islands. Visit the "Sabot-Maker's House" at La Chapelle-des-Marais, or take a trip down the canals on a barge. Explore the rocky coastline with its coves and caves, or spend a few days lazing on the beach at La Baule.

Moving south into Vendée, you will come to the Marais-Poitevin Conservation Park with similar canals and marshlands where you can take a boat-trip. Well worth a visit are Bluebeard's castles, open to visitors all summer and the capital town of La Roche-sur-Yon, planned and laid out by Napoléon in its rigorous style, as it is seen today. The most interesting thing to see here, is probably the stud farm where they breed trotting racehorses. Also worth a visit are the island of Noirmoutier, joined to the mainland by a bridge, and Ile d'Yeu where you can see Pétain's tomb.

Further north, and inland, lies the départment of Mayenne, named after the river flowing through the area. From here you are within easy reach of Châteaubriant, an old town with many interesting features, besides a château. At Laval, the capital town, there is an interesting museum housing works by Rousseau. The neighbouring départe-ment, Sarthe, in the beautiful Loire countryside, is a peaceful and green area with its noisy, capital town, Le Mans, where the famous 24 hour race takes place each June. Although busy and industrial, the old mediaeval city of Le Mans is still partly enclosed by fourth-century ramparts. When you have had enough of the city, spend some time going back in history and visiting the Châteaux of the Loire, not too far away.

Loire-Atlantique

ABBARETZ La Belle Etoile A charming old cottage with traditional furnishings in a quiet rural setting, 3 km from the village. There is a swimming-pool at Nozay (5 km) and in the vicinity are châteaux and standing stones to visit. Sailing at a lake (12 km); riding at 15 km. Living room/kitchenette, 3 bedrooms (4 double and 1 child's bed), shower room, fireplace, enclosed ground. Shopping and restaurant in the village or at Nozay.

Prices: low season F 580
high season F 760/805
8/9 people
IGN 24

Booking: Loire-Atlantique booking service   E

44/15B

AVESSAC La Chataigneraie An unusual old house, renovated and furnished in traditional style, in a wooded area, 2 km from the village. Good fishing in the Vilaine river and a lake and swimming-pool at 10 km. The Atlantic coast is close enough for a day trip (50 km approx.). Living room/kitchenette (1 double divan), 2 bedrooms (1 double, 2 single and 1 child's bed), bathroom, electric central heating, open ground. Shopping and restaurant in the village or at Redon (10 km).

Prices: low season F 515/570
high season F 745/810
6/7 people
IGN 24

Booking: Loire-Atlantique booking service   E

44/VD358

AVESSAC La Hunaudière A pretty stone-built gîte with rustic furnishings, in the heart of wooded countryside, some 4 km from the village. Local forest walks and a swimming-pool at Redon (9 km). Châteaubriant (50 km approx.) with its fine château and many other attractions is well worth a visit. Living room, kitchen, 3 bedrooms (2 double, 2 single and 1 child's bed; 1 single divan on a mezzanine), shower room, electric heating, ground. Shopping and restaurant in the village or at Redon.

Prices: low season F 690/765
high season F 990/1090
7/8 people
IGN 24

Booking: Loire-Atlantique booking service   E

44/VD218

AVESSAC Renihel A very attractive old cottage, furnished in rustic fashion, set on a livestock farm deep in the countryside, 7 km from the village. Fishing at a lake (0.1 km). Redon (15 km) is a busy commercial and pleasure port on the Vilaine river with many leisure facilities. Living room/kitchenette (washing-up machine, 1 single divan), 3 bedrooms (3 double 1 single and 1 child's bed), shower room, heating, garage, garden. Shopping and restaurant in the village or at Redon.

Prices: low season F 520/580
high season F 755/820
8/9 people
IGN 24

Booking: Loire-Atlantique booking service   E

44/229

BESLE-SUR-VILAINE La Croix A traditionally furnished and renovated gîte in a hamlet, 2 km from the village. Many interesting sites in the region, including numerous châteaux and megalithic standing stones. Guéméné-Penfao (7 km) is a pretty little country resort on the river Don, with many leisure facilities. Living room, kitchen, 4 bedrooms (4 double beds), shower room, electric central heating, open ground. Shopping and restaurant in the village or at Redon (26 km).

Prices: low season F 555/610
high season F 805/885
8 people
IGN 24

Booking: Loire-Atlantique booking service   E

44/VD284

Loire-Atlantique

BLAIN La Mercerais A small, traditionally furnished gîte on the ground floor of the owners' stylish old house, 3 km from the country holiday resort of Blain. The département capital of Nantes (40 km approx.) is an interesting university town on the river Loire with a fifteenth century château, cathedral and other sites. Living room/kitchenette, 1 bedroom (2 double and 1 single beds), bathroom, open fire, oil-fired central heating, garden. Shopping and restaurant in Blain or at Nozay (11 km).

Prices:	low season	F 505/540	**5 people**
	high season	F 680/765	*IGN 24*

Booking: Loire-Atlantique booking service   E

44/222

BLAIN La Peaudais An old, traditionally furnished cottage, 1 km from Blain where there is a swimming-pool and tennis courts. This is a pleasant region near the Don Valley with local river fishing, a lake and riding at 5 km and close enough to the coast for a day trip 45 km. Living room, kitchen, 2 bedrooms (1 double and 2 large single beds), bathroom, fireplace, electric central heating, garden. Shopping and restaurant in Blain or at Nozay (15 km).

Prices:	low season	F 505/540	**4 people**
	high season	F 715/760	*IGN 24*

Booking: Loire-Atlantique booking service   E

44/211

BLAIN La Rouaudais An old cottage, traditionally furnished and situated in a hamlet, 8 km from the rural holiday resort of Blain. Fishing nearby in the Nantes-Brest canal and good walks in the Gâvre forest (3 km). Visit the Château de Groulaie, now a museum of local arts and traditions. Living room/kitchenette, 2 bedrooms (1 double and 4 single beds), bathroom, fireplace, electric heating, carport, garden. Shopping and restaurant at Blain.

Prices:	low season	F 705	**6 people**
	high season	F 875/945	*IGN 24*

Booking: Loire-Atlantique booking service   E

44/111

CLISSON Le Moulin de Plessard One of four gîtes in a lovely old building which has been renovated and traditionally furnished. It is 2 km from the medieval town of Clisson, built in italianate style with a thirteenth-century château and fifteenth-century market halls. Guided tours are available in July and August. Living room/kitchenette, 2 bedrooms (1 double and 3 child's beds), shower room, electric central heating, open courtyard. Shopping and restaurant in the town or at Nantes (27 km).

Prices:	low season	F 575/640	**2/5 people**
	high season	F 840/940	*IGN 24*

Booking: Loire-Atlantique booking service   E

44/72A

FEGREAC La Basse Abbaye A well-renovated little gîte with traditional furnishings in a hamlet, 2.5 km from the village. The gîte is just 7 km from the busy port of Redon, there is a golf course at 17 km and the Atlantic coast is an easy drive at 45 km. Living room/kitchenette, 2 bedrooms (1 double and 2 single beds), shower room, open fire, electric central heating, open courtyard with garden furniture. Shopping and restaurant in the village or at Redon.

Prices:	low season	F 515/570	**4 people**
	high season	F 740/805	*IGN 24*

Booking: Loire-Atlantique booking service   E

44/IB337

Loire-Atlantique

FEGREAC Coisnauté Nestling in a hamlet, 7 km from the village, this gîte has been carefully restored and furnished in traditional style. The Gâvre forest (10 km) is well worth exploring; a lake at 11 km has facilities for bathing and sailing and the coast is just 45 km away. Living room/kitchenette (1 double divan), 2 bedrooms (2 double, 1 single and 1 child's bed), bathroom, fireplace, electric central heating, open ground. Shopping and restaurant in the village or at Redon (15 km).

Prices:　low season　　F 645/715　　　　　**7/8 people**
　　　　　high season　F 930/1000　　　　　　*IGN 24*
Booking: Loire-Atlantique booking service　　E

44/IB336

FEGREAC La Grulais A renovated and traditionally furnished single-storey gîte on an arable farm in a rural hamlet, 2 km from the village. Local river fishing (0.5 km). At the port of Redon (11 km) you can take a trip on the river Vilaine or the Breton canals and enjoy the many other leisure facilities. Living room (1 double divan), kitchen, 2 bedrooms (1 double and 2 single beds), bathroom, electric central heating, enclosed ground. Shopping and restaurant in the village or at Redon.

Prices:　low season　　F 505/565　　　　　**6 people**
　　　　　high season　F 730/810　　　　　　*IGN 24*
Booking: Loire-Atlantique booking service　　E

44/IB271

LE GAVRE Vieux Chemin A renovated and traditionally furnished gîte on a mixed farm in truly rural surroundings, 2 km from the village. Nearby is the vast Gâvre forest with many marked footpaths. Other leisure facilities, including swimming-pool and tennis, at the pretty little château town of Blain (7 km), a rural holiday resort. Living room/kitchenette, 2 bedrooms (1 double and 3 single beds), bathroom, fireplace, electric central heating, enclosed ground. Shopping and restaurant in the village or at Blain.

Prices:　low season　　F 510/565　　　　　**5 people**
　　　　　high season　F 725/785　　　　　　*IGN 24*
Booking: Loire-Atlantique booking service　　E

44/VD203

GORGES La Magasin A renovated, traditionally furnished gîte lying amongst Muscadet vineyards on the Nantes-Clisson road, and 2 km from the village centre. Local walks and river fishing. The attractive town of Clisson (3 km) has a château with park, old market halls and other sites, also a swimming-pool and tennis. Living room, kitchen, 3 bedrooms (2 double, 3 single and 1 child's bed), shower room, oil-fired central heating, garage, open ground. Shopping and restaurant in the village or at Clisson.

Prices:　low season　　F 590/645　　　　　**7/8 people**
　　　　　high season　F 870/930　　　　　　*IGN 24*
Booking: Loire-Atlantique booking service　　E

44/220

GUEMENE-PENFAO Le Fondreau A renovated and traditionally furnished gîte, set on farmland, 4 km from the country holiday resort of Guéméné-Penfao in the Don valley. Swimming-pool and tennis in the village, the châteaux of Juzet, Bruc and Boisfleury are just some of the many to see in the region. Living room (1 single divan), kitchen, 2 bedrooms (1 double and 3 single beds), shower room, fireplace, electric central heating, open ground. Shopping and restaurant in the village or at Redon (24 km).

Prices:　low season　　F 555/620　　　　　**6 people**
　　　　　high season　F 805/875　　　　　　*IGN 24*
Booking: Loire-Atlantique booking service　　E

44/VD361

Loire-Atlantique

GUENROUET La Butte des Rochaux A gîte on the first floor of the owners' modern house with contemporary furnishings on their livestock farm, 4 km from the village. It is near the Nantes-Brest canal and the lovely Gâvre forest. A race course at Pontchâteau (16 km) and the coast is at 30 km approx. Living room/kitchenette (washing machine, TV, 1 single divan), 2 bedrooms (1 double, 3 single and 1 child's bed), bathroom, electric central heating, open ground. Shopping and restaurant in the village or at Pontchâteau.

| Prices: | low season | F 705/775 | **6/7 people** |
| | high season | F 1030/1095 | *IGN 24* |

Booking: Loire-Atlantique booking service   E

44/IB323

MOISDON-LA-RIVIERE La Boulais An unusual renovated house with traditional furnishings, 3 km from the village. There are disused slate quarries nearby which have been stocked for fishing; a swimming-pool at 14 km. Châteaubriant (16 km) has a fine mediaeval/Renaissance château, race course and many leisure facilities. Riding at 18 km. Living room, kitchen, 2 bedrooms (1 double, 2 single and 1 child's bed), shower room, fireplace, electric central heating, garden. Shopping and restaurant in the village or at Pontchâteau.

| Prices: | low season | F 555/705 | **4/5 people** |
| | high season | F 945/980 | *IGN 24* |

Booking: Loire-Atlantique booking service   E

44/151

NORT-SUR-ERDRE Vault A well-renovated and traditionally furnished cottage in a rural hamlet, near the pretty river Erdre – popular for fishing and pleasure boating. There is an important race course in the town (3.5 km). Nantes, the historic château town and capital of the département with many leisure facilities (30 km). Living room (TV), kitchen, 2 bedrooms (3 double and 1 child's bed), shower room, fireplace, oil-fired central heating, enclosed ground. Shopping and restaurant in the town.

| Prices: | low season | F 595 | **6/7 people** |
| | high season | F 790/845 | *IGN 24* |

Booking: Loire-Atlantique booking service   E

44/245

NORT-SUR-ERDRE Vault One of three traditionally furnished gîtes in a renovated house in a hamlet, 4 km from the town and centrally situated in the département, within easy striking distance of Nantes, Châteaubriant, Redon and the coast. Living room, kitchen, 2 bedrooms (1 double and 3 single beds), shower room, electric heating, open courtyard. Shopping and restaurant in the town or at Nantes (30 km approx.).

| Prices: | low season | F 545/600 | **5 people** |
| | high season | F 795/855 | *IGN 24* |

Booking: Loire-Atlantique booking service   E

44/389A

LE PALLET La Roche An attractive modern chalet with traditional furnishings at the heart of the Muscadet vineyards – follow the wine road for an interesting tour. The charming old town of Clisson with is italianate architecture is at 7 km. The coast (65 km). Living room/kitchenette, 2 bedrooms (1 double, 1 single and 2 child's beds), shower room, open fire, balcony, terrace, garage, open ground. Shopping and restaurant in the village (1 km).

| Prices: | low season | F 705 | **3/5 people** |
| | high season | F 945/1040 | *IGN 24* |

Booking: Loire-Atlantique booking service   E

44/172

Loire-Atlantique

PAULX La Maquinière An old, traditionally furnished cottage with a table tennis table for your amusement, outside the village (1.5 km). It is 8 km from the rural holiday resort of Mâchecoul (swimming-pool and tennis) and 26 km from the coast where you should visit the delightful Ile de Noirmoutier. Living room (1 double divan), kitchen, 3 bedrooms (3 double and 2 single beds), bathroom, fireplace, electric central heating, garage, enclosed ground. Shopping and restaurant in the village.

Prices:	low season	F 830/925	**10 people**
	high season	F 1235/1300	*IGN 32*

Booking: Loire-Atlantique booking service   E

44/382

PAULX A renovated and traditionally furnished gîte near the village centre. It is 7 km from Mâchecoul which has a swimming-pool and the ruined château of "Bluebeard", Gilles de Retz; Grand Lieu lake is at 20 km. The coast, with good beaches and sailing facilities, is just 25 km away. Living room (1 double divan), kitchen, 1 bedroom (3 double beds), bathroom, open fire, enclosed ground. Shopping in the village (0.2 km) or at Mâchecoul.

Prices:	low season	F 590	**8 people**
	high season	F 760/825	*IGN 32*

Booking: Loire-Atlantique booking service   E

44/223

PETIT AUVERNE Moulin de la Pile One of two gîtes with modern furnishings in a large, renovated house, by a little river where you may fish. Pleasant walks along local marked footpaths. The fine medieval château town of Châteaubriant is at 16 km; a s swimming-pool (16 km); sailing at a lake (20 km). Living room/kitchenette, 2 bedrooms (1 double and 2 child's beds), shower room, fireplace, heating, enclosed ground. Shopping in the village (2 km) and restaurants at Châteaubriant.

Prices:	low season	F 645/720	**2/4 people**
	high season	F 955/1005	*IGN 24*

Booking: Loire-Atlantique booking service   E

44/331B

PIERRIC La Grée du Queux A small, traditionally furnished gîte, one of two in a renovated cottage, 2 km from the village centre. It is close to the vast Gàvre forest and local sites include the Château of Boisfleury and Friguel and the rural holiday resort of Guéméné-Penfao (10 km). Living room, kitchen, 1 bedroom (1 double, 2 single and 1 child's bed), bathroom, electric heating, carport, enclosed ground. Shopping and a restaurant at Derval (5 km).

Prices:	low season	F 565/630	**4/5 people**
	high season	F 825/890	*IGN 24*

Booking: Loire-Atlantique booking service   E

44/UD401A

PLESSE L'Angle A renovated and traditionally furnished cottage, typical of the region, lying in a hamlet, near the Nantes-Brest canal and the delightful Gâvre forest. The country resort of Blain (15 km) has an interesting museum of local arts and traditions, as well as a swimming-pool and tennis. Golf course at 20 km. Living room/kitchenette (1 single divan), 2 bedrooms (4 single beds), shower room, fireplace, electric heating, open ground. Shopping and restaurant in the village (3 km) or at Blain.

Prices:	low season	F 475/515	**5 people**
	high season	F 675/750	*IGN 24*

Booking: Loire-Atlantique booking service   E

44/304

Loire-Atlantique

SAINT-ETIENNE-DE-MER-MORTE Le Tremble A pleasant gîte, renovated and furnished in traditional fashion in a rural hamlet, 1.5 km from the village. The interesting château town of Mâchecoul is at 12 km; swimming-pool and tennis (13 km) and the gîte is very handy for the coast (30 km) and the Ile de Noirmoutier. Living room (1 double divan), kitchen, 2 bedrooms (3 double and 1 single bed), shower room, fireplace, gas central heating, garage, open ground with seesaw and swing. Shopping and restaurant in the village.

Prices: low season   F 625/710   **9 people**
high season F 910/945   *IGN 32*

Booking: Loire-Atlantique booking service   **E**

44/188

SAINT-LUMINE-DE-CLISSON Le Frêne A spacious, renovated house with traditional furnishings. Clisson (8 km) has a château and other historic buildings, many of which are illuminated in summer and offer guided tours. Horse-riding at 10 km; the coast 70 km approx. Living room (1 double divan), kitchen, 4 bedrooms (2 double and 4 single beds), bathroom, open fire, electric central heating, carport, enclosed courtyard. Shopping and restaurant in the village (2.5 km).

Prices: low season   F 660/725   **10 people**
high season F 945/1045   *IGN 33*

Booking: Loire-Atlantique booking service   **E**

44/263

SAINT-MARS-LA-JAILLE La Moulinière A small studio, one of two traditionally furnished gîtes in the owners' attractive modern house at the edge of this rural holiday resort which has a swimming-pool, tennis, river fishing and bathing. Visit the nearby Grison Château with its extensive grounds and lake. Studio room/kitchenette (1 double divan, 1 single bed), bathroom, central heating, garden and open ground. Shopping and restaurant in the village (0.8 km) or at Ancenis (18 km).

Prices: low season   F 480   **3 people**
high season F 600/680   *IGN 24*

Booking: Loire-Atlantique booking service   **E**

44/95A

SAINT-NICOLAS-DE-REDON A ground-floor gîte in the owners' modern house at the edge of the town. Fishing, swimming-pool and tennis are among the many leisure facilities at the interesting port of Redon, set at the crossroads of the Brittany canals. The coast (with sailing facilities) is just 45 km away. Living room (1 double divan), kitchen, 1 bedroom (1 double and 1 child's bed), shower room, oil-fired central heating, terrace, garden. Shopping and restaurant in the town (0.5 km) or at Redon itself (1 km).

Prices: low season   F 570   **4/5 people**
high season F 740/805   *IGN 24*

Booking: Loire-Atlantique booking service   **E**

44/365

VARADES An old, traditionally furnished house near the centre of a small town between Nantes and Angers. It lies near the Loire river (2.5 km) and 12 km from Ancenis (swimming-pool and tennis). There are gastronomic restaurants in the town, so try the fine wines and, 'Beurre Blanc' cuisine. Living room (1 single divan), kitchen, 2 bedrooms (1 double, 2 child's beds), bathroom, fireplace, central heating, garage, enclosed ground. Shopping and restaurant in the town (0.5 km).

Prices: low season   F 530/595   **3/5 people**
high season F 785/845   *IGN 24*

Booking: Loire-Atlantique booking service   **E**

44/301

Mayenne

BRECE Les Mares A well-renovated stone cottage with traditional furnishings in a hamlet, 4 km from the village where you may buy fresh farm produce. At Gorron (6 km), a pretty town on the river Colmont, leisure amenities include a swimming-pool and tennis. Living room, kitchen, 3 bedrooms (3 double and 2 single beds), bathroom, no heating, open ground. Shopping in the village or at Gorron where there is a restaurant.

Prices:	low season	F 500	**8 people**
	high season	F 700	IGN 17

Booking: M FOUGERAY, Lotissement de la Main Gantée, 53120 Gorron. Tel. (43) 04 63 82.

53/118

DESERTINES La Fouberdière A large house, renovated and traditionally furnished on a livestock farm, some 4 km from the village. Fishing at a river near the property; a riding stable at 10 km. Mayenne, with its twelfth-century château and other sites, is an easy day trip at 35 km approx. Living room (1 double divan), kichen, 5 bedrooms (2 double, 3 single and 1 child's bed), bathroom and shower, fireplace, central heating, terrace, garage, open ground. Shopping in the village or at Gorron (10 km).

Prices:	low season	F 730/940	**10 people**
	high season	F 1050/1150	IGN 17

Booking: M GUYARD, Les Douets, Brecé, 53120 Gorron. Tel. (43) 04 64 28.

53/111

LANDIVY A village gîte, well renovated and with country-style furnishings, set in its own enclosed ground with garden furniture for outdoor meals. Visit Fougères (18 km) and see the vast fortified castle walls dating from the thirteenth century. The coast and lovely Mont-Saint-Michel is just 40 km away. Living room (1 double divan), kichen, 1 bedroom (4 single beds), shower room, fireplace, heating. Shopping, farm produce and restaurant in the village.

Prices:	low season	F 620/700	**6 people**
	high season	F 750/800	IGN 17

Booking: Mayenne booking service   **E**

53/99

LARCHAMP La Vieille Cour A small renovated and traditionally furnished cottage on a mixed farm where you may buy fresh farm produce from the owners. The château town of Ernée (6 km) is a rural holiday resort with good leisure facilities, set in a pleasant valley. Living room/kitchenette, 1 bedroom (1 double and 2 single beds), shower room, electric central heating, carport, open ground with garden furniture. Shopping and restaurant in the village (3 km).

Prices:	low season	F 415/524	**4 people**
	high season	F 765/780	IGN 17

Booking: Mayenne booking service   **E**

53/129

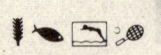

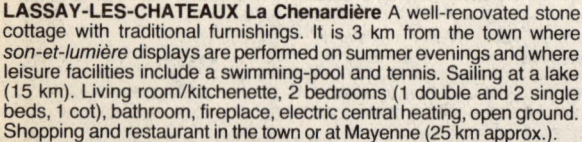

LASSAY-LES-CHATEAUX La Chenardière A well-renovated stone cottage with traditional furnishings. It is 3 km from the town where son-et-lumière displays are performed on summer evenings and where leisure facilities include a swimming-pool and tennis. Sailing at a lake (15 km). Living room/kitchenette, 2 bedrooms (1 double and 2 single beds, 1 cot), bathroom, fireplace, electric central heating, open ground. Shopping and restaurant in the town or at Mayenne (25 km approx.).

Prices:	low season	F 550/650	**5 people**
	high season	F 850	IGN 17

Booking: M BELLARD, 15 rue de Housse, 53110, Lassay-les-Châteaux. Tel. (43) 04 73 40.

53/74

Mayenne

MADRE La Motte A gîte with country-style furnishings in the owners' fine old house, set in extensive grounds, 3 km from the village. The pleasant spa town of Bagnoles-de-L'Orne (16 km) has many leisure amenities including a lake, golf links and a casino. Living room, kitchen, 3 bedrooms (3 double and 6 single beds), bathroom, central heating, garden furniture. Farm produce and other shopping in the village or at Lassay-les-Châteaux (11 km) where there is a restaurant.

Prices:	low season	F 790/895	**12 people**
	high season	F 1050	IGN 17

Booking: M DESLANDES DE FONTENAY, La Motte, Madré, 53250 Javron-les-Chapelles. Tel. (43) 04 73 81

53/18

NEUILLY-LE-VENDIN A large old house, renovated and traditionally furnished, on a mixed farm in the Normandy Regional Park. A swimming-pool, tennis and cinema at the lively town of Pré-en-Pail (10 km); other amenities at the spa town of Bagnoles-de-l'Orne (12 km). Living room (1 double divan), kitchen, 3 bedrooms (1 double, 2 single beds, 1 cot), bathroom, fireplace, open ground. Farm produce, other shopping and restaurant in the village (2 km).

Prices:	low season	F 460/560	**7 people**
	high season	F 820/870	IGN 17

Booking: M G. MARTIN, 12 rue Cazault, 61000 Alençon. Tel. (33) 26 00 14.

53/61

SAINT-MARTIN-DU-LIMET La Renazaie A farm cottage, which has been renovated and furnished in traditional style in an open courtyard, 3 km from the village. The owners are happy to sell their produce. Craon (8 km) has a race course and other leisure facilities include a swimming-pool and tennis. Living room/kitchenette (1 single divan), 2 bedrooms (2 double and 1 single bed), bathroom, fireplace, electric heating. Shopping in the village or at Craon where there is a restaurant.

Prices:	low season	F 550/650	**6 people**
	high season	F 700	IGN 24

Booking: M LAURENT, La Renazaie, Saint-Martin-du-Limet, 53800 Renaze. Tel. (43) 06 17 71.

53/6

LA SELLE-CRAONNAISE La Greslerie A well-renovated house with its own bread oven. It is situated in a hamlet, 2.5 km from the village. Laval (35 km approx.) is a lovely cathedral town with a château, parks and France's only museum of Naive Art. Living room (TV), kitchen, 1 bedroom (2 double and 1 single bed), bathroom, fireplace, electric heating, enclosed ground with garden furniture. Farm produce, other shopping and restaurant in the village or at Craon (7 km).

Prices:	low season	F 575/675	**5 people**
	high season	F 810/870	IGN 24

Booking: Mayenne booking service E

53/35

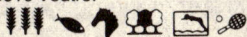

VOUTRE Touchevallier A charming, stone-built house which has been renovated and furnished in country-style, situated in a hamlet, 3 km from the village. Evron (9 km) is a lively country resort where leisure facilities include a swimming-pool, riding and tennis. A forest at 10 km. Living room (TV), kichen (washing machine), 2 bedrooms (2 double and 1 single bed), bathroom, fireplace, electric central heating, enclosed ground with garden furniture. Farm produce and restaurant in the village; shopping at Evron.

Prices:	low season	F 950	**5 people**
	high season	F 1045	IGN 17

Booking: M POISOT, Touchevallier, 53610 Voutré. Tel. (43) 98 17 59.

53/124

Mayenne

BELGEARD Le Closeau de Brive *Chambre d'hôte* accommodation in the owners' lovely old house which has been renovated and furnished in traditional style, on a mixed farm, 2 km from the village. Sailing at a lake (4 km). Mayenne (6 km) is a pleasant old country town where leisure amenities include swimming-pool, tennis and cinemas. Two double rooms available on the first floor with shared bathroom and lounge; central heating, open ground. Farm produce from the owners; other shopping and restaurant at Mayenne.
Prices: on request
4 people
IGN 17
Booking: M LELIEVRE, Le Closeau de Brive, Ancien Bourg, Belgeard, 53100 Mayenne. Tel. (43) 04 14 11.
53/11

GREZ-EN-BOUERE La Chevalerie *Chambre d'hôte* accommodattion in the owners' traditionally furnished old house on a mixed farm where they also have a camp-site. Château-Gontier (14 km) is a rural holiday resort where there is an important cattle market every Thursday; leisure facilities there include a swimming-pool and tennis. Two ground-floor rooms available: bedroom 1 (1 double, 1 single bed); bedroom 2 (1 double bed), shared shower room and lounge, central heating and open ground. Farm produce from the owners; shopping and restaurant in the village (4 km).
Prices: on request
5 people
IGN 25
Booking: M TENDRON, La Chevalerie, 53290 Grez-en-Bouère. Tel. (43) 70 50 64.
53/12

LAIGNE La Grande Forterie *Chambre d'hôte* accommodation in the owners' old house where they have renovated and traditionally furnished two rooms for bed and breakfast guests. It is on a mixed farm where there is also a camp-site. Craon, which has a race course, and Château-Gontier are both 10 km away. Bedroom 1 (1 double bed, private shower); bedroom 2 (1 double, 2 single beds, private shower), lounge and open ground at your disposal; central heating. Shops and restaurant at Château-Gontier.
Prices: on request
6 people
IGN 25
Booking: M ELECHAIS, La Grande Forterie, Laigné, 53200 Château-Gontier. Tel. (43) 07 39 45.
53/13

MONTREUIL-POULAY Le Vieux Presbytère *Chambre d'hôte* accommodation in the owners' former presbytery with country-style furnishings, situated in enclosed ground at the edge of the village (0.7 km). Four rooms available: bedroom 1 (1 double, 1 single bed, private bath); bedroom 2 (1 double bed, private bath); bedroom 3 (2 single beds); bedroom 4 (2 single beds, private bath and WC); shared lounge, central heating. Shopping at Lassay and a restaurant in the village.
Prices: on request
9 people
IGN 17
Booking: Mme C. GERARD, Le Vieux Presbytère, Montreuil-Poulay, 53300 Ambrières-les-Vallees. Tel. (43) 00 83 45.
53/14

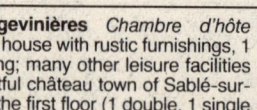

SAINT-LOUP-DU-DORAT Les Angevinières *Chambre d'hôte* accommodation in the owners' fine old house with rustic furnishings, 1 km from the village centre. Local fishing; many other leisure facilities including miniature golf and the delightful château town of Sablé-sur-Sarthe (7 km). One room available on the first floor (1 double, 1 single bed, private shower) lounge and extensive grounds at your disposal; central heating. Farm produce and restaurant in the village; other shopping at Sablé-sur-Sarthe.
Prices: on request
3 people
IGN 25
Booking: Mme E. BOUTIN, Les Angevinières, Saint-Loup-du-Dorat, 53290 Grez-en-Bouère. Tel. (43) 70 83 67.
53/15

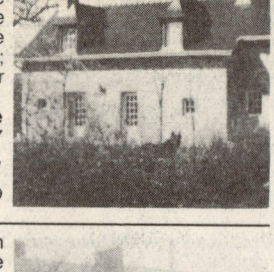

The château du Moulin at Lassay (Mayenne).

Sarthe

AUVERS-LE-HAMON Le Moulin de la Vieille Panne A rustically furnished and spacious gîte in a restored former water mill, 4 km from the village. Fishing right there and local tennis, riding and forest walks. A swimming-pool and other amenities at Sablé-sur-Sarthe (4 km). Living room/kitchenette (1 double bed), 4 bedrooms (2 double, 3 single and 2 child's beds), bathroom, shower room, fireplace, electric heating, terrace, garage, enclosed ground with garden furniture. Linen available. Local farm produce; other shopping and restaurant at Sablé-sur-Sarthe.

Prices:	low season	F 1000	9/11 people
	high season	F 1200	IGN 25

Booking: M G. METAIS, Moulin de la Vieille Panne, Auvers-le-Hamon, 72300 Sablé-sur-Sarthe. Tel. (43) 95 11 02.
72/1

LA CHAPELLE-AUX-CHOUX Les Hêtres A renovated cottage with country-style furnishings on a mixed farm where you may buy fresh produce and hire bicycles. At Le Lude (7 km) see the lovely château where *son-et-lumière* displays are performed in summer. Sailing at Marçon lake (14 km). Living room/kitchenette, 1 bedroom (2 double, 1 single bed), shower room, fireplace, open courtyard. Linen available. Mobile butcher and baker call; other shopping at Le Lude and a restaurant in the village (1 km).

Prices:	low season	F 530/620	5 people
	high season	F 740/760	IGN 25

Booking: M R. BELDENT, Les Hêtres, La Chapelle-aux-Choux, 72800 Le Lude. Tel. (43) 94 67 12.
72/2

LHOMME Lhôpiteau A traditionally furnished and renovated house near a little farming hamlet. A swimming-pool at the old town of La Chartre-sur-le-Loir where you will see dwellings and wine cellars cut into the rock. Sailing at Marçon lake (10 km). Living room (TV, 1 double divan), kitchen, 2 bedrooms (2 double, 2 single and 1 child's bed), bathroom, fireplace, electric heating, terrace, carport, open ground by the river (at 150 metres). Farm produce and shopping in the village (1.2 km); a restaurant at La Chartre-sur-le-Loir.

Prices:	low season	F 500/620	9 people
	high season	F 815/895	IGN 25

Booking: M D. CHEVALLIER, 28 rue Bailleul, 72130 Fresnay-sur-Sarthe. Tel. (43) 97 20 28.
72/3

LUCHE-PRINGE Le Vau An attractively renovated gîte with rustic furnishings, set in its own garden, 3.5 km from the village centre and 8 km from the château town of Le Lude. Visit the zoological garden at the pleasant town of La Flèche (15 km) and the potteries at Malicorne. Living room/kitchenette (1 single divan), 2 bedrooms (2 double, 1 single, 2 child's beds and a cot), bathroom and shower, fireplace (wood supplied), electric heating, garden furniture and swing. Linen available. Farm produce, shopping and restaurant in the village.

Prices:	low season	F 760	6/9 people
	high season	F 900	IGN 25

Booking: M J. THOIN, 14 rue Haute-Justice, 14290 Orbec-en-Auge. Tel. (31) 32 82 55.
72/4

We hope you enjoy your stay —

please leave the gîte clean and tidy for the

next visitors

Thank you

Vendée

LA BOISSIERE DES LANDES La Boutiere A gîte in a modern house set in its own enclosed grounds in the countryside 3 km from the centre of the village. The sea and forests at Jard-sur-Mer (14 km). La Roche-sur-Yon (approx. 15 km), the département capital, was founded by Napoleon in 1804 and lies in the heart of woody countryside. Swimming-pool at 20 km. Living room, (1 double sofa-bed), kitchen (washing machine, dishwasher), 1 bedroom (1 double bed and 2 bunk beds), bathroom, fireplace, electric heating, garage. Shopping at Nieul le Dolent (3 km).

Prices:	low season	F 800	4/6 people
	high season	F 1100	IGN 32

Booking: Vendée booking service E
85/G345

CHAVAGNES EN PAILLERS La Bretaudiere A gîte in a renovated house next to the owner's house in a hamlet, 3 km from the centre of the village. There are pleasant footpaths, a river and tennis courts at 3 km. Saint-Fulgent (approx. 12 km) has a lake for bathing and a sports centre with facilities for table tennis, tennis and petanque. Living room (1 double sofa bed and 1 single bed), kitchen, 3 bedrooms (3 single and 1 child's bed), bathroom, fireplace, carport, ground. Shopping at 3 km.

Prices:	low season	F 450/630	4/7 people
	high season	F 900	IGN 33

Booking: Vendée booking service E

85/G247

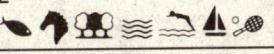

CHAVAGNES EN PAILLERS Les Cinq Moulins A gîte in a new house next to the owner's home in a hamlet 2 km from the centre of the village. The area around Montaigu (approx. 30 km) has some interesting châteaux ruins and the town itself has a museum devoted to the North Vendée; pleasant riverside walks and a lake for windsurfing. The sea is at 50 km. Living room/kitchenette (1 double sofa-bed), 3 bedrooms (1 double, 3 single and 2 bunk beds), shower room, carport, enclosed ground with furniture. Shopping at 1.5 km.

Prices:	low season	F 650/750	7/9 people
	high season	F 1150	IGN 33

Booking: Vendée booking service E
85/G370

LA GARNACHE Le Chiron A gîte in an old, renovated house next to the owner's own home on a livestock farm in a village 5 km from the small town of La Garnache. Footpaths in the village and a chance to try the local wine in Paulx (1.5 km). The sea is at 20 km and forests, bathing and sailing at 25 km. Living room, kitchen, 2 bedrooms (2 double beds and 1 double sofa-bed), shower room, heating, carport, enclosed ground with furniture. Shopping at 5 km.

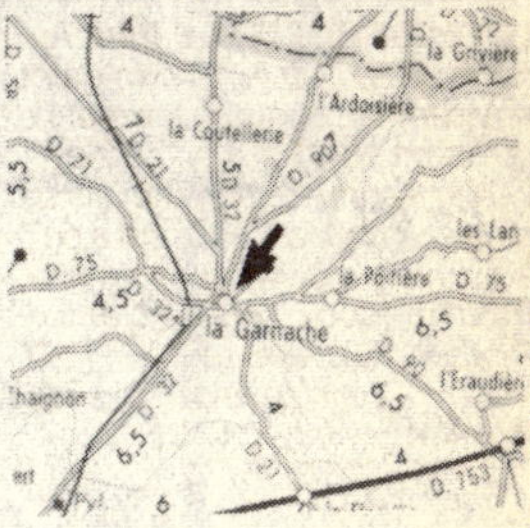

Prices:	low season	F 620/670	4/6 people
	high season	F 1235	IGN 32

Booking: Vendée booking service E

85/G348

MOUCHAMPS La Pagerie A gîte in the owner's well-renovated house, some 5 km from the village. Chantonnay (10 km), noted for its manufacture of traditionally dressed dolls, has a lake (bathing and sailing); see the nearby fifteenth-century Château de Sigournais and Grainetière Abbey. The coast (45 km). Living room/kitchenette (double sofa-bed), 3 bedrooms (1 double, 2 single and 1 child's bed), shower room, electric heating, open communal ground. Shopping and restaurant in the village or at Chantonnay.

Prices:	low season	F 750	6/7 people
	high season	F 910/1020	IGN 33

Booking: Vendée booking service E
85/G056

Carte de Bretagne

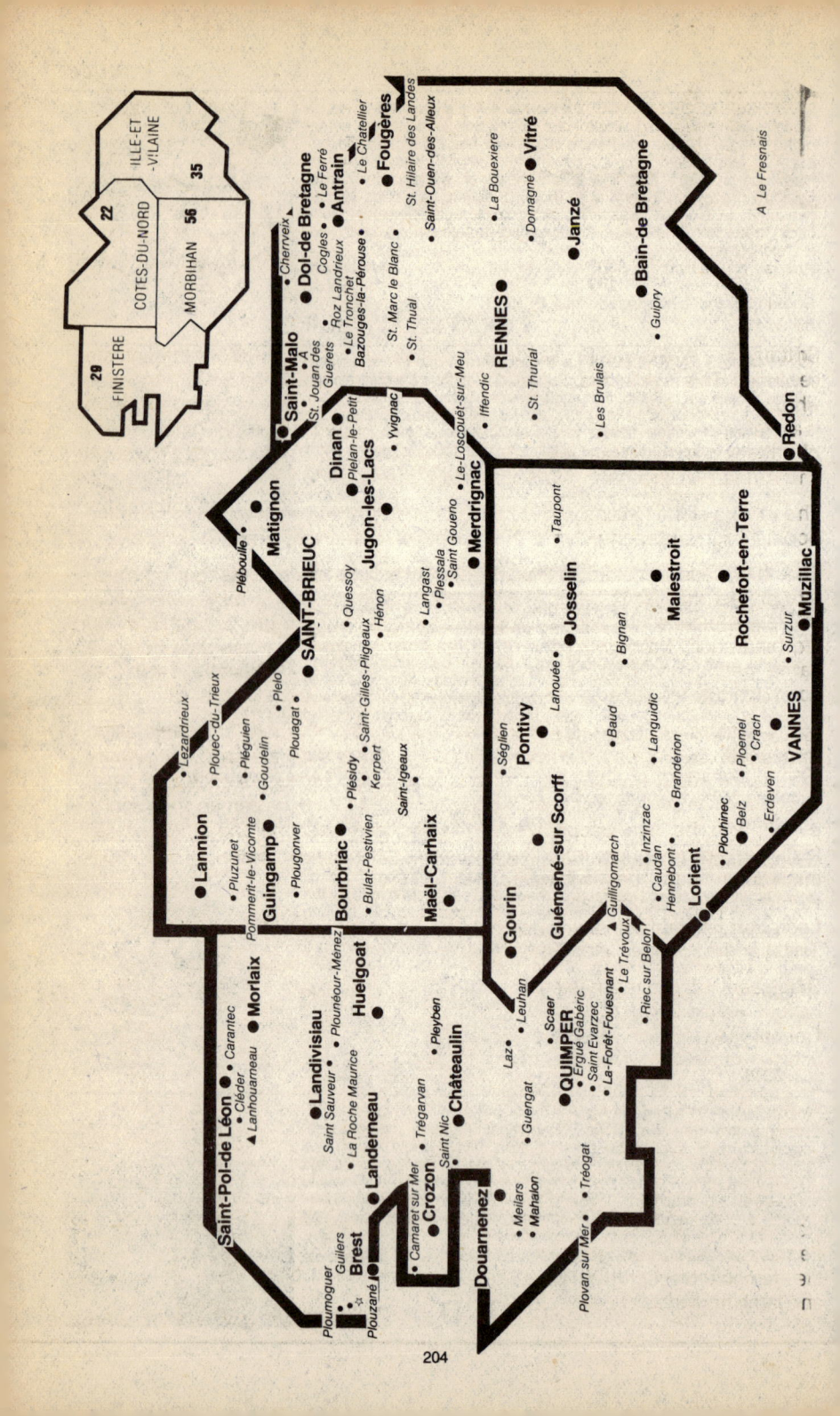

Départements:
- 22 CÔTES-DU-NORD
- 29 FINISTÈRE
- 35 ILLE-ET-VILAINE
- 56 MORBIHAN

Villes principales:

- Saint-Pol-de-Léon
  - Carantec
  - Cléder
  - ▲ Lanhouarneau
- Brest
  - Ploumoguer
  - Guilers
  - ☆ Plouzané
- Morlaix
  - Saint Sauveur
  - Plounéour-Ménez
- Landivisiau
  - La Roche Maurice
- Landerneau
- Huelgoat
- Châteaulin
  - Trégarvan
  - Saint Nic
  - Pleyben
- Crozon
  - Camaret sur Mer
- Douarnenez
  - Meilars
  - Mahalon
  - Trégoat
  - Plovan sur Mer
- QUIMPER
  - Ergué Gabéric
  - Saint Evarzec
  - La Forêt-Fouesnant
  - Guengat
  - Leuhan
  - Scaer
  - Laz
- Lannion
  - Lézardrieux
  - Pluzunet
  - Pommerit-le-Vicomte
  - Plouëc-du-Trieux
  - Péguien
  - Goudelin
- Guingamp
  - Plougonver
  - Plouagat
  - Plélo
- Bourbriac
  - Plésidy
  - Bulat-Pestivien
  - Kerpert
  - Saint-Gilles-Pligeaux
  - Saint-Igeaux
- Maël-Carhaix
- Matignon
  - Pléboulle
- SAINT-BRIEUC
  - Quessoy
  - Hénon
- Dinan
  - Plélan-le-Petit
- Saint-Malo
  - A St. Jouan des Guérets
  - Cherrueix
- Dol-de-Bretagne
  - Le Chatellier
  - Cogles
  - Le Ferré
  - Roz Landrieux
  - Le Tronchet
  - Bazouges-la-Pérouse
- Antrain
- Fougères
  - St. Hilaire des Landes
  - Saint-Ouen-des-Alleux
- Jugon-les-Lacs
  - Yvignac
  - Le Loscouët-sur-Meu
- Merdrignac
  - Langast
  - Plessala
  - Saint Gouéno
  - St. Marc le Blanc
  - St. Thual
- RENNES
  - Iffendic
  - St. Thurial
  - Les Brûlais
  - La Bouëxière
  - Domagné
- Vitré
- Janzé
- Bain-de-Bretagne
  - Guipry
  - A Le Fresnais
- Redon
- Gourin
- Guémené-sur-Scorff
  - Séglien
  - Lanouée
- Pontivy
  - Baud
  - Bignan
- Josselin
  - Taupont
- Malestroit
- Rochefort-en-Terre
- VANNES
  - Languidic
  - Brandérion
  - Ploemel
  - Crach
  - Erdeven
  - Surzur
- Muzillac
- Lorient
  - ▲ Le Trévoux
  - Riec sur Belon
  - Guilligomarch
  - Inzinzac
  - Caudan
  - Hennebont
  - Plouhinec
  - Belz

204

10 BRITTANY

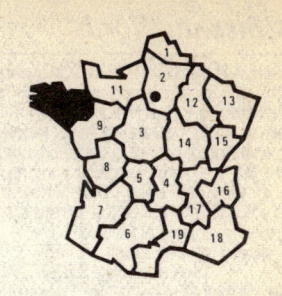

Brittany, like Wales and Scotland, has maintained its Celtic traditions through the centuries. This is reflected particularly in its place names and the Breton language which is still spoken in an everyday manner by the people of lower Brittany. There is an International Celtic Festival at Lorient every August, and even the landscape of Brittany is known by its Celtic names: Armor for the 3500 km of jagged coastline and Argoat (which means woodland) for the interior.

The forests of the hinterland have now given way to wild moorlands similar to the Scottish highlands and with the same feeling of myth and legend.

The landscape is dotted with prehistoric megalithic monuments that go much further back than Celtic times. Menhirs, or standing stones, can be found singly or in groups (cromlechs), such as the famous one on a tiny island, Er Lannic, in the Morbihan gulf. Dolmens, round or rectangular funeral chambers date from the same period and one of the most famous is the "Merchant's Table" at Locmariaquer (Morbihan).

Many Bretons are very religious, as is shown by the "Pardons" that take place throughout the region. The term "Pardon" comes from the fact that plenary indulgence was granted by the church to repentant churchgoers on Saints' days. Every town and village has a patron saint and some Pardons can be spectacular events with the local people dressed in traditional costume and more secular festivities following on from the religious observances. Some of the most interesting can be witnessed at Rumengol (first Sunday after Whitsun), Locronan (second Sunday in July) and Tréguier (first Sunday after 19th May).

Sightseers will find much to enjoy in the historic walled towns of Saint-Malo and Concarneau (which has an unusual fishing museum). The coast is, of course, a great attraction, very popular with yachtsmen, but also offering such diverse activities as wind-surfing, water ski-ing, sand yachting and underwater diving. The visitor is naturally tempted by the huge variety of seafood available: lobsters, oysters, crayfish and also freshwater salmon and trout; but try too the famous crêpes (pancakes), cider and lamb from the salt pasturelands.

Côtes-du-Nord

BULAT-PESTIVIEN Le Château A stone-built renovated house of character, furnished in country fashion and situated 3 km from the village. The rural holiday resort of Callac is at 7 km offering bathing in a small lake, canoeing and tennis. Guingamp (25 km approx.) has excellent sporting facilities (including Breton wrestling!) and a grand dance festival in August. Living room/kitchenette, 1 bedroom (1 double, 2 single and 1 child's bed), shower room, fireplace, open ground. Eggs, chickens and vegetables from the owners (who speak a little English), other shopping at Callac.

Prices: low season F 650
high season F 850/950

4/5 people
IGN 14

Booking: Côtes-du-Nord booking service   E
22/600

GOUDELIN Kerlay A pretty stone-built and renovated ground-floor gîte, rustically furnished, in the owners' house 2.5 km from the village. Guingamp (12 km) offers tennis, swimming, canoeing, riding and guided tours amongst other diversions. The sea is at 16 km. Living room/kitchenette, 1 bedroom (1 double and 1 large single bed), bathroom, no heating, open shared garden. Restaurant in the village, shopping at Guingamp.

Prices: low season F 660
high season F 990

3/4 people
IGN 14

Booking: Côtes-du-Nord booking service   E

22/465

HENON One of two newly built gîtes in the owners' home with modern furnishings close to the village centre (0.2 km). The picturesque town of Saint Brieuc (18 km) offers swimming, tennis, riding, undersea diving and an opportunity to try really fresh seafood and fish. The accommodation consists of 1 large studio, kitchenette, 1 double and 1 single bed, shower room, toilet shared with other gîte, central heating, shared enclosed ground. Shopping and restaurant in the village or at Moncontour (6 km).

Prices: low season F 430/530
high season F 630/700

3 people
IGN 14

Booking: Côtes-du-Nord booking service   E
22/1304B

KERPERT Kéranquéré This little renovated cottage lies in a hamlet, 3 km from the village. There are standing stones and Roman sites in the area; a swimming-pool and tennis at the château town of Saint-Nicolas-de-Pelem (13 km), designated a rural holiday resort. The sea is close enough for a day trip at 45 km approx. Living room/kitchenette, 1 bedroom (1 double, 2 single beds), bathroom, fireplace, electric heating, garden with furniture. Shopping at Bourbriac (13 km).

Prices: low season F 370/420
high season F 725/785

4 people
IGN 14

Booking: Côtes-du-Nord booking service   E

22/926

LANGAST Château de Pontgand. A ground-floor gîte with country-style furnishings in the owner's old, renovated house 2 km from the village. Moncontour (12 km) is an old fortified town (twelfth century) and the fourteenth-century church has some stained-glass windows worth seeing. There is a small lake at 16 km where you may sail and hire pedalos. Living room/kitchenette, 3 bedrooms (1 double and 3 single beds), shower room, electric heating, shared open ground. Restaurant in the village, shopping at Moncontour.

Prices: low season F 615/665
high season F 935/1100

5 people
IGN 14

Booking: Côtes-du-Nord booking service   E

22/1418

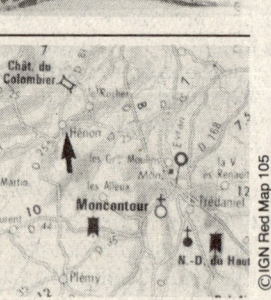

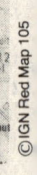

Côtes-du-Nord

LEZARDRIEUX La Mi-Ville A pretty, well-renovated cottage, divided into two gîtes and furnished in country style, lying on a vegetable farm 2.5 km from the village. Paimpol (7.5 km) is a coastal resort with riding, tennis, fishing and sailing, a cinema and pleasant seaside walks. Living room/kitchenette, 2 bedrooms (2 double and 1 single bed), bathroom, no heating, shared courtyard. Restaurant in the village, shopping in Paimpol.

Prices: low season F 705 **5 people**
high season F 1055/1110 IGN 14

Booking: Côtes-du-Nord booking service E

22/252

LE-LOSCOUET-SUR-MEU La Bécelais A renovated and traditionally furnished house standing on a livestock farm 2.5 km from the village. Saint-Méen-le-Grand (3 km) is a small town with some interesting old buildings, including a sixteenth-century château. The area around the gîte offers good opportunities for pleasant walks. Living room/kitchenette (1 double divan), 2 bedrooms (1 double, 2 single and 1 child's bed), shower room, fireplace, electric heating, garage, shared courtyard with child's swing. Eggs, chickens and vegetables from the owner, shopping and restaurant at 3 km.

Prices: low season F 600 **6/7 people**
high season F 800/830 IGN 16

Booking: Côtes-du-Nord booking service E
22/1520

PLEBOULLE Le Fournel One of two spacious gîtes with country-style furnishings in the owners' fine old house on a livestock farm which has been renovated with care. It is near the village centre (0.8 km) and just 6 km from the coast where you may bathe and sail. The popular resorts of Dinard and Saint-Malo are within 30 km. Living room (1 single divan), lounge, kitchen, 6 bedrooms (4 double, 4 single and 1 child's bed), 3 bathrooms, fireplace, central heating, courtyard shared with other gîte. Owners speak a little English. Shopping at Matignon (4 km).

Prices: low season F 1105 **13/14 people**
high season F 1900/2020 IGN 16

Booking: Côtes-du-Nord booking service E

22/1926A

10

PLEGUIEN Kerlan One of two gîtes in a renovated farmhouse, 2 km from the village. A golf links at 5 km and you are just 7 km from the coast with facilities for sailing and bathing, swimming-pool and tennis. Much to see and do at the nearby département capital of Saint-Brieuc (18 km approx.). Living room/kitchenette, 3 bedrooms (1 double, 4 single and 1 child's bed), bathroom, fireplace, courtyard and ground with child's swings shared with the other gîte. Shopping at Lanvollon (1 km).

Prices: low season F 440/565 **6/7 people**
high season F 1395 IGN 14

Booking: Côtes-du-Nord booking service E

22/449B

PLELAN-LE-PETIT La Mariais This gîte is particularly suitable for someone handicapped. It is in a large old renovated house, rustically furnished some 0.5 km from the village and 10 km from Jugon-les-Lacs, a rural holiday resort in the tree-lined valleys of the rivers Arguenon and Rosette. The sea is at 25 km. Living room/kitchenette, 4 bedrooms (3 double, 6 single and 1 child's bed), shower room, fireplace, electric heating, open courtyard. Restaurant in the village, shopping at Jugon-les-Lacs.

Prices: low season F 895 **12/13 people**
high season F 1310 IGN 16

Booking: Côtes-du-Nord booking service E

22/1831

Côtes-du-Nord

PLELO La Croix des Terres An old renovated stone-built cottage, furnished in traditional style on a livestock farm 1.5 km from the village. This is pretty, wooded countryside and Chatelaudren (5.5 km) has a picturesque small lake. Living room, kitchen, 2 bedrooms (1 double, 2 single and 1 child's bed), shower room, heating, garage, enclosed courtyard. Eggs, vegetables and chickens from the owners, restaurant in the village, shopping in Chatelaudren.

Prices:	low season	F 500	4/5 people
	high season	F 1000	IGN 14

Booking: Côtes-du-Nord booking service   E

22/510B

PLESIDY Kerdanet A gîte with rustic furnishings which has been renovated and especially adapted to suit a handicapped person in a wheelchair. It is in a hamlet, in pleasant wooded countryside, 2 km from the village. Swimming-pool, riding and tennis at 16 km and the coast is at 40 km approx. Living room/kitchenette (1 single divan), 2 bedrooms (1 double and 3 single beds), shower room, fireplace, open ground. Fresh eggs, poultry and vegetables from the owners; other shopping at Bourbriac (9 km).

Prices:	low season	F 485/610	6 people
	high season	F 940/1040	IGN 14

Booking: Côtes-du-Nord booking service   E

22/710A

PLESSALA La Ville Josse A nice little stone-built and renovated cottage in a pleasant wooded area with opportunities for walks 4 km from the village where there is a restaurant and shops. Tennis, riding and swimming at 20 km. Guerladan lake (45 km) offers water-skiing, pedalo boats and sailing, together with a small beach. Living room/kitchenette, 1 bedroom (1 double and 3 single beds), shower room, fireplace, open ground.

Prices:	low season	F 595	5 people
	high season	F 800/865	IGN 14

Booking: Côtes-du-Nord booking service   E

22/1412

PLOUAGAT Kerdanet One of two renovated and traditionally furnished gîtes on a livestock farm 2.5 km from the village. The small town of Chatelaudren (4 km) has a picturesque small lake; the sea is at 18 km. This is an attractive forested area with good walks. Living room/kitchenette, 1 bedroom (2 double and 1 child's bed), shower room, fireplace, shared open ground. Eggs, chickens and vegetables from the owners. Restaurant in the village and shopping at Chatelaudren.

Prices:	low season	F 555	4/5 people
	high season	F 680/790	IGN 14

Booking: Côtes-du-Nord booking service   E

22/531B

PLOUEC-DU-TRIEUX A newly built gîte with modern furnishings at the centre of the village. Pontrieux (5 km) has fine views across the Trieux valley, a small harbour and facilities for tennis, canoeing and pedalo hire. The sea and fishing at 25 km. Drive to Paimpol (approx. 20 km) and take a boat trip to the offshore island of Bréhat. Living room, kitchen, 3 bedrooms (3 double beds), bathroom, open ground. Restaurant and shopping in Pontrieux.

Prices:	low season	on request	6 people
	high season	on request	IGN 14

Booking: Côtes-du-Nord booking service   E

22/369

Côtes-du-Nord

PLOUEC-DU-TRIEUX Kermarch A small old house, furnished in traditional style and standing in its own enclosed ground 3 km from the centre of the town of Pontrieux which has a small river harbour, facilities for canoeing, pedalos and tennis. Etables-sur-Mer (35 km approx.) has beautiful beaches, sea fishing and inland trout fishing, golf, table tennis and tennis. Living room/kitchenette, 2 bedrooms (2 double beds), bathroom, fireplace. Shopping and restaurant at Pontrieux.

Prices:	low season	F 580/645	**4 people**
	high season	F 885/945	IGN 14

Booking: Côtes-du-Nord booking service   E

22/354

PLOUGONVER Kervern Situated in a hamlet, 2.5 km from the village, this typical Breton cottage has been renovated and furnished in traditional fashion. The owners speak a little English. Tennis court in the village; bathing and sailing at Callac lake (9 km); the sea and beaches close enough for a day trip at 40 km. Living room (1 double divan), kitchen, 1 bedroom (1 double, 1 single and 1 child's bed), shower room, heating, open ground. Butcher and baker in the village; other shopping and restaurant at Belle-Isle-en-Terre (10 km).

Prices:	low season	F 440/500	**6 people**
	high season	F 790/800	IGN 14

Booking: Côtes-du-Nord booking service   E

22/120

PLUZUNET Bardérou An old renovated gîte, traditionally furnished, 3 km from the village centre. Lannion (10 km) is a most picturesque port with good beaches, rocky coastline and some interesting ruins as well as tennis, swimming-pool and golf. Local specialities include liqueurs, crêpes and the manufacture of distinctive Breton-style furniture. Living room, kitchen, 2 bedrooms (2 double beds), bathroom, electric heating, enclosed ground. Restaurant in the village, shopping at Lannion.

Prices:	low season	on request	**4 people**
	high season	on request	IGN 14

Booking: Côtes-du-Nord booking service   E

22/144

© IGN Red Map 105

10

POMMERIT-LE-VICOMTE St. François One of two gîtes in a renovated building, rustically furnished and 2 km from the village. The sea is 17 km, riding at 12 km and swimming-pool, tennis and fishing within 10 km. Children's games, *boules* and bicycle hire in the village. Living room, kitchen, 2 bedrooms (2 double, 2 single and 1 child's bed), shower room, fireplace, central heating, shared garden.

Prices:	low season	F 585/690	**6/7 people**
	high season	F 1155	IGN 14

Booking: Côtes-du-Nord booking service   E

22/308B

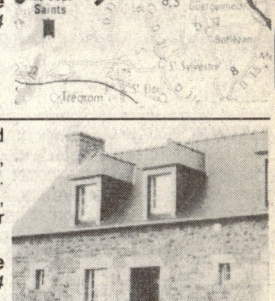

QUESSOY Le Pré Long An attractive stone-built house, now divided into two gîtes and furnished in country style just 2 km from the village. Lamballe (11 km) is a historic town with many interesting buildings, public gardens and walks and facilities for swimming, tennis, riding, cinema and concerts in season. The sea is at 25 km. Living room/kitchenette, lounge, 2 bedrooms (2 double beds), bathroom, fireplace, electric heating, terrace, open courtyard. Shopping and restaurant in the village.

Prices:	low season	F 705	**4 people**
	high season	F 1275	IGN 14

Booking: Côtes-du-Nord booking service   E

22/1328B

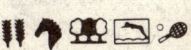

Côtes-du-Nord

SAINT-GILLES-PLIGEAUX La Maisonneuve Lying in a pleasant garden, this traditionally furnished old house is at the edge of the village (1 km). Corlay (10 km) has a fine stud farm and the eleventh-century château of the former Duchy of Rohan. Swimming-pool and tennis at Saint-Nicolas-du-Pelem (10 km). Living room/kitchenette, 3 bedrooms (1 double, 4 single and 1 child's bed), bathroom, electric heating, garage, garden and open ground. Restaurant and some shops in the village; other shopping at Corlay.

Prices: low season   F 650 740
         high season F 850/890

6/7 people
IGN 14

Booking: Côtes-du-Nord booking service   E

22/913

SAINT GOUENO Les Rues Colleu A gîte in the owners' old house, renovated and traditionally furnished. The village is 2 km. Hardouinais forest with its small lake is 12 km – plenty of forest walks in this region and fishing in the village, swimming-pool at 30 km. Living room, kitchen, 2 bedrooms (1 double, 2 single and 1 child's bed), bathroom, central heating, garden and courtyard with child's swing and *boules*. Restaurant at 2 km, shopping at Collinee-Saint-Goueno (4 km).

Prices: low season   F 550
         high season F 800

4/5 people
IGN 14

Booking: Côtes-du-Nord booking service   E

22/1506

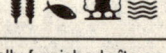

SAINT-IGEAUX Kersaint A renovated and rustically furnished gîte on a farm where the owners offer fresh eggs, poultry and vegetables for sale. It is 1 km from the village and 8 km from Gouarec in whose environs you can visit the Abbaye de Bon Repos and other sites. Sailing at a lake (12 km); the sea (40 km approx.). Living room (1 double divan), kitchen, 3 bedrooms (2 double, 4 single and 1 child's bed), shower room, fireplace, electric heating, open courtyard. Shopping in Gouarec.

Prices: low season   F 805/970
         high season F 1360/1475

10/11 people
IGN 14

Booking: Côtes-du-Nord booking service   E

22/924

YVIGNAC A large old village house owned by the local commune which has been renovated and divided into three rustically furnished gîtes. Pleasant walks in nearby woods (1 km), many small lakes nearby and a reservoir at 12 km. Sailing school and many other facilities at Jugon-les-Lacs (17 km). The sea is at 40 km. Living room, kitchenette, 4 bedrooms (2 double, 5 single beds), bathroom, fireplace, central heating, shared garden with *boules*. Shopping in the village or at Broons (8 km).

Prices: low season   F 570
         high season F 1040

9 people
IGN 14

Booking: Côtes-du-Nord booking service   E

22/1608 B

Finistère

CAMARET SUR MER Kervian A well-renovated, creeper-hung gîte all on the ground floor 3 km from the pretty little fishing port of Camaret sur Mer, where you may hire bicycles, fish, sail and enjoy the fine sandy beaches. Crozon (approx. 11 km) is a larger resort with a lively nightlife, including discothéques and cinema. Living room, kitchen, 4 bedrooms (2 double and 4 single beds), bathroom, fireplace, heating, ground. Restaurant and shopping at Camaret sur Mer.

Prices: low season F 1010/1325   **8 people**
           high season F 2450   IGN 13
Booking: Finistère booking service

29/3.80.762

CARANTEC Kervézec A gîte in an attractive little stone-built cottage adjoining a second gîte 1 km from the village. Morlaix (approx. 15 km) offers sailing, swimming-pool, fishing, windsurfing, riding and marked footpaths and Carantec itself is a small seaside resort and yachting centre; you may hire bicycles here. Living room, kitchen, 2 bedrooms (1 double, 3 single and 1 child's bed), bathroom, fireplace, heating, ground. Restaurant and shopping at Carantec.

Prices: low season F 930/1030   **5/6 people**
           high season F 1630   IGN 13
Booking: Mme A. BOHIC, Kervzec, 29226 Carantec. Tel. 98 67 00 26

29/2.74.453

CLEDER Kérivarc One of two adjoining gîtes in an attractive stone-built cottage set amongst other buildings on a farm 4 km from the village. St Pol de Léon (approx. 13 km) is an old episcopal town now an important centre for the vegetable trade and for the breeding of Breton horses. Living room/kitchenette, 2 bedrooms (1 double and 3 single beds), shower room, fireplace, heating, carport, enclosed ground. Restaurant and shopping at St Pol de Léon.

Prices: low season F 905/1170   **5 people**
           high season F 1695   IGN 13
Booking: Finistère booking service

29/2.81.790

10

ERGUE GABERIC Sulvintin One of two gîtes in an old stone-built house beside other buildings on a farm 3 km from the village. Quimper (approx. 8 km) is the tourist centre of the region and has some interesting old buildings, museums and cultural and sporting facilities. The sea, beaches, sailing and fishing at 20 km. Living room, kitchen, 2 bedrooms (1 double and 2 single beds), shower room, fireplace, heating, ground. Restaurants and shopping at Quimper.

Prices: low season F 590/720   **4 people**
           high season F 1085   IGN 13
Booking: Mme A. LE GOFF, Sulvintin, Ergue Gaberic, 29000 Quimper. Tel. 98 59 51 93

29/7.76.697

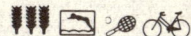

LA FORET FOUESNANT Créac'h an Dû A gîte in a stone-built house amongst other buildings on a farm 4 km from the village. La Forêt Fouesnant is a lively small town with regular folk evenings in the summer, golf, tennis, beaches and a small port where you may hire boats and sailboards. Living room/kitchenette, 3 bedrooms (2 double and 2 single beds), shower room, fireplace, heating, garage, enclosed ground. Shopping and restaurants at Fouesnant (approx. 7 km).

Prices: low season F 900   **6 people**
           high season F 1600   IGN 13
Booking: M J. CARNOT, Créac'h an Dû, 29133 La Forêt Fouesnant. Tel. 98 56 98 61

29/7.79.726

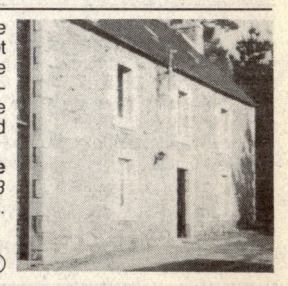

Finistère

GUENGAT Crinquellic A ground-floor gîte in a stone-built cottage set on a farm 2 km from the village. Quimper (approx. 13 km) is a fine old city with several well-preserved streets and buildings (guided tours available from the tourist office), and the Breton museum in the old Bishop's Palace is well worth seeing; excellent sports and cultural activities. Living room/kitchenette, 2 bedrooms (1 double and 2 single beds), shower room, heating, carport and ground. Shopping and restaurants at Quimper.

Prices:	low season	F 530/820	**4 people**
	high season	F 1180	*IGN 13*

Booking: M H. LE ROUX, Crinquellic, Guengat, 29136 Plogonnec. Tel. 98 94 37 20

29/3.CND.030

GUILERS Ker Guen A gîte in a well-maintained stone-built house on a farm in the countryside 1 km from the village. Bicycles for hire locally. Brest (approx. 6 km) is a large military and naval port with splendid beaches close by: guided tours to the arsenal include a visit to a warship. Living room, kitchen, 2 bedrooms (2 double, 2 single and 1 child's bed), bathroom, fireplace, heating, carport and ground. Shopping and restaurants at Brest.

Prices:	low season	F 900/1100	**6/7 people**
	high season	F 1715	*IGN 13*

Booking: M Y. PERES, Ker Guen, 29243 Guilers. Tel. 98 07 63 61

29/1.78.649

LAZ Kergoat A gîte in a stone-built detached house set amongst other buildings on a farm 5 km from the village and approximately 15 km from Châteauneuf du Faou, a rural holiday resort on the Aulne with an attractive park and château, good sports facilities, cycle tracks and marked footpaths. The sea is at 30 km. Living room/kitchenette, 2 bedrooms (2 double, 1 single and 1 child's bed), shower room, heating, carport, ground. Shopping and restaurants at Châteauneuf du Faou.

Prices:	low season	F 680/790	**5/6 people**
	high season	F 1150	*IGN 13*

Booking: Mme H. SINQUIN, Kergoat, 29164 Laz. Tel. 98 59 14 05

29/4.72.268

LEUHAN Carn Hir A gîte in a compact, stone-built cottage 2 km from the village. Rosporden (approx. 21 km) has a summer folk festival and good sports facilities including a sports centre. Local specialities include irresistible Breton *crêpes* and preserved vegetables. The sea and beaches are at 30 km. Living room/kitchenette, 2 bedrooms (3 double beds), shower room, fireplace, heating, enclosed ground. Shopping and restaurants at Châteauneuf du Faou (approx. 15 km).

Prices:	low season	F 750/960	**6 people**
	high season	F 1220	*IGN 15*

Booking: Finistère booking service

29/4.76.583

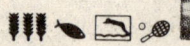

MAHALON Lesmahalon A ground-floor gîte, one of two, in a neat stone cottage set amongst other buildings on a farm 3 km from the village. Audierne (approx. 12 km) is a seaside resort with extensive beaches and a typically Breton fishing port – plenty of really fresh fish and seafood here! Living room/kitchenette, 2 bedrooms (1 double, 2 single and 1 child's bed), shower room, no heating, carport, ground. Shopping and restaurants at Audierne.

Prices:	low season	F 695/835	**4/5 people**
	high season	F 1065	*IGN 13*

Booking: Finistère booking service

29/5.72.273

Finistère

MEILARS Pénesquen Vraz A ground-floor gîte in a stone-built cottage adjoining another holiday home beside other buildings 1 km from the village. Pont-Croix (approx. 6 km) is a small town with eleventh-century origins on the Cap Sizun peninsula at the head of the Goyen estuary. Good beaches and fishing in the area. Markets are held on the first and third Thursdays of each month. Kitchen, 2 bedrooms (2 double and 1 single bed), shower room, fireplace, heating, ground. Shopping and restaurant in Pont-Croix.

Prices: low season F 700/800
high season F 1030
5 people
IGN 13

Booking: Mme M.-J. COLLOREC, Pénesquen Vraz, Confort, Meilars, 29122 Pont-Croix. Tel. 98 70 50 19

29/5.80.768

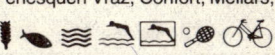

PLEYBEN A gîte in a neat little house on the 'Vieille Route de Châteaulin' in the village itself where there are tennis courts for your use. The picturesque town of Châteaulin, on the river Aulne, is at 10 km and offers good river fishing, canoeing, pedalo hire and opportunities for rambles and cycle trails. Living room/kitchenette, open landing (1 double and 2 single beds), shower room, heating, enclosed ground. Shopping in the village or at Châteaulin.

Prices: low season F 600
high season F 800
4 people
IGN 13

Booking: M R. LE DUFF, 29 Place Charles de Gaulle, 29190 Pleyben. Tel. 98 26 61 19

29/4.70.133

PLEYBEN Lanvézennec A gîte in a well-maintained stone house now divided into two gîtes amongst other buildings on a farm 2 km from the village. Canoeing at 5 km. Châteaulin (approx. 10 km) is a pretty town with good leisure facilities and the sea and beaches are at 22 km. The département capital, Quimper (approx. 30 km), is a fine old city and well worth a visit. Living room/kitchenette, 2 bedrooms (1 double, 2 single and a cot), bathroom, fireplace, heating, carport and ground. Shopping in the village or at Châteaulin.

Prices: low season F 750/855
high season F 1220
4 people
IGN 13

Booking: Finistère booking service

29/4.82.872

PLOUMOGUER Lamber One of three adjoining gîtes set amongst other buildings on a farm 4 km from the village. The sea is just 7 km away and a swimming-pool and riding at 18 km. Brest, one of France's premier naval and military ports, is approximately 24 km and well worth a visit – good beaches and plenty to do. Living room/kitchenette, 2 bedrooms (1 double and 2 single beds), bathroom, fireplace, heating, ground. Shopping and restaurants at Brest.

Prices: low season F 740/855
high season F 1145
4 people
IGN 13

Booking: Finistère booking service

29/1.81.806

PLOUNEOUR MENEZ La Villeneuve A gîte in a pretty stone-built cottage, all on the ground floor, 4 km from the village. Table tennis at the gîte and the sea and sailing at 20 km. Morlaix (approx. 22 km) is an important yachting harbour and offers windsurfing, fishing, tennis and pleasant walks; good beaches at 28 km. Living room/kitchenette, 1 bedroom and 1 bed-sittingroom (4 single beds), bathroom, heating, ground. Shopping and restaurant at Morlaix or Huelgoat (approx. 20 km).

Prices: low season F 540/770
high season F 1035
4 people
IGN 13

Booking: Finistère booking service

29/2.80.778

Finistère

PLOVAN SUR MER Kervouyen A gîte in a neat little cottage, set beside other buildings, on a farm 2 km from the village and just 3 km from the sea and beaches. Quimper (approx. 28 km) is the département capital with a thirteenth-century cathedral and some curious old streets and houses; the Cornouaille Festival, celebrating Breton arts and folklore, takes place here in the summer. Living room/kitchenette, 2 bedrooms (1 double and 3 single beds), shower room, no heating, ground. Shopping and restaurants at Quimper or at Pont l'Abbé (approx. 20 km).

Prices: low season   F 645/855
         high season F 1190/1245

5 people
IGN 13

Booking: Finistère booking service
29/6.82.881

PLOVAN SUR MER Penfrajou One of two adjoining gîtes set amongst other buildings 2 km from the village. The sea and bicycle hire at 2 km. Pont l'Abbé (approx. 20 km) is the capital of the Bigouden country and is famed for its lace, embroidery and dolls – look out for the Breton women wearing typical headgear. Living room/kitchenette, 3 bedrooms (3 double, 1 single and 1 child's bed), shower room, no heating, enclosed ground. Shopping at Pont l'Abbé or at Quimper (approx. 28 km).

Prices: low season   F 900
         high season F 1320

7/8 people
IGN 13

Booking: M G. AUTRET, Penfrajou, Plovan sur Mer, 29143 Plogastel.
Tel. 98 54 42 48
29/6.72.326

RIEC SUR BELON Kerspern A ground-floor gîte in a stone-built cottage amongst other buildings on a farm 2 km from the small town of Riec sur Belon which has a renowned sailing school. Walkers will enjoy the 18 km of coastal footpaths and other walks amongst magnificent scenery. Living room/kitchenette, 2 bedrooms (1 double and 2 single beds), bathroom, fireplace, heating, ground. Shopping and restaurant at Riec sur Belon or at Pont Aven (approx. 6 km).

Prices: low season   F 700/900
         high season F 1200

4 people
IGN 15

Booking: Mme S. JOUAN, Kerspern, 29124 Riec sur Belon.
Tel. 98 06 91 67
29/8.78.666

LA ROCHE MAURICE Ti Ménez A gîte in a substantial stone house beside other buildings 0.3 km from the village centre and approx 5 km from Landerneau on the river Elorn. Facilities here for bicycle and pedalo hire, char-a-banc rides, tennis, golf and other sports in the Lann-Rohou leisure park. Sea, beaches and sailing at 20 km. Living room/kitchenette, 2 bedrooms (1 double and 3 single beds), shower room, fireplace, heating, carport. Shopping and restaurants in Landerneau.

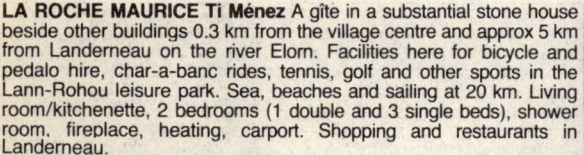

Prices: low season   F 800
         high season F 1250

5 people
IGN 13

Booking: Mme F. LE BIHAN, 10 rue Edmond Michelet, 29220 Landerneau. Tel. 98 21 45 70
29/1.72.266

SAINT EVARZEC Moustoir Vihan One of two adjoining gîtes set amongst other buildings on a farm 1 km from the village. The sea, beaches and sailing are just 5 km and the attractive resort of Fouesnant is approximately 7 km. Quimper, the département capital, with its manifold attractions is approximately 10 km. Living room, kitchen, 2 bedrooms (1 double and 2 single beds), shower room, heating, enclosed ground. Shopping and restaurants at Fouesnant or Quimper.

Prices: low season   F 770/1025
         high season F 1445

4 people
IGN 13

Booking: Finistère booking service
29/7.72.340

Finistère

SAINT NIC Ruyen A gîte in a neat little house set on its own 3 km from the village and just 0.8 km from the sea, beaches and sailing facilities. Swimming-pool at 17 km and the small town of Châteaulin, set in the lush valley of the river Aulne (good for fishing) is approximately 20 km. Look out for the typical Breton cottages scattered around the countryside here. Living room, kitchen, 2 bedrooms (2 double, 2 single and 1 child's bed), bathroom, heating, enclosed ground. Shopping and restaurants at Châteaulin.

Prices:	low season	F 750/850	**6/7 people**
	high season	F 1125/1076	*IGN 13*

Booking: Mme M. CANEVET, Rue du Leuré, Pentrez, Saint Nic, 29127 Plomodiern. Tel. 98 26 51 39

29/3.74.487

SAINT SAUVEUR Kerbunçou A gîte in a pretty, stone-built cottage on a farm 0.5 km from the village and standing in its own enclosed grounds. Landivisiau (approx. 15 km) is on the Elorn river and affords plenty of opportunity to sample the local seafood, fish and delicious Breton *crêpes*. Windsurfing, sailing and other sports at Morlaix (approx. 25 km). Living room/kitchenette, 2 bedrooms and an open landing (2 double and 2 single beds), bathroom, fireplace, heating, carport, enclosed ground. Shopping and restaurant at Morlaix or Landivisiau.

Prices:	low season	F 750/900	**6 people**
	high season	F 1350	*IGN 13*

Booking: M J. CORRE, Kerbunçou, Saint Sauveur, 29230 Landivisiau. Tel. 98 68 73 70

29/2.80.755

SCAER Kergoff Bihan A gîte in a substantial house set on a farm 2 km from the town of Scaer which has a lively summer programme of special events, facilities for tennis, swimming and a forest for picnics. Rosporden (approx. 16 km) hosts a summer folk festival. The sea, beaches and sailing are at 23 km. Living room, kitchen, 3 bedrooms (3 double and 1 single bed), fireplace, heating, carport, ground. Shopping and restaurant at Scaer.

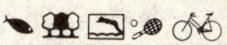

Prices:	low season	F 780/960	**7 people**
	high season	F 1339/1390	*IGN 15*

Booking: M M. THEPOT, Cleubeuz, Mellac, 29130 Quimperlé. Tel. 98 71 83 67

29/8.82.900

TREGARVAN Le Cosquer One of two ground-floor gîtes in a well-maintained stone-built cottage set amongst other buildings 1 km from the village centre. Châteaulin (approx. 13 km) is a pretty town set in a hollow of the Aulne valley. Good walking and cycling country here and canoeing, pedalo hire and fishing facilities. Living room/kitchenette, 1 bedroom and 1 bed-sitting room (1 double and 2 single beds), shower room, fireplace, heating, ground. Shopping and restaurants in Châteaulin.

Prices:	low season	F 960	**4 people**
	high season	F 1275	*IGN 13*

Booking: Finistère booking service

29/3.81.818

TREOGAT Kergroas One of two gîtes in a pretty, stone-built house set amongst other buildings 2 km from the village. Pont l'Abbé (approx. 12 km) is the capital of the Bigouden country and the Bigouden women always wear a distinctive head dress – look out for them in the shady streets of this old Breton town. Sailing at 17 km. Living room/kitchenette, 2 bedrooms (1 double and 2 single beds), shower room, fireplace, heating, ground. Shopping and restaurants at Pont l'Abbé.

Prices:	low season	F 590/895	**4 people**
	high season	F 1275	*IGN 13*

Booking: Finistère booking service

29/6.80.786

10

Finistère

LE TREVOUX Kerfouënnec One of two gîtes set amongst other buildings on a farm 3 km from the village. Quimperlé (approx. 15 km) is a picturesque town set on the confluence of the rivers Elle and Isole and amongst woody countryside. Several old buildings of note here and a visit to the Breton museum is recommended; between May and September the town hosts colourful gatherings of local people wearing the distinctive Breton dress. Living room/kitchenette, 2 bedrooms (1 double and 2 single beds), bathroom, ground. Shopping and restaurants at Quimperlé.
Prices: low season F 875/1025 **4 people**
high season F 1305 IGN 15
Booking: Finistère booking service
29/8.81.836

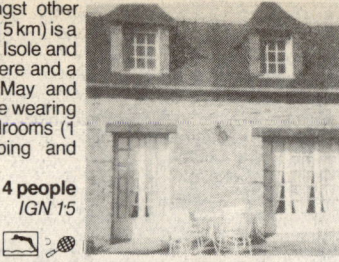

LAZ Kerhuel *Chambre d'hôte* accommodation in the owner's home on a farm 2 km from the village. Châteauneuf du Faou (approx. 12 km) is a rural holiday resort with an excellent range of sporting and cultural activities including an international dance festival; do visit the château and botanical gardens. The sea, beaches and sailing at 30 km. Three rooms with washbasins available: bedroom 1 (1 double and 1 single bed); bedroom 2 (1 double bed); bedroom 3 (1 double and 2 single beds); private bathroom and toilet for the three rooms, central heating. Shopping and restaurants at Châteauneuf du Faou. **9 people**
Prices: 1p F 70, 2p F 97, 3p F 130, 4p F 150 IGN 13
Booking: Mme M. BARRE, Kerhuel, 29164 Laz. Tel. 98 26 84 73

29/4.83.042.3

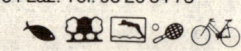

PLOUZANE Lézavarn *Chambre d'hôte* accommodation in the owner's own home on a farm near the village. The city of Brest is just 8 km away and offers an extensive range of entertainments from boat trips and beaches to museums and a wide range of sports; try the local seafood and strawberries in season. Four rooms with washbasins available: bedrooms 1 and 2 (1 double bed); bedrooms 3 and 4 (1 double and 1 single bed), shared bathroom and toilet, central heating. Shopping and restaurants in Brest. **10 people**
Prices: 1p F 85, 2p F 110, 3p F 140 IGN 13
Booking: Mme M. PERROT, Lézavarn, Plouzané, 29290 St Renan. Tel. 98 48 41 28

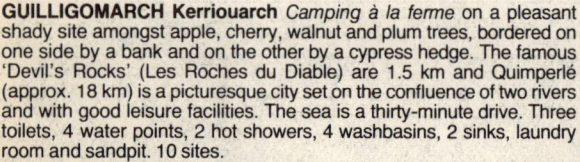

29/1.78.014.4

GUILLIGOMARCH Kerriouarch *Camping à la ferme* on a pleasant shady site amongst apple, cherry, walnut and plum trees, bordered on one side by a bank and on the other by a cypress hedge. The famous 'Devil's Rocks' (Les Roches du Diable) are 1.5 km and Quimperlé (approx. 18 km) is a picturesque city set on the confluence of two rivers and with good leisure facilities. The sea is a thirty-minute drive. Three toilets, 4 water points, 2 hot showers, 4 washbasins, 2 sinks, laundry room and sandpit. 10 sites.
Prices: on request IGN 13
Booking: Mme L. BAHUON, Kerriouarch, Guilligomarch, 29130 Quimperlé. Tel. 98 71 70 12

29/8.78.004

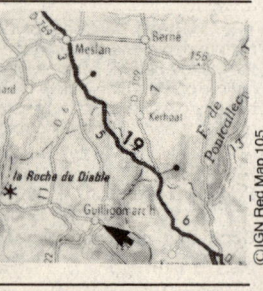

LANHOUARNEAU Mulin de Coat Merret *Camping à la ferme* 4 km from the town and 10 km from the sea on a flat site in a sheltered valley surrounded by trees and with a stream running through the grounds. Lesneven (approx. 14 km) is an attractive old town with some fifteenth-century buildings. Now an important commercial centre, it holds a picturesque weekly Monday market. Three toilets, 2 hot showers, 4 washbasins, laundry room and 2 sinks. 25 sites.
Prices: on request IGN 15
Booking: Mme A. SIOHAN, Moulin de Coat Merret, Lanhouarneau, 29221 Plouescat. Tel. 98 61 62 06

29/2.81.020

Ille-et-Vilaine

BAZOUGES LA PEROUSE Bourdinnais One of three gîtes in an old stone building now renovated and furnished in rustic style on a livestock farm 4 km from the village. Visit the château and forest at Fougères (30 km), the famous Mont Saint Michel (25 km) and Combourg (18 km) offers swimming-pool, château and park. Living room/kitchenette, 2 bedrooms (1 double, 2 single beds), bathroom, fireplace, electric central heating, shared open ground with furniture. Farm produce from the owner, shopping and restaurant in the village or at Combourg.

Prices:	low season	F 486/730	4 people
	high season	F 835/876	IGN 16

Booking: Ille-et-Vilaine Loisirs Accueil E
35/G2433043

LA BOUEXIERE Chataignier An old traditionally furnished stone-built house, stylishly renovated just 2 km from the village. The département capital, Rennes, is well worth a visit at 22 km and there is a swimming-pool and tennis at Cesson Sévigné (17 km). Living room/kitchenette, 4 bedrooms (1 double, 5 single and 1 child's bed), bathroom, open fire, electric central heating, enclosed ground. Fresh farm produce and shopping in the village where there is a restaurant, or at Rennes.

Prices:	low season	F 519/664	7/8 people
	high season	F 914/1016	IGN 16

Booking: Ille-et-Vilaine Loisirs Accueil E

35/G2740132

LES BRULAIS La Barriais An attractively renovated cottage with rustic furnishings, just outside the village (1.5 km). Interesting tourist excursions include Rochefort-en-Terre, a delightful old village of granite houses and a twelfth-century church where a pardon is held in mid-August, and Redon (30 km approx.) which grew up around a ninth-century Benedictine abbey. Living room (1 double divan), kitchen, 3 bedrooms (1 double and 2 single beds), bathroom, fireplace, electric central heating, open ground with garden furniture. Shopping at Maure-de-Bretagne (5 km).

Prices:	low season	F 677/753	6 people
	high season	F 907/1008	IGN 16

Booking: Ille-et-Vilaine Loisirs Accueil E
35/G2671683

LE CHATELLIER Petit Mont Merson A pretty country cottage renovated and furnished in rustic style in an attractive setting, 4 km from the village. The famous Mont St Michel is well worth a trip at 30 km as is the interesting fortress town of Fougères (10 km). Living room (single sofa bed), kitchen, 2 bedrooms (1 double and 2 single beds), bathroom, fireplace, electric heating, large enclosed grounds with barbecue. Shopping and restaurant in the village where fresh farm produce is available or at Fougères.

Prices:	low season	F 827	5 people
	high season	F 953/1017	IGN 16

Booking: Ille-et-Vilaine Loisirs Accueil E

35/G2630267

CHERRUEIX Bas Village One of two gîtes in a substantial old stone house now renovated and furnished in traditional style and situated by the owner's livestock farm 1 km from this seaside village. St Malo (20 km) is a popular coastal resort and there are good beaches at Cancale (18 km). Living room/kitchenette, 2 bedrooms (1 double and 2 single beds), shower room, electric heating, garage, ground (shared). Fresh milk from the owner, shopping and restaurant at Cherrueix or at Cancale.

Prices:	low season	F 761/821	4 people
	high season	F 991/1019	IGN 16

Booking: Ille-et-Vilaine Loisirs Accueil E
35/G2610038

Ille-et-Vilaine

ILLE-ET-VILAINE in Upper Brittany

With its famous coastline – the Emerald Coast: Cancale, Dinard and Saint-Malo.

With its mysterious countryside, covered with heaths and forests.

The Emerald Coast

Ille-et-Vilaine offers you many and varied holidays:

105 1–4-star camp sites
570 hotels
500 gîtes de France and country-cottages
and many holiday lettings.
Here, there are lots of different things to do: sailing, fishing, tennis, golf, riding. . .
Discover Ille-et-Vilaine's rich heritage: museums, châteaux, churches. . .

For general tourist information and documentation:

Comité Départemental du Tourisme d'Ille-et-Vilaine,
1 rue Martenot,
35000 RENNES, France
Tel. (99) 02.97.43.
Telex. 730 808 IVTOUR.

Chateau de Vitré
(Photo: CDT Ille-et-Vilaine)

Special Interest Holidays

RESERVATION LOISIRS ACCUEIL

Ille-et-Vilaine has created a certain number of *Pays d'Accueil* specially in order to welcome its visitors. A *Pays d'Accueil* is an area naturally rich in beauty and culture. Here, the local people and tourist office undertake certain guarantees to their visitors:
– Quality accommodation – Events and activities, even out of season – Above all, a warm and true welcome.
In **Ille-et-Vilaine,** these small natural regions have their own special character.
– Le Pays de Brocéliande – land of legends, moors, forests and ponds.
– Le Pays de Combourg – the Mont St. Michel and the home of romanticism.
– Le Pays d'Accueil de Fougères – the granite kingdom and seat of the *Chouannerie* (Breton Royalists).
– Le Pays de Vilaine – crossroads of the navigable waterways, land of tradition, home of a rich folk culture.

Le Pays d'Accueil de FOUGERES

A granite land, full of tradition, lying within the Breton border, neighbouring Normandy.

Apart from the proximity of famous places, such as St. Malo and Mont St. Michel, its main tourist attractions are its three beautiful forests; the valley of Couesnon and Minette; and a great number of granite-built châteaux and country-houses. In this rich and green countryside, there is something for everyone to do, all the year round, and apart from the various outdoor pursuits, horse-riding, canoeing, etc., Ille-et-Vilaine offers:
– courses in wood-carving and sculpting out of granite
– courses in drawing and painting

Workshop tuition is given by skilled artists and craftsmen and courses of 5 days duration are approx. F 900.

Château de Fougères

Villages d'Accueil
The majority of gîtes and country-cottages are furnished accommodation in old granite farm buildings.

Bazouges-la-Pérouse (less than 25 km from Mont St. Michel and 45 km from St. Malo – 31 gîtes ruraux within a radius of 5 km),

Beuvron (less than 30 km from Mont St. Michel, 7 km from the Sélune Valley, 140 km from Cherbourg and 100 km from the beaches of the Normandy landings),
– 18 gîtes ruraux

The Valleys of Couesnon and Minette (between Fougères and Rennes),
– 23 gîtes ruraux

A gîte in Bazouges-la-Perouse
(Photograph: Office du Pays d'Accueil de Fougeres)

For booking and further information of the gîtes listed on the next page contact:
Loisirs Accueil en Haute-Bretagne – Ille-et-Vilaine,
1 rue Martenot, 35000 RENNES, France. **Tel.** (99) 02.97.41. **Telex.** 730 808 IVTOUR.

NB For fuller information about all Loisirs Accueil services, please see pages 12–13 of this guide.

Ille-et-Vilaine

COGLES Les Buttes A ground-floor gîte in an attractive old stone-built cottage, now renovated and equipped with traditional-style furnishings 3 km from the village. The old fortress town of Fougères (22 km) offers plenty to do including forest walks, riding and a swimming-pool. Living room/kitchenette, 2 bedrooms (1 double and 2 single beds), shower room, fireplace, electric central heating, open ground. Fresh milk and wine from the owner, shopping and restaurant at Cogles or at Fougères.

Prices:	low season	F 742/779	**4 people**
	high season	F 843/902	*IGN 16*

Booking: Ille-et-Vilaine Loisirs Accueil   E

35/G1431014

DOMAGNE La Rivière A ground-floor gîte adjoining the owner's home and furnished in traditional style just 1 km from the village centre. Vitré (16 km) has an interesting old quarter and a château. Living room/kitchenette, 2 bedrooms (2 double and 1 single bed), shower room, fireplace, central heating, garage, grounds shared with the owner and garden furniture. Fresh eggs and chickens from the owner, shopping and restaurant in the village or at Vitré.

Prices:	low season	F 465/583	**5 people**
	high season	F 714/764	*IGN 16*

Booking: Ille-et-Vilaine Loisirs Accueil   E

35/G2561116

LE FERRE Les Vallées A charming little gîte, renovated and furnished in country style, in a hamlet. Fougères (18 km) has a strong fortress built to protect the frontier with Normandy. The town is now known for its shoe trade and there is an annual summer exhibition of the craft in the castle. The sea (25 km approx.). Living room, kitchen, 2 bedrooms-one on an open landing (1 double, 2 single beds), bathroom, fireplace, electric central heating, open ground. Shopping and restaurant in the village (0.4 km).

Prices:	low season	F 476/744	**4 people**
	high season	F 851/993	*IGN 16*

Booking: Ille-et-Vilaine Loisirs Accueil   E

35/G2433332

LA FRESNAIS Bédolière A pretty stone-built cottage, stylishly renovated and traditionally furnished 3 km from the village. The coastal resort of St Malo offers plenty to see and do at 12 km and Cancale (8 km) is worth a visit. Living room/kitchenette, 4 bedrooms (2 double, 5 single and 1 child's bed), bathroom, fireplace, electric heating, open grounds. Fresh dairy produce in the village where there are shops and a restaurant or at Dol de Bretagne (8 km) which has a market on Saturdays.

Prices:	low season	F 1253/1485	**9/10 people**
	high season	F 1739	*IGN 16*

Booking: Ille-et-Vilaine Loisirs Accueil   E

35/G3910304

GUIPRY Chesnaie du Sain An old stone-built, creeper-hung, semi-detached country cottage furnished in traditional style and situated 3.5 km from the village. Guipry itself is a rural holiday resort and offers swimming-pool and tennis and the surrounding countryside is well worth touring. Living room/kitchenette, 2 bedrooms (1 double and 2 single beds), shower room, fireplace, central heating, open grounds. Shopping and restaurant in the village or at Redon (18 km).

Prices:	low season	F 402/514	**4 people**
	high season	F 850	*IGN 24*

Booking: Ille-et-Vilaine Loisirs Accueil   E

35/G2471811

Ille-et-Vilaine

IFFENDIC Croix Cormier A gîte in a substantial stone-built house now renovated and divided into three gîtes with country-style furnishings, 4 km from the village. There is a lovely old abbey at Paimpont and the Brocéliande forest (6 km) offers pleasant walks. Living room/kitchenette (single sofa bed), 4 bedrooms (2 double, 4 single and 1 child's bed), bathroom, fireplace, electric central heating, open ground with garden furniture and children's swings shared with other gîtes. Restaurant at 1.5 km, shopping in the village or at Montfort-sur-Meu (8 km).

Prices:	low season	not available	9/10 people
	high season	F 990/1077	IGN 16

Booking: Ille-et-Vilaine Loisirs Accueil E
35/G2150944

ROZ-LANDRIEUX Vildé Bidon A rustically furnished gîte in a renovated building adjoining another house on farmland just 1.5 km from the village. Fascinating Mont St Michel is 20 km away as are the coastal towns of St Malo and mediaeval Dinan. Living room (TV), kitchen, 2 bedrooms (1 double, 1 single and 1 child's bed), shower room, fireplace, electric heating, garage, enclosed courtyard and grounds with children's swings and garden furniture. Fresh farm produce at the neighbouring farm, shopping (0.2 km) and restaurant in the village or at Dol-de-Bretagne (5 km).

Prices:	low season	on request	3/4 people
	high season	on request	IGN 16

Booking: Ille-et-Vilaine Loisirs Accueil E
35/G2323798

SAINT-HILAIRE-DES-LANDES Grand-Bossart A ground-floor gîte in an old renovated building, with traditional-style furnishings, forming part of a small hamlet. The interesting fortress town of Fougères is at 15 km and Chenedet (15 km) has a lake suitable for bathing. Living room/kitchenette, 2 bedrooms (1 double, 2 single beds), shower room, fireplace, electric central heating, open ground with summerhouse and garden furniture. Dairy produce and wine from the owner, other shopping and restaurant in the village (1 km) or at Fougères.

Prices:	low season	F 476/744	4 people
	high season	F 851/893	IGN 16

Booking: Ille-et-Vilaine Loisirs Accueil E
35/G1433481

SAINT-JOUAN-DES-GUERETS Le Fresne A detached, renovated house with country-style furnishings next to another gîte 0.3 km from the village centre. Excellently situated for visiting the interesting coastal resorts of St Malo (4 km) and Dinard (8 km) which offer plenty to do and see. Living room/kitchenette, 2 bedrooms (1 double and 2 single beds), shower room, fireplace, electric central heating, shared open ground with children's games and garden furniture. Shopping and restaurant in the village or at St Malo (4 km).

Prices:	low season	F 1230/1289	4 people
	high season	F 1505	IGN 16

Booking: Ille-et-Vilaine Loisirs Accueil E
35/G2412138

SAINT-MARC-LE-BLANC Bodinais One of two traditionally furnished gîtes in the owners' own house on a livestock farm 3 km from the village centre. Good country for walking with plenty of marked footpaths and the Fougères forest (15 km) also has a lake. Living room, kitchen, 2 bedrooms (1 double and 2 single beds), shower room, fireplace, electric heating, shared open ground with children's swings and garden furniture. Fresh farm produce from the owners, shopping and restaurant in the village or at Fougères.

Prices:	low season	F 450/578	4 people
	high season	F 702/826	IGN 16

Booking: Ille-et-Vilaine Loisirs Accueil E
35/G1530567

10

Ille-et-Vilaine

SAINT-OUEN-DES-ALLEUX Bouexiere A substantial renovated stone house furnished in rustic style and just 1 km from the village centre. Plenty for outdoor types in the area including a climbing school and canoeing (at 8 km), trout fishing and bicycle hire and a lake at Chenedet (20 km). Living room/kitchenette, 3 bedrooms (2 double, 2 single and 1 child's bed), bathroom, fireplace, electric central heating, open ground. Shopping and restaurant in the village or at Fougères (18 km).

Prices:	low season	F 521/792	**6/7 people**
	high season	F 959/997	IGN 16

Booking: Ille-et-Vilaine Loisirs Accueil   E

35/G2633535

SAINT-THUAL La Motte-Rouxel A renovated house with traditional furnishings situated in a small hamlet. Dinan, a well-preserved fortified mediaeval town, is at 20 km as is Combourg which offers a castle and park. The coast is 40 km away. Living room/kitchenette, 2 bedrooms (2 double, 1 single and 1 child's bed), shower room, electric central heating, garage and shared open ground. Shopping and restaurant at Bécherel (5 km).

Prices:	low season	F 586/650	**6 people**
	high season	F 908	IGN 16

Booking: Ille-et-Vilaine Loisirs Accueil   E

35/G1520980

SAINT-THURIAL Le Frambois Rustically furnished gîte in its own open grounds but adjoining the main house 1 km from the village centre. Tremelin (10 km) has a leisure centre offering various watersports, riding and miniature golf and the abbey at Paimpont (12 km) is well worth a visit. Living room (1 single bed), kitchen, 2 bedrooms (2 double and 1 child's bed), shower room, open fire, heating, garage. Shopping and restaurant in Saint-Thurial or at Plelan le Grand (10 km); a market every Tuesday at Mordelles (8 km).

Prices:	low season	F 471/633	**6 people**
	high season	F 728/788	IGN 16

Booking: Ille-et-Vilaine Loisirs Accueil   E

35/G1551712

LE TRONCHET A ground-floor gîte, traditionally furnished, in an old house sharing an open courtyard and gardens (sun lounge) with other dwellings. The popular resort of Saint-Malo (25 km) has been sympathetically restored since the war with cobbled streets and busy yachting harbour. Living room/kitchenette (1 single sofa bed), 1 bedroom (1 double, 1 child's bed), shower room, open fire, central heating, garden furniture. Shops and restaurant in the village (0.5 km) or at Dol-de-Bretagne (12 km).

Prices:	low season	F 596/719	**3/4 people**
	high season	F 743/804	IGN 16

Booking: Ille-et-Vilaine Loisirs Accueil   E

35/G2310738

LE TRONCHET A ground-floor gîte traditionally furnished, in an old house sharing an open courtyard and gardens (sun lounge) with other dwellings. The popular resort of Saint Malo (25 km) has been château at Combourg are all within 22 km and Mont-Saint-Michel is 30 km. Living room (single sofa bed), kitchen, 1 bedroom (1 double and 1 child's bed), shower room, no heating, open ground and enclosed courtyard with garden furniture. Shopping and restaurant in the village or at Combourg (15 km).

Prices:	low season	F 759	**3/4 people**
	high season	F 853/928	IGN 16

Booking: Ille-et-Vilaine Loisirs Accueil   E

35/G2310266

FOR YOUR HOLIDAYS IN 1986 VISIT MORBIHAN

MORBIHAN
LA BRETAGNE AU NATUREL

Loisirs accueil en Morbihan takes all the strain and risk out of booking the type of accommodation you want leisure activities, or organised holidays...
- top-class service,
- guaranteed prices,
- offices open all year round.

A group of holiday experts from Morbihan County have formed an association called loisirs accueil en Morbihan with a view to providing information and help in choosing the most suitable holiday for you.

The 1986 catalogue will be available as from December 1985.

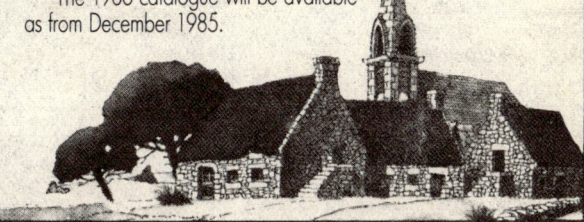

Write to :
LOISIRS ACCUEIL EN MORBIHAN
B.P. 400. 56009 VANNES CEDEX.
Or phone (010.33) 97.42.61.60

RESERVATION LOISIRS ACCUEIL

IT'S THE SURE WAY TO VISIT FRANCE

Morbihan

BELZ Porniscop One of two gîtes in a renovated building, traditionally furnished and situated in its own enclosed garden a short walk from the village centre (1.5 km). Auray (15 km) is a pretty little town with a small harbour on the river Auray—try the oyster and other seafood specialities! The sea is at 3 km. Living room/kitchenette, 2 bedrooms (1 double and 2 single beds), shower room, fireplace, electric heating, terrace, garden furniture. Shopping and restaurant in the village or at Auray.

Prices:	low season	F 780/895	**4 people**
	high season	F 1615	IGN 15

Booking: Morbihan Booking Service   E

56/013-13R

BIGNAN Lande de Kergan A lovely little Breton cottage with rustic furniture, standing in its own extensive, wooded grounds, 5 km from the village and 35 km from the sea. Fishing in the nearby Beaulieu lake; swimming-pool and tennis at Locminé (10 km). Living room, kitchen, 3 bedrooms (2 double, 3 single and 1 cot), bathroom, fireplace, electric heating, carport, garden with outdoor furniture and child's swing. Shopping and restaurant at Saint-Jean-Brevelay (2.5 km) or in Locminé.

Prices:	low season	F 1100	**7 people**
	high season	F 1430	IGN 15

Booking: Morbihan booking service   E

56/017-2R

BRANDERION Le Millédec This attractive stone-built house has been renovated and divided into two traditionally furnished gîtes. Visit the interesting town of Hennebont (6 km) which has many fine old buildings and other architecture, including thirteenth-century prison gates. Sailing and bathing at the coast (18 km). Living room/kitchenette, 2 bedrooms (1 double, 2 single beds and a cot), bathroom, electric heating, enclosed ground with garden furniture. Shopping and restaurant in the village (2 km).

Prices:	low season	F 830	**4 people**
	high season	F 1140	IGN 15

Booking: Morbihan booking service   E

56/021-4R

CAUDAN Kerbihan One of three gîtes in a spacious, well renovated house furnished in traditional style and stiuated 3 km from the village. Hennebont (2 km) has old fortifications and a museum devoted to Breton traditions (July/August); Lorient (approx. 15 km) is an important port and a centre for watersports. Living room, kitchen, 4 bedrooms (1 double and 6 single beds), shower room and bathroom, open fire, electric heating, carport, garden with furniture, barbecue and *boules*. Shopping and restaurant at 3 km or Hennebont.

Prices:	low season	F 1500	**8 people**
	high season	F 2380	IGN 15

Booking: Morbihan Booking Service   E

56/036-12R

CRACH Keruzerh-Brigitte A well renovated and traditionally furnished cottage sheltered by trees in its own enclosed garden, 2 km from Auray, a pretty town with a small harbour. Carnac (10 km) has excellent beaches and is renowned for its prehistoric megaliths. Living room/kitchenette, 2 bedrooms (1 double, 2 single beds and a cot), shower room, fireplace, electric heating, garden with barbecue and furniture. Shopping and restaurant at Auray.

Prices:	low season	F 790/840	**4/5 people**
	high season	F 1520	IGN 15

Booking: Morbihan Booking Service   E

56/046-8R

Morbihan

ERDEVEN Kerhat One of 2 gîtes in an attractive house on a livestock farm 1.5 km from the village and only 2km from the sea. Auray (15 km) offers guided tours round its interesting old buildings and an opportunity to try excellent seafood. Living room, kitchen, 3 bedrooms (2 double and 2 single beds), shower room, fireplace, oil-fired central heating, carport, enclosed garden with furniture. Shopping and restaurant in the village or at Belz (approx. 8 km).

Prices: low season   F 1020/1110   **6 people**
high season   F 1760   IGN 15
Booking: Morbihan Booking Service   **E**

56/054-6R

HENNEBONT Etang de Locoyarn A first-floor gîte in a traditionally furnished house, lying on a mixed farm whose owners may sell fresh produce. A pond nearby (punt available). It is 2 km from the interesting old town of Hennebont, where you can see the remains of its fortifications, basilica and botanic gardens. The sea is just 8 km away. Living room/kitchenette (TV), 2 bedrooms (1 double and 2 single beds), shower room, open fire, electric central heating, grounds with garden furniture seesaw and *boules*. Shopping and restaurant in the village or at Lorient (6 km).

Prices: low season   F 790/830   **4 people**
high season   F 1255   IGN 15
Booking: Morbihan booking service   **E**
56/083-1R

INZINZAC Kerglaw A lovingly restored, stone-built gîte with traditional furnishings, situated in its own enclosed grounds with garden furniture and barbecue for outdoor meals, 2 km from the village centre. Bathing and canoeing in the river (0.6 km). Lorient (10 km) is an important military seaport with a naval museum. Living room, kitchen, 2 bedrooms (1 double, 2 single and 1 cot), bathroom, open fire, electric heating, carport. Shopping and restaurant within walking distance (0.6 km).

Prices: low season   F 710/750   **4/5 people**
high season   F 1100   IGN 15
Booking: Morbihan booking service   **E**

56/090-5R

10

INZINZAC Kerlino A ground-floor gîte, one of two in a renovated and traditionally furnished building on a farm, some 4 km from the village. Forest walks at 2 km. See the botanic gardens at the old town of Hennebont (8 km). The coast is 25 km away. Living room/kichenette, 2 bedrooms (2 double and 1 single bed), bathroom, electric heating, garden and enclosed ground shared with other gîte, garden furniture. Shopping and restaurant at 1 km.

Prices: low season   F 800/870   **5 people**
high season   F 1240   IGN 15
Booking: Morbihan booking service   **E**

56/090-3R

INZINZAC Sainte Geneviève A well renovated and traditionally furnished ground floor gîte on a mixed farm in a small hamlet 7 km from the village. Hennebont (10 km) has some interesting old fortifications and houses and you can join in the *fêtes de nuit* celebrations in July; the sea is 20 km. Living room/kitchenette (1 single bed), 1 bedroom (1 double bed), shower room, fireplace, oil central heating, terrace, open garden with furniture and child's swing. Shops and restaurant at 7 km or at Hennebont.

Prices: low season   F 560   **3 people**
high season   F 970   IGN 15
Booking: Morbihan booking service   **E**
56/090-10R

Morbihan

LANGUIDIC Coet-Colay One of three gîtes in a renovated building with traditional furnishings, situated 4 km from the village. It lies near a forest and river (fishing permitted). The busy port of Lorient (24 km) has a sailing club and all the usual facilities of a seaside resort; try the seafood, particularly lobster. Living room/kitchenette, 2 bedrooms (1 double, 2 single and 1 cot), shower room, electric heating, carport, open ground shared with the other gîtes, garden furniture. Shopping and restaurant in the village.

Prices:	low season	F 625/650	4/5 people
	high season	F 965/1080	IGN 15

Booking: Morbihan booking service   E

56/101-14R

LANOUEE Gué-Aux-Biches A traditionally furnished gîte at the edge of the village (2 km). Local fishing and forest walks; many leisure facilities available at the lovely château town of Josselin (10 km) or at Ploermel where there is a lake (20 km). The sea is 50 km away. Living room/kitchenette, 3 bedrooms (2 double, 2 single and 1 cot), bathroom, open fire, electric heating, open ground. Shopping and restaurant in the village (2 km).

Prices:	low season	F 630/730	6/7 people
	high season	F 1040	IGN 15

Booking: Morbihan booking service   E

56/102-3R

PLOEMEL Kerbrezel One of two gîtes on two floors of this attractive, stone-built house on a mixed farm. Bathing and sailing at the coast (8 km). Visit the narrow peninsula of Quiberon (25 km approx.) with its fine sandy beaches, golf course and four fishing ports. Living room, kitchen, 2 bedrooms (2 double and 1 single bed), shower room, fireplace, gas central heating, open ground shared with other gîtes, garden furniture. Shopping and restaurant in the village (1 km) or at Auray (6 km).

Prices:	low season	F 780/850	5 people
	high season	F 1290	IGN 15

Booking: Morbihan booking service   E

56/161-5R

PLOEMEL Kerganiet A large house, not far from the village centre (0.7 km) and just 7 km from the coast. Auray (7 km) is an unusual little town with a small port and regular market, swimming-pool and tennis court; it is surrounded by pine woods. Living room, kitchen, 3 bedrooms (1 double and 3 single beds), shower room, open fire, gas central heating, terrace, carport, open ground with garden furniture. Farm produce from the owners; shopping and restaurant in the village.

Prices:	low season	F 820/1045	5 people
	high season	F 1490	IGN 15

Booking: Morbihan booking service   E

56/161-3R

PLOUHINEC Kermarhic A renovated and traditionally furnished gîte, one of two, in a small hamlet 2 km from the village. Lorient (15 km) is an important military, naval and fishing port—you might see some submarines! Local specialities include seafood, cider and *crêpes*. Living room/kitchenette, 2 bedrooms (1 double, 4 single and 1 child's bed), shower room, fireplace, electric heating, carport, open ground with garden furniture. Shopping and restaurant in the village or at Lorient.

Prices:	low season	F 680/760	6/7 people
	high season	F 1040	IGN 15

Booking: Morbihan booking service   E

56/169-7R

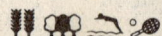

Morbihan

PLOUHINEC Kervelhué A charming, spacious family house with traditional furnishings, outside the village and within walking distance of the coast (1.5 km), where you may fish and sail. Visit the ancient département capital of Vannes (40 km approx.) with its delightful old buildings, cathedral, gardens and other attractions. Living room, kitchen, 4 bedrooms (2 double and 4 single beds), shower room, fireplace, electric heating, terrace, garden and enclosed ground. Shopping and restaurant in the village (2.5 km) or at Belz (8 km approx.).

Prices:	low season	F 1150/1300	8 people
	high season	F 2150	IGN 15

Booking: Morbihan booking service   E

56/169-57R

PLOUHINEC Le Magouër A renovated and traditionally furnished gîte situated on a mixed farm in a hamlet 3 km from the village centre. Lorient (18 km) is an important military and fishing port offering guided tours, bicycle hire, canoeing and several beaches: do try the local seafood specialities and cider! Living room/kitchenette, 2 bedrooms (1 double and 2 single beds), shower room, electric heating, carport, ground with garden furniture. Restaurant at 2 km, shopping at 3 km or at Lorient.

Prices:	low season	F 760/870	4 people
	high season	F 1320	IGN 15

Booking: Morbihan booking service   E

56/169-62R

SEGLIEN Loucouviern Situated on a livestock farm, this attractive gîte has traditional furniture. The lovely Quénécan forest is 10 km; sailing at Guerlédan lake (20 km). The sea and beaches are near enough for a day trip (45 km). Living room, kitchen, 2 bedrooms (4 single beds), bathroom, open fire, electric heating, carport, open ground. Shopping and restaurant in the village (2 km) or at Pontivy (15 km).

Prices:	low season	F 660/770	4 people
	high season	F 1050	IGN 15

Booking: Morbihan booking service   E

56/242-2R

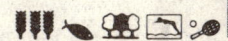

SURZUR Blavazon A neat, well renovated and maintained gîte situated on a mixed farm and furnished in traditional style. Vannes (20 km) has some interesting old fortifications and offers guided tours and boat trips in the Gulf of Morbihan in season as well as good sporting facilities, including tennis, riding and swimming. Living room/kitchenette, 4 bedrooms (2 double and 4 single beds), bathroom, shower room, fireplace, electric heating, open garden with furniture. Restaurant and shopping at 5 km or at Vannes.

Prices:	high season	F 980/1100	8 people
	low season	F 2020	IGN 15

Booking: Morbihan booking service   E

56/248-8R

TAUPONT Quelneuc An attractive stone built house situated in a small hamlet just outside the village. Ploermel (4 km) is a quiet old town with some interesting buildings and the Lac du Duc there has facilities for swimming, sailing, tennis and pedalo hire. The sea is at 50 km. Kitchen, 3 bedrooms (3 double beds), bathroom, central heating, open ground. Shopping in the village or at Ploemel where there is a restaurant.

Prices:	high season	F 700	6 people
	low season	F 800	IGN 15

Booking: Morbihan booking service   E

56/249-3R

10

chambre d'hôte

IN GREAT BRITAIN, YOU HAVE
"BED AND BREAKFAST"
IN FRANCE WE HAVE
"CHAMBRE D'HOTE"

Chambre d'hôte is the name given to Bed and Breakfast in the country, usually in a farm. Chambres d'hôte are classified and regularly inspected by the "gîte de France" board.

"Cidre d'Honneur in a Chambre d'hôte"
An idea of your welcome in a French farm with a "Chambre d'hôte"

Please send me holiday and accommodation information

NAME ——————
Address ——————

WRITE TO: **RELAIS DES GITES DE LA MANCHE (50)**
Préfecture – B.P. F2
50009 SAINT-LO CÉDEX
Tél: (33) 57.52.80

OR TO: **RELAIS DES GITES DE L'ORNE (61)**
60, rue Saint-Blaise – B.P. 50
61002 ALENÇON CÉDEX
Tél: (33) 26.18.71 ou 26.74.00

11 NORMANDY

Normandy will always be indelibly linked in the minds of many British with the liberation of France in 1944.

However, its connection with Britain goes way back to the time of William the Conqueror, the Norman Duke whose invasion of our country is so well depicted on the Bayeux Tapestry (still in remarkably good condition and on view at the museum in Bayeux), now said to have been made in England!

Britain's proximity to the Normandy coast has led to its popularity with British holidaymakers, who flocked to such fashionable and elegant resorts as Deauville at the end of the nineteenth century. Deauville and many other family resorts which, bathed by the gulf stream enjoy a very mild climate, still welcome thousands of British visitors annually.

For those disinclined to spend their days lazing on beaches, Normandy has many fascinating historic sites: Mont-Saint-Michel, Rouen, Lisieux, made famous by pilgrimages to the young Carmelite nun, Saint Theresa, to name but a few. On the coast, the many picturesque fishing ports, such as Honfleur and Tréport, are well worth a visit.

Inland Normandy, divided almost in half by the river Seine, with its landscape of forests, pasturelands and fine half-timbered manor houses, also attracts a good many visitors. But you have to be prepared to abandon all thoughts of dieting during your stay! This is the land of the three "Cs" — cream, cider and calvados — and Normandy cuisine liberally includes all three.

VIEUX CALVADOS   Fine old apple brandy

PAYS D'AUGE
Appelation d'origine controlée

Well-aged spirit from the oldest reserves of the Ouin family, distilled from the 1930's. Also available, cider vinegar, fruit and other farm produce in season. Open daily, except Sunday mornings.

M. Rene Ouin and M. Michel Fernagut,
Rue de la Baronnerie, St Julien le Faucon, 14140 Livarot (Tel: 31.63.81.46)
OR Vieux Pont en Auge, 14140 Livarot (Tel: 31.20.73.00)

Carte de Normandie

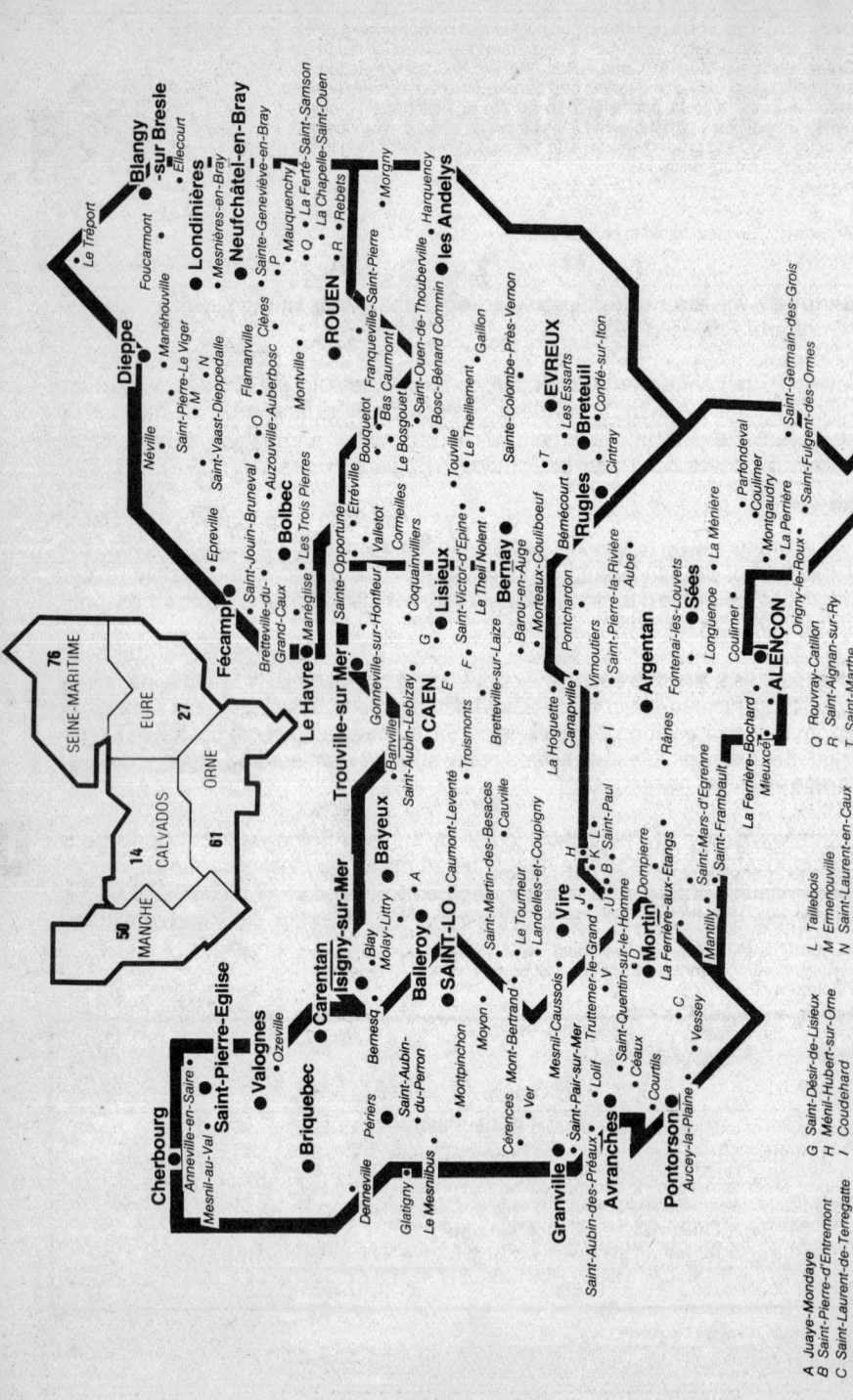

Départements : 76 Seine-Maritime, 27 Eure, 14 Calvados, 61 Orne, 50 Manche

Villes principales
Cherbourg, Saint-Pierre-Eglise, Valognes, Briquebec, Carentan, Isigny-sur-Mer, Bayeux, Balleroy, SAINT-LO, Vire, Mortain, Pontorson, Avranches, Granville, Trouville-sur-Mer, Le Havre, Fécamp, Dieppe, Blangy-sur-Bresle, Londinières, Neufchâtel-en-Bray, les Andelys, ROUEN, Bolbec, Lisieux, CAEN, Bernay, Rugles, Breteuil, EVREUX, Argentan, Sées, ALENÇON

Localités
Le Tréport, Foucarmont, Ellecourt, Mesnières-en-Bray, Sainte-Geneviève-en-Bray, Mauquenchy, La Ferté-Saint-Samson, La Chapelle-Saint-Ouen, Rebets, Morgny, Harquency, Gaillon, Bosc-Bénard Commin, Franqueville-Saint-Pierre, Saint-Ouen-de-Thouberville, Bas Caumont, Le Bosgouet, Bouquetot, Valletot, Cornevilles, Coquainvilliers, Gonneville-sur-Honfleur, Sainte-Opportune, Étréville, Le Theil Nolent, Saint-Victor-d'Épine, Le Theillement, Sainte-Colombe-Près-Vernon, Condé-sur-Iton, Les Essarts, Cintray, Saint-Pierre-la-Rivière, Aube, Fontenai-les-Louvets, Longuenoë, La Ménière, Coulimer, Parfondeval, Montgaudry, La Perrière, Saint-Fulgent-des-Ormes, Saint-Germain-des-Grois, Origny-le-Roux, Vimoutiers, Pontchardon, Barou-en-Auge, Morteaux-Couliboeuf, Bernécourt, Bretteville-sur-Laize, Troismonts, Saint-Aubin-Lebizay, Banville, La Hoguette, Canapville, Rânes, Saint-Paul, Caumont-Leventé, Cauville, Le Tourneur, Landelles-et-Coupigny, Saint-Martin-des-Besaces, Blay, Molay-Littry, Mesnil-Caussois, Loitf, Truttemer-le-Grand, Saint-Quentin-sur-le-Homme, Céaux, Saint-Mars-d'Egrenne, Mantilly, Saint-Frambault, La Ferrière-Bochard, Mieuxcé, La Ferrière-aux-Étangs, Dompierre, Saint-Pierre-du-Regard, Roncherolles-en-Bray, Baons-le-Comte, Saint-Laurent-en-Caux, Ermenouville, Taillebois, Bernesq, Moyon, Montpinchon, Cérences, Mont-Bertrand, Ver, Saint-Aubin-du-Perron, Périers, Saint-Pair-sur-Mer, Ozeville, Anneville-en-Saire, Mesnil-au-Val, Denneville, Glatigny, Le Mesnilbus, Saint-Aubin-des-Préaux, Courtils, Vessey, Aucey-la-Plaine, Épreville, Saint-Jouin-Bruneval, Bretteville-du-Grand-Caux, Flamanville, Auzouville-Auberbosc, Cléres, Les Trois Pierres, Montville, Manéglise, Néville, Saint-Pierre-Le Viger, Saint-Vaast-Dieppedalle, Manéhouville, Touville, Saint-Aignan-sur-Ry, Rouvray-Catillon, Saint-Marthe, Fresnes, Les Loges-sur-Brecey

Légende
- A Juaye-Mondaye
- B Saint-Pierre-d'Entremont
- C Saint-Laurent-de-Terregatte
- D Bellefontaine
- E Saint-Laurent-du-Mont
- F Saint-Désir-de-Lisieux
- G Ménil-Hubert-sur-Orne
- H Coudehard
- I Bernières-le-Patry
- J Saint-Pierre-du-Regard
- K Saint-Pierre-du-Regard
- L Taillebois
- M Ermenouville
- N Saint-Laurent-en-Caux
- O Baons-le-Comte
- P Roncherolles-en-Bray
- Q Rouvray-Catillon
- R Saint-Aignan-sur-Ry
- T Saint-Marthe
- U Fresnes
- V Les Loges-sur-Brecey

230

Calvados

BANVILLE One of six renovated gîtes with modern furnishings, at the centre of the village and just 4 km from the seaside resort of Courseulles-sur-Mer. At Courseulles, the leisure facilities include a swimming-pool; riding and tennis and a museum about oysters (which are, naturally, a local speciality). Living room/kitchenette (2 single beds), 2 bedrooms (1 double and 2 single beds), shower room, central heating, enclosed ground shared with the other gîtes. Shopping in the village or at Courseulles.

Prices: low season   F 750/850   **6 people**
high season   F 1060   IGN 6
Booking: Calvados booking service   E
14/329

BAROU-EN-AUGE A traditionally furnished former farmhouse which has been sympathetically restored to retain its rural character, at the edge of the village. See the former Benedictine abbey and old market halls at Saint-Pierre-sur-Dives (10 km). A small lake and pony rides at Ommoy (12 km). Living room (1 double divan), kitchen, 1 bedroom (1 double bed), bathroom, fireplace, electric heating, enclosed ground. Linen available. Farm produce in the village; other shopping at Morteaux (2 km).

Prices: low season   F 630/700   **4 people**
high season   F 910   IGN 18
Booking: Calvados booking service   E
14/212

BERNESQ Les Helleries A renovated and traditionally furnished gîte outside the village (1.5 km). Molay-Littry (6 km) has an industrial museum and cattle market and is near the Balleroy forest (10 km). The coast (12 km). Living room, kitchen, 4 bedrooms (2 double, 6 single beds and a cot), bathroom, open fire, electric central heating, garage, enclosed ground shared with two other gîtes. Linen available. Farm produce from the owners, shopping in the village, and restaurant at Molay-Littry.

Prices: low season   F 920/1050   **11 people**
high season   F 1270   IGN 6
Booking: Calvados booking service   E
14/435

BERNIERES-LE-PATRY Le Mont A spacious, traditionally furnished, detached house in its own enclosed garden, 2 km from the village. Swimming-pool and tennis at the attractive town of Condé-sur-Noireau (15 km) which has been largely rebuilt since the war. Riding stables at Flers (18 km); the sea is at 75 km. Living room (1 double divan), kitchen, 4 bedrooms (2 double, 2 single beds), shower room, fireplace, electric central heating, enclosed garden. Shopping in the village or at Tinchebray (6 km).

Prices: low season   F 880   **8 people**
high season   F 1260   IGN 17
Booking: Calvados booking service   E
14/489

BLAY One of four traditionally furnished gîtes in a renovated house at the village centre. Local fishing and walks in Balleroy forest (9 km), the sea (8 km). Bayeux (9 km) boasts one of the most beautiful cathedrals in France; other attractions include the botanical gardens and, of course, the tapestry. Living room/kitchenette (1 double divan), 1 bedroom (2 single beds), shower room, electric central heating, open ground shared with the other gîtes (garden furniture). Shopping in the village and restaurant at Trevières (7 km).

Prices: low season   F 610/680   **4 people**
high season   F 850   IGN 6
Booking: Calvados booking service   E
14/440

Calvados

BRETTEVILLE-SUR-LAIZE Château des Riflets One of two traditionally furnished gîtes in a recently renovated house, set in a large wooded park at the edge of the village (0.8 km). The lovely Abbaye Aux Hommes escaped bombing in the war at Caen (15 km) and the city offers many modern facilities. The sea is just 25 km away. Living room, kitchen, 3 bedrooms (2 double, 6 single beds), bathroom, central heating. Linen available. Shopping in the village or at Caen where there is a good choice of restaurants.

Prices:	low season	F 860/1090	**10 people**
	high season	F 1290	*IGN 18*

Booking: Calvados booking service   E

14/467

CAUMONT-L'EVENTE A comfortable apartment in the owners' renovated house which boasts a wealth of exposed beams. The owners keep ponies and are willing to teach young children to ride. At Bayeux (24 km) see the famous tapestry and cathedral. Arromanches and the coast (35 km). Living room/kitchenette (1 double divan), 1 bedroom on an open landing (2 single beds), bathroom, central heating, enclosed garden with garden furniture and barbecue. Shopping in the town or at Bayeux.

Prices:	low season	F 700/800	**4 people**
	high season	F 1000	*IGN 6*

Booking: Calvados booking service   E

14/315

CAUVILLE La Mogisière An old stone house, traditionally furnished and lying in its own enclosed ground with garden furniture and barbecue for outdoor meals. Hang-gliding, climbing and canoeing at Clécy (7 km). See the ruined seventeenth-century château at Thury-Harcourt (10 km), former residence of the governors of Normandy. Living room, kitchen, 4 bedrooms (2 double and 2 single beds), shower room, open fire, oil heating, garage. Linen available. Farm produce and grocer in the village (1 km); other shopping at Thury-Harcourt.

Prices:	low season	F 760/910	**6 people**
	high season	F 1170	*IGN 6*

Booking: Calvados booking service   E

14/317

COQUAINVILLIERS Le Chemin d'Argentelle A pretty, half-timbered house of typical Norman design in its own enclosed garden, 1 km from the village centre. Lisieux (10 km) is famous as a place of pilgrimage to Saint Theresa—you cannot miss the huge basilica built in her honour. The coast and sailing at Cabourg (20 km). Living room (1 double divan), kitchen, 2 bedrooms (1 double, 2 single beds), bathroom, fireplace, electric central heating, garden furniture. Local farm produce; shopping at Manerbe (3 km) or Lisieux.

Prices:	low season	F 850/970	**6 people**
	high season	F 1130	*IGN 7*

Booking: Calvados booking service   E

14/409

GONNEVILLE-SUR-HONFLEUR Just 4 km from the coast, this attractive former farm building has been well renovated and traditionally furnished. The lovely old port of Honfleur (4 km) and Deauville, which has been a fashionable and elegant resort since the last century, is at 13 km. Living room/kitchenette, 1 bedroom (1 double, 1 child's bed), bathroom (small bath), electric central heating, open ground with garden furniture. Shopping in the village (2 km), or at Honfleur where you should try the seafood.

Prices:	low season	F 750/850	**3 people**
	high season	F 980	*IGN 7*

Booking: Calvados booking service   E

14/456

Calvados

LA HOGUETTE Courcelles A delightful old stone cottage with traditional furnishings, 1 km from the village centre. Fishing at the owners' private pond. The market town of Falaise (4 km) was the birthplace of William the Conqueror; the town's huge stone castle is one of the oldest surviving in Normandy. The coast (45 km). Living room (1 double divan), kitchen, 1 bedroom (1 double, 1 single bed), fireplace, electric central heating, garden (furniture and barbecue). Shopping in the village or at Falaise.

Prices:	low season	F 700/880	**5 people**
	high season	F 1000	IGN 18

Booking: Calvados booking service E
14/487

JUAYE-MONDAYE Ferme de l'Abbaye A renovated house with country-style furnishings on a mixed farm outside the village and right next to the Juaye-Mondaye abbey which is open to the public in summer. Visit historic Bayeux (8 km) and the Normandy landing beaches at Arromanches (15 km). Living room/kitchenette, 2 bedrooms (1 double, 3 single beds), shower room, electric central heating, enclosed garden. Linen available. A grocery, bakery and restaurant in the village (1.5 km); other shopping at Tilly-sur-Seulles (6 km).

Prices:	low season	F 700/900	**5 people**
	high season	F 1040	IGN 6

Booking: Calvados booking service E
14/496

LANDELLES-ET-COUPIGNY La Ribaudière A modern, traditionally furnished gîte in peaceful surroundings, 2 km from this small country village. Facilities at La Dathée lake (13 km) including fishing, wind-surfing and miniature golf. At Vire (12 km), see the restored thirteenth-century gateway and Gothic church in an otherwise modern town. Living room/kitchenette (1 double divan), 1 bedroom (1 double, 1 single bed), shower room, central heating, enclosed garden. Shopping in the village or at Saint-Sever (9 km).

Prices:	low season	F 600/730	**5 people**
	high season	F 860	IGN 17

Booking: Calvados booking service E
14/431

LECAUDE La Tibaudière A delightful, typically Norman, half-timbered house, renovated and furnished in traditional style, 2 km from the village and 30 km from the coast (sailing at Trouville). Local forest walks. At Lisieux (12 km), places of interest include the vast basilica, cathedral and former Bishop's Palace. Living room (1 double divan), kitchen, 2 bedrooms (1 double, 2 single beds), bathroom, fireplace, electric central heating, enclosed ground. Local farm produce; other shopping at Crèvecoeur-en-Auge (6 km).

Prices:	low season	F 800/860	**6 people**
	high season	F 1140	IGN 18

Booking: Calvados booking service E
14/280

11

MESNIL-CAUSSOIS Le Beaubis A deceptively spacious village gîte, just 2.5 km from the lovely Saint-Sever forest. The small market town of Saint-Sever itself (2.5 km) has a Benedictine abbey, swimming-pool, riding and tennis. Sailing at La Dathée lake (6 km). The sea (80 km approx.). Living room (TV, 1 single divan), kitchen, 4 bedrooms (2 double, 2 single beds), bathroom, fireplace, electric central heating, enclosed ground. Farm produce from the owners; other shopping at Saint-Sever.

Prices:	low season	F 800/970	**7 people**
	high season	F 1180	IGN 17

Booking: Calvados booking service E
14/234

Calvados

MOLAY-LITTRY One of two gîtes in a modern house owned by the local council, in open ground near the village centre. Bicycles for hire; a mining museum and cattle market in the village (0.8 km). Swimming-pool at historic Bayeux (13 km). The sea and sailing facilities at Saint-Laurent-sur-Mer (18 km). Living room/kitchenette (4 single beds), 1 bedroom (1 double bed), shower room, fireplace, electric central heating, terrace, open ground. Shopping and restaurant in the village.

Prices:	low season	F 780/840	**6 people**
	high season	F 1060	IGN 6

Booking: Calvados booking service   E

14/338

MONT-BERTRAND La Roulandière A traditionally furnished house, near the village centre (0.5 km), ideally situated for touring rural Calvados: Saint-Sever forest (15 km), La Dathée lake (23 km) and Saint-Lô (25 km approx.) where the modern town has grown up around a fortified medieval city; visit too the famous stud farm there. Living room (TV), kitchen (washing machine), 2 bedrooms (2 double, 2 single beds), shower room, fireplace, electric heating, enclosed garden. Shopping at Campeaux (3 km) or Le Bény-Bocage (6 km).

Prices:	low season	F 850	**6 people**
	high season	F 1050	IGN 17

Booking: Calvados booking service   E

14/488

MORTEAUX-COULIBOEUF Le Petit Couliboeuf Situated in a little hamlet with local fishing and marked footpaths, this house has been renovated and traditionally furnished. It will be appreciated by those seeking an active holiday: hang-gliding at 2 km; swimming-pool and tennis (9 km). Visit the historic castle at Falaise (9 km). Living room (TV), kitchen, 3 bedrooms (2 double, 2 single beds), bathroom, fireplace, central heating, enclosed ground. Shopping in the village or at Falaise.

Prices:	low season	F 760/880	**6 people**
	high season	F 1110	IGN 18

Booking: Calvados booking service   E

14/470

SAINT-AUBIN-LEBIZAY Cour L'Epée A large, renovated and traditionally furnished house set in open ground just outside the village (1 km). At Caen (20 km approx.), you can see the tomb of William the Conqueror at the Abbaye-Aux-Hommes. Good leisure amenities at Pont-L'Evêque and the coast (both 15 km). Living room, kitchen, 4 bedrooms (2 double, 2 single and 1 child's bed), bathroom, fireplace, gas central heating, open ground. Shopping at Dozulé (6 km).

Prices:	low season	F 860/980	**7 people**
	high season	F 1210	IGN 7

Booking: Calvados booking service   E

14/459

SAINT-DESIR-DE-LISIEUX A traditionally furnished, detached house in the lovely apple-growing district of Auge, 4 km from Lisieux which rose to fame because of the canonisation of a young Carmelite nun, Theresa Martins. A lake (wind-surfing) at Pont-L'Evêque (17 km); the seaside resort of Houlgate (28 km). Living room (1 double divan), kitchen, 3 bedrooms (2 double, 2 single beds), bathroom, fireplace, electric heating, enclosed ground. Shopping and restaurants at Lisieux.

Prices:	low season	F 740/850	**8 people**
	high season	F 1090	IGN 18

Booking: Calvados booking service   E

14/484

Calvados

SAINT-LAURENT-DU-MONT A charming, half-timbered cottage with traditional, country-style furnishings, in open ground on a livestock farm, in a region dotted with traditional Norman manor houses. Enjoy the fine sandy beaches, golf course and many other amenities at the seaside resort of Cabourg (25 km). Living room (1 double divan), kitchen, 3 bedrooms (2 double, 2 single beds), bathroom, fireplace, electric heating, open ground. Linen available. Shopping at Cambremer (3 km).

Prices:	low season	F 820/940	**8 people**
	high season	F 1180	IGN 18

Booking: Calvados booking service E

14/397

SAINT-MARTIN-DES-BESACES Les Bouillons A traditionally furnished gîte in its own enclosed garden, 2 km from the village centre. A swimming-pool at the modern town of Villers-Bocage (17 km) which has an important cattle market. Tennis at Torigni (10 km) and other leisure facilities (including sailing) at La Dathée lake (25 km). Kitchen, 3 bedrooms (5 single beds), shower room, fireplace, garage, garden furniture. Farm produce from the owners; other shopping in the village.

Prices:	low season	F 800	**5 people**
	high season	F 1000	IGN 6

Booking: Calvados booking service E

14/472

LE TOURNEUR La Terrerie An old, traditionally furnished house on a mixed farm where the owners are happy to sell you fresh produce. Visit Saint-Lô (25 km approx.) which has been largely rebuilt and restored since the war; in particular see the art collection at the Hôtel de Ville and the Cathedral of Notre-Dame. Living room, kitchen, 2 bedrooms (2 double, 1 single bed), shower room, fireplace, electric central heating, enclosed ground. Shopping at Le Bény-Bocage (3 km) or Vire (15 km).

Prices:	low season	F 680/720	**5 people**
	high season	F 900	IGN 17

Booking: Calvados booking service E

14/182

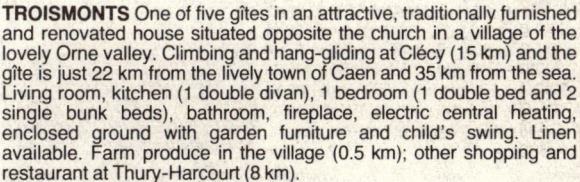

TROISMONTS One of five gîtes in an attractive, traditionally furnished and renovated house situated opposite the church in a village of the lovely Orne valley. Climbing and hang-gliding at Clécy (15 km) and the gîte is just 22 km from the lively town of Caen and 35 km from the sea. Living room, kitchen (1 double divan), 1 bedroom (1 double bed and 2 single bunk beds), bathroom, fireplace, electric central heating, enclosed ground with garden furniture and child's swing. Linen available. Farm produce in the village (0.5 km); other shopping and restaurant at Thury-Harcourt (8 km).

Prices:	low season	F 570/710	**6 people**
	high season	F 830	IGN 6

Booking: Calvados booking service E

14/343

TRUTTEMER-LE-GRAND A rustically furnished old house, set on a mixed farm (where you may buy fresh produce), some 5 km from the village. Swimming-pool and miniature golf at Vire (10 km) and many other amenities at La Dathée lake (15 km). The sea (70 km approx.). Living room/kitchenette, 2 bedrooms (2 double and 1 child's bed), shower room, fireplace, electric heating, open ground. Shopping in the village or at Vire; a restaurant at 7 km.

Prices:	low season	F 570/650	**5 people**
	high season	F 860	IGN 17

Booking: Calvados booking service E

14/191

11

Eure

BAS CAUMONT Rochecôte
A detached, renovated house in a lovely peaceful setting right by the river Seine, 3 km from the village centre. Furnished in traditional rustic style, the gîte is near the owners' home where you may use their private tennis court. It is 65 km from the coast. Living room (1 double divan), kitchen (washing machine), 2 bedrooms (1 double, 2 single beds), bathroom, fireplace, electric heating, open ground (garden furniture). Linen available. Local farm produce available, shopping and restaurant (0.5 km) or at Bourg-Achard (8 km).

Prices: low season F 585/760 **6 people**
high season F 1006 *IGN 7*
Booking: Eure booking service **E**

27/101

BEMECOURT Les Tilleuls
A traditionally furnished gîte in an old, renovated cottage, near the village centre and only 3 km from Breteuil, a town which attracts many visitors on account of its rich and fertile situation only 100 km from Paris. Try to sample the local cider which can be bought in the village. Living room (1 single divan), kitchen, 3 bedrooms (2 double and 2 single beds), shower room, open fire, electric central heating, carport, garden with furniture. Linen available. Farm produce in the village; other shopping and restaurant at Breteuil.

Prices: low season F 649/827 **7 people**
high season F 1053 *IGN 18*
Booking: Eure booking service **E**

27/134

BOSC-BENARD-COMMIN
Situated on a mixed farm, this renovated and traditionally furnished gîte is owned by a couple with a young family. Visitors at the end of August can join in the impressive harvest festival (at 10 km). The attractive town of Bourgtheroulde is at 2 km and the sea (55 km). Living room, kitchen, 3 bedrooms (2 double, 2 single beds), bathroom, fireplace, electric heating, open garden with child's swings. Linen available (F37 per set per week). Farm produce available; shopping and restaurant in the village (2 km).

Prices: low season F 594/770 **6 people**
high season F 1045 *IGN 7*
Booking: Eure booking service **E**

27/155

LE BOSGOUET Le Malmain
A beautifully restored half-timbered building (a former cider press), comprising two gîtes with country-style furnishings, on a mixed farm in a quiet hamlet. Sailing at 15 km. Visit Rouen (25 km) to see its magnificent cathedral and famous clock amongst other sights. Living room (1 double divan), kitchen (washing machine), 2 bedrooms (2 double, 1 single and 2 bunk beds), bathroom, electric heating, open ground. Linen available. Shopping and restaurant at Bourg-Achard (3 km).

Prices: low season F 660/840 **9 people**
high season F 1150 *IGN 7*
Booking: Eure booking service **E**

27/95

LE BOSGOUET Le Verger
A second gîte in the house described above, built in traditional local style, 3 km from Bourg-Achard. The owners have three young children. The delightful Brotonne Regional Park is 5 km away and there is a swimming-pool at 25 km. The coast is near enough for a day trip at 65 km. Living room (1 double divan), kitchen, 2 bedrooms (2 double, 1 single bed), bathroom, electric heating, open ground. Linen available. Farm produce from the owners; other shopping at Bourg-Achard.

Prices: low season F 600/770 **7 people**
high season F 1020 *IGN 7*
Booking: Eure booking service **E**

27/120

Eure

BOUQUETOT Les Rufoux A renovated, half-timbered cottage, near the English-speaking owners' home, 1 km from the village centre. Rouen (30 km approx.) is a fine city with delightful old quarter and an important commercial port. The city boasts some particularly interesting museums; see too the site of Joan of Arc's execution. Living room (1 double divan), kitchen, 1 bedroom (1 double bed), bathroom, open fire, electric heating, enclosed ground. Linen available (F37 per set per week). Farm produce in the village; shopping at Routot (3 km).

Prices:	low season	F 650/800	**4 people**
	high season	F 1050	IGN 7

Booking: Eure booking service   E

27/156

BRETEUIL Cornet-Moulin An old cottage, modestly furnished, formerly the residence of the retired owners who still lovingly maintain the garden attached to the gîte. It is 3 km from Breteuil, a little town on the edge of a forest with plenty of leisure facilities. Living room/kitchenette, 3 bedrooms (2 double, 2 single and 1 child's bed), bathroom, no heating, garage, garden with outdoor furniture. Linen available. Farm produce in the village. Shops and restaurant in Breteuil.

Prices:	low season	F 660	**7 people**
	high season	F 838	IGN 18

Booking: Eure booking service   E

27/106

CINTRAY La Tournevraye A renovated and traditionally furnished former farmhouse near the owners' home where bed-and-breakfast accommodation is also available. Visit the lovely old town of Verneuil-sur-Avre (12 km) with its superb Gothic church (La Madelaine), charming market place and other places of interest. The coast (100 km). Living room/kitchenette (1 double divan), 2 bedrooms (1 double, 3 single beds), shower room, electric heating, open ground. Linen available. Shopping in the village (2.5 km).

Prices:	low season	F 495/660	**7 people**
	high season	F 963	IGN 18

Booking: Eure booking service   E

27/149

CONDE-SUR-ITON Les Brosses A renovated and traditionally furnished gîte on farmland, 10 km from the owners' home, in a lovely area, popular for second home-owners as it is less than 100 km from Paris. Breteuil-sur-Iton (4.5 km) is a little holiday resort in a forest clearing with a swimming-pool and tennis. Living room, kitchen, 2 bedrooms (1 double, 3 single beds), bathroom, open fire, electric heating, enclosed ground. Linen available. Farm produce in the village; other shopping at Breteuil.

Prices:	low season	F 575/745	**5 people**
	high season	F 1010	IGN 18

Booking: Eure booking service   E

27/154

CORMEILLES Les Poiriers This gîte, which has been renovated and traditionally furnished, is ideally situated for touring. Near the town centre, it is 35 km from the lovely seaside resort of Deauville and just 18 km from Lisieux, famous as a centre of pilgrimage to Saint Theresa. Living room, kitchen, 3 bedrooms (2 double, 3 single beds, 1 cot), shower room, electric heating, enclosed ground. Linen available. Shopping and restaurant in the town (0.5 km).

Prices:	low season	F 660/803	**8 people**
	high season	F 1076	IGN 7

Booking: Eure booking service   E

27/140

11

Eure

LES ESSARTS Le Failly A spacious former farmhouse with traditional, country-style furnishings and its own enclosed garden, 2 km from the village centre. Conches-en-Ouches (10 km) is an interesting old market town with a ruined abbey and a fifteenth-century church which boasts some fine stained glass. Living room (1 single divan), kitchen (washing machine), 4 bedrooms (1 double, 7 single beds, 1 child's cot), bathroom, fireplace, electric heating, barbecue. Linen available. Shops at Damville (7 km); mobile baker and grocer call.

Prices:	low season	F 906/1133	**11 people**
	high season	F 1359	IGN 18

Booking: Eure booking service   E

27/128

ETREVILLE An unusual gîte with country-style furnishings in a restored bakery—the kitchen is particularly sunny, in a glass-built extension. It is 5 km from the vast Brotonne Regional Park (sailing at 18 km) and 13 km from the interesting old town of Pont-Audemer. The coast (60 km). Living room, kitchen, 2 bedrooms (2 double, 1 single bed), shower room, fireplace, enclosed garden shared with the owners (garden furniture). Linen available. Farm produce (including cider) and other shopping in the village or at Bourneville (5 km).

Prices:	low season	F 545/650	**5 people**
	high season	F 865	IGN 7

Booking: Eure booking service   E

27/142

GAILLON Domaine de Court-Moulin One of two gîtes with country-style furnishings in a renovated house, situated in extensive wooded grounds. At Gaillon (3 km), see the Renaissance château, formerly the residence of the archbishops of Rouen. A swimming-pool (13 km) and sailing at a leisure centre (20 km). The coast (85 km). Living room (1 double divan), kitchen, 3 bedrooms (1 double, 4 single beds), bathroom and separate shower, fireplace, electric heating, garden furniture. Linen available. Shopping at Gaillon.

Prices:	low season	F 620/770	**8 people**
	high season	F 1050	IGN 8

Booking: Eure booking service   E

27/161

HARQUENCY Travailles A renovated cottage, traditionally furnished, lying on a mixed farm where the owner has carefully restored an old chapel on his land, 3 km from the village. There are two other gîtes on the same farm. Plenty of forest walks in the vicinity, the Seine at 7 km, and sailing, a swimming-pool and tennis in Les Andelys (9 km). Living room/kitchenette, 2 bedrooms (1 double and 3 single beds), shower room, electric heating and oil stove, carport, garden. Linen available. Mobile baker calls; other shopping at Les Andelys, where there are restaurants.

Prices:	low season	F 407/560	**5 people**
	high season	F 747	IGN 8

Booking: Eure booking service   E

27/16

MORGNY Les Lilas A large old house with traditional, country-style furnishings, set in its own pleasant garden in a lovely area of forests, very popular with tourists. The charming little town of Lyons-la-Forêt (9 km) has a covered market hall, fifteenth-century church and pretty, half-timbered buildings. Sailing at 20 km. Living room, kitchen, 4 bedrooms (1 double, 4 single and 1 child's bed), bathroom, fireplace, central heating, garage. Linen available. Shopping and restaurant in the village (0.3 km) or at Etrépagny (10 km).

Prices:	low season	F 565/756	**7 people**
	high season	F 1085	IGN 8

Booking: Eure booking service   E

27/133

Eure

SAINT-OUEN-DE-THOUBERVILLE Le Bosc-Groult A renovated cottage with traditional furnishings on the large estate of a manor house, 1.5 km from the village centre. It lies just near the Brotonne Regional Park (3 km), 20 km from historic Rouen and close enough to the Normandy coast for a day trip (50 km). Living room, kitchen (washing machine), 4 bedrooms (1 double, 5 single beds and a child's cot), bathroom, fireplace, electric heating, carport, garden furniture. Linen available. Shops (0.5 km) or at Bourg-Achard (7 km).

Prices: low season   F 700/800   **8 people**
high season   F 1100   IGN 7
Booking: Eure booking service   **E**
27/115

SAINT-VICTOR-D'EPINE Aubépine A simply furnished village gîte in the retired farming owner's renovated Norman house which has been divided into two. Many pleasant walks nearby. The pretty town of Saint-Georges-du-Vièvre, where there is a swimming-pool, is 5 km away. At Brionne (11 km), there are various leisure facilities, including tennis and a lake. The sea is close enough for a day trip at Honfleur (45 km). Living room/kitchenette, 2 bedrooms (1 double, 2 single beds), shower room, central heating, carport, courtyard with furniture. Linen available. Mobile baker calls; other shopping at Giverville (4 km).

Prices: low season   F 400/460   **4 people**
high season   F 700   IGN 7
Booking: Eure booking service   **E**
27/106

SAINTE-COLOMBE-PRES-VERNON Les Bideaux A pretty, little renovated cottage with rustic furniture, lying on a mixed farm at 0.5 km from the village. There is riding and tennis within 15 km and the interesting towns of Vernon (12 km) with its Château de Bizy and Giverny (15 km) with its Claude Monet museum and gardens. Living room, kitchen, 1 bedroom (1 double, 2 single, and 1 child's bed), shower room, wood-fired central heating, enclosed courtyard (garden furniture). Linen available. Mobile baker and delicatessen call; other shopping in the village or at Vernon, where there are restaurants.

Prices: low season   F 390/500   **5 people**
high season   F 630   IGN 8
Booking: Eure booking service   **E**
27/5

SAINTE-MARTHE Les Deux Sapins A small, simply furnished old farm cottage, owned by a young couple, 0.5 km from the village centre, and 4 km from the attractive market town of Conches. Sailing at a lake (10 km). Visit the busy département capital of Evreux (30 km approx.). The sea (100 km). Living room, kitchen, 2 bedrooms (1 double, 2 single beds), shower room, electric heating, open ground. Linen available (F37 per set per week). A restaurant and farm produce in the village; other shopping at Conches.

Prices: low season   F 420/470   **4 people**
high season   F 700   IGN 18
Booking: Eure booking service   **E**
27/43

SAINTE-OPPORTUNE-LA-MARE La Chaumine A pretty little thatched cottage, sympathetically restored and furnished in traditional style, situated 1 km from a village in the Brotonne Regional Park, just 20 km from the coast. The attractive town of Pont-Audemer (8 km) was an important port in William the Conqueror's time. Living room (1 double divan), kitchen, 1 bedroom (2 single beds), bathroom, electric heating, enclosed ground with garden furniture. Linen available. Shops (3 km) or at Pont-Audemer.

Prices: low season   F 555/670   **4 people**
high season   F 906   IGN 7
Booking: Eure booking service   **E**
27/124

Eure

LE THEIL NOLENT La Blottière A large gîte in a lovely Norman house which has been renovated and traditionally furnished, surrounded by orchards. Fresh farm produce is available from the owners. Leisure activities include tennis at 7 km and a swimming-pool at Bernay (9 km), a typically Norman town of historic and architectural interest. Living room, kitchen, 4 bedrooms (1 double, 6 single and 1 child's bed), bathroom, fireplace, electric heating, enclosed ground (garden furniture). Linen available. Mobile greengrocer calls, other shopping and restaurant at 2 km.

Prices: low season   F 700/875
         high season   F 1135
9 people
IGN 18

Booking: Eure booking service   E
27/79

LE THEILLEMENT Les Mousquetaires A gîte with rustic furnishings in a wing of the owners' fine old house where the author, Alexander Dumas once stayed. Visit Le Bec-Hellouin (20 km approx.) from whose important monastery came three Archbishops of Canterbury. The buildings (dating from the eleventh-century) can be visited. Living room (1 double divan), kitchen, 3 bedrooms (2 double, 2 single and 1 child's bed), bathroom, open fire, central heating, enclosed ground. Linen available. Shopping at Eppreville-en-Roumois (3 km).

Prices: low season   F 610/765
         high season   F 1020
9 people
IGN 7

Booking: Eure booking service   E
27/108

TOUVILLE Le Chalet A chalet-style gîte with traditional furnishings situated in wooded parkland where there are a few animals, at 0.5 km from the centre of the village. Farm produce may be bought from the owners. Plenty of nice walks round about, riding at 5 km and a swimming-pool and a lake at 12 km. Living room/kitchenette, 2 bedrooms (2 double beds), shower room, electric heating, terrace, enclosed ground with garden furniture and a child's swing. Shopping at Boissey-le-Châtel where there is a restaurant (4 km).

Prices: low season   F 524/693
         high season   F 817
4 people
IGN 7

Booking: Eure booking service   E
27/116

VALLETOT Médine A small renovated and traditionally furnished gîte near the owners' house where Shetland Ponies are reared, 1 km from the village centre. Riding is available at the gîte; other activities at Pont-Audemer. Not far away, and worth a visit is the Brotonne Regional Park. Living room (1 single bed), kitchen, 1 bedroom (1 double bed), bathroom, electric heating, garden with outdoor furniture. Linen available. Mobile baker and butcher call; other shopping and restaurant at 2 km, or at Pont-Audemer (10 km).

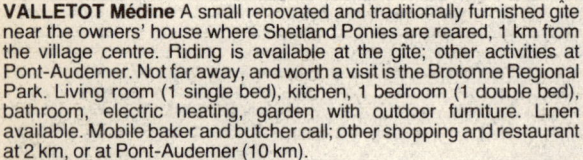

Prices: low season   F 445/572
         high season   F 744
3 people
IGN 7

Booking: Eure booking service   E
27/9

Manche

ANNEVILLE-EN-SAIRE Hameau Poignant A spacious renovated house with country-style furnishings, near the owners' home and just 4 km from the coast. The little fishing port of Barfleur (5 km) has an unusual fortified church. The Gatteville lighthouse nearby, one of the tallest in France, is open to the public. Living room, kitchen, lounge (1 double divan), 3 bedrooms (1 double, 2 single beds), shower room, fireplace, central heating, enclosed courtyard. Farm produce, shopping and restaurant in the village (1 km).

Prices:	low season	F 945/1079	**6 people**
	high season	F 1079/1223	IGN 6

Booking: Manche booking service
50/SR266

AUCEY-LA-PLAINE Le Haut Village A well-renovated, rustically furnished cottage, 2 km from the village centre. Visit the remarkable eleventh-century abbey perched on the rocky outcrop of Mont-Saint-Michel (12 km), reached by a causeway at low tide. The abbey's historic manuscripts are kept in Avranches museum. Living room/kitchenette, 3 bedrooms (2 double, 2 single beds), fireplace, central heating, carport, enclosed garden. Farm produce and a restaurant in the village (2 km); shopping at Pontorson (5 km).

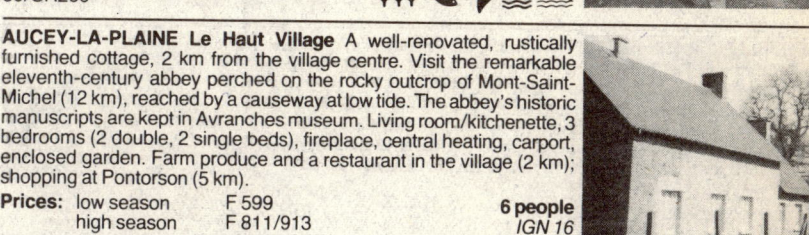

Prices:	low season	F 599	**6 people**
	high season	F 811/913	IGN 16

Booking: Manche booking service
50/SR42

BELLEFONTAINE Sainte-Agathe A purpose-built village of twelve gîtes of attractive design and furnished in country fashion. The 'village' is in open countryside next to a leisure park with a country inn, craft exhibitions, boating, pony rides and other amusements. The coast is at 40 km. Living room (1 single divan), kitchen, 3 bedrooms (2 double, 2 single beds), bathroom, fireplace, electric central heating, open ground. Linen available. Local farm produce and shops at 3.5 km or at Mortain (6 km).

Prices:	low season	F 891	**7 people**
	high season	F 1169	IGN 17

Booking: Manche booking service
50/3

CEAUX Village Athée A renovated cottage with country-style furnishings in a hamlet, 1 km from the village centre. The delightful botanical gardens at Avranches (7 km) afford impressive views over Mont-Saint-Michel. Leisure facilities at this old, fortified town include a swimming-pool, tennis and cinema. The sea (20 km). Living room (1 double divan), kitchen, 2 bedrooms (2 double beds), bathroom, open fire, central heating, garage, enclosed garden. Linen available. A restaurant in the village and shops at Avranches.

Prices:	low season	F 700	**6 people**
	high season	F 880/942	IGN 16

Booking: Manche booking service
50/SR233

CERENCES La Regibe A modernised gîte with country-style furnishings, adjoining the owners' holiday home, 3 km from the village. The coast (sailing facilities) and a golf links (7 km). Granville (17 km), built by the English in the fifteenth century, celebrates a 'Pardon of the Sea' at the harbour in August. Living room, kitchen, 3 bedrooms (3 double, 1 single bed), bathroom, fireplace, electric central heating, carport, enclosed garden with outdoor furniture. Farm produce, shopping and restaurant in the village.

Prices:	low season	F 819	**7 people**
	high season	F 1034/1141	IGN 16

Booking: Manche booking service
50/SR23

11

241

Manche

COURTILS One of three simply furnished gîtes in a fine old presbytery whose garden has swings and a sand-pit for children. It is at the town centre, 30 km from the coast. Do not miss the historic abbey at Mont-Saint-Michel (8 km). Living room, kitchen, 2 bedrooms (2 double, 2 single beds), electric heating, enclosed garden. Farm produce, shopping and restaurant in the town or at Avranches (14 km).

Prices:	low season	F 502/621	**6 people**
	high season	F 873	IGN 16

Booking: Manche booking service

50/SR85

DENNEVILLE Les Kerdes A gîte with rustic furnishings in the owners' renovated house just outside the village (0.8 km). It is within walking distance of the sea and beaches (4 km). At La Haye-du-Puits (10 km), see the Gallo-Roman ruins, twelfth-century keep and Blanchelande Abbey. Living room, kitchen, 3 bedrooms (4 double and 1 child's bed), shower room, oil-fired central heating, garden. Local produce (including seafood and cider), shopping and restaurant in the village.

Prices:	low season	F 643/751	**8/9 people**
	high season	F 901/1009	IGN 6

Booking: Manche booking service

50/SR33

GLATIGNY One of two spacious, traditionally furnished gîtes in a well-renovated village presbytery. Local sites include Blanchelande Abbey, the châteaux of Franquetot and Coigny and the pottery at Vindefontaine. The sea and beaches, a healthy walk at 3 km. Living room (1 double divan), kitchen (washing machine), 4 bedrooms (2 double and 5 single beds), bathroom and shower, fireplace, central heating, garden. Fresh milk, eggs, poultry and a restaurant in the village; other shopping at La-Haye-du-Puits (8 km).

Prices:	low season	F 1060	**11 people**
	high season	F 1342	IGN 6

Booking: Manche booking service

50/SR262

LES LOGES-SUR-BRECEY Les Lardières An old stone cottage with country-style furnishings on a mixed farm, 4 km from Brecey. Visit Saint-Hilaire-du-Harcouët (20 km approx.) which has a lake and a colourful market every Wednesday. The coast is an easy day trip at 35 km. Living room/kitchenette, 3 bedrooms (2 double, 1 single bed), shower room, fireplace, open ground. Farm produce (including cider) available from the owner and in the village. Shopping and restaurant at Brecey.

Prices:	low season	F 535	**5 people**
	high season	F 695	IGN 17

Booking: Manche booking service

50/SR272

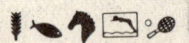

LOLIF Les Belins A first-floor gîte with rustic furnishings in a well-renovated house where the owners' parents occupy the ground floor. At Avranches Museum (5 km) there is a valuable collection of manuscripts dating back as far as the eighth century, most come from the Mont-Saint-Michel abbey. Living room/kitchenette (1 double divan), 3 bedrooms (2 double, 1 single and 1 child's bed), bathroom, electric central heating, enclosed garden with furniture. Linen available. Farm produce and restaurant in the village (2 km), other shopping at Avranches.

Prices:	low season	F 622	**7/8 people**
	high season	F 867/988	IGN 16

Booking: Manche booking service
50/SR238

Manche

MESNIL-AU-VAL Hameau Barville A detached house, furnished in rustic style, in its own garden near the village centre (0.8 km). Ideal for holidaymakers arriving at Cherbourg which is less than 10 km away. Riding stables at Tourlaville (3 km); sailing and a skating rink at 7 km. Living room (1 single divan), kitchen, 2 bedrooms (2 double beds), bathroom, fireplace, electric central heating. Farm produce in the village; other shopping at Tourlaville and a restaurant at 2 km.

Prices:	low season	F 638/746	5 people
	high season	F 808/870	IGN 6

Booking: Manche booking service

50/SR275

LE MESNILBUS La Commanderie A well-renovated and rustically furnished gîte in a hamlet, 0.5 km from the village where the local people provide good holiday entertainment, such as pony and trap rides, bicycle hire and visits to craft workshops. The coast is just 20 km away. Living room (1 double divan), kitchen, 3 bedrooms (2 double, 1 single and 1 child's bed), bathroom, fireplace, electric central heating, enclosed garden. Farm produce and restaurant in the village; shopping at Saint-Sauveur-Lendelin (4 km).

Prices:	low season	F 739	8 people
	high season	F 1100	IGN 6

Booking: Manche booking service

50/SR27M

LE MESNILBUS Hôtel Cousteur A traditionally furnished and renovated house near the centre of a lively village where the amenities include a country inn. River fishing at 2 km and a swimming-pool at 13 km. The sea, an easy day trip at 20 km. Living room, kitchen, 2 bedrooms (4 double beds), bathroom, fireplace, electric central heating, enclosed garden. Farm produce (including cider) from the owners or in the village (0.3 km) where there is a restaurant; shopping at Saint-Sauveur-Lendelin (4 km).

Prices:	low season	F 648	8 people
	high season	F 957	IGN 6

Booking: Manche booking service

50/SR12M

11

MONTPINCHON Le Doucet Situated 1.5 km from the village centre, this renovated house with country-style furnishings has its own enclosed garden with outdoor furniture and swings for children. Coutances (14 km) was founded by the Romans and now boasts a beautiful Romanesque cathedral and attractive public gardens in an otherwise modern town. Living room (1 double divan), kitchen, 2 bedrooms (2 double beds), shower room, fireplace, central heating. Local farm produce available; shopping and a restaurant in the village.

Prices:	low season	F 700	6 people
	high season	F 947	IGN 6

Booking: Manche booking service

50/SR66

MONTPINCHON Le Hameau Durand A large house, renovated and furnished in country style, just 18 km from the coast. Local river fishing (0.4 km); tennis at 3 km. Good modern shopping facilities and other leisure amenities at Coutances (13 km), which has a busy and popular market on Thursdays. Living room, kitchen, 3 bedrooms (3 double and 1 single bed), shower room, open fire, oil stove, enclosed garden. Farm produce, shopping and restaurant in the village (3 km).

Prices:	low season	F 695	7 people
	high season	F 947	IGN 6

Booking: Manche booking service

50/SR269

Manche

MOYON Le Haut Pays Set in extensive open grounds, some 5 km from the village, is this spacious house which has been modernised and furnished in country fashion. Visit the département capital of Saint-Lô (20 km) whose delightful mediaeval quarter has been sympathetically restored since the war. The sea (40 km). Living room, kitchen, 4 bedrooms (4 double and 1 child's bed), bathroom, fireplace, carport, open courtyard. Farm produce in the village (5 km); shops and a restaurant at 3 km.

Prices:	low season	F 818	**8/9 people**
	high season	F 1040	*IGN 6*

Booking: Manche booking service

50/SR236

OZEVILLE L'Ebahy A renovated and traditionally furnished cottage on a mixed farm just outside the village (1 km). It is near the 1944 landing beaches and you can take a day trip from Montebourg (5 km) to the Channel Islands or Mont-Saint-Michel. A golf links at 7 km. Living room (1 double divan), kitchen, 2 bedrooms (2 double, 1 single bed), bathroom, fireplace, central heating, garage, enclosed ground. Farm produce from the owners; a restaurant in the village and other shopping at Montebourg.

Prices:	low season	F 571/679	**7 people**
	high season	F 867/904	*IGN 6*

Booking: Manche booking service

50/SR22

PERIERS La Huche A renovated and simply furnished gîte near the owners' mixed farm where you may buy fresh produce, including cider. It is 15 km from the coast and 22 km from the old fortified town of La Haye-du-Puits: see Blanchelande Abbey and the châteaux of Franquetot and Coigny nearby. Living room/kitchenette, 3 bedrooms (2 double, 1 single and 1 child's bed), shower room, electric heating, enclosed garden. Shopping and restaurant in the village (1.5 km).

Prices:	low season	F 638/731	**6 people**
	high season	F 1009	*IGN 6*

Booking: Manche booking service

50/SR284

SAINT-AUBIN-DU-PERRON A renovated gîte with country-style furnishings, on a mixed farm, 0.5 km from the village centre. Bicycles for hire and other amenities at the attractive village of Le Mesnilbus (2 km); plenty to see and do at the cathedral town of Coutances (13 km). The sea (20 km). Living room (1 double divan), kitchen, 2 bedrooms (1 double and 4 single beds), bathroom, fireplace, central heating, garden. Farm produce from the owners; a restaurant in the village; other shopping at Saint-Sauveur-Lendelin (3 km).

Prices:	low season	F 751	**8 people**
	high season	F 957/1030	*IGN 6*

Booking: Manche booking service

50/SR3M

SAINT-AUBIN-DES-PREAUX Laugny A simply furnished gîte in the owners' renovated holiday home, 1.5 km from the village centre. Granville (8 km) built high on a hill as a stronghold, and whose ramparts remain today, offers superb views of the coastline. Amenities there include yachting, swimming-pool, aquarium and a casino. Living room, kitchen, 2 bedrooms (2 double beds, 2 single), fireplace, electric heating, garden. Farm produce and restaurant in the village; shops at 4 km.

Prices:	low season	F 842/894	**6 people**
	high season	F 1203	*IGN 16*

Booking: Manche booking service

50/SR244

Manche

SAINT-LAURENT-DE-TERREGATTE Le Bel-Orient A traditionally furnished gîte in a purpose-built village of nineteen holiday homes, 2 km from Saint-Laurent. It is set in peaceful wooded countryside with two artificial lakes for sailing, fishing and canoeing. There is a communal room for group activities and miniature golf on the site. Living room/kitchenette, 3 bedrooms (1 double, 4 single and 1 child's bed), central heating, carport, open ground. Linen available (F 22 per set per week). Shops (4 km) or at Avranches (16 km); a restaurant at Saint-Laurent.

Prices:	low season	F 768	6/7 people
	high season	F 1012	IGN 16

Booking: Manche booking service

50/21

SAINT-PAIR-SUR-MER La Hervière A spacious, attractively renovated cottage with country-style furnishings within walking distance of the sea (1 km) where there are sailing facilities. A golf course and flying club at 5 km. Saint-Pair-sur-Mer (0.8 km) is a popular family resort with good leisure amenities. Living room, kitchen, 4 bedrooms (3 double, 2 single and 1 child's bed), 2 bathrooms, open fire, central heating, garage, open garden with outdoor furniture. Farm produce, shopping and restaurant in the town or at Granville (4 km).

Prices:	low season	F 927/1071	8/9 people
	high season	F 1442	IGN 16

Booking: Manche booking service

50/SR198

SAINT-QUENTIN-SUR-LE-HOMME La Robinière A renovated cottage, furnished in country style, in its own enclosed garden, 2 km from the village centre and 4.5 km from the interesting old town of Avranches whose lovely botanical gardens offer impressive views over Mont-Saint-Michel. The coast (25 km). Living room, kitchen, 2 bedrooms (1 double, 2 single beds), bathroom, fireplace, gas central heating, carport. Farm produce (including cider), other shopping and restaurant in the village.

Prices:	low season	not available	4 people
	high season	F 1255/1410	IGN 16

Booking: Manche booking service

50/SR199

VER Le Val d'Airou A village of twelve purpose-built semi-detached gîtes with modern furnishings in a quiet setting by the river Airou, 0.8 km from Ver. You can enjoy walks along country lanes, mushroom picking and tennis locally; the sea is just 15 km away. Living room (1 single divan), kitchen, 2 bedrooms (1 double, 2 single beds), shower room, electric heating, open ground with garden furniture. Linen available (F 22 per set per week). Farm produce and restaurant in the village, other shopping at Gavray (3 km).

Prices:	low season	F 777	5 people
	high season	F 1022	IGN 16

Booking: Manche booking service

50/24

VESSEY La Sennélée A detached house, renovated and furnished in country style in its own enclosed garden, 0.5 km from the village centre. Legend has it that the superb abbey at Mont-Saint-Michel at 15 km was built by command of the Archangel Saint Michael! Living room/-kitchenette (1 double divan), 3 bedrooms (3 double and 1 child's bed), bathroom, open fire, electric central heating, garage. All kinds of farm produce, shopping and restaurant in the village or at Pontorson (7 km).

Prices:	low season	F 551	8/9 people
	high season	F 872/927	IGN 16

Booking: Manche booking service

50/SR173

11

Orne

AUBE La Clémendière This gîte is next door to the owner's house and is furnished in rustic style. It is located in the Ouche region of forests and small lakes. Soligny-La-Trappe at 14 km has a lake where you may swim. Living room (1 single bed), kitchen, 1 bedroom (2 double and 1 child's bed), shower room, oil heating, enclosed ground. Linen available. Farm produce, shopping and restaurant in the village (2.5 km) or at L'Aigle (6 km) where there is an attractive market on Tuesdays. Mobile shops call.

Prices:	low season	F 550/600	**6 people**
	high season	F 670	IGN 18

Booking: M MALLET, La Clémendière, 61270 Aube. Tel. (33) 24 53 90.

61/1

CANAPVILLE La Panetière An attractively renovated gîte with country-style furnishings, surrounded by apple orchards, 2 km from the village. The Auge valley is noted for its farm produce, including Camembert and Calvados, and Vimoutiers (8 km) celebrates an apple fair in October. The sea (50 km). Living room (1 single bed), kitchen, 2 bedrooms (1 double and 2 single beds), bathroom, fireplace, central heating, terrace, open ground with barbecue. Mobile shops call; cider from the owners; other shopping and restaurant in the village.

Prices:	low season	F 650/720	**5 people**
	high season	F 820/900	IGN 18

Booking: Mme DE CARNE, Le Hameau des Vesques, Canapville. 61120 Vimoutiers. Tel. (33) 39 12 96 **E**

61/3

COUDEHARD Le Hanigot A delightful, half-timbered cottage, typical of the region, renovated and furnished in country style, in a lovely spot surrounded by apple trees, 2 km from the village. There is a leisure centre at Vimoutiers (8 km) with lake (bathing), tennis, riding and grass ski-ing. The sea (65 km). Living room, kitchen, 2 bedrooms (1 double, 2 single and 1 child's bed), bathroom, heating, enclosed ground. Linen available. Produce from neighbouring farms; mobile shops call; other shopping and restaurant at 3 km.

Prices:	low season	F 520/650	**5 people**
	high season	F 800/920	IGN 18

Booking: Orne Loisirs Accueil **E**

61/SR26

COULIMER La Bouée A pleasant gîte in a converted stable block 3 km from the village where there is a café. The owners, a young farming couple, are very welcoming and live 1 km away. Mortagne (8 km) offers many leisure and cultural activities as well as its special black pudding, perry and Calvados. Living room, kitchen, 2 bedrooms (2 double, 3 single, 1 child's bed), bathroom, open fire, electric heating, garage and ground. Linen available. The owners will sell you farm produce. A fishmonger and greengrocer call. Shops in the village.

Prices:	low season	F 687/785	**8 people**
	high season	F 960/1000	IGN 18

Booking: M J. YVER, Ferme de l'Hôtel au Roux, Saint-Jouin-de-Blavou, 61360 Pervenchères. Tel. (33) 25 97 31. **E**

61/4

DOMPIERRE La Hélisière An attractively renovated cottage with country-style furnishings, set in pleasant wooded surroundings. Museum of local crafts and courses available in the village (1 km); a folk festival in July at Domfront (8 km). The spa town of Bagnoles-de-l'Orne (lake, golf, casino) is at 12 km. Living room/kitchenette, 3 bedrooms (2 double, 2 single and 1 child's bed), bathroom, open fire, central heating, garden. Linen available. Farm produce, other shopping and restaurant in the village or at Domfront.

Prices:	low season	F 530/610	**7 people**
	high season	F 780/900	IGN 17

Booking: M DANNIEL, La Hélisière, Dompierre, 61700 Domfront. Tel. (33) 38 14 33.

61/5

246

Orne

LA FERRIERE AUX ETANGS Le Bas Bourg A well-renovated gîte with a mix of traditional and modern furnishings. It is just near a small lake (fishing, wind-surfing and pedalo boats available). Bagnoles-de-l'Orne (12 km) is a spa town in the lovely Andaines forest where leisure facilities include golf and a casino. Living room (TV), kitchen, 2 bedrooms (2 double and 2 single beds), bathroom, open fire, electric heating, balcony, garage, enclosed ground with garden furniture. Linen available. Farm produce, shopping and restaurant in the village (0.1 km) or at Flers (10 km). 
Prices: low season   F 840/1050   **6 people**
         high season   F 1260   IGN 17
Booking: Orne Loisirs Accueil   E
61/SR 47

LA FERRIERE-BOCHARD La Guiberdière A pretty, renovated and comfortably furnished gîte with extensive grounds. The busy town of Alençon (12 km) has a School of Lace with fine examples of the craft on show. Sailing at a lake at Sillé-le-Guillaume (25 km). Living room (1 double divan and television), kitchen, 2 bedrooms (1 double and 1 single bed), bathroom, open fire, electric heating, terrace, enclosed ground with garden furniture and barbecue. Linen available. Farm produce, shopping and restaurant in the village (3 km). 
Prices: low season   F 705/805   **5 people**
         high season   F 995/1100   IGN 19
Booking: M M. LEROUX, 31 rue Blériot, B.P. 227, 61000 Alençon.
Tel. (33) 31 05 06.   E
61/6

FONTENAI LES LOUVETS La Savatte A gîte in an old stone-built cottage, recently renovated and furnished in traditional style, lying in a small, quiet town in forested countryside. Local fishing and footpaths. Alençon (15 km) has a museum devoted to lace-making and fine arts and good sports facilities. Living room (1 double divan), kitchen, 3 bedrooms (2 double, 2 single and 1 child's bed), bathroom and shower, fireplace, central heating, garage, enclosed ground. Linen available. Mobile shops call, shopping in the village or in Alençon. 
Prices: low season   F 635/690   **8/9 people**
         high season   F 800/890   IGN 18
Booking: M MONNIER, 4 rue de la Marne, 61250 Damigny.
Tel. (33) 29 00 77
61/2

11

FRESNES La Rivière Situated in a little hamlet, this old stone house has been renovated and furnished in modern style. The owners, who live 2 km away, manufacture the local speciality, *andouilles* (a kind of sausage). See the fifteenth-century abbey at Tinchebray (3 km); the sea (60 km). Living room, kitchen, 1 bedroom and open landing (1 double, 2 single beds), bathroom and shower, fireplace, central heating, garage, enclosed ground. Linen available. Shopping in the village (2.5 km) or from mobile shops. 
Prices: low season   F 605/665   **4 people**
         high season   F 705/790   IGN 17
Booking: M LETOUZEY, La Rivière, Fresnes, 61800 Tinchebray.
Tel. (33) 66 62 34.
61/7

LONGUENOE Les Eves A renovated cottage with country-style furnishings set in a pleasant garden with outdoor furniture, in a peaceful hamlet, just 1 km from the Ecouves forest. Bicycles for hire at 18 km; try your hand at hang-gliding (20 km); sailing and wind-surfing at a lake (35 km). Living room (TV), kitchen, 2 bedrooms (1 double, 1 single, 1 child's bed, 1 single divan), bathroom, fireplace, electric heating, balcony. Shopping and restaurant (2 km) or at Carrouges (7 km); mobile shops call. 
Prices: low season   F 475/570   **5 people**
         high season   F 700/780   IGN 18
Booking: M J. BOUTHEMY, 17 rue Maryse Bastié, 61000 Alençon.
Tel. (33) 29 49 51.   E
61/8

Orne

MANTILLY Le Petit Village A tiny cottage, renovated and furnished in rustic style, standing quite on its own at the end of a country lane. The owners own the village bakery (1.2 km). Visit Saint-Fraimbault (8 km) which has won competitions for 'flowered villages'. A lake at 9 km. Living room/kitchenette (1 double divan), 1 bedroom (1 double bed), shower room, fireplace, electric heating, open ground with garden furniture. Linen available. Local farm produce; other shopping in the village or at Passais-la-Conception (3 km).

Prices: low season   F 420/470   **4 people**
          high season   F 575/685   IGN 17
Booking: Orne Loisirs Accueil   E
61/SR31

LA MESNIERE La Faltière A lovely gîte, recently restored and full of rustic charm, at the edge of a village in the picturesque Perche region. The owner is the local mayor and lives nearby. Bathing and sailing at a lake and tennis at Le Mêle-sur-Sarthe (7 km). Living room (1 single divan), kitchen, 3 bedrooms (2 double, 2 single, 1 child's bed and a cot), bathroom, open fire, heating, open ground. Linen available. Fishmonger calls; farm produce available; shopping and restaurant in the village (1 km) or at Le Mêle-sur-Sarthe.

Prices: low season   F 550/750   **9 people**
          high season   F 880/950   IGN 18
Booking: M R. ODOLANT, La Faltière, La Mesnière, 61560 Bazoches-sur-Hoesne. Tel. (33) 25 10 30.   E
61/9

MENIL-HUBERT-SUR-ORNE Le Bateau Ideal for serious walkers, this renovated gîte lies on the long-distance footpath, GR36, at the heart of the lovely region known as 'Swiss Normandy'. Motor boats available at a lake (20 km); the coast is just 55 km away. Living room (1 double divan), kitchen, 2 bedrooms (2 double, 1 child's bed), shower room, fireplace, electric heating, terrace, open ground (garden furniture). Farm produce (including cider), other shopping and restaurant in the village (1 km) or at Athis-de-l'Orne (8 km).

Prices: low season   F 520/675   **7 people**
          high season   F 830/885   IGN 18
Booking: M G. KLAINE, La Potiche, 14690 Pont-d'Ouilly. Tel. (31) 69 81 12.
61/10

MIEUXCE La Poussinière A very old stone house, well renovated with country style furnishings, lying amongst other buildings near a livestock farm in the village. There is a village festival at Mieuxcé (2 km) in July. Bicycles for hire and many other leisure facilities at the important town of Alençon (6 km). Living room, kitchen, 3 bedrooms (1 double, 3 single beds), bathroom, open fire, gas heating, enclosed ground with barbecue facilities. Linen available. Baker and grocer call; dairy produce from a neighbouring farm; shopping and restaurant at 3 km.

Prices: low season   F 670/800   **5 people**
          high season   F 900/1000   IGN 17
Booking: M M. DIVIER, Le Bourg, Rouperroux, 61320 Carrouges. Tel. (33) 27 20 11.   E
61/11

MONTGAUDRY Biard A renovated gîte, furnished in country style, standing quite alone, surrounded by pastureland, outside a tiny village (0.3 km). A swimming-pool, riding and tennis at 9 km; many other leisure facilities, including a lake, at Le Mêle-sur-Sarthe (13 km). Living room (1 single divan), kitchen, 3 bedrooms (2 double, 2 single, 1 child's bed), bathroom, fireplace, electric heating, enclosed ground with child's swing. Linen available. Farm produce in the village; other shopping and restaurant (3 km) or at Mamers (9 km).

Prices: low season   F 550/590   **8 people**
          high season   F 770/820   IGN 19
Booking: M M. CHARDON, Boisaubert, Marchemaisons, 61170 Le Mêle-sur-Sarthe. Tel. (33) 27 61 50.
61/12

Orne

ORIGNY-LE-ROUX L'Angellerie An old stable block has been beautifully converted into a gîte with country-style furnishings, near the owners' old house where their son, a dairy farmer, lives, 3.5 km from the village. Bathing and sailing at a lake (25 km), or take a trip to the Loire châteaux, 1½ hours' drive away. Living room (1 double divan), kitchen, 2 bedrooms (1 double, 3 single beds), shower room, fireplace, heating, enclosed ground with garden furniture. Linen available. Shopping and restaurant at Mamers (4 km); farm produce available.

Prices:	low season	F 710/790	**7 people**
	high season	F 855/930	*IGN 19*

Booking: Orne Loisirs Accueil E

61/SR35

PARFONDEVAL La Chevairie A renovated and rustically furnished house on a livestock farm by a fishing pond. Bicycles for hire in Mortagne (5 km) which holds a black pudding festival in March. Bathing and sailing at Le Mêle-sur-Sarthe lake (15 km). Living room, kitchen, 2 bedrooms (2 double beds, 2 single), shower room, fireplace, central heating, open ground. Linen available. Shops and restaurant in the village (1.2 km); farm produce available from the owners.

Prices:	low season	F 680/750	**6 people**
	high season	F 840/890	*IGN 18*

Booking: M E. LEVESQUE, La Chevairie, Courgeoust, 61560 Bazoches-sur-Hoesne. Tel. (33) 25 37 71.

61/13

LA PERRIERE Bouvigny A small, renovated cottage, furnished in rustic fashion, standing alone in a forest clearing, 1 km from the lovely village of La Perrière. The owners have an hotel at Le Mêle-sur-Sarthe (20 km) where there is a lake and other leisure facilities. Living room (1 double divan), kitchen, 1 bedroom (1 double, 1 single and 1 child's bed and a cot), shower room, fireplace, electric heating, enclosed ground (garden furniture). Local farm produce (including cider) available; other shopping in the village or at Mamers (9 km).

Prices:	low season	F 650/700	**7 people**
	high season	F 750/800	*IGN 19*

Booking: Orne Loisirs Accueil E

61/SR38

PONTCHARDON Les Grandes-Bruyères A pretty little cottage, set in pastureland, outside a village of the picturesque Pays d'Auge region. The L'Escale du Vitou leisure complex at Vimoutiers (8 km) has a lake, grass ski-ing, swimming-pool, riding centre and tennis. The sea is at 60 km. Living room (1 double divan), kitchen, 2 bedrooms (1 double, 2 single beds and 1 cot), bathroom, open fire, electric heating, extensive enclosed ground. Linen available. Farm produce, shopping and restaurant in the village (2 km).

Prices:	low season	F 620/720	**7 people**
	high season	F 770	*IGN 18*

Booking: M DESLANDES, 1 rue du Val d'Auge, 61120 Vimoutiers. Tel. (33) 39 11 46.

61/14

RANES Le Chêne-Angot A delightful gîte, renovated and furnished in country style, in a quiet spot, 2 km from the village which boasts an eighteenth-century château and where leisure facilities include tennis and miniature golf. Visit Carrouges château (11 km) and the spa town of Bagnoles-de-l'Orne (13 km). Living room/kitchenette, 2 bedrooms (2 double, 1 single bed, 1 cot), shower room, electric heating, carport, enclosed ground. Produce available from a neighbouring farm; other shopping in the village or at La Ferté-Macé (13 km).

Prices:	low season	F 480/540	**6 people**
	high season	F 650/700	*IGN 17*

Booking: Orne Loisirs Accueil E

61/SR12

Orne

SAINT-FRAMIBAULT La Chouanne A well-renovated gîte with country-style furnishings in wooded countryside, 1.5 km from the village which has gained fame in national 'flowered village' contests. At Domfront (15 km), visit the public gardens around the eleventh-century keep; leisure facilities there include miniature golf. Living room, kitchen (washing machine), 2 bedrooms (1 double, 1 single bed, 2 child's cots), open landing (1 double divan), bathroom, fireplace, electric heating, carport, enclosed ground. Shopping and restaurant in the village.

Prices:	low season	F 800/900	**7 people**
	high season	F 1200/1500	IGN 17

Booking: Orne Loisirs Accueil   E

61/15

SAINT-FULGENT-DES-ORMES La Grande Maison A renovated farm cottage with country-style furnishings and its own bread oven. The owners have a cattle farm at 0.5 km. Wind-surfing at a lake (8 km). An hour and a half's drive will take you to the Loire châteaux. Living room (1 double divan), kitchen, 2 bedrooms (1 double, 3 single beds, a child's cot), bathroom, fireplace, electric heating, garage, enclosed ground with garden furniture. Linen available. Farm produce from the owners; a restaurant in the village (0.15 km); shopping at Saint-Cosme (6 km).

Prices:	low season	F 780/850	**8 people**
	high season	F 885/950	IGN 19

Booking: Orne Loisirs Accueil   E

61/SR46

SAINT-GERMAIN-DES-GROIS Heurtebise An old, renovated farm building with country-style furnishings. It is situated on a cereal crops farm 1.5 km from the village. The owners will sell milk and eggs. There are various local festivals during the summer months. Trout fishing at 1 km. Living room (1 single bed), kitchen, 2 bedrooms (1 double, 2 single beds and 1 child's cot), bathroom, fireplace, electric heating, carport, open grounds with garden furniture. Linen available. Restaurant in the village; shopping at Condé-sur-Huisne (3 km).

Prices:	low season	F 580/630	**6 people**
	high season	F 790/840	IGN 19

Booking: Mme A.-M. OLIVIER, Heurtebise, Saint-Germain-des-Grois, 61110 Rémalard. Tel. (33) 73 31 33.   E

61/16

SAINT-MARS-D'EGRENNE La Chauvinière A pretty, half-timbered gîte, carefully renovated with modern furniture. The friendly owners run a business 2 km from the gîte. Domfront at 6 km has a folk festival in July. The lively spa of Bagnoles de l'Orne at 30 km has a lake, golf links and casino. Living room, kitchen, 2 bedrooms (1 double and 2 single beds), bathroom, open fire, electric heating, enclosed ground with child's swing. Linen available. Farm produce, shopping and restaurant in the village (1.5 km) or at Domfront.

Prices:	low season	F 630/690	**4 people**
	high season	F 790	IGN 17

Booking: Orne Loisirs Accueil   E

61/SR53

SAINT-PAUL La Pilonnière A stone house renovated and traditionally furnished, situated on a country road next door to where the retired owners live. Sailing at a lake (2 km), riding and swimming-pool (5 km). See the rhododendron festival at nearby Cérisy-Belle-Etoile. Golf and a casino (35 km); the sea (80 km). Living room, kitchen, 2 bedrooms (1 double and 2 single beds), bathroom, oil and electric heating, garage, ground. Café in the village (0.3 km); shopping at Flers (7 km).

Prices:	low season	F 710/820	**4 people**
	high season	F 870/930	IGN 17

Booking: M DEHAIS, La Pilonnière, Saint-Paul, 61100 Flers. Tel. (33) 66 80 38.

61/17

Orne

SAINT-PIERRE-D'ENTREMONT Le Pont au Moitte A charming thatched house with country-style furnishings, recently restored, near the village centre (0.8 km). Flers (10 km) is a château town with a motor museum and swimming-pool. Sailing and wind-surfing at 12 km. The sea is at 70 km. Living room/kitchenette, 2 bedrooms (1 double, 3 single and 1 child's bed), shower room, open fire, electric heating, extensive enclosed ground. Linen available. Farm produce (including cider), shopping and restaurant in the village or at Flers.

Prices: low season   F 685/890   **6 people**
          high season   F 1030/1090   *IGN 17*
Booking: M GRANGE, Les Prés, Saint-Pierre-d'Entremont, 61800 Tinchebray. Tel. (33) 66 56 96. **E**
61/18

SAINT-PIERRE-DU-REGARD L'Etre An attractive, renovated house with delightful attic rooms in an apple orchard on a mixed farm, 1 km from the village. The owners are welcoming and will sell farm produce. This very picturesque region is called Suisse Normande. Rhododendron festival in May at Cerisy-Belle-Etoile (12 km). Large living room/kitchenette, 3 bedrooms (3 double, 1 single and 1 child's bed), bathroom. fireplace, electric heating, ground. Linen available. Shopping and restaurant at Condé-sur-Noireau (3 km).

Prices: low season   F 950/1000   **8 people**
          high season   F 1050   *IGN 17*
Booking: M V. BUFFARD, L'Etre, Saint-Pierre-du-Regard, 14110 Condé-sur-Noireau. Tel. (31) 69 09 59.
61/19

SAINT-PIERRE-LA-RIVIERE La Laiterie On a mixed farm, 2 km from the village, this gîte has been renovated and furnished in rustic style. Visit the national stud, Haras du Pin, at 10 km; there are three châteaux open to the public within a radius of 20 km; the sea (65 km). Living room, kitchen, 2 bedrooms (2 double, 2 single beds), shower room, fireplace, electric heating, garage, enclosed ground with garden furniture and swings for children. Linen available. Farm produce from the owners; shopping at Chambois (6 km).

Prices: low season   F 570/750   **6 people**
          high season   F 980/1050   *IGN 18*
Booking: M J. BONHOMME, La Boulangerie, Saint-Pierre-la-Rivière, 61310 Exmes. Tel. (33) 35 60 27. **E**
61/20

TAILLEBOIS A renovated and rustically furnished house in a village typical of the lovely Swiss Normandy region. Local leisure activities include canoeing (3 km), hang-gliding (13 km) and water ski-ing (15 km). The sea (70 km). Living room (TV), kitchen, 3 bedrooms (1 double, 2 single, 1 child's bed and a cot), bathroom, fireplace, electric heating, enclosed ground with garden furniture. Linen available. Farm produce, other shopping and restaurant in the village or at Athis-de-l'Orne (7 km).

Prices: low season   F 620/725   **6 people**
          high season   F 805/880   *IGN 21*
Booking: M C. LERAT, 5 rue des Challonets, 14110 Condé-sur-Noireau. Tel. (31) 69 35 15. **E**
61/21

VIMOUTIERS L'Escale du Vitou A country-club-style holiday village and riding centre lying in an orchard in the Pays d'Auge with the town of Camembert, famous for its cheese, 2 km away. Deauville and the Normandy coast (55 km). This is a well-equipped leisure centre whose facilities include a lake, a swimming-pool, tennis courts, a playground, a riding school, grass ski-ing and a restaurant. Sixteen detached gîtes, for 4, 5 or 6/9 people. Living room/kitchenette, 2 bedrooms, shower room. Shopping in Vimoutiers (1.5 km).

Prices: low season   on request
          high season   on request   *IGN 18*
Booking: Centre de Loisirs, L'Escale du Vitou, 61120 Vimoutiers. Tel. (33) 39 12 04. **E**
61/22

11

Seine-Maritime

AUZOUVILLE-AUBERBOSC La Cidrerie One of two rustically furnished gîtes in a typical renovated Norman cottage in a hamlet where there is a fishing pond. Visit the popular seaside resort of Fécamp (20 km), famous for the production of Benedictine liqueur: the distillery is open to the public. Living room/kitchenette, 2 bedrooms (2 double, 1 single bed), shower room, fireplace, electric heating, enclosed garden with outdoor furniture. Shopping and farm produce in the village; a restaurant at Fauville-en-Caux (3 km).

Prices: low season F 564/738
        high season F 850

5 people
IGN 7

Booking: M P. LEVESQUE, Auzouville-Auberbosc, 76640 Fauville-en-Caux. Tel. (35) 96 72 37.
76/139PC

BAONS-LE-COMTE Le Village A charming thatched cottage, 0.5 km from the village centre. A swimming-pool and tennis at Yvetot (4 km). See the mediaeval village of Jumièges with its ruined Benedictine abbey in the Brotonne Regional Park (15 km approx.). The coast (30 km). Living room (1 double divan), kitchen, 2 bedrooms (1 double, 2 single beds), shower room, fireplace, electric heating, enclosed ground with garden furniture. Shopping in the village and a restaurant at Yvetot.

Prices: low season F 584/799
        high season F 1117

6 people
IGN 7

Booking: Mme G. LEMOINE, Le Village, Baons-le-Comte, 76190 Yvetot. Tel. (35) 95 19 32.

76/140PC

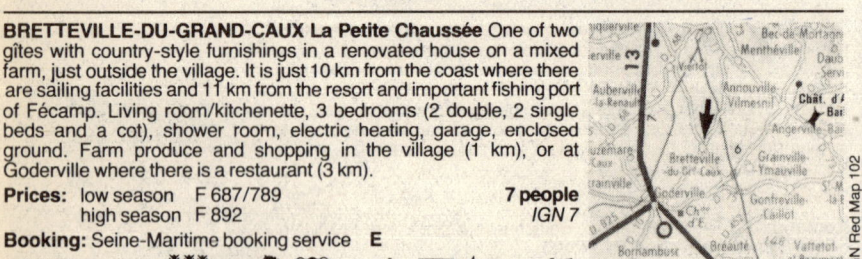

BRETTEVILLE-DU-GRAND-CAUX La Petite Chaussée One of two gîtes with country-style furnishings in a renovated house on a mixed farm, just outside the village. It is just 10 km from the coast where there are sailing facilities and 11 km from the resort and important fishing port of Fécamp. Living room/kitchenette, 3 bedrooms (2 double, 2 single beds and a cot), shower room, electric heating, garage, enclosed ground. Farm produce and shopping in the village (1 km), or at Goderville where there is a restaurant (3 km).

Prices: low season F 687/789
        high season F 892

7 people
IGN 7

Booking: Seine-Maritime booking service E
76/108L

LA CHAPELLE-SAINT-OUEN This old, rustically furnished cottage is in a particularly pleasant rural setting, on a mixed farm, 1 km from the village centre. A pony club at 3 km; the spa town of Forges-les-Eaux, popularised by Cardinal Richelieu, at 15 km, has a swimming-pool, attractive park and pedalo boats for hire. Living room, kitchen, 2 bedrooms (4 single and 2 child's beds), bathroom, fireplace, central heating, enclosed garden. Farm produce in the village, shopping and a restaurant at 12 km.

Prices: low season F 565/644
        high season F 793

4/6 people
IGN 3

Booking: M E. BECQUART, La Chapelle-Saint-Ouen, 76780 Argveil. Tel. (35) 90 83 56.
76/137PB

CLERES Grande Cordellerille This spacious old cottage with country-style furnishings is situated in its own delightful garden and is surrounded by woodland. The market town of Clères (1.5 km) has many tourist attractions including a wildlife park with many rare species; an automobile museum and Renaissance château. The coast (45 km). Living room (TV, 1 double divan), kitchen, 3 bedrooms (2 double, 2 single beds and a cot), fireplace, electric heating, garage, garden furniture. Shopping and restaurant in the town.

Prices: low season F 717/922
        high season F 1127

9 people
IGN 7

Booking: M R. NASSIET, 172 rue Beauvoisine, 76000 Rouen. Tel. (35) 71 59 62
76/126PB

Seine-Maritime

ELLECOURT Ferme de la Quesnay An old house with rustic furnishings on a livestock farm. Good leisure facilities at Aumale and the Eu forest (7 km), including a swimming-pool, tennis and pedalo boat hire. Riding at 25 km. The coast is an easy day trip at 40 km. Living room/kitchenette, 3 bedrooms (3 double, 2 single beds), shower room, fireplace, electric central heating, carport, enclosed garden. Shopping and restaurant at Aumale (7 km).

Prices: low season F 635/738
high season F 840

8 people
IGN 3

Booking: Seine-Maritime booking service **E**

76/107PB

EPREVILLE Guernesey A small gîte with country-style furnishings in the owners' imposing old house on a mixed farm, just 6 km from the seaside resort of Fécamp, which offers all kinds of leisure amenities including bicycle hire to explore this delightful region of coast and countryside. Living room, kitchen, 1 bedroom (2 double beds), bathroom, central heating, enclosed garden. Shopping in the village (1 km) or at Fécamp where there is a choice of restaurants.

Prices: low season F 666/810
high season F 871

4 people
IGN 7

Booking: M Y. GEULIN, Guernesey, Epreville, 76400 Fécamp.
Tel. (35) 29 32 34.

76/125L

ERMENOUVILLE A truly delightful half-timbered thatched cottage set in extensive enclosed grounds near the village centre (0.8 km) where you will find a tennis court and riding stables. Sailing and other amenities at the modern seaside town of Saint-Valéry-en-Caux (8 km). Living room/kitchenette, 2 bedrooms (1 double, 2 single beds, 1 single divan), bathroom, fireplace, electric heating, garden furniture. Mobile shops call; farm produce in the village (0.8 km); other shopping at Saint-Valéry-en-Caux; a restaurant within walking distance (1 km).

Prices: low season F 661/811
high season F 916

5 people
IGN 7

Booking: Seine-Maritime booking service **E**

76/155L

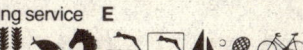

LA FERTE-SAINT-SAMSON La Ruete A small, attractively renovated and rustically furnished gîte in a hamlet, 1 km from the village and 4 km from the spa town of Forges-les-Eaux where you may hire bicycles, visit the casino or try any of the eight different medicinal waters available. The sea (50 km). Living room (1 double divan), kitchen, 1 bedroom (1 double bed), bathroom, fireplace, electric heating, carport, garden with outdoor furniture. Farm produce in the village; other shopping and restaurant at Forges-les-Eaux.

Prices: low season F 600/758
high season F 863

4 people
IGN 3

Booking: Seine-Maritime booking service **E**

76/157PB

FLAMANVILLE Rue Verte A renovated, stone-built house with modern furnishings, set on a mixed farm where you may buy fresh produce (including cider). The busy market town of Yvetot (7 km) has a remarkable round modern church with a wall of stained glass which is the work of Max Ingrand. Living room/kitchenette (TV), 3 bedrooms (2 double, 2 single and 1 child's bed), shower room, fireplace, electric heating, enclosed ground. Shopping in the village (1 km) or at Yvetot where there is a restaurant.

Prices: low season F 507/733
high season F 856

7 people
IGN 7

Booking: M Y. QUEVILLY, Rue Verte, Flamanville, 76970 Motteville.
Tel. (35) 96 81 27.

76/98PC

11

253

Seine-Maritime

FOUCARMONT L'Abbaye A lovely old house, modernised and furnished in country fashion, situated in extensive grounds with private tennis court, 0.5 km from the village centre. The pleasant town of Neufchâtel-en-Bray (15 km approx.), dominated by a huge Gothic church, is noted for its cheese. The sea (30 km). Living room, kitchen, 3 bedrooms (2 double, 2 single and 1 child's bed), bathroom and shower, fireplace, central heating, terrace, garden furniture. Farm produce, shopping and restaurant in the village.

Prices:	low season	F 636/738	**6/7 people**
	high season	F 840	*IGN 3*

Booking: Seine-Maritime booking service **E**

76/57PB

FRANQUEVILLE-SAINT-PIERRE La Paillette A gîte with country-style furnishings in the owners' modernised house. Good shopping and leisure facilities at Rouen (10 km), an important port whose delightful old quarter is pedestrianised and famous landmarks include the ornate clock, cathedral and the site of Joan of Arc's execution. Living room, kitchen, 3 bedrooms (2 double, 2 single and 1 child's bed), shower room, fireplace, central heating, terrace, carport, enclosed garden. Shopping and restaurant in the village (0.5 km).

Prices:	low season	F 784/922	**7 people**
	high season	F 1143	*IGN 7*

Booking: Mme R. LAINEY, La Paillette, Franqueville-Saint-Pierre, 76520 Boos. Tel. (35) 80 60 02. **E**

76/111S

MANEGLISE Les Hellandes A lovingly restored, half-timbered Norman cottage with rustic furnishings, situated on a mixed farm, 1.5 km from the village centre. There is an abbey church at the old fortified town of Montvillers (6 km); a golf course and other amenities at the cliff-top town of Etretat (12 km). Living room/kitchenette (1 double divan), 2 bedrooms (2 double, 1 child's bed), bathroom, fireplace, electric heating, enclosed ground with garden furniture. Shopping and restaurant at Angerville L'Archer (1.5 km).

Prices:	low season	F 548/769	**6/7 people**
	high season	F 897	*IGN 7*

Booking: M P. DECULTOT, Les Hellandes, Manéglise, 76280 Criquetot-L'Esneval. Tel. (35) 20 93 40.

76/42L

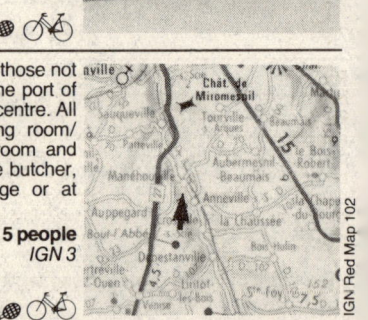

MANEHOUVILLE Hameau de Calnon This gîte is ideal for those not wanting too long a drive as it is situated just 10 km from the port of Dieppe. It is in the owners' old house, 1 km from the village centre. All kinds of leisure and cultural amenities at Dieppe. Living room/kitchenette, 2 bedrooms (1 double, 3 single beds), bathroom and shower, fireplace, electric heating, enclosed ground. Mobile butcher, baker and fishmonger call; other shopping in the village or at Saugueville (2 km) where there is a restaurant.

Prices:	low season	F 687/892	**5 people**
	high season	F 994	*IGN 3*

Booking: Seine-Maritime booking service **E**

76/14L

MAUQUENCHY Le Randillon A detached house with country-style furnishings, set in its own enclosed garden, 2 km from the village centre where you may hire horses or even a pony and trap! Good forest walks at 6 km and other amenities at the country holiday resort of Forges-les-Eaux (6 km). Living room, kitchen, 2 bedrooms (1 double, 2 single beds), bathroom, fireplace, central heating, garage. Fresh milk and eggs from the owners; mobile butcher and baker call; other shopping at Somméry (2 km); several restaurants at Forges-les-Eaux.

Prices:	low season	F 543/646	**4 people**
	high season	F 712	*IGN 3*

Booking: M J. TILMANT, Le Randillon, Mauquenchy, 76440 Forges-les-Eaux. Tel. (35) 90 77 52.

76/85PB

Seine-Maritime

MESNIERES-EN-BRAY Isembertheville A deceptively spacious old cottage, furnished in country fashion, situated on a mixed farm. Local tourist attractions include a riding centre at 10 km, miniature golf at Londinières and sailing (20 km). The coast is just 30 km away. Living room, kitchen, 3 bedrooms (3 double, 1 single, 1 child's bed and a single divan), shower room, fireplace, electric heating, enclosed garden. Fresh milk and eggs from the owners; other shopping in the village (1 km) or at Neufchâtel-en-Bray (9 km).
Prices: low season F 543/759   **9 people**
           high season F 923   IGN 3
Booking: M J. CHEDRU, Isembertheville, Mesnières-en-Bray, 76270 Neufchâtel-en-Bray. Tel. (35) 93 10 23.
76/87PB

MONTVILLE Le Tôt A charming country cottage in a pleasant garden, 1 km from the village centre. Clères (3 km) has much to offer tourists: its zoological park in the grounds of a Renaissance château has flamingoes, deer, gibbons and many other animals roaming at large. Living room, kitchen, 1 bedroom (4 single beds), shower room, fireplace, electric heating. Farm produce, shopping and restaurant in the village, or at Clères.
Prices: low season F 584/687   **4 people**
           high season F 789   IGN 7
Booking: Seine-Maritime booking service   E

76/156PC

NEVILLE Quartier de l'Eglise A thatched cottage, typical of the region, with country-style furnishings and its own enclosed garden, 0.5 km from the village centre. The seaside resort of Saint-Valéry-en-Caux is just 6 km away and you may enjoy a drive along the picturesque coast road. Living room (1 double divan), kitchen, 2 bedrooms (1 double, 1 single and 1 child's bed), bathroom, fireplace, central heating. Farm produce and shopping in the village or at Saint-Valéry-en-Caux where you will find a selection of restaurants.
Prices: low season F 748/789   **6 people**
           high season F 1148   IGN 7
Booking: Seine-Maritime booking service   E

76/114L

REBETS Les Huées A well-renovated and very spacious Norman cottage with country-style furnishings, surrounded by woodland. Bicycle hire, riding and tennis at 12 km; other leisure amenities at the spa town of Forges-les-Eaux (18 km) and the coast, close enough for a day trip at 50 km. Living room (TV), kitchen (washing machine), 7 bedrooms (1 double, 9 single beds), bathroom and shower, fireplace, electric heating, enclosed garden with outdoor furniture. Shopping from mobile stores, in the village (1.5 km) or at Mauquenchy (12 km).
Prices: low season F 811/1022   **11 people**
           high season F 1233   IGN 3
Booking: Seine-Maritime booking service   E
76/152PB

RONCHERELLES-EN-BRAY La Croix du Vieux Bled Situated on a mixed farm (2 km from the village), this attractive house is now divided into two gîtes. Forges-les-Eaux (7 km) has a pleasant park with tennis court and boating lake. There is horse racing in the town on July 14th. Living room/kitchenette, 2 bedrooms (1 double, 2 single and 1 child's bed), shower room, fireplace, electric heating, enclosed garden. Shopping and restaurant at Forges-les-Eaux.
Prices: low season F 476/620   **5 people**
           high season F 748   IGN 3
Booking: Mme A. M. PETIT, Ferme de la Houssaye, Fontaine-sous-Péaux, 76160 Darnetal. Tel. (35) 34 70 64.
76/38PB

11

255

Seine-Maritime

ROUVRAY-CATILLON A terraced house at the village centre where you can buy local cider and other farm produce. Bicycles for hire at Forges-les-Eaux (6 km). The busy town of Dieppe (45 km) has a popular market 3 days a week (Tues., Thurs. and Sat.). Living room, kitchen, 2 bedrooms (2 double, 1 single and 1 child's bed), shower room, fireplace, electric heating, enclosed garden. Shopping in the village or at Forges-les-Eaux where there are restaurants.

Prices:	low season	F 544/683	**5/6 people**
	high season	F 794	IGN 3

Booking: M J. M. MOREL, Rouvray-Catillon, 76440 Forges-les-Eaux. Tel. (35) 90 72 93.

76/128PB

SAINT-AIGNAN-SUR-RY Les Marettes A very attractive renovated Norman cottage with country-style furnishings, set in its own garden, 1 km from the village centre. Visit the motor museum at Ry (4 km), the village where Flaubert wrote *Madame Bovary*; see too the Château de Vascoeuil nearby. The coast (50 km). Living room, kitchen, 3 bedrooms (1 double, 3 single beds and a cot), shower room, fireplace, electric heating, garden with outdoor furniture. Cider and other produce from the owners; other shopping and restaurant at Ry.

Prices:	low season	F 564/718	**5 people**
	high season	F 820	IGN 8

Booking: M G. LESUR, Les Marettes, Saint-Aignan-sur-Ry, 76116 Ry. Tel. (35) 34 03 03.

76/144PB

SAINTE-GENEVIEVE-EN-BRAY Le Mont-Fossé A well-modernised house, furnished in rustic fashion and situated in its own enclosed garden where the English-speaking owners offer rides in a donkey and trap (provided you are insured). Swimming-pool, riding, tennis and bicycle hire all at 10 km. The coast is at 50 km. Living room/kitchenette (1 double divan), 2 bedrooms (1 double, 2 single, 1 child's bed), shower room, fireplace, electric heating, carport, enclosed ground. Mobile butcher, baker and fishmonger call.

Prices:	low season	F 758/916	**6/7 people**
	high season	F 1128	IGN 3

Booking: Seine-Maritime booking service **E**

76/151PB

SAINT-JOUIN-BRUNEVAL Le Village A small rustically furnished old cottage, 1 km from the village centre where there are marked cycle routes (bicycles for hire at 10 km). Etretat (10 km) is an elegant and popular resort, famous for its high cliffs; it has a lovely covered market place and good leisure amenities. Living room (1 double divan), kitchen, 1 bedroom (1 double bed), fireplace, heating, enclosed garden with outdoor furniture. Shopping and restaurant in the village.

Prices:	low season	F 663/769	**4 people**
	high season	F 874	IGN 7

Booking: Seine-Maritime booking service **E**

76/73L

SAINT-LAURENT-EN-CAUX Hameau de Caltot A well-modernised and comfortably furnished gîte near the village centre (0.8 km). It is 15 km from the pleasant seaside resort of Veules-les-Roses where amenities include sailing and golf. Do not miss historic Rouen (35 km) with its fine cathedral and outstanding museums. Living room (1 double divan), kitchen, 1 bedroom (1 double and 1 child's bed), bathroom, fireplace, heating, terrace, garage, enclosed garden with outdoor furniture. Shopping and restaurant in the village.

Prices:	low season	F 640/799	**5 people**
	high season	F 907	IGN 7

Booking: Mme E. GUIUEBERT, Saint-Laurent-en-Caux, 76560 Doudeville. Tel. (35) 96 44 33.

76/22PC

Seine-Maritime

SAINT-LAURENT-EN-CAUX Hameau de Caltot A modern gîte, built in traditional local style, in a hamlet at the edge of the village (1.3 km). At Veules-les-Roses (15 km), enjoy the fine sandy beaches backed by high cliffs, water sports and casino. The interesting towns of Fécamp, Rouen and Dieppe are all within reach. Living room/kitchenette, 2 bedrooms (1 double, 2 single and 1 child's bed), bathroom, fireplace, electric heating, enclosed ground with garden furniture. Shopping and restaurant in the village.

Prices:	low season	F 615/718	**4/5 people**
	high season	F 923	IGN 7

Booking: M A. MAYEUX, Hameau de Caltot, Saint-Laurent-en-Caux, 76560 Doudeville. Tel. (35) 96 65 26.
76/141PC

SAINT-PIERRE-LE-VIGER A gîte set in its own ground, near the centre of the village where you may hire bicycles. It is within walking distance of the coast (4 km) and the picturesque resort of Veules-les-Roses whose beaches offer safe bathing. Living room/kitchenette, 3 bedrooms (2 double, 2 single beds), bathroom, fireplace, electric heating. Linen available. Shopping in the village (0.5 km) or at Veules-les-Roses where there is a choice of restaurants.

Prices:	low season	F 687/892	**6 people**
	high season	F 1097	IGN 7

Booking: Seine-Maritime booking service   E

76/17L

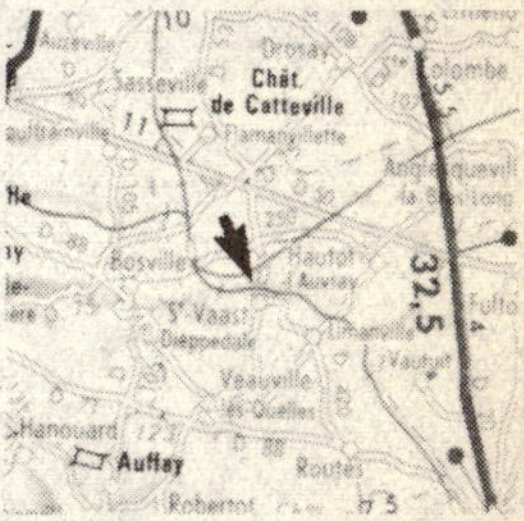

SAINT-VAAST-DIEPPEDALLE Artemare A simply furnished old cottage on a mixed farm, 2 km from the village. Cany-Barville (7 km) has a seventeenth-century château. The picturesque seaside town of Saint-Valéry-en-Caux (10 km) has a yachting harbour and lively nightlife with discotheque, casino and cinemas. Living room/kitchenette, 2 bedrooms (1 double, 3 single beds), shower room, fireplace, central heating, enclosed ground. Local farm produce and shopping in the village or at Cany-Barville where there is a restaurant.

Prices:	low season	F 605/718	**5 people**
	high season	F 840	IGN 7

Booking: Seine-Maritime booking service   E

76/24L

LE TREPORT Les Granges A rustically furnished gîte, situated on a farm where the owners may offer a babysitting service. It is 1 km from the popular seaside resort of Le Tréport which has a pretty fishing harbour and a lift to take visitors from the beach to the top of its steep cliffs. Living room, kitchen, 2 bedrooms (1 double, 2 single and 1 child's bed), shower room, electric heating, enclosed garden with outdoor furniture. Farm produce from the owners; other shopping and restaurant in the town.

Prices:	low season	F 717/892	**4/5 people**
	high season	F 994	IGN 3

Booking: Seine-Maritime booking service   E

76/146L

LES TROIS PIERRES Eroiderue A gîte with country-style furnishings in the owners' attractive old house on a farm where they raise sheep and poultry, and offer fresh produce for sale. Try your hand at gliding (4 km); a discotheque at 4 km. All kinds of other leisure amenities at the coast (15 km). Living room, kitchen, 2 bedrooms (1 double, 5 single and 1 child's bed), shower room, fireplace, electric heating, enclosed garden with child's sand-pit. Shopping in the village (2 km); a restaurant at Saint-Romain-de-Colbosc (4 km).

Prices:	low season	F 705/916	**7/8 people**
	high season	F 1021	IGN 7

Booking: Seine-Maritime booking service   E

76/150PC

11

CHAMPAGNE ARDENNE
the land where life sparkles

More than 50 museums and art collections to visit.
Forests and lakes for nature lovers.
The vineyards and a world famous wine
Champagne ! Gastronomie !

Champagne-Ardenne demands to be discovered. Come and visit our region and get to know it through Its country lanes - Its many facets.
You will fall in love !

- The Meuse valley and its beautiful river-boat trips
- Troyes, knitting City and its museum of Modern Art
- The Champagne vineyards, the famous cellars, Rheims, Epernay
- Langres, the walled town in the heart of the countryside

For further information, please contact :
COMITÉ RÉGIONAL DE TOURISME
CHAMPAGNE-ARDENNE
2 bis, Boulevard Vaubécourt
51000 CHALONS/MARNE FRANCE
Tél. : 26.64.35.92 — Télex : 830 138

NOT TO BE MISSED

12 CHAMPAGNE-ARDENNE

Still very much undiscovered by tourists, Champagne-Ardenne has a tremendous amount to offer.

It is easily accessible from Britain, roughly half a day's drive from the Channel ports and close to Germany and Luxembourg if you want a more varied holiday. The landscape ranges from the heavily wooded Ardennes, rising to pleasant hills and valleys in the Haute-Marne. In the centre is Montagne-de-Reims, a 124,000-acre nature conservation park, covering the Champagne-producing area and stretching between Châlons-sur-Marne, Epernay and Reims. Circular routes offer an interesting tour of the Champagne vineyards, forests and country towns.

This region boasts the largest artificial lake in Europe, the Lac du Der-Chantecoq, and also has a splendid bird reserve at the Lac de la Forêt d'Orient. Both lakes have all kinds of sporting facilities.

Of course, one of the main attractions of the region is simply Champagne. The technique for maturing Champagne is attributed to the blind monk Dom Perignon and later refined by the widow Clicquot. The Champagne-producing area is small and comprises three different sectors, each producing good-quality Champagne: the Montagne de Reims, Marne Valley and the Côte de Blancs. Reims and Epernay are the two Champagne capitals and the tourist offices in both towns will arrange visits to cellars – hundreds of kilometres of chalky caves under the towns and fields. Visitors in May can enjoy the Champagne Festival at Rilly-la-Montagne.

In Epernay, the avenue du Champagne, half a mile of shippers' mansions and the courtyards of their offices/cellars, is well worth a visit. Not to be missed either are the fine cathedral at Reims, the huge fortress of Sedan and the star-shaped fortified city of Rocroi. Other historic towns include Troyes, well preserved with many remarkable churches; Châlons-sur-Marne, dating back to Roman times, and Charleville-Mézières, whose Ducal square is a replica of the Place des Vosges in Paris.

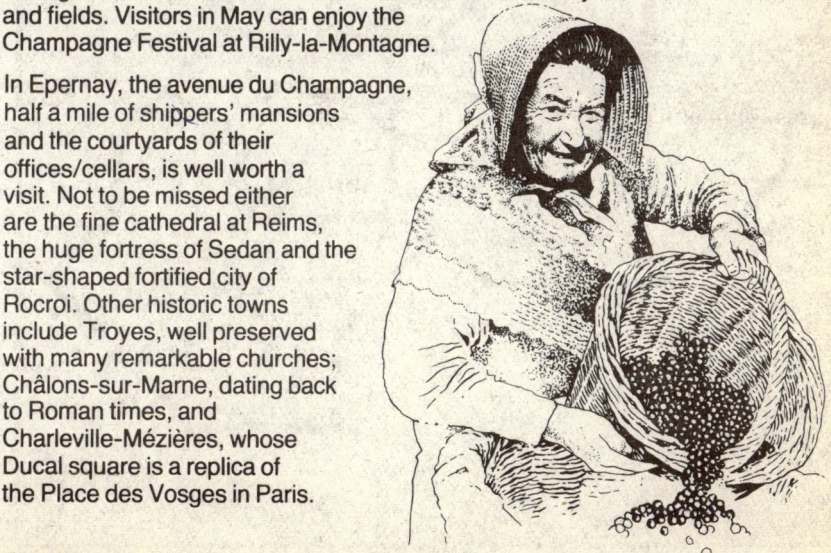

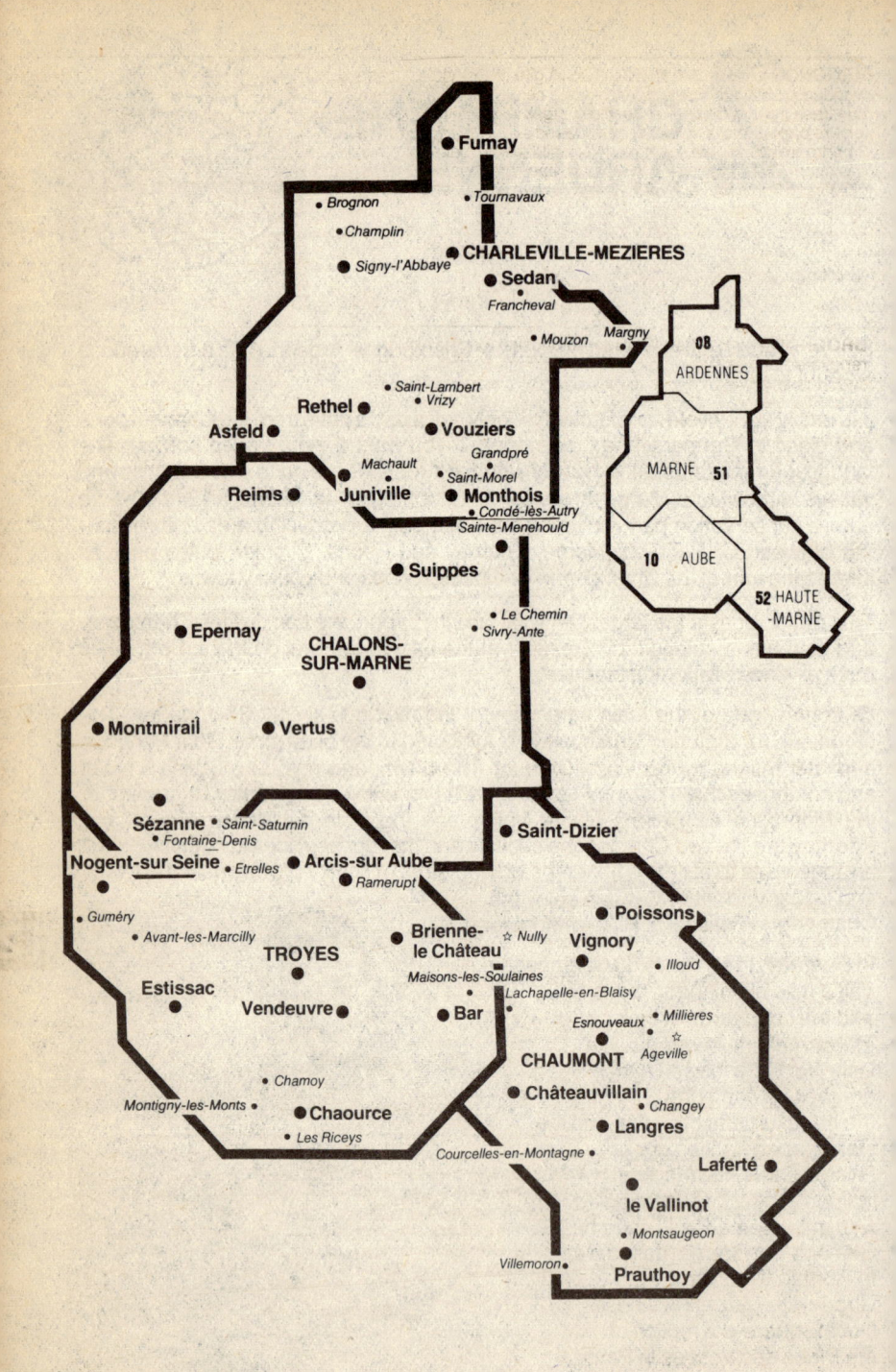

- Fumay
- Brognon
- Tournavaux
- Champlin
- **CHARLEVILLE-MEZIERES**
- Signy-l'Abbaye
- **Sedan**
- Francheval
- Mouzon
- Margny
- Saint-Lambert
- **Rethel**
- Vrizy
- **Asfeld**
- **Vouziers**
- Machault
- Grandpré
- Saint-Morel
- **Reims**
- **Juniville**
- **Monthois**
- Condé-lès-Autry
- Sainte-Menehould
- **Suippes**
- Le Chemin
- Sivry-Ante
- **Epernay**
- **CHALONS-SUR-MARNE**
- **Montmirail**
- **Vertus**
- **Sézanne**
- Saint-Saturnin
- Fontaine-Denis
- **Saint-Dizier**
- **Nogent-sur-Seine**
- Etrelles
- **Arcis-sur Aube**
- Ramerupt
- **Poissons**
- Guméry
- Avant-les-Marcilly
- **Brienne-le Château**
- ☆ Nully
- **Vignory**
- Illoud
- **TROYES**
- Maisons-les-Soulaines
- **Estissac**
- Lachapelle-en-Blaisy
- Millières
- **Vendeuvre**
- **Bar**
- Esnouveaux
- Ageville ☆
- **CHAUMONT**
- Chamoy
- **Châteauvillain**
- Changey
- Montigny-les-Monts
- **Chaource**
- Les Riceys
- **Langres**
- Courcelles-en-Montagne
- **Laferté**
- le Vallinot
- Montsaugeon
- Villemoron
- **Prauthoy**

08 ARDENNES
MARNE 51
10 AUBE
52 HAUTE-MARNE

260

Ardennes

BROGNON Le Brochet A recently built gîte, traditionally furnished, in wooded countryside close to the village centre (1 km) where you may buy fresh eggs and milk. Les Vieilles Forges lake (25 km) provides good leisure opportunities including bathing and sailing. Living room, kitchen, 3 bedrooms (2 double, 2 single and 1 child's bed), bathroom, fireplace, gas central heating, verandah, carport, open grounds with furniture and child's swing. Mobile baker and butcher call, other shopping and restaurant at Signy-le-Petit (4 km).

Prices:	low season	F 538/700	7 people
	high season	F 1049	IGN 5

Booking: Ardennes booking service   **E**

08/94

BROGNON Pré Baptiste Bisque An unusual long, low building, well renovated and furnished in rustic style 1.5 km from the village centre and standing in wooded countryside where there are good walks and ponds for fishing. Les Vieilles Forges lake (25 km) offers good leisure facilities including bathing and sailing. Living room, kitchen (washing machine), 4 bedrooms (4 double and 1 child's bed), shower room, open fires, central heating, terrace, open grounds. Mobile butcher and baker call, shopping and restaurant at Signy-le-Petit (4 km).

Prices:	low season	F 725/828	9 people
	high season	F 1035	IGN 5

Booking: Ardennes booking service   **E**

08/99B

CHAMPLIN A substantial old stone-built house now renovated and equipped with both traditional and modern furnishings belonging to the local council and situated in the village. Good opportunities for walking in the surrounding forests along marked footpaths. Les Vieilles Forges marina at 25 km, swimming-pool at 20 km. Living room (1 double divan), kitchen, 2 bedrooms (2 double and 1 single bed), bathroom, electric central heating, carport, open ground with garden furniture. Mobile butcher and baker call, other shopping (3 km) or at Hirson (20 km).

Prices:	low season	F 753	7 people
	high season	F 814	IGN 5

Booking: Ardennes booking service   **E**

08/85

CONDE-LES-AUTRY Now renovated and furnished in traditional style this pretty pink and white house stands in its own enclosed garden in the centre of the community. There is a swimming-pool at 25 km and tennis at 16 km; Bairon lake (40 km) offers good leisure facilities. Living room (TV), kitchen, 3 bedrooms (2 double, 2 single and 1 child's bed), bathroom, electric central heating, terrace, carport, garden with barbecue and furniture. Mobile butcher, baker and grocer; other shopping and restaurant at (4 km), or at Vouziers (25 km).

Prices:	low season	F 565/678	7 people
	high season	F 849	IGN 10

Booking: Ardennes booking service   **E**

08/87

FRANCHEVAL La Grande-Jonquette One of two gîtes in a spacious old house also occupied by the English-speaking owner and set amongst fields and trees where there is a pony and various children's games for the use of guests. The magnificent Château de Sedan at 10 km; sailing at 35 km. Living room (TV), kitchen (washing machine), 2 bedrooms (1 double, 3 single beds and 1 cot), bathroom, heating, open grounds with furniture. Linen available. Mobile butcher and baker call, shops in the village (0.8 km) or at Sedan.

Prices:	low season	F 576/609	6 people
	high season	F 609	IGN 5

Booking: Ardennes booking service   **E**

08/27A

12

Ardennes

GRANDPRE Centrally situated in this small town on the Aire river, this newly built gîte, furnished in traditional style, is close to shops and restaurant. A swimming-pool at 17 km; Bairon lake is at 25 km, forest walks and fishing locally. Living room, kitchen, 2 bedrooms (2 double, 1 single bed and 1 double divan), bathroom, central heating, balcony, garage, small enclosed courtyard. Farm produce and shopping in the village, other shopping at Vouziers (17 km).

Prices: low season F 776
high season F 906

7 people
IGN 10

Booking: Ardennes booking service E

08/73

MACHAULT Just 1½ hours from Paris this imposing old house, now renovated and furnished in rustic style, has been converted into two holiday homes by the English-speaking owners. Surrounded by extensive grounds (garden furniture and children's swings) and close to the village centre. Close to the Champagne vineyards, watersports at Bairon lake (30 km), riding at 20 km. Living room, kitchen, 3 bedrooms (3 double, 2 single beds and 1 cot), shower room, electric heating, terrace and garage. Farm produce, shops and restaurant at Machault or at Vouziers (16 km).

Prices: low season F 689
high season F 840

9 people
IGN 10

Booking: Ardennes booking service E
08/03

MARGNY An old, renovated house in the village, close to shops where local eggs and milk can be bought. A good touring area in lovely forested countryside with viewpoints, the famous Maginot line at 10 km, Avioth cathedral (6 km) and visits to Belgium—the frontier is only 3 km. The traditionally furnished gîte offers living room, kitchen (washing machine), 3 bedrooms (2 double, 1 single bed), bathroom, fireplace, electric central heating. Mobile butcher and baker call, other shopping locally or at Margut (8 km) where there is a restaurant.

Prices: low season F 538/753
high season F 861

5 people
IGN 5

Booking: Ardennes booking service E

08/82

MOUZON Ferme de Givodeau An attractive gîte, newly built and traditionally furnished, adjoining other buildings on a mixed farm 2 km from the village centre where fresh milk and eggs are available. Good watersports facilities at 10 km including bathing, sailing and boating. Living room, kitchen (washing machine), 2 bedrooms (2 double beds, 1 cot), bathroom, electric central heating, enclosed ground with barbecue for outdoor meals. Shopping and restaurant in Mouzon, or at Sedan (13 km).

Prices: low season F 501/565
high season F 630

5 people
IGN 5

Booking: Ardennes booking service E

08/70

SAINT-LAMBERT A very attractive village house owned by the local community, now renovated and equipped with country-style furnishings. Bairon lake (15 km) offers excellent leisure facilities including canoeing, windsurfing, sailing, tennis and pleasant walks. Living room/kitchenette (washing machine), 2 bedrooms (3 double, 1 single and 1 child's bed), bathroom, heating, enclosed ground with garden furniture. Fresh eggs and milk available in the village. Mobile butcher and baker call, other shopping and restaurant at Attigny (3 km).

Prices: low season F 481/543
high season F 662

8 people
IGN 10

Booking: Ardennes booking service E

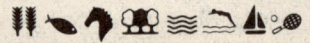

08/40

Ardennes

SAINT-MOREL Corbon A substantial old house, now renovated and converted into two holiday homes, situated on a mixed farm almost 1 km from the village centre. Bairon lake with its excellent leisure facilities is just 20 km away. This ground-floor gîte is furnished in traditional country style and comprises living room, kitchen, 2 bedrooms (2 double and 1 single bed), shower room, fireplace, electric central heating, carport, garden and enclosed grounds with furniture. Mobile butcher and baker, shopping in the village or at Vouziers (9 km) where there is a restaurant.

Prices:	low season	F 639/698	**5 people**
	high season	F 869	*IGN 10*

Booking: Ardennes booking service   **E**

08/72A

SAINT-MOREL Corbon A renovated house with rustic furniture on a livestock farm. The gîte is surrounded by extensive grounds including a pond where you may fish (supplement). Bairon lake is 20 km away and offers bathing, sailing, canoeing, tennis and pleasant walks. Living room (TV, 1 double divan), kitchen, 1 bedroom (1 double bed), bathroom, electric heating, carport, open grounds with garden furniture. Mobile butcher and baker, fresh eggs, milk and other shopping in the village (1 km) or at Vouziers (9 km) where there is a restaurant.

Prices:	low season	F 792/828	**4 people**
	high season	F 895	*IGN 10*

Booking: Ardennes booking service   **E**

08/98

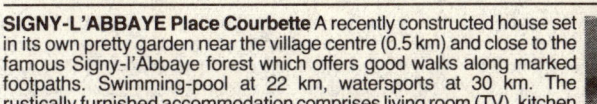

SIGNY-L'ABBAYE Place Courbette A recently constructed house set in its own pretty garden near the village centre (0.5 km) and close to the famous Signy-l'Abbaye forest which offers good walks along marked footpaths. Swimming-pool at 22 km, watersports at 30 km. The rustically furnished accommodation comprises living room (TV), kitchen (washing machine), 3 bedrooms (2 double, 2 single beds and 2 cots), shower room, open fire, heating, terrace, enclosed garden with furniture. Shopping and restaurant locally or at Rethel (22 km).

Prices:	low season	F 484/700	**8 people**
	high season	F 807	*IGN 5*

Booking: Ardennes booking service   **E**

08/83

TOURNAVAUX A newly built gîte, furnished in traditional style, in the owner's own house bordering the Semoy river. There is a camping site adjacent. Canoeing on the Meuse river nearby. Les Vieilles Forges lake (15 km) offers a wide range of watersports plus tennis and rambling. Living room (TV), kitchen, 2 bedrooms (2 double beds), shower room, central heating, carport, enclosed grounds. Mobile butcher and baker call, shopping and restaurant in the village (0.1 km) or at Monthermé (4 km).

Prices:	low season	F 700/753	**4 people**
	high season	F 807	*IGN 5*

Booking: Ardennes booking service   **E**

08/97

12

VRIZY One of two holiday homes in a spacious old house in the village, renovated and furnished in country style. Bairon leisure centre with opportunities for sailing, canoeing, windsurfing, tennis and rambling is just 15 km away—or why not try pétanque in Vrizy itself! Living room, kitchen (washing machine), 4 bedrooms (2 double, 4 single beds, 1 cot and a double divan), bathroom, fireplace, wood central heating, small courtyard. Restaurant, farm produce and shopping locally or at Vouziers (5 km).

Prices:	low season	F 700/1023	**11 people**
	high season	F 1130	*IGN 10*

Booking: Ardennes booking service   **E**

08/76

Country Food and Wine in CHAMPAGNE~ARDENNES

"Where Life Bubbles with Joy"

The name 'Champagne' comes from the old province where this famous wine was first created. The Champagne wine region as designated by French law, is situated 150 km north-east of Paris and is characterised by its very special soil and climate, which give the Champagne grapes a unique and unequalled taste.

The people of Champagne discovered, through their patient work and research, a way of preparing a 'bubbly' wine which is now considered by wine-specialists to be the greatest in the world. The dedication of the people, their loyal and constant respect for the local customs of their craft, have produced exceptional wines which have made the perfumes and flavours of the Champagne countryside famous throughout the world.

In all four corners of the world Champagne wine is an extraordinary ambassdaor for the Champagne-Ardennes region. There, of course, Champagne is everywhere – in the glass and in the dish. In fact cooking with Champagne produces some real delicacies but these represent only a small part of the region's culinary repertoire. Many 'Champagne-Ardennais' recipes are still prepared in a traditional way: cabbage soup; stews, and 'haricots en fricasson' for example.

THE SPECIALITIES OF THE REGION INCLUDE:

Jambon (ham) d'Ardennes, salade au lard, Galette au sucre (a dessert).
Andouillette (sausage) de Troyes, Fromage de Chaource, Potée (stew) champenoise.
Coq au Bouzy, Rognons au champagne, Pieds de porc à la Ste-Ménehould.
Game, fish, cheeses, cakes and pastries (Champardennais, Pavé de l'Aube etc).
The wines of Champagne: red, white and rosé – Champagne, Coteaux Champenois, Vieux Marc, Fine de Marne, Ratafia, Eau de Vie de fruits, Cider (du Pays d'Othe).

Package holiday programmes with such descriptive titles as 'Discovery' and 'Gastronomy' are presented in the brochure 'La Champagne-Ardennes Vous Acceuille' (Welcome to Champagne-Ardennes) available from the Tourism address below.

Please contact the Regional Tourism Dept. about this or for any other assistance or information, at the following address:

COMITE REGIONAL DE TOURISME
DE CHAMPAGNE ARDENNES,
2 Bis, Boulevard Vaubecourt,
51000 CHALONS-SUR-MARNE, France.
Tel: 26.64.35.92

CHAMPAGNE ARDENNE

ARDENNES · AUBE
MARNE · HAUTE-MARNE

Aube

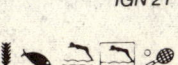

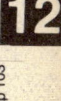

AVANT-LES-MARCILLY Tremblay An old detached cottage with traditional furnishings in the courtyard of an arable farm, 2 km from the village. Plenty of sights in the area, including Le Paraclet, the abbey of Abelard and Heloise, and the eighteenth-century Château de la Motte-Tilly. Living-room (1 double divan), kitchen, 2 bedrooms (1 double and 3 single beds), bathroom, electric central heating, carport, courtyard. Linen available (F20 per set per week). Mobile shops and farm produce available; other shopping at Nogent-sur-Seine (8 km).

Prices:	low season	F 360/515	**7 people**
	high season	F 618	*IGN 22*

Booking: M R. VAN GOETSENHOVEN, Tremblay, 10400 Avant-les-Marcilly. Tel. (25) 39 21 18.
10/46

CHAMOY A detached, renovated and rustically furnished house on the edge of a farming village. Walking on long-distance, marked footpaths (2 km), bicycle hire 3 km and a swimming-pool at 25 km. Living room, kitchen, 2 bedrooms (1 double, 2 single beds), shower room, gas heating, garage, courtyard. Linen available (approx. F20 per set per week). Mobile butcher and fishmonger call; other shopping in the village (0.2 km), or at Ervy-le-Châtel (15 km). Restaurant at 2 km.

Prices:	low season	F 464/515	**4 people**
	high season	F 618	*IGN 22*

Booking: M G. CHAPIER, Chamoy, 10130 Ervy-le-Châtel.
Tel. (25) 42 14 03
10/54

CHAMOY A renovated and traditionally furnished gîte in the village mentioned above. It is just 2 km from the Othe forest where you should try the local cheese and cider. Troyes (24 km) is a fine cathedral city well worth a visit. Sailing at a lake (30 km). Living room (1 double divan), kitchen, 2 bedrooms (1 double, 2 single beds), bathroom, open fire, enclosed garden with outdoor furniture. Linen available. Farm produce and other shopping in the village or at Ervy-le-Châtel (10 km).

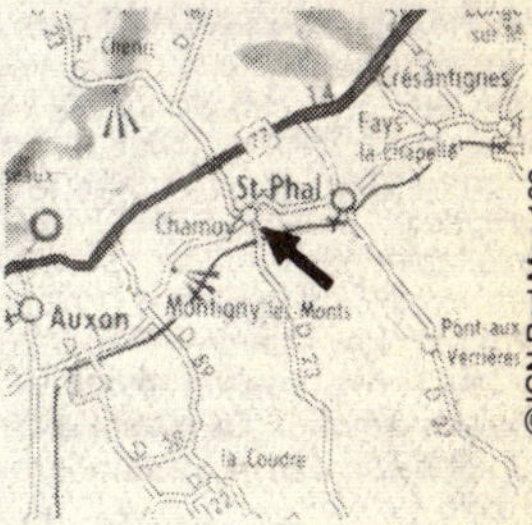

Prices:	low season	F 436/488	**6 people**
	high season	F 561	*IGN 22*

Booking: M G. BOULLE, 64 rue Marcellin-Berthelot, 10000 Troyes.
Tel. (25) 82 25 94.
10/33

ETRELLES A detached renovated gîte with traditional furnishings situated on a cereal farm near the village centre. Local river fishing; riding, tennis and swimming pool within 13 km. Living room, kitchen, 2 bedrooms (1 double, 3 single beds), shower room, fireplace (wood supplied), electric heating, garden, enclosed ground. Linen available (approx. F20 per set per week). Dairy produce is available in the village. Mobile shops call; other shopping and restaurant at Méry-sur-Seine (6 km).

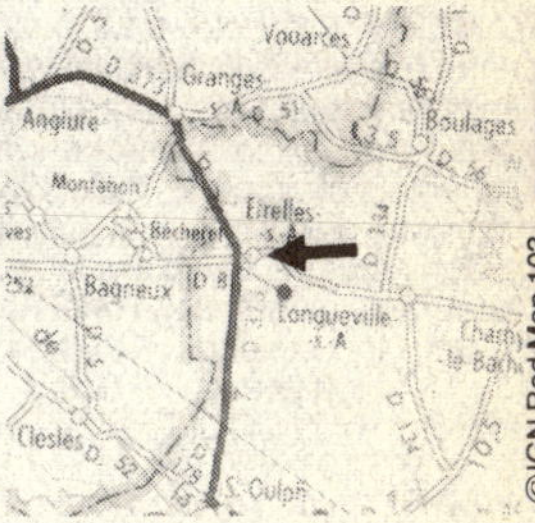

Prices:	low season	F 464/515	**5 people**
	high season	F 588	*IGN 22*

Booking: M C. JEANSON, Etrelles, 10170 Méry-sur-Seine.
Tel. (25) 21 20 29.
10/51

GUMERY Cercy One of two gîtes in a modern house, outside the village (3 km) where the owners also have *chambres d'hôtes* and offer *table d'hôte* meals. It lies 4 km from the Seine Valley, 100 km east of Paris. Local river fishing; a swimming-pool and tennis at 13 km. Living room (1 double divan), kitchen, 1 bedroom (1 double and 1 single bed), shower room, fireplace, electric heating, terrace, open ground with garden furniture. Linen available (approx. F20 per set per week). Shops in the village or at Nogent-sur-Seine (12 km).

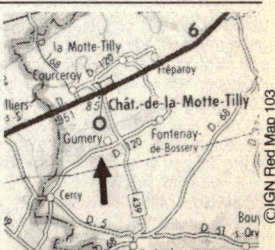

Prices:	low season	F 512/638	**5 people**
	high season	F 682	*IGN 21*

Booking: M R. VISSE, Cercy, 10400 Gumery.
Tel. (25) 39 15 70
10/11

12

Aube

MAISONS-LES-SOULAINES A ground-floor gîte with traditional furnishings in a former village school, owned by the local commune. This is a pretty farming village, 9 km from the interesting old town of Bar-sur-Aube where there is a swimming-pool, tennis courts and other facilities. Forest walks at 2 km. Living room/kitchenette, 2 bedrooms (2 double beds), shower room, electric heating, terrace, garden. Linen available. Shopping and restaurant at Bar-sur-Aube. 
Prices: low season   F 330/412   **4 people**
         high season F 495   *IGN 22*
Booking: Mme LALLEMENT, Commune de Maisons-les-Soulaines, 10200 Bar-sur-Aube.
Tel. (25) 27 28 79.
10/C

MONTIGNY-LES-MONTS An old, detached house with traditional furnishings, near a river, situated in the village. Bicycle-hire and walking on marked, long-distance footpaths at 2 km. Fishing (7 km) and a swimming-pool (28 km). Living room (1 double divan), kitchen, 2 bedrooms (1 double, 3 single beds), shower room, fireplace, electric heating, enclosed ground. Linen available (approx. F20 per set per week). Mobile butcher, baker and greengrocer call; other shopping and restaurant at Auxon (5 km). 
Prices: low season   F 425/485   **7 people**
         high season F 585   *IGN 22*
Booking: M B. JAY, 10130 Ervy-le-Châtel.
Tel. (25) 70 52 53
10/3B

MONTIGNY-LES-MONTS An old stone cottage with country-style furnishings at the edge of the village (1 km) in a pleasant area of woods and farmland. The grounds of the gîte (shared by the owners) run down to a river. Riding (20 km) and sailing at a lake (35 km). Living room/kitchenette, 2 bedrooms (1 double and 2 single beds), bathroom, fireplace, oil-fired central heating. Linen available. Dairy produce available from local farms; other shopping and restaurant at Auxon (5 km) or at Ervy-le-Châtel (10 km).
Prices: low season   F 464/515   **4 people**
         high season F 618   *IGN 22*
Booking: M C. DEHAEMERS, Montigny-les-Monts, 10130 Ervy-le-Châtel. Tel. (25) 42 12 56.
10/56

RAMERUPT An old, traditionally furnished house, 0.1 km from the centre of a village in the Aube valley where the local river is very good for fishing and there are trout farms in the area if you don't want to catch your own! Sailing at a lake (25 km). Living room (1 double divan), kitchen, 2 bedrooms (1 double, 1 large and 1 regular single bed), bathroom, electric heating, garage, enclosed courtyard and ground with garden furniture. Linen available. Mobile shops call; other shopping and restaurants in the village or at Arcis-sur-Aube (12 km).
Prices: low season   F 360/515   **6 people**
         high season F 618   *IGN 22*
Booking: M L. COUFFIGNAL, 10240 Ramerupt.
Tel. (25) 37 61 48.
10/57

LES RICEYS Ricey-Haut An old, traditionally furnished house near the town centre and owned by the director of the tourist office at Troyes, so she should be able to tell you all there is to do in this picturesque region, including visits to local Champagne cellars. Living room, kitchen, 3 bedrooms (2 double and 1 single bed), bathroom, electric heating, courtyard and garden nearby. Local produce (including Champagne) and all other shops in the town or at Bar-sur-Seine (14 km). 
Prices: low season   F 430/482   **5 people**
         high season F 578   *IGN 22*
Booking: Mlle J. RICHARD, 46b Boulevard du 14 Juillet, 10000 Troyes.
Tel. (25) 73 00 36 (office)   **E**
10/43

Marne

LE CHEMIN A renovated and traditionally furnished house in a small village. Visits to local craft studios; bathing at a lake at 10 km. Tennis and swimming-pool at the old town of Sainte-Ménéhould (15 km) where the countryside carries reminders of the battles of the First World War. Living room (1 double and 1 single divan), kitchen (washing machine), 3 bedrooms (2 double, 2 single and 1 child's bed), shower room, central heating, garage, enclosed ground. Linen available. Fresh milk and eggs in the village; other shopping at 10 km.
Prices: low season   F 460/F 600   **9/10 people**
           high season   F 625   IGN 10
Booking: Mme J. FRUIT, Le Chemin, 51800 Sainte-Ménéhould.
Tel. (26) 60 35 39.
51/65

FONTAINE-DENIS A traditionally furnished old house at the centre of the village. The owner has a bicycle shop at Sézanne (12 km) and will hire cycles to explore the locality. A tennis court in the village; a swimming-pool, miniature golf and other amenities at Sézanne. Living room/kitchenette (washing machine), 1 bedroom (3 single beds), bathroom, electric heating, enclosed courtyard with barbecue, garden furniture and table tennis. Linen available (F 15 per set per week). Mobile shops call; other shopping at Sézanne and a restaurant (5 km).
Prices: low season   F 480/500   **3 people**
           high season   F 535   IGN 22
Booking: M R. GAILLARD, 19–23 Rue Paul Doumar, 51120 Sézanne.
Tel. (26) 80 59 03.
51/90

SAINT-SATURNIN A renovated and rustically furnished gîte in its own enclosed garden near the village centre. Take a day trip to Reims (75 km approx), capital of the Champagne trade; visit its fine Gothic cathedral and the Palais de Tau, now a museum. Living room, kitchen, 2 bedrooms (2 double, 1 single and 1 child's bed), bathroom (washing machine), fireplace, electric central heating, terrace. Farm produce available in the village or from the owner; mobile shops call; other shopping (6 km) or at Sézanne (20 km).
Prices: low season   F 605   **5/6 people**
           high season   F 660   IGN 22
Booking: Mme LANCELOT, Vouarces 51260 Anglure.
Tel. (26) 42 71 62.
51/98

SAINTE-MENEHOULD La Vignette One of two apartments with country-style furnishings in a large, renovated house, 1 km from the village at the heart of the Argonne forest. Sainte-Ménéhould (8 km) is a country holiday resort with good leisure amenities; try the local speciality of pigs' trotters at a restaurant there. Living room, kitchen, 2 bedrooms (1 double, 2 single and 1 child's bed), bathroom, heating, terrace, ground. Farm produce, other shopping and restaurant in the village.
Prices: low season   F 550   **4/5 people**
           high season   F 680   IGN 10
Booking: M L. CHRISTIAENS, La Vignette, 55120 Clermont-en-Argonne. Tel. (26) 60 81 91.
51/61

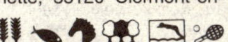

SIVRY-ANTE Ante A well-renovated and traditionally furnished gîte at the village centre, right on the tourist circuit through the Argonne forest (107 km of marked scenic roads altogether). Bathing and sailing at a large lake at Givry-en-Argonne (8 km). Living room/kitchenette (washing machine), lounge (1 double divan), 2 bedrooms (1 double, 3 single beds), bathroom, fireplace (wood supplied), electric central heating, terrace, garage, enclosed ground with garden furniture. Mobile shops call; other shopping and restaurant at Givry-en-Argonne.
Prices: low season   F 575/625   **7 people**
           high season   F 730   IGN 10
Booking: M J. P. SCHLADENHOFF, 37 rue Paul-Louis Courier, 51000 Châlons-sur-Marne. Tel. (26) 64 26 61 (evenings).
51/93

12

Haute-Marne

CHANGEY A sympathetically renovated and traditionally furnished village house, with fishing and bathing at a nearby lake (1 km). The old fortified town of Langres (12 km) has a fascinating old quarter and the town walls offer superb panoramic views; swimming-pool and many other amenities available. Living room/kitchenette, 3 bedrooms (2 double, 2 single and 1 child's bed), bathroom, fireplace (wood supplied), electric heating, garage, enclosed ground. Local honey and farm produce; mobile shops call; other shoppng (6 km); restaurant at 1.5 km.

Prices:	low season	F 400/450	**7 people**
	high season	F 550	IGN 29

Booking: M J. RUPPANNER, Changey, 52360 Neuilly-l'Evèque.
Tel. (25) 85 23 61.
52/75C3

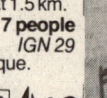

LA CHAPELLE-EN-BLAISY A pretty renovated cottage with country-style furnishings, situated in the village. Chaumont (20 km) is an old town with many historic buildings and a fine viaduct some 600 metres long and 52 metres high. Living room (1 single bed), kitchen, 1 bedroom (1 double and 1 single bed), bathroom, fireplace (wood supplied), electric heating, terrace, garage, garden with outdoor furniture. Shopping at 5 km; mobile shops call.

Prices:	low season	F 335	**4 people**
	high season	F 370/425	IGN 29

Booking: Mme M. JACQUILLET, 59 rue Brancion, 75015 Paris.
Tel. (1) 250 70 29.   E
52/39B2

COURCELLES-EN-MONTAGNE A semi-detached, stone-built house which has been renovated with care and has country-style furniture at the heart of the village. Visit the old walled town of Langres (12 km) with its museums and leisure facilities. Sailing at 15 km. Living room, kitchen, 3 bedrooms (1 double, 3 single and 1 child's bed), shower room, fireplace, electric heating, garage, garden with outdoor furniture. Farm produce in the village; mobile shops call; restaurant (5 km); other shopping at 6 km.

Prices:	low season	F 390/550	**6 people**
	high season	F 620/700	IGN 29

Booking: M M. GINDREY, 5 rue d'Epinal, Jeuxey 88000 Epinal.
Tel. (29) 34 24 31.
52/27B3

ESNOUVEAUX A recently built house with contemporary furnishings, near the village centre (0.3 km). Local river fishing and forest walks at 2 km. A swimming-pool and tennis at 12 km. Chaumont (15 km approx.) is well worth a visit to see its viaduct, thirteenth-century basilica and other attractions. Living room, kitchen, 3 bedrooms (2 double, 2 single and 1 child's bed), bathroom, electric heating, balcony, garage. Mobile shops call; farm produce available; other shopping in the village or at Nogent (12 km); a restaurant at 1 km.

Prices:	low season	F 300/380	**7 people**
	high season	F 500	IGN 29

Booking: M B. PAGE, Esnouveaux, 52340 Biesles. Tel. (25) 01 21 30.
52/30C2

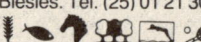

ILLOUD Le Moulin Neuf A renovated and rustically furnished house at the edge of a village (1 km). Local forest walks; a lake and swimming-pool at 20 km. Visit the famous spa town of Vittel (30 km) with its Olympic sports facilities, casino and other night-life. Living room, kitchen, 1 bedroom (1 double and 1 single bed), bathroom, oil heating, garage, garden with outdoor furniture. Mobile butcher and baker call; farm produce, other shopping and restaurant in the village.

Prices:	low season	F 250/420	**3 people**
	high season	F 485/515	IGN 29

Booking: M P. THOMAS, Illoud, 52150 Bourmont.
Tel. (25) 01 12 21.   E
52/36C2

Haute-Marne

MILLIERES A very attractive renovated village house with rustic furnishings, lying in its own pleasant garden. Local forest walks; swimming-pool and riding at 16 km; sailing at a lake (35 km). Living room (1 single bed), kitchen, 2 bedrooms (1 double and 1 single bed), bathroom, open fire, electric central heating, terrace, garage. Mobile butcher and grocer call, fresh farm produce available in the village and other shopping at Nogent-en-Bassigny (16 km).

Prices: low season F 405   4 people
         high season F 425/500   IGN 29

Booking: M E. OLBRECHT, Millières, 52240 Clefmont.
Tel. (25) 01 22 61.

52/48C2

MONTSAUGEON An attractively renovated gîte adjoining the owners' holiday home, with country-style furnishings at the village centre. Plenty of country walks and visits to château, a park with wild boar and archaeological sites (Roman); sailing at a lake (10 km). Living room (TV), kitchen, 2 bedrooms (1 double, 2 single and 1 child's bed), bathroom, fireplace (some wood supplied), electric heating, garage, enclosed ground with garden furniture and swings. Mobile shops call, other shopping and restaurant within 2 km or at Langres (22 km).

Prices: low season F 430/540   5 people
         high season F 700/1760   IGN 29

Booking: Mme O. Du BOULLAY, 25 rue Jean de la Bruyère, 78000 Versailles. Tel. (3) 955 54 14. E
52/50C4

VILLEMORON A fine old house, renovated and rustically furnished, situated on a mixed farm near the village centre. Bathing at a lake (15 km). The lovely old town of Langres (31 km) boasts a wealth of historic treasures and is well worth a visit. Living room (TV, 2 double divans), kitchen (washing machine), 2 bedrooms (1 double, 2 single and 1 child's bed), shower room, fireplace (wood supplied) and oil stove, carport, ground with garden furniture. Mobile shops call and farm produce in the village; other shopping at Auberive (17 km).

Prices: low season F 400   9 people
         high season F 450/500   IGN 29

Booking: M R. LORIMIER, Villemoron, Vals des Tilles 52160 Auberive.
Tel. (25) 84 84 13.
52/80B4

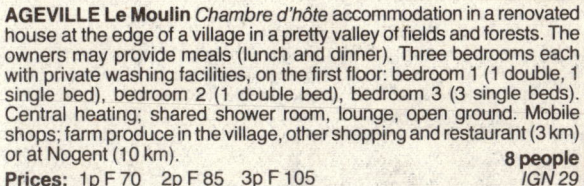

AGEVILLE Le Moulin *Chambre d'hôte* accommodation in a renovated house at the edge of a village in a pretty valley of fields and forests. The owners may provide meals (lunch and dinner). Three bedrooms each with private washing facilities, on the first floor: bedroom 1 (1 double, 1 single bed), bedroom 2 (1 double bed), bedroom 3 (3 single beds). Central heating; shared shower room, lounge, open ground. Mobile shops; farm produce in the village, other shopping and restaurant (3 km) or at Nogent (10 km).

Prices: 1p F 70 2p F 85 3p F 105   8 people
                                          IGN 29

Booking: M F. CHARLET, le Moulin d'Ageville, 52340 Biesles.
Tel. (25) 31 95 16. E
52/9

NULLY *Chambre d'hôte* accommodation in the owners' renovated and traditionally furnished house on a mixed farm at the centre of the village. Walking in nearby forests; river fishing (6 km); tennis and riding (10 km); other leisure facilities at the lovely Lac du Der (20 km). Two bedrooms on the first floor, each with private washing facilities: bedroom 1 (1 double bed, 1 child's bed on request); bedroom 2 (1 double bed). Central heating; shared shower room, lounge and grounds. Meals available. Shopping in the village or at Montier-en-Der (15 km).

Prices: 1p F 65 2p F 80/100   4 people
                                          IGN 22

Booking: Mme M. MOREL, Nully, 52110 Blaiserives.
Tel. (25) 55 40 36.
51/10

ALSACE

THE HAUT-RHIN
THE BAS-RHIN

TOURIST ITINERARIES

The Wine Road (Routes des Vins), the Mountain road through the Vosges (Routes des Crêtes), the Green Road (Route Verte), the Fried Carp Roads (Routes de la Carp Frite), the Flowered Villages Road (Le Route des Villages Fleuris), the Picturesque Villages Road (la Route des Villages Pittoresques), the Road of the Fortified Castles (Routes des Châteaux Forts) . . .

HISTORICAL BUILDINGS AND ART TREASURES

Visit our cathedrals, museums and medieval castles.

THE VOSGES

Where you will discover nature and the panorama of the Alsatian Plain, the Canal d'Alsace and the Black Forest beyond.

ALSACE

Situated in the heart of the Common Market and at the crossroads between Germany and Switzerland, Alsace is a part of France with a long tradition of Tourism. Its rich artistic, cultural and folkloric heritage attracts a growing number of visitors each year.

Turckheim
A typical Alsatian town

13 LORRAINE – VOSGES – ALSACE

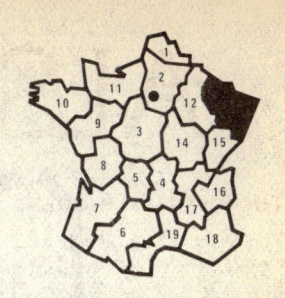

A land of pure air, clear water and the rich green countryside of the Vosges, where the shimmering lakes and colourful, natural fauna attract visitors from springtime until the fall of the first snow. Winter brings its own kind of magic, for lovers of winter sports, when picturesque villages take on their own kind of charm and visitors may well feel they have stepped into a scene from a Christmas card.

Although known as the "wooded hills" as the slopes are covered with beech and fir-trees, the Vosges mountain chain, which is shared by and separates Lorraine and Alsace, has higher peaks than any mountain in Britain. Bordering France and Germany, Alsace is fortunately situated with the Vosges Forest on one side and the Black Forest on the German side, thus providing shelter and promoting the growth of vines.

Still relatively unfrequented by British tourists and largely unspoiled, this region boasts spa towns and various health resorts, in the Moselle Valley, using spring waters. Many local wines are produced here, apart from the well-known *Moselle*, and visitors are invited to sample the wine, stored in the many wine cellars.

A lively atmosphere prevails throughout the region, and visitors may enjoy some of the festivities, as well as the excellent opportunities for fresh air activities. Music lovers may well want to visit the music festival in Strasbourg, which takes place in June. Strasbourg, seat of the European Council, with its cathedral and quaint old streets, is a must for any visitor. The elegant town of Wissembourg has a folk-dance festival on Whit Monday and, if you are going early in the year, there is a daffodil festival at Gérardmer. October is the month for grape harvest festivals throughout Lorraine and the Jazz Festival in Nancy.

272

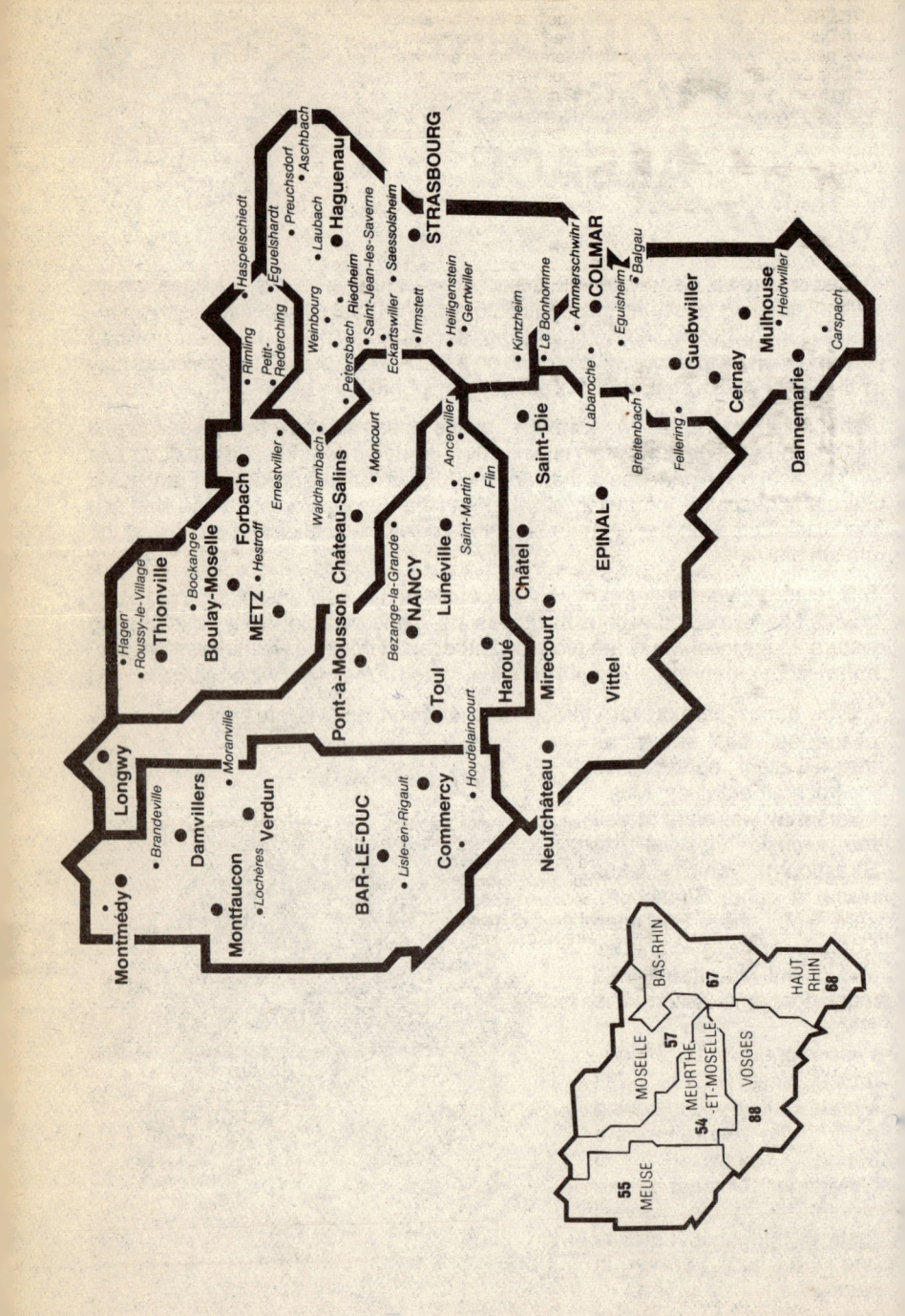

Meurthe-et-Moselle

ANCERVILLER One of two gîtes in a large renovated house on a mixed farm 0.5 km from the village centre. The owner, who has three sons, lives next door. At Badonviller (7 km) there is fishing and other sports, and it is a good starting-point for numerous walks on marked footpaths. Living room, kitchen (TV), 2 bedrooms (2 double, 2 single beds), shower room, electric and wood heating, carport, garden and courtyard. Mobile shops call; grocer's shop in the village; other shops and restaurant at Badonviller.

Prices:	low season	F 400/500	**6 people**
	high season	F 700	IGN 12

Booking: M B. COLIN, 4 rue de la Treille, Ancerviller, 54450 Blamont. Tel. (8) 342 13 88. **E**

54/26

ANCERVILLER A second gîte with rustic furnishings in the renovated house described above, lying on a farm near the village centre. Local forest walks; swimming-pool, riding and tennis at 13 km. Living room (1 double divan), kitchen, 1 bedroom (1 double and 1 child's bed), shower room, open fire, heating, terrace, garage, garden with barbecue. Mobile shops call; grocery in the village, other shopping and restaurant at Badonviller (7 km).

Prices:	low season	F 450/550	**5 people**
	high season	F 750	IGN 12

Booking: M B. COLIN, 4 rue de la Treille, Ancerviller, 54450 Blamont. Tel. (8) 342 13 88. **E**

54/25

BEZANGE-LA-GRANDE Moulin-Sainte-Marie A detached renovated house with traditional furnishings 0.5 km from the owners' farmhouse, in a lovely setting. Bicycles for hire at the interesting university town of Nancy (20 km). Try the local wine and quiche lorraine. Living room, kitchen (washing machine), 4 bedrooms (2 double, 4 single beds, extra bedroom available for a supplement), bathroom, solid fuel heating, balcony, carport, courtyard and ground with child's swing. Mobile shops call; other shopping at 12 km.

Prices:	low season	F 725	**8 people**
	high season	F 775	IGN 11

Booking: M R. VIRIOT, Bezange-la-Grande, 54370 Einville. Tel. (8) 372 93 34.

54/30

FLIN A gîte in the owners' former farmhouse which has been renovated and traditionally furnished. Local fishing and forest walks; sailing at 30 km. Visit Baccarat (9 km), renowned for its crystal; see the Gallo-Roman Bacha tower and other old buildings; swimming-pool. Living room/kitchenette (1 double divan), 2 bedrooms (2 double, 1 single and 1 child's bed), shower room, central heating, open grounds. Farm produce from the owners, other shopping at Baccarat.

Prices:	low season	F 380/400	**8 people**
	high season	F 550	IGN 12

Booking: M E. GASPARD, 3 rue Général Leclerc, Flin, 54120 Baccarat. Tel. (8) 372 65 37.

54/38

SAINT-MARTIN A large, simply furnished gîte near a river where you can fish. Local forest walks, swimming-pool and riding within 17 km, see the *son et lumière* at Lunéville château (20 km). Living room (1 double divan), kitchen, 3 bedrooms (2 double, 2 single and 1 child's bed), bathroom, electric heating, garage, enclosed grounds. Try local specialities, such as honey, cheese and quiche lorraine; mobile shops call; other shopping (7 km). Restaurant at 1.5 km.

Prices:	low season	F 480/520	**9 people**
	high season	F 580	IGN 12

Booking: M B. PIERRON, 1 Grande rue, Halloville, 54450 Blamont. Tel. (8) 342 35 67.

54/50

13

Meuse

BRANDEVILLE A nice old house, furnished in country style near the village centre where there are shops and a restaurant. The old fortified town of Montmedy (16 km) offers superb views over the Chiers valley and walks round the citadel – access by drawbridge! Facilities here for tennis, table tennis and fishing in a small lake. Living room (1 double divan), kitchen, 4 bedrooms (3 double and 2 single beds), shower room, fireplace, terrace. Fresh farm produce from the owners, mobile butcher, baker, grocer and *charcutier* call.

Prices:	low season	F 463/618	**10 people**
	high season	F 875	IGN 10

Booking: Meuse booking service   **E**

55/232

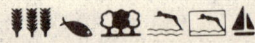

HOUDELAINCOURT A gîte in an old, renovated building, furnished in traditional style and standing close to the village centre (0.2 km). Ligny-en-Barrois (23 km) is a medium size town with a pleasant park bordered by the river Ornain and facilities for swimming, tennis, riding and trout fishing. Living room, kitchen, (washing machine), 3 bedrooms (1 double, 3 single and 1 child's bed), bathroom, electric heating, garage, enclosed courtyard. Fresh dairy produce and vegetables, mobile shops call, shopping and restaurant in the village.

Prices:	low season	F 427	**5/6 people**
	high season	F 438	IGN 23

Booking: Meuse booking service   **E**

55/210

LISLE-EN-RIGAULT An unusual old building with modern furnishings near the centre of the village. Bar-le-Duc (10 km) is an ancient fortified city with an outstanding and well-preserved collection of buildings and excellent sporting facilities. Home of the unique Bar-le-Duc currrant jam! Living room/kitchenette, sitting room (1 double divan), 2 bedrooms (1 double, 1 single and 1 child's bed), bathroom, central heating, terrace, garden. Mobile shops call, farm produce, shopping and restaurant in the village.

Prices:	low season	F 566/670	**5/6 people**
	high season	F 824	IGN 23

Booking: Meuse booking service   **E**

55/194

LOCHERES A traditionally furnished gîte in a renovated building close to the village centre. The owners speak a little English. Clermont-en-Argonne (10 km) has some interesting mediaeval buildings and there are pleasant forest walks along marked footpaths here; try the local *quiche lorraine* and *pâté*. Living room (1 double bed), kitchen, 1 bedroom (1 double and 2 single beds), shower room, heating, terrace. Mobile shops call, fresh dairy produce and vegetables in the village, shopping and restaurant in Clermont-en-Argonne.

Prices:	low season	F 561/566	**6 people**
	high season	F 623	IGN 10

Booking: Meuse booking service   **E**

55/219

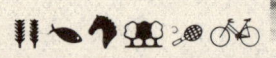

MORANVILLE A ground-floor gîte with traditional furnishings in a renovated house near the village centre. Owner speaks some English. Verdun (16 km) has a fascinating subterranean citadel and museums and exhibitions devoted to the town's role in the 1914–18 war; sports here include miniature golf, tennis, riding and swimming. Living room, kitchen, 1 bedroom (1 double and 3 single beds), bathroom, central heating, terrace, garage, ground. Mobile shops call, fresh farm produce in the village, other shopping at Etain (10 km).

Prices:	low season	F 463/510	**5 people**
	high season	F 623	IGN 11

Booking: Meuse booking service   **E**

55/87

Moselle

BOCKANGE A renovated house with country-style furnishings outside the village. Use of the owners' tennis court; sailing and bathing at Burtoncourt lake (5 km). At the old fortified town of Boulay (12 km) try the macaroons – a local speciality. Living room, kitchen, 3 bedrooms (2 double, 2 single beds), bathroom and shower, central heating, garage, enclosed ground with garden furniture. Shopping and restaurant in the village (3 km).

Prices:	low season	F 500/600	**6 people**
	high season	F 700	IGN 11

Booking: M J. P. EVRARD, 32 rue Principale, Bockange, 57220 Boulay. Tel. (8) 779 70 40.

57/100

EGUELSHARDT A first-floor gîte, one of two in the owners' renovated and traditionally furnished house in the village. Leisure amenities in the area include sailing at a lake and a forest. Visit the crystal works at Saint-Louis-lès-Bitche (15 km approx.). Living room, kitchen, 2 bedrooms (3 double beds), bathroom, central heating, balcony, enclosed ground. Shopping and restaurant at Bitche (7 km).

Prices:	low season	F 390/440	**6 people**
	high season	F 490	IGN 12

Booking: Moselle booking service

57/10

ERNESTVILLER A ground-floor gîte, one of two in a renovated and rustically furnished former farmhouse in the village. Many leisure facilities at Sarreguemines (8 km) where there is a wealth of historic architecture ranging from Romanesque to late Renaissance. Living room/kitchenette, 2 bedrooms (1 double, 3 single beds and 1 child's bed), bathroom, central heating, garage, enclosed ground. Shopping and restaurant at Sarreguemines.

Prices:	low season	F 400/440	**6 people**
	high season	F 490	IGN 12

Booking: Moselle booking service

57/12

HAGEN A village house which has been renovated and traditionally furnished and adapted to suit the needs of a handicapped guest. Local leisure facilities include a swimming-pool and tennis. The gîte is just 13 km from Luxembourg; visit too, the old fortified town of Thionville (20 km). Living room, kitchen, 2 bedrooms (3 double and 1 child's bed), bathroom and shower, wood and electric heating, garage, enclosed ground with garden furniture. Shopping at Hettange-Grande (10 km).

Prices:	low season	F 440/490	**7 people**
	high season	F 540	IGN 11

Booking: Moselle booking service

57/17

HASPELSCHIEDT An attractive, modern house with traditional furnishings, at the edge of a village in the Northern Vosges Regional Park, so plenty of good walks. Fishing and canoeing are possible at the old fortified town of Bitche (6 km). Sarreguemines at 41 km also warrants a day trip. Living room, kitchen, 3 bedrooms (1 double, 4 single and 1 child's bed), bathroom and shower, fireplace, central heating, enclosed courtyard with garden furniture. Shopping and restaurant at Bitche.

Prices:	low season	F 650/710	**7 people**
	high season	F 820	IGN 12

Booking: Moselle booking service

57/18

Moselle

HESTROFF A renovated and traditionally furnished village house, set in its own enclosed ground with garden furniture. Visit Metz (27 km), an historic town on the river Moselle, close to the German border; see in particular its fine cathedral and important Gallo-Roman collection at the museum. Living room, kitchen, 2 bedrooms (2 double, 1 single and 1 child's bed), bathroom, central heating. Fresh fruit and vegetables from the owners; other shopping and restaurant in the village or at Bouzonville (10 km).

Prices:	low season	F 390/440	**6 people**
	high season	F 540	IGN 11

Booking: M L. FANTIN, 2 rue des Tilleuls, Hestroff, 57320 Bouzonville. Tel. (8) 778 51 12.

57/105

MONCOURT A renovated and traditionally furnished gîte at the village centre, in the Lorraine Regional Park. Sailing at a lake (5 km). Visit the old salt-works at Château-Salins (20 km); see the Lunéville Château (23 km), a scaled-down version of Versailles, with gardens designed by Le Nôtre. Living room, kitchen, 3 bedrooms (2 double, 2 single and 1 child's bed), bathroom, central heating, enclosed ground. Fresh farm produce, shopping and restaurant in the village.

Prices:	low season	F 420/470	**7 people**
	high season	F 520	IGN 11

Booking: Moselle booking service

57/29

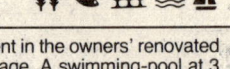

PETIT-REDERCHING A first-floor apartment in the owners' renovated and traditionally furnished house in the village. A swimming-pool at 3 km. Take a trip to Sarrebourg (45 km approx.) and see the largest stained glass window ever executed by Marc Chagall at the Chapelle des Cordeliers. Living room, kitchen, 2 bedrooms (2 double and 1 child's bed), bathroom, central heating, balcony, open courtyard with garden furniture. Shopping and restaurant at Bitche (12 km).

Prices:	low season	F 520/570	**5 people**
	high season	F 670	IGN 12

Booking: Moselle booking service

57/34

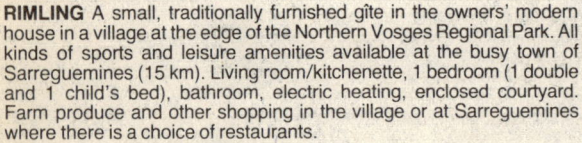

RIMLING A small, traditionally furnished gîte in the owners' modern house in a village at the edge of the Northern Vosges Regional Park. All kinds of sports and leisure amenities available at the busy town of Sarreguemines (15 km). Living room/kitchenette, 1 bedroom (2 double and 1 child's bed), bathroom, electric heating, enclosed courtyard. Farm produce and other shopping in the village or at Sarreguemines where there is a choice of restaurants.

Prices:	low season	F 340/390	**3 people**
	high season	F 440	IGN 12

Booking: Moselle booking service

57/35

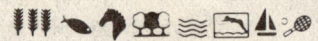

ROUSSY-LE-VILLAGE A ground-floor gîte with country-style furnishings, in a renovated house on a mixed farm. Ideal for a truly European holiday as it is close to the borders of Belgium, Germany and Luxembourg. Visit too the site of the Maginot line nearby. Living room, kitchen, 2 bedrooms (1 double, 4 single and 1 child's bed), bathroom, electric and wood heating, garage, enclosed ground. Shopping at Hettange-Grande (8 km).

Prices:	low season	F 450/500	**7 people**
	high season	F 550	IGN 11

Booking: Moselle booking service

57/6

Bas-Rhin

ASCHBACH An attractive gîte situated in a flat adjoining the owners' home, in a charming village, typically Alsatian with its quaint houses. The village lies in the Outre-Forêt region to the north of Strasbourg. Living room, kitchen, 2 bedrooms (1 double divan, 2 single and 1 child's bed), shower room, electric heating and wood-burning stove, terrace, lawn and ground for parking. Mobile butcher calls; baker and grocer in the village; other shopping and restaurant at Hatten (approx. 6 km) or Soultz-sous-Forêts (approx. 10 km).

Prices: low season   F 558/644   **5 people**
        high season   F 845   IGN 12
Booking: Bas-Rhin booking service
67/380

ECKARTSWILLER A spacious, renovated and traditionally furnished house in the northern Vosges forest. Good leisure facilities at the attractive little town of Saverne (3 km) whose château, now a museum, was the former residence of the prince-bishops of Strasbourg. Living room (TV), kitchen, 4 bedrooms (2 double, 2 single beds), bathroom, oil and electric heating, enclosed garden. Linen available (F25 per set per week). Mobile shops call and farm produce available locally; other shopping at Saverne.

Prices: low season   F 634/733   **6 people**
        high season   F 863   IGN 12
Booking: M VIRTEL, 74 rue des Jésuites, 67100 Strasbourg.
Tel. (88) 40 15 60.
67/462

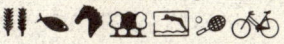

GERTWILLER A first-floor gîte, one of two in a modern house with traditional furnishings, on a vineyard where the owners offer *table d'hôte* meals. The old town of Barr is at the heart of the wine-producing region and visitors in July can enjoy its wine festival. Living room/kitchenette (1 double divan), 2 bedrooms (1 double, 2 single beds), shower room, electric heating, enclosed courtyard. Linen available. Farm produce available in the village; other shopping at Barr (1 km).

Prices: low season   F 780   **6 people**
        high season   on request   IGN 31
Booking: M MAULER, 77 rue de l'Eau, 67140 Gertwiller.
Tel. (88) 08 04 72.
67/629

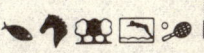

HEILIGENSTEIN A lovely old village house, typical of the region, which has been carefully renovated and furnished in traditional style. Local fishing and forest walks; a swimming-pool, riding and tennis at Barr (2 km) which has an interesting museum. Living room, kitchen, 3 bedrooms (6 single beds), bathroom, electric and oil heating. Linen available (F25 per set per week). Shopping, farm produce and restaurant in the village.

Prices: low season   F 900/950   **6 people**
        high season   F 1100   IGN 31
Booking: M MECKERT, 7 rue Principale, 67140 Heiligenstein.
Tel. (88) 08 96 97.
67/743

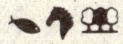

13

IRMSTETT A traditionally furnished gîte in the owners' old house where you have the use of the garden and barbecue. It is in a little farming village on the Alsace wine route, 5 km from the old fortified town of Molsheim which has good leisure and sports facilities. Living room, kitchen, 2 bedrooms (5 single and 1 child's bed), bathroom, central heating, garage, courtyard, enclosed garden. Mobile butcher and grocer call; other shopping at Marlenheim (3 km).

Prices: low season   F 700   **6 people**
        high season   F 800   IGN 12
Booking: M VAN FUHREN, 36 rue de l'Eglise, 67310 Irmstett.
Tel. (88) 50 66 87.
67/75

Bas-Rhin

KINTZHEIM A gîte in the owners' traditionally furnished and renovated house. Kintzheim boasts one of the best-preserved châteaux in Alsace (dating back to the thirteenth century). Sélestat (4 km) has a delightful old quarter and was once the haunt of Humanist scholars; its acclaimed Humanist Library was founded in the fifteenth century. Kitchen, 2 bedrooms (1 double, 2 single beds), shower room, electric heating, carport, enclosed garden. Linen available. Farm produce in the village; shopping at Sélestat.

Prices: low season   F 850/900   **4 people**
          high season   F 1000   IGN 31
Booking: M BLUMBERGER, 4 rue de la Liberté, 67600 Kintzheim.
Tel. (88) 82 09 37.
67/636

LAUBACH A renovated and traditionally furnished house, typical of the region, sharing a courtyard with the owners' house. Niederbronn-les-Bains (10 km approx.) is a lively spa town with parks, sports facilities (including miniature golf, fishing and tennis) and a casino. Living room, kitchen, 2 bedrooms (1 double, 2 single and 1 child's bed), bathroom, wood and oil heating, courtyard with children's games. Grocer, mobile butcher, baker and restaurant in the village, other shops and services at Mertzwiller (3 km).

Prices: low season   F 580/644   **5 people**
          high season   F 716   IGN 12
Booking: Bas-Rhin booking service

67/183

PETERSBACH A detached house, in a quiet spot with good views. The terrace has a table and chairs for outdoor meals. It lies in a small farming village in the Northern Vosges Regional Park, so plenty of good walks. A zoo and châteaux to see in the vicinity. Living room (1 double divan), kitchen, 2 bedrooms (1 double and 2 single beds), bathroom, fireplace, central heating, terrace, garage, garden. Shopping in the village or at Petite-Pierre (5 km).

Prices: low season   F 598/716   **6 people**
          high season   F 776   IGN 12
Booking: Bas-Rhin booking service

67/237

PREUCHSDORF A lovely old house with country-style furnishings and good leisure amenities within a radius of 10 km. It is not more than 25 km from the German border. Visit the historic town of Wissembourg (15 km approx.) which has an interesting museum of local history. Kitchen, 3 bedrooms (4 single and 1 child's bed), bathroom, wood heating, enclosed meadowland with barbecue and child's swing. Farm produce in the village and other shopping at Merckwiller (3 km).

Prices: low season   F 675   **5 people**
          high season   F 725   IGN 12
Booking: M BECK, 19 rue de l'Eglise, 67250 Preuchsdorf.
Tel. (88) 80 70 22.
67/506

RIEDHEIM A first-floor gîte in the owners' house in a typical Alsatian farming village. Forest walks on marked footpaths; swimming-pool, tennis and riding within 7 km. The attractive old town of Bouxwiller (2 km) has a museum of local arts and traditions. Strasbourg (45 km approx.) makes an interesting day trip. Living room (2 single beds), kitchen, 2 bedrooms (1 double, 1 single bed), bathroom, oil heating, garage, courtyard and garden. Linen available. Mobile butcher and baker call; grocer in the village; other shopping and restaurant at Bouxwiller.

Prices: low season   F 517   **5 people**
          high season   F 580   IGN 12
Booking: Bas-Rhin booking service
67/42

Bas Rhin

SAESSOLSHEIM A well-appointed gîte in a half-timbered house in a small village which boasts a beautiful Romanesque church. Local footpaths, a swimming-pool at Hochfelden (8 km), tennis, riding, fishing and other leisure amenities in Saverne (12 km). Living room (with separate alcove with 2 single beds), kitchen, 2 bedrooms (3 single beds), shower room, solid fuel stove and electric heating, enclosed courtyard, garden. Mobile butcher and fishmonger call. Baker, grocer and a restaurant in the village. Other shopping in Hochfelden.

Prices:	low season	F 541/634	**5 people**
	high season	F 789	IGN 12

Booking: Bas-Rhin booking service

67/150

SAINT-JEAN-LES-SAVERNE One of two gîtes in a charming, traditionally furnished house at the heart of the forest. At Saverne (4 km), visitors in mid-June can enjoy the Rose Festival; see too the botanical and rose gardens there and the Château Rohan. Living room, kitchen, 2 bedrooms (3 single beds), shower room, electric heating, courtyard and ground. Shopping and restaurant at Saverne.

Prices:	low season	F 725	**3 people**
	high season	F 875	IGN 12

Booking: M WEINBORN, 10 rue de Haegen, 67700 Saint-Jean-les-Saverne. Tel. (88) 91 32 00.

67/468

WALDHAMBACH A pretty little chalet with modern furniture, in an isolated position at the edge of a forest in the Northern Vosges Regional Park. In the vicinity are châteaux to visit and troglodyte dwellings at Graufthal. Other leisure facilities at La Petite-Pierre (10 km approx.). Living room/kitchenette (1 single divan, 1 child's bed), 1 bedroom (1 double bed), bathroom, electric heating, terrace, garage, garden with conservatory. Shopping at Diemeringen (3 km).

Prices:	low season	F 778	**4 people**
	high season	F 829	IGN 12

Booking: Bas-Rhin booking service

67/169

WEINBOURG A gîte in the owners' fine old house which has been renovated and traditionally furnished. It is in a pleasant garden with barbecue, garden furniture and children's swings at your disposal. A swimming-pool and riding (3 km); see the fortified château at Lichtenberg (7 km) and the nearby subterranean lake. Living room (TV), kitchen, 2 bedrooms (1 double, 4 single and 1 child's bed), bathroom, electric heating, balcony, enclosed garden. Linen available. Shopping at La Petite-Pierre (14 km).

Prices:	low season	F 1200/1300	**7 people**
	high season	F 1400	IGN 12

Booking: M FEURER, 62 rue Mercière, 67340 Weinbourg. Tel. (88) 89 49 71.

67/537

HELP!
to keep **RABIES** out of Britain

Just one smuggled animal could import this terrible and fatal disease into Britain

Haut-Rhin

AMMERSCHWIHR A modern, traditionally furnished house near the town centre. It is just 8 km from Colmar where you should visit the beautifully restored Tanners' Quarter and the Bartholdi Museum in the former home of the Statue of Liberty's designer. Ski-ing at Bagnelles (15 km). Living room/kitchenette, 3 bedrooms (1 double and 4 single beds), shower room, oil heating, balcony, garage, garden. Linen available. Farm produce, shopping and restaurant in the village.

Prices:	low season	F 1070	**6 people**
	high season	F 1070	*IGN 31*
	winter season	F 1070	

Booking: M P. ADAM, 25 rue du Lt. Mourier, 68770 Ammerschwihr. Tel. (89) 78 23 07.
68/29

BALGAU A renovated and traditionally furnished gîte on the owners' cereal crops farm (fresh milk and eggs available), 0.7 km from the village centre. Fishing on the Alsace canal (2 km). The interesting old fortified town of Neuf-Brisach (8 km) has a museum and other attractions. Kitchen, 3 bedrooms (1 double and 5 single beds), bathroom, electric and oil heating, garden. Linen available. Shopping and restaurant in the village.

Prices:	low season	F 858	**7 people**
	high season	F 1072	*IGN 31*
	winter season	F 1072	

Booking: Haut-Rhin booking service E

68/4

LE BONHOMME One of two gîtes in the owners' renovated and traditionally furnished house in a mountain hamlet (altitude 900 metres), 2 km from the village centre. Local ski-ing and forest walks. A swimming-pool at Kayserberg (12 km) where you can visit the birthplace of Dr Albert Schweitzer. Living room/kitchenette, 2 bedrooms (1 double and 4 single beds), shower room, gas heating, open courtyard. A restaurant within walking distance. Farm produce and other shopping in the village or at Colmar (22 km).

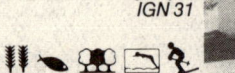

Prices:	low season	F 800	**6 people**
	high season	F 1000	*IGN 31*
	winter season	F 1000	

Booking: Haut-Rhin booking service E

68/141

BREITENBACH A traditionally furnished gîte, adjacent to the owners' old house outside the village (1 km) in a quiet spot in the Vosges mountains (altitude 500 metres). A swimming-pool and many other amenities at Munster (3 km) famous for its cheese. Ski-ing at 10 km. Living room (1 double divan), kitchen, 1 bedroom (3 single beds), bathroom, electric central heating, terrace, garage, open ground with garden furniture. Shopping (0.5 km) and restaurant in the village.

Prices:	low season	F 858	**5 people**
	high season	F 1072	*IGN 31*
	winter season	F 1072	

Booking: Haut-Rhin booking service E

68/322

CARSPACH An attractive old house with traditional furnishings, typical of the region and set on a livestock farm (fresh milk and eggs available), at the village centre. Swimming-pool and riding facilities at the interesting old town of Altkirch (2 km). Ski-ing at 28 km. Living room, kitchen, 5 bedrooms (1 double and 7 single beds), bathroom, wood heating, carport, garden. Shopping and restaurant in the village or at Altkirch.

Prices:	low season	F 912	**9 people**
	high season	F 1139	*IGN 31*
	winter season	F 1139	

Booking: Haut-Rhin booking service E

68/239

Haut-Rhin

EGUISHEIM A gîte with country-style furnishings, in the owners' attractive old house, set on a vineyard. Eguisheim has a fascinating history, going right back to the fourth century; the Pope Leon IX was born in its former eighth-century château and its museum boasts the skull of Cro-Magnon man found near there. Living room (1 double divan), kitchen, 1 bedroom (1 double bed), bathroom, central heating, garage, garden. Farm produce, shopping and restaurant in the village or at Colmar (6 km).

4 people
IGN 31

Prices: low and high season F 910
winter season F 910

Booking: M A. HERTZ, 3 rue du Riesling, 68420 Eguisheim.
Tel. (89) 41 30 32.
68/46

FELLERING A gîte with country-style furnishings, adjacent to the owners' renovated house in a village of the Upper Thur valley. The historic town of Thann, which was a centre for pilgrimage in the Middle Ages, is at 12 km. Ski-ing at 20 km. Living room, kitchen, 3 bedrooms (1 double and 3 single beds), shower room, electric heating, ground with river at the bottom for fishing; garden furniture. Farm produce, other shopping and restaurant in the village (0.5 km).

5 people
IGN 31

Prices: low season F 858
high season F 1072
winter season F 1072

Booking: Haut-Rhin booking service E
68/398

HEIDWILLER A large old village house with traditional furnishings. Local fishing and walks along marked footpaths. Riding and swimming at the medieval town of Altkirch. The Swiss border (40 km approx.) is close enough for a day trip. Living room (1 double divan), kitchen, 1 bedroom (1 single bed, 1 single divan), electric heating, open courtyard. Farm produce in the village; other shopping at Altkirch; a restaurant at 5 km.

4 people
IGN 31

Prices: low season F 676
high season F 845
winter season F 845

Booking: Haut-Rhin booking service E
68/469

LABAROCHE A traditionally furnished gîte, one of three in a renovated house, typical of the region, at an altitude of 750 metres and 0.5 km from the village centre. Riding facilities nearby and many other amenities, including tennis and museums at Colmar (18 km). A swimming-pool at 20 km and ski-ing (30 km). Living room/kitchenette, 2 bedrooms (1 double, 3 single and 1 child's bed), bathroom, electric heating, open ground. Farm produce, shopping and restaurant in the village.

6 people
IGN 31

Prices: low season F 800
high season F 1000
winter season F 1000

Booking: Haut-Rhin booking service E
68/289

13

281

FREE RANGE   SPECIALLY FED
Order Now from France!
FAMOUS AND
UNIQUE
BRESSE CHICKEN

Comité Interprofessionel de la
Volaille de Bresse
14 Avenue du 8 Mai 1945,
71500 LOUHANS, France.
Tel: 16 (85) 75.10.07

Specially bred Bresse Chickens are reared in limited and controlled numbers in small flocks under free-range conditions. Commercial fat-free feedstuffs are used for the first few weeks of rearing and for over a month before sale, maize and milk products only are fed. Prepared for the table after 16 weeks rather than the 8–12 weeks for most mass-produced poultry, the Bresse Chicken is a legally protected trademark. Each bird has its own numbered leg-ring and a red, white and blue seal carrying the name of the person who prepared and sold the chicken.

All poultry from the Bresse region is not necessarily 'Bresse Chicken', which is the product exclusively of the Committee.

Bresse Chicken is not cooked just like any factory-farmed poultry. Here is a recommended basic recipe:

ROAST BRESSE CHICKEN

For 8 servings: 1 **Bresse Chicken** weighing 2kg; 100g butter; salt and pepper; 1 cup water.

Truss the chicken, salt and pepper on inside. Place a sprig of thyme and a bay leaf to taste. After covering with butter, place in an earthenware dish greased beforehand. Set oven to thermostat 7. After cooking for 20 minutes, turn it over and add salt and pepper, add one cup hot water. Baste several times and leave to cook for another 40 minutes.

HOW TO ORDER A BRESSE CHICKEN

You can of course buy Bresse Chicken in good foodshops by asking for the authentic product and trademark. Bresse chicken can be sent to you by applying to:

Comité Interprofessionel de la Volaille de Bresse,
14 Avenue du 8 Mai 1945, 71500 LOUHANS, France.
Tel: 16 (85) 75 10 07

14 BURGUNDY

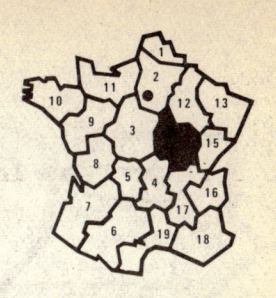

Archaeological finds in Burgundy have shown the existence of early civilisations in the region. Through the ages, Burgundy has been a crossroads for the movement of populations and the region reached the height of its importance during Roman times. One of the most interesting of the towns that grew up around this period is Autun (Saône-et-Loire), the Roman Augustodunum, and its enormous Roman gateways and temple of Janus, part of the former theatre, bear witness to its earlier glory. Unfortunately, at Auxerre (Yonne), there is nothing to show its Roman history, but this, one of the oldest towns in France, has some fine mediaeval architecture.

Although much of Burgundy shares a common history, it lacks a physical or geographical cohesion, but its very contrasts give the region its character.

In the granite uplands of the Morvan Conservation Park, beautiful lakes contrast with untamed countryside, forests and moors. In the park there are wildlife preserves where deer and wild boar roam at will; there is yachting on the Lac de Settons and visitors may enjoy riding at one of the five centres there.

Burgundy is perhaps best known for its wines and gastronomic reputation. The very mention of food brings to mind delicious snails in garlic butter, Bresse poultry and of course, Dijon mustard. World-famous names, such as Beaujolais, Chablis, Côtes de Beaune and Côtes de Nuits are just some of the fine wines produced in the region. At Beaune, the charitable hospital, Hospices de Beaune, a building worth visiting for its architectural splendour, is run solely on the proceeds from their annual wine auction in November. If you want to see just how seriously the Burgundians take food and wine, visit the Arts of the Table Museum at Arnay-le-Duc and the wine-making museum at Beaune. The National French Wines Fair takes place on the third Monday in May at Mâcon.

Do not leave the region without seeing the magnificent flamboyant Gothic church at Brou, near Bourg-en-Bresse; Nevers on the river Loire, with a reputation for the manufacture of fine china; and Dijon, the historic capital of Burgundy.

Map of Burgundy region

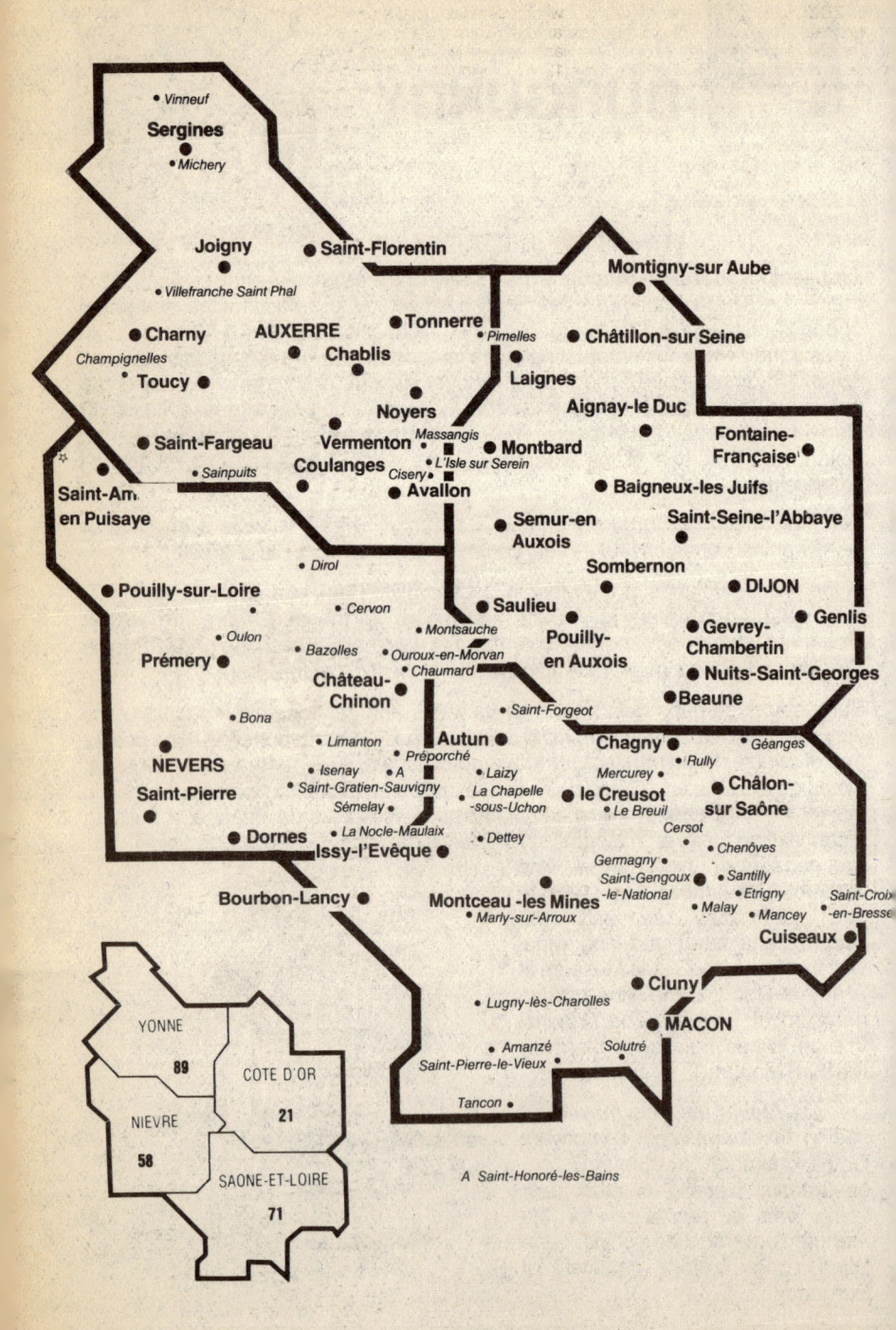

Towns and places shown on the map:

- Vinneuf
- Sergines
- Michery
- Joigny
- Saint-Florentin
- Montigny-sur Aube
- Villefranche Saint Phal
- Charny
- AUXERRE
- Tonnerre
- Pimelles
- Châtillon-sur Seine
- Champignelles
- Chablis
- Toucy
- Laignes
- Noyers
- Aignay-le Duc
- Saint-Fargeau
- Vermenton
- Massangis
- Montbard
- Fontaine-Française
- Coulanges
- L'Isle sur Serein
- Sainpuits
- Cisery
- Baigneux-les Juifs
- Saint-Am-en Puisaye
- Avallon
- Semur-en Auxois
- Saint-Seine-l'Abbaye
- Dirol
- Sombernon
- Pouilly-sur-Loire
- Cervon
- Sautieu
- DIJON
- Montsauche
- Gevrey-Chambertin
- Prémery
- Oulon
- Bazolles
- Ouroux-en-Morvan
- Pouilly-en Auxois
- Genlis
- Château-Chinon
- Chaumard
- Nuits-Saint-Georges
- Saint-Forgeot
- Beaune
- Bona
- Limanton
- Autun
- Chagny
- Géanges
- NEVERS
- Préporché
- Mercurey
- Rully
- Saint-Pierre
- Isenay
- A
- Laizy
- le Creusot
- Châlon-sur Saône
- Saint-Gratien-Sauvigny
- La Chapelle-sous-Uchon
- Le Breuil
- Sémelay
- Cersot
- Chenôves
- Dornes
- La Nocle-Maulaix
- Dettey
- Germagny
- Santilly
- Issy-l'Evêque
- Saint-Gengoux-le-National
- Malay
- Etrigny
- Mancey
- Saint-Croix-en-Bresse
- Bourbon-Lancy
- Montceau-les Mines
- Marly-sur-Arroux
- Cuiseaux
- Cluny
- Lugny-lès-Charolles
- MACON
- Amanzé
- Solutré
- Saint-Pierre-le-Vieux
- Tancon

Legend (département map):
- YONNE 89
- COTE D'OR 21
- NIEVRE 58
- SAONE-ET-LOIRE 71

A Saint-Honoré-les-Bains

284

Nièvre

BAZOLLES Baye A ground-floor gîte with traditional furnishings in a renovated house in its own enclosed garden, 3.5 km from the village. The gîte is good for water sports enthusiasts as there is a canal and lake nearby. Bicycles for hire at Corbigny (12 km). Living room (1 double divan), kitchen, 1 bedroom (2 double beds), shower room, electric heating. Farm produce (including honey) in the village; mobile shops call; other shopping at Corbigny and a restaurant within walking distance (50 metres).

Prices:	low season	F 600/700	6 people
	high season	F 1000/1200	IGN 36

Booking: Mme O. MAREJUS, Bazolles, 58110 Châtillon-en-Bazois. Tel. (86) 38 97 57.
58/179

BONA Lichy A traditionally furnished and renovated cottage on a mixed farm where you may buy fresh produce from the owners. Local forest walks. Visit Nevers (25 km), the département capital, famed for its fine porcelain (see the porcelain museum). Sailing at a lake (30 km). Living room/kitchenette, 2 bedrooms (2 double, 1 single and 1 child's bed), shower room, oil and electric heating, carport, enclosed ground with garden furniture. Mobile shops call; other shopping at Saint-Saulge (10 km); a restaurant in the village (2 km).

Prices:	low season	F 650/850	6 people
	high season	F 950	IGN 36

Booking: Mme O. GOURY, Lichy-Bona, 58330 Saint-Saulge. Tel. (86) 58 60 03.
58/233

CERVON Viry A renovated gîte with country-style furnishings on a farm where sheep and poultry are raised. Situated outside the village, the gîte is ideal for country-lovers with lovely waterside and forest walks. Tennis and other leisure amenities at Corbigny (4 km) which has an old abbey. Living room, kitchen, 3 bedrooms (3 double, 1 single and 1 child's bed), bathroom, fireplace, electric heating, terrace, carport, enclosed ground with garden furniture and barbecue. Linen available. Shopping from mobile stores or at Corbigny.

Prices:	low season	F 620/710	8 people
	high season	F 920	IGN 28

Booking: M C. RENARD, Viry, 58800 Corbigny. Tel. (86) 20 12 23.
58/4

CHAUMARD Vissingy An old house with country-style furnishings, next to a forest and some 9 km from the village. Visit the interesting old town of Château-Chinon (8 km), built in circular form on the side of a hill, where there is a folklore and costume museum, tennis and fishing. Living room, kitchen, 1 bedroom (1 double, 3 single and 1 child's bed), shower room, solid-fuel stove, balcony, courtyard. Mobile butcher, baker and grocer call; other shopping and restaurant at Château-Chinon.

Prices:	low season	F 650/700	6 people
	high season	F 800	IGN 36

Booking: M R. BROSSARD, Remoillon Charin, 58120 Château-Chinon. Tel. (86) 85 01 34.
58/14

DIROL A modern, single-storey gîte lying in an open courtyard, near the village centre (0.5 km). Bathing and fishing nearby at the Nivernais Canal. Tannay (10 km approx.) is a very old town overlooking the Yonne valley, where ceramics is a major industry. Living room/kitchenette (1 single divan), 2 bedrooms (2 double and 2 single beds), shower room, electric heating. Farm produce in the village; mobile butcher, baker and grocer call; other shopping and a restaurant (1.5 km) or at Corbigny (8 km).

Prices:	low season	F 500/600	7 people
	high season	F 700	IGN 28

Booking: M R. LOZANO, Dirol, 58190 Tannay. Tel. (86) 20 02 18.
58/214

14

Nièvre

ISENAY Baudin A renovated cottage with country-style furnishings on a livestock farm, 2 km from the village centre. Saint-Honoré-les-Bains (11 km) is a spa resort with good leisure amenities, including a casino, miniature golf, etc. Sailing at a lake (14 km). Living room (1 double divan), kitchen, 3 bedrooms (3 double, 1 single and 1 child's bed), shower room, fireplace, heating, enclosed ground with garden furniture and barbecue. Linen available. Mobile baker and grocer; other shopping at Saint-Honoré-les-Bains.
Prices: low season F 550/800   **10 people**
high season F 1000   *IGN 36*
Booking: M P. LAFAYE, Baudin, Isenay, 58290 Moulins-Engilbert. Tel. (86) 50 55 57.
58/81

LIMANTON Pannegot A renovated house with traditional furnishings, situated near the town centre where you may hire bicycles to explore the surrounding countryside. Local fishing and tennis. At Moulins-Engilbert (6 km) see the ruined feudal château and Roman sites. Sailing at a lake (20 km). Living room, kitchen, 3 bedrooms (3 double and 1 single bed), bathroom, central heating, enclosed courtyard. Shopping and restaurant in the town or at Moulins-Engilbert.
Prices: low season F 750/780   **7 people**
high season F 830   *IGN 36*
Booking: Mme Y. PERRUCHOT, Pannegot, Limanton, 58290 Moulins-Engilbert. Tel. (86) 84 25 85. **E**
58/106

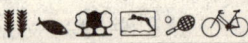

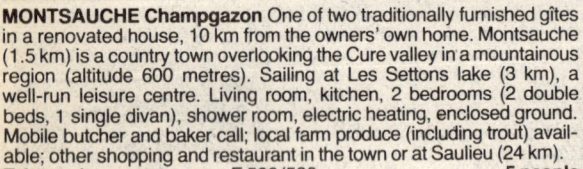

MONTSAUCHE Champgazon One of two traditionally furnished gîtes in a renovated house, 10 km from the owners' own home. Montsauche (1.5 km) is a country town overlooking the Cure valley in a mountainous region (altitude 600 metres). Sailing at Les Settons lake (3 km), a well-run leisure centre. Living room, kitchen, 2 bedrooms (2 double beds, 1 single divan), shower room, electric heating, enclosed ground. Mobile butcher and baker call; local farm produce (including trout) available; other shopping and restaurant in the town or at Saulieu (24 km).
Prices: low season F 500/580   **5 people**
high season F 800   *IGN 36*
Booking: M M. REGNIER, Ouroux-en-Morvan, 58230 Montsauche. Tel. (86) 78 23 03.
58/166

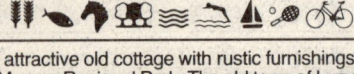

LA NOCLE-MAULAIX An attractive old cottage with rustic furnishings at the southern end of the Morvan Regional Park. The old town of Luzy (13 km) on the river Alène, has some druidic stones and a museum of ancient history in the tower of the old château. Living room (TV), kitchen (washing-up machine), 2 bedrooms (1 double and 3 single beds), fireplace, shower room, electric central heating, covered terrace, enclosed garden with furniture and barbecue. Linen available. Farm produce, shopping and a restaurant in the village (1.5 km).
Prices: low season F 800/950   **5 people**
high season F 1200   *IGN 36*
Booking: M D. BIGEARD, 141 rue des Montapins, 58000 Nevers. Tel. (86) 36 21 06.
58/231

OULON Marolles A pretty, renovated cottage, furnished in rustic style, next to a farm where the owner will take you to see his herd of Charolais cattle. Sailing at Baye lake (16 km). Living room/kitchenette (TV, washing machine, 1 double divan), 3 bedrooms (1 double, 4 single beds), shower room, fireplace (wood supplied), electric central heating, garden with furniture, barbecue, sand-pit and swing for children (table tennis also available). Linen available. Mobile shops call; other shopping and restaurant in the village (3 km) or at Prémery (7 km).
Prices: low season F 710/860   **8 people**
high season F 1210   *IGN 36*
Booking: M B. BITAULT, Marolles, Oulon, 58700 Prémery. Tel. (86) 68 16 25.
58/129

Nièvre

OUROUX-EN-MORVAN A renovated gîte with country-style furnishings, just 0.1 km from the lively town centre; visitors at the beginning of August can enjoy the local town festival. Good riding centre in the town; bathing at a lake (7 km). Altitude 600 metres. Living room/kitchenette, 2 bedrooms (2 double beds), shower room, open fire, gas and electric heating, courtyard with garden furniture. Farm produce, shopping and restaurant in the town or at Château-Chinon (24 km).

Prices:	low season	F 690/850	**4 people**
	high season	F 1050	*IGN 36*

Booking: Mme C. POMPELE, Jasseron, 01250 Ceyzeriat. Tel. (74) 30 02 79.

58/142

PREPORCHE Achez A gîte with country-style furnishings in a renovated building on a mixed farm at the edge of the village (1.5 km). Bicycles for hire at the spa resort of Saint-Honoré-les-Bains (4 km) where a riding centre and swimming-pool number among its many leisure amenities. Living room, kitchen, 2 bedrooms (1 double, 1 single bed), bathroom, fireplace, central heating, ground with garden furniture and barbecue. Mobile shops call; farm produce, other shopping and restaurant in the village.

Prices:	low season	F 760	**3 people**
	high season	F 980	*IGN 36*

Booking: M J. M. LEMOINE, Préporché, 58360 Saint-Honoré-les-Bains. Tel. (86) 30 75 74.

58/223

SAINT-GRATIEN-SAUVIGNY Domaine-de-l'Isle Situated on a private lane leading to the owners' farm, this old cottage has country-style furnishing and enclosed ground. Visit the picturesque old town of Decize (20 km) on the banks of the Loire, where places of interest include the Promenade des Halles. Living room, kitchen, 2 bedrooms (1 double, 3 single beds, 1 double divan), shower room, fireplace, electric heating, carport. Mobile baker calls; farm produce in the village; other shopping and restaurant at Cercy-la-Tour (2 km).

Prices:	low season	F 500/700	**7 people**
	high season	F 900/1000	*IGN 36*

Booking: Mme M. SAYET, Domaine de l'Isle, Saint-Gratien-Sauvigny, 58340 Cercy-la-Tour. Tel. (86) 50 54 50.

58/218

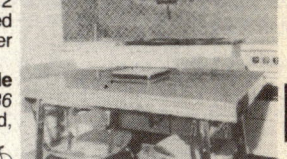

SAINT-HONORE-LES-BAINS A ground-floor gîte, one of four in a renovated house at the centre of this popular spa resort in the Morvan Regional Park, with good leisure amenities. Plenty of interesting day trips possible: the caves at Arcy-sur-Cure; the château town of Larochemillay (22 km). Living room, kitchen, 1 bedroom (1 double, 2 single beds), bathroom, electric heating, covered terrace, enclosed courtyard and garden with furniture. Linen available (F25 per set per week). Shopping and restaurant in the town.

Prices:	low season	F 820/995	**4 people**
	high season	F 1400	*IGN 36*

Booking: M MARTINACHE, La Renaudière, 1 rue Henri Renaud, 58360 Saint-Honoré-les-Bains. Tel. (86) 30 71 13.

58/245

14

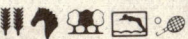

SEMELAY Le Martray An old, simply furnished cottage on a livestock farm, 2 km from the village which has an interesting Romanesque church. It lies at the edge of the Morvan Regional Park, so good walks. Other leisure facilities, including a swimming-pool and tennis, at the attractive old town of Luzy (12 km). Living room, kitchen, 1 bedroom (1 double, 3 single and 1 child's bed), shower room, fireplace, electric heating, terrace, enclosed ground with garden furniture. Farm produce, shopping and restaurant in the village.

Prices:	low season	F 600	**6 people**
	high season	F 800	*IGN 36*

Booking: M G. D'ETE, Semelay, 58360 Saint-Honoré-les-Bains. Tel. (86) 30 75 70.

58/26

Saône-et-Loire

AMANZE A well-renovated and traditionally furnished, single-storey cottage at the town centre. La Clayette (10 km) boasts a fourteenth-century château and a lake for fishing. Visit Charolles (15 km) an interesting old town which gave its name to the local breed of cattle and sheep. Living room (1 double divan), kitchen, 2 bedrooms (2 double, 2 single beds), shower room, fireplace, electric heating, enclosed ground. Shopping (5 km) and a *ferme auberge* (farm inn) at 1 km.

Prices:	low season	F 500/600	**8 people**
	high season	F 750/800	IGN 43

Booking: Commune d'Amanzé, 71610 Saint-Julien-de-Civry.
Tel. (85) 28 20 77.

71/225

AUTUN Saint Pierre This typical Burgundian house has been renovated and traditionally furnished and is situated near the owners' home in a rural hamlet. Autun (2 km) is an ancient town, more important in Roman times than today, with many historic treasures; take a walk around its medieval ramparts. Living room, kitchen, 2 bedrooms (1 double, 2 single beds), bathroom, electric heating, enclosed garden with outdoor furniture and barbecue. Shopping and restaurants in the town (1.5 km).

Prices:	low season	F 850/900	**4 people**
	high season	F 950	IGN 36

Booking: M J. C. COLLINET, 2 rue Saint-Etienne, 71400 Autun.
Tel. (85) 52 13 74.

71/263

LE BREUIL Les Lavriots A renovated gîte with traditional furnishings near the owners' home on their mixed farm, 3 km from the village centre. At 6 km, Le Creusot (where the saucepans come from!) is famous for its metallurgical works, and its factories accept visits from the public. Living room/kitchenette (1 double divan), 1 bedroom (1 large single and 1 child's folding bed), shower room, central heating, garden. Linen available (F 30 per set per week). Farm produce from the owners; shopping and restaurant at 2 km.

Prices:	low season	F 600	**3 people**
	high season	F 650	IGN 37

Booking: M C. VARIOT, Les Lavriots, 71670 Le Breuil.
Tel. (85) 55 15 14.

71/26

CERSOT Le Mâconnais Set in its own garden, near the owners' home, this renovated and traditionally furnished cottage is right at the centre of the village. At Buxy (7 km), enquire at the Tourist Office for a visit to the wine cellars for a tasting of the Côte Chalonaise wine. Living room (1 double divan), kitchen, 2 bedrooms (2 double, 1 single bed), bathroom, heating, balcony, garden. Linen available. Shopping at 4 km or at Buxy where there is a restaurant.

Prices:	low season	F 570/685	**7 people**
	high season	F 800	IGN 37

Booking: Mme M. F. LAPORTE, Cersot, 71390 Buxy.
Tel. (85) 96 10 38.

71/147

LA CHAPELLE-SOUS-UCHON Toulongeon A renovated and traditionally furnished gîte on a working farm, 2.5 km from the village centre. Autun (15 km) is a busy town, noted for its many Gallo-Roman remains, some of which you can see in the museum, others still standing such as the theatre. Living room (1 double divan), kitchen, 2 bedrooms (4 large single beds), bathroom, electric heating, terrace, garage, enclosed ground with garden furniture and barbecue. Linen available. Shopping and restaurant at 3 km.

Prices:	low season	F 655	**6 people**
	high season	F 850	IGN 36

Booking: M R. PATRU, La Chapelle-sous-Uchon, 71190 Etang-sur-Arroux. Tel. (85) 54 43 87.

71/178

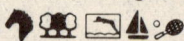

Saône-et-Loire

CHENOVES La Baitière A delightful country cottage, renovated to provide two traditionally furnished gîtes on a mixed farm. Visit the medieval city of Saint-Gengoux-le-National (5 km approx.) with its old wooden houses and other interesting architecture. Chalon-sur-Saône and Mâcon are both within 40 km and warrant a day trip. Living room/kitchenette, 3 bedrooms (1 double, 3 single beds, a child's bed on request), shower room, gas heating, balcony, open ground. Shopping at Saint-Gengoux-le-National.

Prices: low season   F 600/620   **5 people**
         high season   F 650   IGN 37
Booking: Mme P. COLLIN, La Baitière, Chenôves, 71940 Saint-Boil.
Tel. (85) 44 03 76.
71/14

CLUNY La Murgère A renovated and traditionally furnished gîte in its own enclosed ground near the owners' home. Cluny (1 km) is an important spiritual and intellectual centre in the Middle Ages. Its great abbey was destroyed during the Revolution and today just the cloisters and a few other remains can be seen. Living room/kitchenette (1 double divan), 2 bedrooms (3 single beds), shower room, electric heating, balcony, enclosed ground. Linen available (F 30 per set per week). Shopping and restaurant in Cluny.

Prices: low season   F 540/700   **5 people**
         high season   F 815   IGN 43
Booking: M J. FONTERAY, La Murgère, La Cras, 71250 Cluny.
Tel. (85) 59 11 25.
71/265

DETTEY La Montagne This small gîte is one of two in a renovated and traditionally furnished building, situated in the country, 1.5 km from the village centre. Local forest walks; a pond for fishing at 3 km. The lovely sixteenth-century bridge is a noted landmark at Toulon-sur-Arroux (11 km). Living room/kitchenette, 1 bedroom (2 double, 1 single bed), shower room, gas heating, enclosed ground. Linen available. Farm produce in the village; other shopping and a restaurant at 10 km.

Prices: low season   F 450   **5 people**
         high season   F 630/680   IGN 36
Booking: M M. BONNOT-BICHET, route de Gueugnon, 71320 Toulon-sur-Arroux. Tel. (85) 79 42 70.
71/16

ETRIGNY Champlieu This traditionally furnished house has been carefully renovated to preserve its old character. It is on a mixed farm outside the village. All the facilities of a large modern town at Chalon-sur-Saône (28 km), birthplace of the early photographer, Nièpce. Living room/kitchenette (1 single divan), 1 bedroom (2 double, 2 single beds), shower room, fireplace, central heating, balcony. Linen available. Shopping in the village (1.8 km) and a restaurant (8 km). Farm produce from the owners.

Prices: low season   F 450/460   **7 people**
         high season   F 480   IGN 37
Booking: M M. BRETHENET, Etrigny, 71240 Sennecey-le-Grand.
Tel. (85) 92 21 94.
71/68

GEANGES Le Mebiadot One of two traditionally furnished apartments in this renovated house on a farm at the edge of the village (0.8 km). At Beaune (9 km), a centre for the wine trade, the Hospices de Beaune is a celebrated example of Renaissance architecture; in November this charitable hospital auctions the wine from its vineyards. Living room, kitchen, 2 bedrooms (1 double, 3 single and 1 child's bed), shower room, central heating, terrace, garden with furniture and barbecue. Linen available. Shopping and restaurant (2 km).

Prices: low season   F 700/760   **6 people**
         high season   F 820   IGN 37
Booking: M M. FAIVRE, Géanges, 71133 Saint-Loup-de-la-Salle.
Tel. (85) 49 47 19.
71/112

14

Saône-et-Loire

GERMAGNY A renovated and traditionally furnished cottage at the centre of the town with local fishing and marked footpaths at 5 km. Tennis at Buxy (10 km), a small town, flanked by the mountains, with a twelfth-century church. Living room (1 double divan), kitchen (washing machine), 2 bedrooms (1 double, 2 single and 1 child's bed), shower room, central heating, balcony, enclosed ground. Local farm produce; shopping and restaurant in the town.

Prices:	low season	on request	**7 people**
	high season	on request	*IGN 37*

Booking: M J. DESCOMBIN, Germagny, 71460 Saint-Gengoux-le-National. Tel. (85) 49 27 74.

71/148

LAIZY An attractive, spacious house, carefully renovated and situated in its own enclosed ground with garden furniture, barbecue and table tennis at your disposal. Sailing (11 km) and good leisure facilities at the historic town of Autun (11 km) which has a wealth of Gallo-Roman monuments. Living room (TV), kitchen (washing machine), 3 bedrooms (4 single beds), bathroom, electric heating. Farm produce and other shopping in the town and a restaurant at 5 km.

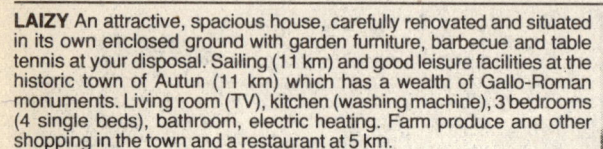

Prices:	low season	F 650/770	**4 people**
	high season	F 770/825	*IGN 36*

Booking: M H. LARCHEY, 16 avenue M. L. King, 78230 Le Pecq. Tel. (1) 958 49 24.

71/286

LUGNY-LES-CHAROLLES Les Cadolles Situated 2 km from the village centre, this country cottage has been well renovated and furnished in traditional style. It is in an important stock-rearing district, famous for its Charollais cattle and sheep. Plenty of leisure amenities at Charolles itself (6 km). Living room, kitchen, 2 bedrooms (2 single beds, 1 double divan), bathroom, central heating, garage, enclosed garden. Farm produce in the village; shops (3 km) or at Charolles where there is a restaurant.

Prices:	low season	F 670	**4 people**
	high season	F 750	*IGN 43*

Booking: M H. DURY, 15 rue Sergent Laforêt, 71600 Paray-le-Monial. Tel. (85) 81 02 64.

71/188

MALAY A renovated and traditionally furnished gîte near the owners' home at the town centre. See the lovely Renaissance Château de Cormatin (1 km). Do not miss historic Cluny (17 km), a mediaeval town which grew up around its vast abbey, second only in size to Saint Peter's in Rome. Living room/kitchenette, 2 bedrooms (2 single beds, 1 single divan), shower room, central heating. Linen available (F 30 per set per week). Shopping and restaurant at Cormatin.

Prices:	low season	F 320	**3 people**
	high season	F 375	*IGN 37*

Booking: Mme M. C. BOUILLIN, Malay, 71460 Saint-Gengoux-le-National. Tel. (85) 50 11 65.

71/190

MANCEY An attractive little gîte, renovated and traditionally furnished, in a rural hamlet. The ancient town of Tournus (6 km) with its cobbled streets and old houses, is a delight to the eye and boasts one of the earliest Romanesque churches in France. Living room, kitchen, 1 bedroom (1 double, 2 single beds), shower room, oil heating, enclosed ground. Linen available (F 30 per set per week). Mobile baker and butcher call; farm produce in the village; other shopping (5 km) and a restaurant at 1 km.

Prices:	low season	F 600	**4 people**
	high season	F 620	*IGN 37*

Booking: Mme S. LAVAL, Mancey, 71240 Sennecey-le-Grand. Tel. (85) 51 10 30.

71/89

Saône-et-Loire

MARLY-SUR-ARROUX Mazoncle An unusual house with its own particular style and character which has been renovated and furnished in traditional fashion. It is situated 3 km from the village and approximately 15 km from Digoin, an old town on the rivers Loire and Arroux, which boasts an aqueduct and Byzantine church. Living room (1 single divan), kitchen, 3 bedrooms (1 double, 4 single beds), shower room, wood stove, garage, garden. Farm produce in the village; other shopping and restaurant at Gueugnon (7 km).

Prices:	low season	F 710	**7 people**
	high season	F 850	*IGN 36*

Booking: M F. DE SAINT-TRIVIER, Mazoncle, Marly-sur-Arroux, 71420 Perrecy-les-Forges. Tel. (85) 79 30 03.
71/140

MERCUREY Grande-Rue This renovated and traditionally furnished gîte is near the owners' home on their vineyard where you may try and buy their product. Near the village centre (0.5 km), it is just 10 km from the bustling town of Chalon-sur-Saône. Local forest walks and tennis (1 km). Living room/kitchenette, 3 bedrooms (4 single and 3 child's beds), bathroom, fireplace, electric heating, enclosed ground with garden furniture and barbecue. Shopping and restaurant in the village.

Prices:	low season	F 1050	**7 people**
	high season	F 1200	*IGN 37*

Booking: M M. JUILLOT, 71640 Mercurey. Tel. (85) 45 27 27.

71/285

RULLY Grande-Rue A renovated and traditionally furnished farm building on a vineyard at the village centre. Fishing, tennis, riding and swimming-pool are all within 5 km of the gîte. Plenty of other leisure and cultural pursuits at the cathedral town of Chalon-sur-Saône (15 km). Living room/kitchenette, 2 bedrooms (1 double, 6 single beds), bathroom, electric heating, terrace, courtyard. Wine from the owners; other shopping and restaurant in the village.

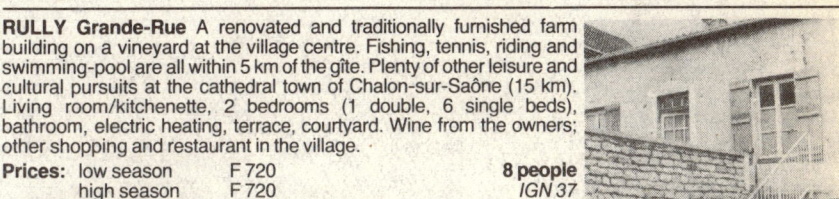

Prices:	low season	F 720	**8 people**
	high season	F 720	*IGN 37*

Booking: M M. BRIDAY, Grande-Rue, Rully, 71150 Chagny. Tele. (85) 87 07 90.

71/267

SAINT-CROIX-EN-BRESSE A traditionally furnished apartment in the owners' renovated village house where you may have the use of their barbecue facilities for outdoor meals. It is in the Bresse district, noted for its delicious corn-fed poultry. Visit Louhans (7 km) with its attractive arcaded streets and fourteenth-century hospital. Living room, kitchen, 2 bedrooms (2 double and 1 child's bed), shower room, central heating, garden. Farm produce, shopping and restaurant in the village.

Prices:	low season	F 435/540	**5 people**
	high season	F 620	*IGN 37*

Booking: M H. JEANNOT, Saint-Croix-en-Bresse, 71470 Montpont-en-Bresse. Tel. (85) 74 81 43.

71/105

SAINT-FOREGEOT La Revenue A ground-floor gîte in a renovated and traditionally furnished terraced house next to the owners' home at the village centre. Places of tourist interest at Autun (5 km) include the Roman sites, the twelfth-century cathedral and the Rolin Museum, housing a good collection of paintings and sculpture. Living room, kitchen, 2 bedrooms (1 double, 3 single beds), bathroom, fireplace, central heating, garden with outdoor furniture and barbecue. Linen available. Farm produce in the village; shops at Autun.

Prices:	low season	F 900	**5 people**
	high season	F 1100/1200	*IGN 36*

Booking: Mme T. EHRET, Saint-Foregeot, 71400 Autun. Tel. (85) 52 30 50.
71/82

Saône-et-Loire

SAINT-GENGOUX-LE-NATIONAL La Chassagne An interesting old house, renovated to preserve its local character, and furnished in traditional style, 1 km from the centre of this mediaeval town. Saint-Gengoux (1 km), lies at the very heart of the département so is ideally situated for trips to Cluny, Autun, Mâcon, etc. Living room/kitchenette (2 single divans), 2 bedrooms (1 double, 1 single bed), shower room, electric heating, enclosed ground. Linen available. Mobile baker calls; local farm produce and shopping in the town.

| Prices: | low season | F 390/465 | **5 people** |
| | high season | F 570/620 | *IGN 37* |

Booking: M M. JOLY, La Chassagne, 71460 Saint-Gengoux-le-National. Tel. (85) 92 64 89.
71/96

SAINT-PIERRE-LE-VIEUX La Place A spacious gîte, renovated and traditionally furnished, on a mixed farm where you may buy fresh eggs and cheese. A swimming-pool and tennis at 8 km; other leisure facilities at historic Cluny (20 km) where the remains of a vast abbey are open to the public. Living room/kitchenette, 3 bedrooms (1 double, 3 single beds), bathroom, oil heating, balcony, garage, enclosed garden. Shopping in the village (1 km) and a restaurant at Matour (8 km).

| Prices: | low season | F 330/430 | **5 people** |
| | high season | F 630 | *IGN 43* |

Booking: M F. FOUILLOUX, Saint-Pierre-le-Vieux, 71520 Matour. Tel. (85) 50 43 64.

71/100

SANTILLY A traditionally furnished gîte in a renovated farm building in its own enclosed ground at the village centre and 4 km from the delightful little mediaeval town of Saint-Gengoux-le-National. Riding (8 km) and a swimming-pool at 15 km. Living room/kitchenette, 2 bedrooms (1 double, 2 single, 2 child's beds and a double divan), bathroom, wood heating, balcony, garage, enclosed garden. Linen available (F 30 per set per week). Farm produce from the owners; other shopping and restaurant at Saint-Gengoux.

| Prices: | low season | F 380/400 | **8 people** |
| | high season | F 450 | *IGN 37* |

Booking: M H. JUSSEAU, Santilly, 71460 Saint-Gengoux-le-National. Tel. (85) 47 63 74.
71/76

SOLUTRE La Grange du Bois In a hamlet, 3.5 km from the village, this renovated and traditionally furnished house enjoys a view of a famous prehistoric site. The Solutré discoveries are displayed at the Museum in Mâcon (13 km), an attractive old city and an important centre for the wine trade. Living room/kitchenette (1 double divan), 2 bedrooms (2 single beds), bathroom, electric heating, enclosed courtyard. Linen available. Shopping and farm produce in the village and a restaurant nearby.

| Prices: | low season | F 320/600 | **4 people** |
| | high season | F 760 | *IGN 43* |

Booking: Mme G. FAVIER, Solutré, 71960 Pierreclos. Tel. (85) 37 82 08.
71/202

TANCON Le Chélut A detached house, renovated and traditionally furnished, and situated in its own garden, some 2.5 km from the village in a fertile valley where local sights include the Mussy viaduct. A swimming-pool and tennis (5 km); other amenities at Chauffailles (6 km). Living room, kitchen, 2 bedrooms (2 double, 2 single beds), shower room, fireplace, heating, carport, enclosed ground. Farm produce available in the village; other shopping and restaurant at Chauffailles.

| Prices: | low season | F 550/650 | **6 people** |
| | high season | F 800 | *IGN 43* |

Booking: M B. ROUX, 2 rue François-Bariquand, 71170 Chauffailles. Tel. (85) 26 12 85.

71/58

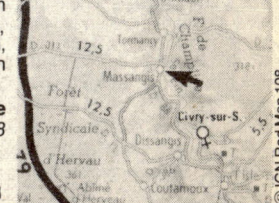

Yonne

CHARNY Champcorgeon A ground floor gîte, simply furnished, and situated 2.5 km from the village. Auxerre (approx. 45 km) has many well-preserved medieval buildings; sporting facilities here include canoeing, riding, tennis, swimming and pleasure boating. This is the Chablis wine area so be sure to try some! Living room, kitchen, 3 bedrooms (2 double and 2 single beds), shower room, fireplace (logs supplied), oil stove, terrace, garage, garden with furniture. Shopping in the village or at Aillant-sur-Thone (approx. 20 km).

Prices:	low season	F 870	**6 people**
	high season	F 870/985	*IGN 27*

Booking: Yonne booking service   E

89/108

CHAMPIGNELLES Les Maisons Blanches One of two gîtes in an old farm building in a hamlet 3 km from the village. The old château town of Toucy (12 km) on the Ouanne has a traditional Saturday market, some interesting old streets and fifteenth century houses. Auxerre (approx. 32 km) has good sports facilities and shops. Living room, kitchen, 2 bedrooms (1 double, 2 single and 1 child's bed), 1 double divan, bathroom, fireplace (logs supplied), ground with child's swing. Shopping in the village or at Toucy.

Prices:	low season	F 800	**6/7 people**
	high season	F 850	*IGN 27*

Booking: Yonne booking service   E

89/104

CISERY An attractive stone-built village gîte standing in its own enclosed ground on a mixed farm. A lake for sailing at 25 km. Avallon (approx 20 km) is a picturesque town overlooking the Cousin valley; swimming, riding and pleasant walks on marked footpaths. Living room (TV), kitchen (washing machine), 3 bedrooms and a mezzanine (2 double and 4 single beds, 1 double divan), bathroom and shower room, fireplace, electric heating, carport, garden furniture, barbecue and child's swing. Shopping and restaurant in the village.

Prices:	low season	F 870/950	**10 people**
	high season	F 1100	*IGN 28*

Booking: Yonne booking service   E

89/96

L'ISLE SUR SEREIN A substantial old house, now renovated and rustically furnished, near the village centre where you may buy fresh farm produce. A lake for sailing at 30 km. Avallon (15 km) has beautiful views across the Cousin valley, medieval fortifications and a fifteenth century clock tower. Living room, kitchen (washing machine), 2 bedrooms (2 double, 2 single and 1 child's bed, double divan), shower room, fireplace, electric heating, terrace, enclosed ground with barbecue and swings. Linen available.

Prices:	low season	F 600/750	**8/9 people**
	high season	F 950/1000	*IGN 28*

Booking: Yonne booking service   E

89/59

MASSANGIS Tormancy A gîte in a hamlet a short walk from the village centre (1 km). Noyers-sur-Serein (6 km) is an old fortified town, surrounded by a tributary of the Serein, with some unusual thirteenth century wooden houses. Living room (TV), kitchen (washing machine), 3 bedrooms (3 double and 1 single bed, 1 double divan), shower room, fireplace (wood supplied), terrace, garage, enclosed garden with furniture, barbecue and child's swing. Shopping at Noyers-sur-Serein.

Prices:	low season	F 735/860	**9 people**
	high season	F 975	*IGN 28*

Booking: Yonne booking service   E

89/90

14

Yonne

MICHERY A well maintained, renovated and rustically furnished house in a hamlet a short walk from the village centre (0.250 km) where you may buy fresh farm produce. Pont-sur-Yonne (4 km) has an old aqueduct and bridge and a thirteenth century church. Sens (approx. 12 km) offers good sporting facilities. Living room (TV), kitchen, 3 bedrooms (1 double and 3 single beds), bathroom and shower room, fireplace (wood supplied), oil central heating, terrace, enclosed garden with furniture and barbecue. Linen available. Owner speaks English. Shopping at Pont-sur-Yonne.

Prices: low season   F 900
           high season   F 980
Booking: Yonne booking service   E
89/119

5 people
IGN 21

PIMELLES La-Grange-aux-Mahes A ground floor gîte on a farm set in open ground with furniture, child's swing and barbecue for outdoor meals. The village is at 3 km. A lake for sailing at 25 km and swimming pool at 20 km. Living room (TV), kitchen (washing machine), 3 bedrooms (3 double, 1 single and 1 child's bed), shower room, fireplace (wood supplied), electric heating, garage. Shopping in the village or at Ancy-le-Franc (10 km).

Prices: low season   F 480/580
           high season   F 850
Booking: Yonne booking service   E

89/31

7/8 people
IGN 28

SAINPUITS An old renovated country cottage, situated in the village and with accommodation all on the ground floor. A river and sailing at 25 km. Burgundy, of course, is noted for its fine food and wines and regional delicacies include snails and corn-fed Bresse chickens. Living room/kitchenette, 2 bedrooms (1 double and 2 single beds), bathroom and shower room, gas heating, garage, enclosed garden with furniture, child's swing and barbecue. Shopping in the village or at Entrains-sur-Nohain (7 km).

Prices: low season   F 800
           high season   F 1000
Booking: Yonne booking service   E

89/16

4 people
IGN 28

VILLEFRANCHE SAINT PHAL Francheville An old, long, low building, furnished in traditional style 2 km from the village where there are shops and a restaurant. Auxerre (approx. 50 km) is a fine medieval town on the river Yonne with good sports facilities and shops. A lake at 35 km. Visit too the old Burgundian town of Joigny (30 km). Living room, kitchen (washing machine), 2 bedrooms (1 double, 3 single and 1 child's bed, 1 double divan), shower room and bathroom, fireplace, electric heating, carport, ground with furniture, child's swing and barbecue.

Prices: low season   F 900
           high season   F 1000
Booking: Yonne booking service   E
89/101

7/8 people
IGN 21

VINNEUF Champeond A well renovated gîte furnished in traditional style on a farm 5 km from the village. The owners speak good English. Sens (23 km) has good leisure facilities, some interesting old churches and a museum devoted to Napoleonic relics. Living room/kitchen (TV, washing machine), 1 bedroom (1 double and 1 child's bed), bathroom, electric heating, enclosed courtyard with garden furniture, barbecue and child's swing. Eggs from the owners, shopping in the village or at Sens.

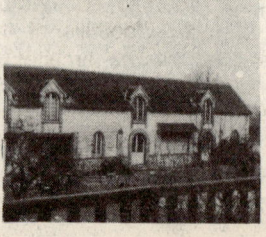

Prices: low season   F 800
           high season   F 800
Booking: Yonne booking service   E

89/120

2/3 people
IGN 21

15 FRANCHE-COMTE

Reminiscent of Switzerland and decidedly influenced by its neighbour, this upland region, still relatively unknown to tourists, has some beautiful mountain scenery. The snow and the mountains offer some excellent opportunities for winter sports, the more popular resorts being Les Rousses, Col de la Faucille and Mijoux. However, all the year round, a fresh climate and rain, provide constant refreshment to the greenery and give many agricultural benefits.

Naturally, this mountain region has its spas and health resorts, such as Divonne-les-Bains, near the Swiss border. Its springs were discovered and used as far back as Roman times and it is an ideal spot for trips to Lake Geneva.

The Loue Valley attracts visitors to its picturesquely winding river, with a large cave at its source and charming little towns along its banks. One such town is Ornans, the birthplace of the artist, Courbet, who was fond of painting the river and its surrounding scenery.

The impressive valley of the Doubs has a large waterfall, beautiful gorges and possesses two towns of importance: Montbéliard has many interesting old buildings and a fine fifteenth-century château and Besançon, set in a loop of the river and enclosed by hills. This university town is now known for the watch and clock-making industry. It was the birthplace of Victor Hugo and is indeed a most attractive town.

It would be unfair to leave this region without mentioning the spectacular scenery found in the valleys of Ain, Dessoubre and the striking Valserine Valley, with some of the highest peaks in the Jura rising up on either side. There are also many *reculées*, particularly steep-sided valleys, cutting their way through the hillsides, ending in a *cirque* (corrie), where you may find caves set deep in the rock face.

At any time of year, you will be impressed by the upland scenery, soothed by the green pastures and rolling foothills of the Vosges, perhaps puzzled by the architecture reflecting former occupying nations: the Romans, Spaniards, Hungarians and Prussians, and tempted by the wide variety of cheese, gleaned from the rich pasture-lands of the Jura and the Vosges.

Map

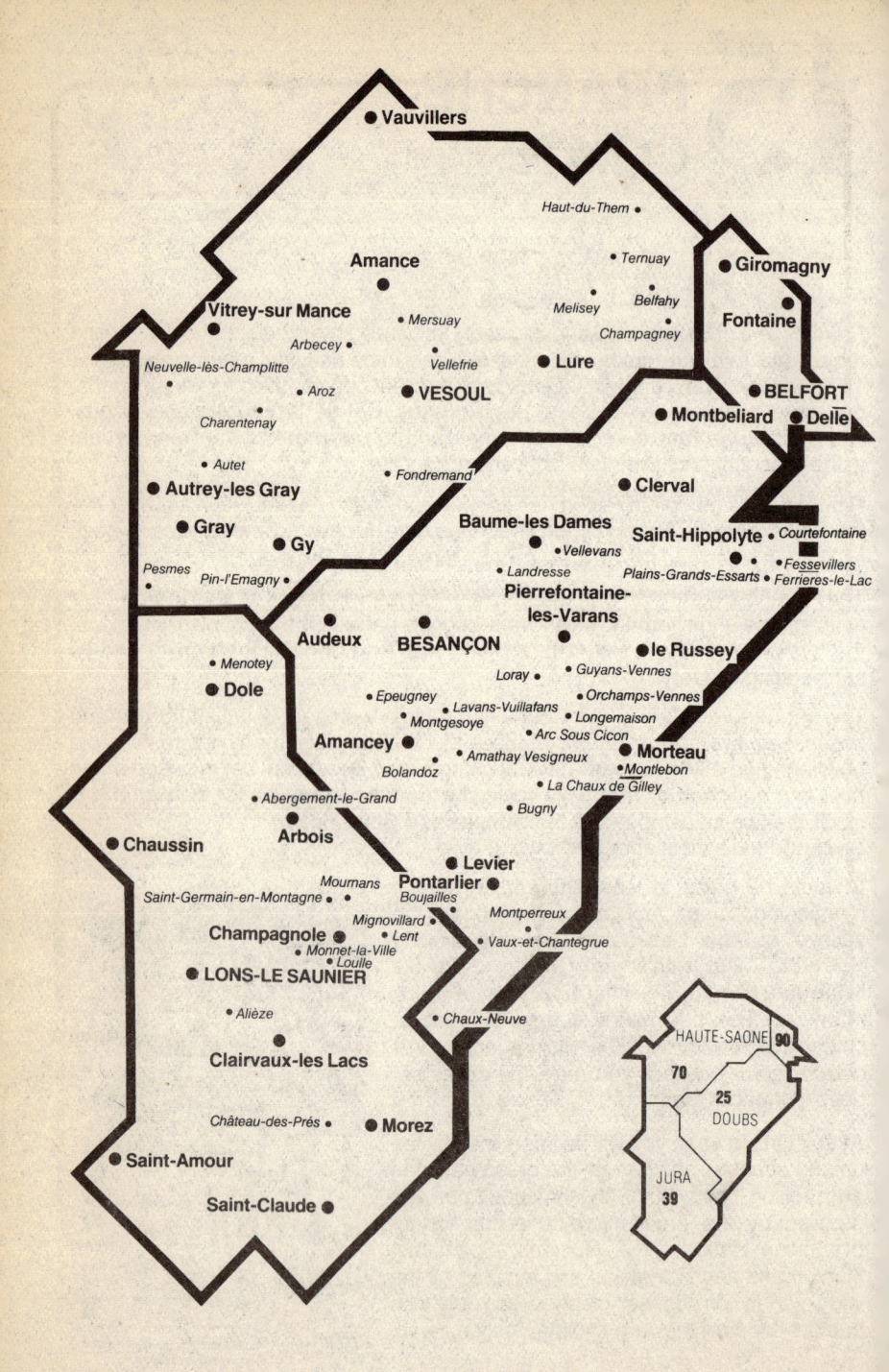

- Vauvillers
- Haut-du-Them
- Amance
- Ternuay
- Giromagny
- Vitrey-sur Mance
- Mersuay
- Melisey
- Belfahy
- Fontaine
- Arbecey
- Vellefrie
- Champagney
- Neuvelle-lès-Champlitte
- Aroz
- VESOUL
- Lure
- BELFORT
- Charentenay
- Montbeliard
- Delle
- Autet
- Fondremand
- Clerval
- Autrey-les Gray
- Baume-les-Dames
- Saint-Hippolyte
- Courtefontaine
- Gray
- Vellevans
- Gy
- Landresse
- Plains-Grands-Essarts
- Fessevillers
- Pesmes
- Pin-l'Emagny
- Pierrefontaine-les-Varans
- Ferrieres-le-Lac
- Audeux
- BESANÇON
- le Russey
- Menotey
- Loray
- Guyans-Vennes
- Dole
- Epeugney
- Lavans-Vuillafans
- Orchamps-Vennes
- Montgesoye
- Longemaison
- Amancey
- Arc Sous Cicon
- Morteau
- Bolandoz
- Amathay Vesigneux
- Montlebon
- Abergement-le-Grand
- La Chaux de Gilley
- Chaussin
- Arbois
- Bugny
- Mournans
- Levier
- Saint-Germain-en-Montagne
- Pontarlier
- Boujailles
- Montperreux
- Champagnole
- Mignovillard
- Lent
- Vaux-et-Chantegrue
- Monnet-la-Ville
- Louile
- LONS-LE SAUNIER
- Aliéze
- Chaux-Neuve
- Clairvaux-les Lacs
- Château-des-Prés
- Morez
- Saint-Amour
- Saint-Claude

Inset: HAUTE-SAONE 70 / 90 / DOUBS 25 / JURA 39

FRANCHE-COMTE

Haute-Saône & Doubs

The most unique feature of the Franche-Comté is its greenness; the dark green of the pine forests, the lighter green of the enormous pastures; peaceful green, ever-changing green, reflected by the lakes, enlivened by the rushing waters and sparkling waterfalls.

For further information, write to the Comité Régional de Tourisme de Franche-Comté, Place de la 1re-Armée-Française, 25000 BESANÇON. Tel: 80 92 55.

Doubs

AMANCEY A newly built gîte right in the village centre, all on the ground floor and furnished in traditional style. Altitude 600 m. Besançon, (30 km), the département capital, has many fine buildings, museums (including one on the Resistance movement) and good sporting facilities. Living room, kitchen, 1 bedroom (1 double bed), shower room, electric central heating, enclosed garden grounds with furniture. Farm produce, restaurant and shopping in the village or at Ornans (15 km).

Prices:	low season	F 655/675	**2 people**
	high season	F 780	*IGN 38*

Booking: Doubs Loisirs Accueil　　E

25/03

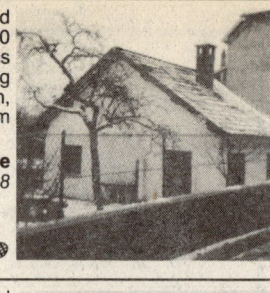

AMATHAY VESIGNEUX Les Nades A new gîte in its own enclosed grounds with child's swing 2 km from the centre of the village, altitude 650 m. Pontarlier (32 km) offers canoeing, karting and aero-club amongst other sporting facilities and Besançon (40 km) offers all the amenities of a large town. Living room, kitchen, 2 bedrooms (1 double and 2 single beds), shower room, electric central heating, balcony, garage. Farm produce and shopping in the village or at Ornans (12 km).

Prices:	low season	F 540/600	**4 people**
	high season	F 740	*IGN 38*

Booking: Doubs Loisirs Accueil　　E

25/05

ARC SOUS CICON One of two gîtes in a spacious chalet on the edge of the village, altitude 850 m. A lake at 30 km and Pontarlier (18 km) has an eleventh-century château, a weapons museum and good sports facilities for winter and summer. Living room/kitchenette (1 double divan), 1 bedroom (1 double and 1 single bed), shower room, electric central heating, open grounds. Farm produce, shopping and restaurant in the village or at Pontarlier.

Prices:	low season	F 575/600	**5 people**
	high season	F 740/760	*IGN 38*

Booking: Doubs Loisirs Accueil　　E

25/08

BOLANDOZ A recently built house, with country-style furnishings, near the village centre. Local forest walks and cross-country and traditional ski-ing. Ornans (13 km) is in the lovely Loue valley, the backdrop for many of the artist Courbet's paintings. Altitude 700 metres. Living room, kitchen, 2 bedrooms (1 double, 2 single, 1 child's bed), bathroom, central heating, garage, open ground. Mobile grocer and baker call; other shopping at 4 km.

Prices:	low season	F 690/730	**5 people**
	high season	F 800/865	*IGN 38*

Booking: Doubs Loisirs Accueil　　E

25/20

BOUJAILLES A gîte in the retired owners' renovated and traditionally furnished village house. Fishing locally, walking in nearby forests; riding and tennis (9 km), and swimming-pool at the lovely old town of Pontarlier on the river Doubs (25 km), noted for its cheese and chocolate. Altitude 820 metres. Living room, kitchen, 2 bedrooms (1 double, 2 single and 1 child's bed), bathroom, gas heating, garage, small garden. Mobile shops call; farm produce and restaurant in the village.

Prices:	low season	F 715	**5 people**
	high season	F 790	*IGN 38*

Booking: Doubs Loisirs Accueil　　E

25/24

Doubs

BUGNY A gîte on the first floor of the owners' completely modern house in a quiet position at the edge of the village (altitude 850 metres). Pontarlier (10 km) is a busy town, but picturesque, with a variety of leisure and cultural amenities; see the twelfth-century Montbenoit Abbey nearby. Kitchen, 2 bedrooms (1 double, 2 single and 1 child's bed), bathroom, central heaating, open ground. Mobile butcher, baker and grocer call; farm produce in the village; other shopping (6 km).

Prices: low season   F 610   **5 people**
         high season   F 745   IGN 38

Booking: Doubs Loisirs Accueil   E

25/27

LA CHAUX-DE-GILLEY A ground-floor gîte, one of two in the owners' traditionally furnished and renovated village house (altitude 900 metres). Local forest walks and ski-ing. Pontarlier (16 km) is a busy town where leisure facilities include a swimming-pool and skating rink; see the nearby eleventh-century Château du Joux. Kitchen, 2 bedrooms (1 double and 2 single beds), bathroom, central heating, open ground. Mobile butcher calls; farm produce and other shopping in the village.

Prices: low season   F 595/650   **4 people**
         high season   F 780/800   IGN 38

Booking: Doubs Loisirs Accueil   E

25/40

CHAUX-NEUVE One of six traditionally furnished gîtes in a recently renovated building at the village centre (altitude 1000 m). Ideally situated for walking and ski-ing in the Jura mountains. Bathing, sailing and other leisure amenities at Saint-Point lake at Malbuisson (20 km). Living room/kitchenette, 2 bedrooms (1 double and 2 single beds), shower room, electric heating, garden and enclosed ground. Mobile butcher, baker and grocer call; other shopping in the village or at Pontarlier (35 km).

Prices: low season   F 610/620   **4 people**
         high season   F 800/980   IGN 38

Booking: Doubs Loisirs Accueil   E

25/43

COURTEFONTAINE One of two traditionally furnished gîtes in a large old house which has been recently restored and is set in quiet surroundings outside the village (altitude 850 metres). Tennis, riding and ski-ing within 15 km; other amenities at Maîche (12 km) where you can visit a cheese factory. Living room/kitchenette, 2 bedrooms (1 double and 2 single beds), bathroom, fireplace, electric heating, open ground. Shopping in the village (2 km) or at Maîche.

Prices: low season   F 550/560   **4 people**
         high season   F 665/710   IGN 38

Booking: Doubs Loisirs Accueil   E

25/51

EPEUGNEY A first-floor gîte in a well-renovated substantial old house in the centre of the village. The fine old town of Besançon on the river Doubs, the birthplace of Victor Hugo, is 18 km away and offers excellent sporting and cultural activities. Kitchen, 2 bedrooms (1 double and 2 single beds), shower room, electric central heating. Farm produce, shopping and restaurant in the village or at Besançon.

Prices: low season   F 615/625   **4 people**
         high season   F 790   IGN 38

Booking: Doubs Loisirs Accueil   E

25/68

15

Doubs

FERRIERES-LE-LAC A traditionally furnished, ground-floor gîte, one of two in the owners' attractive, renovated house at the centre of a small village near the Swiss border. River fishing (4 km) and ski-ing at 6 km. Tennis and other amenities at Maîche (12 km), noted for its clock industry. Altitude 800 metres. Living room/kitchenette, 2 bedrooms (1 double and 4 single beds), shower room, central heating, open ground. Mobile butcher, baker and grocer call; other shopping at 6 km.

Prices: low season   F 745/830   6 people
         high season F 920   IGN 38

Booking: Doubs Loisirs Accueil   E
25/71

FESSEVILLERS Le Plain One of two simply furnished gîtes adjoining the owners' renovated house on their livestock farm. It lies in an isolated spot, 2 km from the village, but has the benefit of beautiful surroundings. Maîche (14 km) has leisure amenities for winter and summer: riding, tennis, ski-ing. Altitude 650 metres. Living room/kitchenette, 1 bedroom (2 double and 2 single beds), bathroom, heating, open ground. Mobile butcher, baker and grocer call; farm produce from the owners; other shopping at 6 km; restaurant at 1 km.

Prices: low season   F 520/645   6 people
         high season F 745   IGN 38

Booking: Doubs Loisirs Accueil   E
25/73

GUYANS-VENNES Les Geys A traditionally furnished gîte adjoining the owners' house on a farm overlooking open countryside at the edge of the village (0.4 km). At Morteau on the river Doubs (12 km), a town noted for the manufacture of clocks and chocolate, see the Renaissance Château Pertusier. Altitude 740 metres. Kitchen, 2 bedrooms (2 double beds), shower room, central heating, open ground. Farm produce from the owners; mobile butcher, baker and grocer call; other shopping at 3 km.

Prices: low season   F 520   4 people
         high season F 625   IGN 38

Booking: Doubs Loisirs Accueil   E
25/97

LANDRESSE A traditionally furnished gîte in an old house at the village centre, surrounded by forests (altitude 600 metres). At Pierrefontaine-les-Varans (9 km), see the Reverotte gorges. Cross-country ski-ing (9 km); riding (15 km) and a swimming-pool and tennis at 18 km. Living room (1 double divan), kitchen, 1 bedroom (1 double, 1 single and 1 child's bed), shower room, wood heating, garage, enclosed ground. Farm produce and other shopping in the village.

Prices: low season   F 730/760   5/6 people
         high season F 845   IGN 38

Booking: Doubs Loisirs Accueil   E
25/104

LAVANS-VUILLAFANS A renovated house containing three gîtes at the centre of the village (altitude 640 metres). The charming town of Ornans on the river Loue (12 km) has a museum dedicated to the artist Gustave Courbet, in the house where he was born, and many leisure amenities. Living room (1 double bed), kitchen, 1 bedroom (1 double and 1 child's bed), bathroom, central heating, open ground. Mobile shops call; other shopping and restaurant at Ornans.

Prices: low season   F 540   4/5 people
         high season F 640/680   IGN 38

Booking: Doubs Loisirs Accueil   E
25/106

Doubs

LONGEMAISON A first-floor gîte above the owners' cafe/restaurant in a quiet little village surrounded by forests. Morteau (20 km) has a Renaissance château and is an important centre for the manufacture of clocks and chocolate. Altitude 830 metres. Kitchen, 2 bedrooms (2 double, 1 single and 1 child's bed), bathroom, oil-fired central heating, balcony, enclosed ground. Mobile butcher calls; fresh farm produce and other shopping in the village.

Prices:	low season	F 470	**5/6 people**
	high season	F 590	IGN 38

Booking: Doubs Loisirs Accueil   E

25/112

LORAY An old renovated cottage modestly furnished in traditional style on the edge of the village, altitude 750 m. Morteau (24 km) is on the Doubs and famous for cheeses, butter and smoked ham and offers excellent sporting facilities. Living room/kitchenette, 2 bedrooms (2 double beds), shower room, electric central heating, garage, open grounds. Mobile baker and butcher call. Restaurant and shopping in the village or at Valdahon (12 km).

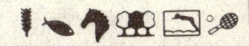

Prices:	low season	F 575	**4 people**
	high season	F 780	IGN 38

Booking: Doubs Loisirs Accueil   E

25/119

MONTGESOYE A ground-floor gîte in the owner's own holiday home, a substantial renovated building in the centre of the village. Besançon, the département capital, is 29 km and offers all the sporting and cultural facilities of a large town – try the local confectionery! Living room/kitchenette (1 double divan), 1 bedroom (1 double bed), bathroom, central heating, garage, enclosed ground. Restaurant and shopping in the village or at Ornans (4 km).

Prices:	low season	F 545/625	**4 people**
	high season	F 735/745	IGN 38

Booking: Doubs Loisirs Accueil   E

25/140

MONTLEBON Les Mourlets A first-floor gîte in a large chalet-type house (shared with a permanent resident) 2 km from the village centre (altitude 725 m). Morteau (4 km) is an attractive town surrounded by pine forests and open countryside and there are facilities for fishing and forest walks in the village; ski slopes at 2 km. Living room, kitchen, 3 bedrooms (2 double and 2 single beds), shower room, fireplace, electric central heating, open grounds. Restaurant and shopping in the village or at Morteau.

Prices:	low season	F 720/905	**6 people**
	high season	F 960/1020	IGN 38

Booking: Doubs Loisirs Accueil   E
35/142

MONTPERREUX Chaudron An attractive chalet (altitude 1,000 m) divided into two gîtes; the village is 3 km away. Malbuisson (3 km) is a rural holiday centre and there is sailing and other watersports on the Saint Point lakes. Living room/kitchenette, 2 bedrooms (1 double and 3 single beds), shower room, fireplace, central heating, balcony, garage, open ground. Shopping and restaurant at Malbuisson.

Prices:	low season	F 975	**5 people**
	high season	F 1125/1165	IGN 38

Booking: Doubs Loisirs Accueil   E

35/148

15

Doubs

ORCHAMPS-VENNES Les Courbottes One of two traditionally furnished gîtes on the ground floor of a building, typical of the region. Ideal for country-lovers as it is in an isolated spot, surrounded by a pine forest, some 8 km from the village. Many leisure facilities available at Morteau (18 km). Altitude 917 metres. Living room/kitchenette (1 double divan), 2 bedrooms (2 double and 1 single bed), bathroom, electric heating, open ground. Shopping in the village, or at Morteau.

Prices: low season   F 530
high season   F 665

7 people
IGN 38

Booking: Doubs Loisirs Accueil   E

25/159

PIERREFONTAINE-LES-VARANS Le Creusot A ground-floor gîte with traditional furnishings, one of two in an old farmhouse, typical of the region, which has been renovated. It lies in an isolated spot in the country, but just 0.8 km from the village (altitude 750 metres). Local ski-ing; riding (23 km). Kitchen, 1 bedroom (1 double and 4 single beds), shower room, electric heating, open ground. Farm produce from the owners; other shopping in the village.

Prices: low season   F 490/520
high season   F 675

6 people
IGN 38

Booking: Doubs Loisirs Accueil   E

25/170

PLAINS-GRANDS-ESSARTS This gîte, with traditional country-style furnishings, adjoins the owners' attractive renovated house on a mixed farm near the village centre (0.1 km). It is 12 km from Maîche, where local sites include the Waroly caves, Doubs gorges and the Montalembert Château. Altitude 730 metres. Living room (1 single divan), kitchen, 2 bedrooms (2 double, 2 single and 1 child's bed), bathroom, wood heating, ground. Mobile butcher, baker and grocer call; other shopping at 3 km.

Prices: low season   F 385/545
high season   F 710

7/8 people
IGN 38

Booking: Doubs Loisirs Accueil   E

25/174

VAUX-ET-CHANTEGRUE A ground-floor gîte in a large old former farmhouse, which has been renovated and converted into nine holiday apartments. It is in the village, near Saint-Point lake and 8 km from Malbuisson (swimming-pool, tennis, winter sports). Altitude 900 metres. Living room/kitchenette, 1 bedroom (1 double, 5 single and 1 child's bed), shower room, central heating, balcony, enclosed ground. Farm produce in the village; other shopping and restaurant in Malbuisson.

Prices: low season   F 550/615
high season   F 675/715

7/8 people
IGN 38

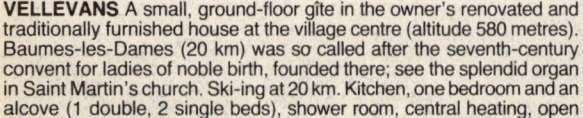

Booking: Doubs Loisirs Accueil   E

25/190

VELLEVANS A small, ground-floor gîte in the owner's renovated and traditionally furnished house at the village centre (altitude 580 metres). Baumes-les-Dames (20 km) was so called after the seventh-century convent for ladies of noble birth, founded there; see the splendid organ in Saint Martin's church. Ski-ing at 20 km. Kitchen, one bedroom and an alcove (1 double, 2 single beds), shower room, central heating, open ground. Mobile shops call; other shopping at Sancey-le-Grand (8 km).

Prices: low season   F 620
high season   F 645

4 people
IGN 38

Booking: Doubs Loisirs Accueil   E

25/196

Jura

ABERGEMENT-LE-GRAND A gîte with country-style furnishings in the owners' old house near the centre of a village in a region of vineyards. Local forest walks; see the Planches caves nearby. Swimming-pool and other amenities at the little old town of Arbois (7 km) where there is a wine museum. Living room (1 double divan), kitchen, 1 bedroom (1 double and 1 single bed), bathroom, central heating, terrace, open garden with outdoor furniture. Mobile shops call; other shopping and restaurant at 3 km.

Prices:	low season	F 550	**5 people**
	high season	F 770	*IGN 37*

Booking: Jura booking service   E

39/532

ALIEZE Les Roches A gîte in the owners' modern house, 0.5 km from the village centre. It is just 13 km from the splendid 4000-acre Vouglans lake with facilities for all kinds of water sports. Many other leisure amenities at the spa town of Lons-le-Saunier (12 km). Altitude 600 metres. Living room (1 double divan), kitchen (washing machine), 2 bedrooms (2 double beds), bathroom, electric central heating, garage, open ground. Mobile butcher, baker and grocer. Farm produce in the village; other shopping and a restaurant at 7 km.

Prices:	low season	F 695	**6 people**
	high season	F 920/985	*IGN 37*

Booking: Jura booking service   E

39/314

CHATEAU-DES-PRES One of two gîtes in a renovated village house with traditional furnishings. Bathing and sailing at a lake (4 km) and local cross-country ski-ing. Many other leisure facilities at the picturesque cathedral town of Sainte-Claude, famous for the manufacture of briar pipes (20 km approx.). Altitude 950 metres. Living room/kitchenette, 2 bedrooms (1 double, 2 single and 1 child's bed), bathroom, electric heating, courtyard. Mobile shops call; other shopping (3 km) or at Saint-Laurent-en-Grandvaux (13 km).

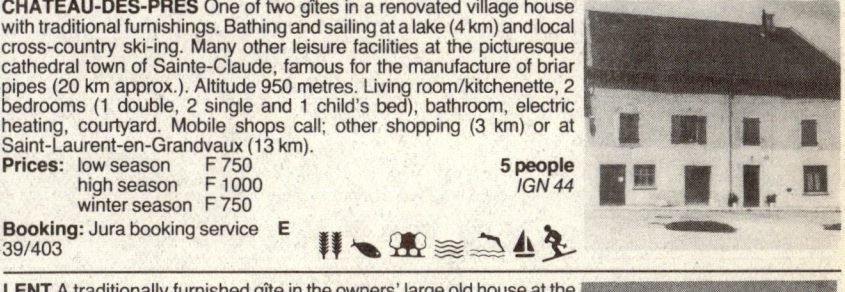

Prices:	low season	F 750	**5 people**
	high season	F 1000	*IGN 44*
	winter season	F 750	

Booking: Jura booking service   E

39/403

LENT A traditionally furnished gîte in the owners' large old house at the village centre. Good trout fishing at the small industrial town of Champagnole (9 km), in a picturesque wooded area where local tourist attractions include the Bellefrise Gardens and monumental fountains. Altitude 700 metres. Living room/kitchenette, 2 bedrooms (2 double and 1 single bed), shower room, wood heating, courtyard. Mobile shops; dairy produce in the village; other shopping and a restaurant at 4 km.

Prices:	low season	F 625	**5 people**
	high season	F 750/810	*IGN 38*
	winter season	F 625	

Booking: M H. TISSOT, 3 Ruelle Baudin, 39300 Champagnole. Tel. (84) 52 29 34.

39/89

LOULLE A ground-floor gîte with country-style furnishings, one of two in a house near the village centre (altitude 690 metres). Good leisure amenities at Champagnole at the foot of Mount Rivel (6 km) and at Domaine de Chalain lake (bathing and sailing, 8 km). Living room/kitchenette, 1 bedroom (1 double and 2 single beds), shower room, fireplace (wood supplied), electric heating, terrace, open ground. Linen available (F20 per set per week). Shopping from mobile stores or at Champagnole; a restaurant at 4 km.

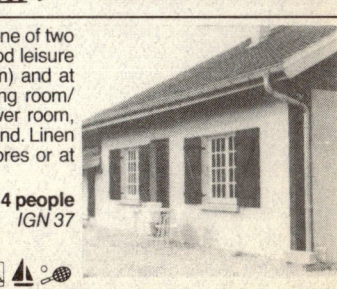

Prices:	low season	F 735	**4 people**
	high season	F 840	*IGN 37*

Booking: Jura booking service   E

39/162

15

Jura

MENOTEY A traditionally furnished, ground-floor gîte in a village house near the forest (1 km). Dole (7 km) is a delightful town with narrow, winding streets on the river Doubs, birthplace of Louis Pasteur (see the Pasteur Museum); leisure amenities include swimming-pool and tennis. Living room, kitchen, 2 bedrooms (2 double, 1 single and 1 child's bed), bathroom, central heating, enclosed garden. Linen available. Shopping in the village or from mobile stores; a restaurant at 5 km.

Prices:	low season	F 660	6 people
	high season	F 880/990	IGN 37

Booking: Jura booking service **E**

39/533

MIGNOVILLARD Froidefontaine A traditionally furnished, ground-floor gîte in an attractive old house, situated in a rural hamlet (altitude 875 metres). The medieval town of Nozeroy (6 km) has some interesting old architecture, including its ramparts and clock tower. Skiing locally; a lake (bathing and sailing at 20 km). Kitchen, 2 bedrooms (4 double beds), bathroom, central heating, garden and courtyard. Fresh dairy produce, other shopping and restaurant in the village (2 km); mobile shops call.

Prices:	low season	F 550	8 people
	high season	F 770	IGN 38
	winter season	F 550	

Booking: Jura booking service **E**

39/296

MONNET-LA-VILLE A gîte in the owners' village house (altitude 550 metres), near the local dairy where you can buy fresh cheese. Bathing and sailing at Chalain lake (5 km); a riding centre at 7 km; other leisure facilities at the small town of Champagnole (12 km). Living room, kitchen, 2 bedrooms (2 double, 1 single and 1 child's bed), bathroom, central heating, courtyard. Mobile shops call; other shopping and restaurant in the village.

Prices:	low season	F 625	6 people
	high season	F 810/875	IGN 37

Booking: M L. BAUD, Monnet-la-Ville, 39300 Champagnole.
Tel. (84) 51 21 21. **E**

39/449

MOURNANS One of three gîtes with country-style furnishings in a modern house at the village centre (altitude 760 metres). Take a day trip to the spa town of Lons-le-Saunier (30 km approx.) and enjoy its public gardens, arcaded streets and many leisure amenities. Living room/kitchenette, 2 bedrooms (1 double, 3 single beds), shower room, electric central heating, garage, open ground. Mobile shops call; other shopping at Champagnole (6 km); a restaurant at 3 km.

Prices:	low season	F 750	6 people
	high season	F 1030	IGN 38

Booking: M C. DENISET, Mournans, 39250 Nozeroy.
Tel. (84) 51 15 51. **E**

39/379

SAINT-GERMAIN-EN-MONTAGNE A gîte in the owners' house right at the village centre (altitude 650 metres) and 5 km from Champagnole with its range of leisure facilities. Visit the delightful old spa town of Salins-les-Bains (25 km approx.) where the natural salty water is popular for cures. Living room, kitchen (washing machine), 2 bedrooms (2 double and 1 child's bed), bathroom, central heating, open ground. A restaurant in the village and shopping at Champagnole, or from mobile shops.

Prices:	low season	F 685	5 people
	high season	F 945	IGN 38

Booking: Jura booking service **E**

39/580

Haute-Saône

ARBECEY A large, detached house with rustic furniture, in the village, set in grounds large enough to give complete peace and quiet. There are forests within 1 km of the gîte; fishing and bathing at a lake (5 km). Living room, kitchen, 4 bedrooms (1 double, 4 single and 1 child's bed), shower room, wood heating, garage, grounds. Mobile shops call, other shopping (5 km) or at Jussey (12 km).

Prices:	low season	F 460/710	7 people
	high season	F 740/825	IGN 30
	winter season	F 740	

Booking: Haute-Saône Loisirs Accueil   E

70/030

AROZ A renovated house in the centre of the village only 2 km from the peaceful river Saône where you can enjoy bathing and fishing. Tennis, swimming-pool or a visit to the museum in the old town of Vesoul (12 km), sailing at a lake (12 km). Living room, kitchen, 2 bedrooms (2 double and 2 single beds), shower room, oil heating, garage. Mobile grocer, baker and butcher call. Shops and restaurant (2 km) or at Vesoul.

Prices:	low season	F 460/710	6 people
	high season	F 740/825	IGN 30

Booking: Haute-Saône Loisirs Accueil   E

70/036

AUTET This new house comprises a simply furnished gîte and one other apartment. It lies at the centre of the village at the edge of the Saône valley – a region renowned for its gastronomy and fishing. At 10 km is the château of Ray-sur-Saône. Living room, kitchen, 2 bedrooms (2 double, 2 single and 1 child's bed), bathroom (washing machine), central heating, garden with children's swings. Mobile baker, butcher and grocer call; other shopping and restaurants at Dampierre-sur-Salon (3 km).

Prices:	low season	F 380/540	7 people
	high season	F 710/740	IGN 30

Booking: Haute-Saône Loisirs Accueil   E

70/042

BELFAHY One of four apartments with modern furnishings in a renovated house at the edge of a small village in the Vosges mountains (altitude 900 metres). Local forest walks and downhill and cross-country ski-ing at 1 km. Bathing at Champagney lake (15 km). Living room, kitchen, 1 bedroom (1 double and 3 single beds), shower room, oil-fired central heating, open ground. Mobile butcher calls; grocer's shop and restaurant in the village; other shopping at 9 km.

Prices:	low season	F 540	5 people
	high season	F 710/740	IGN 31
	winter season	F 710	

Booking: Haute-Saône Loisirs Accueil   E

70/83

15

CHAMPAGNEY One of four holiday apartments in a large house on the edge of a village which is ideal for tourists because of its numerous leisure facilities and beautiful surrounding countryside. The gîte, which has modern furniture, is 15 km from the interesting old town of Lure. Living room/kitchenette, 1 bedroom (1 double and 1 single bed), shower room, central heating, garden. Shopping in the village or at Belfort (20 km).

Prices:	low season	F 350/400	3 people
	high season	F 525/580	IGN 31
	winter season	F 525	

Booking: Haute-Saône Loisirs Accueil   E

70/175

Haute-Saône

CHARENTENAY An old, traditionally furnished house whose owner, Monsieur Paris, keeps an inn (auberge rurale) where he serves the local speciality, 'Pochouse' – a kind of fish stew. He has one other gîte and accommodation for users of the river Saône (100 metres). Fresne-le-Mont leisure park is at 7 km. Kitchen, 3 bedrooms (2 double, 2 single and 1 child's bed), shower room, heating, open ground. Mobile butcher, baker and grocer call; farm produce and shopping in the village (3 km).

Prices:	low season	F 460/710	**7 people**
	high season	F 740/825	IGN 30
	winter season	F 740	

Booking: Haute-Saône Loisirs Accueil E

70/187

FONDREMAND A modern, chalet-style house with traditional furnishings, set in open ground within walking distance (0.5 km) of the village where you may hire a raft at the source of the Romaine. A swimming-pool at Rioz (8 km) and the historic town of Besançon (25 km approx.) is well worth a visit. Living room/kitchenette (1 single divan), 2 bedrooms (1 double and 2 single beds), shower room, central heating, balcony, open ground. Mobile butcher and grocer call and local farm produce available. Other shopping at Rioz; a restaurant in the village.

Prices:	low season	F 400/540	**5 people**
	high season	F 710/740	IGN 30
	winter season	F 710	

Booking: Haute-Saône Loisirs Accueil E

70/311

HAUT-DU-THEM La Pile A modern detached house traditionally furnished with an outlook on gently rolling wooded hills. Cross-country ski-ing (8 km), 10 km to Faucogney, an ancient fortified town with a château. Riding (15 km), swimming-pool (20 km). Living room, kitchen, 3 bedrooms (2 double, 1 single and 1 child's bed), bathroom, central heating, balcony, garage and ground. Mobile baker and butcher call, other shops and restaurant in the village (1 km) or at Le Thillot (8 km).

Prices:	low season	F 460/710	**6 people**
	high season	F 740/825	IGN 31
	winter season	F 740	

Booking: Haute-Saône Loisirs Accueil E

70/451

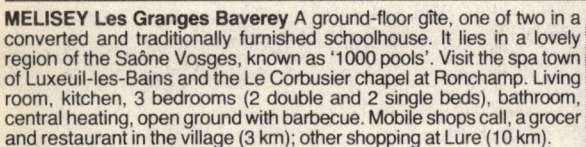

MELISEY Les Granges Baverey A ground-floor gîte, one of two in a converted and traditionally furnished schoolhouse. It lies in a lovely region of the Saône Vosges, known as '1000 pools'. Visit the spa town of Luxeuil-les-Bains and the Le Corbusier chapel at Ronchamp. Living room, kitchen, 3 bedrooms (2 double and 2 single beds), bathroom, central heating, open ground with barbecue. Mobile shops call, a grocer and restaurant in the village (3 km); other shopping at Lure (10 km).

Prices:	low season	F 460/540	**6 people**
	high season	F 710/740	IGN 31
	winter season	F 710	

Booking: Haute-Saône Loisirs Accueil E

70/658

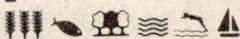

MERSUAY A traditionally furnished gîte adjoining the owners' well-renovated house at the centre of a village on the river La Lanterne, 10 km from the Saône valley. Bathing and sailing at a lake (0.5 km). Vesoul, capital of the département, is at 20 km approx. Living room/kitchenette (1 double divan), 3 bedrooms (3 double and 1 single beds), bathroom, terrace, garage, open ground with garden furniture. Shopping and restaurant in the village or at Faverney (4 km).

Prices:	low season	F 540/710	**9 people**
	high season	F 740/825	IGN 30
	winter season	F 740	

Booking: Haute-Saône Loisirs Accueil E

70/662

Haute-Saône

NEUVELLE-LES-CHAMPLITTE Detached renovated house on a cattle farm, in wooded countryside near a river. Bathing, tennis and riding (17 km), an eighteenth-century château and fifteenth-century chapel in Gray (17 km). Living room/kitchenette, 2 bedrooms (3 double beds), shower room, oil and gas heating, enclosed garden. The owner can sell you eggs, milk and poultry, mobile baker, butcher and grocer call, other shopping and restaurant (3 km) or in the town of Gray.

Prices:	low season	F 460/540	6 people
	high season	F 710/740	IGN 30
	winter season	F 710	

Booking: Haute-Saône Loisirs Accueil E

70/702

PESMES A traditionally furnished, old house at the heart of the village. Guided visits of the village are possible, bicycles for hire (enquire at the Syndicat d'Initiative). Gray (19 km) has a château, museums and all the facilities of a large town. Kitchen, 2 bedrooms (2 double and 2 single beds), bathroom, central heating, interior courtyard. Shopping and restaurants in the village.

Prices:	low season	F 400/540	6 people
	high season	F 710/740	IGN 30
	winter season	F 710	

Booking: Haute-Saône Loisirs Accueil E

70/739

PIN-L'EMAGNY One of two gîtes with modern furniture in this renovated house in the centre of the village. River bathing and fishing at 1 km, tennis (8 km), riding (12 km). Besançon (15 km) is well worth a visit with its famous clock, cathedral, numerous churches and seventeenth-century buildings, birthplace of Victor Hugo and the Lumière brothers. Living room/kitchenette, 2 bedrooms (2 double and 1 single bed), shower room, central heating. You can shop in the village which has a café or in Besançon.

Prices:	low season	F 400/540	5 people
	high season	F 710/740	IGN 30
	winter season	F 710	

Booking: Haute-Saône Loisirs Accueil E

70/755

TERNUAY Saint-Hilaire This detached, renovated house is situated in the region of "1000 pools". The owner has his own fishing pond where visitors may enjoy free fishing. Swimming-pool and tennis (18 km); ski-ing (20 km). Living room (1 double divan), kitchen, 2 bedrooms (1 double, 2 single and 1 child's bed), bathroom, oil heating, grounds. Mobile shops in the village (2 km); shopping (8 km) or at Lure (18 km).

Prices:	low season	F 460/710	7 people
	high season	F 740/825	IGN 31
	winter season	F 740	

Booking: Haute-Saône Loisirs Accueil E

70/928

VELLEFRIE One of three gîtes in this renovated detached house, equipped with modern furniture. It is within the village and you can fish in the local river. Riding (4 km), tennis, sailing and a swimming-pool (12 km). Living room (1 double divan), kitchen, 2 bedrooms (1 double and 2 single beds), bathroom, central heating, grounds. Mobile butcher, baker and grocer call, there is a café in the village and shops at 3 km. Other shops in the town of Vesoul (12 km).

Prices:	low season	F 380/540	6 people
	high season	F 710/740	IGN 30
	winter season	F 710	

Booking: Haute-Saône Loisirs Accueil E

70/982

15

Map

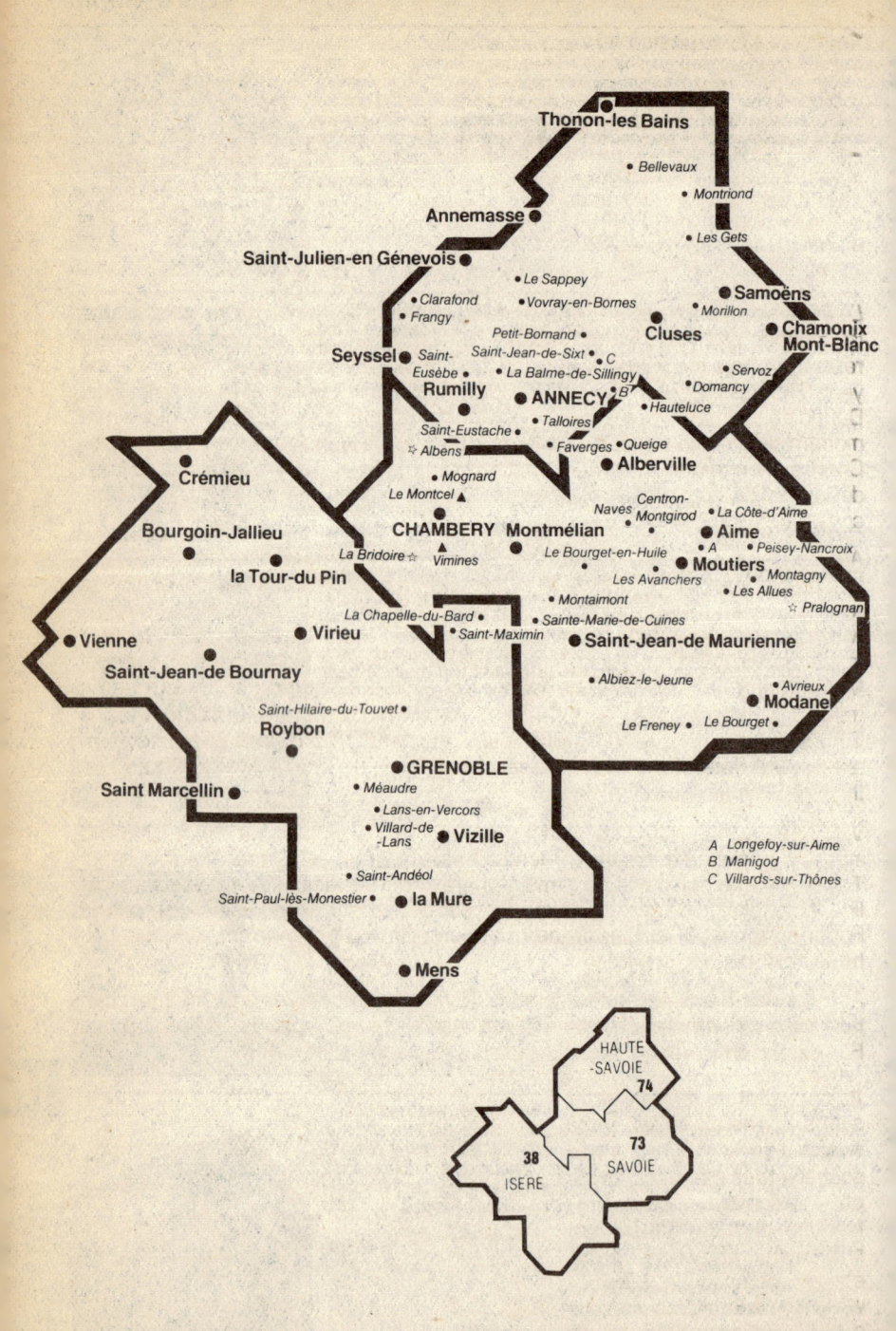

- Thonon-les Bains
- Bellevaux
- Montriond
- Annemasse
- Les Gets
- Saint-Julien-en-Génevois
- Le Sappey
- Samoëns
- Clarafond
- Vovray-en-Bornes
- Morillon
- Frangy
- Petit-Bornand
- Cluses
- Chamonix Mont-Blanc
- Seyssel
- Saint-Jean-de-Sixt
- Saint-Eusèbe
- C
- Servoz
- Rumilly
- La Balme-de-Sillingy
- Domancy
- B
- ANNECY
- Saint-Eustache
- Talloires
- Hauteluce
- ☆ Albens
- Faverges
- Queige
- Crémieu
- Mognard
- Alberville
- Le Montcel ▲
- Centron-Montgirod
- La Côte-d'Aime
- Bourgoin-Jallieu
- Naves
- Aime
- CHAMBERY
- A
- Peisey-Nancroix
- La Bridoire ☆
- Vimines
- Montmélian
- Le Bourget-en-Huile
- Moutiers
- Montagny
- la Tour-du-Pin
- Les Avanchers
- Les Allues
- ☆ Pralognan
- Montaimont
- La Chapelle-du-Bard
- Sainte-Marie-de-Cuines
- Vienne
- Virieu
- Saint-Maximin
- Saint-Jean-de-Maurienne
- Saint-Jean-de-Bournay
- Albiez-le-Jeune
- Avrieux
- Saint-Hilaire-du-Touvet
- Modane
- Roybon
- Le Freney
- Le Bourget
- Saint-Marcellin
- GRENOBLE
- Méaudre
- Lans-en-Vercors
- *A* Longefoy-sur-Aime
- Villard-de-Lans
- Vizille
- *B* Manigod
- *C* Villards-sur-Thônes
- Saint-Andéol
- Saint-Paul-lès-Monestier
- la Mure
- Mens

HAUTE-SAVOIE 74
38 ISERE
73 SAVOIE

16 FRENCH ALPS

Le Pays des quatre saisons (the land of four seasons), famed for its breathtaking landscapes of snow covered mountains, lush green valleys, parks and nature reserves where the fresh air and mountain climate can be enjoyed throughout the year. The bustling, university town of Grenoble, former capital of the old province, Dauphiné, is renowned for the nineteenth-century travellers who pioneered modern ski-ing and alpinism; situated by the river Isère and backed by the Grande-Chartreuse mountains, there are many splendid views. Take a cable-car to Fort-de-la-Bastille from where you can see the old quarter and the Olympic Village, constructed in 1968 for the Winter Olympics.

Aix-les-Bains is a lovely town situated on the shore of the largest lake in France, Lac du Bourget. Once a Roman settlement, this modern day health resort has retained several features from the Roman era including the remains of the baths which can be seen within the spa buildings, and a Gallo-Roman museum, located in the former Temple of Diana. Haute-Savoie boasts the highest peak in Europe, Mont Blanc (4807 metres) and the winter resort of Chamonix at the foot of the mountain is also worth a visit. From here, you can make your way to the Mont Blanc Tunnel (toll charge), open all year round, shortening the distance from northern and central France and western Switzerland into Italy, useful during winter when the high Alpine passes are closed.

Visit Annecy, an ancient town on the edge of the lake, known for the bell-making industry: it was here that the 19-ton bell was made for the Sacré-Coeur in Paris. The old town is particularly charming where picturesque houses in narrow streets line the banks of the canals. Enjoy also, some of the local food and wine, such as Fondue Savoyarde, as the cuisine in this border region has been greatly influenced by its neighbouring countries.

At Evian-les-Bains, where the famous "Evian" mineral water is bottled, you can take trips round Lake Geneva, calling at some forty-six places on the shore in France and Switzerland. The complete tour lasts 10 hours.

If you want to enjoy winter sports or merely enjoy some spectacular mountain scenery, then the resort towns of Mégève, Chamonix, Morzine and Val d'Isère will hold many attractions being equally beautiful in summer when the mountains are still capped with snow.

Isère

LA CHAPELLE-DU-BARD Beauvoir The local council have converted this old school into two gîtes with modern furnishings. Allevard-les-Bains (9 km) is a popular spa where leisure amenities include a casino, miniature golf and a ski station for winter visitors. Altitude 860 metres. Living room, kitchen, 2 bedrooms (1 double, 5 single beds), bathroom, electric central heating, enclosed courtyard with garden furniture. Linen available. Grocer in the village; other shopping and restaurant at Allevard-les-Bains.

Prices: low season F 610
high season F 940
winter season F 1015/1440

7 people
IGN 53

Booking: Isère booking service E
38/335.100

LA CHAPELLE-DU-BARD Beauvoir A second gîte with modern furnishings on the ground floor of the renovated school described above, 7 km from the village (altitude 860 metres). Good sports facilities at Allevard-les-Bains (9 km). The delightful château town of Chambéry at 20 km approx. is worth a visit. Living room, kitchen, 1 bedroom (5 single beds), bathroom, electric central heating, enclosed courtyard with garden furniture. Linen available (F30 per set per week); grocer in the village and other shopping at Allevard-les-Bains.

Prices: low season F 500
high season F 790
winter season F 830/1235

5 people
IGN 53

Booking: Isère booking service E
38/335.200

LANS-EN-VERCORS Bouilly A traditionally furnished gîte, one of two in a renovated house, outside the village (altitude 1000 metres). Plenty of leisure facilities at Villard-de-Lans (5 km). The university town of Grenoble, with theatre, museum and other places of interest, is at 26 km. Living room (1 double divan), kitchen, 3 bedrooms (2 double, 3 single beds), bathroom, electric central heating, terrace, garage, open ground. Farm produce, shopping and restaurant in the village (3 km).

Prices: low season F 720
high season F 1305
winter season F 1205/1855

9 people
IGN 52

Booking: Isère booking service E

38/909.100

MEAUDRE Les Morets A traditionally furnished gîte in the owners' renovated house, on a livestock farm, 2 km from Méaudre (altitude 1000 metres), a centre for cross-country ski-ing. The town also has a nightclub, swimming-pool, tennis and downhill ski runs. Do not miss Grenoble (36 km). Living room/kitchenette, 2 bedrooms (2 double, 2 single beds), bathroom, central heating, terrace, open ground. Local farm produce available; shopping in the town and a restaurant at 1.5 km.

Prices: low season F 700
high season F 1130
winter season F 1310/1720

6 people
IGN 52

Booking: Isère booking service E
38/934.100

SAINT-ANDEOL A house comprising two purpose-built gîtes in a group of holiday homes owned by the local council in the lovely Vercors regional park, 1 km from the village (altitude 1020 metres). At La Mure (20 km approx.) see the Château Delphinal and fourteenth-century market halls (market day—Monday). Living room/kitchenette (2 single divans), 2 bedrooms (1 double, 2 single beds), bathroom, electric central heating, open ground. Farm produce in the village; mobile grocer calls; other shopping at Monestier-de-Clermont (12 km).

Prices: low season F 480
high season F 950
winter season F 630/1030

6 people
IGN 52

Booking: Isère booking service E
38/956.100

Isère

SAINT-HILAIRE-DU-TOUVET Les Gaudes A lovely modern chalet, comprising two traditionally furnished gîtes outside the village (altitude 1000 metres). Take the steep funicular railway for a view over the Belledonne range. Leisure activities organised by the local tourist office include gliding, climbing and pot-holing. Living room, kitchen, 1 bedroom (1 double, 4 single beds), bathroom, electric central heating, balcony, enclosed ground. Shopping in the village or at Grenoble (25 km).

Prices: low season   F 805   **6 people**
high season   F 1250   IGN 53
winter season   F 1035/1350

Booking: Isère booking service   **E**
38/618.200

SAINT-HILAIRE-DU-TOUVET Granet A modern, traditionally furnished chalet, set in a group of houses, 2 km from the village (altitude 1000 metres), which is surrounded by forests with ski-ing facilities and other amenities. The lively département capital of Grenoble, with twelfth-century cathedral and other places of interest, is 25 km away. Living room/kitchenette (2 single divans), 2 bedrooms (1 double, 2 single beds), shower room, electric central heating, balcony, carport, open ground. Shopping in the village; a restaurant (1.5 km).

Prices: low season   F 790   **6 people**
high season   F 1300   IGN 53
winter season   F 1035/1420

Booking: Isère booking service   **E**
38/607.100

SAINT-MAXIMIN A traditionally furnished ground-floor gîte, one of two in a large old house, 2 km from the village. At Pontcharra (2 km), see the Château Bayard and take the little tourist train over the Gorges de Breda. Ski-ing at 20 km. Living room, kitchen, 2 bedrooms (1 double, 6 single beds), bathroom, oil-fired central heating, garden with furniture and child's swing. Farm produce in the village; other shopping and restaurant at Pontcharra.

Prices: low season   F 770   **8 people**
high season   F 1340   IGN 53
winter season   F 1110/1440

Booking: Isère booking service   **E**
38/350.100

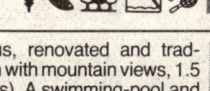

SAINT-PAUL-LES-MONESTIER A spacious, renovated and traditionally furnished house set in an open garden with mountain views, 1.5 km from the village centre (altitude 870 metres). A swimming-pool and tennis at Monestier-de-Clermont (2 km); water sports at Avignonet-Monteynard lake (12 km); ski-ing at 13 km. Living room/kitchenette, 3 bedrooms (3 double, 2 single beds), shower room, electric central heating, terrace. Farm produce, other shopping and restaurant in the village, or at Monestier-de-Clermont.

Prices: low season   F 745   **8 people**
high season   F 1310   IGN 52
winter season   F 960/1310

Booking: Isère booking service   **E**
38/250.100

VILLARD-DE-LANS Pont de l'Essarton One of two gîtes with country-style furnishings in the owners' modern chalet, 1 km from the town centre where there is a skating rink, miniature golf and child-minding facilities. A ski station at 5 km. Take a day trip to the interesting town of Grenoble (30 km). Living room/kitchenette (washing and washing-up machines), 3 bedrooms (1 double, 4 single beds), bathroom, central heating, courtyard. Local farm produce; other shopping and restaurant in the town.

Prices: low season   F 700   **6 people**
high season   F 1390   IGN 52
winter season   F 1360/1930

Booking: Isère booking service   **E**
38/979.100

16

Savoie

AIME Villaroland One of two gîtes in the owners' modern chalet with traditional furnishings, 1 km from the village (altitude 720 metres). Aime lies in a valley at the foot of the Pourri and Bellecôte glaciers and has gallo-roman ruins, a Romanesque basilica and museum. Swimming-pool and canoeing at 16 km. Living room/kitchenette, 2 bedrooms (1 double, 3 single beds), shower room, central heating, open ground. Farm produce, shopping and restaurant in the village or at Moutiers (12 km approx.).

Prices:	low season	F 1080	**5 people**
	high season	F 1200	IGN 53
	winter season	F 1080/1200	

Booking: Savoie Loisirs Accueil E
73/2921

ALBIEZ-LE-JEUNE One of three traditionally furnished gîtes in a renovated house at the village centre (altitude 1350 metres). Local forest walks (1 km) and downhill and cross-country ski-ing at 5 km. Saint-Jean-de-Maurienne (17 km) is an attractive cathedral city with swimming-pool, tennis and other amenities. Living room/kitchenette (1 double divan), 2 bedrooms (1 double and 3 single beds), bathroom, electric heating, open ground. Farm produce and shopping in the village; a restaurant at 5 km.

Prices:	low season	F 700	**7 people**
	high season	F 1235	IGN 53
	winter season	F 965/1340	

Booking: Savoie Loisirs Accueil E
73/1607

LES ALLUES A traditionally furnished ground-floor gîte, one of three in an attractive chalet near the village centre (altitude 1000 metres). Meribel (5 km) is a popular winter and summer resort where leisure facilities include grass ski-ing, hang-gliding, golf and of course winter ski-ing. Living room/kitchenette (2 single beds), 1 bedroom (1 double bed), bathroom, electric heating, open ground. Shopping and farm produce in the village; a restaurant at 5 km.

Prices:	low season	F 1000	**4 people**
	high season	F 1200	IGN 53
	winter season	F 2200/2400	

Booking: Savoie Loisirs Accueil E
73/3405

LES AVANCHERS La Charmette A ground-floor gîte in the owners' modern, traditionally furnished house, 3 km from the village (altitude 1300 metres). It lies in the Tarentaise region with good ski-ing resorts and at the edge of the Vanoise National Park. Visit the cathedral town of Moutiers (10 km). Kitchen (1 double divan), 1 bedroom (3 single beds), shower room, electric heating, open ground. Shopping, farm produce and restaurant in the village or at Moutiers.

Prices:	low season	F 628	**5 people**
	high season	F 937	IGN 53
	winter season	F 1761/2153	

Booking: Savoie Loisirs Accueil E
73/2960

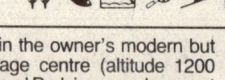

AVRIEUX A ground-floor gîte, one of two in the owner's modern but traditionally furnished chalet near the village centre (altitude 1200 metres). Modane (5 km) in the Vanoise National Park is a popular resort both in winter and summer; visit the panoramic restaurant at 2200 metres. Living room/kitchenette (1 double divan), 1 bedroom (1 double bed), shower room, electric heating. Farm produce in the village; other shopping and restaurant at Modane.

Prices:	low season	F 800	**4 people**
	high season	F 900	IGN 53
	winter season	F 800/1150	

Booking: Savoie Loisirs Accueil E
73/1721

Savoie

LE BOURGET A small, traditionally furnished gîte, one of three in a renovated house (altitude 1150 metres). Modane (5 km) lies in the Vanoise Regional Park with exceptional flora and fauna. You can see the monumental entrance to the first alpine tunnel there; good ski-ing. Kitchen, 1 bedroom (1 double and 1 single bed), shower room, central heating, enclosed courtyard. Farm produce and other shopping in the village; a restaurant at Modane.

Prices:	low season	F 610	3 people
	high season	F 800/860	IGN 53
	winter season	F 855/1050	

Booking: Savoie Loisirs Accueil E
73/2813

LE BOURGET-EN-HUILE A small, traditionally furnished gîte, one of four in a renovated house at the village centre (altitude 840 metres). This is a delightful hilly region of vineyards, small lakes and feudal châteaux. Swimming-pool and tennis (12 km); ski-ing at 20 km. Living room/kitchenette (2 single beds), 1 bedroom (1 double bed), shower room, central heating, ground. Mobile shops call and fresh dairy produce in the village; other shopping (6 km) or at Pontcharra (20 km).

Prices:	low season	F 650	4 people
	high season	F 800	IGN 53
	winter season	F 900	

Booking: Savoie Loisirs Accueil E
73/324

CENTRON-MONTGIROD A traditionally furnished gîte in the owners' modern house, near the village centre. Fishing and canoeing nearby. Many other leisure facilities including cinema, tennis and climbing at the lively town of Bourg-Saint-Maurice (15 km approx.). Ski-ing at 23 km. Kitchen, 2 bedrooms (2 double, 1 single bed, 1 double divan), shower room, central heating, open ground. Farm produce in the village; other shopping and restaurant at Aime (4 km).

Prices:	low season	F 565	7 people
	high season	F 675/725	IGN 53
	winter season	F 565/825	

Booking: Savoie Loisirs Accueil E
73/3163

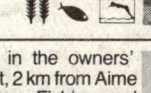

LA COTE D'AIME Le Villard A ground-floor gîte in the owners' renovated and traditionally furnished house in a hamlet, 2 km from Aime which has a museum, Roman ruins and other sites. Fishing and canoeing in Aime; a swimming-pool at 9 km and ski-ing at 18 km. Altitude 800 metres. Kitchen, 3 bedrooms (3 double and 1 single bed), bathroom, central heating, balcony, carport, open ground. Linen available. Farm produce available, shopping and restaurant in Aime.

Prices:	low season	F 960	7 people
	high season	F 1080	IGN 53
	winter season	F 1200/1540	

Booking: Savoie Loisirs Accueil E
73/3252

LE FRENEY A traditionally furnished, ground-floor gîte, one of four in a renovated village house (altitude 1040 metres). The gîte is just 3 km from Modane, a popular ski resort in the Vanoise Regional Park; try the local honey and take a day trip to Montcenis lake (40 km approx.). Living room/kitchenette, 2 bedrooms (1 double and 4 single beds), shower room, electric heating, open ground. Mobile butcher, baker and grocer call; other shopping and restaurant in Modane.

Prices:	low season	F 975	6 people
	high season	F 1020	IGN 53
	winter season	F 1000/1320	

Booking: Savoie Loisirs Accueil E
73/2065

16

Savoie

HAUTELUCE Col des Saisies A traditionally furnished studio, one of eight apartments in a modern block outside the village (6 km). Local riding and ski-ing; swimming-pool at 17 km. Albertville (32 km) is a fortified medieval city, former seat of the Savoy Dukes with many interesting sites and attractions. Altitude 1650 metres. Studio room/kitchenette (4 single beds), bathroom, central heating, balcony. Farm produce available and shops at 150 metres; a restaurant at 17 km.

Prices:	low season	F 750	**4 people**
	high season	F 940/1185	*IGN 53*
	winter season	F 1250/2320	

Booking: Savoie Loisirs Accueil E

73/1390

HAUTELUCE Col des Saisies A ground-floor gîte, one of twenty apartments in modern chalets, some 6 km from the village (altitude 1650 metres). Hauteluce is a winter and summer resort which enjoys good snow and has views over Mont Blanc; ski school and ice skating available. Visit historic Albertville (32 km). Living room/kitchenette (1 double bed), 1 bedroom (4 single beds), bathroom, electric heating, terrace. Farm produce and other shopping at 150 metres; a restaurant at 17 km.

Prices:	low season	F 875	**6 people**
	high season	F 1112/1195	*IGN 53*
	winter season	F 1600/2830	

Booking: Savoie Loisirs Accueil E

73/1335

LONGEFOY-SUR-AIME Montalbert One of three gîtes in a traditionally furnished, modern house near the village centre, with ski-ing right there. Local forest and fishing (2 km). Canoeing at the pleasant town of Aime (8 km), and a swimming-pool at 9 km. Altitude 1250 metres. Living room/kitchenette (2 single beds), 1 bedroom (2 double beds), bathroom, open fire, electric heating, balcony, open ground. Farm produce and other shopping in the village and a restaurant at Aime.

Prices:	low season	F 650	**6 people**
	high season	F 950	*IGN 53*
	winter season	F 1400/2200	

Booking: Savoie Loisirs Accueil E

73/3350

MOGNARD One of four traditionally furnished gîtes in a renovated house at the village centre. Do not miss the lovely old spa town of Aix-les-Bains (10 km), with its Roman baths and other historic sites. The varied leisure facilities there include water ski-ing, yachting and a casino. Kitchen, 1 bedroom (1 double and 2 single beds), shower room, electric heating, enclosed ground. Farm produce available in the village; other shopping at 6 km and a restaurant at 3 km.

Prices:	low season	F 515	**4 people**
	high season	F 615/695	*IGN 53*
	winter season	F 570/660	

Booking: Savoie Loisirs Accueil E

73/62

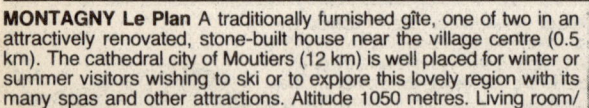

MONTAGNY Le Plan A traditionally furnished gîte, one of two in an attractively renovated, stone-built house near the village centre (0.5 km). The cathedral city of Moutiers (12 km) is well placed for winter or summer visitors wishing to ski or to explore this lovely region with its many spas and other attractions. Altitude 1050 metres. Living room/kitchenette (1 double divan), 2 bedrooms (5 single beds), bathroom, electric heating, terrace, open ground. Farm produce available; shopping at 1.5 km and a restaurant at 5 km.

Prices:	low season	F 1000	**7 people**
	high season	F 1250	*IGN 53*
	winter season	F 1000/1250	

Booking: Savoie Loisirs Accueil E

73/3484

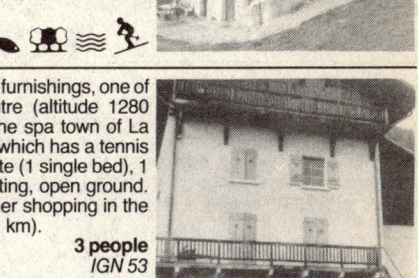

Savoie

MONTAIMONT La Pontchéry One of five small, traditionally furnished gîtes in a renovated house near the village centre with local downhill and cross-country ski-ing and forest walks. Fishing (3 km) and a lake at 6 km. Many other leisure amenities at the interesting old cathedral city of Saint-Jean-de-Maurienne (19 km). Altitude 1100 metres. Kitchen, 1 bedroom (1 double, 3 single beds), shower room, central heating, open ground. Farm produce and restaurant in the village other shopping at Saint-Jean-de-Maurienne.

Prices:	low season	F 750	**5 people**
	high season	F 1000/F1110	IGN 53
	winter season	F 1110/1940	

Booking: Savoie booking service E
73/2330

NAVES Fontaine A ground-floor gîte with traditional furnishings, one of three in a renovated chalet near the village centre (altitude 1280 metres). Local cross-country ski-ing (2 km). Visit the spa town of La Lechère-les-Bains (11 km) in the Tarentaise valley which has a tennis court and swimming facilities. Living room/kitchenette (1 single bed), 1 bedroom (1 double bed), shower room, central heating, open ground. Mobile grocer and baker call; farm produce and other shopping in the village; a restaurant at Notre-Dame-de-Briançon (11 km).

Prices:	low season	F 835	**3 people**
	high season	F 960/1040	IGN 53
	winter season	F 1000/1220	

Booking: Savoie Loisirs Accueil E
73/3539

PEISEY-NANCROIX A traditionally furnished gîte, one of two in a modern house near the village centre (altitude 1300 metres). Local tennis (0.2 km); climbing at 3 km and other leisure facilities at the lively town of Bourg-Saint-Maurice (20 km). Kitchen, 2 bedrooms (1 double, 2 single beds and 1 single divan), shower room, electric heating, balcony, garage. Shopping and fresh farm produce in the village or at Landry (12 km); a restaurant at 2 km.

Prices:	low season	F 545	**5 people**
	high season	F 686/765	IGN 53
	winter season	F 1125/1605	

Booking: Savoie Loisirs Accueil E
73/3564

QUEIGE A traditionally furnished studio, one of two gîtes on the ground floor of the owners' renovated house on a mixed farm near the village centre. Fishing and tennis locally and a swimming-pool at 8 km. At the historic town of Albertville see the well-preserved medieval Conflans quarter. Altitude 580 metres. Studio room/kitchenette (1 double and 3 single beds), shower room, electric heating, terrace, open ground. Farm produce and other shopping in the village (0.5 km); a restaurant at 8 km.

Prices:	low season	F 600	**5 people**
	high season	F 1000	IGN 53
	winter season	F 900/1300	

Booking: Savoie Loisirs Accueil E
73/1475

SAINT-MARIE-DE-CUINES La Cour One of three gîtes, traditionally furnished, in a renovated house near the village centre. A swimming-pool at Saint-Jean-de-Maurienne (7 km); ski-ing and a lake at 15 km. You are close enough for a day trip to the interesting town of Grenoble (50 km approx.) where chocolate is a speciality. Living room/kitchenette, 1 bedroom (1 double, 2 single beds), shower room, electric heating, balcony, carport, enclosed ground. Farm produce and shopping in the village; a restaurant at Saint-Jean-de-Maurienne.

Prices:	low season	F 675	**4 people**
	high season	F 900/950	IGN 53
	winter season	on request	

Booking: Savoie Loisirs Accueil E
73/2530

16

Savoie

ALBENS Pégis *Chambre d'hôte* accommodation in the owners' renovated and traditionally furnished house on a mixed farm where you may purchase fresh produce, 2 km from the village. Sailing and canoeing on the lake at the lovely spa town of Aix-les-Bains (13 km); whilst there take a boat across the lake to Hautecombe Abbey. Two rooms available on the first floor: bedroom 1 (1 double, 1 single bed), bedroom 2 (1 double bed); shared bathroom and open ground. A restaurant in the village and shops at Aix-les-Bains. 
Prices: on request **5 people**
IGN 53
Booking: M A. ANDRE, Pégis, 73410 Albens. Tel. (79) 63 03 15.

73/4600

LA BRIDOIRE *Chambre d'hôte* accommodation in the owners' modern house with traditional furnishings, where there is also a gîte, at the village centre. Fishing and tennis in the village; bathing at a lake (3 km); ski-ing at 20 km. Chambéry, capital of the département, is at just 15 km. Four rooms available on the second floor: 1 room has 1 double and 1 single bed and 3 rooms have 1 double bed each. Central heating; shared bathroom, shower, and kitchen. Shopping and restaurant in the village (0.1 km). 
Prices: on request **9 people**
IGN 53
Booking: M L. DE MARCO, 73520 La Bridoire. Tel. (79) 31 13 47.

73/4635

PRALOGNAN Les Granges *Chambre d'hôte* accommodation in a renovated and traditionally furnished building on a mixed farm, where there are also five gîtes, 1 km from the village (altitude 1430 metres). Pralognan is a winter sports resort at the heart of the Vanoise Regional Park. Four rooms available with private washing facilities: bedrooms 1 and 3 have 1 double and 1 single bed each, bedroom 2 (1 double, 2 single beds), bedroom 4 (1 double bed). Lounge, recreation room and open ground at your disposal. Main meals available or a restaurant and shopping in the village. **12 people** 
Prices: on request
Booking: M H. BLANC, Les Granges, 73710 Pralognan.
Tel. (79) 08 72 14.
73/4760

LE MONTCEL Les Mermoz *Aire naturelle de camping* on flat, partly shaded grassland on a mixed farm, 0.5 km from the village centre (altitude 560 metres). Many sites and amenities at Aix-les-Bains (8 km), including the Roman baths, sailing, tennis, etc. One hot and 2 cold showers, recreation room (table tennis), swings for children, laundry room. Farm produce from the owners; other shopping in the village or at Aix-les-Bains where there are restaurants. 
Prices: on request IGN 53
Booking: M H. MAILLAND, Les Mermoz, 73100 Le Montcel.
Tel. (79) 61 24 46.

73/24

VIMINES Le Roncin *Aire naturelle de camping* on a pleasant site—a partly shaded flat field, some 2.5 km fromm the village (altitude 550 metres). You are no more than 10 km from historic Chambéry with its wealth of leisure and cultural amenities. At 18 km is the splendid Le Bourget lake with facilities for sailing and other water sports. One hot and 1 cold shower, recreation room, laundry room. Farm produce available from the owners; other shopping and restaurant at Cognin (6 km). 
Prices: on request IGN 53
Booking: M G. DENARIE, Le Roncin, 73160 Vimines.
Tel. (79) 69 33 78.

73/25

Haute-Savoie

LA BALME-DE-SILLINGY La Bonasse A simply furnished, first-floor gîte, one of two in the owners' renovated house on a mixed farm where you may buy fresh milk and eggs. Annecy with its vast château and famous lake is at 12 km. Ski-ing (28 km). Altitude 500 metres. Living room/kitchenette (1 double divan), 1 bedroom (1 double, 1 single bed), bathroom, electric heating, balcony, open courtyard. Shopping and restaurant in the village (3 km).

Prices:	low season	F 688	**5 people**
	high season	F 941	IGN 45
	winter season	F 693	

Booking: Haute-Savoie booking service

74/5076

BELLEVAUX La Chèverie A recently-built chalet containing four gîtes with modern furnishings, and the owners' own holiday apartment. There is a ski school in the village (8 km). The spa town of Thonon-les-Bains on Lake Geneva is well worth a visit (33 km). Altitude 1100 metres. Living room/kitchenette (1 double divan), 2 bedrooms (1 double, 4 single bunk beds), shower room, electric heating, balcony, open ground. Farm produce, shopping and restaurant in the village.

Prices:	low season	F 995	**8 people**
	high season	F 1519/1722	IGN 45
	winter season	F 1257/2011	

Booking: Haute-Savoie booking service

74/9082

BELLEVAUX La Cluse A simply furnished, ground-floor gîte, one of two in the owners' modern house, 3.5 km from the village centre (altitude 1000 metres). Good mountain and forest walks on marked footpaths locally; a swimming-pool at 13 km. Many other leisure amenities at Thonon-les-Bains (23 km). Kitchen, 1 bedroom (1 double, 2 single bunk beds), shower room, central heating, terrace, open ground. Farm produce, other shopping and restaurant in the village or at Thonon-les-Bains.

Prices:	low season	F 802	**4 people**
	high season	F 995/1048	IGN 45
	winter season	F 1048/1487	

Booking: Haute-Savoie booking service

74/9086

BELLEVAUX Le Frêne A simply furnished gîte on the ground floor of a renovated chalet in a hamlet outside the village (altitude 1000 metres). Ski-ing at Bellevaux-Hirmentaz (7 km). Hire bicycles at Thonon-les-Bains (28 km) to explore this lovely region in summer. Kitchen, 3 bedrooms (2 double and 2 single beds), shower room, central heating, open ground. Linen available (F30 per set per week). Shopping and restaurant in the village or at Boëge (15 km).

Prices:	low season	F 642	**6 people**
	high season	F 1123	IGN 45
	winter season	F 642/1498	

Booking: Haute-Savoie booking service

74/9057

CLARAFOND A small, renovated and simply furnished village gîte (altitude 500 metres). Swimming-pool and tennis at Clarafond (2 km); sailing at Lake Genissiat (3 km). Other leisure amenities (including trout fishing) at Frangy (9 km) which enjoys an exceptionally mild alpine climate. Living room (2 single beds), kitchen, 1 bedroom (1 double bed), shower room, wood stove, balcony, garage. Shopping in the village or at Frangy; a restaurant at 1 km.

Prices:	low season	F 770	**4 people**
	high season	F 936	IGN 45

Booking: Haute-Savoie booking service

74/5230

16

Haute-Savoie

DOMANCY Letraz A ground-floor gîte with modern furnishings in a renovated house on the owners' village farm with splendid views over the Mont Blanc range (altitude 570 metres). The town of Sallanches (3 km) was first established in Roman times and now boasts a swimming-pool, tennis and riding among its leisure facilities. Ski-ing at 6 km. Kitchen, 2 bedrooms (1 double, 2 single and 1 single folding bed), bathroom, central heating, garage, open ground. Farm produce in the village; other shopping and restaurant at Sallanches.

Prices:	low season	F 535	**5 people**
	high season	F 952/1102	IGN 45
	winter season	F 1123/1551	

Booking: Haute-Savoie booking service
74/8222

DOMANCY La Plaine One of three simply furnished gîtes in the owners' house on their mixed farm, 2 km from the village centre (altitude 570 metres). Chamonix (20 km) at the foot of the Mont Blanc range, offers all kinds of winter sports and plenty of amenities for summer visitors, including golf. Kitchen, 2 bedrooms (1 double and 2 single beds), bathroom, central heating, open ground. Fresh farm produce available; other shopping and restaurant at Le Fayet (3 km).

Prices:	low season	F 749	**4 people**
	high season	F 909	IGN 45
	winter season	F 963/1230	

Booking: Haute-Savoie booking service
74/8215

FAVERGES One of two gîtes (this one on the ground floor), furnished in simple, modern style in the owners' home (altitude 600 metres). Bicycle hire, tennis and ski-ing at Faverges (4 km) which is just 8 km from the beautiful Annecy lake; Annecy itself is at 26 km. Living room/kitchenette (1 double divan), 1 bedroom (1 double bed), bathroom (small bath), central heating, terrace, open garden. Linen available (F30 per set per week). Shopping and restaurant in the village.

Prices:	low season	F 802	**4 people**
	high season	F 1016	IGN 53

Booking: Haute-Savoie booking service

74/5476

FRANGY Champagne A second-floor gîte in the owners' modern farmhouse, 2 km from the town which lies on the river Usses (good trout fishing). It is ideally situated for day trips to Annecy lake (25 km), Geneva (34 km) and the old spa town of Aix-les-Bains (42 km). Living room/kitchenette, 2 bedrooms (2 double and 2 single beds), bathroom, electric heating, open ground. Shopping, farm produce and restaurant in the village or at Bellegarde (16 km).

Prices:	low season	F 749	**6 people**
	high season	F909/963	IGN 45

Booking: Haute-Savoie booking service

74/5503

FRANGY Moisy An old house with simple, country-style furnishings near the owners' mixed farm (fresh produce available) outside the town. Bicycles for hire and sailing at a lake at La Balme-de-Sillingy (16 km). Do not miss the beautiful old town of Annecy (26 km). Living room, kitchen, 2 bedrooms (2 double and 1 single bed), bathroom (washing machine), no heating, small enclosed ground. Shopping and restaurant in the village or at La Balme-de-Sillingy.

Prices:	low season	F 771	**5 people**
	high season	F 1062	IGN 45

Booking: Haute-Savoie booking service

74/5502

Haute-Savoie

LES GETS Les Mouilles A renovated chalet with country-style furnishings, situated in a group of other houses, but some 4 km from the town which has good ski-ing facilities (altitude 1000 metres). Bicycle hire, swimming-pool, skating rink and other amenities at Morzine (2.5 km), another ski resort. Living room, kitchen, 2 bedrooms (1 double, 2 single beds), bathroom, fireplace (wood supplied), electric heating, terrace, open ground with garden furniture. Shopping and restaurant at Morzine.

Prices:	low season	F 888	**4 people**
	high season	F 1234/1465	IGN 45
	winter season	F 1401/2501	

Booking: Haute-Savoie booking service 74/7203

MANIGOD Les Combes A spacious, modern chalet, 2 km from Manigod—an old Savoie village with good trout fishing and noted for its cheeses (reblochon, chevrotin, etc.). Swimming-pool, riding and tennis at Thônes (9 km). A visit to Annecy (25 km), with its château, theatre, lake and other attractions, is a must. Altitude 1000 metres. Living room, kitchen, 3 bedrooms and mezzanine landing (3 double and 1 single bed), bathroom, central heating, balcony, garage, open ground. Linen available. Shopping and restaurant in the village or at Thônes.

Prices:	low season	F 984	**7 people**
	high season	F 1391/1540	IGN 45
	winter season	F 1444/2247	

Booking: Haute-Savoie booking service 74/5685

MANIGOD Nant-de-Joux A simply furnished, ground-floor gîte in a renovated chalet where the owners have their own holiday apartment on the first floor. Ski-ing at La Croix Fry—Manigod (9 km); bicycle hire and other leisure amenities at Thônes (8 km); sailing at Annecy lake (30 km). Altitude 1000 metres. Living room (1 child's divan), kitchen, 2 bedrooms (2 double, 1 single bed), bathroom, electric heating, terrace, open ground. Farm produce, other shopping and restaurant in the town (2 km).

Prices:	low season	F 1284	**6 people**
	high season	F 1498/1712	IGN 45
	winter season	F 1284/1926	

Booking: Haute-Savoie booking service 74/5675

MONTRIOND Les Plagnettes A ground-floor gîte with rustic furnishings, one of four in a modern chalet in a peaceful spot, 2 km from the village (altitude 1000 metres). The international ski resort of Avoriaz (8 km). Cluses (25 km approx.) is noted for its clock manufacture and even has a National School of Clock-making. Living room/kitchenette, 1 bedroom (1 double, 2 single beds), bathroom, central heating, terrace, open ground. Shopping and restaurant in the village or at Morzine (3 km).

Prices:	low season	F 1167	**4 people**
	high season	F 1420	IGN 45
	winter season	F 1195/1366	

Booking: Haute-Savoie booking service 74/9494

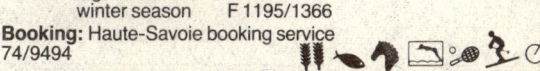

MORILLON A ground-floor gîte in the owners' modern house in the village. Morillon is a small ski resort with child-minding facilities. Plenty to see and do at Samoëns (4 km) including a swimming-pool, tennis, a cinema, botanical gardens and miniature golf. Altitude 700 metres. Living room/kitchenette, 2 bedrooms (2 double beds), shower room, open fire, electric heating, open ground. Shopping, farm produce and restaurant in the village (0.2 km).

Prices:	low season	F 1005	**4 people**
	high season	F 1070/1230	IGN 45
	winter season	F 1348/2193	

Booking: Haute-Savoie booking service 74/7320

16

Haute-Savoie

PETIT-BORNAND Termine A simply furnished first-floor gîte, one of two in a renovated house, 3 km from the village. Ski-ing, skating, bicycle hire and other facilities at Grand-Bornand (11 km) where you should try the reblochon cheese and local ham. Altitude 730 metres. Kitchen, 2 bedrooms (2 double and 1 single bed), shower room, electric and wood heating, open ground. Farm produce from the owners; other shopping and restaurant in the village or at Saint-Pierre-en-Faucigny (5 km).

Prices:	low season	F 609	**5 people**
	high season	F 775	*IGN 45*
	winter season	F 888/995	

Booking: Haute-Savoie booking service

74/7368

SAINT-EUSEBE Thusel A simply furnished gîte in the owners' renovated farmhouse, 2 km from the village centre (altitude 550 metres). Rumilly (10 km) is an agricultural town, very picturesque with arcaded squares and old houses, situated at the confluence of the rivers Chéran and Nephaz. Kitchen, 2 bedrooms (1 double, 2 single beds), bathroom (small bath), no heating, terrace, open ground with garden furniture. Farm produce in the village; other shopping and restaurant at Vallières (5 km).

Prices:	low season	F 684	**4 people**
	high season	F 1070/1134	*IGN 45*

Booking: Haute-Savoie booking service

74/5910

SAINT-EUSTACHE A village gîte, renovated and simply furnished, in an open courtyard (altitude 728 metres). At Saint-Jorioz lake (6 km) there are facilities for water ski-ing and other sports. Visit Albertville (30 km approx.) and see the well-preserved medieval quarter of Conflans. Living room (1 double divan), kitchen, 2 bedrooms (1 double, 3 single beds), bathroom, electric heating, balcony, garage. Linen available. Farm produce and a restaurant in the village; shopping at Saint-Jorioz.

Prices:	low season	F 642	**7 people**
	high season	F 963/1123	*IGN 53*

Booking: Haute-Savoie booking service

74/5918

SAINT-JEAN-DE-SIXT Forgeassoud A simply furnished, ground-floor gîte in the owners' modern chalet, 1 km from the village centre (altitude 980 metres). La Clusaz (4 km) is a popular mountain resort for both winter and summer visitors, where leisure amenities include ski-ing, ice-skating, tennis and miniature golf. Living room/kitchenette (1 double divan), 2 bedrooms (1 double, 2 single beds), shower room, central heating, terrace, open ground. Linen available. Shopping in the village or at Thônes (8 km).

Prices:	low season	F 936	**6 people**
	high season	F 1209/1332	*IGN 45*
	winter season	F 1000/2097	

Booking: Haute-Savoie booking service

74/5978

SAINT-JEAN-DE-SIXT Forgeassoud A first-floor gîte with simple, traditional furnishings in the owners' modern house near the centre of the village at the foot of the Massif des Aravis. Annecy, with its delightful narrow arcaded streets and canals crossed by little bridges, is at 30 km. Kitchen, 2 bedrooms (1 double, 3 single beds), bathroom, central heating, balcony, open ground. Farm produce, other shopping and restaurant in the village (0.8 km) or at Thônes (7 km).

Prices:	low season	F 866	**5 people**
	high season	F 1096/1230	*IGN 45*
	winter season	F 877/2065	

Booking: Haute-Savoie booking service

74/5970

Haute-Savoie

LE SAPPEY A first-floor gîte in the owners' modern house which enjoys superb Alpine views (altitude 900 metres). The old fortified town of Cruseilles (9 km) has a ruined chateau, lake and other leisure amenities; try the local honey and Gruyère cheese. Geneva is just 20 km away. Living room (1 double divan), kitchen, 2 bedrooms (1 double and 2 single beds), bathroom, central heating, balcony, open ground. Farm produce, groceries and a restaurant in the village; other shopping at Cruseilles.

Prices:	low season	F 888	**6 people**
	high season	F 1134	IGN 45
	winter season	F 856/1070	

Booking: Haute-Savoie booking service
74/6030

SERVOZ A simply furnished, ground-floor gîte in the owners' modern chalet where you can wake up to a magnificent view of Mont Blanc (altitude 816 metres). Chamonix (12 km) is a superbly equipped ski resort and boasts Europe's highest cable car (3800 metres). Living room/kitchenette (1 double divan), 2 bedrooms (1 double, 2 single beds), shower room, central heating, terrace, open ground with garden furniture. Linen available (F30 per set per week). Farm produce, shopping and restaurant in the village (0.5 km).

Prices:	low season	F 856	**6 people**
	high season	F 1284/1498	IGN 45
	winter season	F 1444/2204	

Booking: Haute-Savoie booking service
74/8441

TALLOIRES Perroix A spacious, traditionally furnished modern house, 1.8 km from the village centre where you may enjoy varied leisure facilities including sailing at a lake, tennis and fishing. A golf course at Echarvine (1 km) and ski-ing at 25 km. Altitude 500 metres. Living room, kitchen, 4 bedrooms (1 double, 4 single and 1 child's bed), bathroom and shower, central heating, garage (washing machine), enclosed ground with garden furniture. Farm produce, shopping and restaurant in the village or at Annecy (11 km).

Prices:	low season	F 1123	**7 people**
	high season	F 1765/1872	IGN 53

Booking: Haute-Savoie booking service
74/6136

VILLARDS-SUR-THONES Carrouge A ground-floor gîte with simple furnishings in the owners' modern house on a main road just outside the village (0.8 km). All kinds of leisure facilities at Thônes (5 km) where you can also visit a museum of local folklore. Ski-ing at 8 km; Annecy lake (25 km). Altitude 800 metres. Living room/kitchenette (1 double divan), 2 bedrooms (1 double, 2 single beds), bathroom, central heating, small open ground. Linen available. Shopping and restaurant at Thônes; farm produce in the village.

Prices:	low season	F 661	**6 people**
	high season	F 1322/1432	IGN 45
	winter season	F 1013/1983	

Booking: Haute-Savoie booking service
74/6264

VOVRAY-EN-BORNES Chez Baudy A simply furnished, first-floor gîte in the owners' modern chalet, 1 km from the village centre (altitude 840 metres). Cruseilles (5 km) is an interesting old town surrounded by beautiful pine forests with many places of interest including Dronières Park and the fourteenth-century Maison de Fésigny. Kitchen, 3 bedrooms (2 double and 1 single bed), bathroom (washing machine), central heating, terrace, open ground with child's swing. Farm produce in the village; shopping and restaurant at Cruseilles.

Prices:	low season	on request	**5 people**
	high season	F 1551	IGN 45

Booking: Haute-Savoie booking service
74/6325

16

Map

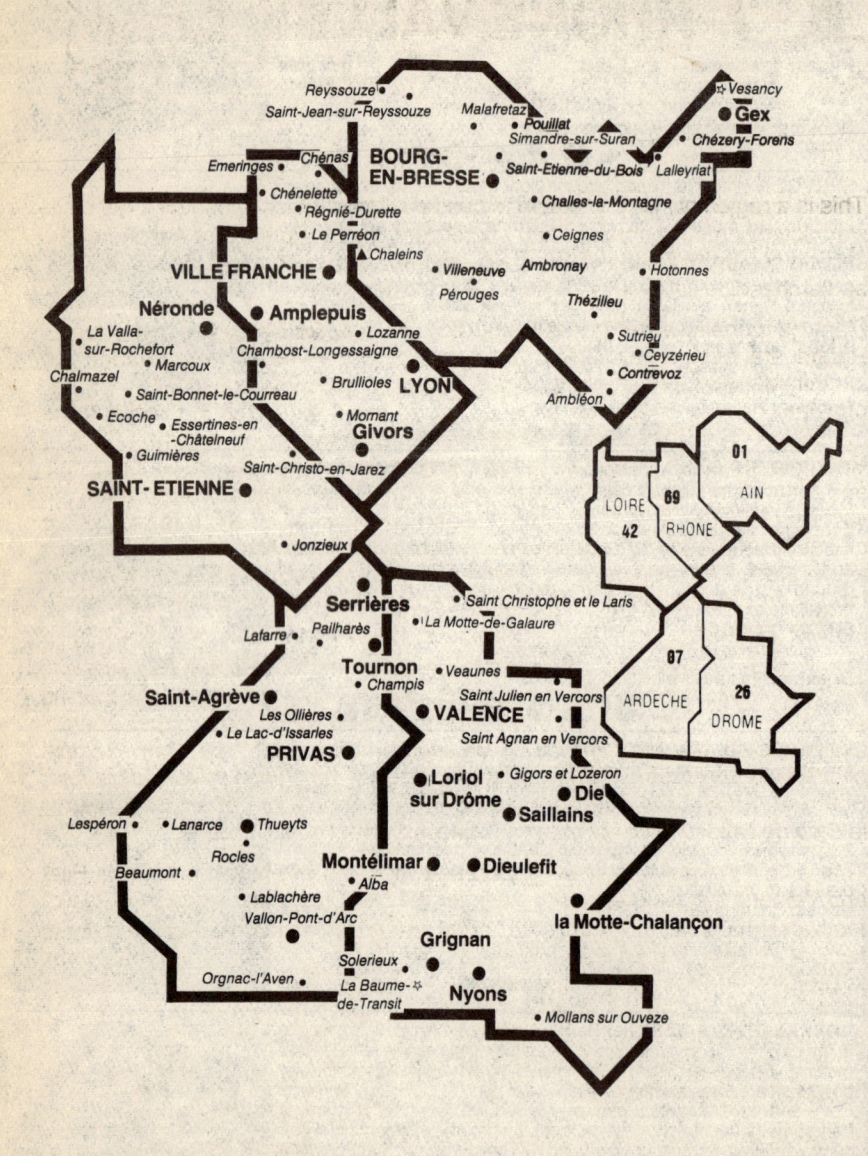

Ain (01) / Rhône (69) / Loire (42) / Ardèche (07) / Drôme (26)

- Reyssouze
- Saint-Jean-sur-Reyssouze
- Malafretaz
- Pouillat
- Simandre-sur-Suran
- ☆ Vesancy
- ● Gex
- Chézery-Forens
- Emeringes
- Chénas
- **BOURG-EN-BRESSE**
- Saint-Etienne-du-Bois
- Lalleyriat
- Chénelette
- Régnié-Durette
- Challes-la-Montagne
- Le Perréon
- ▲ Chaleins
- Ceignes
- **VILLE FRANCHE**
- Villeneuve
- Ambronay
- Hotonnes
- Pérouges
- Thézilleu
- Néronde
- ● Amplepuis
- La Valla-sur-Rochefort
- Lozanne
- Sutrieu
- Chambost-Longessaigne
- Ceyzérieu
- Chalmazel
- Marcoux
- Brullioles
- Contrevoz
- Saint-Bonnet-le-Courreau
- **LYON**
- Ecoche
- Essertines-en-Châtelneuf
- Mornant
- Ambléon
- Guimières
- ● Givors
- **SAINT-ETIENNE**
- Saint-Christo-en-Jarez
- Jonzieux
- ● Serrières
- Saint Christophe et le Laris
- Lafarre
- Pailharès
- La Motte-de-Galaure
- ● Tournon
- Champis
- Veaunes
- **Saint-Agrève**
- Saint Julien en Vercors
- Les Ollières
- ● **VALENCE**
- Le Lac-d'Issarles
- Saint Agnan en Vercors
- **PRIVAS**
- ● Loriol sur Drôme
- Gigors et Lozeron
- ● Die
- Lespéron
- Lanarce
- Thueyts
- ● Saillans
- Beaumont
- Rocles
- ● Montélimar
- ● Dieulefit
- Lablachère
- Alba
- Vallon-Pont-d'Arc
- la Motte-Chalançon
- Orgnac-l'Aven
- Solerieux
- Grignan
- La Baume-de-Transit
- Nyons
- Mollans sur Ouveze

322

17 RHONE VALLEY

This is a region of hills and valleys carved out by the River Rhône as it wends its way southwards. Conquered and appreciated by the Romans at the end of the second century B.C., the valley is still scattered with numerous Roman vestiges, and archaeological excavations are still going on.

Many gastronomical delights and famous wines, of which Beaujolais and Côtes du Rhône are but two examples, make this a land loved by both visitors and inhabitants. At the heart of the region lies Lyon, the third largest city in France, popular because of its ideal situation, being equidistant from the sea and the mountains. The Beaujolais vineyards lie to the north of Lyon and the Côtes du Rhône to the south. There are many wine tasting activities organised for visitors and a tour round the Wine University, where they confer labels on the wine and give visitors the history of wine, is recommended. Lyon, famed for silk, has twenty-four museums and among these, an unusual one to visit, is the Ancient Fabric Museum where there is a collection of fourteenth- to eighteenth-century Italian and Spanish fabrics and also some of Lyon's own beautiful materials, from the seventeenth century onwards.

The Ardèche is appreciated by ramblers and climbers for its lovely, hilly scenery, and the River Ardèche flowing through the département attracts canoeing enthusiasts. The western part of the Ardèche is also well loved by cross-country skiers. Ain too, offers some good ski-ing and the *traversée de l'Ain* is one example of cross-country ski-ing that forms just one stage of the *grande traversée du Jura*. Bourg-en-Bresse, the chief town, is known by gourmets for its famous chickens, *le Bleu de Bresse* (blue cheese) and various types of goats' cheese.

With a lovely climate, interesting food and wine, the two regional parks of Pilat and Vercors, the sweet-smelling lavender fields of Drôme and a continual flow of festivals throughout the year, there is little possibility of boredom. Visit the puppet festival in Lyon, the Lavender Festival in Lesches-en-Dios and the magnificent caves at Orgnac where you can see enormous stalagmites. Take time to explore and discover this valley with its unlimited possibilities.

Ain

AMBLEON A renovated gîte in a small village. Belley (12 km) is a quiet town in a delightful region of forests, mountains, lakes and waterfalls. It has a Gothic-Romanesque cathedral and the chief local industry is tanning and leatherwork; leisure facilities there include tennis and a swimming-pool. Living room (1 double divan), kitchen, 2 bedrooms (3 double beds), shower room, solid fuel stove, terrace, carport, garden and ground. Mobile grocer and baker call; other shopping at 3 km.

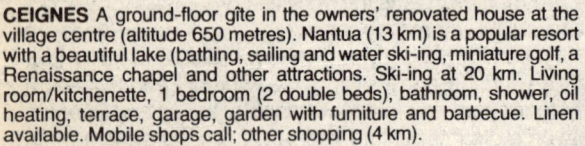

Prices:	low season	F 600	**8 people**
	high season	F 690	IGN 44
	winter season	F 550	

Booking: M L. BERTHELET, Ambléon, 01300 Belley.
Tel. (79) 81 24 38.
01/006.087

AMBRONAY Au Mollard A renovated gîte with traditional country-style furnishings, 3 km from the village. Bathing and sailing from shady beaches on the river Ain at Ambérieu-en-Bugey (6 km). Do not miss Pérouges (15 km approx.) a medieval fortified hill-top village which has been preserved almost intact. Living room/kitchenette, 2 bedrooms (1 double, 2 single and 1 child's bed), shower room, heating, open ground. Mobile shops call and farm produce in the village; other shopping and restaurant at Ambérieu-en-Bugey.

Prices:	low season	F 725	**4/5 people**
	high season	F 780	IGN 44

Booking: Ain booking service   E
01/007.897

CEIGNES A ground-floor gîte in the owners' renovated house at the village centre (altitude 650 metres). Nantua (13 km) is a popular resort with a beautiful lake (bathing, sailing and water ski-ing, miniature golf, a Renaissance chapel and other attractions. Ski-ing at 20 km. Living room/kitchenette, 1 bedroom (2 double beds), bathroom, shower, oil heating, terrace, garage, garden with furniture and barbecue. Linen available. Mobile shops call; other shopping (4 km).

Prices:	low season	F 550	**4 people**
	high season	F 650	IGN 44
	winter season	F 600	

Booking: M J. DELEAZ, Ceignes, 01430 Maillat. Tel. (74) 75 13 19.
01/067.005

CEYZERIEU Le Chavolley One of two gîtes in a renovated house, some 3 km from the village, with local fishing and forest walks. Belley (7 km), at the southern edge of the Jura mountain range, has a swimming-pool and tennis court. A lake at 8 km; ski-ing (30 km). Living room, kitchen, 2 bedrooms (2 double and 1 single bed), bathroom, fireplace (wood supplied), heating, garden. Mobile baker and butcher call; farm produce, other shopping and restaurant in the village.

Prices:	low season	F 850	**5 people**
	high season	F 950	IGN 44
	winter season	F 850	

Booking: Ain booking service   E
01/073.894

CHALEINS One of two gîtes in this renovated and traditionally furnished house in the village, next to the young owners' house and wood-working studio. Stroll by the river Saône (5 km); visit the Château de Flechères (2 km) and the nearby Motor Museum at Rochetaillé. Living room/kitchenette, 2 bedrooms (2 double and 1 single bed), shower room, electric heating, open ground. Farm produce, other shopping and restaurant in the village (0.1 km) or at Villefranche (10 km).

Prices:	low season	F 512	**5 people**
	high season	F 718	IGN 44

Booking: Ain booking service   E
01/075.009

Ain

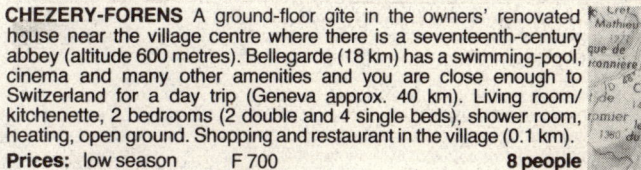

CHALLES-LA-MONTAGNE Sameyriat A renovated house with rustic furnishings, 2 km from the village centre. Poncin (6 km) is an old town with a château dating back to the fourteenth century. All kinds of water sports at Nantua lake (7 km); visit the Roman temple at Izemore (15 km). Ski-ing (20 km). Living room (1 double divan), kitchen, 2 bedrooms (2 double and 1 single bed), bathroom and shower, electric heating, terrace, ground with garden furniture. Mobile shops call; other shopping and restaurant in the village (2 km).

Prices: low season   F 770   **7 people**
         high season   F 840   IGN 44

Booking: M R. ARPIN, Challes-la-Montagne, 01450 Poncin. Tel. (74) 37 22 76.
01/077.121

CHEZERY-FORENS A ground-floor gîte in the owners' renovated house near the village centre where there is a seventeenth-century abbey (altitude 600 metres). Bellegarde (18 km) has a swimming-pool, cinema and many other amenities and you are close enough to Switzerland for a day trip (Geneva approx. 40 km). Living room/kitchenette, 2 bedrooms (2 double and 4 single beds), shower room, heating, open ground. Shopping and restaurant in the village (0.1 km).

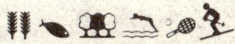

Prices: low season   F 700   **8 people**
         high season   F 900   IGN 44
         winter season   F 1500

Booking: Ain booking service   E
01/104.902

© IGN Red Map 109

CONTREVOZ Mont Brézieu A lovely old renovated stone cottage in a hamlet, where the owners may sell you their wine. Fishing and bathing at a lake (5 km). Swimming-pool and tennis at Belley (8 km), birthplace of Brillat-Savarin, seventeenth-century author of a classic text on gastronomy. Living room (1 double divan), kitchen, 2 bedrooms (2 double and 1 child's bed), bathroom, shower, fireplace, wood stove, terrace, garage, garden. Shopping and restaurant in the village (1.3 km).

Prices: low season   F 620   **7 people**
         high season   F 720   IGN 44

Booking: M J. BERNE, Ambléon, 01300 Belley. Tel. (79) 81 33 50
01/116.901

HOTONNES Les Plans One of four gîtes in a large, renovated and simply furnished house, some 5 km from the village (altitude 1000 metres). Local ski-ing and forest walks. Hauteville (20 km) is a popular health resort and local sites there include the Charabotte waterfall, caves and other geological curiosities. Living room/kitchenette (1 double divan), 2 bedrooms (1 double, 3 single and 1 child's bed), bathroom, shower, fireplace, electric heating, open ground. Shopping and restaurant in the village.

Prices: low season   F 740   **7/8 people**
         high season   F 740   IGN 44
         winter season   F 1270

Booking: Ain booking service   E
01/187.019

LALLEYRIAT Le Rys One of three gîtes in a renovated and traditionally furnished chalet owned by a local carpenter. This is a lovely region ideal for cross-country ski-ing and hang-gliding. Nantua, with its beautiful lake, at 12 km. Altitude 850 metres. Living room, kitchen, 3 bedrooms (2 double, 3 single and 1 child's bed), bathroom and shower, central heating, balcony, open ground. Mobile shops call; other shopping and restaurant in the village (1.8 km).

Prices: low season   F 700   **8 people**
         high season   F 850   IGN 44
         winter season   F 1150

Booking: M E. DURRAFOUR, Lalleyriat, 01130 Nantua.
Tel. (74) 76 08 46.   **E**
01/204.183

17

Ain

MALAFRETAZ Costal A pleasant cottage, situated on a mixed farm, 2 km from the village. Bourg-en-Bresse (12 km) is a busy market town Do not miss the splendid Flamboyant Gothic church in the suburb of Brou. Living room/kitchenette (1 double divan), 2 bedrooms (2 double and 1 single bed), bathroom, shower, fireplace, gas central heating, terrace, carport, open ground. Mobile butcher and grocer call; farm produce; other shopping and restaurant in the village.

Prices:	low season	F 755	
	high season	F 1060	**7 people**
	winter season	F 1010	IGN 44

Booking: M R. GUILLEMAUD, Malafretaz, 01340 Montrevel.
Tel. (74) 32 42 57.
01/229.077

PEROUGES Rapan A small gîte in the owners' renovated house in a hamlet, 2.5 km from the well-preserved mediaeval town of Pérouges which has a museum and craft studios. Take a trip to the bird sanctuary and park at Villars-les-Dombes (25 km) in the region of 'one thousand lakes'. Living room, kitchen (washing machine), 1 bedroom (1 double and 1 child's bed), shower room, gas central heating, terrace, garage, garden with garden furniture and barbecue. A restaurant nearby (0.8 km); farm produce and other shopping in Pérouges or at Meximieux (2.5 km).

Prices:	low season	F 1100	**3 people**
	high season	F 1100	IGN 44

Booking: Ain booking service   E
01/290.891

POUILLAT A gîte in the owners' attractively renovated house at the heart of the village with local forest walks on marked footpaths. Treffort (15 km) is a pleasant old town with a ruined feudal château and prehistoric caves. Sailing at Nantua lake (20 km). Altitude 500 metres. Living room/kitchenette, 2 bedrooms (1 double and 2 single beds), bathroom, shower, heating, small enclosed ground with garden furniture and barbecue. Mobile butcher, grocer and baker call; farm produce in the village; other shopping and restaurant at 1 km.

Prices:	low season	F 865	**4 people**
	high season	F 930	IGN 44
	winter season	F 920	

Booking: Ain booking service   E
01/309.900

REYSSOUZE Le Biolay A ground-floor gîte in the owners' modern home, set in open ground at the edge of the village (0.8 km). Visit Macon (15 km), a quiet town on the river Saône, crossed by a fourteenth-century bridge, at the heart of this famous wine-producing region. Living room/kitchenette (1 double divan), 1 bedroom (1 double bed), bathroom, shower, oil heating, open ground. Shopping and restaurant in the village or at Pont-de-Vaux (5 km approx.).

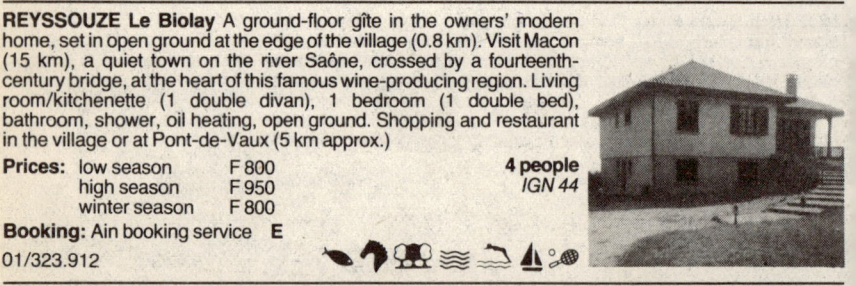

Prices:	low season	F 800	**4 people**
	high season	F 950	IGN 44
	winter season	F 800	

Booking: Ain booking service   E
01/323.912

SAINT-ETIENNE-DU-BOIS Le Châtelet A renovated gîte at the edge of the village (1 km) where you can buy the local speciality, corn-fed Bresse chickens. Bourg-en-Bresse (10 km), the capital of the département, has many gastronomic restaurants. Sailing at Montrevel lake (20 km). Living room/kitchenette, 3 bedrooms (2 double, 4 single and 2 child's beds), shower room, heating, verandah, carport, enclosed courtyard and open ground with garden furniture and barbecue. Shopping in the village or at Bourg-en-Bresse.

Prices:	low season	F 1100	**8/10 people**
	high season	F 1400	IGN 44
	winter season	F 1600	

Booking: Ain booking service   E
01/350.034

Country Food and Wine in AIN

For Country Food, Accommodation and Camping Sites

FERME AUBERGE DU GRAND-RONJON

Amongst the forests and pasturelands of this district, famous for Bresse chickens and blue cheese, the Farm Inns of Ain are well-maintained and offer good, simple home cooking. Near Cormoze, midway between Louhan and Bourg en Bresse, M and Mme Claude Guyon offer a range of country hospitality in a lively farm setting.

The ferme auberge includes in its specialities Bresse frogs' legs, farm chickens a la creme, rabbit, Bresse tart and pigeon. It is advisable to book in advance and the Inn is open every day except Wednesday evening.

You can also make 'chambre d'hôte' bookings at Le Grand Ronjon for bed and breakfast accommodation or enjoy the goats and ponies, geese and chickens which range free near the farm camp-site.

For enquiries, information and bookings for accommodation, sites or meals, please contact:
**M and Mme Claude Guyon,
Le Grand Ronjon, Cormoz,
01270 Coligny, France.
Tel: 74.51.23.97.**

Ain

SAINT-JEAN-SUR-REYSSOUZE Varennes A ground-floor gîte in the retired owners' home with private tennis court. The village is in the heart of the Bresse region (famous for poultry). The leisure centre at Montrevel (12 km) has a lake for water sports and riding facilities. Living room, kitchen, 2 bedrooms (1 double, 3 single and 1 child's bed), shower room, fireplace, gas central heating, carport, open grounds. Linen available. Restaurant, farm produce and shopping in the village (1 km) or at Pont-de-Vaux (12 km).

Prices:	low season	F 755	**5/6 people**
	high season	F 970	IGN 44
	winter season	F 510	

Booking: Ain booking service E
01/364.037

SIMANDRE-SUR-SURAN Petit Simandre A well-renovated and rustically furnished gîte, with a trout river running nearby. It is in a pleasant hilly region at the beginning of the Jura mountains. Much to see (Brou church) and do at Bourg-en-Bresse (17 km), capital of the département. Living room, kitchen, 3 bedrooms (2 double and 2 single beds), bathroom, shower, open fire, electric heating, terrace, garage, enclosed ground with garden furniture. Farm produce, shopping and restaurant in the village (0.6 km).

Prices:	low season	F 1110	**6 people**
	high season	F 1440	IGN 44
	winter season	F 1310	

Booking: Ain booking service E
01/408.041

SUTRIEU Charancin A renovated cottage in a hamlet, 3.6 km from the village (altitude 700 metres). Visit the nearby Cormaranche forest and Cerveyrieu waterfall. Swimming-pool at 6 km and other facilities, at the health resort of Hauteville (12 km). Ski-ing at 25 km. Living room (1 double divan), kitchen, 3 bedrooms (3 double, 1 single and 1 child's bed), bathroom, electric heating and wood stove, terrace, carport, enclosed ground. Farm produce from the owners; butcher and grocer call; other shopping (6 km).

Prices:	low season	F 750	**9/10 people**
	high season	F 870	IGN 44
	winter season	F 870	

Booking: Ain booking service E
01/414.043

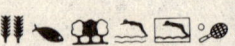

THEZILLIEU Hameau du Genevray One of five purpose-built wooden gîtes at the edge of the village (1 km). Fishing, forest walks and cross-country ski-ing. This region is known as Le Valromey with châteaux and picturesque villages to visit. Altitude 850 metres. Living room/kitchenette, 3 bedrooms (2 double and 4 single beds), shower room, electric heating, open ground. Mobile shops call; farm produce in the village; a restaurant at 4 km; other shopping at Cormaranche (7 km).

Prices:	low season	F 700	**8 people**
	high season	F 805	IGN 44
	winter season	F 805	

Booking: SIVOM, Ancienne Mairie de Lompnes, 01110 Hauteville.
Tel. (74) 35 39 73. E
01/417.004

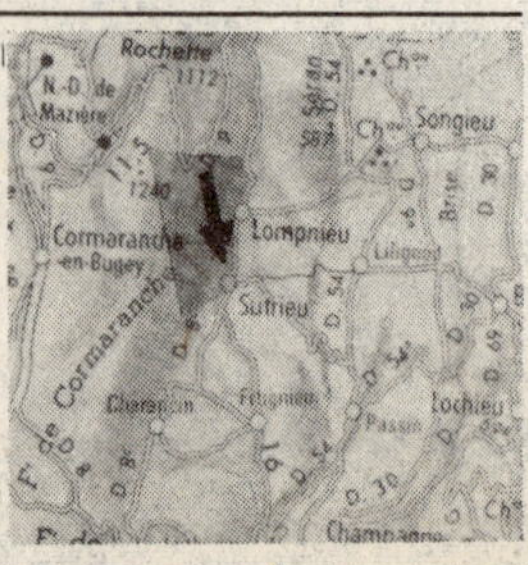

SUTRIEU Fitignieu *Chambre d'hôte* accommodation in the owners' home in a hamlet at 4 km from the interesting old town of Champagne, with its unusual eleventh-century church where you can see Roman capitals and sculptures. Leisure activities include a swimming-pool and tennis courts at 3.5 km; riding at 12 km and ski-ing at 15 km. One double bedroom available with washhand basin, electric heating. Shopping and restaurant at Champagne.

Prices:	on request		**2 people**
			IGN 44

Booking: M G. BASSIEU, Fitignieu, Sutrieu, 01260 Champagne.

01/20

© IGN Red Map 109

Ain

VESANCY La Combette *Chambre d'hôte* accommodation in the enterprising owners' large house where they also have two gîtes and a *ferme-auberge* (meals available). The farm, where they raise geese and ducks, is situated 4 km from the spa town of Divonne-les-Bains which has a lake (bathing) and a casino. Altitude 700 metres. On the first floor: bedrooms 1 and 3 (1 double, 1 single bed each); bedroom 2 (1 double, 2 single beds); bedrooms 4 and 5 (1 single bed each), with private washing facilities; central heating. Shops in the village (0.5 km).
Prices: on request
12 people
IGN 45
Booking: M G. DE ANTONI, Ferme 'La Combette', Vesancy, 01170 Gex. Tel. (50) 41 64 17.
01/21

CHALEINS Sapeins *Aire naturelle de camping* on a flat, shady field, 100 metres from the owners' house on a mixed farm, some 4 km from the village and 5 km from the river Sâone which offers pleasant walks and fishing. Villefranche-sur-Saône (10 km) is an attractive old town, centre of the Beaujolais wine region (follow the Beaujolais wine route for an interesting tour). Two hot showers, electric current for caravans, camping gas available; recreation room. Fresh vegetables and other produce available from the owners; other shopping in the village and a restaurant at 2 km.
Prices: on request
IGN 44
Booking: M G. THETE, Sapeins, Chaleins, 01480 Jassans-Riottier. Tel. (74) 67 82 85.
01/22

HOTONNES Les Plans *Gîte d'Etape* Overnight hostel accommodation for walkers and riders (and their horses) in the owners' renovated and traditionally furnished house on a livestock farm, some 7 km from the village (altitude 1100 metres). Local cross-country and downhill ski-ing; swimming-pool at 10 km and a lake at 20 km. Living room, kitchen, dormitory (15 people), shower room, fireplace (wood supplied), central heating. *Table d'hôte* meals available; otherwise shopping and restaurant in the village or at Hauteville (15 km).
Prices: on request
15 people
IGN 44
Booking: Mme C. DALIN, Les Plans d'Hotonnes, 01260 Champagne. Tel. (79) 87 68 46.
01/23

MALAFRETAZ La Citerne *Gîte équestre* Full-board accommodation in the owners' home on a mixed farm and riding centre (horses for hire) where they also have a camp-site. Local fishing; tennis, bathing and sailing at Montrevel lake (2 km). Many other cultural and leisure amenities at Bourg-en-Bresse (15 km). Four rooms available; bedrooms 1 and 2 (1 double bed each), bedroom 3 (1 double, 2 single beds), bedroom 4 (4 single beds); shared shower room and lounge, central heating. *Table d'hôte* meals at the farm, or shopping and restaurant in the village (2 km).
Prices: on request
12 people
IGN 44
Booking: M J. CRETIN, Malafretaz, 01340 Montrevel. Tel. (74) 30 81 19.
01/9

VILLENEUVE Gressieu *Gîte d'enfants* Accommodation for unaccompanied children in the owners' renovated house on a farm in the west of the département, 13 km from Villefranche-sur-Saône. Activities offered include games, learning about animals and the rural surroundings, bicycle rides and music. Three bedrooms with 2 single beds in each; shared bathroom and shower. Full-board accommodation (vegetarian meals available if required).
Prices: on request
6 people
IGN 44
Booking: M J. Y. SOBOUL, 01480 Jassans-Riottier. Tel. (74) 00 76 20.

01/4

Ardèche

ALBA L'Esplanade A ground-floor gîte adjoining the owners' home at the centre of the village where there is a fifteenth-century château. Altitude 650 metres. Visit the château town of Montélimar (20 km approx.), famous for its nougat – enquire at the tourist office for a visit to the factories of production. Living room, kitchen, 1 bedroom (1 double bed), shower room, central heating, enclosed ground (not adjoining the gîte). Shopping and restaurant in the village or at Villeneuve-de-Berg (10 km approx.).

Prices: low season F 765/870
high season F 1075

2 people
IGN 52

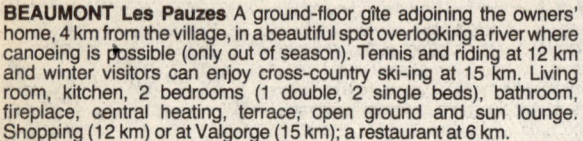

Booking: Ardèche booking service
07/5.005R002

BEAUMONT Les Pauzes A ground-floor gîte adjoining the owners' home, 4 km from the village, in a beautiful spot overlooking a river where canoeing is possible (only out of season). Tennis and riding at 12 km and winter visitors can enjoy cross-country ski-ing at 15 km. Living room, kitchen, 2 bedrooms (1 double, 2 single beds), bathroom, fireplace, central heating, terrace, open ground and sun lounge. Shopping (12 km) or at Valgorge (15 km); a restaurant at 6 km.

Prices: low season F 645/845
high season F 1245/1345
winter season F 645/845

4 people
IGN 59

Booking: Ardèche booking service
07/4.029R003

CHAMPIS A wing of the town hall has been converted into three gîtes, this one on the ground floor. Visit historic Tournon (15 km approx.) where the château of the former Counts is now a museum; visitors in late August can enjoy its popular fair. Living room/kitchenette, 2 bedrooms (2 double, 1 single bed), shower room, open courtyard shared with the other gîtes. A restaurant in the village; shopping at Saint-Sylvestre (2 km).

Prices: low season F 510
high season F 655

5 people
IGN 52

Booking: Ardèche booking service

07/1.052R003

LABLACHERE Sebet-Haut A first-floor gîte in a renovated stone house in a hamlet, 2 km from the village. Bathing and fishing at Joyeuse (4 km) where there is a carnival on July 14th. Do not miss the lovely medieval château town of Largentière (15 km approx.). Living room/kitchenette, 2 bedrooms (2 double, 2 single beds), shower room, central heating, terrace, carport. Shopping and restaurant in the village or at Joyeuse.

Prices: low season F 705/805
high season F 1145
winter season F 705/845

6 people
IGN 59

Booking: Ardèche booking service
07/4.117R019

LE LAC-D'ISSARLES A small, first-floor gîte, one of two in the owners' home at the village centre (altitude 1000 metres), situated at the edge of a large natural lake where you may hire pedalo boats and enjoy other leisure amenities including tennis. Local cross-country ski-ing. Living room/kitchenette, 2 bedrooms (2 double beds), shower room, central heating, open courtyard. Shopping and restaurant in the village or at Coucouron (12 km).

Prices: low season F 695/725
high season F 895/905
winter season F 695

4 people
IGN 50

Booking: Ardèche booking service
07/3.119R001

Ardèche

LAFARRE A ground-floor gîte in a renovated building housing the town hall next door, and a public meeting room above the gîte. Altitude 720 metres. Local forest walks and cross-country ski-ing. From Lamastre (15 km approx.), take a special tourist train through the Doux Gorge to Tournon. Living room/kitchenette, 2 bedrooms (2 double, 1 single beds), shower room, electric and gas heating, open courtyard. A restaurant (4 km); shopping at Lalouvesc (9 km) or at Saint-Félicien (15 km).

Prices:	low season	F 665/695
	high season	F 750/810
	winter season	F 665/745

5 people
IGN 52

Booking: Ardèche booking service
07/1.124R001

LANARCE Le Rayol One of four gîtes in a building owned by the local forestry authorities and situated in the forest itself, 4 km from the village (altitude 1080 metres). Local fishing, bathing and cross-country ski-ing. A swimming-pool and tennis at 10 km. Living room/kitchenette, 2 bedrooms (1 double, 2 single beds), shower room, oil stove, open ground. Shopping and a restaurant in the village or at Coucouron (17 km).

Prices:	low season	F 395/653
	high season	F 875/987
	winter season	F 395/611

4 people
IGN 59

Booking: Ardèche booking service
07/3.130R001

LESPERON One of four gîtes in a modern house at the village centre (altitude 1000 metres). Take a day trip to the lovely old town of Aubenas (45 km approx.) which has a twelfth-century château and other places of interest; try the local speciality of *marrons glacés*. Living room/kitchenette, 3 bedrooms (1 double, 4 single beds), shower room, fireplace, central heating, garage, terrace, open ground and courtyard. Shopping and restaurant at Pradelles (7 km).

Prices:	low season	F 869
	high season	F 1075
	winter season	F 869/1075

6 people
IGN 59

Booking: Ardèche booking service
07/3.142R011

© IGN Red Map 111

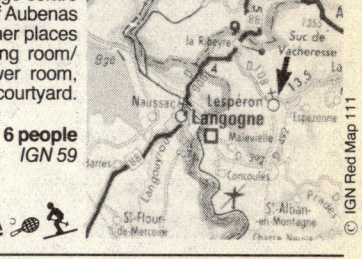

LES OLLIERES Les Vallats A very spacious detached house at the village centre where there are facilities for river fishing, bathing and canoeing. Plenty to see and do at the département capital of Privas (15 km); visit the Verdus agricultural museum, 4 km from the town. Lounge, living room, kitchen, 5 bedrooms (4 double, 2 single beds), bathroom, enclosed ground, covered terrace and balcony. Shopping and restaurant in the village or at Privas.

Prices:	low season	F 1345/1595
	high season	F 1795

10 people
IGN 52

Booking: Ardèche booking service

07/2.167R002

ORGNAC-L'AVEN A ground-floor gîte in an old village house containing another apartment on the first floor. The village is a popular tourist site, established around marvellous natural caves, 600 metres long and some 100 metres deep, with stalactites and stalagmites. Other leisure facilities in the village include a swimming-pool and tennis. Bed-sitting room (1 double divan, 1 single bed), kitchen, shower room, electric heating, open ground (not adjoining the gîte). Shopping and restaurant in the village or at Barjac (9 km).

Prices:	low season	F 745/805
	high season	F 915

3 people
IGN 59

Booking: Ardèche booking service
07/5.168R019

Ardèche

PAILHARES This village school has been converted into eight gîtes (this one on the ground floor). Visit the lovely old town of Tournon (30 km) which boasts some fine Renaissance architecture; take a trip on a tourist train from there through the delightful Doux valley to Lamastre. Altitude 700 metres. Living room (1 double divan), kitchen, 2 bedrooms (2 double, 1 single bed), shower room, oil stove, carport, open courtyard shared with other gîtes. A restaurant in the village; shopping at Saint-Félicien (7 km).

Prices:	low season	F 605/705	**7 people**
	high season	F 945/975	*IGN 52*

Booking: Ardèche booking service
07/1.170R003

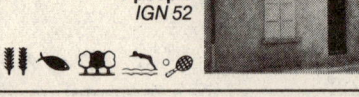

PAILHARES Another ground-floor gîte in the former school described above where there are seven more holiday apartments (altitude 700 metres). Local fishing and forest walks; tennis at 14 km and a swimming-pool (35 km). Places of tourist interest in the vicinity include Rochefort Château and the Daronne Gorge. Living room/kitchenette (1 double divan), 2 bedrooms (2 double, 1 single and 1 child's bed), shower room, no heating, carport, open courtyard shared with other gîtes. Shopping at Saint-Félicien (7 km); a post-office in the village.

Prices:	low season	F 605/705	**8 people**
	high season	F 945/975	*IGN 52*

Booking: Ardèche booking service
07/1.170R005

ROCLES Le Jal An attractively renovated stone cottage, lying at an altitude of 500 metres, near the village centre. Largentière (12 km) is a charming medieval town with a fine château. At 25 km there are facilities for downhill and cross-country ski-ing. Living room/kitchenette, 2 bedrooms (2 double, 1 single bed), bathroom, central heating, terrace, open ground with games room and barbecue. Shopping and restaurant in the village or at 10 km.

Prices:	low season	F 595/795	**5 people**
	high season	F 1145/1245	*IGN 59*
	winter season	F 595/795	

Booking: Ardèche booking service
07/4.196R010

THUEYTS A development of several gîtes in renovated buildings at the centre of the village. Thueyts is an attractive old village, a centre for cross-country ski-ing and organised walks along marked footpaths. Visit the lovely old château town of Aubenas (25 km approx.). Living room/kitchenette (1 single bed), 1 bedroom (1 double bed), shower room, central heating, enclosed ground. Shopping and a restaurant in the village or at Aubenas.

Prices:	low season	F 612	**3 people**
	high season	F 715	*IGN 59*
	winter season	F 612	

Booking: Ardèche booking service
07/4.322R002

VALLON-PONT-D'ARC Le Colombier A ground-floor gîte, one of four in a beautifully restored old house, 1 km from the centre of the village. It is ideally situated for exploring the fascinating natural phenomena of the region, including the Ardèche Gorge. A swimming-pool at 17 km. Living room/kitchenette (1 single bed), 2 bedrooms (1 double, 2 single beds), bathroom, fireplace, central heating, terrace, open ground. Washing machine, telephone and garden furniture shared with the other gîtes. Shopping and restaurant in the village or at Barjac (10 km).

Prices:	low season	F 1295/1610	**5 people**
	high season	F 1940	*IGN 59*
	winter season	F 1295/1595	

Booking: Ardèche booking service
07/5.330R036

Drôme

GIGORS ET LOZERON Peyrache A gîte in a detached house 6 km from the village, altitude 900 m. Romans (approx. 35 km) has an unusual footwear museum and a museum of the Resistance Movement, several riding schools and an Olympic swimming-pool. Tennis at 25 km. Living room, kitchen, 3 bedrooms (2 double and 2 single beds, 1 double divan), bathroom, no heating, terrace, garage, ground. Shopping at Beaufort sur Gervanne (13 km).

Prices:	low season	F 500	**8 people**
	high season	F 730	IGN 52

Booking: Drôme booking service   **E**

26/376

MOLLANS SUR OUVEZE Le Clos de Veaux An old gîte in a detached house 4 km from the village where there are shops. Buis-les-Baronnies (12 km) is famous for its limes and has a lime-flower festival the first Wednesday in July. River fishing in the village. Living room, kitchen, 2 bedrooms (1 double and 2 single beds, 1 double divan), shower room, fireplace, electric heating, open ground.

Prices:	low season	F 897	**6 people**
	high season	F 1207	IGN 60
	winter season	F 897	

Booking: Drôme booking service   **E**

26/19

LA-MOTTE-DE-GALAURE Les Cornets A modern gîte with traditional furnishings, surrounded by farm buildings at 0.8 km from the village. A swimming-pool at 4 km; at 9 km is the charming pottery-making town of Saint-Vallier with its château, once the residence of Guillaume, the last count of the Valentinios and brother of Diane de Poitiers. Living room, kitchen, 3 bedrooms (2 double and 3 single beds), bathroom, central heating, terrace, garage, courtyard and open ground. Shopping at Saint-Vallier.

Prices:	low season	F 520/675	**7 people**
	high season	F 830	IGN 51
	winter season	F 520/675	

Booking: Drôme booking service   **E**

26/355

SAINT AGNAN EN VERCORS Le Rousset One of two gîtes in a renovated stone building 5 km from the village. Altitude 960 m. La Chapelle-en-Vercors (12 km) is a rural holiday resort with some interesting caves and good sporting facilities including organised walks and two ski stations. Living room, lounge, kitchen, 2 bedrooms (4 double beds), bathroom, electric central heating, terrace, garage, courtyard. Shopping in La-Chapelle-en-Vercors.

Prices:	low season	F 860/910	**8 people**
	high season	F 1020/1155	IGN 52
	winter season	F 1110/1380	

Booking: Drôme booking service   **E**

26/229

SAINT CHRISTOPHE ET LE LARIS Le Breuil A large old chalet-type house furnished in country style at the edge of the village (1 km). Saint Donat (11 km) has an international Bach festival from 28th July to 12th August and a large lake with facilities for bathing, sailing and pedalos. Living room, kitchen, 2 bedrooms (2 double and 2 single beds), shower room, fireplace, electric and wood heating, carport, open ground. Shopping at St Donat.

Prices:	low season	F 500/700	**6 people**
	high season	F 800	IGN 52

Booking: Drôme booking service   **E**

26/357

17

Drôme

SAINT JULIEN EN VERCORS La Martelière A substantial house situated near the centre of the small town of St Julien en Vercors. The larger town of La-Chapelle-en-Vercors (approx. 15 km) has something to interest all tastes from caving, fishing, bicycle hire and skiing to cinema and museums. Living room, kitchen, 4 bedrooms (4 double and 2 single beds), shower room, electric and wood heating, terrace, garden and courtyard. Shopping at St Martin en Vercors (3 km).

Prices:	low season	F 1000/1100	**10 people**
	high season	F 1350/1450	IGN 52
	winter season	F 1000/1550	

Booking: Drôme booking service E

26/320

SOLERIEUX One of two gîtes in an old village house. Saint-Paul-Trois-Châteaux (4 km) has open and covered swimming-pools, exhibitions of painting and craft workshops, skating rink and an archaeological museum amongst other attractions. Visit the châteaux at Grignan (approx. 24 km) and Suze-la-Rousse (approx. 28 km). Living room/kitchenette, 2 bedrooms (1 double and 3 single beds), shower room/fireplace, electric heating, carport, open ground. Shopping in Saint-Paul-Trois-Châteaux.

Prices:	low season	F 800/1000	**5 people**
	high season	F 1200	IGN 59
	winter season	F 800	

Booking: Drôme booking service E

26/182

SOLERIEUX A second gîte in the old village house described above. Montelimar (approx. 35 km) has all the facilities of a large town – don't leave without trying the famous nougat, factory visits can be arranged at the tourist offices. Living room/kitchenette, 2 bedrooms (1 double and 3 single beds), shower room, fireplace, electric heating, carport, open ground. Shopping at Saint-Paul-Trois-Châteaux (4 km).

Prices:	low season	F 800/1000	**5 people**
	high season	F 1200	IGN 59
	winter season	F 800	

Booking: Drôme booking service E

26/183

VEAUNES A new village house, furnished in traditional style, adjoining the owners' home. Tain l'Hermitage (7 km) has magnificent views over the Rhone valley, swimming-pool, lake for sailing and interesting organised walks. Living room/kitchenette, 1 bedroom (1 double and 1 single bed, 1 double divan), shower room, oil and electric heating, balcony, courtyard with garden furniture. Shopping in the village or at Tain l'Hermitage.

Prices:	low season	F 700	**5 people**
	high season	F 855	IGN 52

Booking: Drôme booking service E

26/360

LA BAUME-DE-TRANSIT Le Gas-du-Rossignol *Chambre d'hôte* accommodation in the owner's renovated stone house in an isolated spot surrounded by magnificent trees. The owner will hire bicycles. 5 rooms available: each bedroom has one double bed and private bathroom. Use of kitchen, sitting room, games room (table tennis and darts). Fruit and vegetables, as well as honey, herbs and lavender from the owner. Shops and restaurant 4 km, or in Saint-Paul-Trois-Châteaux (8 km).

10 people
IGN 59

Prices: 1p F 130, 2p F 160, 3p F 190

Booking: M L. CORNILLON, Ferme Saint Luc, La Baume-de-Transit, 26130 Saint-Paul-Trois-Châteaux. Tel. (75) 98 11 51. E

26/10

Loire

CHALMAZEL Le Supt One of two traditionally furnished gîtes in a renovated house on a mixed farm (altitude 1000 metres). It is set in the forest with plenty of marked footpaths and ski-ing at 2.5 km. There is an eighteenth-century château in the village (3 km). Living room/kitchenette, 2 bedrooms (2 double and 1 child's bed), bathroom, central heating, balcony, open ground. Farm produce from the owners; other shopping and restaurant in the village or at Boën-sur-Lignon (12 km). 
Prices: low season   F 630   **5 people**
           high season   F 750   IGN 50
           winter season F 630/750
Booking: M M. MARCHAND, Le Supt, 42920 Chalmazel.
Tel. (77) 24 80 47.
42/7

ECOCHE La Quicherie An attractively renovated stone house with country-style furnishings, set in open ground on a mixed farm, 4 km from the village (altitude 600 metres). This is a lovely wooded, hilly region where Charolais cattle are reared. Historic Lyon is just 35 km away. Living room, kitchen, 2 bedrooms (3 double and 2 single beds), shower room, fireplace, electric heating. Fresh dairy produce and vegetables from the owners; other shopping at Belmont (10 km) and a restaurant in the village. 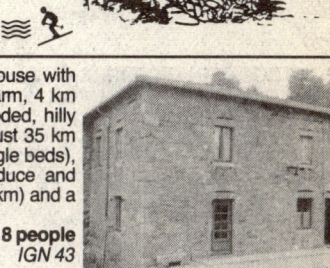
Prices: low season   F 400/525   **8 people**
           high season   F 700/760   IGN 43
Booking: M GOUJAT, La Quicherie, Ecoche, 42670 Belmont.
Tel. (77) 63 61 67.
42/146

ESSERTINES-EN-CHATELNEUF Aux Faux A traditionally furnished gîte in the owners' renovated house on their livestock farm, 2 km from the village in the Forez mountains (altitude 750 metres). There is an interesting Doll Museum and other attractions at Montbrison (10 km). Visit, too, the Château de la Bastie d'Urfé nearby. Living room, kitchen, 2 bedrooms (3 double and 1 child's bed), shower room, central heating, balcony, garage, enclosed courtyard. Farm produce and restaurant in the village; other shopping at Montbrison. 
Prices: low season   F 520   **7 people**
           high season   F 650/680   IGN 50
Booking: M G. RONDEL, Aux Faux, Essertines-en-Châtelneuf, 42600 Montbrison. Tel. (77) 76 20 15.
42/38

GUMIERES Mursant A renovated cottage, set in open ground near a hamlet, and some 3 km from the town (altitude 950 metres). The gîte benefits from a splendid view over the Forez plain. A swimming-pool and tennis at the interesting old town of Montbrison (20 km). Living room, kitchen, 4 bedrooms (3 double, 2 single and 1 child's bed), bathroom, fireplace, electric heating, carport. Farm produce in the village; other shopping and restaurant at 15 km. 
Prices: low season   F 520/600   **9 people**
           high season   F 750   IGN 50
Booking: M H. MONDON, Querezieux, Ecotay-L'Oime, 42600 Montbrison. Tel. (77) 58 04 48.
42/41B

JONZIEUX A modern house with traditional furnishings near a livestock farm where the owners keep a *ferme auberge* in the Pilat Regional Park. There is an unusual museum of *passementerie* (gold and silver braid, etc.) in Jonzieux (2 km). Saint-Etienne is at 25 km. Altitude 980 metres. Living room/kitchenette, 2 bedrooms (2 double and 3 single beds), bathroom, fireplace, oil-fired central heating, open ground. Dairy produce from the owners, other shopping in the village; meals available at the farm. 
Prices: low season   F 525/630   **7 people**
           high season   F 820   IGN 51
Booking: Mme M. BAR, Pimbert, Jonzieux, 42660 Saint-Genest-Malifaux. Tel. (77) 39 90 09.
42/179b

Loire

MARCOUX Jomard This gîte is in a village of the Forez plain, 0.5 km from the owners' farm. It has been renovated and furnished in rustic style. Local forest walks and riding stables nearby (0.5 km). Plenty of leisure facilities at Noirétable (30 km approx.). Living room/kitchenette, 2 bedrooms (2 double and 1 single bed), bathroom, fireplace, electric heating, garage, open garden. Farm produce in the village; other shopping and restaurant at Boën-sur-Lignon (5 km).

Prices:	low season	F 460/520	**5 people**
	high season	F 730	*IGN 50*

Booking: M M. GOURE, Les Merlins, Marcoux, 42130 Boën-sur-Lignon. Tel. (77) 97 47 35.

42/66

SAINT-BONNET-LE-COURREAU Grand Ris A lovely old stone house which has been renovated and furnished in rustic fashion, situated in the forest, overlooking the Forez plain. Possibility of visiting a local cheese-making dairy. Altitude 830 metres. Living room, kitchen, 4 bedrooms (4 double and 1 single bed), bathroom, fireplace, electric heating, garage, enclosed ground. Farm produce, other shopping and restaurant in the village (3 km).

Prices:	low season	F 630/680	**9 people**
	high season	F 860/950	*IGN 50*
	winter season	F 630/800	

Booking: M M. BEAL, Grand Ris, 42940, Saint-Bonnet-le-Courreau. Tel. (77) 76 80 97.

42/103

SAINT-BONNET-LE-COURREAU Le Palais A renovated house with rustic furnishings, high in the Forez mountains (altitude 1150 metres), at the edge of a wood. Local ski-ing (5 km). At Montbrison (15 km) enquire at the tourist office about guided tours of the old quarter of the town. Living room/kitchenette, 3 bedrooms (2 double and 1 single bed), bathroom, fireplace, central heating, open ground with garden furniture. Farm produce, shopping and restaurant in the village (6 km).

Prices:	low season	F 680	**5 people**
	high season	F 890	*IGN 50*
	winter season	F 680/735	

Booking: M A. BEAL, Tournel, Champdieu, 42600 Montbrison. Tel. (77) 58 11 41.

42/105B

SAINT-CHRISTO-EN-JAREZ Albuzy A renovated and traditionally furnished gîte set in open ground in a little hamlet, 7 km from the village. The retired owner speaks some English. The university town of Saint-Etienne (15 km) has many leisure and cultural amenities. Altitude 650 metres. Living room/kitchenette, 2 bedrooms (1 double and 2 single beds), shower room, electric heating, open ground. Farm produce and restaurant in the village; shops at 7 km.

Prices:	low season	F 315/520	**4 people**
	high season	F 690	*IGN 51*

Booking: Loire booking service **E**

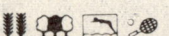

42/SR20

LA VALLA-SUR-ROCHEFORT Col des Brosses One of two traditionally furnished gîtes in a renovated house, set in open ground in an isolated spot at the edge of the forest (altitude 980 metres). River fishing (6 km) and tennis court at 12 km; other amenities at the château town of Boën-sur-Lignon (10 km). Living room, kitchen, 2 bedrooms (2 double and 1 single bed), shower room, central heating, balcony, garden furniture. Restaurant in the village (1.5 km); shopping at Boën-sur-Lignon.

Prices:	low season	F 450/546	**5 people**
	high season	F 725	*IGN 56*
	winter season	F 450/725	

Booking: M H. BERTHIER, rue Déchelette, 42130 Boën-sur-Lignon.

42/56

Rhône

BRULLIOLES Montizuel A gîte on a mixed farm at the edge of the village (altitude 600 metres). It is just 40 km to Lyon, France's second city — visit the fascinating museums of Fabrics and Decorative Arts and Puppetry, and the delightful Renaissance quarters of the town. Living room (1 single divan), kitchen, 2 bedrorooms (1 double and 2 single beds), shower room, solid fuel heating, ground with barbecue. Farm produce, shopping and restaurant in the village (0.6 km).

Prices:	low season	F 600	5 people
	high season	F 600	IGN 43

Booking: M J. DUPIN, Brullioles, 69690 Bassenay.
Tel. (74) 70 52 95.

69/1

CHAMBOST-LONGESSAIGNE La Loire A renovated gîte on a former farm near the owners' home (although they're frequently away). It is set in hilly countryside (altitude 550 metres). Fishing at a lake; Lyon (60 km approx.) is close enough for a day trip, but worthy of several days' exploration. Living room/kitchenette (1 single divan), bathroom (small bath), 1 bedroom (2 double, 1 single bed, 1 cot), oil stove, courtyard and open ground with garden furniture. Shopping in the village (2.5 km).

Prices:	low season	F 500	6 people
	high season	F 600	IGN 43

Booking: Mme M. GOUBIER, Le Tronchil, Sainte-Consorce, 69260 Charbonnières. Tel. (7) 887 14 70.

69/2

CHENAS Les Brureaux A ground-floor gîte in a renovated and traditionally furnished house in a famous wine-producing area. The wines of Juliénas (2 km) are particularly prized. Mâcon (12 km) is worthy of a visit for the old town itself and you can taste the wines at the Maison des Vins there. Living room, kitchen, 3 bedrooms (1 double, 5 single beds), bathroom, central heating, carport, courtyard and enclosed ground. Wine from the owners; other shopping and restaurant at Juliénas.

Prices:	low season	F 600	7 people
	high season	F 800/1000	IGN 43

Booking: M A. JULLIEN DE POMMEROL, 1 place Gaulleton, 69002 Lyon. Tel. (7) 837 17 40.

69/3

CHENAS Le Seignaux A lovely old house with simple country-style furnishings, at the edge of the village where you may buy the local wine. Leisure facilities at Thoissey (9 km) include a swimming-pool, sailing and tennis. Mâcon (18 km) also has much to offer its visitors. Living room, kitchen, 3 bedrooms (1 double and 4 single beds), shower room, oil and gas heating, terrace, carport, open courtyard with garden furniture. Mobile baker calls; other shopping and restaurant in the village (0.8 km).

Prices:	low season	F 400/500	6 people
	high season	F 600	IGN 43

Booking: M DRU, 22 rue Juliette Lancher, 75017 Paris.
Tel. (1) 766 58 33. **E**

69/4

CHENELETTE La Nuizière A ground-floor gîte in the owners' well-renovated house with rustic furnishings, 2.5 km from the village centre (altitude 660 metres), surrounded by woodland. Enjoy the local village fêtes in the region during the summer. Beaujeu (12 km) has a folk museum with a collection of traditional dolls. Living room/kitchenette, 2 bedrooms (1 double, 2 single beds), bathroom, central heating, terrace, carport, open ground. Shopping in the village; a restaurant at 5 km.

Prices:	low season	F 900	4 people
	high season	F 900	IGN 43

Booking: M J. FAYARD, La Nuizière, Chênelette, 69230 Beaujeu.
Tel. (74) 03 61 55.

69/5

17

Rhône

EMERINGES Le Complet An unusual gîte which has been renovated and traditionally furnished, set on a vineyard near the village centre. It is 18 km from the interesting old town of Mâcon which has many leisure and cultural amenities; try your hand at wind-surfing at a lake (25 km). Living room/kitchenette (TV, 1 single divan), 2 bedrooms (1 double, 4 single beds), shower room, solid fuel stove, garage, open courtyard. Mobile shops; other shopping (3 km); restaurant in the village (0.5 km).

Prices: low season F 500/700 **7 people**
high season F 800 IGN 43

Booking: M P. BOIN, Le Complet, Emeringes, 69840 Juliénas. Tel. (74) 04 41 56.

69/6

LOZANNE Aux Gouttes A renovated gîte with country-style furnishings adjacent to a farmhouse where the English-speaking owners raise Dartmoor ponies. The village (1 km) lies at the edge of the Beaujolais wine-producing district and is just 20 km from the important city of Lyon. Sailing at a lake (25 km). Living room/kitchenette, 2 bedrooms (1 double, 2 single beds, extra beds and linen available on request), shower room, electric heating, open garden with furniture. Shopping and restaurant in the village.

Prices: low season F 300/400 **4 people**
high season F 500 IGN 43

Booking: M ANGER, Aux Gouttes, 69380 Lozanne.
Tel. (7) 843 74 32 **E**
69/7

MORNANT La Grange a Gonin A renovated house on a farm where the owners are happy to sell fresh eggs, milk and cheese. A swimming-pool at 2 km; the little town of Givors on the Rhône (10 km) has a ruined feudal château. Lyon is just 30 km approx. away. Living room/kitchenette, 2 bedrooms (1 double, 2 single beds, 1 single divan), shower room, central heating, terrace, Linen available. Shopping and restaurant in the village (2 km).

Prices: low season F 450/500 **5 people**
high season F 650 IGN 51

Booking: M J. BAJARD, La Grange a Gonin, 69440 Mornant.
Tel. (7) 884 10 41

69/8

LE PERREON Le Perrin A renovated house with traditional furnishings on a vineyard 0.5 km from the village which has fresh produce available at the Thursday market. Concerts and cycle rides are organised locally in summer. The interesting old town of Villefranche-sur-Saône is at 14 km. Living room/kitchenette, 4 bedrooms (1 double, 3 single, 3 child's beds and a cot), bathroom, gas central heating, balcony, carport, enclosed courtyard with garden furniture and barbecue. Shopping and restaurant in the village.

Prices: low season F 580/650 **9 people**
high season F 780 IGN 43

Booking: M M. JACQUET, Ecole de Filles, Le Perréon, 69460 Saint-Etienne-les-Oullières. Tel. (74) 03 22 07 **E**
69/9

REGNIE-DURETTE Les Forchets A lovely old stone house with country-style furnishings at the heart of Beaujolais country (the owners themselves produce wine); many local cellars offer tastings. Villefranche-sur-Saône (25 km) has much fine Renaissance architecture and good cultural and leisure amenities. Living room/kitchenette, 3 bedrooms (2 double, 4 single and 1 child's bed), bathroom, electric heating, terrace, carport, enclosed ground. Shopping and restaurant in the village (0.5 km).

Prices: low season F 500/600 **9 people**
high season F 700 IGN 43

Booking: Mme F. PLASSE, Régnié-Durette, 69430 Beaujeu.
Tel. (74) 04 31 50.
69/10

18 COTE D'AZUR PROVENCE –

The hot, sandy beaches, bustling ports, marinas and casinos line the glittering coast of the riviera, making it a lively playground for sun-lovers and water sports' enthusiasts. However, the contrasting hinterland could hardly be more surprising. Leaving the fashionable resorts behind, the sleepy villages of the Loup Valley and Haute-Provence, often perched high on hilltops, and the prolific vineyards of Provence provide a welcome change to visitors from the coast. This is a land of contradiction: where else in France can you ski in the morning and bathe in the Med in the afternoon?

Even the industry in this area is not unattractive. With a mild climate and plenty of sunshine, mimosa, jasmine, carnations and roses bloom early. The flowers and lavender are usually destined for the large perfume industry and flower markets around the world.

The South of France has always attracted artists and Paul Cézanne's studio is open to the public at his birthplace, Aix-en-Provence. This is the former capital of the region, with many Roman remains, reminding us that Provence was the first province of Rome. Visitors in July and August may also appreciate the lively atmosphere of the International Music Festival.

Arles, an important city, in Roman Gaul, now known as the gateway to the Camargue, was greatly appreciated by Van Gogh, who painted the surrounding area in its vivid colours. Visitors to Arles in summer may spectate at a bull-fight in the ancient Roman arena.

Even some of the hilltop villages have a tale to tell. Les Baux-de-Provence balances on a rocky outlet to the sea, a marvellous sight for anyone around. Once the home of troubadours, then part of Provence, it was eventually given to France. However, its inhabitants were mainly protestant, unlike the monarchy, so the town's fortifications were destroyed by Louis XIII and the people were fined and moved out. The old village is no longer inhabited and can only be reached on foot.

Do not leave without a taste of Provence. Try some of the local dishes, such as *bouillabaisse* (fish soup), *ratatouille* (vegetable casserole), *tourte aux blettes* (sweet spinach pie) and the almond-flavoured biscuit, *calisson*, from Aix-en-Provence. According to the people of Marseille, food should be accompanied with local *Cassis* wine!

Map of Provence-Alpes-Côte d'Azur region

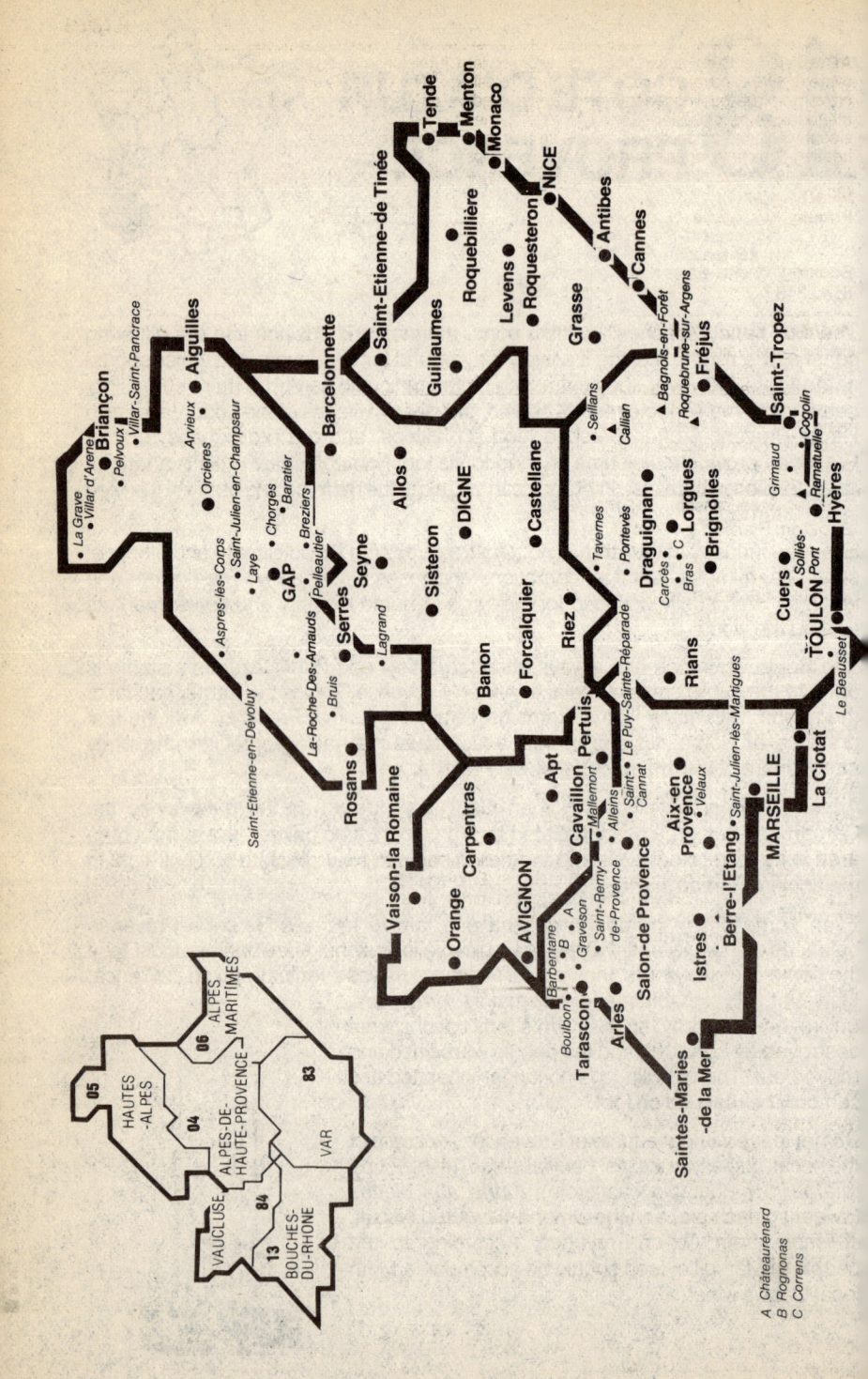

Départements:
- 05 HAUTES-ALPES
- 04 ALPES-DE-HAUTE-PROVENCE
- 06 ALPES-MARITIMES
- 84 VAUCLUSE
- 13 BOUCHES-DU-RHÔNE
- 83 VAR

Localités:

Briançon, La Grave, Villar-d'Arène, Pelvoux, Villar-Saint-Pancrace, Aiguilles, Arvieux, Orcières, Aspres-lès-Corps, Saint-Julien-en-Champsaur, Chorges, Laye, Baratier, Bréziers, Saint-Étienne-en-Dévoluy, La Roche-Des-Arnauds, Pelleautier, GAP, Serres, Seyne, Bruis, Lagrand, Rosans, Barcelonnette, Allos, Saint-Étienne-de-Tinée, Guillaumes, Roquebillière, Tende, Menton, Monaco, NICE, Levens, Roquesteron, Grasse, Antibes, Cannes, DIGNE, Sisteron, Forcalquier, Banon, Castellane, Riez, Tavernes, Pontevès, Sellans, Callian, Bagnols-en-Forêt, Roquebrune-sur-Argens, Fréjus, Saint-Tropez, Grimaud, Cogolin, Ramatuelle, Draguignan, Lorgues, Brignolles, Carcès, Bras, Hyères, Cuers, Solliès-Pont, TOULON, Le Beausset, La Ciotat, MARSEILLE, Aix-en-Provence, Pertuis, Apt, Cavaillon, Mallemort, Alleins, Le Puy-Sainte-Réparade, Cannat, Velaux, Saint-Julien-lès-Martigues, Rians, Berre-l'Étang, Salon-de-Provence, Istres, Saintes-Maries-de-la-Mer, Arles, Tarascon, Boulbon, Barbentane, Graveson, Saint-Rémy-de-Provence, AVIGNON, Carpentras, Orange, Vaison-la-Romaine

A Châteaurenard
B Rognonas
C Correns

Hautes-Alpes

ARVIEUX Le Coin A first-floor gîte with modern furnishings in the owner's old, renovated house 1 km from the village. The owner is a craftsman making wooden toys and furniture and the gîte is situated in the Quey as regional park. Living room/kitchenette, 1 bedroom and 1 sleeping-alcove (1 double and 3 single beds), shower room, central heating, balcony, open courtyard. Mobile shops call, farm produce (including honey), shopping and restaurant in the village or at Guillestre (20 km).

Prices: low season   F 640/690
         high season   F 980
         winter season   F 1170/1855

5 people
IGN 54

Booking: Hautes-Alpes booking service
05/Q.349

ARVIEUX Le Coin A second gîte with contemporary furnishings in the owner's renovated house described above, this one on the second floor. Altitude 1500 m. Guillestre (20 km) is an important town overlooking impressive mountainous scenery. Canoeing at 4 km and swimming-pool at 20 km. Living room/kitchenette (1 double divan), 1 bedroom (3 single beds), shower room, central heating, balcony, open courtyard. Farm produce, shopping and restaurant in the village.

Prices: low season   F 530/640
         high season   F 900
         winter season   F1060/1800

5 people
IGN 54

Booking: Hautes-Alpes booking service
05/Q350

ASPRES-LES-CORPS One of three gîtes in the owners' substantial new house, furnished in traditional style, on a livestock farm a short walk from the village (0.8 km). (Altitude 900 m). The gîte lies on the edge of the Ecrins national park; cross-country skiing at 16 km. Living room/kitchenette, 4 bedrooms (4 double and 2 single beds), shower room, oil central heating, open courtyard. Mobile butcher calls, farm produce in the village, shopping and restaurant at St Firmin (5 km).

Prices: low season   F 1060
         high season   F 1210
         winter season   F 1060/1280

10 people
IGN 54

Booking: Hautes-Alpes booking service
05/V303

BARATIER An old renovated house with traditional furnishings in an orchard 0.6 km from the village, altitude 860 m. Embrun (1.5 km) offers excellent sporting facilities, both winter and summer, including skiing, archery and watersports. Summer concerts in the cathedral. Living room (TV), kitchen, 4 bedrooms (2 double and 2 single beds), fireplace, central heating, terrace, garage, open ground with furniture. Fruit from the owner, farm produce in the village, restaurant and shopping at Embrun.

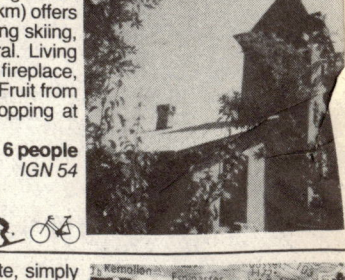

Prices: low season   F 900/1330
         high season   F 1880
         winter season   F 1220/1880

6 people
IGN 54

Booking: Hautes-Alpes booking service
05/E131

BREZIERS Chandarêne An old, renovated ground-floor gîte, simply furnished, on a livestock farm 1 km from the village, altitude 850 m. Gap (25 km) is an important town with excellent sports facilities including an Olympic pool and a skating rink. Living room/kitchenette, 1 bedroom (1 double and 2 single beds), shower room, oil central heating, open courtyard. Farm produce and local wine in the village, shopping and restaurant at 4 km.

Prices: low season   F 770
         high season   F 940

4 people
IGN 54

Booking: Hautes-Alpes booking service
05/G741

Hautes-Alpes

BRUIS A ground-floor gîte in an old, renovated house on a livestock farm 1 km from the village (650 m). Serres (25 km) is a picturesque fortified town built on a rocky promontory and with good sports facilities. Living room, kitchen, 2 bedrooms (1 double and 2 single beds), shower room, wood stove, terrace, open courtyard. Mobile baker calls, farm produce from the owners, restaurant at 3.5 km and shopping in Serres.

Prices: low season   F 690/750
         high season F 1040

4 people
IGN 60

Booking: Hautes-Alpes booking service

05/B711

CHORGES Le Bourget One of three gîtes in an attractive chalet-type house on a livestock farm, now renovated and traditionally furnished, and 3.5 km from the village (altitude 1150 m). Riding and ski slopes at 20 km. Gap (22 km) is an important town with good sports facilities all year round. Living room/kitchenette, 3 bedrooms (2 double and 2 single beds), oil and electric heating, open courtyard. Farm produce, restaurant and shopping in the village or at Savines (14.5 km).

Prices: low season   F 690/810
         high season   F 960
         winter season F 640/770

6 people
IGN 54

Booking: Hautes-Alpes booking service

05/G593

GAP Saint Mens A rustically furnished, renovated gîte only 1 km from Gap where there are leisure activities, such as a swimming-pool, tennis and riding. Ski-ing at 18 km and 5 km, sailing and bathing in a lake at 22 km. Altitude 750 m. Living room/kitchenette, small studio (1 double and 1 large single bed), shower room, open fire, electric heating, balcony, ground. Shopping and a choice of restaurants at Gap.

Prices: low season   F 780/830
         high season F 1010

3/4 people
IGN 54

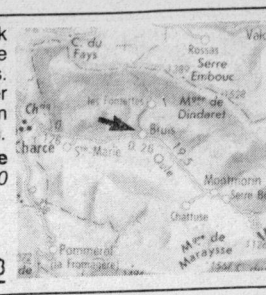

Booking: Hautes-Alpes booking service

05/G021

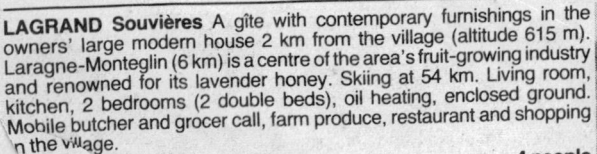

LAGRAND Souvières A gîte with contemporary furnishings in the owners' large modern house 2 km from the village (altitude 615 m). Laragne-Monteglin (6 km) is a centre of the area's fruit-growing industry and renowned for its lavender honey. Skiing at 54 km. Living room, kitchen, 2 bedrooms (2 double beds), oil heating, enclosed ground. Mobile butcher and grocer call, farm produce, restaurant and shopping in the village.

Prices: low season   F 720
         high season F 1090

4 people
IGN 60

Booking: Hautes-Alpes booking service

05/B421

LA GRAVE Les Hières An attractive renovated gîte of typical local design with traditional furnishings, outside (3.5 km) the popular winter sports resort of La Grave (altitude 1760 metres). Summer leisure amenities at La Grave include tennis and horse-riding. Living room/kitchenette, 1 bedroom (1 double and 2 single beds), bathroom, central heating, terrace, open ground. Farm produce, other shopping and a restaurant at La Grave.

Prices: low season   on request
         high season   on request
         winter season on request

4 people
IGN 54

Booking: Hautes-Alpes booking service

05/0554

342

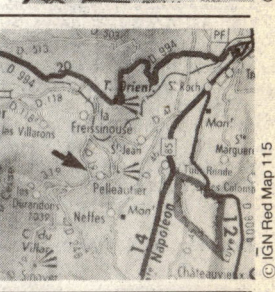

Hautes-Alpes

LA-ROCHE-DES-ARNAUDS A pretty little gîte in the owners' traditionally furnished, modern home at the edge of the village where there are the ruins of a château, once the family home of Arnaud de Flotte. Caves nearby to explore, fishing, ski-ing at 9 km and Gap at 14 km. Living room/kitchenette, 1 bedroom (1 double and 1 single bed), bathroom and shower, electric heating terrace, enclosed ground. Shopping and restaurant in the village or at Gap.

Prices:	low season	F 700/860	**3 people**
	high season	F 970	*IGN 54*
	winter season	F810/920	

Booking: Hautes-Alpes booking service

05/G152

LAYE Pic de l'Aiguille One of two gîtes in the owners' newly built chalet-type holiday home with modern furnishings 1.5 km from the village, altitude 1250 m. A lake for sailing at 31 km. This is a picturesque mountain region with plenty of good walks. All-year-round sports at Gap (12 km). Living room/kitchenette, studio (1 double and 1 single bed), shower room, fireplace, electric heating, open ground. Farm produce and restaurant in the village, shopping at St Bonnet (approx. 5 km).

Prices:	low season	F 640/770	**3 people**
	high season	F 940	*IGN 54*
	winter season	F 875/1300	

Booking: Hautes-Alpes booking service

05/C.801

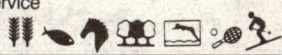

ORCIERES Prapic A gîte in the owners' old, renovated village house, furnished in traditional style. Altitude 1540 m. This is a mountainous region and the gîte lies on the edge of the Ecrins national park which has some splendid scenery. Gap (37 km) has excellent sports facilities and shopping. Living room/kitchenette, 1 bedroom (1 double and 2 single beds), shower room, fireplace, electric heating. Farm produce and restaurant in the village, shopping at 5 km.

Prices:	low season	F 750/800	**4 people**
	high season	F 1040	*IGN 54*
	winter season	F 800/1010	

Booking: Hautes-Alpes booking service

05/C.053

PELLEAUTIER Les Blâches An old, renovated gîte, traditionally furnished, on a livestock farm 3 km from the village. Altitude 925 m. A lake for sailing at 25 km; cross-country skiing at 17 km and ski slopes at 15 km. Living room/kitchenette (1 double divan), 1 bedroom (1 double and 1 child's bed), shower room, electric and wood heating, open ground. Linen available F35 per pair per week. Farm produce from the owners, mobile shops call, restaurant in the village and shopping at Gap (12 km).

Prices:	low season	F 750/830	**4/5 people**
	high season	F 980	*IGN 54*
	winter season	F 750/925	

Booking: Hautes-Alpes booking service

05/G.282

SAINT-ETIENNE-EN-DEVOLUY Le Courtil A ground-floor gîte with modern furnishings, one of two in a renovated house on a farm 2.5 km from the village. Saint-Etienne is a winter sports resort, also popular in summer with swimming-pool, tennis, riding and a golf course. Altitude 1240 metres. Living room/kitchenette (1 double divan), 1 bedroom (1 double bed), shower room, electric heating, open ground. Shopping and restaurant in the village.

Prices:	low season	F 510/690	**4 people**
	high season	F 930	*IGN 54*
	winter season	F 620/1090	

Booking: Hautes-Alpes booking service

05/D447

18

Hautes-Alpes

SAINT-JULIAN-EN-CHAMPSAUR Chantaussel A ground-floor gîte, owned, renovated and simply furnished by the local community 2 km from the village at an altitude of 1150 m. The gîte lies at the edge of the Ecrins national park which has some outstanding mountain scenery with lakes and waterfalls. Living room, kitchen, 2 bedrooms in a recess (2 double and 2 single beds), shower room, oil heating, carport, enclosed courtyard. Farm produce and restaurant in the village, shopping at St Bonnet (5.5 km).

Prices: low season   F 430/630   **6 people**
           high season   F 865   IGN 54
           winter season   F 320/865

Booking: Hautes-Alpes booking service
05/C.691

SAINT SAUVEUR Vabres A gîte in a house in a small hamlet 3 km from the village. Altitude 1100 m. Embrun (8 km) offers good all-year sports facilities, forest walks and mountain rambles – enquire at the tourist office for suggested routes. Car trips could include a visit to Italy through some stunning scenery. Living room, kitchen, 3 adjoining bedrooms (4 double and 1 single bed), bathroom, electric heating, courtyard. Shopping at Embrun.

Prices: low season F 700/980   **9 people**
           high season F 1500   IGN 54
           winter season F 840/1500

Booking: Hautes-Alpes booking service
05/E981

SERRES The owners of this old, renovated house have converted the second floor into a gîte furnished in country style just 0.2 km from the small town of Serres, altitude 680 m. A swimming-pool at 17 km, lake at 19 km and Gap (42 km) has good sports facilities. Living room/kitchenette, 1 bedroom (1 double and 1 large single bed), shower room, no heating, loggia. Farm produce, restaurant and shopping in Serres.

Prices: low season   F 530/660   **3/4 people**
           high season   F 820   IGN 60

Booking: Hautes-Alpes booking service

05/B.506

VILLAR D'ARENE An old renovated stone-built house with simple modern furnishings just 0.50 km from the village, altitude 1650 m. This is splendid mountainous countryside on the edge of the Ecrins national park with good marked footpaths. Various sports at the old fortified town of Briançon. Living room/kitchenette (TV, small washing machine), 3 attic bedrooms (2 double, 2 single and 1 child's bed), fireplace, central heating, open ground. Farm produce and restaurant in the village, shopping at La Grave (3 km).

Prices: low season   F 1060/1280   **6/7 people**
           high season   F 1700   IGN 54
               F 1490/2340   winter season

Booking: Hautes-Alpes booking service
05/0.106

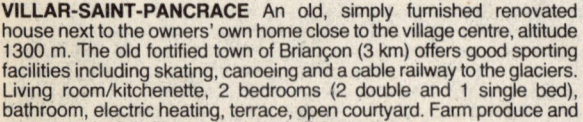

VILLAR-SAINT-PANCRACE An old, simply furnished renovated house next to the owners' own home close to the village centre, altitude 1300 m. The old fortified town of Briançon (3 km) offers good sporting facilities including skating, canoeing and a cable railway to the glaciers. Living room/kitchenette, 2 bedrooms (2 double and 1 single bed), bathroom, electric heating, terrace, open courtyard. Farm produce and restaurant in the village, shopping in Briançon.

Prices: low season   F 690/850   **5 people**
           high season   F 1510   IGN 54
           winter season   F 1060/1510

Booking: Hautes-Alpes booking service
05/R.904

Bouches-du-Rhône

ALLEINS A simply furnished gîte, one of two in the home of the owners who speak good English, near the village centre. At 10 km is Salon-de-Provence, whose most famous citizen was Nostradamus. Sailing at 10 km; the coast 60 km. Living room/kitchenette, 1 bedroom (2 double beds), shower room, oil stove, small enclosed garden with barbecue. Farm produce, shopping and restaurant in the village (0.1 km) or at Salon-de-Provence.

Prices:	low season	F 667	**4 people**
	high season	F 667	*IGN 67*

Booking: Bouches-du-Rhône Loisirs Accueil   **E**

13/R63

ARLES One of two traditionally furnished gîtes in the English-speaking owners' old house on a farm at the heart of the Camargue, on the edge of Vaccarès lake, and just 10 km from the Mediterranean sea. Visit Arles (25 km) to see its fine Roman theatre, arena and other sites. Living room, kitchen, 3 bedrooms (1 double, 4 single beds), shower room, central heating, terrace, open farmland, garden furniture. Shopping and restaurant in the village (2 km) or at Arles.

Prices:	low season	F 1218/1545	**6 people**
	high season	F 1771	*IGN 66*

Booking: Bouches-du-Rhône Loisirs Accueil   **E**

13/R29

BARBENTANE One of two gîtes with traditional furniture in an old house situated on a farm at the edge of the village. Fresh farm produce is sold in the village and there are pleasant country walks in the vicinity. Fishing in local river (3 km), tennis, riding and a swimming-pool at Avignon (8 km). Living room, kitchen, 2 bedrooms (1 double and 2 single beds), shower room, electric heating, open ground with outdoor furniture. Shopping and café in the village (2 km); other shopping at Avignon.

Prices:	low season	F 1161/1510	**4 people**
	high season	F 1766	*IGN 66*

Booking: Bouches-du-Rhône Loisirs Accueil   **E**

13/R48

CHATEAURENARD A small old house with traditional furnishings on a farm, 2.5 km from the old town of Châteaurénard whose eleventh-century château is open to the public. Do not miss historic Avignon (10 km) where an international festival of drama and music is held every July. Kitchen, 1 bedroom (1 double, 1 single bed), shower room, electric heating, enclosed courtyard. Linen available. Fresh fruit from the owners; other shopping and restaurant in the town.

Prices:	low season	F 716/820	**3 people**
	high season	F 983	*IGN 66*

Booking: Bouches-du-Rhône Loisirs Accueil   **E**

13/R59

LA CIOTAT One of three traditionally furnished gîtes in the owners' imposing old house, 2 km from the resort of La Ciotat. There are vast dockyards in the town, but it also has an attractive fishing harbour and good leisure facilities including sailing, water ski-ing and casino. Living room, kitchen, 2 bedrooms (2 double, 2 single beds), shower room, central heating, terrace, spacious enclosed grounds (shared with other gîtes), garden furniture. Farm produce available; shopping and restaurants at La Ciotat.

Prices:	low season	F 1280/1680	**6 people**
	high season	F 1975	*IGN 67*

Booking: Bouches-du-Rhône Loisirs Accueil   **E**

13/R66

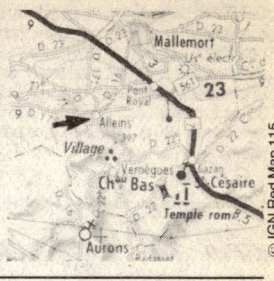

18

Bouches-du-Rhône

GRAVESON A small apartment with contemporary furnishings in the owners' modern home, 1 km from the village at the heart of Provence. At historic Avignon (18 km), see the famous fourteenth-century bridge, the Papal Palace and other sites; the sea (70 km). Living room/kitchenette (1 double divan), 1 bedroom (1 double bed), bathroom, electric heating, open ground with garden furniture, shared with the owners. Linen available. Farm produce, shopping and restaurant in the village.

Prices: low season F 1112/1157 **4 people**
high season F 1270 IGN 66
Booking: Bouches-du-Rhône Loisirs Accueil **E**

13/R67

MALLEMORT La Mascotte A modern gîte in the owners' home, set in open ground, 4 km from the town where you will find a swimming-pool and tennis courts. Ideally situated for exploring Provence: Avignon, Aix, Arles and the coast are all within a radius of 50 km. Kitchen, 2 bedrooms (2 double beds), bathroom, central heating, terrace, open garden. Farm produce, other shopping and restaurant in the village or at Salon-de-Provence (20 km).

Prices: low season F 940/1003 **4 people**
high season F 1218 IGN 67
Booking: Bouches-du-Rhône Loisirs Accueil **E**

13/R19

LE PUY-SAINTE-REPARADE Saint-Canadet A small studio with country-style furnishings, one of two gîtes in the owners' modern house with private swimming-pool and tennis court. It is 2 km from the village centre and 55 km from the coast. The delightful old town of Aix-en-Provence is just 15 km away. Living room/kitchenette (1 double, 1 single bed), shower room, central heating, terrace, open ground and garden furniture shared with the other gîte and owners. Farm produce in the village (2 km); other shopping at Le Puy-Sainte-Réparade (5 km).

Prices: low season on request **3 people**
high season on request IGN 67
Booking: Bouches-du-Rhône Loisirs Accueil **E**

13/R07

ROGNONAS An old, traditionally furnished house on a farm, 2 km from the village centre. At Avignon (4 km), see in particular the Papal Palace, cathedral and the Calvet museum with its impressive collection of French paintings. The Mediterranean coast is close enough for a day trip at 70 km. Living room, kitchen, 2 bedrooms (2 double beds, 1 single divan), shower room, electric heating, terrace, open courtyard with garden furniture. Linen available. Farm produce, shopping and restaurant in the village.

Prices: low season F 757/870 **5 people**
high season F 1043 IGN 66
Booking: Bouches-du-Rhône Loisirs Accueil **E**

13/R53

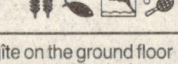

SAINT-CANNAT A small, traditionally furnished gîte on the ground floor of an old farmhouse on a vineyard. At Aix-en-Provence (10 km), do not miss the Granet museum, the Pavillon de Vendôme and the Atelier Cézanne where the painter died. Sailing at a lake (20 km). Living room, kitchen, 1 bedroom (2 single beds, a child's bed on request), shower room, fireplace, electric heating, open ground with garden furniture shared with the owners. Farm produce, shopping and restaurant in the village (4.5 km).

Prices: low season F 880/1003 **2 people**
high season F 1105 IGN 67
Booking: Bouches-du-Rhône Loisirs Accueil **E**

13/R40

Bouches-du-Rhône

SAINT-JULIEN-LES-MARTIGUES One of two simply furnished gîtes in the owners' renovated house on a vineyard where there are footpaths leading down to the beach (5 km). Martigues (7 km) was much appreciated by nineteenth-century painters such as Corot; now a large industrial town, it retains its waterfront charm and has good leisure facilities. Living room/kitchenette, 3 bedrooms (2 double and 1 single bed), bathroom, central heating, small open courtyard with garden furniture. Shops (2 km) and a restaurant in the village (5 km).

Prices:	low season	F 886/1105	5 people
	high season	F 1218	IGN 66

Booking: Bouches-du-Rhône Loisirs Accueil E

13/R08

SAINT-REMY-DE-PROVENCE A modern, traditionally furnished house in a lovely setting, 1.5 km from Saint-Rémy-de-Provence, a delightful little town with a swimming-pool, tennis and riding facilities. It is close enough to the sea for a day trip (60 km). Living room, kitchen, 3 bedrooms (2 double and 2 single beds), bathroom, fireplace, central heating, terrace, open courtyard with garden furniture. Farm produce, shopping and restaurant in the town.

Prices:	low season	F 993/1218	6 people
	high season	F 1433	IGN 66

Booking: Bouches-du-Rhône Loisirs Accueil E

13/R20

SAINT-REMY-DE-PROVENCE A traditionally furnished gîte in the owners' modern house, 2 km from the town, an important centre for market gardening. The sixteenth-century astrologer Nostradamus was born there. Do not miss historic Arles, erstwhile home of Vincent Van Gogh, with its famous Roman sites (25 km). Living room, kitchen, 1 bedroom (1 double, 2 single beds), shower room, electric heating, use of the owners' enclosed garden and outdoor furniture. Linen available. Shopping and restaurant in the town.

Prices:	low season	F 773/886	4 people
	high season	F 1105	IGN 66

Booking: Bouches-du-Rhône Loisirs Accueil E

13/R69

TARASCON One of two traditionally furnished gîtes in an attractive and unusual old house on a mixed farm, 3 km from the town where leisure amenities include sailing. See the fifteenth-century château and the Abbaye de Frigolet nearby. The town stages regular bull runs and is 60 km from the sea. Living room (1 single bed), kitchen, 2 bedrooms (3 double beds), bathroom, fireplace, electric heating, terrace, open garden with outdoor furniture. Farm produce shopping and restaurant in the town or at Boulbon (3 km).

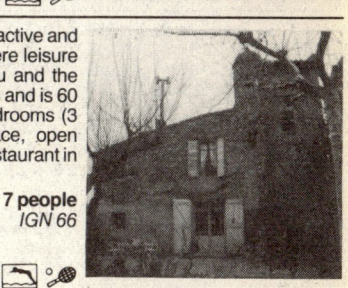

Prices:	low season	F 1105/1440	7 people
	high season	F 1545	IGN 66

Booking: Bouches-du-Rhône Loisirs Accueil E

13/R70

VELAUX A ground-floor gîte in the owners' modern house, 2 km from the village centre. Bathing and sailing on a lake (10 km) and the Mediterranean coast is just 25 km away. Visit the fascinating town of Marseilles (30 km), a blend of old and new, with its bustling port and good shopping facilities. Living room, kitchen, 2 bedrooms (1 double, 1 single and 1 child's bed), shower room, electric heating. Use of the owners' enclosed garden and garden furniture. Linen available. Farm produce, shopping and restaurant in the village.

Prices:	low season	F 932/1043	4 people
	high season	F 1157	IGN 67

Booking: Bouches-du-Rhône Loisirs Accueil E

13/R61

Var

LE BEAUSSET Les Concades A comfortably furnished gîte in the owner's modern home in the fragrant Provence hills, 0.5 km from the centre of a pleasant little town. See the thirteenth-century chapel at Old Beausset. Bandol (9 km) is an attractive seaside resort; take a boat from there to the fascinating Calanques (creeks) at Cassis. Living room/ kitchenette (1 double divan), sleeping area (1 double, 1 single bed), shower room, electric heating, terrace, garden with furniture. Shopping in the town or at Toulon (15 km).

Prices: low season   F 950
         high season   F 1260/1370
Booking: Var booking service   E

5 people
IGN 67

83/225

BRAS A very pleasant gîte with country-style furnishings set on a vineyard at the edge of the village. Local fishing and forest walks; swimming-pool (9 km). At the old town of Brignoles (14 km) visit the museum, formerly the eleventh-century château of the Dukes of Provence. The sea (60 km). Living room, kitchen, 3 bedrooms (2 double and 2 single beds), shower room, fireplace, electric central heating, terrace, carport, ground with child's swing. Farm produce, shopping and restaurant in the village.

Prices: low season   F 1184
         high season   F 1534/1699
Booking: M J. HERMITTE, Quartier des Routes 83149 Bras.
Tel. (94) 78 73 73.   E

6 people
IGN 68

83/455

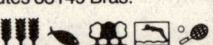

CARCES Saint-Jean An old, renovated gîte with rustic furnishings, in the owner's large farmhouse, set in a vineyard at 6 km from the village centre. There is a swimming-pool on the farm and you may hire bicycles from the owner. Visit Brignoles (10 km), a town famed for bauxite mines. Living room (1 double divan), kitchen, 2 bedrooms (2 double and 1 single bed), bathroom, oil-fired central heating, terrace, garden, outdoor furniture and swings. Shopping and restaurants at 3 km.

Prices: low season   F 968
         high season   F 1184/1287
Booking: Mme BARGES, Mas Saint-Jean, Chemin Départemental 45, 83570 Carces. Tel. (94) 59 59 31.

7 people
IGN 68

83/427

CARCES Saint-Jean A traditionally furnished, modern gîte, lying on a vineyard at 3 km from Montfort-sur-Argens and 6 km from Carces, itself. Farm produce may be purchased from the owners, in the village or from the neighbouring farm. Bathing in a river at 0.2 km, tennis (6 km) and riding (8 km). The sea is at 56 km and is close enough for a day trip. Living room, kitchen, 2 bedrooms (2 double and 2 single beds), bathroom, open fire (wood supplied), heating, terrace, open ground. Shopping and restaurant at 3 km or 6 km.

Prices: low season   F 968
         high season   F 1184/1287
Booking: M L. MAILLE, 42 avenue Ferrandin, 83570 Carces.
Tel. (94) 04 50 97.

6 people
IGN 68

83/39

COGOLIN One of several modern, purpose-built gîtes on a livestock farm 2 km from the village centre. Riding and tennis are at 1 km; the sea and the beach are only 6.5 km and the busy holiday resort of Saint Tropez is at 10 km. Living room/kitchenette, 1 bedroom (2 single beds), bathroom, electric heating, covered terrace. Shopping and restaurant at Cogolin.

Prices: low season   on request
         high season   on request
Booking: M J. SENEQUIER, Le Merle, Chemin de la Graviere, 83310 Cogolin. Tel. 94 54 43 90

2 people
IGN 68

83/284

Var

CORRENS La Praderie An attractive modern gîte with traditional furnishings, on a vineyard outside the village. Brignoles (15 km) is a modern town, but its old quarter is being sympathetically restored and is worth a visit. The coast is an easy day trip at 50 km. Living room/kitchenette (1 double divan), 1 bedroom (1 double bed), shower room, open fire, electric heating, terrace, open ground with garden furniture. Farm produce, other shopping and restaurant in the village (2.5 km), or at Brignoles.

Prices:	low season	F 1100	**4 people**
	high season	F 1420/1570	*IGN 68*

Booking: Var booking service **E**
83/252

GRIMAUD Les Vigneaux A simply furnished ground-floor gîte in the owner's modern house where there are 3 other gîtes, outside the village. Only 3 km from the sea, and 10 km from the world-famous resort of Saint-Tropez. Sailing, tennis and riding in the area, local wines and sea-food. Living room/kitchenette (2 single beds), 1 bedroom (1 double bed), bathroom, central heating, terrace, carport, ground. Shopping and restaurant in the village (2 km).

Prices:	low season	F 1030	**4 people**
	high season	F 1359/1483	*IGN 68*

Booking: M V. MOLAS, Quartier des Vigneaux, 83360 Grimaud.
Tel. (94) 43 23 91.
83/349

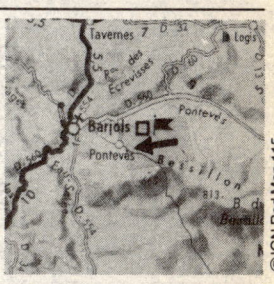

PONTEVES La Chouètte A charming, rustically furnished, cottage-style gîte in a fairly isolated spot, some 5 km from the village. Various leisure facilities, including a swimming-pool and riding at Barjols (5 km), a very attractive village with fountains, and waterfalls in the surrounding woods. Living room/kitchenette, 3 bedrooms (1 double, 1 single, 1 child's bed and 1 double divan), shower room, open fire, gas-fire heating, terrace, garden. Linen available. Shopping and restaurants in either Pontevès or Barjols.

Prices:	low season	F 824	**6 people**
	high season	F 1030	*IGN 68*

Booking: M P. GLAZENER, La Chouètte, Pontevès 83670 Barjols.
Tel. (94) 77 02 24. **E**
83/410

SEILLANS La Fabrique A well-renovated gîte with modern furnishings in an unusual old village which centres on its feudal château. Swimming-pool and tennis in the village; try gliding at Fayence (10 km), an old town whose clock tower offers superb views of the surrounding countryside. The coast (30 km). Studio room/kitchenette (washing machine, 1 double and 1 single bed), shower room, electric heating. Local farm produce available; other shopping and restaurant in the village or at Fayence.

Prices:	low season	F 895	**3 people**
	high season	F 1100/1190	*IGN 68*

Booking: Var booking service **E**
83/773

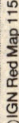

TAVERNES Quartier les Peyronèdes A traditionally furnished, modern gîte in enclosed ground with barbecue facilities, 1.5 km from the village centre. Barjols (5 km) is a picturesque town where local places of interest include the Château de la Reine Jeanne, a Carmelite convent, caves and waterfalls. The sea (70 km). Living room, kitchen (washing machine), 3 bedrooms (3 double beds), fireplace, electric heating, terrace, garage. Farm produce, other shopping and restaurant in the village.

Prices:	low season	F 1100	**6 people**
	high season	F 1420/1570	*IGN 68*

Booking: Var booking service **E**
83/380

18

Var

BAGNOLS-EN-FORET Les Clos *Aire naturelle de camping* in a grassy meadow. The site is partially in the shade and the ground is flat in places and slopes in others, at a distance of 150 metres from the owners' home. The village centre is at 0.4 km, where you may buy fresh farm produce. Tennis in the village; riding at 11 km. The sea and sailing at Fréjus or Saint-Raphaël (20 km). Four hot showers, electricity for caravans, laundry facilities, iron available on request. Shopping and restaurant in the village.

Prices: on request *IGN 68*

Booking: M R. MAGAIL, Camping des Clos, 83600 Bagnols-en-Fôret.

83/AN4

CALLIAN Plaine de Mirur *Camping à la ferme* on a fruit farm, where the owners also raise geese. They have one gîte and one *chambre d'hôte* on their property. The site is partially shaded on flat, grassy ground at 100 metres from the farmhouse, far from the main roads and at 2 km from Callian. Bathing, sailing at a lake (8 km); riding and a swimming-pool (10 km); the sea is at 27 km. One hot shower, meals available on request (approx. F 50). Fresh strawberries, dairy produce and poultry from the owners; other shopping and restaurant at Callian.

Prices: on request *IGN 68*
Booking: M SCAGLIA, Camping Plaine de Mirur, Callian, 83440 Fayence.

83/CF6

RAMATUELLE Les Fondudes *Camping à la ferme* on a vineyard. The site is by a stream on partially shaded flat grassland at 150 metres from the owners' house and 2 km from the village. Evening entertainment is provided for the campers. The sea and beach are at 2 km and leisure facilities are available at the famous resort of Saint-Tropez (9 km). Four hot showers, electricity, garage space available. Farm produce in the village. Nearest restaurant at 0.7 km.

Prices: on request *IGN 68*

Booking: M A. BATTINI, Camping des Fondudes, 83350 Ramatuelle.

83/13

IGN Red Map 115

ROQUEBRUNE-SUR-ARGENS Vaudois *Camping à la ferme* on a cereal farm and vineyard. The site is partially shaded on flat grassland at 4 km from the village and the sea. The lovely, historic town of Fréjus, where there is an amphitheatre and the remains of the walls round the old city, is at 5 km. Six hot showers, electricity, recreation room for children, swings, volleyball, bowling and mini-football, laundryroom, iron and carport. Meals on request. Shopping and restaurant in the village.

Prices: on request *IGN 68*
Booking: Mme G. GONZALEZ, Camping de Vaudois, 83520 Roquebrune-sur-Argens.

83/CF18

SOLLIES-PONT Le Cros de Castel *Camping à la ferme* on a fruit farm and vineyard. The site is by a stream on partially shaded, flat grassland by the owners' house where there are 2 gîtes, and at 2.5 km from the village. Tennis in the village; other activities at Toulon, France's major naval base, and the beach at 20 km. Two hot showers, electricity, children's games, and a sand-pit. Fresh farm produce from the owners; shopping and restaurant in the village.

Prices: on request *IGN 68*
Booking: M CAMBRAY, 'Le Petit Réal', Camping à la ferme, Le-Cros-de-Castel, 83219 Solliès-Pont.

83/CF27

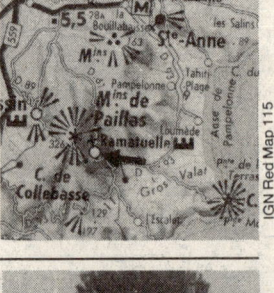

19 LANGUEDOC-ROUSSILLON

The old province of Languedoc stretched much further than the present day region and its name derives from the provençal language of Oc – *oc* meaning yes.

Although now more confined, the region still has a widely varying landscape: the peaks of the Cévennes and Pyrénées; the Causses plateau; the *garrigue* moorlands (also known as the *maquis*, the name adopted by the French resistance of the region); the coastal plains, known as the Midi and the splendid Gorges du Tarn in the Cévennes National Park, where a road runs through picturesque villages, the length of the canyon, giving spectacular views.

The coast is a blend of new resorts, such as Cap d'Agde, Port Camargue and Port Leucate, and old villages and fishing ports, e.g. Collioure, the small fishing port where the Fauvism movement was initiated in 1905 by such artists as Picasso, Dufy and Matisse.

The region is noted for its seafood, including oysters and anchovies; try *Nîmes Brandade* – salt cod blended with garlic, oil and cream. Other specialities include olives, fruit, honey, full fruity red wines and some delicious dessert wines such as *Muscat de Frontignan*.

There are several spa towns (Perrier water comes from Vergèze in Gard) and ski resorts, the highest being Eyne and Puigmal in the Pyrénées. For cross-country ski-ing, go to the Lozère.

Languedoc-Roussillon has some splendid towns which are a must for any itinerary: Carcassonne with its superbly preserved fortified old city; Nîmes which boasts a Roman amphitheatre and other sites; Montpellier, an excellent shopping centre; and Alès, at the heart of the still prosperous silk trade. Also worth a visit are the automobile and railway museum at Uzès (Gard) and the museum of underwater discoveries at Agde (Hérault).

Visitors in February can enjoy the Mardi Gras festival in the village of Palada, near Amelie-les-Bains. August sees the Wine Festival at Banyuls-sur-Mer and the Théâtre Midi Festival at Collioure. The *Corride de Muerte* with Spanish matadors are held in May and September at the Nîmes amphitheatre.

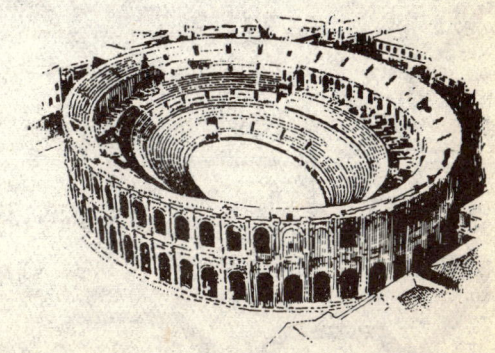

Départements

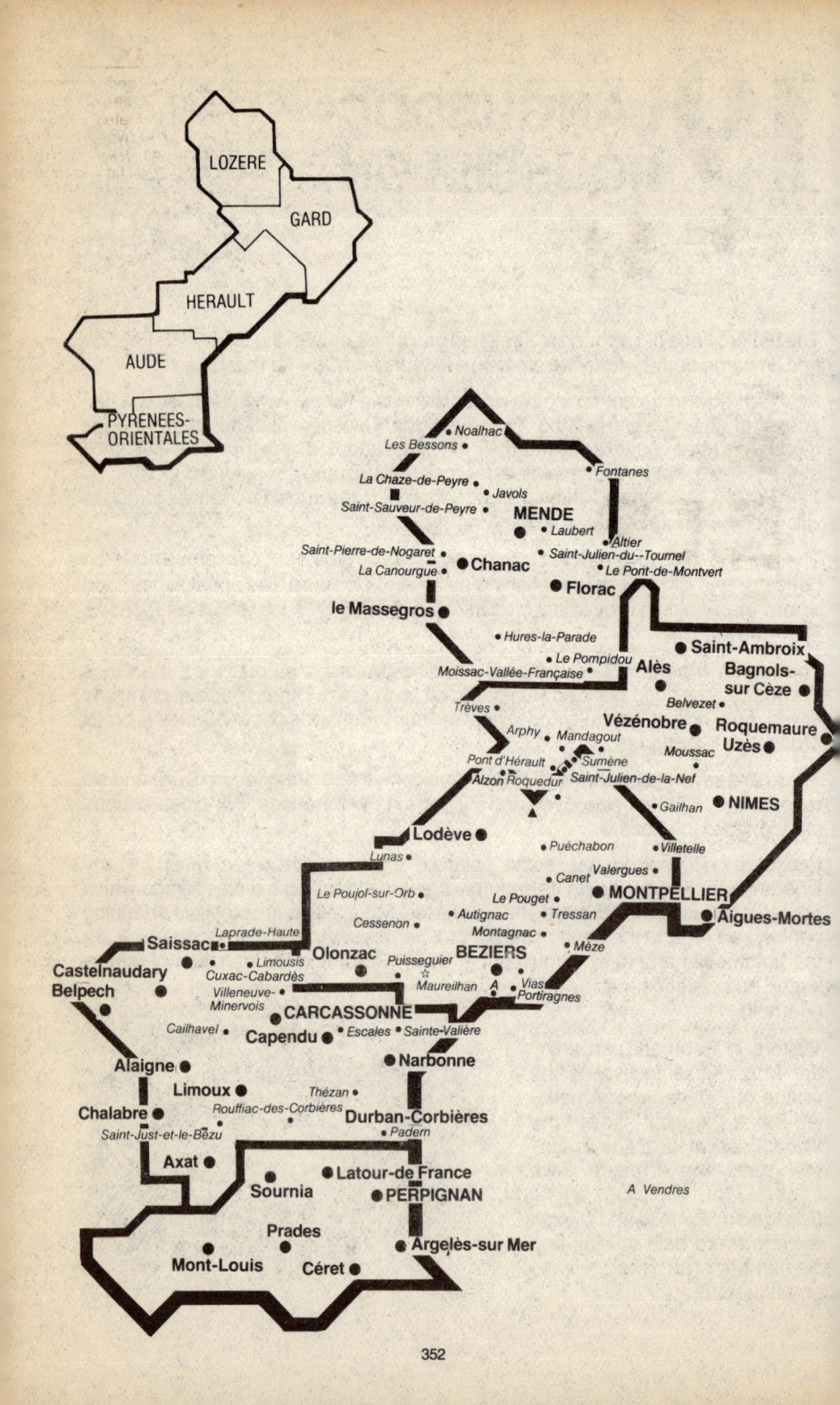

- LOZÈRE
- GARD
- HÉRAULT
- AUDE
- PYRÉNÉES-ORIENTALES

Localités

- Noalhac
- Les Bessons
- Fontanes
- La Chaze-de-Peyre
- Javols
- Saint-Sauveur-de-Peyre
- **MENDE**
- Laubert
- Altier
- Saint-Pierre-de-Nogaret
- Saint-Julien-du-Tournel
- La Canourgue
- Chanac
- Le Pont-de-Montvert
- Florac
- le Massegros
- Hures-la-Parade
- Le Pompidou
- **Saint-Ambroix**
- Moissac-Vallée-Française
- Alès
- **Bagnols-sur Cèze**
- Belvezet
- Trèves
- Vézénobre
- **Roquemaure**
- Arphy
- Mandagout
- Moussac
- Uzès
- Pont d'Hérault
- Sumène
- Alzon
- Roquedur
- Saint-Julien-de-la-Nef
- Gailhan
- **NIMES**
- Lodève
- Puéchabon
- Villetelle
- Lunas
- Canet
- Valergues
- Le Poujol-sur-Orb
- Le Pouget
- **MONTPELLIER**
- Cessenon
- Autignac
- Tressan
- **Aigues-Mortes**
- Laprade-Haute
- Montagnac
- Mèze
- Saissac
- Limousis
- Olonzac
- Puisseguier
- **BÉZIERS**
- Castelnaudary
- Cuxac-Cabardès
- Maureilhan
- Belpech
- Villeneuve-Minervois
- Vias
- Cailhavel
- **CARCASSONNE**
- Portiragnes
- Capendu
- Escales
- Sainte-Valière
- Alaigne
- Narbonne
- Limoux
- Thézan
- Chalabre
- Rouffiac-des-Corbières
- Durban-Corbières
- Saint-Just-et-le-Bézu
- Padern
- Axat
- Latour-de France
- Sournia
- **PERPIGNAN**
- A Vendres
- Prades
- Mont-Louis
- Céret
- Argelès-sur Mer

352

Aude

CAILHAVEL A modern gîte with traditional furnishings at the village centre where you can enjoy walks in the surrounding forest. Swimming-pool, riding and tennis at 12 km. Limoux (18 km) has some interesting Renaissance architecture. Try Blanquette, reputed to be the world's oldest sparkling wine. Visit Alet-les-Bains (28 km approx.), a spa town with a twelfth-century abbey. Living room, kitchen, 2 bedrooms (2 double beds), bathroom, electric heating, terrace, enclosed ground. Mobile shops call; other shopping at 6 km.

Prices:	low season	F 980	**4 people**
	high season	F 1090	IGN 71

Booking: Aude Loisirs Accueil **E**

11/310

LAPRADE-HAUTE Pas-du-Rieu A renovated gîte with traditional furniture, one of two on a farm 4 km from the village (altitude 890 metres). Local river fishing and marked footpaths and forest walks. A lake, swimming-pool, riding and tennis (15 km). The well-preserved fortified mediaeval town of Carcassonne (40 km). Living room, kitchen, 2 bedrooms (2 double, 2 single beds), shower room, open fire, electric heating, terrace, open ground. Baker, butcher and grocer call; restaurant near the gîte, shops in the village.

Prices:	low season	F 655	**6 people**
	high season	F 835	IGN 64

Booking: Aude Loisirs Accueil **E**

11/1073

LAPRADE-HAUTE Pas-du-Rieu A second gîte in the attractive, renovated farm building described above. It lies in the Aude plain where sites include fabulous châteaux (Saissac, Lastours, etc.), Limousis caves (35 km) and the superbly preserved city of Carcassonne (40 km). Altitude 890 metres. Living room, kitchen, 2 bedrooms (2 double and 1 single bed), shower room, open fire, electric heating, terrace and open ground. Shopping from mobile shops or in the village (4 km).

Prices:	low season	F 655	**5 people**
	high season	F 835	IGN 64

Booking: Aude Loisirs Accueil **E**

11/1073b

LIMOUSIS A renovated gîte with traditional furniture in the village where you can visit interesting underground caves. Four bicycles at your disposal, local footpaths. The small town of Villeneuve-Minervois with imposing oak and pine forests and famed wine only 6 km away; Carcassonne (25 km). Living room/kitchenette, 2 bedrooms (3 double and 1 large single bed), shower room, open fire. Baker, butcher and grocer call. Shops and restaurant in Villeneuve-Minervois.

Prices:	low season	F 670	**7 people**
	high season	F 915	IGN 64

Booking: Aude Loisirs Accueil **E**

11/130

ROUFFIAC-DES-CORBIERES A small, renovated, traditionally furnished gîte at the heart of a pleasant village enjoying a Mediterranean climate (the sea at 60 km). The Corbières region is noted for its wine and Cathar châteaux. Riding and tennis (20 km); the département capital of Perpignan (45 km); the Sigean African Reserve (70 km) is also worth a visit. Living room/kitchenette, 2 bedrooms (2 double beds), and alcove (1 single bed), shower room, oil stove, and garden. Shopping in the village or at Perpignan.

Prices:	low season	F 460	**5 people**
	high season	F 720	IGN 72

Booking: Aude Loisirs Accueil **E**

11/295

19

Aude

SAINT-JUST-ET-LE-BEZU En Bec A renovated gîte with traditional furnishings, on a vineyard, 2 km from the village. A forest nearby and ancient monuments to visit. Quillan (10 km), is a town rich in history; there you may fish for trout in the River Aude and use the tennis courts, swimming-pool and other amenities. The sea (70 km). Altitude 557 metres. Living room/kitchenette, 3 bedrooms (3 double, 2 single beds), shower room, open fire, central heating, balcony, garden. Baker, butcher and grocer call, shops and restaurant in Quillan.

Prices:	low season	F 650	**8 people**
	high season	F 1160	IGN 72

Booking: Aude Loisirs Accueil   E

11/809

SAINTE-VALIERE A renovated and traditionally furnished village gîte in the lovely hilly region of Corbières. It is just 15 km from the lively town of Narbonne and 35 km from the Mediterranean Sea. Do not miss historic Carcassonne (45 km); other sites include the Galamus gorge, Cathar châteaux and Lagrasse and Saint-Hilaire abbeys. Living room/kitchenette, 2 bedrooms (2 double and 1 single bed), shower room, no heating. Shopping in the village or at Narbonne.

Prices:	low season	F 560	**4/5 people**
	high season	F 860	IGN 72

Booking: Aude Loisirs Accueil   E

11/398

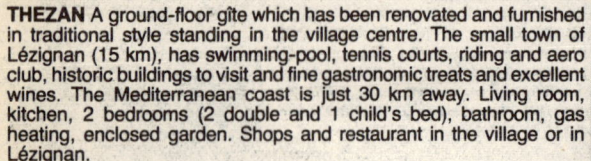

THEZAN A ground-floor gîte which has been renovated and furnished in traditional style standing in the village centre. The small town of Lézignan (15 km), has swimming-pool, tennis courts, riding and aero club, historic buildings to visit and fine gastronomic treats and excellent wines. The Mediterranean coast is just 30 km away. Living room, kitchen, 2 bedrooms (2 double and 1 child's bed), bathroom, gas heating, enclosed garden. Shops and restaurant in the village or in Lézignan.

Prices:	low season	F 435	**4/5 people**
	high season	F 850	IGN 72

Booking: Aude Loisirs Accueil   E

11/961

VILLENEUVE-MINERVOIS A pleasant gîte on the first floor of the owner's renovated house, furnished in traditional style only 0.3 km from the village centre, where there is a river for fishing; marked footpaths nearby. Swimming-pool and tennis (10 km). A visit to the spectacular fortified city of Carcassonne (20 km) is a must. Living room/kitchenette, 2 bedrooms (2 double, 1 single bed), shower room, terrace, courtyard. Farm produce, local wine, shops and restaurant in the village.

Prices:	low season	F 535	**5 people**
	high season	F 660	IGN 72

Booking: Aude Loisirs Accueil   E

11/211

VILLENEUVE-MINERVOIS An attractive gîte, renovated and traditionally furnished, at the village centre. This is a region of picturesque villages (e.g. Caunes-Minervois), Romanesque churches and vineyards. See, too, the fortified Cistercian farm at Fontcalvi. The sea and sailing facilities at 65 km. Living room/kitchenette, 2 bedrooms (2 double and 1 single bed), shower room, fireplace, terrace, courtyard. Shopping in the village or at Carcassonne (20 km).

Prices:	low season	F 525	**5 people**
	high season	F 835	IGN 72

Booking: Aude Loisirs Accueil   E

11/1171

Gard

ALZON Valcroze One of two gîtes in a renovated house in a farming hamlet of the Cévennes National Park (altitude 700 metres). Local fishing and walks on marked footpaths. The lovely old town of Le Vigan (20 km) on the river Arre, has a swimming-pool, tennis and other attractions. Ski-ing (23 km) and the sea (100 km). Living room, kitchen, 2 bedrooms (3 double and 1 single bed), shower room, fireplace, terrace. Shopping locally or at Le Vigan.

Prices: low season   F 700   **7 people**
          high season   F 1300   IGN 65

Booking: Gard booking service   **E**
30/A12

ARPHY Galary A first-floor gîte, one of two, furnished in rustic fashion, in an old Cevenol house in a pretty hamlet, 2 km from the village. A swimming-pool nearby; Le Vigan (7 km) has tennis courts and a twelfth-century bridge. Ski-ing at 25 km; the sea (75 km). Living room/kitchenette, 1 bedroom (1 double, 1 child's bed and 4 single beds on mezzanine landings), shower room, open fire, oil heating, terrace. Mobile baker; farm produce available; other shopping at 3 km; a restaurant within walking distance (0.3 km).

Prices: low season   F 750   **7 people**
          high season   F 1270   IGN 59

Booking: Gard booking service   **E**
30/V131

BELVEZET Pujet A well-renovated stone house with contemporary furnishings, on a vineyard in a farming hamlet, 1 km from the village. At the interesting old town of Uzès (10 km) there is a motor and railway museum, swimming-pool, tennis and other amenities. The sea is at 80 km. Living room/kitchenette, 2 bedrooms (2 double and 4 single beds on a mezzanine), shower room, open fire, electric heating, terrace, garage, garden. Shopping and restaurant at Uzès.

Prices: low season   F 820   **8 people**
          high season   F 1550   IGN 59

Booking: Gard booking service   **E**

30/L12

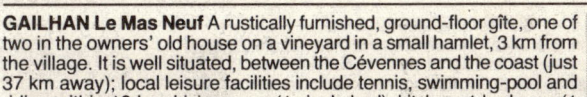

GAILHAN Le Mas Neuf A rustically furnished, ground-floor gîte, one of two in the owners' old house on a vineyard in a small hamlet, 3 km from the village. It is well situated, between the Cévennes and the coast (just 37 km away); local leisure facilities include tennis, swimming-pool and riding within 10 km. Living room (1 single bed), kitchen, 1 bedroom (1 double, 1 single bed), bathroom, oil heating, terrace, open ground. Linen available. Local wine available and mobile baker calls; other shopping and restaurant at Quissac (6 km).

Prices: low season   F 670   **4 people**
          high season   F 1210   IGN 66

Booking: Gard booking service   **E**
30/Q12

MANDAGOUT L'Arboux A renovated stone house in the local style, traditionally furnished, perched on the side of a hill in a Cevenol valley, at the edge of the Cévennes National Park. Sea at 70 km. Living room/kitchenette, 3 bedrooms – reached by an outside staircase (2 double beds, 1 single), shower room, fireplace, gas heating, terrace. Garden with a stream. Mobile baker calls; farm produce and shopping in the village (4 km) or at Le Vigan (7 km).

Prices: low season   F 560   **5 people**
          high season   F 1200   IGN 59

Booking: Gard booking service   **E**

30/V13

Gard

MANDAGOUT L'Arboux One of two gîtes with traditional, country-style furnishings, in a renovated house in a large hamlet in the Cévennes National Park. River bathing and fishing and forest walks close by (0.2 km). There is a museum of local arts and traditions and many other leisure facilities at Le Vigan (7 km). Living room/kitchenette, 2 bedrooms (1 double and 3 single beds), shower room, fireplace, electric heating, terrace, enclosed courtyard. Mobile baker calls, farm produce in the village; other shopping and restaurant at Le Vigan.

Prices:	low season	F 650	**5 people**
	high season	F 1190	IGN 59

Booking: Gard booking service   E

30/V133

MANDAGOUT Beaulieu One of two traditionally furnished gîtes in a lovely old village presbytery which has been well renovated and is set in a pretty garden surrounded by the Cevenol countryside and mountains (altitude 550 metres). Swimming-pool, and tennis at the old town of Le Vigan (10 km). Living room (2 single beds), kitchen, 1 bedroom (1 double bed), shower room, fireplace, heating, garden. Farm produce and other shopping in the village or at Le Vigan where there are restaurants.

Prices:	low season	F 630	**4 people**
	high season	F 1025	IGN 59

Booking: Gard booking service   E

30/V118

MANDAGOUT Beaulieu A modern house, one of three recently built gîtes just outside the village in the Cévennes near the Massif Aigoual. Natural sites in the region include many caves and gorges; leisure facilities at Le Vigan (9 km) include swimming-pool and tennis. Ski-ing at 40 km. Living room, kitchen, 2 bedrooms and mezzanine landing (3 double, 1 child's bed), shower room, fireplace, electric heating, terrace, carport, courtyard and open ground. Farm produce available; other shopping and restaurants at Le Vigan.

Prices:	low season	F 700	**7 people**
	high season	F 1300	IGN 59

Booking: Gard booking service   E

30/V127

MOUSSAC A village gîte in a wing of a renovated village house with traditional, country-style furnishings. It lies in a wine-producing region between Nîmes, Alès and Uzès – all fascinating towns to visit. At Nîmes in particular (22 km), see the famous Roman sites. Local fishing, bathing and tennis (0.5 km); the sea (60 km). Living room, kitchen, 2 bedrooms (3 double and 1 single bed), shower room, open fire, electric heating, terrace. Shopping in the village or at Nîmes.

Prices:	low season	F 710	**7 people**
	high season	F 1300	IGN 59

Booking: Gard booking service   E

30/B12

PONT D'HERAULT Le Mas de Lègue Four purpose-built and simply furnished tiny gîtes in a lovely spot, slightly isolated, on a farm 1.5 km from the village. The gîtes are ideal for a group as they have a communal lounge and terrace, although each gîte also has its own small living and cooking area. Five bedrooms altogether (4 double and 3 single beds), 2 shower rooms, open fire, oil heating, terrace, garden and enclosed ground with garden furniture. Mobile fishmonger calls; other shopping and restaurant in the village or at Le Vigan (7 km).

Prices:	low season	F 1300	**11 people**
	high season	F 2335	IGN 59

Booking: Gard booking service   E

30/S115

ROQUEDUR Roquedur-le-Haut A gîte in the owners' lovely old, renovated house, typical of this region and lying 3 km from the village, between the Causses plateau and the Cévennes National Park (altitude 600 metres). Local forest walks; swimming-pool and other leisure facilities at Le Vigan (7 km). The sea (60 km). Living room/kitchenette, 3 bedrooms (1 double, 3 single and 1 child's bed), shower room, open fire, terrace. Shopping and restaurant at Le Vigan (7 km).

Prices: low season F 730
high season F 1320

6 people
IGN 59

Booking: Gard booking service E

30/V144

SAINT-JULIEN-DE-LA-NEF Piedcourt A truly rural gîte with traditional furnishings in a renovated house in a hamlet, 1 km from the village. Ganges (6 km) is an industrial town, known for its silk manufacture; see the ruined château and octagonal church there. The sea is an easy day trip at 50 km. Living room/kitchenette (2 single beds), 2 bedrooms (2 double and 2 single beds), shower room, fireplace, electric heating, terrace. Mobile baker calls; other shopping at Ganges or Le Vigan (10 km) where there are restaurants.

Prices: low season F 685
high season F 1310

8 people
IGN 65

Booking: Gard booking service E

30/S145

SUMÈNE Le Castanet One of two simply furnished gîtes (this one on the ground floor) in a renovated house in a farming hamlet of the mountainous region of the Cévennes National Park – so good for walking. There is a feudal château at Saint-Hippolyte-du-Fort (15 km approx.). Altitude 550 metres. Living room/kitchenette, 3 bedrooms (2 double, 2 single and 1 child's bed), shower room, fireplace, central heating, terrace and courtyard. Farm produce in the village and shopping in Sumène (5 km) or at Le Vigan (10 km).

Prices: low season F 700
high season F 1300

7 people
IGN 59

Booking: Gard booking service E

30/S14

SUMÈNE Le Castanet A slightly isolated, modern house, built on the side of a hill in a hamlet, 4.5 km from Sumène, near the foothills of the Massif d'Aigoual (altitude 570 metres). Take a trip to the fine old town of Montpellier (50 km approx.) or just a little further to the coast (65 km). Living room, kitchen, 3 bedrooms (2 double, 1 single bed), shower room, open fire, heating, open ground. Farm produce in the village and shopping at Sumène; restaurant at Le Vigan (10 km).

Prices: low season F 750
high season F 1400

5 people
IGN 59

Booking: Gard booking service E

30/S114

TREVES A gîte, one of two in a renovated village house which has rustic furnishings, at the heart of the Cévennes National Park (altitude 600 metres). Trèves is surrounded by high wooded hills and has a little Romanesque church. Visit the nearby gorges. Swimming-pool, riding and ski-ing in winter (20 km). Living room/kitchenette, 2 bedrooms (1 double, 2 single bunk beds), shower room, terrace, enclosed ground. Shopping in the village or at Le Vigan (40 km).

Prices: low season F 63
No high season booking.

4 people
IGN 58

Booking: Gard booking service E

30/T12

...GNAC One of two gîtes in a stone-built house at the centre of the ...age in a wine-growing district (the owners will sell their own *appellation controlée* wine). A swimming-pool at 4 km and it is just 30 km from the sea and the mountains. Living room/kitchenette (1 double divan), 1 bedroom (1 double bed), shower room, electric heating, garage, open ground with garden furniture (shared with the other gîte). Linen available (F 35 per set per week). Mobile shops call; shopping and restaurant in the village or at Béziers (18 km).

Prices: low season   F 800/1100   **4 people**
           high season   F 1400   *IGN 65*
Booking: M C. HORTER, 10 avenue de Beziers, Autignac 34480 Magalas. Tel. (67) 90 26 79.
34/018.3

BEZIERS Montimas A renovated cottage with traditional furnishings, on a vineyard, 3 km from Béziers which dates back to Roman times, and has a splendid cathedral. The *corrida de muerte* is held in the amphitheatre there regularly during the summer. The sea (10 km). Living room (1 single divan), kitchen, 2 bedrooms (2 double and 1 child's bed), shower room, fireplace, electric heating, courtyard, enclosed ground with garden furniture. Linen available. Farm produce from the owners; other shopping and restaurant at Béziers.

Prices: low season   F 700/750   **6 people**
           high season   F 1000/1100   *IGN 65*
Booking: M J. MOREAU, Domaine des Oliviers, Montimas, 34500 Béziers. Tel. (67) 76 20 94   **E**
34/321.02

CAMPAGNAN Mas Soyris A renovated gîte on a vineyard outside the village (1 km). The interesting old Roman town of Pézenas (12 km), at the heart of this wine-growing region, has a ruined château. The playwright Molière had his début there and is commemorated by a statue. The sea (35 km). Living room/kitchenette, 2 bedrooms (3 double and 1 child's bed), shower room, fireplace (wood supplied), central heating, terrace, garage, garden with outdoor furniture. Mobile baker calls; local wine from the village; other shopping at 3 km.

Prices: low season   F 650/700   **7 people**
           high season   F 800/850   *IGN 65*
Booking: M P. H. SOYRIS, rue de l'Eglise, Campagnan, 34230 Paulhan. Tel. (67) 25 04 43.
34/047-1

CANET A renovated house with country-style furnishings on a vineyard at the village centre. Local river fishing, bathing and tennis. See the keep and towers of the feudal château at the medieval town of Clermont-L'Hérault (5 km) which has an important grape market (for eating, not wine!). The coast 30 km. Living room/kitchenette, 2 bedrooms (1 double, 2 single beds), bathroom, electric heating, garden with outdoor furniture. Shopping (including local fruit) and restaurant in the village.

Prices: low season   F 600/700   **4 people**
           high season   F 1000   *IGN 65*
Booking: Mme J. HENRY, 63 Grande-Rue, Canet, 34800 Clermont-l'Hérault. Tel. (57) 95 70 51.
34/051.6

CESSENON Mas de Raties One of two gîtes in a renovated house with traditional, country-style furnishings on a farm surrounded by pine woods, situated between the sea (35 km) and the mountains (40 km). There is a beach by the river in the village at 1.5 km (bathing and fishing). Living room, kitchen, 3 bedrooms (2 double, 1 single, 2 child's beds and a cot), fireplace, heating, terrace, garage, open ground with garden furniture and barbecue. Shopping and restaurant in the village or at Béziers (20 km).

Prices: low season   F 1000/1100   **8 people**
           high season   F 1250   *IGN 65*
Booking: M L. ROBERT, 7bis rue de la Source, 34460 Cessenon. Tel. (67) 89 61 91.
34/074.7

Hérault

CESSENON Mas de Raties A second gîte in the renovated farm building described above, in a lovely spot, 1.5 km from the village. Bicycles for hire at Béziers (20 km), an interesting hill-top town with good leisure amenities; see the amphitheatre there. Living room (TV, 1 double divan), kitchen, 2 bedrooms (2 double and 1 child's bed), shower room, fireplace, heating, terrace, garage, open ground, shared with the other gîte (garden furniture and barbecue). Shopping and twice-weekly visiting market in the village. 
Prices: low season F 1000/1100 **7 people**
         high season F 1250 *IGN 65*
Booking: M L. ROBERT, 7bis rue de la Source, 34460 Cessenon. Tel. (67) 89 61 91.
34/074.8

MEZE Domaine de Geyrols A traditionally furnished, ground-floor gîte in the owners' renovated house on a vineyard, just 10 km from the Mediterranean sea. Try the local oysters and mussels. Visit Sète (20 km), which has a picturesque old port; see in particular the important art collection in the Musée Paul Valéry. Living room/kitchenette, 1 bedroom (1 double, 1 single bed), shower room, electric heating, terrace, carport, extensive open ground (garden furniture). Linen available. Mobile baker and shopping in the village (5 km). 
Prices: low season F 600/800 **3 people**
         high season F 980 *IGN 65*
Booking: Mme J. BEMAU, Domaine de Geyrols, 34140 Mèze. Tel. (67) 43 80 82.
34/157.1

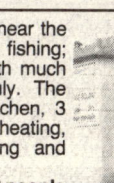

MONTAGNAC A fine old house with traditional furnishings, near the village centre, with tennis court right there. Local river fishing; swimming-pool (5 km). Pézenas (6 km) is an old town with much interesting architecture. It stages a drama festival in July. The Mediterranean coast is just 25 km away. Living room, kitchen, 3 bedrooms (2 double and 2 single beds), shower room, gas heating, balcony, garage, garden with outdoor furniture. Shopping and restaurant in the village (0.1 km). 
Prices: low season F 1200 **6 people**
         high season F 1500 *IGN 65*
Booking: M J. BERT, 14 rue Jean-Jaures, 34530 Montagnac. Tel. (67) 98 33 57.
34/162-1

PORTIRAGNES This old farmhouse has been converted to provide several simply furnished gîtes (this one on the ground floor). It is 4 km from the village but less than 1 km from the sea (bathing and sailing). The modern resort of Cap d'Agde is just 10 km away. Kitchen (washing machine), 2 bedrooms (2 double, 2 single beds), shower room, heating, garden with barbecue and child's swing. Linen available (F 20 per set per week). Shopping in the village or at Béziers (10 km); a restaurant within walking distance (0.5 km). 
Prices: low season F 620/635 **6 people**
         high season F 1130/1170 *IGN 65*
Booking: Mme R. SICARD, Gîtes Ruraux, Domaine de Cassafières, 34420 Portiragnès. Tel. (67) 90 90 32.
34/209.16

PORTIRAGNES A second, simply furnished gîte in the house described above on a mixed farm, ideally situated for day trips to the Pyrenees, Cathar châteaux and the many Mediterranean resorts. The old fishing port of Agde, just along the coast, has an unusual fortified castle. Kitchen, 2 bedrooms (1 double, 3 single beds), shower room, central heating, garden with barbecue and swing. Linen available. Shopping in the village (4 km) or at Béziers (10 km).
Prices: low season F 610/705 **5 people**
         high season F 1055/1155 *IGN 65*
Booking: Mme R. SICARD, Gîtes Ruraux, Domaine de Cassafières, 34420 Portiragnès. Tel. (67) 90 90 32.
34/209.17

19

Hérault

LE POUGET A renovated and traditionally furnished house in a village where you can visit the mysterious standing stones. Clermont-L'Hérault (9 km) is a small town with ruined château and fortified church; swimming-pool and riding facilities and sailing on Salagou lake near the town. Living room/kitchenette, 1 bedroom (1 double, 2 single and 1 child's bed), shower room, gas heating, garage, garden with outdoor furniture. Linen available. Shopping and restaurant in the village (0.3 km), or at Gignac (9 km).

Prices:	low season	F 650/700	**5 people**
	high season	F 1050/1100	IGN 65

Booking: Mme M. A. VENEUR, 10 rue des Caves, Le Pouget, 34230 Paulhan. Tel. (67) 96 76 98.
34/210-2

LE POUJOL-SUR-ORB A renovated and simply furnished house near the village centre. Visitors in July can see the annual art exhibition at the pleasant little spa town of Lamalou-les-Bains (2 km) where leisure amenities include tennis, riding and a casino. The coast is an easy day trip at 50 km. Kitchen (small washing machine), 2 bedrooms (2 double beds, 1 child's bed available), shower room, fireplace, heating, terrace, garage, open ground. Mobile fishmonger and *charcutier*; other shopping and restaurant in the village.

Prices:	low season	F 600	**4 people**
	high season	F 700/769	IGN 65

Booking: M F. CAZALS, Le Poujol-sur-Orb, 34600 Bédarieux.
Tel. (67) 95 66 58.
34/211.1

PUECHABON An old house with country-style furnishings at the village centre, surrounded by woods. Montpellier (28 km) is a fine old town where you should see in particular the Arc de Triomphe, the Promenade du Peyrou and the Château d'Eau, the pavilion at the end of the aqueduct. The sea (40 km). Living room, kitchen, 3 bedrooms (3 double and 1 child's bed), shower room, oil stove, balcony, garage, outdoor furniture. Linen available. Farm produce and other shopping in the village; a restaurant at 4 km.

Prices:	low season	F 520/585	**7 people**
	high season	F 877/906	IGN 65

Booking: M A. SANIER, 26 avenue de Gignac, Aniane, 34150 Gignac.
Tel. (67) 57 78 15.

34/221.2

PUISSEGUIER A large old house which has been renovated to provide two gîtes with traditional, country-style furnishings. It is in a peaceful spot near the village centre at the foot of the Cevennes mountains. Visit the Sigean Wildlife Reserve at 25 km. Living room/kitchenette (TV, 1 double divan), 4 bedrooms (3 double, 1 single bed and a cot), shower room, electric heating, small terrace and open ground shared with the other gîte. Linen available (F 80 per set per week). Shopping in the village or at Béziers (18 km).

Prices:	low season	F 650/900	**10 people**
	high season	F 1200	IGN 65

Booking: M J. ASSET, 24 avenue de Béziers, 34620 Puisseguier.
Tel. (67) 93 74 01.
34/225.1

TRESSAN Visitors to this renovated gîte in late August can join in the fun at the local village festival. Sailing at Salagou lake (9 km); other leisure amenities at the pleasant market town of Clermont-L'Hérault which has a ruined château and fortified church. Living room/kitchenette, 2 bedrooms (1 double, 2 single, 1 child's bed, a cot also available), shower room, electric heating. Mobile fishmonger, charcutier and greengrocer call; other shopping in the village.

Prices:	low season	F 800	**5 people**
	high season	F 1000	IGN 65

Booking: Mme O. CHAUVET, 10 place du Jeu-de-Ballon, Tressan, 34230 Paulhan. Tel. (67) 96 74 31.

34/313.2

Hérault

VENDRES Les Arbousiers A modern holiday home with traditional furnishings 1 km from the village centre, and right by the sea. Béziers (15 km) is an ancient town at the junction of the river Orb and the Canal du Midi; see the wine museum there in a former Dominican church. Living room (1 double divan), kitchen, 3 bedrooms (3 double beds), bathroom, electric central heating, terrace, enclosed garden with outdoor furniture. Linen available (F 150 per set per week). Shopping and restaurant in the village. 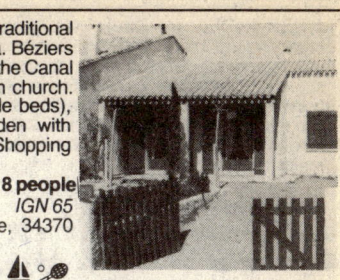
Prices: low season   F 600/800   **8 people**
         high season   F 1800   IGN 65
Booking: M FABRE-BARTHEZ, impasse de la pharmacie, 34370 Maureilhan.
34/329.3

VIAS A modern house bordering the Canal du Midi near the town centre which has a market on Wednesday and Saturdays. It is just 2 km from the sea and 4 km from the old town of Agde. The nearby Cap d'Agde is a modern resort becoming increasingly popular with tourists. Living room/kitchenette, 1 bedroom (1 double, 2 single beds and a cot), shower room, central heating, open courtyard. Shopping and restaurant in the town (1.5 km), in Agde or at Béziers (16 km). 
Prices: low season   F 770/875   **5 people**
         high season   F 1000   IGN 65
Booking: M H. PASTRE, Les Oeillets, 34450 Vias.
Tel. (67) 94 00 62. **E**
34/332.13

VIAS Domaine Saint-Louis A small gîte with traditional, country-style furnishings in the owner's renovated house on a vineyard, just 2 km from the town centre (where you can hire bicycles) and the coast; try the superb local seafood. There is a village carnival o the Sunday following Mardi Gras. Living room/kitchenette, 1 bedroom (3 single and 1 child's bed), shower room, electric heating, terrace, open ground with garden furniture. Linen available. Shopping and restaurant in the village or at Agde (5 km). 
Prices: low season   F 670/890   **4 people**
         high season   F 1100   IGN 65
Booking: M C. PLUCHET, Domaine Saint-Louis, Route de la Plage, 34450 Vias. Tel. (67) 94 01 81. **E**
34/332.18

VILLETELLE A first-floor apartment in the owners' old village house. At Lunel (7 km), a town noted for its Muscat wines, see the charming public gardens (laid out by Lenôtre). One of the town's traditions is the shoeing of Camargue bulls in May. Living room (1 single divan), kitchen, 1 bedroom (1 double, 1 large single and 1 child's bed), shower room, balcony, enclosed garden. Mobile butcher and fishmonger call; other shopping in the village (including local wine); a restaurant at 3 km. 
Prices: low season   F 530/700   **5 people**
         high season   F 850   IGN 66
Booking: M F. BOURGUET, Place du Porche, Villetelle, 34400 Lunel.
Tel. (67) 71 35 60.
34/340.02

MAUREILHAN Chambre d'hôte accommodation in the owners' renovated, traditionally furnished house on a village vineyard where you may buy the owners' wine and honey. Béziers (9 km) has a fortified cathedral and good museums. The sea (20 km). Five rooms available four with private bath or shower. Bedrooms 1 and 2, 2 double and 1 single bed; bedroom 3, 2 double beds; bedroom 4, 1 double bed; bedroom 5, 2 single beds. Lounge, garage, and garden at your disposal. Main meals available (F 45 each), shopping in the village. 
Prices: F 630/800 per week   **13 people**
                                                          IGN 65
Booking: M L. FABRE-BARTHEZ, Les Arbousiers, Maureilhan, 34370 Cazouls-lès-Béziers. Tel. (67) 90 52 49.
34/155

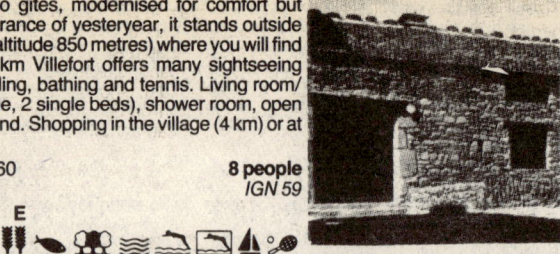

Lozère

ALTIER La Pigeyre One of two gîtes, modernised for comfort but preserving the charm and appearance of yesteryear, it stands outside the village near a livestock farm (altitude 850 metres) where you will find fishing and forest walks. At 15 km Villefort offers many sightseeing opportunities and a lake with sailing, bathing and tennis. Living room/kitchenette, 3 bedrooms (3 double, 2 single beds), shower room, open fire, oil central heating, open ground. Shopping in the village (4 km) or at Villefort.

Prices: low season   F 760/960
         high season   F 1280

8 people
IGN 59

Booking: Lozère Loisirs Accueil E
48/G1333822

LES BESSONS Moulin de la Vedrine A comfortable former mill house on a livestock farm in a pleasant, isolated setting, with nearby river, forests, fishing and hunting. Saint-Chély-d'Apcher (6 km) has interesting old buildings, druidic stones, tennis. Altitude 1000 metres. Living room/kitchenette, 2 bedrooms (2 double beds, 2 single), shower room, fireplace, oil central heating, ground. Farm produce available locally; shopping and restaurant in Saint-Chély-d'Apcher.

Prices: low season   F 845/1040
         high season   F 1420
         winter season F 1040

6 people
IGN 58

Booking: Lozère Loisirs Accueil E
48/2

LA CANOURGUE Le Domal A stone house sensitively modernised and furnished traditionally 3 km outside the village (altitude 840 metres). At La Canourgue (12 km) you may swim, fish, play tennis and go for excursions to the famous Gorges du Tarn or the many archaeological digs and sites which abound. Living room, kitchen, 2 bedrooms (2 double, 2 single beds), shower room, open fireplace, central heating, grounds. Shopping at La Canourgue.

Prices: low season   F 845/1040
         high season   F 1420
         winter season F 1040

6 people
IGN 58

Booking: Lozère Loisirs Accueil E
48/G2796639

LA CHAZE-DE-PEYRE Grandviala A pretty stone house in a tiny hamlet on the Margeride Plateau (altitude 1000 metres). Tennis at Aumont-Aubrac (6 km) where there are Roman ruins. Sailing at a lake and cross-country ski-ing (10 km). A swimming-pool at the fortified town of Marjevols (23 km). Living room, kitchen, 3 bedrooms (2 double, 3 single beds), shower room, fireplace, central heating. Shopping and a restaurant at Aumont-Aubrac.

Prices: low season   F 625/760
         high season   F 910
         winter season F 760

7 people
IGN 58

Booking: Lozère Loisirs Accueil E
48/G0201525

FONTANES One of two gîtes with country-style furnishings in a well-renovated house at the village centre. Bathing and sailing at nearby lake Naussac. Tennis and other leisure facilities at the attractive old market town of Langogne (7 km). Altitude 7000 metres. Living room/kitchenette (1 single bed), 2 bedrooms (1 double, 2 single beds), shower room, fireplace, heating, enclosed ground. Shopping at Longogne.

Prices: low season   on request
         high season   on request
         winter season on request

5 people
IGN 50

Booking: Lozère Loisirs Accueil E
48/C1062520

Lozère

HURES-LA-PARADE Nivoliers One of two gîtes in a rustically furnished house, near the Gorges du Tarn and just 1 km from the gliding centre at Chanet. Also in the vicinity, visit the Château d'Ayres and the fascinating pot-holes at Argilan and Aven-Armand. Living room/kitchenette, 2 bedrooms (1 double, 3 single beds), shower room, fireplace, electric heating, enclosed courtyard with garden furniture. Farm produce available locally; shopping and restaurant at Meyrueis (12 km).

Prices: low season — on request
high season — on request
winter season — on request

5 people
IGN 58

Booking: Lozère Loisirs Accueil E
48/6

JAVOLS Longuessagne A renovated house comprising two gîtes with country-style furnishings (altitude 1000 metres). Mende (25 km approx.), the département capital, has a fine cathedral in the picturesque old quarter of the town; a zoo at Chastel-Nouvel, 6 km from Mende. Living room (1 single bed), kitchen, 2 bedrooms (1 double, 2 single beds), shower room, fireplace, heating, open ground. Shopping and restaurant at Aumont-Aubrac (4 km).

Prices: low season — on request
high season — on request
winter season — on request

5 people
IGN 58

Booking: Lozère Loisirs Accueil E
48/G0391532

LAUBERT Gourgons One of two gîtes with rustic furnishings in a small hamlet, surrounded by forest (good for walking and fishing). Take a drive down to the interesting old town of Florac and the Cévennes Regional Park (35 km approx.). Altitude 1200 metres. Living room, kitchen, 4 bedrooms (1 double, 7 single beds), shower room, fireplace, central heating, open ground (separate from the gîte). Shopping at Châteauneuf-de-Randon (5 km approx.).

Prices: low season — on request
high season — on request
winter season — on request

9 people
IGN 59

Booking: Lozère Loisirs Accueil E
48/C1072826

MOISSAC-VALLEE-FRANCAISE Appias A charming little gîte with country-style furnishings, at the heart of the Cévennes. River fishing, bathing and canoeing at 5 km. Take a drive along the breathtaking Corniche des Cévennes which runs near the gîte, from Florac to Saint-Jean-de-Gard. Living room/kitchenette, 1 bedroom (1 double, 2 single beds), shower room, fireplace, heating, open ground. Shopping and restaurant at Saint-Croix-Vallée-Française.

Prices: low season — F 740/895
high season — F 1215
winter season — F 895

4 people
IGN 59

Booking: Lozère Loisirs Accueil E
48/G1834637

NOALHAC Le Bécus An old stone-built house, carefully renovated to preserve its local character, with rustic furnishings, on a farm, 4 km from the château town of Fournels which has a sports centre. Local forest walks and winter ski-ing. Altitude 1000 metres. Living room/kitchenette, 3 bedrooms (2 double, 2 single beds), shower room, fireplace, central heating, enclosed courtyard with child's swings. Local farm produce available; shopping and restaurant at Fournels.

Prices: low season — on request
high season — on request
winter season — on request

6 people
IGN 58

Booking: Lozère Loisirs Accueil E
48/10

19

Lozère

LE POMPIDOU
Situated in a hamlet, right on the Corniche des Cévennes, this gîte enjoys impressive views over the surrounding countryside. Local cross-country ski-ing; tennis and fishing at 10 km. Plenty of other leisure facilities at the attractive old town of Florac (30 km). Altitude 760 metres. Living room/kitchenette (1 single bed), 2 bedrooms (1 double, 2 single beds), shower room, open fire, heating, terrace, enclosed ground. Shopping and restaurant in the hamlet.

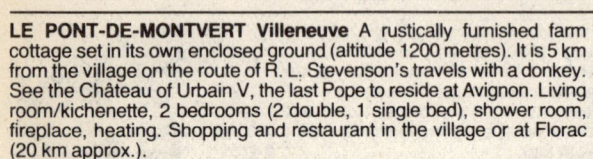

Prices:	low season	on request
	high season	on request
	winter season	on request

5 people
IGN 59

Booking: Lozère Loisirs Accueil   E
48/11

LE PONT-DE-MONTVERT Villeneuve
A rustically furnished farm cottage set in its own enclosed ground (altitude 1200 metres). It is 5 km from the village on the route of R. L. Stevenson's travels with a donkey. See the Château of Urbain V, the last Pope to reside at Avignon. Living room/kichenette, 2 bedrooms (2 double, 1 single bed), shower room, fireplace, heating. Shopping and restaurant in the village or at Florac (20 km approx.).

Prices:	low season	on request
	high season	on request
	winter season	on request

5 people
IGN 59

Booking: Lozère Loisirs Accueil   E
48/G1623537

SAINT-JULIEN-DU-TOURNEL Les Sagnes
A well-renovated old stone cottage with country-style furnishings in a hamlet on Mont-Lozère (altitude 1200 metres), at the edge of a forest with marked footpaths where you can pick wild fruits and mushrooms. The small spa resort of Bagnols-les-Bains is at 6 km. Living room/kitchenette (1 single bed), 2 bedrooms (2 double beds), shower room, fireplace, central heating. Shopping and restaurant at Bagnols-les-Bains.

Prices:	low season	F 680/820
	high season	F 1100

5 people
IGN 59

Booking: Lozère Loisirs Accueil   E
48/G1613538

SAINT-PIERRE-DE-NOGARET Le Besset
A spacious gîte, renovated and furnished in rustic fashion, 8 km from the village (altitude 980 metres). Hire bicycles at La Canourgue (17 km) to explore this fascinating region where you will come across many prehistoric monuments (enquire at La Canourge tourist office for a list of sites). Living room/kitchenette (1 single bed), 3 bedrooms (1 double, 4 single beds), shower room, fireplace, central heating, open ground. Shopping and restaurant in the village.

Prices:	low season	on request
	high season	on request
	winter season	on request

7 people
IGN 58

Booking: Lozère Loisirs Accueil   E
48/G0681643

SAINT-SAUVEUR-DE-PEYRE La Randèche
A renovated and rustically furnished farm building, 3 km from the village. In the eighteenth century, the legendary beast of Gévaudan (probably a wolf or bear), terrified the inhabitants of this region: see its statue at the old fortified town of Marjevols (15 km approx.). Living room, kitchen, 3 bedrooms (1 double, 5 single beds), shower room, fireplace, heating, ground. Shopping and restaurant in the village or at Aumont-Aubrac (8 km approx.).

Prices:	low season	on request
	high season	on request
	winter season	on request

7 people
IGN 58

Booking: Lozère Loisirs Accueil   E
48/G0731745

Established in 1955 to promote rural tourism

Federation Nationale des Gîtes Ruraux de France

9, avenue Georges V
75008 PARIS
Tel: 723.77.30

Gîtes de France Ltd.
178 Piccadilly
LONDON W1V 0AL

Complaints and Problems with your Gîte de France

As mentioned at the beginning of this book, all the *Gîtes de France* described here are selected by the *Relais Départemental*. The publishers rely on them for the accuracy of the descriptions, and the information given for each *Gîte de France* is printed in good faith and correct at the time of going to press.

Problems and discrepancies can however sometimes occur, fortunately very seldom, but if you are unlucky enough to find that your *Gîte de France* does not match up to your expectations, then there is a procedure to follow which is laid down by the *Fédération Nationale des Gîtes Ruraux de France*. Please do ensure, first of all, that you have serious grounds for complaint before going ahead. It is sometimes difficult for town dwellers to appreciate how different life in a country cottage can be. French country people do not, in general, go in for luxurious furnishings and fittings (although of course these should always be adequate and as described in the inventory). If you are on a farm, it is quite likely that you may get the occasional curious field mouse or other creature inspecting your *gîte* – try not to be alarmed – but if mice are a nuisance then you should inform the owner.

Procedure

If anything is seriously wrong, in the first instance tell the owner. If he or she cannot or will not settle the matter to your satisfaction, contact the local *Relais Départemental des Gîtes de France* immediately, even if you rented the *gîte* direct from the owner (the addresses are given at the back of this book). As mentioned in the rent agreement on page 374, all complaints must be registered within the first three days of occupancy of the *gîte*. The *Relais* will do everything possible to solve your problem and if necessary find you an alternative *gîte*, although of course, this could be difficult at the height of the season. If you still feel that you have been badly treated write as soon as possible to the head office of the:

> **Fédération Nationale des Gîtes Ruraux de France,**
> **9 avenue Georges V,**
> **75008 Paris.**

Please send a copy of your correspondence to ourselves so that we can ensure that the *gîte* in question does not appear in the guide in future. If you experience difficulties with the *Fédération*, we will of course, give you any assistance we can, but please bear in mind that the dispute remains a matter to be resolved between yourselves and the *Gîtes de France* and that we, as publishers, cannot be held responsible for the accommodation provided.

FEDERATION NATIONALE DES GITES RURAUX DE FRANCE
9 Avenue Georges V, 75008 PARIS

CHARTER of the GITES DE FRANCE

1. The welcome offered to hirers
The best of welcomes must be offered to the people who come to stay in your gite. They should be treated as paying guests, everything should be done to make their stay agreeable, to provide them with all sorts of facilities and satisfy their travel and information needs, be they touristic or of any other kind. Close collaboration with the *Syndicat d'Initiative* (Tourist information office) or any other tourist organisation is highly recommended.

2. Fittings
1 The premises offered for rent must be self-contained and equipped to the following minimum standards:
- electric light in all rooms,
- a sink with running water on tap,
- an inside lavatory (with flush and ventilation),
- washing facilities (shower and washbasin),
- shuttered or curtained windows.

2 The walls must be painted or papered and floors covered with tiles or any other easily cleaned material.
3 The interior of the holiday accommodation must be kept clean and in a perfect state of hygiene and painted regularly.
4 Each bedroom must contain at least a full sized bed, a table, two chairs, a wardrobe, preferably a closet and a wall-cupboard where possible.
5 The living room must be equipped, in addition to the basic furniture (cupboard, table and chairs), with kitchen fixtures necessary for a family, cooking facilities (wood, coal, oil, gas or electricity), a sink, a closet or wall-cupboard. In mountainous regions, adequate means of heating must also be provided. Shopping must be made easy for hirers, by all useful means.
6 The tenancy, whether seasonal, monthly, fortnightly or daily, must include, as per the charges in the rent agreement, limited quantities of water, electricity and cooking facilities, calculated on the basis of the number of people to be lodged according to the same rent agreement.

7 The inside fittings and furniture, as well as kitchen fixtures, must be in good condition and maintained.
8 The house front must be decorated with care and good taste.
9 Special care must be taken with the w.c. It must be suitably situated, easily accessible, well lit, ventilated and with a septic installation.
10 Household facilities must be available to help the tenants wash and iron their clothes and house linen (also a washtub, brushes, etc.).
11 The interior of the accommodation must be in a good state of upkeep and must be nicely decorated. The surroundings must be neat and have, where possible, a quiet area and a play spot for children.
12 The holiday home should be completely cleaned and ventilated after each tenancy, and the welcoming of new tenants should be carried out by the owner or a person authorised by him or her.

3. Prices
Prices will be established in advance, and will be inclusive of any supplements, rates or taxes, that is, they will cover all costs as evaluated in the rent agreement (**see page 419**). These prices will be forwarded to the authorities of the *Gîtes de France* organisation and strictly respected afterwards, with the exception of specific cases. These prices will be calculated and advertised on a weekly basis.

4. Other provisions
1 The owners are obliged to have all useful information and prices printed in the annual brochure of the *Gîtes de France*. This is the French official document which certifies, for the public authorities, accommodation which has been approved as a *'Gîte de France'*.
2 The plans or lay-out of a *Gîte de France* cannot be modified without previous notification to the *Relais départemental des Gîtes de France*.
3 In the case of a sale, the owner must inform the *Féderation* or the *Relais départemental*, or *Relais régional* concerned, and the premises will no longer be covered by the *'Gîtes de France'* sign. The sale is only permitted if the *Fédération* certifies that the selling owner's financial commitments are in order.
4 The *'Gîtes de France'* sign must be affixed at the door of all accommodation. The sign is offered, with no charge, by the *Relais départemental* once it has given its approval.
5 It is expressly forbidden to use the registered sign *'Gîtes de France'* to rent any other place or furnished accommodation which has not duly been authorised. Legal action may be taken.
6 The subscriptions are fixed each year by the *Fédération Nationale des Gîtes de France*, which takes on the representation, verification and promotion, and which works towards the development of the organisation.
7 The *'Gîtes de France' (Relais départementaux and Fédération Nationale)* will only take up the defence of the rights and interests of the owners if they have fulfilled the obligations set out above, and rented their properties, using the rent agreement created for this purpose and completed in due form.
8 All publicity carried out by a private person or by a group and making use of the *Gîtes de France* sign or of the fact that he belongs to the organisation must receive the prior agreement of the *Relais départemental*, the *Relais régional*, or the *Fédération Nationale*.

FEDERATION NATIONALE DES GITES RURAUX DE FRANCE
9 Avenue Georges V, 75008 PARIS

Extracts from the CHARTER of the GITES CHAMBRES D'HOTE

1. Definition
The *chambres d'hôte* are rooms individually fitted and furnished, on a farm or in a village, with a view to offering overnight accommodation and breakfast to travellers. They are not situated on main routes, but are, in all cases, in a rural area or on the tourist track. They can also be near restaurants or country inns.

2. Basic conditions
To attain the status of *Gîtes de France—Chambre d'Hôte* and the advantages that go with this appellation, the owners must:

1 Be a farmer, or eligible under the provisions of the French Ministry of Agriculture...
2 Offer country accommodation restored and maintained according to the standards laid down...
3 Have heating in all rooms.

3. Equipment
The *chambre d'hôte* must have
- a minimum floor area of 12 square metres (to permit an optional child's bed).
- adequate windows.
- floors and walls in good condition.
- a wash basin (h/c) a mirror, shelf and towel rail in each room.
- a complete set of linen, in good condition.
- a wardrobe or cupboard with an adequate number of coat-hangers and racks.

4. Other provisions
In all cases, the number of *chambres d'hôte* in one house is limited to 5. Where there are only 1-2 rooms, it is permissible for the owners to use the communal living room and toilet facilities (w.c. and shower-room)...With 3-5 rooms, the owners are obliged to provide a separate communal room and toilet facilities for their guests...It is obligatory for the owner to keep the *chambres d'hôte* up to standard, day-by-day... Any additionals (child-minding, extra meals) are charged extra.

5. Reception and other arrangements
The welcoming of guests, accommodation and prices are explained in the Charter of the *Gîtes de France* (pages 12-13), and the owners must strictly adhere to its provisions. The owners must, in any case, have signed an engagement, and agreed to the terms of the Federation...

FEDERATION NATIONALE DES GITES RURAUX DE FRANCE
9 Avenue Georges V, 75008 PARIS

Extracts from the CHARTER of the GITES CAMPING-CARAVANING A LA FERME

A *'Gîte Camping-Caravaning à la Ferme'* is a site on a farm that is open to campers and caravanners... under conditions laid down by the Charter of the *Gîtes des France*.

1. Situation
A *'Gîte Camping-Caravaning à la Ferme'* must not only conform to general French regulations on camping (notably those enacted 9 Feb 1968), but must also be situated:
- in suitable rural areas.
- outside any areas of possible disturbance, and away from main roads and railways.
- on level, grassy ground, near the farmhouse, in order to favour contact between the farmer and the campers or caravanners.

2. Area and number of campers
The minimum area (except in special cases) for each camping or caravanning site is 300 square metres, and there is a maximum of 6 such sites per farm, and a maximum of 20 people. (See note on page 9).

3. Installations
A *'Gîte Camping-Caravaning à la Ferme'* must have covered and lighted facilities at a distance of not more than 100 metres, including:
- drinking water • a wash-room, with an electric point, wash-basin, shower and flushing lavatory • a sink • a refuse bin • a table and chairs • a portable fire extinguisher. Additionally, it is desirable to provide electric points at caravan sites.

4. Prices
The general rule (with certain exceptions) is that rentals are weekly during the high season (15 June to 15 September), and can be for the weekend, or even for one day, at other times of the year. The price charged must not exceed the maximum tariffs currently in force under French regulations... Site-rental charges are net, include local taxes, the water supply, and electricity. All additional charges (child-minding, farm produce, farm meals) are a matter for amicable agreement between the farmer and the camper.

Booking And Deposits

BOOKING

The **French Farm and Village Holiday Guide** offers the widest possible choice of *gîtes de France* throughout rural France in 1986. Readers have the option of making a telephone booking and knowing straight away if the *gîte* selected is free. Booking instructions given below are straightforward and we also give further guidance by publishing a sample booking letter on page 373. The method of booking any *gîte* is given in the individual description of the *gîte*. When writing, please print your name and address **clearly**, in capital letters. In all cases mention the **French Farm and Village Holiday Guide** and quote the *gîte* reference number shown bottom left on each description.

1. By telephone

When the address of the owner or booking service is marked **E**, you can telephone and book in English, if not, you will need to speak French. Dial 010 33 followed by the number given. For most of the year France is 1 hour ahead of Great Britain. As most booking services open between 8 and 9 am it is advisable to 'phone between 7.30 and 8 am to take advantage of the cheap rate. For owners, call either in the early morning or evening. Please do not phone owners too late in the evening – farmers generally have to get up early! For fuller information see page 372.

2. Booking through regional and *départemental* **booking services**
(Sample booking letter page 373).

Write to the regional or *départemental* booking service mentioned in the description. If the *gîte* is already booked at the date you require, the booking service will send you a choice of 1, 2 or 3 *gîtes* corresponding as closely as possible to your choice, or further up-to-date information to help you find another *gîte*.

3. Booking directly with the owner
(Sample booking letter page 373).

Write directly to the owner at the address given in the description. If the *gîte* is already booked at the date you require, the owner will pass on your request to his or her *Relais départemental* which will then send you a choice of 1, 2 or 3 *gîtes* corresponding as closely as possible to your choice, or further up-to-date information to help you find another *gîte*.

4. Booking through Loisirs Accueil booking services

Some *gîtes* and all activity holidays are bookable through a *départemental* Loisirs Accueil booking service which normally have English-speaking staff. Write or telephone the booking service concerned, just as you would for any other *gîte*. For more information, please see pages 12–13 of this guide.

5. Booking any other *gîte*.
(Sample booking letter page 373)

If you cannot find a *gîte* in this book which corresponds to your needs and pleases your fancy, you can write to any regional or *départemental* booking service or to any other *Relais départemental*. You will receive back a choice of 1, 2 or 3 *gîtes* corresponding as closely as possible to your requirements, or further up-to-date information to help you find another *gîte*.

Chambres d'hôte, camping-caravaning à la ferme, gîtes equestres and *gîtes d'enfants* must normally be reserved for a minimum stay of seven days (Saturday to Saturday). They must be booked in advance in the same manner as a *gîte*. It is also advisable to book a *gîte d'étape* in advance if possible.

The addresses of all the booking services and the list of *Relais départementaux* are given on pages 376–380.

IMPORTANT: BOOKINGS IN JULY AND AUGUST WILL NORMALLY ONLY BE ACCEPTED FOR THE FIRST AND SECOND FORTNIGHTS IN THE MONTH, AND THIS FROM SATURDAY TO SATURDAY.

DEPOSITS

Having written or telephoned, and if the *gîte* is free at the date you want, you will receive two copies of the rent agreement (this is often printed in French only, so you will find for your guidance an exact translation on page 374, with the amount of the deposit made out clearly. Sign them, keep one copy and send back the other accompanied by the deposit—a banker's draft in French francs, made payable to THE OWNER named on the rent agreement.

To obtain the banker's draft, take one of the signed rent agreements to your bank and ask for a banker's draft in French francs, for the amount stated on the rent agreement. If your bank cannot deliver the draft immediately or within a day or two, ask for a receipt and send the receipt off with the signed copy of the rent agreement. The receipt will hold your booking until the draft itself can be sent. Be sure to make your deposit payment for the correct sum and in French francs.

BALANCE DUE

The balance of the rent due is normally payable to the *gîte* owner on arrival at your holiday destination. However, in most of the *départements* now operating a **Loisirs Accueil** booking service, this service has also taken over responsibility for booking *gîtes de France*. This means that **Loisirs Accueil** booking conditions apply (see pages 12–13), and the balance of the rent will be payable thirty days before the start of your holiday.

Please enclose an international reply coupon with all correspondence. These are available from all Post Offices.

Although postage between France and Great Britain generally works very well, we suggest that the deposit be sent to France by registered post.

PRICES

Price controls imposed by the French Government affect and often delay the fixing of *gîtes* prices. We have quoted the prices as given to us by the *Relais départementaux*, although some owners have preferred to leave their prices "on request".

We regret that in the circumstances, the publishers cannot accept responsibility for any changes to the prices made by the *Relais départementaux* after the publication of this guide.

For all correspondence, always enclose an international reply coupon – obtainable from the Post Office.

Make all drafts and deposits payable to the OWNER.

Use registered post when sending deposits.

Don't forget to sign both copies of your rent agreement.

Book by phone

Don't be afraid to book by phone. Where you see the symbol **E**, it means English is spoken. Simply dial 010 33 followed by the number given. Ignore brackets, you should normally dial 8 digits after 010 33. For dialling from Britain, therefore, the French number (73) 90 11 87 is treated exactly as 73.90.11.87.

The Booking Service offices are often in large Chambers of Agriculture or in the Prefectoral or other administrative offices. The telephonist receiving your call may not speak English: in this case ask clearly for Le Service des Gîtes or, where appropriate, Le Service Loisirs Accueil. If possible, give the extension (poste) number required.

If you speak even a little FRENCH, do not hesitate to phone, as most people in the reservation service speak a little English.

When making a reservation, mention the FRENCH FARM AND VILLAGE HOLIDAY GUIDE as all Relais have a copy of the book. Quote the reference number of the gîte de France you wish to book.

Booking directly with an owner: the **E** symbol also applies where an owner speaks English. He will probably be delighted to receive your call! Speak clearly and say you are calling from England to book their gîte de France

SAMPLE BOOKING LETTER

TO A GITE OWNER OR RELAIS DÉPARTEMENTAL.
A un propriétaire de gîte ou Relais départemental.

ENCLOSE 1 INTERNATIONAL REPLY COUPON   *DELETE WHERE NECESSARY
Inclure 1 coupon-réponse international   **Rayer les mentions inutiles*

DEAR SIR OR MADAM,
*Cher Monsieur/Chère Madame,**

I WISH TO SPEND MY HOLIDAYS IN YOUR/THE* GITE No. ..... LISTED IN THE FRENCH
J'aimerai passer mes vacances dans votre/le gîte no. ..... mentionné dans le "French*

FARM AND VILLAGE HOLIDAY GUIDE 1985 FOR A PERIOD OF ..... WEEKS
Farm and Village Holiday Guide 1985 pour une durée de ..... semaines

FROM ..... (DATE OF ARRIVAL) TO ..... (DATE OF DEPARTURE).
de ..... (date d'arrivée) à ..... (date de départ).

MY FAMILY/GROUP* INCLUDES ..... ADULTS AND ..... CHILDREN (..... BOY(S)
Ma famille/groupe comprend ..... adultes et ..... enfants (..... garçon(s)*

AGED ..... AND ..... GIRL(S) AGED ......).
de ..... ans et fille(s) de ..... ans).

OR TO A RELAIS DEPARTEMENTAL ONLY: I HAVE NOT BEEN ABLE TO FIND A GITE
Ou au Relais départemental seulement: N'Ayant pas pu trouver de gîte convenant

TO SUIT MY FAMILY'S NEEDS IN THE FRENCH FARM AND VILLAGE HOLIDAY GUIDE.
aux besoins de ma famille dans le "French Farm and Village Holiday Guide", je vous

PLEASE SEND ME A SELECTION OF 1-2-3 OTHER GITES AS RECOMMENDED
prie d'avoir la gentillesse de me faire parvenir une sélection de 1-2-3 gîtes comme il est

IN THE GUIDE.
recommandé dans le guide.

YOURS SINCERELY,
Veuillez accepter, Cher Monsieur/Chère Madame, mes salutations les meilleures.*
NAME .... ADDRESS ....
Nom. .... Demeurant à ....
                 (WRITE IN CAPITALS)   *(Ecrire en majéscules)*

SUPPLEMENTARY QUESTIONS – *Questions supplémentaires:*
CAN WE HIRE SHEETS AND/OR* HOUSE LINEN? YES/NO* – COST: FF ..... PER WEEK PER BED.
Pouvons-nous louer les draps et/ou le linge de maison? Oui/Non* – Coût: FF ..... à la semaine.*
CAN YOU PROVIDE ANOTHER BED? YES/NO* – COST: FF ..... PER WEEK.
Pouvez-vous nous fournir un lit supplémentaire? Oui/Non – Coût: FF ..... à la semaine.*

THIS SAMPLE IS DESIGNED TO FACILITATE PRELIMINARY BOOKING AND THE
Ce modèle de lettre de réservation est destiné à faciliter les premières démarches
PUBLISHERS CANNOT ASSUME LIABILITY FOR THE RESULT.
pour la réservation et l'éditeur n'engage aucun responsabilité quant au résultat.

FEDERATION NATIONALE DES GITES RURAUX DE FRANCE
9 Avenue Georges V, 75008 PARIS

RENT AGREEMENT
To be filled out in duplicate

Relais Departemental des Gîtes Ruraux de: ....

In the case of litigation arising from a rental, the *Federation* or the *Relais départementaux* can only intervene if this agreement has been signed by the owners and the tenant and the complaint made within the first three days of occupancy (postmark accepted).

The following has been agreed between the undersigned ....
Owner's name: M ....
address ....
                                                                            Telephone ....
Owner of the Gîte Rural de France in the commune of ....
Département ....
Gîte no. .... listed in the annual guide of Gîtes Ruraux de France in the département of ....
LETS this Gîte Rural de France to:
Name of tenant: M ....
Address ....
                                                                            Telephone ....

Conditions of tenancy (this section to be completed by the owner)

1. **Period of tenancy:** from .... 19..... at ..... hours to .... 19..... at ..... hours.
2. **Rental:** The rent is fixed at .... francs.
   ☐ This price includes the supply for the gîte of:
      – 500 litres cold water per day   ⎫ or the equivalent,
      – 4 kWh electricity per day for lighting   ⎬ depending on type of
      – 4 kg butane gas per week/1 bottle for 3 weeks ⎭ energy used, that is ....
   ☐ This price includes heating as well as supplies mentioned above.
   ☐ Heating will be charged extra, that is ....
   ☐ This price includes all charges.
3. **Number of people:** .... adults; .... children between 5 and 14 years; .... children under 5.
   The number of people occupying the gîte may not, under any circumstances, exceed the number stated in the annual guide of the Gîtes Ruraux de France. If this number should be exceeded, the owner reserves the right to modify or cancel this contract.
4. **Terms of tenancy:** The tenant receives 2 copies of the contract, duly completed and signed by the owners. Having noted the description and inventory overleaf, the tenant signs the contract, keeps one copy and returns one copy to the owner. The owner has no obligation to the tenant until he has received the signed contract, within .... days, together with a deposit of a maximum of 30% of the total rent, that is .... francs (postmark accepted).
   The tenant formally agrees to pay the owner direct the balance of rent due, that is .... francs, on arrival at the premises. It is understood that the inventory comes into force at the tenant's arrival until his departure from the premises. All losses or breakages to be paid for by the tenant.
   Family pets are/are not (delete where applicable) permitted.
   In the case of cancellation "force majeure" by the tenant, the deposit remains with the owner, except if the latter finds a new tenant for the same period. In the case of cancellation by the owner's default, he repays a sum of twice the amount of deposit taken. A deposit against breakages, fixed at .... francs will be requested and returned at the end of the tenancy.

Tenant's name M .... agrees to this rental after having read this information, given by the owner.

At.......... date..........
(*)
(Owner's signature)

At.......... date..........
I declare that I am insured for my tenancy with the following insurance company:†
....
(*)
(Tenant's signature)

(*) Translator's note: when signing, the words *"lu et approuvé"* (read and agreed) must be inserted by hand.

To the best of our knowledge, it is not possible to insure a *gîte* or holiday villa, when booked directly from the United Kingdom, through any U.K. insurance company. Please therefore strike out this paragraph before signing.

GITE DE FRANCE
(description and inventory)
(Please delete the items not applicable and complete the description)

...is GITE DE FRANCE includes:

1 entrance hall with ....

	Room No 1	Room No 2	Room No 3	Room No 4
...ble				
...airs				
...pboard or wardrobe				
...ngle bed .... cm.				
...uble bed .... cm.				
...ild's bed				

Full bedding (except sheets), in good condition, with a minimum of two woollen bed-covers per bed.

...l lounge-kitchenette including: water (hot and cold) on tap — cooker, type ....
...set — cupboard — dresser, table for .... people and .... chairs — refrigerator — and the ...owing kitchen utensils: ....

...well as all the equipment listed on the inventory fixed inside the gite.

...separate kitchen with: water (hot and cold) ...tap — cooker, type ....set or cupboard — table and .... stools .... chairs — the following kitchen utensils: ....

1 separate lounge with: table, seating .... people and .... chairs — dresser, closet or cupboard — divan with the necessary bedding for 1 or 2 people — refrigerator — miscellaneous ....

1 shower-room (with or without hot water): shower — wash-basin ....
1 separate internal toilet with w.c.
1 clothes washing facility including: basin, boiler, with .... brushes and clothes line.
...her utensils ....
...ating (if necessary, type): ....

...coration and miscellaneous ....
....
....

...closed garden — enclosed orchard — cellar — inside courtyard — garage
...elete items not applicable)
...xtures regularly checked and guaranteed in good order, with all the necessities for the daily needs of a family .... adults and .... children.

Day of arrival: the .... Agreement after inventory The owner The tenant	Day of departure: the .... Agreement after inventory The owner The tenant

Relais Departementaux

Addresses and Booking Services

We list below the addresses of all the *Relais Départementaux des Gîtes de France* for the *départements* whose *gîtes* are featured in this guide. Those *départements* marked **B.S.** offer a booking service, those marked **B.S.E.** offer a booking service with English speaking staff. In those *départements* marked with an * *gîtes* are bookable through the *Loisirs Accueil Booking Service* (addresses on page 380). For all other *départements*, *gîtes* must be booked direct through the owner. Please note that the method of booking each *gîte* is given in the individual description. When writing to the addresses below always write to the Relais Départemental des Gîtes Ruraux de (*département*).

01 – AIN B.S.E.
1, place Georges-Clémenceau
01000 BOURG-EN-BRESSE
Tel: (74) 23.61.96

02 – AISNE B.S.E.
1 rue Saint Martin, B.P. 116
02006 LAON
Tel: (23) 23.24.53

03 – ALLIER B.S.E.
35 rue de Bellecroix, B.P. 50
03400 YZEURE
Tel: (70) 44.41.57

05 – HAUTES-ALPES B.S.
8ter, rue Capitaine-de-Bresson, B.P. 55
05002 GAP Cedex
Tel: (92) 51.31.45

07 – ARDECHE B.S.
8 cours du Palais, B.P. 221
07002 PRIVAS Cedex
Tel: (75) 64.04.66

08 – ARDENNES B.S.E.
Chambre d'Agriculture
1 avenue du Petit Bois, B.P. 331
08000 CHARLEVILLE-MEZIERES Cedex
Tel: (24) 33.38.66 (mornings only)

09 – ARIEGE B.S.E.
Préfecture de l'Ariège
14, rue Lazéma
09000 FOIX
Tel: (61) 65.01.15

10 – AUBE
Chambre d'Agriculture
2 bis, rue Jeanne d'Arc, B.P. 4080
10014 TROYES Cedex
Tel: (25) 73.25.36

11 – AUDE*
70, rue A. Ramon
11001 CARCASSONNE
Tel: (68) 47.09.06

12 – AVEYRON B.S.E.
A.P.A.T.A.R., Carrefour de l'Agriculture,
12006 RODEZ Cedex
Tel: (65) 68.11.38

13 – BOUCHES-DU-RHONE*
Domaine du Vergon
13370 MALLEMORT
Tel: (90) 59.18.05

14 – CALVADOS B.S.E.
4, promenade Madame-de-Sévigné
14039 CAEN Cedex
Tel: (31) 84.47.19

15 – CANTAL (see regional booking service)
Préfecture, B.P. 8
15018 AURILLAC Cedex
Tel: (71) 48.53.54

16 – CHARENTE*
Chambre de Commerce
Place Bouilland
16021 ANGOULEME
Tel: (45) 92.24.43

17 – CHARENTE-MARITIME B.S.E.
2, rue avenue de Fétilly, B.P. 32
17002 LA ROCHELLE Cedex
Tel: (46) 67.34.74

18 – CHER B.S.E.
Préfecture, Place Marcel Plaisant
18014 BOURGES Cedex
Tel: (48) 24.14.95 (ext 445)

19 – CORREZE B.S.*
35, ave du Général de Gaulle
19000 TULLE Cedex
Tel: (55) 20.24.54

22 – COTES DU NORD B.S.E.
5, rue Baratoux, B.P. 556
22010 SAINT-BRIEUC Cedex
Tel: (96) 61.82.79

23 – CREUSE*
Chambre d'Agriculture
1, rue Martinet, B.P. 89
23011 GUERET
Tel: (55) 52.55.75

24 – DORDOGNE*
16, rue Wilson
24000 PERIGUEUX
Tel: (53) 53.44.35

25 – DOUBS*
15 Avenue E. Droz
25000 BESANCON
Tel: (81) 80.38.18

26 – DROME B.S.E.
boulevard Vauban B.P. 121
26001 VALENCE
Tel: (75) 43.01.70

27 – EURE B.S.E.
5, rue de la Petite-Cité, B.P. 882
27008 EVREUX Cedex
Tel: (32) 39.53.38

28 – EURE-ET-LOIR
Maison de l'Agriculture
10, rue Dieudonné Coste,
28024 CHARTRES
Tel: (37) 34.52.09

29 – FINISTERE B.S.
Maison de l'Agriculture
Stang-Vihan, 5 allée Sully, B.P. 504
29109 QUIMPER Cedex
Tel: (98) 95.75.30

30 – GARD B.S.E.
Comité Départemental du Tourisme
3, place des Arènes, B.P. 122
30011 NIMES
Tel: (66) 21.02.51

31 – HAUTE-GARONNE*
31 rue de Metz
31066 TOULOUSE Cedex
Tel: 61 33.43.69

32 – GERS B.S.E.
Maison de l'Agriculture
Route de Mirande, B.P. 99
32003 AUCH Cedex
Tel: (62) 63.16.55

33 – GIRONDE
38 rue Ferrere
33000 BORDEAUX
Tel: 56.81.54.23

34 – HERAULT
Chambre d'Agriculture-Bat 3
Place Chaptal
34076 MONTPELLIER Cedex
Tel: (67) 92.88.00

35 – ILLE-ET-VILAINE*
Préfecture de Région
1, rue Martenot, 35000 RENNES
Tel: (99) 02.97.41

36 – INDRE
Hôtel du Département
Place de la Victoire et des Alliés
36020 CHATEAUROUX
Tel: (54) 27.00.28

37 – INDRE-ET-LOIRE B.S.
Chambre d'Agriculture
38, rue Augustin-Fresnel, B.P. 139
37171 CHAMBRAY-LES-TOURS Cedex
Tel: (47) 27.01.63

38 – ISERE B.S.E.
Maison du Tourisme
14, rue de la République
B.P. 227, 38000 GRENOBLE Cedex
Tel: (76) 54.34.36

39 – JURA B.S.E.
Hôtel du Département
55, rue St. Desiré
39021 LONS LE SAUNIER Cedex
Tel: (84) 24.19.64

40 – LANDES B.S.
Chambre d'Agriculture, Cité Galliane
B.P. 279, 40000 MONT-DE-MARSAN
Tel: (58) 46.10.45

41 – LOIR-ET-CHER
11, place du Château
41000 BLOIS
Tel: (54) 78.55.50

42 – LOIRE
Chambre d'Agriculture
43, avenue Albert-Raimond
Saint-Priest-en-Jarez, B.P. 50
42272 SAINT-ETIENNE Cedex
Tel: (77) 79.15.22

43 – HAUTE-LOIRE
Comité Départemental du Tourisme
Hôtel du Département
4, avenue Charles de Gaulle
43000 LE PUY EN VELAY
Tel: (71) 09.26.05

44 – LOIRE-ATLANTIQUE
Maison de l'Agriculture
47 bis, rue des Hauts Pavés, B.P. 1141
44024 NANTES Cedex
Tel: (40) 76.39.90

45 – LOIRET*
3, rue de la Bretonnerie
45000 ORLEANS
Tel: (38) 66.24.10

46 – LOT*
Association Départementale de
Tourisme Rural
Chambre d'Agriculture du Lot
430, avenue Jean Jaurès
46004 CAHORS Cedex
Tel: (65) 22.55.30

47 – LOT-ET-GARONNE B.S.E.
Chambre d'Agriculture
rue Péchabout
47000 AGEN
Tel: (53) 96.44.99

48 – LOZERE B.S.E.
Place Urbain V-B.P. 4
48002 MENDE
Tel: (66) 65.34.55

50 – MANCHE B.S.
Préfecture B.P. F.2
50009 SAINT-LO Cedex
Tel: (33) 57.52.80

51 – MARNE
Complexe agricole de Mont-Bernard
Bâtiment F
route de Suippes, B.P. 1505
51002 CHALONS-SUR-MARNE Cedex
Tel: (26) 64.08.13

52 – HAUTE-MARNE
Hôtel du Conseil Général
89, rue Victoire de la Marne
52011 CHAUMONT Cedex
Tel: (25) 03.65.00

53 – MAYENNE B.S.E.
9, rue de l'Ancien-Evêché, B.P. 723
53002 LAVAL Cedex
Tel: (43) 53.27.40 (ext. 377)

54 – MEURTHE-ET-MOSELLE
Chambre d'Agriculture
5, rue de la Vologne
54520 LAXOU
Tel: (8) 396.49.58

55 – MEUSE B.S.E.
Hôtel du Département
55012 BAR LE DUC Cedex
Tel: (29) 79.00.02

56 – MORBIHAN B.S.E.
11 place Maréchal Joffre
B.P. 318, 56403 AURAY Cedex
Tel: (97) 56.48.12

57 – MOSELLE B.S.
64, avenue André-Malraux
57045 METZ Cedex
Tel: (8) 763.13.25

58 – NIEVRE
Préfecture, 58019 NEVERS
Tel: (86) 57.80.25

59 – NORD
14, square Foch
59800 LILLE
Tel: (20) 57.00.61

60 – OISE B.S.E.
1, rue Villiers-de-L'Isle-Adam, B.P. 222
60008 BEAUVAIS Cedex
Tel: (4) 448.16.87

61 – ORNE
Comité départemental du Tourisme
60, rue Saint Blaise, B.P. 50
61002 ALENCON Cedex
Tel: (33) 26.74.00

62 – PAS-DE-CALAIS*
44, Grande-Rue
62200 BOULOGNE-SUR-MER
Tel: (21) 30.32.51

63 – PUY-DE—DOME
(see regional booking service)
69, Boulevard Gergovia
63038 CLERMONT-FERRAND Cedex
Tel:' (73) 93.84.80

64 – PYRENEES-ATLANTIQUES B.S.
Maison de l'Agriculture
124, Boulevard Tourasse
64000 PAU
Tel: (59) 80.19.13

65 – HAUTES-PYRENEES*
6, rue Eugène Tenot
65000 TARBES
Tel: (62) 93.03.20

67 – BAS-RHIN B.S.
103, route de Hausbergen
67300 SCHILTIGHEIM
Tel: (88) 62.45.09

68 – HAUT-RHIN B.S.E.
3 Place de la Gare
69000 COLMAR
Tel: (89) 41.35.33

69 – RHONE
4 Place Gensoul,
69287 LYON Cedex 1
Tel: (7) 842.65.92

70 – HAUTE-SAONE*
Maison du Tourisme, B.P. 117
Rue des Bains, 70002 VESOUL Cedex
Tel: (84) 75.43.66

71 – SAONE-ET-LOIRE
A.D.T.R., Chambre d'Agriculture
B.P. 522, bd Henri-Dunant
71010 MACON Cedex
Tel: (85) 38.50.66

72 – SARTHE
Comité départemental du Tourisme
B.P. 515, Préfecture
72017 LE MANS Cedex
Tel: (43) 84.96.00 (ext. 3430)

73 – SAVOIE B.S.E.
24 Boulevard de la Colonne
73000 CHAMBERY
Tel: (79) 33.22.56

74 – HAUTE-SAVOIE B.S.
52, avenue de Iles, B.P. 327
74037 ANNECY Cedex
Tel: (50) 57.82.40

76 – SEINE-MARITIME B.S.E.
A.D.T.E.R., Chambre d'Agriculture
Chemin de la Bretêque, B.P. 59
76232 BOIS-GUILLAUME
Tel: (35) 60.48.60

79 – DEUX-SEVRES B.S.E.
70 rue Alsace-Lorraine
79000 NIORT
Tel: (49) 24.00.42

80 – SOMME*
21, rue Ernest Cauvin
80000 AMIENS
Tel: (22) 92.26.39

81 – TARN B.S.
Maison des Agriculteurs
B.P. 89, 81003 ALBI Cedex
Tel: (63) 54.39.81

82 – TARN-ET-GARONNE
Chambre d'Agriculture
440, avenue Monclar
82000 MONTAUBAN
Tel: (63) 63.30.25

83 – VAR
Conseil Général
1, boulevard Foch
83007 DRAGUIGNAN
Tel: (94) 67.10.40 or 68.55.43

85 – VENDEE B.S.E.
124, boulevard Aristide Briand, 26X
85001 LA ROCHE-SUR-YON
Tel: (51) 62.33.10

86 – VIENNE*
11, rue Victor Hugo
86000 POITIERS
Tel: (49) 41.58.22

87 – HAUTE-VIENNE*
Chambre d'Agriculture
32, avenue General Leclerc
87036 LIMOGES Cedex
Tel: (55) 77.70.27

89 – YONNE B.S.
Chambre d'Agriculture
14 bis, rue Guynemer
89000 AUXERRE
Tel: (86) 46.47.48

Other Relais Départementaux

For details of Gîtes de France in départements not featured in this book, write to the Relais Départementaux des Gîtes ruraux de France et du Tourisme Vert at the addresses given below:

04 – ALPES-DE-HAUTE-PROVENCE
Maison du Tourisme
Rond-Point du 11 Novembre
04000 DIGNE
Tel: (92) 31.52.39

06 – ALPES-MARITIMES
55, promenade des Anglais
06000 NICE
Tel: (93) 44.39.39

20 – CORSE
22, Boulevard Paoli
20000 AJACCIO
Tel: (95) 20.51.34

21 – COTE-D'OR
Hôtel du Département
B.P. 1601, 21035 DIJON Cedex
Tel: (80) 73.81.81

49 – MAINE-ET-LOIRE
B.P. 852
49008 ANGERS Cedex
Tel: (41) 88.23.85

66 – PYRENEES-ORIENTALES
Centrale Loisirs Accueil
C.D.H.R.
30, Pierre Bretonneau, B.P. 946
66020 PERPIGNAN
Tel: (68) 55.33.55

69 – RHONE
4, place Gensoul
69287 LYON Cedex 1
Tel: (78) 42.65.92

77 – SEINE-ET-MARNE
Maison du Tourisme
2, avenue Galliéni
77000 MELUN
Tel: (6) 437.19.36

84 – VAUCLUSE
Chambre Départementale du Tourisme
La Balance, B.P. 147
84008 AVIGNON Cedex
Tel: (90) 85.45.00

88 – VOSGES
13, rue A-Briand, B.P. 405
88010 EPINAL Cedex
Tel: (29) 35.50.34

90 – TERRITOIRE-DE-BELFORT
3, rue de la République
90000 BELFORT
Tel: (84) 21.27.95

971 – GUADELOUPE (WEST INDIES)
Office du Tourisme
5, Square de la Banque
Place de la Victoire
97110 POINTRE A PITRE
Tel: (590) 82.09.30

972 – MARTINIQUE (WEST INDIES)
Caserne Bouillé
B.P. 1122
97209 FORT-DE-FRANCE
Tel: (596) 73.67.92

974 – REUNION (INDIAN OCEAN)
2, avenue de la Victoire
97400 SAINT-DENIS
Tel: (262) 20.31.90

Regional Booking Service

For Gîtes de France in Puy-de-Dôme and Cantal use the Auvergne booking service:

Service Réservation des Gîtes ruraux d'Auvergne
45, avenue Julien, B.P. 395
63011 CLERMONT-FERRAND Cedex
Tel: (73) 93.04.03   E

Loisirs Accueil Booking Services

For gîtes and activity holidays bookable through these services, write to: Service-Reservation Loisirs Accueil – addresses given below:

11 – AUDE
70, rue Aimé-Ramon
11001 CARCASSONNE
Tel: (68) 47.09.06
Telex: LARA 500 370

13 – BOUCHES-DU-RHONE
Domaine du Vergon
13310 MALLEMORT
Tel: (90) 59.18.05   E

16 – CHARENTE
Place Bouillaud
16021 ANGOULEME
Tel: (45) 92.24.43   Telex: 791 607   E

17 – CHARENTE-MARITIME
11, bis rue des Augustins, B.P. 1301
17000 LA ROCHELLE Cedex
Tel: (46) 41.43.33   Telex: 790 712

19 – CORREZE
Quai Baluze
19000 TULLE
Tel: (55) 26.46.88
Telex: CCITUL 590 140   E

23 – CREUSE
43 Place Bonnyaud
23000 GUERET
Tel: 55.52.87.50

24 – DORDOGNE
16, rue Wilson
24000 PERIGUEUX
Tel: (53) 53.44.35   E

25 – DOUBS
15 Avenue E. Droz
25000 BESANCON
Tel: (81) 80.38.18

31 – HAUTE-GARONNE
31 Rue de Metz
31066 TOULOUSE Cedex
Tel: 61.33.43.69

32 – GERS
Maison de l'Agriculture, B.P. 99
Route de Mirande
32003 AUCH Cedex
Tel: (62) 63.16.55   E

33 – GIRONDE
21, Cours de l'intendance
33000 BORDEAUX
Tel: (56) 52.61.40
Telex: 541 523 GIRTOUR

35 – ILLE-ET-VILAINE
1, rue Martenot
35000 RENNES
Tel: (99) 02.97.41
Telex: 730 808 IVTOUR

41 – LOIR-ET-CHER
11, place du Château
41000 BLOIS
Tel: (54) 78.55.50   Telex: 751 375

42 – LOIRET
3, rue de la Bretonnerie
45000 ORLEANS
Tel: (38) 62.04.88   Telex: 780 523   E

46 – LOT
Chambre de Commerce
107, Quai Cavaignac
46000 CAHORS
Tel: (65) 35.67.01

48 – LOZERE
Place Urbain V,
B.P. 4, 48002 MENDE
Tel: 66 65 34 55

56 – MORBIHAN
B.P. 400
56009 VANNES Cedex
Tel: (97) 54.06.56

62 – PAS-DE-CALAIS
44, Grande Rue
62200 BOULOGNE-SUR-MER
Tel: (21) 31.66.80

65 – HAUTES-PYRENEES
6, rue Eugène Tenot
65000 TARBES
Tel: (62) 93.03.30
Telex: COMTOUR 530 535

70 – HAUTE-SAONE
Maison du Tourisme
B.P. 117, rue des Bains
70002 VESOUL Cedex
Tel: (84) 75.43.66   Telex: 361 250

80 – SOMME
21, rue Ernest-Cauvin
80000 AMIENS
Tel: (22) 92.26.39
Telex: 140 754   E

82 – TARN-ET-GARONNE
Hôtel des Intendants
Place du Mal-Foch
82000 MONTAUBAN
Tel: (63) 63.31.40
Telex: 531 705

85 – VENDEE
8, place Napoleon
85000 LA ROCHE-SUR-YON
Tel: (51) 62.08.24
Telex: 700 747

86 – VIENNE
11, rue Victor Hugo
86000 POITIERS
Tel: (49) 41.58.22   E

87 HAUTE-VIENNE
16 Place Jourdan
87000 LIMOGES
Tel: 55.34.70.11
Telex: 580 915 GECOMEX

Gîte Map Special Offer

McCARTA LTD., 122 King's Cross Rd., London WC1X 9DS 01-278 8278

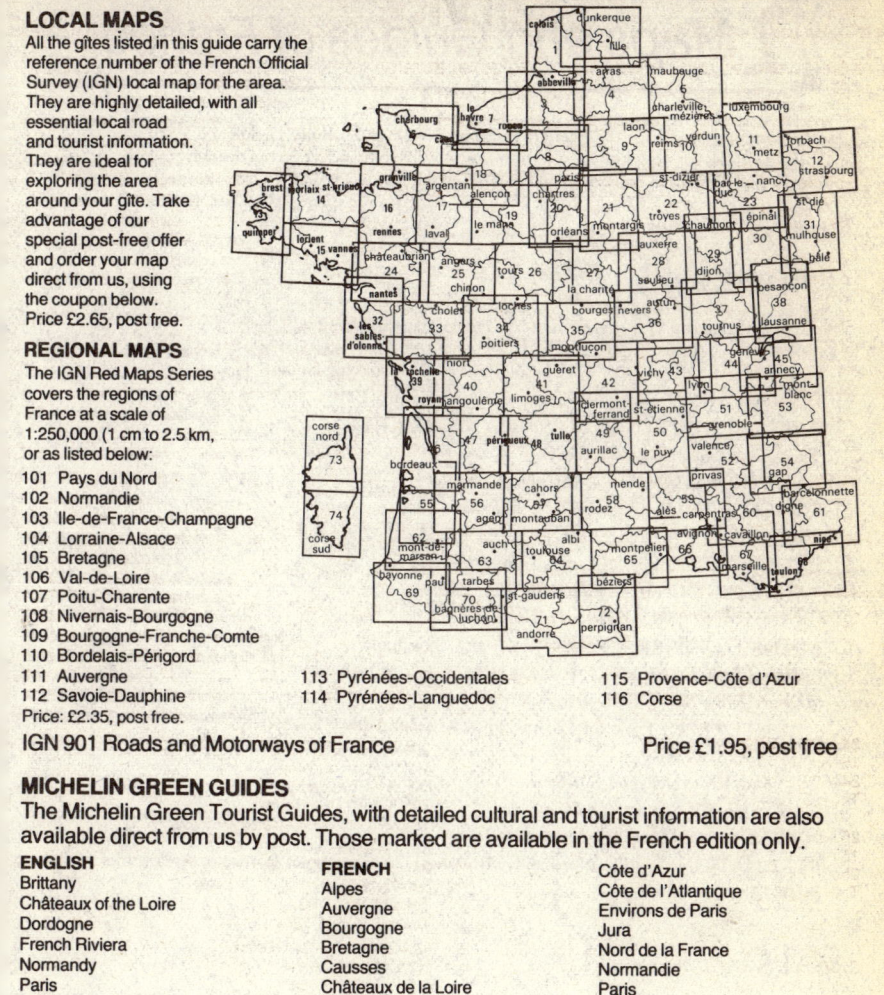

LOCAL MAPS

All the gîtes listed in this guide carry the reference number of the French Official Survey (IGN) local map for the area. They are highly detailed, with all essential local road and tourist information. They are ideal for exploring the area around your gîte. Take advantage of our special post-free offer and order your map direct from us, using the coupon below. Price £2.65, post free.

REGIONAL MAPS

The IGN Red Maps Series covers the regions of France at a scale of 1:250,000 (1 cm to 2.5 km, or as listed below:

101 Pays du Nord
102 Normandie
103 Ile-de-France-Champagne
104 Lorraine-Alsace
105 Bretagne
106 Val-de-Loire
107 Poitu-Charente
108 Nivernais-Bourgogne
109 Bourgogne-Franche-Comte
110 Bordelais-Périgord
111 Auvergne
112 Savoie-Dauphine
Price: £2.35, post free.

113 Pyrénées-Occidentales
114 Pyrénées-Languedoc
115 Provence-Côte d'Azur
116 Corse

IGN 901 Roads and Motorways of France   Price £1.95, post free

MICHELIN GREEN GUIDES

The Michelin Green Tourist Guides, with detailed cultural and tourist information are also available direct from us by post. Those marked are available in the French edition only.

ENGLISH
Brittany
Châteaux of the Loire
Dordogne
French Riviera
Normandy
Paris
Provence

FRENCH
Alpes
Auvergne
Bourgogne
Bretagne
Causses
Châteaux de la Loire
Corse

Côte d'Azur
Côte de l'Atlantique
Environs de Paris
Jura
Nord de la France
Normandie
Paris
Périgord

Price: £3.90 each, plus postage.

Please send me the following:

IGN Green Map nos. ....
............................at £2.65, post free £
IGN Red Map nos. ....
............................at £2.35, post free £
IGN 901 Roads and Motorways of France ....
............................at £1.95, post free £
Michelin Green Guide(s) ....
............................at £3.60 (plus p&p) £

Total £

Please send cheque/p.o. payable to McCarta Ltd.

Name ....

Address ....

....

Send to
McCARTA LTD., 122 King's Cross Rd.,
London WC1X 9DS

Bradt Enterprises Inc
95 Harvey St., Cambridge, MA O2140, USA.
Maps and Guides of France

North American agent for the **French Farm and Village Holiday Guide** and a full range of Maps and Guides for your holiday and/or business visits to France. You can order from your local bookseller or directly by mail or telephone, following the details on the Order Forms below and opposite. Payment by Check, Money Order; American Express, Visa and Master Charge accepted. US funds only.

GUIDEBOOKS

Important: Please add $1.50 per item ordered for postage and handling.

- ☐ THE CANAL DU MIDI & THE LANGUEDOC Sightseeing Guide & How to . . . $12.95
- ☐ TOUR OF MONT BLANC Walking Guide. A Harper, 1984 $9.95
- ☐ WALKING THE FRENCH ALPS: GR5   M Collins, 1984 $12.95

    The Visitors Guide Series. Paperback. each $9.95

- ☐ THE FRENCH COAST   M Collins, 1985
- ☐ THE SOUTH OF FRANCE   N Brangham, 1985
- ☐ BRITTANY   N Lands, 1984
- ☐ THE DORDOGNE   N Lands, 1983
- ☐ WALKING IN THE ALPS   B Spencer, 1983
- ☐ GRAPE EXPEDITIONS: Bicycle Tours of the Wine Country $8.95
- ☐ A TOUCH OF PARIS: 1985 Edition   An insider's guide $9.95
- ☐ PARIS CONFIDENTIAL   New, 1985 $9.95

    Meaker's Travel Tapes. Each 60 minutes. each $9.95

    ROUTE TAPES: From the Channel Ports & Around the
- ☐   South of Paris
- ☐   South Paris to Chalon-Sur-Saone
- ☐   Chalon-Sur-Saone to Orange
- ☐   The Riviera: Marseilles to Menton
- ☐ DESTINATION TAPES: Normandy; Brittany; The Camargue; Bordeaux Area (order by title)

MAPS

Important: Please add $1 per item ordered for postage and handling.

- ☐ FRANCE 1: 1 Million Scale   Freytag Berndt $5.95
- ☐ D-DAY MAP Various Scales   IGN France $5.95
- ☐ PARIS STREET MAP 1:14,000 Scale   Blay Plans $5.95
- ☐ PARIS L'INDESPENSABLE ATLAS 1:10,000   Thumb indexes, pocket-size $10.95

Tick as required and send with the Order Form opposite to:

BRADT ENTERPRISES INC., 95 Harvey St., Cambridge MA 02140 USA
Tel: (617) 492-8776

Bradt Enterprises Inc
95 Harvey St., Cambridge, MA 02140, USA.
Maps and Guides of France

READERS IN THE USA

French Farm And Village Holiday Guide 1987

ORDER YOUR 1987 EDITION NOW!

- ☐ **Please send** .... copy(ies) of the 1987 French Farm and Village Holiday Guide and charge to American Express / Visa / Master Charge (Please delete which do not apply)

    Card number ....

- ☐ Please send price and publication date of the **1987 French Farm and Village Holiday Guide** so that I can order (By check, Money Order – US funds only).

Maps and Guides of France (See page opposite also)

ORDER NOW!

- ☐ Please send Maps and Guides as marked on the attached Order Form (see opposite page).

    I enclose Check/Money Order for .... (US funds only).

OR

- ☐ Please charge to American Express/Visa/Master Charge (Please delete which do not apply)

    Card account number...

- ☐ Please send me further details of French Maps and Guides

NAME...

ADDRESS...

....

Send to
BRADT ENTERPRISES INC.,
95 Harvey St. Box H,
Cambridge, MA 02140,
USA
Tel: (617) 492-8776

MOORLAND
Holiday handbooks
Touring Guide to Europe

- Touring itineraries
- 460 pages packed with information
- Ideal for motorists, ramblers, and cyclists

PLUS! The *Visitor's Guides*

France:	Brittany
	The Dordogne*
only	The French Coast
£4.95	The Loire
	Normandy*
	The South of France
Austria:	The Tyrol
Germany:	The Black Forest

Italy: Tuscany and Florence
Iceland
Walking in the Alps

PLUS! *The Road to Compostela*

Travel Guide through historic France and Spain on a 1,000 mile pilgrims' road. £8.95

Make the most of your holiday with a Moorland holiday guide.

* Available in 1986

8 Station Street,
Ashbourne,
Derbyshire
Tel: (0335) 44486

MOORLAND PUBLISHING

FRENCH FARM GUIDE 1987. ORDER NOW!

Complete and send to:

FARM HOLIDAY GUIDES LTD., ABBEYMILL BUSINESS CENTRES, SEEDHILL, PAISLEY PA1 1JN (041-887-0428)

☐ Please send prices and publication dates of the **1987 French Farm and Village Holiday Guide**

☐ Please send details of **IGN official survey** and other maps of France

Name ....

Address ....

....